Planning Academic and Research Library Buildings

Scholar at His Book Wheel.
From Agostino Ramelli's *Le Diverse et Artificiose Machine*, Paris, 1588.

KEYES D. METCALF

Librarian of Harvard College, Emeritus

Planning Academic and Research Library Buildings

SPONSORED BY The Association of Research Libraries
AND The Association of College and Research Libraries
UNDER A GRANT BY The Council on Library Resources

MᶜGRAW-HILL BOOK COMPANY

New York   San Francisco   Toronto   London   Sydney

To E. E. W., J. F. C., and E. G. M., who each in a different way
made a major contribution toward the transformation of this volume from a dream
to a reality.

Preface

Library architecture has been during recent years the subject of many publications; these include highly valuable works, a number of which are listed in the Selective Annotated Bibliography in Appendix D of this volume. No single publication, however, has been designed to serve as a comprehensive manual dealing with the problems involved directly or indirectly in the planning and construction of academic and research libraries. This book has been written in an attempt to fill that gap. The Association of College and Research Libraries and the Association of Research Libraries believed that a manual was needed, and the Council on Library Resources, by making a grant to the two associations for the preparation and publication of such a book demonstrated that it agreed.

There are three major theoretical and practical reasons for a manual of this kind.

1. Planning an academic or research library building is an important undertaking.

2. It will confront many institutions during the next few years.

3. It is all too often the responsibility of persons who have little or no experience in this field.

The importance of library buildings is obvious, regardless of whether one is thinking of the institution's teaching and research program or of its budget. A poor building can seriously handicap students and professors; a good one can contribute to the intellectual health of the whole institution. Buildings are expensive, and a poor building is an enduring monument to many wasted dollars; moreover, a poorly planned and constructed building may force a library year after year to spend much more on operation and maintenance than would be required by a better one.

Sooner or later nearly every college and university must plan a new library building. A relatively few are resisting pressures to enroll increasing numbers of students, but even these institutions have constantly growing book collections. The others need space for more students as well as for more books. As the nation's population grows and as an ever-increasing percentage of the total will not be content with only a high school education, new colleges are springing up, each of which must have a library building. A recent estimate of the Office of Education indicates that in the United States fully 504 new library buildings will have been built on college and university campuses in the five-year period 1961 to 1965, at a cost of approximately $466,600,000, or at an average of over $93,000,000 a year. This does not include state, Federal, and other research libraries that are not in academic institutions.

Despite the fact that college and university library building is proceeding at this rate, a large percentage of the new buildings are planned by architects, librarians, and other persons who have never before been responsible for designing a building of this kind. Until quite recently only one architect out of every ten who was called upon to design college or university library buildings had ever done so before. With the increasing number of new libraries since the Second World War, this percentage has increased considerably but is still not large. Few chief librarians have more than one opportunity to work with architects on a new building. The others who may be involved—donors, university administrators, members of faculty committees, builders, and contractors—are even less likely to have had previous experience in this particular field.

Planning a library building is a complicated matter. This book does not attempt to provide answers to all the problems that may arise; but it does try to identify the more important ones, to break them down into their component parts, and to indicate the factors that ought to be taken into account in arriving at solutions. Mistakes may be made after careful consideration of a problem; but the most serious mistakes are likely to be those made when no one realizes that any problem exists.

This volume, then, is intended to provide, in so far as it can, a substitute for first-hand experience. Its preface can properly give some indication of what experience the author himself brings to the task; an autobiographical note seems to be in order.

My first years in library work, at Oberlin College from 1905 to 1908, came at a time when the librarian, Professor Azariah S. Root, was planning a new building, which proved to be one of the best college libraries constructed up to that time. The contrast between this building and its predecessor was a convincing proof to me of the importance of good planning. My twenty-four years in administrative positions at the New York Public Library provided experience in rearrangement of space and equipment in several parts of its central building, but many hours of work on plans for an addition, while they contributed to my education, led to no construction.

During eighteen years at Harvard, however, I dealt with plans for three new buildings. One was the New England Deposit Library, a building designed to be as simple, inexpensive, and functional as possible, on which I had the pleasure of working with Mr. Henry Shepley. The second was the Houghton Library for rare books and manuscripts; I worked closely with the architect, Mr. William Graves Perry and the librarian who was to be in charge of the collection, Mr. William A. Jackson. The third was the Lamont Library for undergraduates; Mr. Shepley and I discussed tentative plans for this library over a period of more than eight years before the generous gift from Mr. Thomas W. Lamont made construction possible.

Since Harvard had more than 80 special and departmental libraries, I had many occasions during my eighteen years as director to deal with alterations, additions, rehabilitation, and repair. Moreover, because the Lamont building was well received, invitations to serve as a consultant on building problems elsewhere began to come to me in increasing numbers. Indeed, since my retirement from Harvard in 1955, I have served as a building consultant to more than 250 libraries on six continents and have spent some fifteen months studying library problems in countries other than the United States.

It would require more experience than this to learn how to solve all problems of library architecture, but I believe I may fairly assert that there are few problems in the field that I have not encountered.

This volume would not have been possible as a one-man independent enterprise. Fortunately, the Association of Research Libraries and the Association of College and Research Libraries, a division of the American Library Association, were prepared to sponsor it and to apply to the Ford Foundation's Council on Library Resources for adequate financial support; this support was forthcoming. The author has thus been enabled to spend a considerable portion of his time in work on the preparation of the volume for a period of over four years; to pay for secretarial, editorial, and bibliographical help, as well as to engage a competent professional draftsman and to pay the expenses of an advisory committee representing the two sponsoring library groups.

That committee consisted of the following:

Professor Curtis Bradford of Grinnell College, who had been chairman of the Grinnell Library Building Committee while that college's Burling Library was planned and constructed, and who represented the faculty point of view.

Mr. Verner W. Clapp, president of the Council on Library Resources and formerly chief assistant librarian of the Library of Congress, whose work with the council has kept him in touch with recent library developments and needs throughout the world and to whom I am greatly indebted for support and encouragement.

Dr. Ralph E. Ellsworth, director of the Library of the University of Colorado and formerly director of the Iowa State University Library, who was largely responsible for the planning of library buildings at both of those universities, each of which was an important milestone in the history of American academic library architecture. He has also served as consultant on a large number of other library buildings.

Mr. Richard Harwell, librarian of Bowdoin College, who is now engaged in planning a new library for that institution and who, as executive secretary of the Association of College and Research Libraries before he went to Bowdoin, had wide contacts with academic libraries and their building needs.

Dr. William H. Jesse, director of Libraries of the University of Tennessee and one of the two university librarians (Dr. Ellsworth is the other) who have done more library building consultation work than any other librarians now serving in university libraries. He has made important contributions to academic library building planning.

Dr. Stephen A. McCarthy, director of Libraries at Cornell University, who deserves great credit for his work on planning the fine new Olin Library at Cornell and the successful rehabilitation of the seventy-year-old unsatisfactory central library of the same university into the Uris Undergraduate Library, which has given a remarkable demonstration of how popular and useful an old library building can be made. He has also presided over the Cornell library system for the decade during which every unit in it has been reorganized and provided with new quarters.

Col. F. B. Rogers, formerly director of the National Library of Medicine and now professor of medical bibliography at the University of Colorado Medical School, who was in charge of the National Library of Medicine during the long years that its new building was being planned and who had much to do with bringing it to a successful conclusion.

Miss Eileen Thornton, librarian of Oberlin College, who has been interested in library building planning for many years, first at Vassar and then at Oberlin, and who represented on the committee the woman's point of view and, of greater importance, the views of a first-class liberal arts college librarian.

Dr. Frederick H. Wagman, director of the University of Michigan Library and (in 1963 to 1964) president of the American Library Association, who has contributed a great deal to the storage library building at his university and to the delightful undergraduate library there.

The author could not have asked for a better and more competent advisory committee. It has met regularly at the annual and midwinter conferences of the American Library Association during 4½ years, as well as at specially called meetings lasting one or two full days on three other occasions. Its advice helped tremendously in setting the tone of the whole work and in making suggestions for inclusions and exclusions; each of the members has also helped by reading, commenting on, and criticizing drafts of the text. Professor Bradford has read a large percentage of the text, and each of the others has spent long hours in working over the sections in which he had special knowledge, interest, and competence. While inevitably it was not possible to take all the advice offered by each member, the committee has made a major contribution.

In preparing the volume, the author has not hesitated to call for help and advice from others besides the advisory committee. Notices in the *Library Journal* and *College and Research Libraries* asked for comments in regard to triumphs and blunders in library architecture, particularly in buildings constructed since the Second World War. While the author was disappointed in the number of comments received as a result of these notices, help was given by a considerable number of librarians and is gratefully recorded. Preliminary drafts of five sections of this book were printed in *College and Research Libraries,* one in the *Library Journal,* and one in *College and Business Administration,* each with a request for criticisms and suggestions. Although help was received, a wider response would have been welcome. The comments of those who did write are gratefully acknowledged.

Appreciation should also be expressed to a considerable number of authors and publishers who gave permission for the inclusion in this volume of material which was already in print and which has been acknowledged in connection with the quotations used.

Special thanks are due to my part-time secretary, Mrs. Esther MacSwan, who typed the manuscript and in many cases typed the same matter over again as many as six times, making major or minor changes, always without complaint.

Mr. Willard Thompson, lighting engineer and consultant, read two different drafts of the section on lighting and contributed greatly by catching factual errors and giving valuable advice, which, it is only fair to state, was not always taken, but which was gratefully received. Dr. David G. Cogan, Harvard's Henry Willard Williams Professor of Ophthalmology and its director of the Howe Laboratory of Ophthalmology, also read drafts of this section, made useful comments, and gave words of encouragement, as did Mr. William M. C. Lam, well-known consultant and specialist in the coordination of lighting and architecture.

Dr. Wolfgang M. Freitag of Stanford University, and now at Harvard, prepared the first draft of the glossary, did much of the organization and analysis of the literature on the subject of library building planning, and also made other indirect but valuable contributions to the work.

Mr. Richard DeGennaro, assistant director of the Harvard University Library and assistant librarian of Harvard College, did the basic work on the Selective Annotated Bibliography, and, with Dr. Freitag, on organizing the literature of library building planning, and also stood by ready to help at all stages of the preparation of the book.

Miss Edna E. Voigt of the Library Bureau Division of Sperry Rand, read and made valuable comments on Section 7.1, dealing with book stacks, and on the section on furniture in Chapter 10, which are gratefully acknowledged. Her comments prevented errors in terminology and judgment, but she should not be held responsible for any of the conclusions reached by the author.

Mr. Robert B. O'Connor and Mr. Walter H. Kilham, Jr., of the firm of O'Connor and Kilham, made comments on Chapter 2, dealing with architectural problems, which resulted in important changes in that chapter.

The late Mr. Henry R. Shepley, head of the firm of Shepley, Bulfinch, Richardson, and Abbott, who had encouraged the author, arranged before his death to enable Mr. James Ford Clapp, Jr., a senior partner in the firm, to make a contribution that cannot be exaggerated. Mr. Clapp read every word of the text from start to finish and a good deal of it on two or more occasions; he wrote out his comments, called attention to errors of fact, and suggested changes. He spent nearly seventy-five Saturday mornings going over the text with the author, explaining desirable additions and deletions. He supervised the preparation of the drawings for the whole volume, sketching them out himself first. He made contacts with engineers in various fields— lighting, ventilation, construction, etc.—that enabled the author to include useful information that would otherwise have been missed. And, finally, he prepared in detail the outline and first draft of the parts of Section 10.1, on plumbing and on hardware, and of Section 16.4, which deals with specifications and working drawings. If it were not for the fact that Mr. Clapp's advice was not always taken, it would have been proper to include his name on the title page as a co-author, but it should be made evident that his contribution was great and was made without expectation of financial compensation.

Mr. Edwin E. Williams, counsellor to the director on the collections of the Harvard University Library, with whom I have worked closely for twenty-five years, helped to edit the text of the volume for style and content. I often state that Mr. Williams knows what I want to say better than I do and knows how to say it much better. He too often finds me stubborn and unwilling to take his advice, and while he has made great contributions to the organization, as well as the wording of the volume, he should not be held responsible for the repetition of important points, often three times, in the main parts and then again in the appendix. He did succeed in getting what I was determined to say in intelligible form. My indebtedness to him in this work, as on many previous occasions, defies description and cannot be exaggerated.

And, finally, grateful thanks should be given to Elinor G. Metcalf, who has suffered for nearly five years while her husband, who is no longer young, has for the first time attempted to prepare for publication what can be called a major enterprise. Her patience and her help, together with that of those mentioned above, have made the completion possible.

But in spite of all this help and advice which contributed so much to the volume, it should be made clear that only the author, whose name appears on the title page, can be held responsible for the conclusions reached and the statements made.

Keyes D. Metcalf

Contents

part 1

Basic Information on Library Building Planning

Introduction

This volume deals with the planning of academic and research library buildings. Library buildings house library collections of various kinds, chiefly books and other printed matter; seating accommodations and other facilities for library users; quarters for the library staff that acquires, catalogues, and serves the collections; and, in addition, architectural or what is preferably known as non-assignable space. (If there is space left over after caring for the above needs, it is sometimes assigned for other purposes.)

Before a library building is constructed or even planned, a number of tasks should be carried out. The persons directly concerned should in some way become acquainted with the basic problems involved in library building planning. They may include a good many different individuals: the architect selected for the task, the librarian and often several members of his staff, representatives of the library committee, and other persons whom the institution asks for help in the planning or whom it employs for the work, as well as administrative officers and governing board representatives. Since the library is built primarily for those who are to use it, their needs should be kept in mind; although possibly they should be represented in the planning, ordinarily their interests are to be looked out for by one or more of the individuals or groups already mentioned. The architect is probably not just one individual. He may have associates and draftsmen. He may call in help on the engineering and mechanical aspects of his task.

Altogether a great variety and number of persons will be directly or indirectly involved in the planning process. Often very few if any of them have ever before dealt with a library building planning enterprise. It is hoped that everything in this volume will be of use to one or more of those concerned, but in order to provide the information that may be useful to each, much will be included that is not pertinent to all. The writer is a librarian, not an architect or an engineer, and it is only fair to admit that he was attracted to this phase of library work not because of any special interest or talent in architecture or engineering, but because he was looking for ways to stretch the library dollar so that more of it would be left over and made available for book acquisition and service. He will not attempt to tell the architect and the engineer about their professions, but will try to explain to them the architectural and engineering features that help to make a building a functional library.

The volume is divided into two parts made up of seventeen chapters, which are followed by five appendixes.

Behind the whole problem of planning library buildings is a generally recognized fact, which is so important that it bears repeating and emphasizing. Libraries and those responsible for them have never found a satisfactory way of preventing or even slowing up the growth in library space requirements.

After many years of building inadequate libraries, too often because of a failure to understand the growth problem, architects, librarians, and administrators have finally realized that library collections grow and will probably continue to do so. Academic and research libraries, until they become what may be called mature institutions, tend to grow at the rate of 4 or 5 per cent a year, doubling in perhaps sixteen or seventeen years. This has been true in this country for at least two centuries. In due course libraries may become mature, and the growth rate will slacken. It may go down to 2 per cent a year, doubling in thirty-five to forty years, instead of in half that time, but in general this does not occur until the library is so large that even 2 per cent is a serious matter. Two per cent amounts to 140,000 or more volumes a year at Harvard, requiring some 10,000 sq ft of floor space for additions to the book collection alone. The Library of Congress is still growing far more rapidly than that, as it is still what might be called immature, having become a national library in recent years. This growth must slow up on a percentage basis, but not in terms of volumes added.

Although the wise man in the Bible says that "of making many books there is no end," it seems that they cannot go on multiplying indefinitely. If they do, the financial implications for libraries will become unbearable. As libraries become larger, they tend to become more complex, and unit costs increase; that is, the time and expense involved in making a new volume available or serving a reader become greater. As the number of libraries increases, a shortage of desirable older publications develops. As a result of the law of supply and demand, prices have risen rapidly in recent years. Expensive reprinting becomes necessary. On the other hand, methods of microreproduction reduce bulk, and modern techniques of communication should help; but so far these improvements seem to have had little effect on growth rates, although they have increased total resources. The author believes that growth will slow down in the years ahead but that the process will be fairly gradual. Libraries should expect space demands for collections to increase rapidly enough so that buildings should be planned whenever possible for book collections of at least twice their present size. There will, of course, be exceptions to this rule.

The demands for space for readers in academic and research libraries will tend to increase more rapidly in the next fifteen years than in the past, because of the great increase in the number of research workers and of college and university students and faculty members. As space for books and readers increases, staff requirements will increase at least proportionately or even more rapidly, because unit costs, as already noted, tend to increase.

One might almost say that total space requirements in libraries will increase as much as the traffic will bear. This may be the limiting factor, and it behooves those responsible to realize that, while libraries are not a luxury, there is a limit to the funds that can be or should be devoted to them, considering all the circumstances, and that those who are interested in books and library service should do everything possible to make the funds invested in libraries go as far as possible. We pride ourselves in making two grains of corn grow where one did before if the quality is kept up. If we can get more out of library square footage by careful planning and make 1,000 sq ft go twice as far or even half again as far as in the past, the effort will be very much worth while. How do we want to invest our funds? A handsome library building certainly has its value. Let us not be content with anything less, but if beauty and utility can both be obtained economically, why not economize? Much of this book is devoted to an attempt to show how a maximum of utility in library buildings can be achieved for the funds available, without sacrificing beauty.

This volume is addressed to at least six different groups. Each group is interested primarily in different aspects in the planning of academic and research library buildings, although the objectives may be almost identical. Each group wants a good functional library that will attract use, will not cost too much to erect and to operate, and will at the same time be satisfactory aesthetically. Each group will have a particular interest in different factors, but a better building should result if each group has some comprehension of the problems of interest to each of the others. This point has been kept in mind as the volume has been written, as will be shown in the paragraphs addressed to each of the groups which follow.

1. *Presidents, governing boards, and administrative officers.* Whatever their natural interests may be, most presidents, members of governing boards, administrative officers, and even business managers, cannot be expected to become acquainted with all the technical details of planning library buildings. Generally they will have a particular interest in matters that affect the future usefulness of the building, aesthetics, and costs, problems dealt with in Chapters 1 to 3. They are also inevitably involved in the criticisms that may arise if the building does not function properly. They have the final responsibility for finances. Module sizes, considered in Chapter 4, and the width of stack aisles, the depth and height of shelving, discussed in section 8.1, are subjects that they may, at first thought, be inclined to leave to the architects and librarians. But if they

realize that a change in any one of the points just mentioned may easily affect the total cost of the building by 5 per cent and that all of these matters together may change the total by 10 to 25 per cent without changing the building's appearance or usefulness, they cannot help but be interested. They cannot avoid all responsibility for architectural style and interior decoration. They may prefer to leave the final decision on these points to the architect or some adviser, but a knowledge of the problems involved and their effect on costs will place them in a better position to act before final plans are approved and to deal with criticism when it inevitably arises.

If the building is so planned that it becomes difficult if not impossible to control exits, which are discussed in section 6.1, and if books begin to disappear on a large scale, they may be in an embarrassing position, to put it mildly. This volume has been written with the president and governing boards and those who have final responsibility for results very much in mind, and points that will affect them are brought out again and again. Each of the 17 chapters should contain something pertaining to their interests, but it is suggested that, if they are not prepared to study the volume in detail, they review the table of contents and ask the librarian, the business manager, or architect, with each of whom it is hoped they will keep in touch directly or indirectly during the planning process, to call to their attention pertinent problems that come up and that will affect decisions in which they may be involved.

2. *Library building planning committees.* There may be one planning committee appointed to aid in the process of planning the library building, or there may be as many as five, as will be seen in section 12.1. It is suggested that the governing board, the administrative officers, the faculty and the students in an academic institution, and the library staff be represented on the committee or committees. If each of the groups has a separate committee, the parts of the volume of special interest to each will differ somewhat, although at least a casual reading of the whole volume may be profitable for committee members. Special attention on the part of committee representatives of the governing boards is called to Chapters 1 to 3 and 5 to 11. The administrative representatives and faculty and student committee members will be interested in the same sections. Each person should be expected to deal with other sections in which he has special interest and competence.

3. *Librarians and their staffs.* The volume is written by a librarian. It is addressed as a whole to librarians, and any librarian engaged in planning a library building will presumably be sufficiently interested in all the problems involved to become acquainted with it from beginning to end. The features of library building planning of which the librarian may well be ignorant but for which he has particular responsibility are emphasized throughout. Chapters 2 and 3, on aesthetics and financial matters respectively, will, it is hoped, give a useful background for these problems where the librarian is vitally affected but is perhaps not primarily responsible. Too few librarians have realized the importance and effect on costs of module sizes, and it is hoped that Chapter 4 will make available for the first time a detailed technical statement about them. Few librarians have ever dealt with the complicated problem of height, considered in Chapter 5, for which, of necessity, decisions must be in the form of a compromise. But the right compromise may improve both the functional operation of the library and its appearance; it will inevitably affect costs. Similar situations are found in most of the other chapters, particularly in section 6.4, on spatial relationships. Chapters 9 and 10 on mechanical and construction problems are not technical in character and should be readily understood by the layman with the aid of the Glossary in Appendix E. Chapters 4 to 11 as a whole try to set forth in simple terms the theoretical problems involved in library building planning and to enable the librarian to bring informed judgment to bear upon them. Chapters 12 to 14, on the program, should prove useful to any librarian who assumes responsibility for preparation of that basic document. The last three chapters have been prepared especially for the librarian who is entering new territory for which earlier guidebooks have had little to contribute.

The Selective Annotated Bibliography, Appendix D, should make it easy for the librarian to seek out additional information if the need arises, and the other four appendixes should reduce to some extent the difficulties arising during the period of planning and construction.

4. *Library schools, library school students, and other librarians interested in administration.* For this group the volume may well be considered a textbook on the planning of library buildings interpreted

in the broadest terms. It should be a suitable addition to the personal library of any librarian who expects to take part in the administrative or business aspects of his profession.

5. *The library building planning team.* The desirability of a planning team, representing the different groups involved in library building planning, is discussed in Chapter 12. At least one and preferably all members of the planning team should be as well acquainted as possible with the problems discussed in each of the chapters. It may be possible to assign primary responsibility for different sections to different members of the team. This point may well be discussed after they have all had an opportunity for casual examination of the whole volume.

6. *Architects, engineers, and consultants.* As indicated earlier, a considerable part of this book deals directly or indirectly with architectural and engineering problems on which members of those professions involved in the library building operation undoubtedly have more detailed information than the author of this volume. However, the various sections have approached these problems from the library point of view, and since few architects or engineers have had close connection with library building planning, this book should bring out the points where library needs differ from those with which they are familiar. It is hoped that architects and engineers will become acquainted with the special library requirements in module and height problems, traffic patterns, spatial relationships, and the housing of books, readers, and library staffs, and so on. At least a casual examination of the whole volume should be useful to members of this group, who can then readily pick out special sections where they can expect to find desired information.

While the volume is directed primarily to academic and research libraries, several points at which it should be useful for other types of libraries should be noted.

1. Those responsible for planning any library must realize that it is a matter of first importance to understand the institution which is to use the building, its organization, its objectives, and the community which it serves. Much of library planning is involved in examining and explaining problems that arise in this connection.

2. Any building, to be reasonably successful, must have an architect, and the problems in his selection are very similar, whatever kind of library is to be designed.

3. All libraries face the financial problems involved in building planning, and these may differ as much from one academic library to another as from an academic to a public library or to one of any other kind.

4. The preparation of a program for a library building is generally, if not always, the most important single contribution by the institution's representatives, and seating accommodations, book storage, furniture and equipment, and aesthetics must be dealt with in any type of library. The details are different, of course, but the general principles are the same.

With the above four points in mind, the author has tried to emphasize the similarities and differences in the problems to be faced by different types of libraries. One of the great dangers in all planning of library buildings is that in searching for formulas and rules, the librarian, the planning team, and the architect will make the mistake of adopting blindly what has been used by others. This is perhaps the basic reason why we all too often find a college library equipped with tables whose dimensions are entirely suitable for public libraries but which do not provide enough square feet of reading surface so that college students will fill all the seats. Similar problems come up in other areas of planning. For instance, open-access shelves in a public library should have wider and shorter aisles than in a university library with a very large collection and a limited student body. This volume tries to bring out points of this kind in the hope that it may help to prevent apparently obvious mistakes which are far too often perpetrated by intelligent librarians and architects who are not specialists in this particular field. Here, as elsewhere, a little knowledge may be a dangerous thing.

The author has studied library building problems for many different types of libraries in many countries, in the belief that he would learn about possible solutions and would be enabled to broaden his background and outlook and obtain a better perspective. As a result, he hopes that this volume will be useful throughout the world. It is written from the American point of view, but it has tried to avoid a dogmatism that would limit its usefulness. No two libraries are alike, but they have much in common whatever their type, clientele, and nationality.

1

Looking Ahead

This volume has been prepared to help persons who have or expect to have something to do with planning library buildings. Anyone in that position wants to plan the best possible building for the use to which the structure is to be put. Much of the volume will deal with the question of what is the "best possible." Chapter 2 will consider the aesthetic aspects and their relation to quality, function, and cost. Chapter 3 will deal with the more specific financial problems, and the following chapters will take up the physical aspects of building planning.

One major part of the question relates to time. Best possible for when? When the building is completed, of course. But what about the years beyond that? We live in a changing world. If the past can be taken as a guide, it is obvious that the requirements for a library in 1975 will be quite different from those in 1965. If the apparently ever-accelerating pace of our technological and economic development continues, as there is good prospect of its doing, the needs for the year 2000 will have changed from those in 1965 far more than they have changed between, let us say, 1876, the year when the American Library Association was organized and the history of the modern library might be said to have begun, and today. We know libraries planned in 1876 are so outmoded today as to be questionable assets, this in spite of exceptions that might be said to prove the rule, such as the Redwood Library in Newport, Rhode Island, the Boston Athenaeum in Massachusetts, a very few others in this country, and perhaps more elsewhere.

One of the first questions a library planner must answer is how many years will the building probably be used for the purposes for which it is being planned? As in practically all the other problems that will be discussed in this volume, circumstances alter cases. No two institutions are alike; no two face exactly the same problems. Each must to a considerable extent be a law unto itself. But usually it is safe to say that libraries and other institutional buildings are generally planned on the basis that they should go on as long as possible—whatever that means. Colleges and universities do not expect to follow the business and industrial practice of planned obsolescence with depreciation in value to the zero point and replacement in a limited period of years, perhaps no more than twenty-five to fifty at the most. They may go on for over 200 years, as the oldest buildings at Harvard University have done with the aid of periodic rehabilitation. At any rate, this question of useful life for a new library should be kept in mind during the planning stage.

The cost of a new library building today is so great and represents such a large percentage of an institution's total library investment in books, service, and buildings, that it is generally unwise to build deliberately for a few years only. Evidently, then, the building should be one that can be used to advantage for other than library purposes or for a library with needs in the future very different from those of today. In other words, the building should be as flexible as possible.

What is flexibility? It means adaptability to

changing needs. What are the characteristics of a flexible library? They may be summed up as follows:

As large a percentage of the floor space as possible should be usable for any of the primary functions of a library: reader accommodations, service to readers, space for staff activities, and housing for the collections. It follows that:

1. Atmospheric and other comfort conditions, such as ventilation and lighting, must be suitable for any of these purposes.

2. Floors must be capable of bearing loads up to 150 pounds per square foot, which is the bookstack requirement, in all areas of the building.

3. Floor heights must be adequate for any of these purposes, preferably not less than 8 ft 4 in. (see Chapter 5 for fuller discussion).

4. All library areas must be readily accessible; it is undesirable to have load-bearing interior walls in places where they might interfere with traffic patterns later.

5. Interior arrangements must not seriously interfere with satisfactory capacity for books, for readers, and for shelving.

It must be realized, of course, that in any library building, even if only one level high, there must be supports to hold up the roof, and in most buildings some interior columns are a necessity. With more than one level, vertical transportation, ventilation, and plumbing facilities, at least semipermanent in character, are required and will limit complete flexibility. It might be added that, though flexibility is a requirement, this does not mean that the use of the space should not be carefully planned for the original installation. It should also be realized that these requirements are likely to add to con-

struction costs and that the excuse for them is that they can be expected to save money in the long run.

The above can be summed up by saying that interior masonry or plastered walls which are messy and difficult to remove and permanent built-in installations of all kinds should be avoided as far as practicable. Heating and ventilation ducts, toilet facilities, and vertical transportation should be provided in places where they are least likely to interfere with prospective changes in library-space assignments. Even in a large building the number of what are known as "core" areas that are fixed should be limited and, other things being equal, the fewer cores, the better. A large building with up to 50,000 sq ft or more on each level can be planned with only one central core, and any stairwells, elevators, ducts, toilets, and so forth, not within this core can be placed near the building's periphery, where they will be as unobtrusive as possible. Some architects have gone to an extreme in this connection and have placed secondary stairs and other permanent features outside the main building structure as protrusions from it (see Fig. 1.1) and have been able to fit them into the architectural arrangements without damaging the aesthetic appearance or even have made them an important aesthetic feature. Outside constructions can simplify interior traffic patterns and arrangements but should not be considered essential, because with many buildings they would not be suitable architecturally.

One other important factor in flexibility may prolong the useful life of a library and prevent unnecessary expenditures later: to plan the building in such a way that later additions can be made without undue expense for alterations and rearrangements and without damaging it functionally or aesthetically. This can be accomplished only by providing for these additions in the basic plan adopted.

What changes in library needs can be anticipated? The author is not a prophet, but it seems obvious that the way to attack this problem is to consider what can be learned from the past and what can be deduced from studying the present.

Lessons from the Past

A study of the past makes it obvious that pre-Second World War library buildings, to say nothing of earlier ones, were very different from

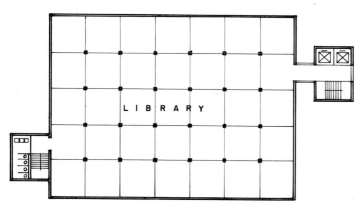

FIG. 1.1 Secondary stairs outside main walls. This arrangement can simplify traffic patterns.

those planned more recently. A brief summary should suffice. One hundred years ago thick bearing exterior and interior walls held up the buildings, which were planned with little thought of flexibility. No library had electric or hydraulic elevators, metal shelving, electric lighting, telephones, or air conditioning. Card catalogues were just beginning to come into use on a small scale. The catalogue in book form was standard. There were no visible indexes. There were no typewriters or other copying machines; no photostats, to say nothing of Xerox 914s. There were no mechanical gadgets for accounting or for charging systems and no microreproductions of any kind.

Individual seating on a large scale was unknown. Compact storage, as we conceive it today, or in fact concentrated stack shelving had not been thought of. Except in libraries with a very limited clientele, there was to all intents and purposes no open access to the collections. It was not customary for readers to have accommodations close to the books, except in a few libraries where there were alcoves surrounded by books with a table in the center.

Of perhaps greater importance from the point of view of building, the largest collections in the United States in 1850 numbered about 100,000 volumes. By 1900 the number had grown to a million. Today, leaving out the large public library circulating collections, there are between 40 and 50 academic and research libraries of that size in the United States, with the total increasing annually. The number of readers in academic libraries, in particular, has increased at a somewhat similar rate, because of the tremendous growth of the number of students in institutions of higher learning and the increasing emphasis on individual work and wider reading and a deemphasis on textbook instruction.

The changes in the physical structure of libraries, which are the direct or indirect result of the different requirements just noted, are of interest. We no longer have to have functionally great reading areas reaching up to 50 ft in height in order to provide ventilation and natural light. This alone has reduced cubage in areas open to the public by 50 per cent or more. With a good quality artificial light available at a reasonable cost, libraries can be open and comfortable on dark days and after sunset. Daylight can be, and it is to be hoped will continue to be,

available in parts of the buildings for psychological purposes, if not for reading. Artificial lighting and windows are discussed in section 9.1, and heating, ventilation, and air conditioning in section 9.2.

These changes make it practicable and often desirable for the sake of reducing outside wall areas and costs and shortening and simplifying traffic lanes to plan a squarish building instead of a relatively long, narrow, and irregular one. The choice, it must be admitted, may complicate the aesthetic problems.

Ceiling heights can now be determined by factors other than natural light and ventilation. Multitier buildings are practicable. Height problems of all kinds are dealt with in Chapter 5.

What then have we learned from the past? Three things among others:

1. Changes in construction methods and in provision for comfort and convenience have come about, and more of them will undoubtedly be made in the future. This reemphasizes the necessity for a new building to be as flexible as possible. It must be admitted, however, that complete flexibility cannot be obtained; efforts to obtain it undoubtedly add to costs and even tend to lower the quality of the space, because none of it can be "custom-built" for a specific purpose. A major step in the development of flexible space has brought into use the modular system which is discussed in Chapter 4.

2. Libraries have grown rapidly in the past in the size of their collections and can be expected to continue to do so in the future. On the average, collections in institutions of higher learning are doubling every sixteen to eighteen years today, and while the rate of growth tends to slow up as they become larger, this effect is apparent only in the very largest and what might be called "mature" or "static" institutions. Even the Library of Congress, our largest library, perhaps the largest in the world, is still growing at a rate of some 4 per cent annually, which will result in doubling its collection in twenty years. Space demands for shelving seem likely to continue to increase.

3. The demand made on academic libraries for seating accommodations has continued to increase. Very few institutions have been able to put a definite limit on the number of students admitted, and the number of persons of college age and the percentage of those interested in a

college and postgraduate education has steadily increased and can be expected to continue to do so in the future. The situation is further complicated by the fact that, although there are only twenty-four hours in the day, past experience indicates that a larger percentage of those hours are spent in the library by students as the years go by, primarily because of changes in methods of instruction and in the curriculum, encouragement from the teaching staff, a more serious student population, and dormitory and home conditions that are not conducive to study. Space demands for reading accommodations will apparently continue to increase.

4. The quality of accommodations has tended to rise, and more comfortable and convenient study conditions have been provided. These have included better temperature and humidity control, improved quality of lighting, a larger percentage of individual seating, and semiprivate accommodations. None of these improvements have as yet reached their limits. The atmospheric conditions and controls now available have been found to be very useful for the preservation of books, and continued improvements in this respect will undoubtedly be made. It might be said that any building built today without what is now regarded as satisfactory control of atmospheric conditions is already outmoded, and many would say that twenty-five years from now a non-air-conditioned academic library would be a thing of the past. The same holds for other provisions for comfort of readers and staff.

If past experience means anything, we can then say that:

1. Since physical changes of many kinds can be expected to take place as the years go by, the utmost possible flexibility is required.

2. Since increase in space demands for collections and reader accommodations is almost inevitable, a building, if it is to continue to be useful, must be so placed and planned that it can be readily enlarged. The question of growth is considered in greater detail in section 13.7.

3. Since accommodations will rise in quality, at least as far as those for the comfort of the occupant and the preservation of the collections are concerned, over-economizing is unwise; if the financial situation dictates a certain economy, the plans may be laid so that later improvements will not be unduly expensive.

Deductions from the Present

What can be deduced from the present that will help in planning for the years ahead? What are the signs for the future? Obviously, there is today a tremendous interest in new scientific developments, photographic and electronic as well as those more strictly mechanical in character. A growing number of library schools are specializing in the field, because of the evident need of providing trained personnel with knowledge of these developments; one has appointed as dean an electronic expert, instead of a man with a library background; another has specialized in information retrieval; and a third has as a senior member of its staff a leading expert in the field. Others will undoubtedly follow these leads.

The Council on Library Resources, with large sums placed at its disposal by the Ford Foundation, is spending literally millions of dollars trying to develop ways and means through mechanisms of various kinds to improve library resources and services. It has a special interest in the development and study of new techniques of general applicability. These include among many others a study of the mechanization of the production of printed copy for catalogues and bibliographies; the employment of computers for storage, indexing, and retrieval of information, and automated procedures for indexing. Edge-notched cards, machine-sorted punched cards, superimposable punched cards, are being investigated, the latter in a form that can be reduced to microfilm for inexpensive dissemination and use by others. The applicability of computer techniques to serial record management is being ascertained. Mechanical storage, closed-circuit television for library use, and other developments may not be far away. A careful study of the survey sponsored by the Council on Library Resources, under the title *Automation and the Library of Congress,* published by the Library of Congress in 1963, may be as good an approach to this problem as any. The continued development of copying devices will undoubtedly take place. A number of libraries are already using IBM computers to control better their circulation records.

The Airlie Conference held at Warrenton, Virginia, on May 26 to 29, 1963, discussed libraries and automation with librarians, engineers, systems men, computer representatives, information and communication experts in attendance. The librarian tended to say to the technician, "Let us know what you can do, and we will tell you if we can apply it to the library." The technicians are inclined to invite the librarian to tell them just what is needed, and they will determine whether a machine can be applied to the problem.

Conference after conference is working on these problems, and someone connected with the planning of each new library building, particularly if it is a large university library which is growing rapidly and where space needs are likely to change, should be assigned to the task of studying the field and the effect of the probable or possible mechanical developments on the program for a new building.

A great deal of attention is being paid to the problem of deteriorating paper, which seriously threatens a large percentage of all our existing records on paper, particularly those printed during the present century. It may be too early to say whether the answer to this difficulty will be the treatment of currently available materials which may increase their space requirements; or their reproduction in facsimile; or microreproduction, which may save space for storage of collections in many libraries, even if the original is preserved somewhere; or all of these and possibly new developments in interlibrary cooperation.

The American Library Association Library Technology Project is making studies of all kinds of library equipment, hoping to improve their quality and usefulness, and real progress has already been made, as is shown by the reports of that organization.

It seems not incorrect today to say that a machine can be devised to do almost anything if someone is ready and able to explain just what is wanted, and ready and able to pay for it. The critical point is, when does it become financially practicable to build the machine, and what are the things that need to be cared for mechanically?

There is no question but that an IBM circulation control system is available and practical today. James R. Cox of the University of California in Los Angeles, on page 492 in the November, 1963, number of *College and Research Libraries* has stated:

There are two generalizations often made about data processing in libraries which are worthy of attention, particularly as they may apply to circulation procedures. They are at opposite poles and represent extreme viewpoints. One is that university libraries should automate their circulation systems because they will save money. The other is that university libraries should not automate their circulation systems because it costs too much and is not worth it in the end. Both viewpoints are probably wrong, or, at least, they are inaccurate. . . . it depends upon what is being discussed. If one is talking of dollars and cents, the first statement is particularly fallacious. As more and more libraries become involved to a greater or lesser degree with automatic systems or plans for them, it is becoming more widely understood that it does cost more to automate, from the pure dollars and cents standpoint. On the other hand, if we could translate faster book shelving and filing, more accurate records and . . . therefore, better . . . service into dollars and cents, automation does clearly save money.

If the above statement is true today, it seems fair to say that, with the increase in salary scales that seems bound to continue, there will be more and more automation of library record keeping and a new library building should be planned to make it convenient to install the machines.

It can be added that without question more and more microreproductions of one kind or another will be used. Because of the cost of the reading machines required to use these microreproductions, they will generally be read in the library, although with the various enlarging machines already available, it is possible at a much more reasonable price than was formerly charged to have the material enlarged on paper and used elsewhere. Whether or not it will become economically practicable to send reproductions of books by wire or wireless from one library to another on a large scale is still a question.

But the author feels that greater development in interlibrary cooperation is bound to come about in the years ahead. Efforts to collect little-used material by the average academic library will be reduced, and copies in cooperative storage or in specialized collections elsewhere will be counted upon instead. Centralized or co-operative cataloguing should expand, as should interlibrary loan work and joint-acquisition programs.

It is suggested that this interlibrary cooperation will mean that the use of materials by readers in the library will increase, not decrease, as the years go by and that the average amount of square footage used per reader will increase in order to make provision for the special equipment required; that with the persistent increase in the productions of the printing press, library collections will continue to grow in spite of the increased use of reproductions and interlibrary borrowing. But the percentage of increase in the size of collections in their original form will gradually slow up as more and more libraries have acquired good basic collections in the fields that they cover and are reasonably adequate for the demands they intend to supply.

The author makes the following prognostications with the full realization that they are dangerous, that details can be easily confuted, and that they should not be taken too literally or specifically for any one institution. It should be emphasized that each institution is and should be different from others and a law unto itself as far as is financially practicable.

1. The average strictly undergraduate library will continue to grow in the size and bulk of its collections and therefore its storage requirements, but its net increase, certainly by the time it approaches the half million mark, will, because of new developments, such as interlibrary cooperation, greater reliance on other libraries for little-used material, microreproductions of one kind or another, and other mechanical developments, be reduced to something like 2 per cent a year. The increase in demand for square footage for seating accommodations will for the next twenty-five years go up at the rate of something like 1 per cent a year, in addition to the increase in the number of students, this in order to make provision for increased intensity of use and for new equipment. Staff-area needs will go up at least as rapidly as the average of the other two and probably more so.

2. The average university library will increase in its space needs for collections more rapidly than will a library for undergraduates for the next twenty-five years, and until any particular collection reaches at least 2,500,000 volumes, that rate is likely to be not less than 4 per cent per annum over that of the year before. The percentage of increase thereafter may well slow up. As was the case with the college library, an increase of 1 per cent of its seating accommo-

dation areas in addition to the percentage increase in the number of students will be required. Increased staff needs will be at least as high as the increase in the collections and in reader accommodations. New machines will take as much space as is used for the staff that will be replaced by the machines.

3. The average large research library, that is, one with over 2,500,000 volumes, if it is already attempting to cover practically the whole field of knowledge, may increase no more rapidly than the undergraduate library group discussed under 1 above, except for an institution such as the Library of Congress, which takes responsibility for the country as a whole. There the increase in the size of the collections will still be rapid, if it has recently broadened its fields of responsibility for collecting and for the service provided for those who do not come to the library itself. The National Library of Medicine now serves something like 10 per cent of its clientele at the library, and a major part of its work is done by mail, interlibrary loan, and through microreproductions; its staff may well have to grow more rapidly than its collections.

As already indicated, these predictions should be considered very rough and should be questioned carefully by each library. They are made not as a guide for a specific library which is planning a new building but as a basis for discussion. Each institution should consider its own special situation, the present size of its collections and their adequacy, the prospects for changes in the quality and size of the student body, the quality of instruction, and particularly its present stage of development and prospects for the years ahead.

One other and very vital phase of the question remains for consideration. How should these prospective changes, particularly those that deal with mechanical installations, affect the planning of the building structure? They require flexibility, because no one knows just what these machines will be, where they will be installed, or the amount of space they will occupy. There is little prospect of their being so heavy or so large that they will require a stronger structure, that is, one that will have to bear heavier loads than standard book stacks. They may well require heavier wiring conduits for electric current, and it will be desirable to have electrical outlets available in more places

FIG. 1.2   Michelangelo's study for the stalls seen in the Laurentian Library (1525–1533), Florence, Casa Buonarroti, no. 94A.

than would have been planned for in the past.

It may mean that in each of the extensive work areas of a large library building perhaps 200 sq ft should be reserved to be made available when required for mechanical installations, one, for instance, at the circulation desk for sorting machines in connection with the circulation work, one in the business offices for business machines of various kinds, and one in the catalogue room for card reproduction. Certainly in a large library, provision should be made for the installation later if not now of a photographic laboratory. This might make greater demands on square footage than any of the other proposals. In the past plumbing connections would have been required there, although they seem to be less important now.

Machines of many kinds tend to produce heat and also require controlled temperature and humidity conditions. They are apt to be noisy, and the walls to their housing should be acoustically treated. It should be repeated, however, that in many cases these installations do not

have to be immediately adjacent to the sections that use them, as the transportation of records may not be a serious problem. But on the whole it is desirable to be able to install them next to the persons who will use the records concerned. The possible requirements for mechanical storage, closed-circuit television equipment, and other developments not yet thought of, should not be forgotten.

This whole chapter then can be summed up somewhat as follows: Libraries will continue to grow; the rate of growth will depend upon local circumstances. The building should be made so flexible that any part of it can be used for any purpose. There are, of course, other general principles to be kept in mind, and they will be considered in the chapters that follow.

Three final suggestions may be made in connection with looking ahead:

1. Read Alvin Toffler's chapter on libraries found on pages 69 to 98 in the report from the Educational Facilities Laboratories, Inc., on College Planning and Building, entitled *Bricks*

and Mortarboards, published by the Laboratories, 477 Madison Avenue, New York 22, N.Y., in 1964.

2. It will not help to make your building a success if you take the attitude of Mary Ellen Chase's father, recorded on page 22 of her *A Goodly Heritage,* Henry Holt and Company, Inc., New York, 1932: "Above all he detested the changes which even in his day he saw creeping steadily over the face of the society he knew. He regarded innovation as a lack of courtesy toward what was old and tried and he set himself to right such disrespect wherever he could."

3. The changes that are ahead of us are not always as new and revolutionary as we think. Michelangelo's study for the stalls (carrels they are called today) seen in the Laurentian Library, 1525–33 (see Fig. 1.2), and the vignette of Ramelli's of the scholar at his book wheel which serves as a frontispiece to this volume and goes back at least to 1588, show that modern library developments have their roots well in the past.

2

Library Objectives and Their Relation
to Aesthetic Problems, Quality of Construction,
Function, and Cost

Introduction

Those concerned with the planning of a new library building should welcome the opportunity that it affords them to face the problem of what the library should do for those who use it. Obviously the building should house the library's collections and the staff and provide accommodations for the readers. But these alone are not enough. Other problems must be dealt with in planning a new structure, and they can rarely be solved without deciding on priorities, which in turn should be based on the objectives of the institution. It can readily be agreed that the library should not be ugly. But how important is its architectural style? Should a minimum of attention be given to the appearance, or should an effort be made to have it harmonize with that of other buildings in the vicinity; or should the architect aim to create an outstanding structure on the campus? Should special attention be paid to its interior design and decoration? Should the construction be of such high quality that the structure will still be sound after a hundred years, or should its life be thought of in terms of a limited period, on the assumption that it will be outdated and not worth preserving after, for instance, twenty-five years? Costs too often must have more influence than one might wish in determining the answers. Financial problems will be discussed in

detail in Chapter 3 and will be treated here only incidentally.

The author is very much interested in all these questions. They must be kept in mind, and during the planning process they must be answered by the institution for which the building is to be planned, either explicitly or indirectly. This volume will not ignore these matters, although it will emphasize functional problems primarily in the hope of assuring proper attention to them. But this chapter, after outlining briefly the essential factors in planning a functional library building, will discuss the relationships between architectural and aesthetic problems and quality, function, and cost, with the objective of making it easier for those who have the responsibility for the decisions to understand what is involved; it will not suggest what the decisions should be, because they must depend on the financial, educational, and other conditions existing in an institution.

In planning a functional building, those responsible must consider certain essential points:

1. Providing quarters that will as far as possible ensure the preservation of the collections. Proper atmospheric conditions—temperature, humidity control, and filtered air—are important here. Optimum conditions can be very expensive, and it must be decided how much emphasis on such matters is warranted by the quality of the collections. The presence of rare

and irreplaceable materials may make the answer obvious. But atmospheric conditions alone will not necessarily preserve the collections. Arrangements that will prevent their loss by vandalism and theft must not be neglected, and again planning is directly involved.

2. Comfort of the readers and staff. Comfort, to oversimplify, might be said to require conditions that enable the occupant to forget about such matters as temperature, humidity, drafts, lighting, visual and auditory distraction, and to go about his work oblivious to his physical surroundings.

3. Convenience. Planning should make it unnecessary for readers and staff to waste time in traveling unnecessary distances or in waiting unduly for service. Traffic patterns, floor-level areas, stairs, and elevators are involved.

4. Space utilization. The fundamental question is how much it will cost to house *satisfactorily* a given number of readers, services to readers, collections, and staff, and how much it will cost to operate and maintain the building during the years to come. This is of much greater importance than the cost per square foot of floor space or of cubage.

Much of this volume will consist of discussion of the problems related to these requirements, that is, the preservation of the collections and the comfort and convenience of readers and staff. Marcus Vitruvius Pollio, the Roman architect and engineer, wrote in his *De Architectura Libri Decem* at the time of the Emperor Augustus, of the three essentials in building which he called *firmitas, utilitas, venustas,* in that order. They might be translated, strength, function, beauty. This chapter will deal with the third and its relation to the first two, quality and function, and also to cost.

2.1 General Comments

No attempt will be made to write dogmatically on architectural style and aesthetics, important as these are in determining the success or failure of a library building. Few librarians, if any, are qualified to decide on them, although some may believe that they are. Often others, directly or indirectly involved in planning, who are no better equipped in this respect than the librarians, have decided opinions on these matters and do not hesitate to express them.

Architectural propriety and aesthetics are not based on an exact science. The struggle to deal with them too often results in more confusion, complaints, and emotional unhappiness than almost any other phase of planning library buildings. They are basic, and they should not be completely subordinated to the functional aspects of building; but the beauty of a building should not interfere with its satisfactory operation. James Thayer Gerould wrote: "A college is, after all, an educational institution rather than an exhibit of architecture," but he went on to say, "There is no incompatibility between beauty and proper functioning."[1] A recent statement by Nikolaus Pevsner, the British author and critic, is pertinent: "Architectural quality is of course aesthetic quality but it is not aesthetic quality alone. The work of architecture is the product of function and art. If it fails in either, it fails in quality."[2]

At the convention of the American Institute of Architects in May, 1963, Dr. Pevsner said that the great ages of architecture have depended "as much on knowledgeable clients as on the flowering of architectural genius," and added that today "clients tend to be too timid." They "take the architect's vision with rather less checking of the fulfillment of the brief than they ought to do."

On the other hand, Donald Canty wrote:

For every architect who follows his vision to the disadvantage of the building's function, there are others who are pushed by the client into doing things which they know are mistakes.

The client must strike a rather delicate balance. On the one hand, he cannot let himself be "controlled" on this point where the building becomes no longer his, but solely the architect's. On the other hand, presuming that he has chosen an architect of some talent, he should not hamstring that talent to the point where he is no longer getting his money's worth in terms of design quality.

In the same article Mr. Canty reports:

The architect stands somewhere in the midst of a diamond. The four corners of the diamond are aesthetics (what the building should look and feel like), technology (how it can be built and its interior environment controlled), economics (the limitations of the budget), and function (what the building is to do).

[1] James T. Gerould, *The College Library Building,* Charles Scribner's Sons, New York, 1933, pp. 20–21.

[2] *Architectural Forum,* 120: 13, January, 1964.

Each corner exerts a magnetic force on the architect, and his outlook depends largely on his response to the tugs of one over the others.

There is nothing in the rules to say that the client can't do a little tugging too, provided he knows what he is about.[3]

A building, even if handsome to look upon, will always be regretted if it is not successful functionally, just as will one which is successful functionally but unattractive or so extreme in its architecture that it becomes outdated while still youthful. This does not mean that a good library building must be traditional in style; quite the contrary—the use of imagination and a contemporary outlook in the planning and design may make a significant contribution toward the success of the building.

Architectural propriety and aesthetics and the program for a new building also, it should be remembered, must be governed to some extent by the financial situation. Dollars go a long way toward determining space both in terms of quality and quantity. To avoid unpleasant controversy which, combined with other complaints, may have deplorable consequences, it is suggested that the architect be told when receiving his assignment that the institution wants as handsome a building as possible, but that there is a definite limit to available funds; within these limits the requirements stated in the program must be provided for and the results must be functionally satisfactory. One of the important considerations in the selection of an architect is the belief that he will be able to design a building that is handsome as well as functional and that at the same time can be built within an agreed-upon budget. The more difficult the problem, the greater the challenge to the architect, and he can properly be told that he was selected because he was believed capable of doing the job required. He should also understand that even what seems on the surface to be good architecture will be unacceptable if it is not functional from the library point of view. He should, however, be prepared to speak up promptly if he is asked to perform a miracle and produce something that cannot be built within the proposed budget.

It is obvious that sooner or later, and probably the earlier the better, some kind of an agreement should be reached as to who makes the final decisions relating to architectural style, aesthetics, and function. Often five different individuals or groups may be directly involved:

1. The architect
2. The librarian
3. The donor, if there is one
4. The institution's administration represented by the president, or, through him, the board of trustees
5. A special committee appointed by the administrative authorities to take the responsibility

Which one of these individuals or groups should have the last word? Certainly, architecture is primarily the responsibility of the architect, but it is obvious that the administrative heads of the institution cannot avoid their share of responsibility and in the final analysis must approve decisions by the architect or others. The institution may, if it desires, delegate the authority and responsibility to a special committee made up of administrative officers, perhaps members of its own board, other officers of the institution, one or more consultants, or a faculty group. It may defer to the donor or may even leave the matter to the librarian. Whatever is arranged, the architect should keep in touch with the librarian or some other person assigned to the task of thoroughly acquainting him with the functional needs of the library, with the understanding that any disagreement which they cannot adjust should be referred to the administrative authorities. The architect should be the one finally to recommend the methods of satisfying these functional necessities as well as the appropriate style and aesthetics. He should of course be selected on the basis of his architectural philosophy, as well as his competence and acquaintance with the problems involved. He is or at any rate should be the "expert" on the team for these matters. His recommendation should be submitted to and approved by the responsible person or persons designated. The functional aspect of the building should be regarded by the architect with as much seriousness as it is by the institution. However, generally, though not always, the librarian or consultant is more familiar than the architect with the details of the functional aspects. The two can, if they cooperate, be of immeasurable assistance to each other.

In all too many cases deference to the donor has brought results which are not always happy.

[3] *Architectural Forum,* 119: 94–95, December, 1963.

This does not mean that the donor's wishes should not be given full consideration or that he should not be kept in touch with the situation. He certainly is entitled to an explanation if it proves impossible or undesirable to conform completely to his wishes. Unfortunately, not enough donors take the attitude that the late Thomas W. Lamont took in connection with Harvard's Lamont Library. The plans and model of the proposed building were placed before him, and he was asked to express his opinion. His reply was simply, "I like it, but if I didn't, I wouldn't say so. I want what the College decides that it needs."

But to go back to the administrative authorities. They have a responsibility to the institution. It is to them ordinarily that complaints will come if the results are not satisfactory. With the shift in recent years from what is often called traditional architecture to a variety of contemporary and modern styles, many alumni of academic institutions have been upset by new buildings. Some of them are tempted to withdraw financial support. Some write letters to the alumni magazines and to the newspapers, doing what they can to arouse antagonism in the hope that it will bring about changes. This statement makes no attempt to claim that architectural atrocities have not been perpetrated in library planning in recent years, but it seems to be true that as one becomes more accustomed to new styles he is less likely to be offended by them.

It should be added that one of the great arguments for modern or contemporary architecture, as some prefer to call it, has been that it can be simple, with good lines, functional, and relatively inexpensive to build and to keep in repair, and that it expresses future needs and hopes. But if the architect goes to extremes in an attempt to produce something different and the results are not functional, are more expensive, and do not stand up physically, there is little excuse for his efforts.

The author is impelled to state, albeit with some hesitation, that he has a distinct impression, gained from wide personal experience and from conversations with other librarians and library consultants, that there has been an unfortunate tendency in recent years (reversing the trend of the first decade after the Second World War) on the part of some of our more capable and well-known architects to attempt to attract attention by glamorous and exciting buildings which subordinate function to other features. They ignore the fact that most academic institutions must choose between a building which is primarily functional and quarters that will quickly be outgrown, will be more expensive, and will be difficult to explain a generation hence when they will require an addition or a replacement. Without question, we need new architectural concepts. We should not object to these concepts just because they are new and different. There is no excuse for unattractive libraries. But is it not still true that form follows function in truly great architecture?

University Hall at Harvard, planned early in the second decade of the nineteenth century by Bulfinch, is now considered one of the finest examples of architecture to be found in any academic institution. It is interesting to note that some twenty years after its completion an authority on college architecture condemned it, writing, "We doubt whether the world contains any other architectural abortion to be compared to this."[4] But he was thinking not of its functional qualities but of its aesthetic aspects at a time when Gothic was in style.

Sooner or later the institution must face the problem of the effect of architectural style on costs. To build a Gothic library today is so expensive as to make its desirability questionable. Anyone who has seen the library in the University of Pittsburgh's Gothic cathedral of learning or the Sterling Library at Yale will understand this point and will also realize the functional problems that may arise from such a design today.

If the architect proposes a slanting roof with unusable attic space not required for the mechanical services and it adds a small percentage to the net cost, its desirability should at least be questioned. If the architect recommends a building that is practically all glass, that will require double windows and also sun protection of some kind on the inside or out or both, the net results in comfort and operating costs should be carefully considered. If irregular exteriors are planned with unduly large amounts of expensive outside wall areas which add to the construction costs, their desirability should be weighed. These points are brought up to state

[4] *North American Review,* 43: 362, October, 1836.

the facts and to call attention to decisions to be made, not to object to any particular style of architecture. It may well be that the additional expenditures are worth while, but they should be incurred with open eyes.

To go back for a moment to the question of who has the responsibility for architectural style and aesthetic problems, it is obvious that in the final analysis responsibility lies with the institution's administration, but that it may be delegated by the administration to any individual or group that it chooses. Leaving the responsibility in the hands of the donor, as we have said, too often brings about unhappy results. If the task is assigned to a librarian or a business manager who has no interest in aesthetics, the end product will suffer. The best solution is probably to select the right architect. He will sincerely want to provide the institution with what is proper. However, he may honestly differ with its representatives on the weight to be given to any particular factor under consideration. Cooperation and understanding of each other's problems by the two groups are prerequisites for the best results. A lack of understanding—that is, misunderstanding—and an unwillingness to consider other points of view are the sources of most difficulties that arise. An architect should not be selected unless the institution is convinced that he will understand these problems. A good architectural or library consultant can sometimes help to bring about a meeting of minds.

From the librarian's point of view, if the building planning can start from the inside, the result should be a better building functionally. For the architect to plan the building with the facade uppermost in his mind before he knows something about the functional requirements, can be a serious mistake. Some architects may be inclined to think that function is secondary and that planning from the inside out is impossible and unwise. While something can be said for their point of view, the result is unlikely to be as useful a library as one that is planned with function uppermost in mind. Functional planning should be considered a challenge. Compromises may have to be made in connection with it, but they should be reached only after the persons directly involved have given full consideration to the consequences.

The Lamont Library building was planned almost completely from the inside out. The architect, when asked to comment on this statement, wrote as follows:

The architect's point of view on "planning from the inside out" should and I am sure does consider that a building is ideally a complete and homogeneous entity and has no inside that can be separated from the outside, any more than natural objects have bones or veins that can be separate from the skin. That the exterior of Lamont fits the inside is not a result of accident but of the disposition of the functional elements inside so that their expression on the outside results in some architectural unity.[5]

This principle held true regardless of the style chosen. The basic disposition of the planned elements was decided long before any final decision was reached in regard to the style of the facades. The architect then made several studies and models, some more contemporary than others, which were presented for review at a meeting of the governing board. From these studies a final exterior design was selected and approved, but this was not done until some time after the major part of the inside planning was finished. The building has proved to be satisfactory functionally, but one well-known architect has commented, "I am afraid it will get no architectural awards." Arguments on aesthetics are like those on religion; they often deal with intangibles.

Perhaps the surest sign of a first-class architect is his ability to design a building which is functional and also distinguished architecturally. But no architect can be expected to accomplish this unless he understands the institution, its objectives, and requirements, and has a satisfactory program on which to base his work.

Selection of the site is an important decision. This will be discussed in section 15.2. The outside of the building should show that it is a library within. Books should be in sight from outside and immediately on entrance. It should be inviting from the outside so as to attract the student to enter. An entrance level no more than one step up will be desirable, and there should be a ramp at the side or another entrance for the use of students in wheel chairs or on crutches.

Other problems are discussed in their appropriate places later in this volume, but attention is called here to several in order to emphasize a

[5] H. R. Shepley, statement prepared for use in this volume.

few basic points that apply to any library. It should be a comfortable place in which to study. It should be well ventilated, well lighted, and quiet. A feeling of restlessness should be avoided, and it should be so arranged that good library service can be provided easily, quickly, and inexpensively. It should be a building in which one can find his way about easily. But these various factors may differ in importance in different parts of a building, according to the specific activity to be carried on in each part.

One of the important aesthetic features is the use of color. Libraries until comparatively recent years were too often drab in their general effect. The walls, the book stack, floors, and furniture, all tended to have an institutional aspect. This conventionality was completely unnecessary. Different colors on different walls of the room can give an effect of larger size. Book stacks of different colors on different levels can add to attractiveness, to say nothing of making it easier for students who go to sleep to recognize where they are when they wake up. There is a good deal of disagreement among librarians and architects and others as well as to whether the colors used should be bright or pastel. Two examples can be named here: the Undergraduate Library at Michigan and Lamont at Harvard. Lamont used more color than was customary thirteen years ago, but colors used in the Michigan Undergraduate Library are much more striking; it is asserted that this stimulates the students and that more study results. On the other hand, some persons believe that quieter colors are more suitable in a library. The matter is for local decision, and that decision is not necessarily irrevocable. Repainting, after all, is possible.

The question of proper proportions and lines is another problem. In general, it has been felt that most rooms should be rectangular, usually not square, and that the height of rooms should properly be related to the other dimensions. In connection with shape, it should be noted that round or triangular, or for that matter, octagonal rooms are wasteful of space, as furniture and equipment—this includes accommodations for readers, services to readers, and shelving—do not fit into them economically. In spite of the unfortunate experiences at the British Museum, the Library of Congress, the Brotherton Library at the University of Leeds, the State Library in Melbourne, Australia, and many others, each

generation of architects again tries out areas that are not rectangular.

Large reading rooms for many years were almost always more than two stack stories high. Smaller reading rooms might be confined to two levels. It was not until thirty years ago, when the University of Virginia Library was constructed at Charlottesville, that a great reading room was built only two stack levels in height. The New York Public Library and the Cleveland Public Library and others built earlier had secondary but still large reading rooms of that height. It has been found in recent years that ceiling heights of 9 ft 6 in. up to 11 ft are entirely adequate for rooms over 125 ft long particularly with the aid of interior decoration, including screens, which reduces the impression of great distance. The fact that many of us have lived in houses with low ceilings in recent years has also had its effect. A further discussion of ceiling heights is undertaken in section 5.1.

Other aesthetic and functional problems of planning library buildings will be discussed later in this chapter. However, it seems desirable first to emphasize some of the important problems that are dealt with in other parts of the volume. Simple lines are aesthetically satisfying. Direct traffic lanes—circulation patterns, as they might be called—are a matter of first importance functionally and aesthetically. Lighting fixtures and lighting effects can make a great deal of difference. Furniture design should not be ignored. Crowded rooms and congestion are no more satisfactory aesthetically than functionally. An open feeling, even if there are no windows, helps to prevent claustrophobia.

The foregoing general comments on architectural style will, it is to be hoped, set the stage for a consideration of special problems which arise in connection with the relationship of architectural style and functional planning. No one questions the importance of producing a building that is pleasant to look at and work in, one that will attract readers, give inspiration, and foster an appreciation of things beautiful. At the same time, no one should question the importance and the desirability of providing a library that is functionally satisfactory. In the last analysis, the architect and the librarian should be equally interested in both, although there is a proper division of responsibility between them. As has already been indicated by the quotation from Mr. Gerould, there is no incompatibility between the two, and in spite of Charles A. Cutter's too well-known statement to the contrary, architects and librarians should *not* be considered natural enemies. If the architect and the librarian really understand each other, there should be no conflict of opinion. The architect, realizing that he must take the first responsibility for beauty and rarely being an authority on the proper functioning of libraries, should leave to the expert on that aspect of library planning at least part of the responsibility and should defer to him in that connection. The author's experience with architects on over two hundred different library buildings has led him to believe that when trouble develops, as he must admit it does on occasion, it is due almost entirely to a lack of complete understanding of the problem by those involved, rather than to their natural incompatibility or to any deliberate crossing of the other's wishes, desires, and hopes.

2.2 Special Problems

Most of the difficulties and misunderstandings that arise between architects and library planning teams stem from comparatively few problems. Eleven of these will be discussed here, not so much in the hope of suggesting definite solutions, as of explaining the difficulties and helping to show what the different points of view are. Some of these questions have already been hinted at, and some of those discussed briefly here are dealt with in more detail in other parts of the book. Other more or less similar problems may arise, and, as has been indicated, the solution should come from an understanding of the basic reasons for the divergence of views. It should be realized, too, that solutions will and should differ as local circumstances differ.

Monumentality. Library buildings have tended traditionally to be monumental in character. This goes back to the importance attributed to them, which has often resulted in a library that is the central, most conspicuous, and largest building on the campus. The donor, wanting perhaps to perpetuate his name, asks for an architectural gem and incidentally a monument. The governing board takes advantage of an opportunity to do something quite special on a campus otherwise pretty well filled with utilitarian buildings and approves, at least in theory, of a monumental structure. The library is probably used regularly by a larger percentage of the students and faculty than any other building, with the possible exception of the chapel in a church-affiliated institution. The architect naturally takes advantage of an unusual opportunity for a fine building. The Widener Memorial building, finished in 1915, has about twice the cubage of a more modern and less monumental building that could be constructed today, which would comfortably house more books and readers and at the same time would be equally satisfactory functionally and aesthetically. Some persons, it should be admitted, will prefer Widener, just as others prefer a more contemporary building. Monumental stairs, which take space and are expensive, can be found in most of the older large university libraries, to say nothing of many of the smaller ones, built before the Second World War.

The librarian frequently goes along with the architect until he finds that funds to provide the monumentality are needed to provide useful square footage for library purposes; then he protests. Instead of permitting an acrimonious debate to arise, the various points of view should be assembled and some agreement reached on what is most important for the particular institution as a whole. If each one is given an opportunity to present his opinion, he should be willing to consider and understand the divergent views.

Irregular Building Shapes. A rectangular building, whether plain or ornamental, may seem to be more difficult to make distinctive than one with irregular walls which can emphasize patterns and bring light and shadow into play. A large building with a projecting wing on each side may be considerably more attractive than a plain rectangle, but it can have perhaps 50 per cent additional expensive outside wall which could increase over-all costs by perhaps up to 5 per cent without increasing square footage within. In the final analysis, the shape question should be determined by what the institution wants and is prepared to pay for, with the full realization that irregularity may be desirable because of the site selected, its effect on the scale of the structure, or for other reasons. Just because paperbacks are cheaper than hardcover books, one does not always buy them.

Interior or Open Courts. In the past, large libraries were often built around one, two, or even as many as four courts, as was the first of the Library of Congress buildings. This was done in order to provide more natural light and better ventilation, but, of course, it involved more wall area and increased the cost per net square foot. With modern lighting and air conditioning, arrangements of this kind are no longer necessary, and in a considerable number of library buildings, courts have been filled in during recent years to provide more square footage, although because of difficult structural problems involved, the added space generally turns out to be expensive. At the same time it may be space which will increase the usability and, therefore, the value of the existing spaces adjacent to it. The first Library of Congress building and the Vassar College Library are examples of libraries where courts have been filled in. Serious consideration has been given to filling in the courts of the central building of the New York Public Library and of Harvard's Widener building. The Hayden Library of the Massachusetts Institute of Technology with a large interior court open to the sky is an example of traffic-pattern difficulties stemming from an open court. The plan was made necessary by foundation problems. But as a result, one sometimes is required to go around three sides of the building in order to reach a room only a few feet away, because of the court and the desirability of controlling much of the library from one desk. Sometimes in an unattractive urban area an open court is preferable to other outside views.

In recent years an interior court going up two or more floors above the ground level with a roof over it, has been used with good effect aesthetically at Colorado College, and is being planned elsewhere, sometimes in the form of what is known as a "book court" lined with books on two or more levels. This can be very attractive and can give a sense of spaciousness, as does a two- or three-level reading room with mezzanines on one or more sides, but it may present acoustic problems if the lower level is a noisy entrance lobby. It may use up valuable, comparatively expensive, potential floor space without increasing capacity. What is perhaps of greater importance, it may interfere with normal traffic patterns and require additional corridor areas and may increase total construction costs for a given number of assignable square feet, by between 5 and 10 per cent.

The decision in regard to roofed-over or uncovered interior courts is one for local decision when all the arguments for and against are understood. Two advantages that might not be realized at first thought are that they preserve the area for future use and that there will be no architectural style conflict if they are used.

Glass Boxes or Windowless Walls. With the widespread tendency of recent years toward all-glass facades, architects sometimes propose tremendous amounts of glass for libraries. This can be very attractive from the outside, particularly after dark when the lights are on. But librarians have found that very large amounts of glass are not suitable for libraries. They require protection for the comfort of the user. Draperies, vertical or horizontal venetian blinds, tinted glass, wide overhangs, outside screens of metal, concrete, or other substance can, of course, be used to counteract the excess light from the glass, but they are expensive to install and to maintain and at best might be termed "corrective measures." Other incidental problems arise. An excess of glass increases the requirements for the intensity of the artificial lighting. Sunlight is injurious to book paper and bindings. The glass, even special types of it, does not keep out the cold in winter and the heat in summer as well as masonry of almost any kind, and the more there is of it the greater the problem. But some architects in pursuit of the desired effect continue to recommend the all-glass walls.

Examples of an excessive percentage of glass are easy to find: the Air Force Academy at Colorado Springs, the University of Chicago Law School Library, the Brandeis University Library, the north and south facades of the Grinnell College Library, the undergraduate part of the University of Miami Library, and so on. Many feel that these buildings are aesthetically good, but few librarians who have to operate them will vigorously defend this extensive use of glass.

Other architects, however, go to the opposite extreme and propose no glass at all or a very minimum of it, claiming that, with modern lighting and ventilation, outside light is unnecessary. The arguments against glass outlined above are used as an excuse for doing something different. The problem of too much or too little glass is discussed in more detail in sections 9.1 and 9.2 and section 10.1, which deal with lighting, ventilating, and windows, respectively. It is suggested that the comfort of the library users, the preservation of the books, and the costs of lighting and heating can often be deciding factors without any undue sacrifice of the importance of the facade aesthetically and architecturally. Certainly there must be a happy medium which can be found between these two extremes.

Stair Location. Everyone involved will readily admit that the placing of stairs is important both aesthetically and functionally. Stairs can be one of the architectural features of a building, but if so, they must be placed where they can be seen. They are important functionally also and should be easy to find. So far there is agreement. But other problems arise. The position of the stairs should help rather than hinder the control of readers. They should not interfere with traffic. They should not be a disturbing factor, adding noise and restlessness to the scene. Fire prevention, public-safety regulations, and building codes come into play. The design of stairs also brings up architectural and functional problems. In a word, a variety of interests and decisions are involved. Stairs are discussed in section 6.2, dealing with vertical transportation, and in section 10.2, dealing with hazards. They are mentioned here because they are one of the problems where architects' and librarians' ideas tend to clash.

Reduction of Space on the Entrance Level for Architectural Reasons. Another area where architects' desires and functional needs may not coincide is in the size and arrangement of the entrance level of a library. In recent years it has been quite common in office and other buildings, in order to provide a desired architectural effect, but also with functional advantages, to have the outside wall of the entrance level set back from those above and probably those below it, in case there are one or more basements. This practice goes back to Le Corbusier and was promoted by the success of the Lever Brothers building on Park Avenue, New York City. Among other things, it makes possible covered colonnades around a building, providing protection from the weather. It makes the building lighter in appearance, almost as though it floated. It can be very attractive. But it may present a special problem because it reduces the square footage on the entrance level, square

footage that from the library point of view may be the most valuable in the building. One of the great problems in planning library buildings is to make room on the entrance level for the central services. These include control, circulation and reference desks, the reference and bibliographical collections and services, the catalogue, the staff that works closely with the catalogue, and also the current periodicals and the reserve books, to say nothing of as large a part of the seating accommodations and shelving for the collections as possible. As shown in section 5.4, in the discussion of the size and number of levels in a library building, the size of the entrance level is a matter of first importance. If there is a setback here, something inside may have to give, and ideal functional arrangements may become impossible. The Olin Library at Cornell, in order to provide a satisfactory first floor, has one three times as large as the floor levels above it. (See Fig. 2.1.) On the other hand, the Louisiana State University Library in Baton Rouge (Fig. 2.2), and the Washington University Library in St. Louis (Fig. 2.3), for very good reasons, make use of a setback on the first-floor plan. The whole problem is further complicated by the fact that, with an adequate entrance lobby, occupying space on the first floor, the net square footage for space for books, readers, and services is less than on other levels. Additional and undesirable stair climbing, with the resulting noise, confusion, and restlessness may result. No answer is proposed here, but it is suggested that, if the architect understands what is involved, he will in most cases find some means of solving his problems other than with a main-floor setback.

Symmetry. Architects have frequently tended to plan symmetrical buildings, with the main entrance central in one facade. The main stairs were often placed straight ahead in front of the entrance, leading up to a landing where they split and went on to the second floor with somewhat narrower treads on each side. This made it natural to place the main reading room over the main entrance with a central reference desk in it, and sometimes with the circulation desk across the hall from the reading room. On the entrance floor small reading rooms were often placed on each side of the entrance. The book stack generally occupied the rear on all levels. A symmetrical building resulted. In recent years the size of the main reading room has often been

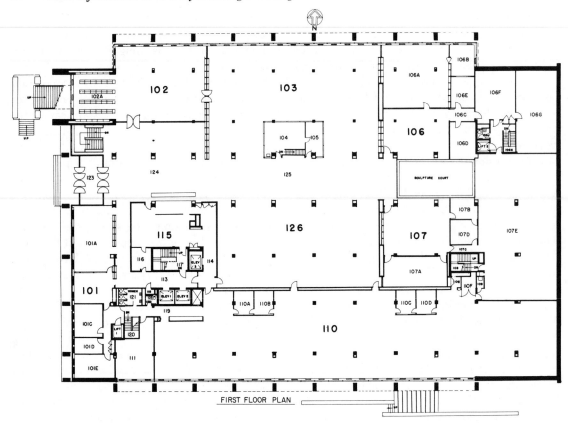

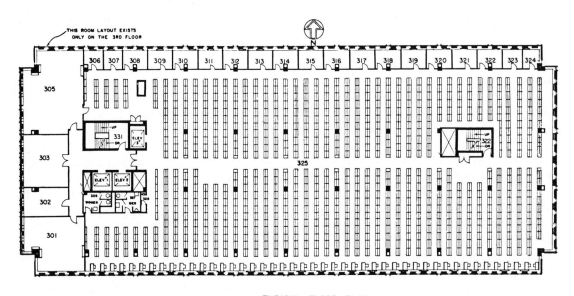

FIG. 2.1 Olin Library, Cornell University. Entrance level and a typical upper floor. The entrance level has more than three times the area of any one of the six floors above it in order to enable it to house the central services and three important special collections. First floor: 102—current periodicals; 103—reference; 110—technical services; 115—circulation; 126 —catalogue and bibliography; 101, 106, 107—special collections. Typical upper floor: 301–305—seminar and study rooms; 306–324—faculty studies; 325—stacks.

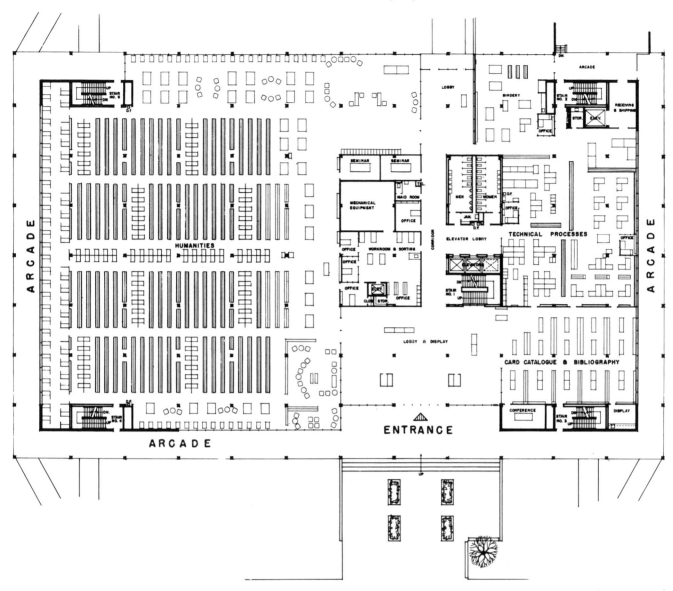

FIG. 2.2 Louisiana State University Library, Baton Rouge. Entrance level with arcade on three sides, reducing square footage badly needed for technical processes.

reduced and the desk brought down to the first floor, but the centrally located entrance, a monumental stair in the center, and a symmetrical entrance lobby still tend to remain and to affect other functional arrangements. No one can deny the aesthetic value of the symmetry. Symmetry has characterized many great styles in architecture and in other arts as well. It should not be lightly abandoned.

But no one can deny that library functions do not always fit into a symmetrical pattern. One can admit the advantages of the Dewey decimal classification with its regular subdivisions with-

out adopting it or continuing its use, and many libraries have come to realize that the Library of Congress classification, which does not have regularity, has its advantages. The problem to decide is whether symmetry or function is more important. In recent years a good many architects have given up symmetry as a prime requisite for the library building as a whole. Lamont's main entrance is not centered. Its circulation desk is at the right of the main exit as one leaves. On the other hand, its three large reading rooms are symmetrical with pleasant results. If a building as a whole is not symmetrical, this character-

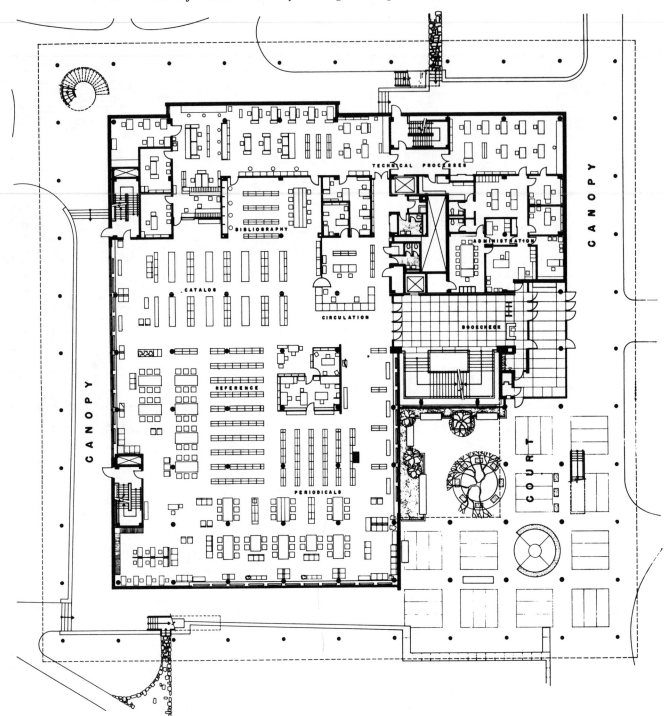

FIG. 2.3 John M. Olin Library, Washington University. Entrance level. This level encloses 55 bays. Levels 1 and 2 below it enclose 84, level 4 encloses 60, and level 5 the equivalent of 67. The entrance level is very effective aesthetically, but the essential services there are unduly restricted, something which could have been avoided if the colonnade area were available for library use.

istic should not interfere with a clear and logical traffic pattern.

Symmetry may be a little more difficult to achieve in a small college library than in a university library, because one side of the entrance level may not contain an area sufficient to house the largest single space required. On the other hand, the Grinnell College Library is symmetrical and is functionally satisfactory in most ways. Symmetry in architecture is important, but it should not interfere with satisfactory functioning, and it is certainly less in vogue than in the past. However, in a not inconsiderable number of new buildings, architects are still advocating symmetry and insisting that it is a prime necessity.

Nonavailability of Certain Space Due to Architectural and Mechanical Requirements. One problem that arises in this connection is generally the result of the librarian's not having made clear to the architect the value of wall space, particularly for the provision of individual seating. The prevalence of this problem is not surprising as the space has been used for seating on a large scale only in recent years, and it has been taken for granted by architects that walls should be used for windows, shelving, and heating and ventilating services. This use of wall space required an aisle for access to the books if there were any on the walls and to the tables and chairs on the other side of the aisle. With the increased use of glass on outside walls, too often going all the way down to the floor, the need for heating in the form of radiators or registers at or near the floor level decreased the space available for shelving and made it necessary to place readers at least 18 in. away from the wall and sometimes considerably farther. The author recently saw plans for a building where on one floor, because of excess glass and the arrangements for heating, a full 5 ft of space all the way around the 700 ft of the periphery could not be used for books or seating accommodations, thus wasting some 3,500 sq ft of space which would cost up to $100,000 to construct. The possibility of placing individual tables 4 to 5 ft apart on centers at right angles to the walls and sometimes fastened to them, should be recognized. Up to 10 sq ft of floor space can be saved for each seat so provided if heating services can be installed so that they will not interfere.

Another problem comes from the lack of realization on the part of the planning team that a considerable percentage of the total building area, generally between one-fourth and one-third, is inevitably unavailable for strictly library space assignments for readers, services to readers, staff, and housing of collections, and must be used for architectural and mechanical space. Non-assignable space is a better term. This is discussed in section 16.2. Be sure that everyone concerned realizes these facts of life and understands their significance, but also be sure that non-assignable space does not take up needlessly large areas.

The Question of an Addition. The architect and the librarian, who quite properly are trying to make the structure they are planning as nearly perfect as possible, sometimes find it difficult to realize that the surest thing about a library is that its space needs will grow. In due course and generally in no very long time ahead and long before the building is worn out or outmoded, new space will be required, and the need for a new wing or additional areas provided in some other way will be a matter of importance. A really flexible building is one that can be added to inexpensively, functionally, and without damaging it aesthetically. It is a serious error to plan an architectural gem in such a way that any addition will spoil it.

Two prerequisites to an addition must be kept in mind: space on the site on which to place it and a building that can be added to without serious aesthetic, construction, or functional complications.

No architect should be selected without first making sure that he realizes the desirability and, indeed, the necessity of planning so that a satisfactory addition can be developed later; he must be prepared to plan a building which can be enlarged.

The Differences among Public, Research, College, and University Libraries. Occasionally an architect who is experienced in planning public-library buildings receives an assignment for an academic or research library without fully appreciating that each type of institution has its own distinctive objectives and requirements. Unfortunate features may be frozen into his plans without realization of their functional effect. To mention but a few, a bay size which may be suitable for an open-access college or public library may have 10 per cent smaller book capacity per square foot of floor space than it should have when used for a research or university library with a very large book collection. A module system or a room suitable in dimension for public-library tables 3 feet across and providing 2½ feet on each side for a reader may be a serious mistake for a college and, particularly, a university or research library. A public library may find that high-intensity light in the entrance lobby will attract users, while a college or university library may find that a lower intensity in that part of the building is more suitable, so that the reader will be satisfied with the higher but still comparatively low intensity he finds in the reading areas and book stacks. The public library may, from a functional point of view, get by comfortably with a smaller lobby and shorter circulation desk than a college library with the same capacity, because the peak loads in the former are ordinarily spread over a longer period than they are in a college where students pour in and out at the change of class periods. These are examples of matters to be watched. Each library should be planned with its pattern of use in mind. Unless the architect is briefed, he cannot be expected to avoid what might seem obvious blunders to the experienced librarian or library consultant.

Standard Sizes. Savings in cost can result from the use of standard dimensions throughout the building. One hesitates to call attention to this problem, as it is one where the layman can be expected to be uninformed and the architect to be knowledgeable; yet too many architects and librarians fail, in their search for perfection in the final results, to give proper weight to the financial implications of using nonstandard sizes in construction, furniture, and equipment. Here the solution can come only if the institution, through its president or business manager, makes it clear that, while the institution wants, as does the architect and the librarian, a handsome functional building, it also wants as much for its money as possible without interfering with these results.

To these eleven special problems can be added one that is occasionally even more serious. Unfortunate developments sometimes arise, more often in a public, tax-supported institution than in a private one, where the governmental authority or the source of the building funds and the institution's administration, without consultation with the librarian or faculty library com-

mittee, decide on the amount of money to be made available for a new library, select the architect and the building site, fail to provide time for the preparation of a program or the employment of consultants, and make basic irreversible decisions that almost inevitably bring about poor planning, an unsatisfactory library building, and a waste of funds. If the architect has had experience in library building planning, some of the hazards may be avoided, but if he has had no experience and in addition is not instructed to discuss the problems which are bound to arise with the librarian or a library planning committee, the results can be and have been disastrous. Fortunately, these occasions are rare, but they still take place, generally because of ignorance rather than malice.

Closely related is the problem that has been expressed to the author by a well-known librarian in these words:

> There is still an all too great tendency for a library building to be regarded as an administrative function, as perhaps a job to be assigned to an assistant to a president to undertake it with little regard being paid to practical librarianship. . . . It is far easier to get money for a monumental or memorial style building than for one providing for the day-to-day needs which will make it live as a library. I doubt if this would be the case if the librarian or someone else who could speak with authority was prepared and able to explain the situation clearly and dispassionately to the institution's administration.

Summary

As was indicated at the beginning of this chapter, there is no necessary conflict between functional and aesthetically good architecture. The architect, the librarian, and the planning team should come to understand each other's problems and position and realize that they are working together toward a common goal. Each will have important contributions to make, and each should respect and honor the professional points of view of the others. Such cooperation will eliminate most sources of difficulty between them, which are almost always the result of misunderstanding. It is to be hoped that this discussion of the problems presented above will help prevent such misunderstandings.

3

Financial Matters

Introduction

Financial problems in library building planning fall naturally into four quite different categories: (1) the provision of the funds required; (2) the costs involved in the new construction; (3) the special items which affect building costs; and (4) the financial implications arising from new construction. They are discussed in this chapter in that order.

The author suggests that in dealing with each group librarians keep in mind the widely quoted statement, "The librarian profession as such puts little emphasis on economy; the pressure comes from college presidents and deans when they make up the annual budget." He also suggests that academic presidents have their attention called to the letter of Louis Round Wilson, the dean of American university librarians, written in 1954 for use at the Monticello Conference of the Association of Research Libraries. In it Mr. Wilson says that the presidents need somehow to be convinced that university librarians are not out to see just how much money they can spend but how they can forward the work of teaching, research, and service to which the higher institutions are committed. The author further suggests that architects keep in mind that academic institutions and their librarians are interested in and appreciate the importance of handsome and attractive surroundings, but that they are always under financial pressure to acquire more books and provide better library service. If a choice must be made, function, comfort, and sturdiness must come first, but in spite of this preference, no fundamental conflict exists between architect and librarian if they have good will, a true sense of proportion, and a willingness to consider, as a whole, the problems that they face in planning a new library.

3.1 Provision of Funds

Ordinarily an institution does not go far with planning until funds are in sight, or until it is believed that they will be readily available. There are cases, however, where preliminary building plans should be made as part of the preparation for a campaign to obtain funds. The need for the new structure certainly must be made clear in order that support from one or more sources can be solicited and can reasonably be expected to be forthcoming. A description of services which the building should provide will also be useful.

In the financing of a governmental institution funds may come from taxation—and then the authorities must be persuaded of the necessity—or for private institutions they may come from private sources. Some libraries in tax-supported institutions have, of course, been built with private funds. Federal legislation in the United States now makes government support available, either by loan or outright gift, to private institutions for library building construction, and state and municipal bodies have on occasion provided funds for this purpose. If the funds are to come from a government, generally various hurdles must be taken. The legislative one is perhaps the most difficult, but boards of regents and finance and education departments must not be forgotten. Ordinarily the president of the institution, with the authorization of his governing board, originates the request to the government authorities. Often the question of priority arises between the library and other needs of the institution, and here the decision will probably be made by the governing board, but the librarian should be prepared to present his case clearly and succinctly. One of the first problems involved is whether the building now under consideration will be constructed at one time or whether it will be in stages. This is a matter of considerable importance. The latter plan, if adopted, makes planning more difficult, but it may also have advantages.

If the funds come from a government body, ordinarily a considerable hierarchy must be dealt with before the plans can be completed and approved. They may include not only the chief administrative officers of the government concerned, the legislature, the finance and education departments, and the administrative officers of the institution, but also one or more government architects who are official representatives of the government bodies involved, sometimes as many as four different ones; and, finally, there is the architect selected to work on the actual project. Threading one's way through this maze is difficult, and the institution's administrative officers and librarian should seek all the help they can get to prevent the whole enterprise from bogging down.

Government participation, whether it be Federal, state, or municipal, also brings with it acceptance by the institution of a number of rules and procedures which may add something to the cost and with some of which the institution or its agent may not agree.

If government funds are not available, private funds must be sought. In spite of the unprecedented large gifts to institutions of higher learning in recent years, funds are ordinarily not easy to come by for new library construction. Many factors are involved. If the present library was named for a donor who is still alive, he may not be interested in repeating a gift; he may even be opposed to a new building because his name would not be attached to it. Another prospective donor may well hesitate to give to an enterprise which apparently, judging from past experience, will outgrow its quarters in a short genera-

tion; he may feel that the gift will not perpetuate his name for more than a comparatively brief period.

The rapid growth of libraries brings another problem in its train. A new library tends to be the largest building on the campus and naturally the most expensive, and only a comparatively few persons have the funds to give the whole amount required. Large gifts tend to come as bequests, and a bequest seldom provides for a library because the donor does not know, when a will is made, what the institution's needs will be when the bequest becomes available, and he is more likely to leave his donation to endow a professorship, scholarships, or a new dormitory, which he understands will be welcome at almost any time.

It must be remembered that it is not easy to name a building after a group of donors. We have very few buildings with compound names. The Smith, Jones, Brown, Robinson, and Johnson Library would certainly in time lose all but one name. Sometimes a donor, wanting to gain fame as inexpensively as possible, will offer to pay for a minor percentage of the cost of a new library if the institution agrees to name it after him, but, if his offer is accepted, it probably will be difficult to persuade Messrs. Jones, Brown, Robinson, and Johnson to give large sums to make the Smith Library possible. Certainly, if an institution agrees to name a building for a donor who gives less than the full amount required for the construction, the donation should be accepted with the understanding that the names of the men who make up the total sum required will be recognized by a tablet in the entrance lobby or perhaps better still, with reading rooms, book stacks, or other sections ascribed to them with suitable plaques posted at the entrances of the areas. This arrangement has been used successfully at the Princeton University Library, where up to a thousand individual gifts are recognized in this way, and at the Brandeis University Library, where it was adopted on a large scale. These individual gifts may vary all the way from a few hundred dollars to several hundred thousand. This plan has been used frequently in recent years.

Often in fund raising an arbitrary square-foot value is put on the space occupied by a stack section, a reader, a carrel, a table, an alcove, or a room. This value may properly be based on the project cost, including non-assignable space, rather than the construction cost of the equipment or the specific rooms; that is, the cost of unsalable areas of the building, such as toilets, stairs, mechanical rooms, corridors, etc., can be prorated through the salable areas. The fundraising project then itemizes these proposed gifts perhaps as follows:

Double stack section	. . . . $ 600
Open carrel	 1,000
Typing booth	 1,500
Faculty study	 3,000
Seminar room	 10,000

These gifts are recognized with suitable plaques. The employment of professional fund raisers who know different methods of presentation and appeal may be useful.

In some institutions the library, after having been assigned priority on the list of new buildings, has been made the recipient of funds raised through a special building campaign among alumni and others. If such a campaign is to be successful, it is obvious that it must be well planned and that the needs of the library must be set forth in as interesting and enticing a manner as possible. The librarian must be prepared, if he has any talents in this direction, to do his share or more of the fund raising.

The desirability of obtaining an endowment for a new building, as well as the funds for its construction, should not be forgotten. After Mr. Lamont's munificent gift of $1,500,000 for Harvard's Lamont Undergraduate Library, the Alumni Fund Council agreed to accept responsibility for raising the endowment for the operating costs of the library, and another $1,500,000 was secured for the purpose, thereby relieving the university of a large part of the additional current expenditures resulting from the new building. This question of endowment may be a matter of first importance.

Another possible source of funds for a new building is one or more of the foundations which have become so numerous in recent years. The foundations best known to academic and research libraries—Ford, Rockefeller, and Carnegie—are seldom prepared to make grants for new buildings, but it should be remembered that there are hundreds of other foundations, some of which might be interested in the proposal of a new building.

A well-prepared brochure explaining needs and requirements can be very useful. If a persuasive voice of someone who has a real knowledge of the situation can be added at the critical and decisive moment, it may turn the tide. If the brochure is not printed, at least the required information should be readily available in some form. The experience of President A. Lawrence Lowell of Harvard should be kept in mind. When he was called upon by Mr. Edward Harkness, he was able to pull out of a desk drawer a prepared statement outlining what became, as a direct result of this visit, the Harvard House Plan. Many a college president and even some librarians can tell similar stories on a smaller scale.

3.2 Costs Involved in Construction

The costs involved in new construction may be divided into six, namely for the following:
1. The structure itself, including finishes
2. Electrical and mechanical installations
3. Furniture and movable equipment
4. Bringing utilities to the building and landscaping
5. Architectural and other fees
6. Administrative costs of various kinds

Each of these costs may be affected by the geographical location of the building and most of them by the time—that is, the economic climate prevailing—when bids are taken and when the contract is let. Is it a high-cost area? What are the local wage rates for the various construction trades? Are the demands for new construction great at the time in the particular locality? The effect of the architectural style selected and the quality of construction must not be forgotten, as these may represent a considerable percentage of the total cost.

The Basic Structure. The largest single factor in the cost of a new building is the structure itself. In general in the United States, this will be cheaper in the South than in the North because, on the average, labor rates are lower there, and because heating requirements tend to be lower, although air-conditioning equipment may be a larger item, as may be the cost of transporting to the site material fabricated at a distance. It must be remembered that the midsummer temperature is little if any hotter in the American South than elsewhere in the United States, but since cooling equipment, if available, will be used for longer periods of time there, the charges for electric current and maintenance may be larger. Living standards in the area, as well as the mechanical installations, are important factors.

In general, costs are reduced by distance from large cities where the labor rates tend to be higher, but it is sometimes found that, because there is a shortage of local labor, the workers must be imported from a nearby city day by day or for the duration of the construction period and that city rates prevail and sometimes "portal-to-portal" charges are involved. Some rural areas, therefore, may be more expensive than urban.

If plans are submitted for bids at a time of great or prospective labor shortage, quotations are likely to be high. If the work must be rushed for one reason or another and overtime work is expected, its effect must be considered. In some places where there is a labor shortage, unions may insist on overtime with its increased costs. An important factor in determining costs may be the need of the contractors who are bidding for work to hold a labor force together in slack periods. Under some circumstances they are ready to submit bids which produce a comparatively small profit or none at all. In a few cases institutions are able to take advantage of the fact that a contractor is available who for one reason or another is prepared to make little or no profit on the job. He may reduce his bid because he is an alumnus of the institution, because he has religious or other affiliations, or because he hopes that this assignment will lead to later ones. It should be realized, however, that a contractor who for any reason bids too low and is in danger of losing money may skimp and require special watching if quality work is to be expected. Beware also of the inexperienced or inadequately financed contractor who may not be able to produce and so may involve himself, as well as the institution, in a complicated, expensive, and embarrassing situation.

The clarity of the plans and specifications may have a considerable effect on bids. If the bidders cannot be absolutely sure of just what will be expected of them, they may quite properly add a contingency figure to their estimates in preparing bids or make their own interpretation of the details—a proceeding which is generally inadvisable. This results in extras, and the final budget cost may be 5 per cent or more higher than it would have been with better-prepared working drawings and specifications.

The effect of soil conditions on the cost of ex-

cavations and foundations must not be forgotten. The Massachusetts Institute of Technology Library, built over what might be called tidal muck, presented a serious and costly foundation problem. The Institute had to decide between going down several hundred feet for a firm base or floating the building on a concrete slab. The latter method was selected, and this made it necessary to distribute the weight evenly and build around a handsome court, which unavoidably interfered with traffic patterns and restricted the book stack to one level. The Louisiana State University Library in Baton Rouge, built on Mississippi River delta land, which has low weight-bearing capacity, was forced to excavate a basement to lighten the load, although the construction resulted in a difficult waterproofing problem. The Cornell University Library, placed where rock was close to the surface, found the excavation of basement space expensive, and on that account limited its extent.

Another problem in connection with costs is how to estimate them with reasonable accuracy in advance before the drawings and specifications are sent out for bids. The architect from his experience should be able to make fair cost estimates during the development of the sketches and plans. When the plans are nearly complete it is also wise, even if the procedure is at the institution's expense, to ask the architect to submit them to a professional estimator in whom he and the institution have confidence. This final estimate will then be based on an actual quantity survey, rather than on a cubic-foot or square-foot approximation. Quantity survey estimates of this kind are usually required under architectural agreements for government projects. Estimating is at best an informed forecast; with rapidly changing economic conditions such as have been prevalent since the war, and with inflation an almost constant threat, it is far from an exact science.

Several factors, then, result in different costs under different conditions—location, time, and the need of the contractor for work or his interest in getting the job at the time when the contract is bid. While each of these is important and should be kept in mind, the primary considerations are what the drawings and specifications call for. Those who must provide the funds want to know what the final total expenditures will be. They will be interested also in estimates in terms of square feet, cubic feet, or, more important still, the number of readers to be served and the number of volumes housed. The answers will depend on the quality of construction, the type of architecture selected, and the use made of the space more than on any other factors.

It has already been indicated that construction costs vary widely in different locations. They may be 15 per cent higher in Washington or Boston than in southern Virginia or central Maine. But it must not be forgotten that in any location, stone outside walls for a Gothic building will increase the wall cost perhaps to 75 per cent more than brick, or 100 per cent more than concrete. Of course, the walls may involve only 10 per cent of the total construction cost. It should be kept in mind that air conditioning may add to the total as much as 10 per cent over a ventilation system or 15 per cent over a heating system alone because of space used by ducts and the price of the mechanical equipment. Lighting installations, though they may vary widely in cost, represent only a comparatively small percentage of the total. The floor covering costs may vary tremendously. The same holds for furniture. Further comment will be made in the sections dealing with these specific items. But remember that, if proper care is used, you get what you pay for, and you must decide what is worth while under your particular circumstances. You can pay for beauty, for utility, for comfort, for spaciousness, and for long life. You can pay for monumentality that gives little in the way of function or capacity for books and readers, but may be desirable for other reasons. Many persons who are interested in the aesthetic features and quality of construction doubt that monumentality is ever justified. You should select what you want and can afford; but always remember that in the long run, square footage is the primary item. Great care should be taken to use space to advantage. If you can increase stack capacity 25 per cent by careful planning without interfering with function or giving a congested effect, do it. If you can plan a reading room with one reader for every 25 sq ft that looks just as well and is as functional and spacious in appearance as one with 30 sq ft per reader, why not? If an extra $1,000 worth of time spent in more careful planning will save $10,000 in costs, why not spend it?

Construction costs can be examined from another point of view and divided into eight categories. It seems desirable to discuss these briefly and set them in their proper places.

1. *The inevitable basic costs of the essential features of the building.* Do everything possible to get the most for the money expended. Engage a good architect and obtain a satisfactory bid from a good contractor, who will carry out the work efficiently and without waste motion. Consider carefully the materials selected and the construction methods used. Reach considered and clear decisions and do not wait until the last minute to reach them. Hastily reached decisions are apt to be retracted or modified and can have a serious effect on construction costs.

2. *The costs resulting from monumentality for its own sake.* There may sometimes be a place for monumentality, but many will doubt its appropriateness in a library project. The question here is, are you ready to pay for it if the architect proposes it? The world would be poorer if it had no monuments, but much if not most aesthetic satisfaction comes from beauty and distinction, not from monumental spaciousness that adds little else. Particularly if funds are scarce, monumentality may be seriously questioned, unless its value for the over-all objectives of the building is clearly shown. It may be well to remember the horrors that have been perpetrated in the name of monumentality.

3. *Costs arising from nonfunctional beauty and distinguished architecture.* This, it is suggested, is a difficult problem and the returns, while still a matter of choice, may be so clear and evident that they are often more defensible and desirable than those for monumentality.[1] The costs should be known and understood and weighed against what could be accomplished by using the funds in another way. If one has to choose between marble walls and space for the storage of 50,000 more volumes or an air-conditioning installation, a decision must be made. Those responsible should listen to the architect's proposal, be sure that they understand what is involved, and then act. If an extra $50,000 for architectural distinction will result in students using the library more, it may well be worth the expense. If it will provide stimulation and foster a love for the

---

[1] One correspondent, after reading this chapter, wrote, "Is true beauty ever nonfunctional?"

finer things of life, it may be more important than the space for additional books which are not yet at hand, but for which construction will inevitably be needed later. The answer is not an easy one to find, but the decision should not go by default.

4. *Costs for additional comfort.* These costs may provide comfortable chairs, for instance, or quieter rooms through the use of acoustic materials, that will enable one to forget about the surroundings; lighting as satisfactory as possible; better air conditioning, heating, and ventilation. All these help one to forget about physical things which too often interfere with concentration in study. Some may say that students studied just as much and as well by candlelight or kerosene lamps, with hard uncomfortable chairs, and that the temperature and humidity in all libraries until recent years was certainly secondary to a place to sit. But there is general agreement that, with the knowledge we now have, solid comfort obtained at a reasonable cost is worth while. Again the suggestion is to weigh the costs and know what you are spending your money for if you have to decide, not between two evils, but two goods.

5. *Costs for utility and function.* Utility and convenience, as it might be called, are a bit more tangible. Anything within reasonable limits that will provide arrangements so that books can be found more easily seems unquestionably worth while. Convenient methods of transportation for books from one floor to another save time for the staff and therefore money for the institution. Individual tables which encourage study can be included in this category.

6. *Costs for sturdiness, long life, and lower maintenance.* This is often not fully considered. There are two sharply conflicting points of view. One may say that if, by spending $50,000 more on construction, the annual upkeep and maintenance cost will be reduced by $3,000, the expenditure will be desirable, and if, at the end of twenty-five years the building is physically as good as it is now, so much the better. The other philosophy is that within twenty-five years the building at best will be outmoded and no longer functional because of changing educational methods and demands and that the common business practice of counting on a depreciating asset and inevitable obsolescence should be followed.

Harvard has tended to take the first point of view and sets up a maintenance reserve against each building, through the use of which funds are always available for repair and emergency, and there is no limit to a building's length of life. Massachusetts Hall may be taken as an example. That 245-year-old structure is as good as ever, and indeed, as a result of modernization, far better. It is not the function of this volume to tell the reader which is the preferable philosophy, but to point out the problem and suggest that each institution make its own decision. If it is ready to have its chairs considered expendable and to throw them out after fifteen years and replace them with chairs made late in the 1970s, all right; the point is that this should be a conscious decision.[2]

7. *Costs resulting from wasted effort and space.* This is something a little less concrete and is perhaps easier to point out by hindsight than foresight. It is the opposite of but closely related to the final point—costs of special planning. If lack of planning provides a module size that reduces capacity for books by 10 per cent, little or nothing can be done about it after the bids are let. If poor planning necessitates extensive rearrangement and alterations within a few years, it entails money lost. Sometimes the waste and unfortunate expenditures result from ignorance with no one really to blame. A floor covering proves to be of poor quality because of a change of formula or materials available to the manufacturer. Perhaps research simply had not gone far enough. The writer remembers one of his larger blunders when he recommended cork tile for the sub-subbasement of Lamont, which is 36 ft below the entrance level and well under ground. While he knew that it was not customary to lay cork in such a place, he also knew that it had been used successfully in the Houghton Building, almost as far beneath the ground and less than 100 ft away, and his technical adviser did not discourage him. It proved a bad gamble, with resulting large expenditures for replacement.

8. *Costs of special planning which may save on the*

---

[2] An advisory committee member suggests: "Collegiate institutions should reject the prevailing business philosophy on construction. It just does not fit. If one is dealing with an architect who has many business clients, it may take a while to get him to approach your problems from an institutional point of view."

items mentioned above. To give proper consideration to each category will take time and will cost money but should be well worth the effort. One thousand dollars worth of time and study that results in a module size that saves $10,000 is a bargain. The same amount used in preparing the layouts for seating accommodations is money well spent if it makes available 50 more seats without reducing aisle widths or table space per reader or causing a feeling of congestion. This list could be lengthened almost indefinitely, but the desired results will not be forthcoming without the availability of knowledge, experience, time, and patience. It is hoped that the information presented in this volume will help.

If these eight points are kept in mind and there is a reasonable meeting of minds between the architect and the institution in regard to the needs of the latter, misunderstanding or complications need not arise. Each of the expense categories may involve disagreements, unless the problems have been talked out thoroughly. The architect should, of course, be in a position to advocate changes in the institution's point of view, but in the long run, once the problem is clearly understood, the latter's needs should prevail.

Electrical and Mechanical Installations. These installations in the library may involve from 20 up to as much as 35 per cent of the total cost. The chief factors are lighting, plumbing, heating, ventilating, and mechanical transportation. In each case there is a question of the original cost of installation, as well as costs for maintenance, replacement, and operation.

Even in the American Deep South, heating of some kind is necessary today, and this is true in most parts of the world outside of the United States, although until comparatively recently many libraries in Australia, New Zealand, South Africa, India, and even the British Isles had little in the way of satisfactory provision for heating. Since the Second World War, air conditioning has come into accepted use in many parts of the United States and to a lesser extent elsewhere. It may add 10 per cent or even more to the total cost of the building, although it may make possible certain savings through making practicable lower ceilings, more fixed windows, less outside wall, and more regular shapes. Moreover, even if the need for human comfort does not convince one of the necessity for cooling, its usefulness in prolonging the life of the book and manuscript collections should at least be considered.

Plumbing is another expensive item, but its cost may be reduced if the building is planned so that the pipes are limited in number and shortened by being largely vertical.

Mechanical transportation by means of elevators, book lifts, conveyors, escalators, and pneumatic tubes is the final large item included in the mechanical group. Very large libraries may require a number of elevators. Unless they are automatic, as they generally are today, they necessitate a large labor expense for operation, but automatic elevators are apt to require more maintenance— although not so much now as heretofore—unless they are little used. In this connection it should be noted that heating and ventilating systems, as well as vertical transportation, are more and more operated by automatic equipment, and this in turn means that a specially trained repairman needs to be readily available. To be fully effective, book lifts involve staff members at both ends of the line. Endless-belt conveyors present difficulties, unless they are kept down to the simplest possible terms. Escalators are in use in a few libraries but are expensive to operate and to construct and use a great deal of space. Pneumatic tubes are not without their difficulties. What are known as "intercom systems" are also often installed.

Each of these items is complicated and may involve a not negligible percentage of the total cost of the building. A fuller discussion of these problems will be found as follows: in section 9.1 on lighting; section 9.2, on heating and ventilation; section 10.1 on plumbing; and section 6.2 on vertical transportation.

Movable Equipment, Book Stacks, and Furniture. Movable equipment in a library is no minor matter; it may represent up to 15 per cent of the total cost of the new structure and may exceed that considerably if the book stack, which is largely free-standing in most new buildings, is extensive and is included. Shelving cost in a library with large collections may by itself run to a considerable figure. For instance, if a double-faced section of shelving costs $50 and with the aisles that provide access to it occupies 17 sq ft of floor space, this means $3 a square foot for the shelving. Shelving is discussed in detail

in Chapter 8. In addition to stack shelving, other particularly important and expensive equipment includes such items as special shelving, often of wood, placed in the various reading areas, service desks for the circulation department, the reference librarian, the control desk, and so on. Office equipment, special shelving for periodicals, indexes, and catalogue cases must not be forgotten. The last of these is very expensive and may cost considerably more than 1 cent for each card that can be housed. Tables and chairs for readers generally constitute the largest single item after the book stack. Two to three dollars for each gross square foot in the building is probably a fair average for movable equipment costs, although they occasionally run higher.

The following general comments on equipment costs may be made. They tend to require a larger percentage of the total cost in a low-wage area, and unless equipment can be locally designed and fabricated, it may be more expensive there than in otherwise high-cost areas. India might be taken as an example because steel shelving and other items have in the past had to be imported.

The larger the amount of equipment of any kind that is purchased, the lower the cost per piece should be. In many small libraries the number of chairs, tables, catalogue trays, and other items required in each group is so small that they will probably be too expensive to design and build locally. This means that the library must depend on the standard library-equipment houses. This procedure has many real advantages. The quality and the design, while not always aesthetically pleasing to those belonging to either the rear or the advance guard, will be sound and sturdy. You can count on the equipment's long life, but you can be sure that the cost will be high, partly because the overhead of the concerns involved is large. Fortunately, there is generally enough competition to maintain costs at a reasonable level.

Two of the basic questions to be decided are whether to deal with a standard library-equipment house and whether to select metal or wood for this equipment. These and other furniture and equipment problems are dealt with in Chapter 11.

Utilities and Landscaping. In many institutions today the heating and refrigerating equipment will not be housed in the new library, but in the institution's central heating plant. (Ventilation fans and air-cleaning equipment must still be provided for in the library.) A new library, however, may make it necessary to enlarge a central heating plant or even to install a new one. Wherever the library is located, water, electric power, storm and sanitary sewers, steam if provided from outside, and sometimes chilled water for air conditioning must be brought to or into the building. If the distance is great or if there are special problems in connection with the new installations, these costs may be considerable. It must also be realized that the air-conditioning machinery and other mechanical apparatus will use considerable valuable space, in terms of both square and cubic footage.

Construction of any kind is bound to require more or less extensive landscaping, which should be provided in a satisfactory manner. The total cost is ordinarily not large in proportion to that of the building as a whole. In some cases the institution may do the landscaping with special funds provided for this purpose and with its own building maintenance force, but ordinarily the cost is assigned to the building budget.

Architectural and Other Fees. A major part of the fees are those for architectural and engineering service. (Consultants' fees, which are discussed in section 12.2, should not be forgotten.) The figure varies with the size and complexity of the project. Many if not most of the state chapters of the American Institute of Architects have prepared statements and recommendations in regard to architectural services and compensations. The rates differ from state to state and also with the total cost of the project and the complexity of its architectural and mechanical character. Much of the following is taken from the Massachusetts State Association of Architects' publication,[3] and while rates elsewhere may be higher or lower it indicates a typical situation.

The architect's compensation is customarily based on a percentage of construction cost, although it may be a set fee plus office costs, a multiple of the technical payroll costs, a lump-sum agreement, or a per diem or hourly rate. Usual services performed by the architect for the average building operation include, in addition to

[3] *Architectural Services and Compensation. A Statement and Recommendations of the Massachusetts State Association of Architects, a Chapter of the American Institute of Architects, Adopted Oct. 31, 1951,* The Association, Boston, 1952.

the architectural concept and planning of the library, engineering services for structural, plumbing, heating, ventilation, and electrical work. This work may be performed within the architect's organization or by outside engineers employed by the architect. What are known as "usual" architectural services are ordinarily divided into three groups:

1. Preliminary services, which include: (*a*) conferences to determine the scope of the project, the problems to be solved and the general approach, and the preparation of schematic drawings; and (*b*) sketches, which include preliminary structural and mechanical design, preparation of preliminary drawings of the approved solution together with outline specifications listing the materials to be used, and preliminary estimates of cost.

2. Working drawings and specifications, which include preparation of working drawings and specifications describing and illustrating in detail the work to be done, the workmanship, and the materials to be used; the preparation of structural and mechanical working drawings and specifications; and assistance in preparing proposal and contract forms in securing bids and in awarding contracts.

3. Execution of work, which includes preparation of additional large-scale and full-size detail drawings; general supervision of the work and necessary shop inspections; checking of samples, shop drawings, and models submitted by contractors and subcontractors; issuing orders for changes in the work required and approved by the owner; and checking of contractors' requisitions, issuance of certificates for payments, and final inspection of the work.

The architect's agreement with his client should make clear that the drawings and specifications, as instruments of service, are the property of the architect, whether the work for which they are made be executed or not, and are not to be used on other work except by agreement with the architect. However, in certain types of public work the authority involved sometimes stipulates that the original plans and specifications are the property of the public authority in question. This is also the case for many academic and research institutions. It should be added that no service, oral, written, or graphic, should be furnished by the architect without assurance of adequate compensation.

When the compensation for the "usual serv-ices" is a percentage of construction cost, it is commonly based on a percentage of the final construction cost, including fixed equipment and book stacks, called the "basic rate." Compensation for supplementary services is added to this.

In the schedule of minimum basic rates recommended by the Massachusetts chapter of the American Institute of Architects, the building types are stated in general terms. The particular character of any project must be judged individually to determine where it should be established on the rating scale. A building of a simple architectural character may involve complex mechanical services and a variety of technical problems. The extent of these complications and the study required for their solution should be considered in fixing the applicable rate. (See Table 3.1 for the Massachusetts AIA schedule.) This schedule might be said to represent a fair minimum, below which complete and adequate architectural services cannot reasonably be expected under ordinary circumstances. A preliminary basic rate for a given project can be arrived at by interpolation, both vertically and horizontally across the schedule. Among other factors, long experience and outstanding reputa-

TABLE 3.1. MASSACHUSETTS CHAPTER OF THE AMERICAN INSTITUTE OF ARCHITECTS, RECOMMENDED MINIMUM BASIC RATES*

Construction cost	A rate†	B rate‡	C rate§	D rate¶
$ 100,000	7.0%	8.5%	10.0%	12.0%
250,000	6.8	8.3	9.8	11.8
500,000	6.6	8.1	9.6	11.6
750,000	6.3	7.8	9.3	11.3
1,000,000	6.0	7.5	9.0	11.0
2,500,000	5.0	6.5	8.0	10.0
5,000,000	4.0	5.5	7.0	9.0
For alterations add . .	2.0	2.5	3.0	3.5

* Seven-tenths of each rate is its approximate cost factor, and three-tenths is its approximate fee factor.

† A rate: For structures of simple architectural character, such as industrial plants, garages, warehouses, and repetitive dwelling units.

‡ B rate: For structures of usual architectural character, such as apartments and hotels, banks, institutional buildings, schools, stores and theaters. (Libraries are generally included in this group.)

§ C rate: For structures of individual or complex requirements, such as churches, hospitals, laboratories, and residences.

¶ D rate: For structures of unusual artistic importance, such as memorials, monumental work, and decorative furnishings.

tion in a given field of work may entitle an architect to higher compensation.

Remember that the recommended minimum basic rates noted above are for Massachusetts and that they may differ in your state or country.

Payments for architectural services based on a percentage of construction cost ordinarily become due as follows:

1. Ten per cent of the estimated fee is due as a retainer for services to be rendered in connection with the initial conferences and preliminary studies, at the time the architect is engaged.

2. An additional 15 per cent of the basic rate computed on a reasonable estimated cost should be paid upon completion of the preliminary studies.

3. Monthly payments aggregating, at the completion of the period of preparation of specifications and general working drawings, to 50 per cent of the fee computed on a reasonable cost estimated on such completed specifications and drawings, or if bids have been received, then computed on the lowest bona fide bid or bids.

4. Payments are due from time to time during the execution of the work and in proportion to the amount of service rendered by the architect, until the aggregate of all payments equals the amount of the final fee computed on the basis of the actual total cost of the work including all change orders. The final installment becomes due when the work is substantially completed. No portion of any compensation should be withheld or reduced on account of penalties, liquidated damages, or other sums withheld from payments to contractors.

Reimbursements for incidental expenses and extra compensation for supplementary services become due when the expenses are incurred or the extra work is performed. These are generally considered to include expenses incurred for transportation and living, long-distance telephone calls and telegrams, reproductions of drawings and specifications in excess of five copies, and other disbursements on the architect's account approved by the owner. When the building problem requires them, the architect offers certain supplementary services, such as those below, and he should be paid in proportion to the value of the services rendered.

1. Site development, including unusual or complex engineering design for underground and overhead utilities, grading, streets, walks, planting, water supply, and sewage disposal

2. General surveys of existing conditions to aid in establishing the building program

3. Detailed surveys and preparation of measured drawings of existing structures preparatory to alterations

4. Special analysis or design in connection with exceptional foundation conditions or with unusual structural and mechanical problems

5. Study of special or complex acoustical problems

6. Research reports, cost and income analyses, expert testimony, preparation of special drawings or developed scale models

7. Preparation of record drawings, showing structures as actually built

This long statement is provided to give the layman some comprehension of the financial and other problems involved in an architect's contract. It should not be considered definitive in scale or scope.

Administrative Costs. It should not be forgotten that there are other expenditures which, while representing a comparatively small percentage of the total, may have to be provided for. These include expenditures for the writing of the program and preparing a master plan. Compensation for architectural, engineering, and library consultants should be included here, unless assigned to the architectural and other fees group. The cost of a clerk of works, if one is to be employed, should not be forgotten. Blueprints, the printing of specifications, advertising for bids, soil borings, and also travel costs for the architects or other professional advisers involved in visiting other buildings may also fall under this category of expenditure. Building permits are generally the responsibility of the general contractor. Moving the books to the new structure and other related library costs, as well as the expenses of the planning team, must be budgeted somewhere.

The total of these six groups represents the project cost as contrasted with the construction cost. The latter is usually the major part and, therefore, the one which should be determined with the greater accuracy. But all of them should be estimated as closely as possible. The project cost must at best be an informed forecast. Estimating is an art, not an exact science. Unless a satisfactory estimate can be made, the institution may find when the bids are opened that the cost is greater than anticipated and that it is impossible to go ahead with the building, or that its size or quality must be cut down at the last moment; to curtail either may be disastrous.

Estimating Procedures. A good estimating procedure in a library project might include the following:

1. With the schematic sketches, a square-foot construction estimate is made based on buildings similar as far as size and complexity and layout and location are concerned, together with a mechanical-installation-cost forecast prepared by the engineers.

2. At the time of completing sketches, a professional estimator or a responsible general contractor should be engaged to prepare an actual quantity survey from the architect's sketches. The engineers at this time may also consult with mechanical subcontractors and prepare a revised estimate for their work.

3. When the working drawings are about three-fourths completed, the estimator should be engaged to recheck the estimate he had previously prepared against the later developments in the architectural drawings and specifications, and the engineers should again resurvey the work against their sketch estimate.

In all of these estimates a proper contingency should be used which should be as high as 10 per cent in the preliminary figures and could be as low as 5 per cent in the final estimates. It is believed that if this estimating is done conscientiously by competent persons, a project will rarely be unable to proceed because of the need for additional funds. It is wise in all cases, however, to have the plans so prepared that some part of the building or finish or equipment may be omitted if estimates run somewhat higher than anticipated.

If there is some question at the time of bidding as to the building market, alternates are frequently included in the bidding which will indicate accurately the monetary value of the construction or finishing of some specified part or parts of the proposed building.

In any case, a careful and accurate estimate must be made at some time, based on a quantity survey, rather than on square-foot costs, in order to insure the institution as far as possible against finding when the bids are opened that the construction cost is greater than anticipated and that it is difficult or impossible to go ahead with the project.

To attempt to give here any precise cost figures is extremely dangerous, because it is practically impossible to avoid misunderstanding and misinterpretation. Wishful thinking too often leads those involved to think that costs can just as well be less than should be expected. But beyond this human failing are three cogent and concrete reasons for misunderstanding:

1. Anything that is true and accurate today may not and probably will not be true tomorrow. Whether we like it or not, we are living in an inflationary age; ever since the middle thirties costs have tended to go up several per cent almost every year, and there is good reason to expect this trend to continue. If bids for your proposed new structures are not to be called for until three years from now, it is wise to add to your best estimate of present cost a contingency figure for this purpose.

2. Costs may vary considerably from place to place because of local labor conditions and building codes, to say nothing of building practices.

3. Each institution does and should decide for itself, with the aid, of course, of the architect, what type of construction and architecture and materials it is prepared to use; these have a great influence on costs.

A rare-book library, planned as an architectural gem to attract gifts, may properly cost much more per square foot than a one-story library structure for a poor struggling rural college that will have few if any irreplaceable volumes in its collection and may be able to use non-fire-resistant construction without building-code restrictions.

Some college and university libraries have been built since the war for as little as $15 per square foot of floor space when all six categories of costs are included; for others the figures have been over $40 for the same amount of space. The differences have been caused for the most part by the three variables just mentioned.

The total project cost can be estimated on an over-all basis, or it can be broken down into separate figures for each of the six categories. The final results, in addition to being recorded as six separate figures or a single total, may also be reported for the sake of comparison with other buildings as so much per cubic foot of enclosed space—the general practice in the past —or, as is more often the case today, as so much per square foot of floor space. Of perhaps even greater usefulness from the librarian's point of view, in the writer's opinion, is the cost per reader and volume housed satisfactorily. It is suggested that emphasis be placed on the word "satisfactorily." A building that has accommodations for 200 readers but can seat comfortably only 150 is not recommended, any more than one which, because its stack capacity has been exaggerated by overestimating the number of volumes that can be shelved in a standard section, claims to be able to house 200,000 volumes when it will be uncomfortably full with 150,000. Self-deception on items like these seldom helps anyone.

The cubic-foot figure was in common use early in the century. Since then, with the reduction in cubage because of the low ceilings made possible by modern lighting and ventilation, the shift to square footage has become almost universal. With it, largely because of increased costs, which have been all too difficult to meet in many institutions, has come more and more emphasis on improved utilization of square footage. Some economically minded librarians and architects have wisely become interested in the square footage required to house readers and books and provide the services for them in a completely satisfactory manner. For instance, if one new library provides accommodations for 200 readers and 60,000 volumes in 17,000 sq ft at the cost of $20 a square foot or $340,000, while another has a more attractive and better-constructed building just as spacious in appearance, with the same accommodations for readers and books, with only 14,000 sq ft, costing $22.50 a square foot, or $315,000, the latter is to be preferred. In fact, it is this emphasis on better planning and better use of space—both cubic and square footage—that represents the greatest change and advance in library planning in recent years. A library today may house twice as many readers and volumes per 1 million cu ft as one built before the First World War, and may house up to 50 per cent more per square foot of floor space than many built before the Second World War. It should be remembered, however, in this connection, that better utilization of space increases the total cost per square foot because of the additional furniture and equipment —mechanical and other—required; but, if it decreases even more the cost per volume and per reader housed, it provides a net gain. Some observers would venture to say that the results are as good architecturally as in earlier days. The new buildings seem almost as spacious. Their span of life is as great, and at the same time they are functionally better buildings and more attractive to the average student and are more heavily used.

After all these warnings and qualifications, what can be expected in the way of costs per square foot of floor space or for each reader accommodated and 1,000 volumes shelved?

One definite thing can be said. Costs are generally and on the average at least 40 per cent higher per square foot than they were twelve to fourteen years ago. A careful study of average costs around the country indicates that the average academic library built today involves a total project expenditure of approximately $2,000 for each reader housed, plus another $2,000 for each 1,000 volumes of estimated book capacity. This is average. The $2,000 for each reader charges against him not only reading-area space, but that required for the staff that services the readers, the non-assignable architectural space, and also the special facilities such as auditoriums, exhibition rooms, audiovisual areas, etc., which vary greatly from library to library. In a low-cost area with very plain buildings, strictly limited special facilities, inexpensive construction, and careful planning, both figures may be reduced to $1,500. In other areas and with different objectives, they may be increased to $2,500 or even more.

These figures will represent the total project cost. They provide for a reasonable number of special accommodations for faculty studies, a limited number of seminars, a map room and a rare-book room in the larger buildings, and possibly a small auditorium and facilities for audiovisual work. Please remember that these are indications only.

The average building even today probably costs at least 10 per cent more than it would if it were more carefully planned with a carefully selected bay size.

Other warnings seem necessary. A library with a small book collection to which a large student body has completely free access should not shelve as many volumes to the square foot as a research library with comparatively few books in open stacks. The percentage of non-assignable or architectural space may well be larger in the small library. The addition of special facilities to a small library seems to add more rapidly to the percentage of space not useful for housing of readers and books than it does in a large library. On the other hand, small libraries on one or two floors may cost less per square foot of floor space than a larger building. These are but a few of the complications that must be kept in mind. A good library consultant can often be useful at this stage in explaining pitfalls that may be encountered and possible ways of avoiding them.

One final word on estimating costs. Remember that wishful thinking is a natural tendency for many persons. Too often many costs are underestimated even by professionals, either because of a desire to encompass the total program within a predetermined budget or because of an unwillingness to face facts. On the other hand, to overestimate and not use all available funds sometimes results in leaving out a much needed extra stairwell or such an essential facility as a service elevator and in providing a book lift in its stead. Every effort should be made to strike a happy medium in estimating. The architect should realize that good estimating will raise his standing with his clients and prospective clients. A librarian who is even indirectly involved in underestimating may lose face with his superiors and find it even more difficult to obtain additional sums later for other library purposes.

Library building costs have been tabulated from time to time in various forms and places. Those for individual libraries are often recorded in library periodicals. While these may be helpful, it should always be remembered that they may not include each of the six categories of expenditure discussed in this chapter and are too often on that account not comparable to each other. And do not forget the three basic cost factors: (1) time of construction and the economic climate when bids are submitted, which result in wide variations; (2) the location of the building and the site problems; and (3) the type of architecture and the quality of materials used. In other words, it is difficult and seldom useful to compare apples with pears, to say nothing of peaches.

3.3 Special Factors Which Affect Building Costs

With one exception this section will not discuss in detail special factors which affect building costs. It will list a limited number of them only—there are, of course, others—with just enough comment to explain their importance. The author does not oppose the use of funds for these purposes. Any of them may be desirable, and under some circumstances essential. They all cost money, and under some conditions can be avoided or omitted. The point to be emphasized is that an institution should understand what it is spending its always inadequate funds for, and should choose intelligently if any choice is available.

Some of the factors were discussed briefly in Chapter 2. Others were dealt with in section 3.2, and most of them will be considered again, perhaps from a different point of view, in later chapters of this volume.

The cost estimates that are recorded here are at best rough and should be checked locally.

The total cost of a building goes back primarily, of course, to the number of square feet that it contains, but other closely related factors should be kept in mind. The first has to do with the construction methods and materials used. The higher the quality of each, other things being equal, the better the results and the greater the cost. Outside walls of a building involve both methods and materials. On the average, outside-wall costs may amount to 9 or 10 per cent of the construction as a whole, but there can be tremendous variations according to the type of wall used, not all of which directly affect the prospective length of life of the building. Some of them are of interest primarily because of aesthetic considerations. Here are some wall-cost figures, obtained from one of the large construction companies, that could be applied to the Boston area in 1963. Remember they may be different in other areas and in other years. The figures given are per running lineal foot for a 10-ft-high outside masonry wall.

Per lineal foot

1. Hollow wall. This is a wall with a 4-in. face layer of brick, separated by at least a 2-in. air space from the inside masonry layer, which may be as little as 4 in. thick $35

Per lineal foot

2. A parged wall. That is a wall consisting of two or three horizontal layers of 4-in. bricks with cement parging between the face brick and the inside layers or backup bricks. The backup bricks are sometimes replaced by terra cotta or cinder or cement block masonry units $40

3. A furred wall. That is a wall similar to either of the other two, with furring, and in the case of an air-conditioned building, a vapor barrier on the inside. Furring may be either masonry-block units or metal lath or wood or steel furring strips $50

4. If any of the above walls are faced outside with stone instead of brick, depending upon the quality and thickness of the stone desired, add . . . . $25–$35

5. Precast-concrete walls are also coming into use, but it is difficult to predict their cost. If a more extensive finish than normal is required, such as sandblasting, bushhammering, or special form work, add $2.50 for each side of the wall so finished to an estimated base of $42.50

In recent years a great deal of outside wall construction is of a type known as a curtain wall. A curtain wall consists of a self-supporting metal or other frame faced on the exterior by panels of glass and metal and on the inside, where required, by prefabricated insulating panels. Masonry walls can also be faced with prefabricated panel materials. The comparable figures per running lineal foot for a 10-ft-high wall of other than masonry or concrete construction are as follows:

1. An insulated curtain wall construction may be built complete with supporting frame for $60
2. If large parts of the outside walls are of glass, a single sheet of plate glass will cost $35
3. A sheet of double glazing or thermopane will cost $60

The above gives some indication of the great variation in costs resulting from different types of walls.

It should be remembered that there is another cost factor, based primarily on the ratio of the length of the exterior wall to the inside area. Curved walls and walls with many corners are somewhat more expensive than straight walls. A square building might be said to make the most efficient use of the exterior wall per square foot of floor space enclosed, although it will be longer than a curved wall. For each corner that is turned, a distance of approximately 2 ft should be added to the length of the wall in order to record comparable relative costs. The shape of the building will, therefore, affect the total cost of construction. To use a specific ex-

ample, a building with 20,000 sq ft on each floor with a wall 10 ft high all around would, if square, be just under 141½ ft long on each of the four sides (see Fig. 3.1*A*). There would be four corners, and the complete outside wall would measure 566 ft, plus 8 ft, adding 2 ft for each of the corners; the cost should be figured on 574 ft.

A rectangular building measuring 200 by 100 ft would also have 20,000 sq ft of floor space, but its walls would be 600 ft long, plus 8 ft for

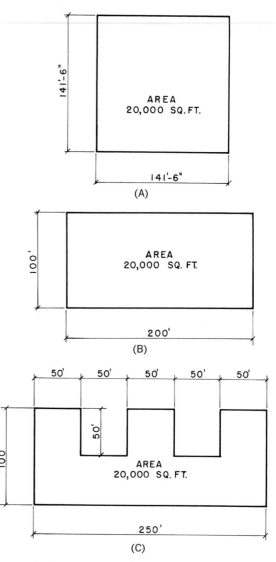

FIG. 3.1 The effect of irregular walls on costs. *A*, *B*, and *C* each have an area of 20,000 sq ft. The length of the outside walls, adding 2 ft extra for each corner, measures as follows: *A*, 574 ft; *B*, 608 ft; *C*, 924 ft. If the cost of the outside wall for *A* is estimated at 10 per cent of the total for the construction, that for *B* will be increased by 6 per cent of 10 per cent, or 6/10 of 1 per cent. The cost of *C* over *B* will be 50 per cent of 10 per cent, or 5 per cent of the total. That of *C* over *A* will be 60 per cent of 10 per cent, or 6 per cent of the total.

four corners, making 608 ft in all, or approximately 6 per cent more (see Fig. 3.1*B*). If the total wall cost of the square building is 10 per cent of the total construction cost, the cost for the second building would be about three-fifths of 1 per cent greater than that for the square building.

If the building were E shaped, as shown in Fig. 3.1*C*, 250 ft long, with a depth of 100 ft in each of the three projections, with the two partially enclosed courts each 50 × 50 ft, the wall would be 900 ft long with 12 corners, so that it should be figured on the basis of 924 lineal ft. This would mean that the outside wall for the E-shaped building would be considered, as far as cost was concerned, just over 60 per cent longer than that for the square building with the same content—or an increase of 61 per cent in the outside wall, or some 6 per cent of the cost of the whole construction. If the construction cost without equipment is $15 a square foot, or $1,500,000 for the 100,000 sq ft in the square building five levels high, the extra three-fifths of 1 per cent for the rectangular one would amount to only $9,000, but for the E-shaped building it would be $90,000, a very considerable figure. It should not be forgotten, however, that changes in the type of wall construction might make an equal or greater difference; that is, the cost of a fine stone building, even if square, might be greater than that of the E-shaped building faced with brick or with one of the other less expensive methods of wall construction.

This statement is not presented in order to argue that the building should be square in order to save $9,000, or that it should not be E shaped to save $90,000. The point to be made is simply that, as this example illustrates, costs mount up. A square building provides more square footage in contents than buildings of other shapes, other things being equal. But the difference between the E-shaped building and the square building costs is little greater than the difference between a first-class brick building and one with inexpensive stone walls. It should also be remembered that the E-shaped building has almost no space more than 25 ft from a window, and its lighting and ventilation problems may be lessened with certain incidental savings in costs. At the same time, its heat loss through the outside wall may be increased considerably in cold weather. The E shape will also increase somewhat the cost of floor and roof

construction. A simple shape in plan and elevation will always cost less than a more complicated one. Those responsible must decide, given all the factors, which they prefer to select.

Interior courts, which used to be common in large libraries, such as the Library of Congress main building, the New York Public Library, the Widener building at Harvard, and the Sterling Library at Yale, go back to the days when natural light and ventilation were much more important than they are today. Such courts are often proposed today, not so much for light and ventilation as for aesthetic or what might be called humanistic purposes, affording a spatial relief to the library as a structure and an intimate attractive outlook for the reader. This may be of special importance in an unattractive urban environment. They reduce available square footage, increase expensive wall areas, and interfere with traffic patterns. When an old library with courts is relighted and air-conditioned, there is a natural temptation, if more space is needed, to fill in the courts, as this provides square footage where it is greatly appreciated and seems a natural development. It has been done in three of the four Library of Congress courts, and more recently in two courts at Vassar, and has been considered at the New York Public Library and the Widener building at Harvard. It turns out, however, that filling in the space is more expensive for each square foot made available than a new wing would be. But the excuse for filling in courts is that the location may make the square footage worth the difference because (1) there may be no other land available, or (2) the space in the heart of the existing building may be more valuable and usable than the same amount of space elsewhere.

The following paragraphs discuss more briefly other items to be watched out for and show where money can be saved. This does not necessarily mean that it should be, but the possible savings should be carefully weighed and decision reached as to which procedure is better to choose.

A cheap flooring material may cost 50 cents a square foot less throughout the whole building than another that might be chosen. If the building has 100,000 sq ft, this may make a difference of $50,000. It should be remembered, however, that the cheaper flooring may be unsatisfactory from the acoustic point of view. It may be unsatisfactory because the cost of maintenance is greater or because it will wear out and have to be replaced in a comparatively few years, and the cost of replacement may be greater than the savings in the original installation.

When it comes to other acoustical material, the question may be a little more difficult to decide. A cheaper variety may last just as long and require no more upkeep; but the problem is whether it satisfactorily performs its other functions and is fireproof.

Increased lighting intensity will in many cases mean a higher original installation cost and greater cost for the replacement of tubes or bulbs; in addition, the increased cost of current may be even greater than the other factors. On the other hand, no one wants to build a building with unsatisfactory lighting.

The cost of monumental stairs may be in the stair construction itself, but a more important consideration is likely to be the amount of square footage involved, which might be used for other purposes. This problem will be dealt with later in this section.

An entrance lobby with 2,000 sq ft of space where 1,000 would be sufficient may, if figured at the rate of $15 a square foot, mean an additional $15,000. On the other hand, if the lobby houses the check-out, control, circulation, and reserve-book desks, for instance, and it is too small to handle the peak loads without congestion, the insufficient space is a serious fault and often one that cannot be corrected later. The lobby should be large enough to provide a satisfactory distribution point from which stem the circulation traffic patterns for the building as a whole.

Complete air conditioning can be expected to add several per cent, sometimes up to as much as 15 per cent, to the net construction cost, even if one takes into consideration the savings in cubage that it may make possible by reducing ceiling heights, but it may be of vital importance in connection with the preservation of books and in making the library an inviting place for students and faculty.

Each additional elevator or book lift has a price attached, although it should always be remembered that it is cheaper to install one at the time of construction than later and that a shortage of service elevators may be very expensive in staff time.

The cost of shelving can be reduced up to 30 per cent by stripping it of finished bases, end panels, and canopy tops, and reducing shelf depths to a minimum, but in many cases economies of this kind are not desirable, and it should be remembered that the cost of the square footage occupied by the equipment is much more important than the cost of the equipment itself. The fact that cheaper shelving is possible does not mean that commercial shelving should be used in regular book stacks; it is more difficult to adjust, and its appearance is much less satisfactory. In most cases the decision can well be based on utility and appearance rather than on cost.

A similar comment can be made regarding equipment of all kinds—tables and chairs and the finishes to be applied to them, circulation desk, catalogue cases, and so on.

All of the above discussion relates to only one of at least five aspects of the whole story. The second one deals with the utilization of the space. If only 60 per cent of the total gross square footage is what is known as assignable or net usable space, you get no more use from a 100,000-sq ft building than from one with 80,000 sq ft where 75 per cent is net usable space as far as the library is concerned. The differences in construction costs alone between an 80,000-sq ft building and a 100,000-sq ft building may come to $300,000 or more, which is greater than any possible difference in costs between the various types of outside walls, floor coverings, shelving, etc. A rough estimate would place the maximum difference between the best interior and exterior finishes and the most economical but feasible ones at only 15 per cent; much more than that often is wasted by an unnecessarily low per cent of net to gross square footage.

This is one of the places where it helps to plan carefully with costs in mind. The extra square footage occupied by a monumental stair, by a circular stair, by an entrance lobby larger than required to take care of peak loads, unless it is used also for exhibition purposes and makes a separate exhibition room unnecessary, may be considerable. A corridor, unless used as multipurpose space, that is longer or wider than is necessary to handle the traffic and to be satisfactory aesthetically, is another example of square footage that does little good. See also section 16.2 on non-assignable or architectural space.

A third important factor is the use made of the square footage available for library purposes. This has already been mentioned incidentally. Here are a few examples:

If reading-room areas are so arranged that one reader can be housed in 25 sq ft of floor space instead of 30, and 1,000 readers are to be seated in the building, this makes a difference of 5,000 sq ft, which at $15 a square foot means $75,000. Of course, if allowing only 25 sq ft per reader results in unsatisfactory accommodations and many seats will not be filled because they are uncomfortable and inconvenient, it makes no sense to crowd them in. But if, by careful planning, readers can be seated just as satisfactorily as in the larger amount of space, why not do it? In this connection, it should be remembered that an increase or decrease of a reading area without changing the number of seating accommodations does not affect proportionately the other facilities of the building; they will still require the same amount of furniture and equipment, the same number of doors, corridors, windows, stairs, toilets, and similar added costs, which prorate themselves over the total square footage of the building.

The same holds for book storage. If, by careful planning and without causing any inconvenience, fifteen volumes can be stored per square foot instead of twelve, and 900,000 volumes are to be provided for, the difference will be 15,000 sq ft, and there may be a saving of $225,000, at the rate of $15 a square foot, in the cost of the whole building.

Sometimes space can be utilized to better advantage by using it for different purposes at different times, that is, making it multipurpose space. For instance, a small auditorium, if properly designed, can be used for a reading area during the examination period when pressure for reading space will be at its peak. Collapsible tables can be stored in a very small area and be made available quickly. Main corridors can serve as satisfactory exhibit areas or can house open-access reserve books if they are made a little wider. It is reported that British schools have been able in the last fifteen years to reduce the square footage requirements per pupil by one-third and the cost per pupil by more than one-fifth, partly by better space utilization in classrooms and partly by the dual use of space.

A fourth cost factor deals with cubic rather than square footage and comes in connection with the height of rooms. Chapter 5 deals with this problem, but it should be noted here that if, in order to place reading areas, book storage, and staff anywhere in a building, greater total height is required, it will cost money. But if the book stacks are all on certain floors with low ceilings and all the areas requiring higher ceilings are on other floors, height and money will be saved. This does not mean that a building should be planned inconveniently for use by readers and staff in order to save cubage, but the difference in cost should be kept in mind in making the decision.

A closely related factor is that if the services to readers are concentrated in one part of a building and heavy book and other storage in another, floors with a lower load-bearing capacity can be used for the former group, and a considerable sum of money can be saved in a large building. On the whole, however, librarians tend to feel that it is better to make all space available for any purpose, in order to obtain more complete flexibility, and those who have tried to economize in this way have too often lived to regret it.

The effect on costs of the column spacing that is selected should not be forgotten. Other things being equal, the closer the column spacing the cheaper the floor construction, but the columns themselves are expensive, and a building 110 ft square with bays 27 ft square will have just over one-half as many columns as one of the same size with bays 18 ft square and only a little over one-third as many interior ones. It is not easy to pick the most economical size bay. As will be shown in Chapter 4, dealing with the Module System, the column spacing may have a great effect on the capacity of the building for housing readers and books, particularly the latter.

The economic factors to be reckoned with here are (1) the maximum use of the resulting net space (a library factor), and (2) the cost of the columns and footings versus the cost of the floor slabs and beam spans (a structural factor), discussed in section 10.1.

Closely related to the column-spacing problem is that of the coordination of sizes of building materials and equipment on a basic standard module of 4 in., which is common in construction work. It can result in considerable savings in field-labor costs on the job by making it possible to use materials produced on a production line in a factory without alteration.

It is suggested then that these five different factors in construction and equipment costs should be kept in mind:

1. Those that deal with the construction itself which are affected by the type and cost of materials used, the amount of outside wall that it takes to enclose the desired area, and the size selected for column spacing.

2. The percentage of architectural or non-assignable space that cannot be used for library purposes; this space includes that occupied by walls, columns, ducts, and pipes, as well as by lobbies, corridors, stairs, elevators and lifts, mechanical rooms, and toilets. It is discussed in section 16.2.

3. The utilization of the space that is available for library purposes to the greatest advantage.

4. Ceiling heights.

5. Load-bearing capacity throughout the building.

These five factors are far from being the only ones. Each member of the building team should be on the lookout for others that should be weighed and discussed so that all concerned will know and understand just what is involved.

To all of these may well be added the costs which stem from asking for bids at what proves to be a disadvantageous time. If contractors are already overwhelmed with work, they are not likely to bid as closely as in times when they are finding it difficult to keep a staff together because of lack of work. Unfortunately, institutional and architectural schedules may not permit speed up or delay to meet the situation. In general, contractors tend to bid low on work in late fall or winter and contracts awarded early in the year often result in lower bids than later ones and may have the additional advantage of making it possible to get the building enclosed before bad weather sets in later in the year. Knowledge of local economic and building conditions may help in selecting the opportune moment.

3.4 Financial Implications of New Construction

Too many institutions become involved in planning new library quarters without considering all the financial implications of the under-taking. Sections 3.1, 3.2, and 3.3 have dealt with the obvious considerations: funds must be provided; an estimate of construction and equipment costs must be made; and ways by which construction costs can be reduced should be considered, although not necessarily adopted.

But there are two other groups of expenditures which may result from a new building and which, in the long view, are often as great as or greater than those already discussed and as difficult to finance. The first of these depends directly on how well the building has been planned as a structure. The second results from the increased use of and demands on the library, which are apparently the inevitable and indeed exceedingly desirable results of an attractive, convenient, and comfortable building. Too often, unfortunately, sufficient attention is paid to neither.

Financial Effects of the Planning Itself. A building can be well planned from most functional points of view, but become overnight a white elephant. Many librarians, particularly those belonging to the older generation, brought up in the days when every library room was supposed to be supervised from the time it was opened until closing, fail to understand the savings that can be obtained by limiting the number of service points that need to be manned during all hours of opening. They have assumed that full-time staff members must be kept at the circulation desk, the reference desk, the reserve-book desk, the periodical room, the rare-book room, and, in a large library, at a number of other areas assigned for special subjects, such as public documents, fine arts, music, a microfilm room, audiovisual facilities, and perhaps divisional reading rooms for humanities, social sciences, and sciences. It is not an overestimate to say that each desk requiring full hours of service results in an addition to the payroll of a sum approximately equal to the salary of a full professor. This is more likely to be the case today with the very long hours of opening which prevail in the average academic library than it was a generation ago; then many libraries closed during the lunch and dinner hours and at 9 or 10 o'clock on weekday evenings, instead of being open from early morning to midnight, as they often are today. Sunday hours of opening are more prevalent and longer than they used to be. Altogether, 90 to 100 hours a week is not unusual. Since there are more and more summer schools, third semesters, or fourth quarters, three shifts of staff are required throughout the year. In view of all this increased use and of badly needed increases in salaries, it is evident that the cost of an additional service desk can well equal a professor's salary.

Careful planning should hold the number of service points to a minimum that will permit the desired type of service to be given. This is not an attack on the divisional plan, for instance, if the institution is convinced that it is worth the cost. It does not mean that students can serve themselves completely, and that there is no such thing as a disciplinary problem today, but it does mean that a considerable amount can be saved if the new library can be planned so that during half the hours of opening, for instance, when the reference load is comparatively light, all types of reference service can be provided from one desk instead of two, or from two instead of four.

If one control instead of two will suffice, so much the better. Seating may be so arranged that reading rooms do not require supervision and an exit check is enough; individual seating, which is used so much today, is a great help in this connection. Microreproduction and record rooms can possibly be served from a desk used for other purposes. A building plan that requires a service staff to travel unnecessarily long distances naturally increases the size of the staff that is needed. Going up and down stairs frequently is a matter of particular importance; it takes strength, energy, and also time, which is always costly. If a library is not a large and very busy one, and the reference, reserve-book, and circulation desks can be fairly close together, one or two assistants may be able to serve all three during meal hours and other quiet times of day.

Efforts should always be made to house members of the processing staff whose work takes them to the public catalogue many times a day on the same level and as close to that catalogue as possible, without upsetting other features of the plan that might be even more important. This point will be dealt with in more detail in the discussion of spatial relationships in section 6.4. It may be that none of these economies would be wise in a particular library, but they should be kept in mind in planning.

The second type of expenditure that may be curtailed by proper planning comes in connection with maintenance and repair costs. Many

of them will be mentioned later in the sections of this volume dealing with the particular features involved, but they are noted briefly here.

1. Items that may reduce or increase building maintenance and operations cost:

a. Janitor's closets with water connections and space for cleaning utensils on each level.

b. Furniture designed so that cleaning under and around it is not complicated and lighting fixtures that can be easily cleaned.

c. Floors that can be kept in order easily without constant buffing and waxing.

d. Window shades, venetian blinds, and draperies that are not constantly requiring repair or replacement or staff attention for opening or closing.

e. Maintenance operations planned so that as large a share as possible of the cleaning can be done during daytime or evening, rather than during night hours when wages may be higher and supervision less satisfactory; janitor's closets placed so they can be used without entering reading areas; and restricted hours of opening for certain areas.

f. The avoidance of too much glass, inadequate insulation, and unsatisfactory protection from the sun through lack of shades, blinds, draperies, awnings, overhangs, etc., each of which affects heating, ventilating, and air-conditioning costs.

g. Lighting costs increased by unnecessarily high intensities, or by too few light switches, making it difficult to cut off light when it is not needed. Time switches, which are expensive in themselves, may prove to be worth while with some installations.

h. Elevators requiring an operator.

i. Mechanical installations so complex that an engineer must be on duty all the time.

j. Too many or too few telephones, which add to current operating expenses.

2. Items which affect repair and replacement costs:

a. Furniture that will not stand up, such as chairs, tables, and catalogue trays with joints that weaken or with finish so poor that it must constantly be renovated.

b. Lighting installations which make it difficult and expensive to change tubes and bulbs.

c. Heating and ventilation problems resulting from inadequate installations, which make necessary constant repairs, to say nothing of opening and closing of windows.

d. Leaking roofs and windows.

e. Floors or floor coverings that require frequent replacement, expensive repairs or refinishing.

The cost of servicing the building and keeping it in good condition may be double in one library what it is in another with the same area. Better planning and quality of construction, although it may increase the original cost considerably, may reduce the total capital expenditures if the long-term view is taken. Remember that if a 100,000-sq ft building has no more useful space than a 75,000-sq ft building, it is better to choose the latter and to improve the quality of the construction.

In connection with this consideration of maintenance and repair expenditures, it is strongly recommended that whenever possible in endowed institutions an additional sum of money beyond the cost of the building and amounting to 20 per cent of it be set aside as endowment to be invested, and the income used to maintain and repair the structure. If there is a single donor and he can be persuaded to add endowment to his donation, so much the better. But remember that munificent and important gifts can become a millstone around the neck if provision for maintenance is not readily available.

Results of Increased Use. A fine new building almost inevitably increases the demands made on the facilities, to such an extent that the staff must be increased. When the Lamont Library for undergraduates at Harvard was made available it was heavily used from the start, but the reduction in use of the old building, Widener, was negligible, and use there is now greater than ever. When the new library at Louisiana State University in Baton Rouge was occupied, the use of the library by students more than doubled immediately. At Cornell the latest reports are that the Uris Library, the old central building which is now used by undergraduates, has an attendance some 50 per cent larger than it did when it was the central library of the university, while the new Olin Library is used by approximately the same number that formerly used the old building, so that there is a net increase in the use of over 150 per cent. At Grinnell the new library has been used several times as much as the old one. The same story can be told about a large number of the buildings erected in recent years. Remember that this may and probably will happen in your institution, and be prepared for the additional demands and the cost of the additional service that will be required.

One might go farther and add that as the library use increases there is also inevitably a demand for a larger collection, which again costs more. The author refuses to admit that this is a vicious circle, although some harrassed treasurers and trustees might be inclined to refer to it in that way. But it does mean that every effort should be made to plan a new building, not only so that it will be functional, but so that its maintenance and service costs will be held to a reasonable figure.

The Modular System

4.1 What It Is and Why It Is Desirable

Under the modular system, as the term is used here, a building is supported by columns placed at regular intervals. Nothing within the building is weight-bearing except the columns, though the outside walls may be. It follows in theory that nothing within the building is fixed and immovable except the columns, though in fact it is generally impracticable if not impossible to shift the location of stairways, elevators, heating facilities, ducts, and plumbing.

A rectangle—usually, but not always, a square—defined by four adjacent columns, is known as a *bay*. The modular building, then, is made up of identical bays, any one of which may be furnished as part of a reading area, filled with ranges of shelving, or divided by partitions into offices; or combinations of two or even three of these may be used. No difficult structural alterations are required when a bay that has been serving one of these purposes is assigned to another; furniture, shelving, and partitions, which may be "dry" and demountable, or "wet" and more difficult to remove, can be shifted.

This flexibility is a major virtue of the modular system, and it appeals greatly to those who have attempted to adapt to changing needs one of the traditional structures characterized by massive interior walls and multitier stacks. There has been a revolution during recent years, thanks in large part, as far as libraries are concerned, to the efforts of the late Angus Snead MacDonald, Ralph Ellsworth, other forward-looking librarians, architects, and

builders; the modular system is now prevalent, although not universally used. It is not strange that a librarian who has been accustomed to and suffered with an inflexible building and then has an opportunity to help plan a new library should be anxious to have it so designed that in the years ahead it will not cause him or his successors to suffer as he has done. He may well decide that while free-standing stacks may be a little more expensive than multitier ones, they may have offsetting advantages, and that inside bearing walls are unnecessary and undesirable and do not reduce construction costs. To sum up, a building consisting largely of space that can be used for almost any purpose without extensive or expensive alterations should in the long run save money and prevent complications which so often arise as space requirements change. The modular system or some adaptation of it is now standard practice in libraries as well as in other buildings.

Like most innovations, however, the modular system is not a panacea; it has its faults and its pitfalls. The fundamental objection is that no one column spacing or bay size is ideal for all purposes; the module that is almost perfectly adapted to one function, such as book storage, will not be equally well suited to another. The writer once suggested that it might be desirable to construct one-third of a library in modules designed for book storage, one-third in a module well adapted to reading areas, and one-third in a reasonably satisfactory all-purpose size. This seemed a more promising procedure at the time it was proposed than it does today, when there is

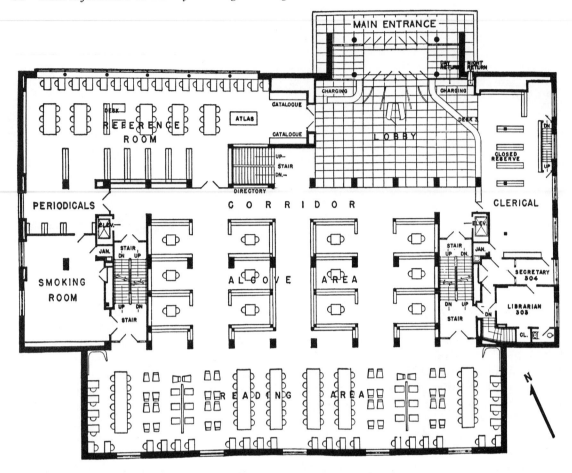

FIG. 4.1 Lamont Library, third level, showing irregular column spacing. The columns are irregularly spaced so as to make possible large reading areas and a lobby without obstructions, but the building is basically modular with columns 13 ft on centers from east to west.

an increasing tendency to bring books and readers together in a single area. A combination of different bay sizes was used in the Lamont Library (see Fig. 4.1) as a means of taking advantage of the useful features of the modular system and at the same time avoiding the handicaps that it often brings in its train. The attempt to obtain flexibility entails certain sacrifices; and some inflexible features, such as columns at regular intervals, remain in any case. At best, the modular system represents a series of compromises, with too often mediocre results.

A closely related complication arises in determining the distances between floors, a problem which will be considered in the next chapter. Here it should be sufficient to point out that, if all space is to be adaptable to all purposes, each floor will have to be high enough for readers, which may entail substantial waste of cubage in stack areas.

Further, if the optimum module size for a new library is based on the present nature of the library's collection and its clientele, it must be recognized that many institutions change and change so rapidly that the size desirable today may be wasteful ten years hence. There may then be an 8 to 10 per cent loss in space utilization, particularly if an addition without change in bay sizes is built. For instance, if a bay size suitable for an open-shelf undergraduate collection with stack ranges 4 ft 6 in. on centers[1] is used for what becomes a large research collection where 4 ft 2 in. on centers may be adequate, some 8 per cent of the stack area will be devoted to unnecessary aisle space.

[1] "On centers" is the distance between the uprights in one range and the uprights in the next parallel range. The term is also used in connection with table and carrel spacing, where it is the distance between the edge of one and the corresponding edge of the next one parallel to it.

Cases could also be cited in which the modular system has caused a librarian to suppose that, since his building was to be completely flexible, layouts did not need to be planned carefully in advance so long as the total floor space was sufficient. The result has been a great deal of shifting that ought not to have been necessary; and it is expensive, even with the modular system, to replace floor coverings, change lighting fixtures, and move temporary partitions.

Modular buildings have sometimes encountered serious acoustical problems because the movable partitions and bookcases on which they depend to divide up each floor have not been adequate barriers to sound.

Finally, it should not be forgotten that the columns themselves are inflexible and may get in the way of stack ranges, tables, aisles, and other features. Very careful consideration of module sizes is recommended as a means of avoiding as many as possible of these complications. Here it should be noted that architects, on occasion, like to use columns as decorative features, but columns that are placed where they will be seen are likely to get in the way.

In spite of these difficulties, the modular system has undoubtedly arrived in library planning, is here to stay, and should be used in most new library construction if it is used with care. But it does necessitate more careful planning if the results are to be satisfactory. Its advantages can be summarized as follows:

1. It simplifies the task of estimating costs and makes the result more accurate.

2. It saves time on the site because materials are acquired in suitable sizes, and it largely eliminates cutting, patching, and wasting materials.

3. It simplifies supervision, as much of the work is routine.

4. It should improve the finished product because more of the work is done under factory controls instead of field conditions.

5. It provides more flexible space adapted for any likely purpose.

6. With prefabrication coming into use more and more, each of these advantages will become more important in the future.

If the modular system is to be used, what should the column spacing be? No one has been able to find an ideal size for all libraries or, indeed, for all parts of even one library, and it is doubtful if anyone ever will. Circumstances

often alter cases in this phase of library building planning, as in so many other conditions. Spacing depends on the library and the use to which it is to be put. If the library is to be primarily for undergraduates, with a very large seating capacity and a small book collection that can be shelved chiefly in the reading areas, spacing is quite a different problem from that which exists in the library that is primarily for advanced research work, with a tremendous stock of books and comparatively few accommodations for readers. It should be repeated also that if a primarily undergraduate college becomes a research institution, what was once a suitable module size will then no longer be entirely satisfactory.

An examination of the module sizes selected in recently constructed libraries shows a tremendous variation from as low as 13 ft in the short dimension to as high as 33 ft or more in the other. On top floors in those instances where only the roof needs to be supported, a much wider space, of course, is practicable. This was the case in the Rutgers University Library main reading room, where there are spans of 83 ft. Recent developments in trusses and concrete have made available very large spans, which are not unduly expensive under some circumstances. In the new Illinois Institute of Technology John Crerar Library in Chicago, much of the weight of the building is hung from tremendous steel roof beams which make possible bays of over 2,000 sq ft and an area without columns on the first floor of some 20,000 sq ft.

The new Lafayette College Library with the aid of special construction methods has been able to obtain spaces as large as 45 × 99 ft separated by smaller areas. Larger module sizes may well be used more frequently in the future.

If the modules are square, with standard construction, they may vary from 16 ft 6 in. in each direction to 27 ft, or in a limited number of cases, even more than that. Almost every imaginable combination between 18 and 27 ft in one or both directions can be found. Some dimensions selected seem to have been accidents rather than the result of deliberate decisions. Some were chosen for reasons which are now obscure and may have been based primarily on the fact that the architect, because he wanted the building to be so many feet long by so many feet deep, adopted a module size to fit those dimensions. The size in more than one library has been de-

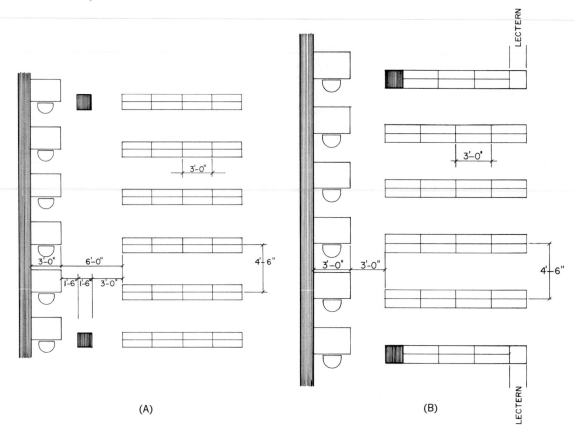

FIG. 4.2 Cantilevered construction in a book stack. (*A*) A cantilevered construction providing 4½ ft beyond the outside columns. This is not wide enough for a carrel and an aisle. (*B*) The cantilever provides 6 ft in the clear beyond the columns, which is room enough for a carrel 3 ft wide and a 3-ft aisle, with book stacks reaching to the outside line of the column. This saves square footage amounting to from 1½ to 3 times the length of the area. Note the use of lecterns in the column ranges at the right.

termined by the size in adjacent buildings, since this may affect facade designs.

Dimensions of the module need not be determined by the total length and breadth of the building; it is possible to cantilever out beyond the outside columns up to at least one-third of the distance between columns and thus increase the over-all building size up to two-thirds of a bay in both directions. This creates no serious engineering problems, but aesthetic involvements should not be forgotten, and careful planning is required to make sure that all the cantilevered space will be useful. (See Fig. 4.2*A* and *B*.)

Perhaps because of the difficulty of deciding on the optimum module size, some architects and librarians have reached the conclusion that almost any size can be adapted to library use and have selected one arbitrarily, failing to realize that the one chosen may reduce bookstack or reading accommodations by perhaps as much as 10 per cent or in some cases even more. If this loss is only 3 per cent in a $4,000,000 building, the $120,000 involved could be used to better advantage, and if, for instance, it took even 10 per cent of this saving to figure out a better size, it would be money well spent.

The other sections of this chapter deal with the problems involved and attempt to state as clearly as possible the points on which the decision should be based. No attempt will be made, however, to find a solution for all libraries or even for any one of them; a choice must be made for each library with its specific requirements in mind.

In a majority of cases in university and research libraries, as distinct from college libraries, bay sizes and column spacing have been determined by book-stack needs, although, as will be seen in section 4.3, they are a factor in other areas. Perhaps the commonest module used in libraries has been 22 ft 6 in. × 22 ft 6 in., with columns preferably no more than 14 in. in diameter. This gives five stack ranges in a bay if they are placed 4 ft 6 in. apart and room for seven 3-ft sections in each range between columns. (See Fig. 4.3.)

Fig. 4.4 shows a 25 ft 6 in. × 25 ft 6 in. column spacing in a book stack. This is a good spacing for a middle-size university with collections of over 500,000 volumes, with a relatively small number of students, not more than 5,000 for instance, or a larger one with access to the stack limited to faculty and graduate students.

Under many circumstances, one of these sizes, 22½ × 22½ ft or 25½ × 25½ ft, is as close to an ideal as can be found. Columns are not too numerous with bays this large, yet the bays are small enough to make it unnecessary to increase the cost of construction and to provide inconviently large columns and thick floors. Because they are square, they permit shelving to be turned in either direction. Other things being equal, they represent economical bay sizes.

But there are many other problems that have been ignored so far, and a much more detailed study seems desirable because bay sizes are basic to all library building planning. This may well start with the book stack.

4.2 The Module Size and Book Stacks

The decision in regard to bay sizes for book stacks might seem to be easier and simpler to make than for reading areas, because in general one part of the book stack differs from another less than one reading area from another; taken as a whole, however, it is the most complicated of the module-size problems, because of the possibility and often the desirability of different depths of shelving and widths of aisle in different parts of the stack. If this were not so, multi-tier fixed stacks, which are discussed in section 8.1, might well be preferable. Since stack layouts will be dealt with in section 16.3, here only the problem of the best theoretical size of the stack module will be discussed. The ten following points should be kept in mind, and it is desirable to delay the final decision until the effect of each on the whole has been considered. This does not mean that the architect must wait for the best solution of all ten to be reached before he starts work. He will probably want to begin making rough sketches that will show him the possible effect of the decisions made later on

the different points and on other areas of the building. It is hoped that this chapter will help both the architect and the librarian to decide what they would like to do. Here, as elsewhere, compromises will inevitably have to be made. The ten points are:

1. The size and shape of the supporting columns
2. Arrangements for housing ventilating, mechanical, and wiring services
3. The length of the stack section
4. The length of the stack ranges before cross aisles are used
5. The depth of shelves and ranges
6. The width of the stack aisles between ranges
7. The width of the main and cross aisles

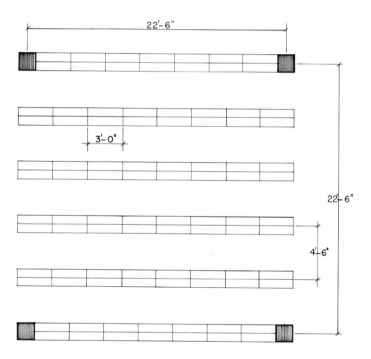

FIG. 4.3 22 ft 6 in. × 22 ft 6 in. column spacing in book stack. A 22 ft 6 in. × 22 ft 6 in. module with standard shelving provides 74 single-faced stack sections,* and 4 ft 6 in. between range centers. (Cross aisles are not included in this figure.) This gives 506²⁵/₁₀₀ sq ft per bay, or 6⁸⁴/₁₀₀ sq ft per section. If 110 sq ft are added for cross aisles, it will amount to 8⅓ sq ft per section, which may well be considered standard. The columns in one bay occupy altogether the space of one section or 1⅓ per cent of the shelving that would be available without columns. Two square columns in the same range occupy the space of one double section. For middle-sized college libraries, that is, those from 800 to 1,500 students and up to 250,000 volumes, this is a suitable size.

* Unless the term double-faced section is used, a section will designate a single-faced section.

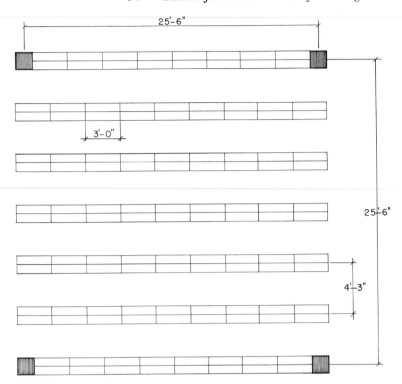

FIG. 4.4   25 ft 6 in. × 25 ft 6 in. column spacing in a book stack. A 25 ft 6 in. × 25 ft 6 in. module with standard shelving provides for 101 single-faced stack sections 4 ft 3 in. between range centers. This gives 650²⁵⁄₁₀₀ sq ft per bay or 6⁴⁴⁄₁₀₀ sq ft per section. If 130 sq ft are added for cross aisles, stairs, and an elevator, it will be approximately 7¾ sq ft per section. The columns occupy the space of one section, and 1 per cent more shelving that would be available without columns. The net increase in capacity over 22½ ft square bay amounts to well over 6 per cent per square foot.

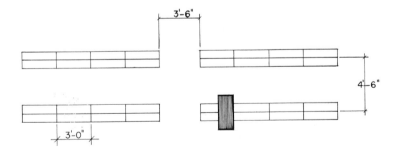

FIG. 4.5   Columns wider than a range. Columns in a book stack should always be in line with the ranges and not so large as to project into a stack or a cross aisle as they do here. They present a fixed obstacle in a traffic artery and sooner or later will inevitably be bumped into by a reader, a staff member, or a book truck. They also often necessitate a stack section of irregular length.

8. The direction in which the stacks run, now or later

9. The clear ceiling heights

10. The type of lighting

These will be discussed in the order listed above, and several of them will be dealt with in other connections elsewhere in this volume. It should be repeated with emphasis that a decision on each of the ten may affect one or more of the others. They are interrelated. Column spacing should be decided with all ten problems in mind.

1. *Column Sizes:* The size of the columns in a library building depends on: (*a*) technical requirements based on the loads to be carried; (*b*) the type of construction; (*c*) whether they enclose heating and ventilation services; and (*d*) their shape.

Older library buildings in general were supported not by columns but by load-bearing walls, both external and internal, except for the concentrated book-storage area in multitier stacks, where the section uprights supported all the stack levels above and sometimes, in addition, the top floor, which was used for other than book-storage purposes, as in Widener at Harvard and the New York Public Library central building. They may support the roof also if stacks go up to it. Multitier stacks are still used and in most cases will be somewhat less expensive than free-standing ones, but the latter are recommended because of the flexibility they provide.

It should be noted that the size of the columns is of importance anywhere in a library, because the larger they are the more they tend to get into the way of activities, services, and equipment. The effect on seating arrangements and other facilities will be dealt with in section 4.3. It is obvious that the columns in a book stack should always come in the line of the stack ranges, not in between, where they would partly or completely block the aisles. It is also evident that if the column is thicker through than the book range, it will partially block an aisle and tend to get into the way of the readers, staff, and book trucks passing through the aisles. Sooner or later one or more of the three will collide with the column and may be injured even if the column is not. This means that the first requirement, if it can be managed, is to keep the columns no wider than the ranges in the direction at right angles to the latter. (See Fig. 4.5.) Range widths will be discussed under 5 below, which deals with shelf depths.

a. WEIGHT-BEARING REQUIREMENTS: The heavier the weight to be carried by the columns, other things being equal, the larger the column must be. The weight to be carried includes the dead load, that is, the floors themselves, which, of course, are heavy, and the live load—equipment, books, and persons—which the floors may be called upon to support. This weight, of course, depends largely on the size of the bay. Books and standard book stacks are heavy. Maps and map cases may be even heavier. Compact storage of any kind, which is discussed in section 8.3, increases the load. Certain machinery is in the same category, but heavy equipment can often be placed on the lowest level, where it may not present a problem. The architect and the builder and engineers should understand the weight requirements and provide for them. Building codes always require a safety margin. If construction provides for 125 to 150 pounds live load per square foot throughout all parts of the library, the floors will hold anything required of them with few exceptions. If bay sizes get much beyond 25 to 27 ft in each direction, the column dimensions and floor thickness may have to be increased and the cost of construction tends to rise correspondingly. If flexibility is desired—and in most cases it should be —it is suggested that the whole building, with the possible exception of cantilevered space, be designed for 150-pound live loads. The extra cost will rarely be as much as 1 per cent of the total cost of the finished building and its equipment.

b. THE TYPE OF COLUMN CONSTRUCTION: Columns are generally of reinforced concrete or of steel covered with concrete or vermiculite for fire protection. Building codes generally forbid the use of steel alone unless protected by concrete, because fire in the building might cause the steel to buckle. It may be impossible to hold a reinforced concrete column to the desired size of 14 in. in diameter if a large bay size is selected or if there is a multistory stack. There are then four variables: the size of the columns, the construction of the columns, the size of the bay, and the total weight to be carried. One or more may have to be changed to suit the situation. A reinforced concrete column takes more space than a steel column protected by concrete, but almost always costs less. The larger the bay, the

stronger and the larger the columns must be, other things being equal. The more floors in the building, the heavier the total load on the columns on the lower levels will be. But remember that a larger column may get in the way and decrease capacity and should be avoided if possible.

c. LOCATION OF SERVICES: Another factor closely related to column sizes deals with whether or not they are to include heating and ventilating ducts. Angus MacDonald recommended that these services be placed in the center of hollow steel columns, thereby taking little or no space that could be used for other purposes and making the services available in each bay or even in each corner of each bay. Most building codes forbid this use of columns because of the fire hazard it would present. Types of column construction and arrangements for services in them are shown in Fig. 4.6.

Types *C* and *F* in Fig. 4.6 require more space than do *A*, *B*, *D*, and *E* and will necessitate more than 14 in. in at least one direction. *D* may also if the number of levels is more than four. In a range that includes two 14-in. columns, the two take the place of one 3-ft section. Thirty-two inches over-all the long way should be sufficient in many cases for *C* and *F*, although at least one

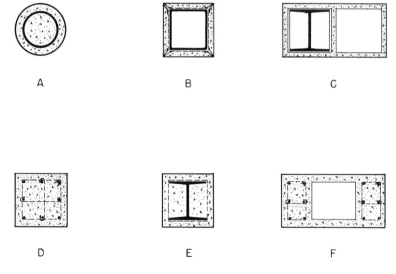

FIG. 4.6 Types of column construction. (*A*) Lally column; (*B*) hollow steel column protected by concrete with services in center; (*C*) divided column with left-hand section of reinforced concrete or steel protected by concrete, and right-hand section enclosing a duct for services protected by reinforced concrete; (*D*) reinforced concrete column; (*E*) steel column protected by concrete; (*F*) column similar to *D* with duct in center with structural reinforced concrete column on each side.

library has columns which include ducts and have a long dimension of almost 6 ft. If 15 in., or better still, 14 in. proves impossible, 32 to 34 in. is a convenient length in the direction of the book ranges, because the column then takes the place of one 3-ft stack section, and irregular length shelf sections are avoided.

Fourteen and 32 in. are used instead of 18 and 36 in., because that leaves a margin of two full inches on each side to provide for irregularities which occasionally appear in column sizes and for the end upright and a finished end panel of the book stacks if one is used.

It should be remembered that if ducts are largely vertical, whether in the columns or elsewhere, they take only a comparatively small amount of square footage, whereas if they are horizontal, they require thicker floors which, in some libraries, have been up to 5 ft in thickness over-all. These very thick floors enable the builder to run the ducts any place he likes without careful planning, but they take a tremendous amount of expensive cubage, and in addition may make a multistory building considerably taller than was anticipated or was necessary. This will be good or bad architecturally as the case may be.

d. THE SHAPE OF THE COLUMN: Should the columns be square (or perhaps round) so that the ranges can be turned in either direction? Or should they be a nonsquare rectangle, longer in the direction of the ranges so that they can be large enough to carry the required weight (and, if desired, the ventilation services) and yet not interfere with the aisles? The question of range direction will be discussed under 8 below. The columns, with occasional exceptions, should be square or round if the ranges are to run in different directions in different parts of the book stack now or later, because, as already shown in Fig. 4.5, they should be no wider than the ranges.

A rectangular column occupying the space of a full section (36 in.) of shelves has the advantage, however, of making the ranges, whether they contain columns or not, end at the same line without the use of odd-length sections and permitting cross aisles at the end of any section instead of only after two 14-in. columns are included in a range. (Since it takes two 14-in. columns to occupy the space of one section, there must be two of them in each range if the measurements are to come out even.)

One other comment about the shape of columns is pertinent. Often a circular column is cheaper than a rectangular one, and in some places it will look better. In a book stack, either one will leave spaces which are difficult to keep clean, unless fillers are used to cover the gaps. In reading areas, furniture frequently does not fit curves. Yet the corners of rectangular columns are particularly vulnerable to bumping and disfiguration. In this connection it should be stated that any column covered by plaster, whether it be round, square, or rectangular, is impracticable in an exposed position, adjacent to a traffic artery of any kind, unless it is protected in some way. It can be covered with plastic cloth, sheet rubber, or even by metal protecting surfaces, preferably noncorrosive, up to the height of a book truck, if not higher. A wide base, which may protect it from most collisions, may be a hazard in other ways.

The problem of column sizes might be summed up by saying that they must be large enough to hold up the building and, if full flexibility is desired, large enough so that any part of the building can be used for any desired purpose. If the building is to be fireproof, they should be either reinforced concrete or steel covered by concrete. The decision on this point may depend upon the cost, but if steel is used, it will be easier to hold the columns to desired sizes, and the additional stack capacity made possible may make up for all or most of the additional cost. If the columns contain most of the heating and ventilating ducts, to say nothing of electric conduits and plumbing lines, they may involve the use of more square footage but considerably less cubage than if these services run horizontally. If the services go up the center of a hollow steel column, they will take little square footage and not nearly as much cubage as when they run horizontally; but this may be forbidden by building codes.

The columns can be square, rectangular, or round. A square or round column will not get in the way of stack ranges if it is no greater in diameter than the depth of the ranges and will result in greater flexibility than a nonsquare rectangular one. Each such rectangular column will probably take the space of a double-faced stack section in each bay, whereas a square or a round one may well occupy only one-half that amount of floor space and may thereby make available one more single-faced section of shelving in many bays. If rectangular columns that are not square are used, the direction of the stack ranges cannot be changed later without inconvenience and loss of space. The bay sizes also are affected because in this case, as shown in Fig. 4.7, they should be multiples of 3 ft, not of 3 ft plus 1½ ft.

It is sometimes possible to reduce the size of most of a column by making it expand near the ceiling. This will not cause trouble, except in a book stack with shelving going all the way to the ceiling. Columns that project into aisles are not completely impossible, particularly if the stack is little used by the public and if the aisles beside them are wide enough to permit passing; but, as will be shown in 6 below, every inch added to a stack aisle reduces stack capacity by approximately 2 per cent. The additional cost of a steel column protected by concrete, beyond that of reinforced concrete, may be less than the value of the space lost by widening stack shelving so that the columns will not project into the aisles, or by widening the aisles to make the projecting columns less dangerous to the users and the equipment.

A further statement relating to column sizes and their effect on column spacing is presented after the other factors which determine module sizes have been discussed.

2. Arrangement for Housing Services: This has been discussed under 1 above, and no further comment is required here.

3. The Length of the Stack Section: The length of what has come to be known as the standard stack section is 3 ft on centers. This gives shelves approximately 35 in.[2] in length, with the thirty-sixth inch used for space required at the end for the intermediate uprights. This is an easy length with which to figure, particularly in connection with the customary 4½-ft distance between range centers, which is discussed in 5 and 6 below, because 3 × 3 is 9 and 2 × 4½ is 9. But 3 ft is not obligatory, as will be seen in section 8.1.

As already noted, if the columns are 14 in. in diameter, two of them, plus the recommended margin for the upright next to the column, will take as much space as a 3-ft section, and with the clear distance between columns being a multiple of 3 ft, there will be practically no waste space. The ranges will come out even with those

[2] This may vary from 34 in. to well over 35¼ in., a difference of more than 3 per cent of the total stack capacity—something worth keeping in mind in selecting the type of shelving.

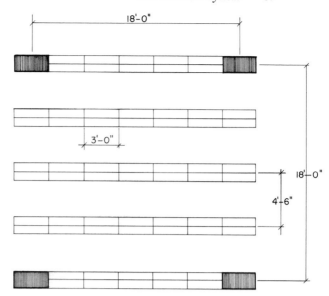

FIG. 4.7 Effect of long rectangular columns on bay sizes. The capacity is reduced by two instead of one section in each bay. The ranges all come out even. The distance between centers in both directions should be a multiple of 3 ft, not a multiple of 3 ft plus 1½ ft.

where there are no columns. The latter have one more standard length section than those which have two square or round columns in the range. This was shown in Figs. 4.3 and 4.4.

There is one difficulty with this proposal, however. The main cross aisles tend to be limited to a few widths, and no one of them may be just right. This problem will be discussed under 7 below.

All of these problems can be simplified if the library is ready to accept odd-length sections when they are required by the column spacing. A 14-in. column may require an 18-in. shelf section to fill out the range. (See Fig. 4.10.) There is nothing impossible about this arrangement, except that an 18-in. section may cost about as much as a 36-in. one, and it complicates planning for shifts of books. It is sometimes advisable to fill out the range, which is 18 in. or less too short because only one square or round column is in it, by hanging a lectern from the end of the last stack section and thus providing a convenient standup reading accommodation for persons examining books at the nearby shelves. This should generally be done in the column ranges only, as a lectern is rarely worth while at the end of more than one range in a bay. But the important point to note here is that if possible the distance between columns should be an exact multiple of the shelf sections' length, plus extra space for stack uprights.

4. *The Length of the Ranges:* There are several problems in connection with range lengths. The first, obviously an important one, is a question as to what length of ranges can be permitted without undue inconvenience to the reader and staff. This matter will be discussed again in section 8.1. It is sufficient here to say that: (*a*) range lengths should vary with circumstances; (*b*) ranges longer than those that have been considered standard are possible, particularly in large installations where the use is light; (*c*) long ranges may increase total stack capacity up to 10 per cent or more; and (*d*) other things being equal, the longer the range or the heavier the use, the wider the stack aisle should be.

A second problem, which deals with column sizes, was discussed under 1 above, where it was stated that if column size in the direction of the range is 14 in. and the range, before a cross aisle is reached, includes two columns, it will not interfere with the cross aisle.

The third problem is that if the module size is based on the distance between columns and

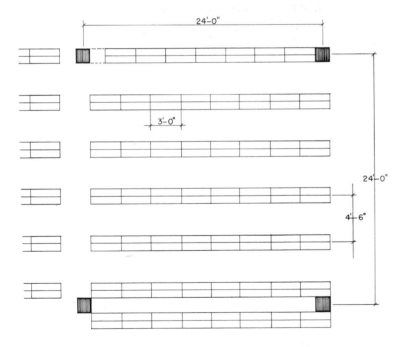

FIG. 4.8 Columns and range spacing fail to gear together. A 24-ft square bay with ranges 4½ ft on centers shows the disastrous results of improper spacing. Ranges with a 24-ft bay should be 4 ft or 4 ft 9⅗ in. on centers, but there is still trouble in the direction of the ranges, unless the columns are a long rectangle and occupy the space of a full section.

hence is a multiple of 3 ft, the width of cross aisles will also normally be a multiple of 3 ft, that is, 3, 6, or 9 ft. This is dealt with in 7 below. But as was noted in 3 above, range length should normally be a multiple of the section length adopted.

5. and 6. *The Depth of Shelving and Width of Stack Aisles:* On first thought one might fail to see why the bay sizes are affected by the shelf depth or, for that matter, the stack-aisle width. But they are, and affected greatly. This is because, if space is to be used to advantage, the distance between columns should be an exact multiple of the distance from the center of one range to the center of the next, and this distance should be determined by two things: the optimum depth from front to back of each range and the optimum width of the aisles. Fig. 4.8 shows the results when this rule is not followed. Many stack layouts have been unsatisfactory and uneconomical because this necessity has not been kept in mind in deciding on the column spacing. The question of range depth is considered in section 8.1, where it is suggested that 16 to 18 in. should be practicable throughout most of the stack.

Aisle widths are also discussed in section 8.1. It is noted there that in libraries with comparatively small collections but with large numbers of students and faculty using open-access shelves, 3-ft wide stack aisles are indicated, and ranges 4 ft 6 in. on centers might be called standard. Any distance up to 5 or even 6 ft may be desirable in locations where reference books or other very heavily used collections are stored.

If 4 ft 3 in. on centers (with a range 16 or 18 in. deep and with a 35- or 33-in. stack-aisle width) is selected, the bay sizes can be 25 ft 6 in., with six ranges installed in each bay, and in the other direction eight 3-ft sections between columns. (See Fig. 4.4 in this section.) A bay of this size has a further advantage. If more compact storage is required later, seven ranges can be placed in a 25 ft 6 in. bay instead of six, giving 3 ft 7⅝ in. from center to center, which is fairly comfortable and certainly possible in the case of little-used material with closed access. On the other hand, with this same 25 ft 6 in. bay, it is possible to use only five ranges 5 ft 1 in. on centers, a useful arrangement in a heavily used section or for oversize books on deeper than standard shelves. In the case of reference books in a reading room, or a newspaper stack, four ranges can be installed, giving 6 ft 4 in. on centers with this column spacing.

A smaller size bay which fits many stack situations and one that, as already indicated, has probably been used more than any other in libraries constructed in recent years is 22 ft 6 in. in each direction. (See Fig. 4.3.) This is the next possible square bay that is smaller than 25 ft 6 in. and is a multiple of 3 ft, plus 1½ ft. It gives approximately 6 per cent less capacity per square foot because the ranges will be 4 ft 6 in. on centers, instead of 4 ft 3 in. It will make possible an increase from five to six ranges which will be 3 ft 9 in. on centers, if at a later time more compact storage is desired, or a decrease to four ranges 5 ft 7 in. on centers for reference books or in other heavily used sections. Other possible bay sizes will be considered later in this chapter.

It should be repeated here that unless range spacing is changed correspondingly, an increase of 1 in. in range depth decreases the aisle width by 1 in. or decreases stack capacity and incidentally increases construction costs by 2 per cent. But it may still be desirable in order to avoid crowded conditions.

7. *The Width of the Main and Subsidiary Cross Aisles:* Here a problem arises in a modular stack that can be avoided in a multitier stack. In a multitier stack it is possible to arrange for aisles of any width desired, so long as those above and below use the same layout. They can be found from as narrow as 2 ft 6 in. or even less for a subsidiary or side cross aisle up to 6 or even 7 ft for the main central aisle. But in a modular stack, if the plan is based on 3-ft stack sections and a multiple of 3 ft between columns, these aisles apparently must be 3, 6, or 9 ft wide. It seems obvious that 3 ft, minus the extra inches occupied by the adjacent uprights, while wide enough for a subsidiary aisle, will not be satisfactory for the main aisle of a heavily used stack. Six feet may be wider than necessary, although in a very large, heavily used stack it may be ideal. Each needless 6 in. in aisle width will decrease capacity of the adjacent bays. In other words, a 4 ft 6 in. cross aisle in place of a 6-ft one will, if the ranges are 30 ft long, increase capacity by 2½ per cent. A 3-ft aisle would save another 2½ per cent, but as already noted, it is not wide enough for a main cross aisle, although it will do very well for a secondary one which is comparatively little used. A width of 4½ ft, or halfway in between 3 ft and 6 ft, is entirely adequate, but ordinarily will not work out if the distance between columns is a multiple of 3 ft. There are two possible remedies to this situation.

a. Make the distance between columns in the direction of the ranges multiples of 3 ft plus 1½ ft in every other bay, and place the cross aisles in those bays as shown in Fig. 4.9, but make no change in the column spacing in the other direction. This does away with the advantageous square bay and flexibility suffers.

b. Use a lectern to fill out any column range that includes only one column. This will permit a 4 ft 6 in. wide main aisle, as shown in Fig. 4.10.

8. *The Direction in Which Stacks Run:* If the column spacing is so designed that the stacks must always run in one direction, a certain amount of flexibility is lost. Is this serious? It may well be, particularly when portions of the stack are used for reading areas, and shelving meeting at right angles would be useful. If the bay is square, there is no reason why all the shelving in any bay should not be turned at will at right angles to that in other bays, except that it may affect both the natural and artificial lighting and will probably necessitate replacement of the floor covering that is used. (See 10 below in connection with the lighting arrangements.) The architect and the librarian must decide whether the extra flexibility, made available by a square bay with its other advantages in economy, is worth while.

Many librarians prefer to have all main-stack shelving run in the same direction and find that if a comparatively small amount of shelving is wanted in other areas with a different orientation it can well have different range spacing and that at worst the book capacity lost is comparatively negligible. A stack with shelving all running in the same direction tends to make the traffic patterns somewhat simpler.

It should be noted that a stack range parallel and adjacent to an outside wall is undesirable if that wall has windows and is so oriented that the sun will shine on the books. This problem can be solved by changing the direction of stack ranges on that side of the building. But such a change may turn out to be a complicated affair, because it also changes the direction of the cross aisles and the traffic lanes. A row of carrels along the window wall and then an aisle may help to solve

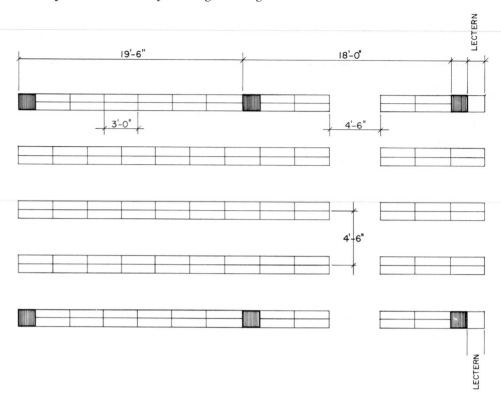

FIG. 4.9   Cross-aisle width controlled by increasing or decreasing column spacing. This figure shows that if the distance between column centers is changed or staggered in the direction of the ranges, with every other row of columns 1½ ft farther apart or closer together than in the next bay, 4 ft 6 in. main aisles become possible instead of 3-ft or 6-ft aisles, but the bays will not be square.

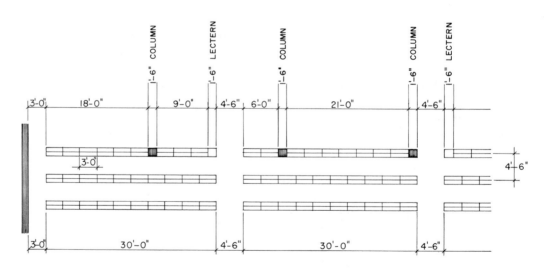

FIG. 4.10   Use of a lectern to fill out a column range. While 1 ft 6 in. is reserved for columns here, the column itself should not be more than 14 in. in order to provide space for stack uprights and a margin for irregularities.

the problem without changing the range direction.

9. *Ceiling Heights:* The clear height of a stack level between the finished floor and the finished ceiling is a bay-size problem only indirectly, but it may be a matter of importance in connection with cubic footage in the building. The lowest ceiling that will permit seven shelves 12 in. apart on centers is just under 7 ft 6 in. (See section 5.1 for a full discussion.) But any space for shelving above 7 ft 6 in. in the clear is useless, except for dead storage, because the top shelf will be 6 ft 4 in. above the floor, and only a tall man can reach it.

It should be noted that a number of recently constructed libraries have built their stack rooms 8 ft 4 in. or 8 ft 6 in. in clear height, with the idea of inserting an extra shelf for "dead storage." This will, of course, increase the gross capacity by nearly 15 per cent, but it is confusing to the reader if it is done in an open-access stack. The extra height may, however, be useful for two purposes other than increasing book capacity. The first is discussed in the next paragraph. The second is that the additional height makes the space available for multiple-seating accommodations.

10. *Lighting:* The effect of lighting in the determination of the size of a stack bay relates to ceiling heights and also to the number of fixtures to a bay and their spacing. In a modern book stack there must be artificial light available in every stack aisle. Normally, the lighting is installed down the center of each aisle in lines parallel to the ranges. If this practice is followed and at a later time capacity is increased by providing an additional range in each bay, the wiring and fixtures must be changed. Or, if it is decided to turn the shelves at right angles for one reason or another, the lighting must also be changed if the ceiling height is only 7 ft 6 in. If the clear height of the ceiling is 8 ft 4 in. or 8 ft 6 in. or more and fluorescent lighting in long strips is used, it can be placed at right angles to the ranges, and the shelves will still be illuminated even if the range spacing changes. The new library at John Carroll University in Cleveland and the Wellesley College Library are examples of this arrangement.

Summary. This discussion of the ten points that affect module sizes in a book stack has brought out the principal problems involved, indicated the interrelationships, and shown that

final decision on column spacing should be made after consideration of all factors. No one column spacing is suitable for all library stacks.

The matter might be summed up as follows: if columns can be held to 16 to 18 in. in the direction at right angles to the ranges, they will not project into the stack aisles or make trouble that way.

If complete flexibility is wanted and the stack is more than four levels high and the columns are more than 27 ft apart on centers, they may have to be of steel, rather than of reinforced concrete, in order to keep them down to a size where they will not interfere with the stack installation. If columns are used for services and these services, because of building codes, cannot be run through the centers of a hollow steel column, they will have to be more than 18 in. in at least one direction, and stack-range direction cannot be changed without the columns interfering with the aisles. The same situation holds if the stack has so many levels that the columns, even if of steel with their concrete covering, must be larger. If the possibility of changing range direction is given up, the columns can be wider in the direction of the range. If they are to be over 14 in., they might just as well be up to 32 in. so as to take the space of a full 3-ft-long shelf section. Of course, if sections of uneven length are permissible or if lecterns are used to fill out range lengths, this problem will be minimized and may be more or less left out of consideration.

The possibility of lengthening shelf sections should not be forgotten. It is discussed in section 8.1, but it would require a complete recalculation of bay sizes.

Each inch added to the thickness of a stack range reduces the width of the aisle between ranges or reduces capacity by approximately 2 per cent. Very few books, except folios and a few deep quartos—probably not over 3 per cent—are more than 10 in. deep, the depth possible with a range with bracket shelving 18 in. from front to back; and comparatively few, 6 per cent, are more than 9 in. Ranges in general should, therefore, be 16 to 18 in. in depth, except for those required for oversize volumes, and these can well be concentrated and space provided for them by reducing the number of ranges in one or more bays by one or, in the case of newspapers, two.

The longer the stack aisles and the more they

are used by students and faculty, the wider the aisles should be, other things being equal. In a very large stack it is possible to have much longer aisles than are considered standard, with an aisle only 30 to 34 in. wide, if use is not too heavy and if range ends are properly labeled to show contents. Each inch by which an aisle width or range depth is decreased can add approximately 2 per cent to stack capacity if the column spacing is right. Every 3-ft cross aisle eliminated will increase capacity by the percentage that 3 ft is of the total range length; that is, a 3-ft cross aisle down the center of 33-ft long ranges reduces capacity by 9 per cent. A 4 ft 6 in. cross aisle adds one-half to this figure and a 6-ft one doubles it. But do not compromise convenience unreasonably because of money savings.

If complete flexibility for the placing of ranges is to be obtained, columns must be square or circular. A clear floor height of something over 8 ft—preferably 8 ft 4 in.—is required if shelving is 7 ft 6 in. high, and the range spacing is to be changed without rearranging the lighting fixtures. If this extra flexibility is not desired, a clear stack height of approximately 7 ft 6 in. is still necessary to obtain seven shelves without relegating over 10 per cent of the volumes to oversize shelving.

What does all this add up to in terms of column spacing? As so often said in this volume, circumstances alter cases. It is suggested as a basis for discussion, however, that in a large university library of over 1 million volumes with limited stack access for undergraduates, construction be such that columns can be held to 14 in. in the direction of the ranges and no more than 18 in. at right angles to them. If, because of heavy loads to be carried, they must be larger than that in one direction, they can be extended up to 32 in. in the line of the ranges. In this case the ventilation and heating ducts may be included in them if legally permissible or separately enclosed for fire protection and placed beside them, but the direction of the ranges cannot be changed later.

Fluorescent light is advisable if artificial light is to be used during a good proportion of the library hours. If the stack area is as much as 8 ft 4 in. in height or a little less, careful consideration should be given to placing lighting at right angles to the range aisles. The parallel rows of tubes can then be as much as 6 ft apart

on centers, and the distance between ranges can be readily adjusted as desired.

With these suggestions as a basis, the following points in connection with bay sizes may well be kept in mind:

1. Other things being equal, the larger the bay, the better, if it does not increase construction costs unduly or necessitate columns more than 14 in. square, or 18 by 32 in. if they are to include the ducts and if the direction of the ranges is not to be changed.

2. Other things being equal, square bays tend to be more economical and to give more flexibility, but they are not essential. The architect may find good reasons for making some of them, if not all, long rectangles, in order to provide larger reading areas without columns or to house to better advantage stairwells, elevators, toilets, and other services requiring interior partitions or nonbearing walls.

3. Except for top floors or in some cases where the use of prestressed concrete is desirable, it is probable that 27 × 27 ft will be the upper limit for square bays, unless columns are to be more than 14 × 18 in. if rectangular, or 18 × 32 in. if much longer in one direction.

4. If the smaller column is selected, the distance between columns should be a multiple of 3 ft, plus 4 in. for the 2-in. extra space on either side of the column for the last upright. Since the column takes 18 in., this will give bay sizes of 25 ft 6 in., 22 ft 6 in., 19 ft 6 in., 16 ft 6 in. as possibilities. A bay size of 25 ft 6 in. will permit six ranges 4 ft 3 in. on centers to a bay. This arrangement is suitable for large collections not too heavily used, with the length of the ranges running up to 30 ft or even 36 ft. A bay size of 22 ft 6 in. would be better for a heavily used, open-access undergraduate stack collection, with ranges 4 ft 6 in. on centers and range lengths from 15 to 30 ft, varying according to the amount of use in relation to the size of the collection.

If 19 ft 6 in. is chosen, it will provide a stack for very limited access, with 5 ranges 3 ft 11 in. on centers and ranges preferably 16 in. from front to back and certainly no more than 18 in., or for four ranges 4 ft 10 in. on centers for undergraduate collections with extremely heavy use. Ranges up to 20 in. from front to back would be permissible in the latter circumstances but would rarely be warranted.

For a limited-access and research library 16 ft 6 in. is possible, but is generally unnecessary and undesirable because the columns become so numerous and will get in the way in nonstack areas. It will provide for four ranges 4 ft 1¼ in. on centers.

5. If the rectangular 14 to 18 × 32-in. column is selected, any column spacing divisible by three will be feasible, and 27 × 27 ft, 24 × 24 ft, 21 × 21 ft, and 18 × 18 ft should be considered.

An ideal size for an undergraduate collection is 27 × 27 ft, which will give six ranges to a bay, 4 ft 6 in. on centers.

If the stack ranges are 16 to 18 in. in depth and if aisles 30 to 32 in. in width are acceptable, 24 × 24 ft is useful. This will provide the same six ranges per bay as the 27 × 27-ft arrangement and increase capacity per square foot by nearly 13 per cent. But—and it is a big "but"—this bay is not satisfactory unless the use is comparatively light or unless you are ready to have only five ranges to a bay which, of course, reduces capacity by one-sixth.

With 21 × 21-ft spacing, the possibilities are four ranges 5 ft 3 in. on centers; or five ranges 4 ft 2⅖ in. on centers; or six ranges 3 ft 6 in. apart. The first is too large except for an exceedingly heavily used open-shelf collection in a combined stack and reading area. The second is quite satisfactory for a large university or research collection with limited open access. (The Widener Library ranges are 4 ft 2 in. on centers.) The third, if 18-in.-deep ranges are used, will leave only 24-in. aisles, which are suitable for very little-used storage collections only. Unless local conditions make a bay this size desirable, a different one would seem to be indicated.

An open-access liberal arts college library may find 18 × 18 ft entirely satisfactory, but the columns will be about twice as many in number as with a 27-ft spacing, will take a somewhat larger percentage of the total space, and will have more of a tendency to get in the way. The reduced construction cost of the smaller bay is generally not sufficient to make it worth while, unless it is important to provide the thinner floors which small bays will make possible. This bay size is ordinarily not desirable for a large collection, as the 4 ft 6 in. range spacing is unduly generous, and 3 ft 7 in. on centers, which would result if five ranges to a bay are

used, is too little for anything but closed-access storage.

6. Up to this point only square bays with sections 36 in. long have been dealt with. Even so, as has been noted, a number of combinations are possible. If bays that are not square are to be considered, but with 36-in. shelf sections used, it would seem that the number of combinations would be multiplied almost indefinitely if range spacing can be greater or less than 4 ft 6 in. This is true unless it is considered necessary to be able to turn the stacks at right angles later on without changing the range spacing. With this restriction, only bays 13 ft 6 in. × 22 ft 6 in., or 22 ft 6 in. × 31 ft 6 in. are possible with 4 ft 6 in. range spacing; and it must also be remembered that only small square or round columns can then be used because long rectangular ones would interfere with the aisles, if the stacks were turned.

It will be found that in most cases the range spacing will have to be changed if section lengths are changed.

If, however, range spacing can be other than the 4 ft 6 in. and stacks are never to change direction, it not only is possible but in some cases may be desirable to use other long rectangular sizes for large collections. To give but a few examples, with the small square or round columns, if the spacing is 16 ft 6 in., 19 ft 6 in., or 22 ft 6 in. in one direction, and if ranges are to be 4 ft on centers, a 16-, 20-, 24-, or 28-ft column spacing in the other direction is possible, and a similar series can be developed for other range spacings, such as 4 ft 1 in., 4 ft 2 in., 4 ft 3 in., 4 ft 4 in., and 4 ft 5 in., for example, to say nothing of those involving fractions of inches between 4 ft and 4 ft 6 in.

To go one step farther, if different length sections are agreed upon, new possibilities arise without changing range spacing, and many more if different range spacing is to be considered. These possibilities are too complicated to be discussed here.

4.3 The Module Size and Other Accommodations

Space for purposes other than concentrated book storage is dealt with throughout this volume. But only rarely is such space seriously affected by column spacing. There may be some inconvenience if the areas required are larger in both directions than the bay size selected, as columns will be required in those areas instead of around the periphery. Likewise, bay sizes should be taken into account if there are numerous identical small units that ought to fit evenly into the module if space is not to be wasted.

The areas so large that they may be affected by columns if the wrong bay size is selected might include the following:

1. Large reading areas for any use, such as for reference collections, current periodicals, reserve books, public documents, divisional reading, maps, large special-subject rooms, and night-study areas

2. Public areas around service desks and the card-catalogue room

3. The processing room or rooms

4. Classrooms and auditoriums; audiovisual rooms and library-school areas

5. Non-assignable space for lobbies, mechanical areas, and stairwells

Small areas that might cause difficulty because two or more of them should fit in between columns should not be forgotten.

Most of the areas in both groups can be disposed of without difficulty. As will be noted elsewhere, the tendency is away from large reading rooms, but with the tremendous seating capacity still required in a large library, some may still be unavoidable. A reading room 18 ft the short way (this is generally the smallest bay recommended) can be extended to 72 ft in length through four bays without seeming completely out of proportion. With the larger bays, 22½, 25½, and 27 ft, rooms 90, 102, and 108 ft in length, respectively, can be available without columns. If the room is next to the outside wall and additional width is wanted without a row of columns down the center, it can be obtained by cantilevering out beyond the last row of columns for 6 to 9 ft and widening the room in that way. On the other side, space for an aisle required under any circumstances can be included, making a room up to 30 ft wide the narrow way with an 18-ft column spacing and perhaps 42 or more feet wide with a 27-ft column spacing.

There are at least five other methods of providing larger areas unbroken by columns.

1. Place the room on the top floor with no weight but the roof, supported by special trusses, overhead. Interior columns can then be left out,

as was done in the very large reference room at the Rutgers University Library.

2. Make the room high enough so that heavier beams can be used in the ceiling. As is noted in section 5.2, which discusses mezzanines, this will not necessarily require high rooms elsewhere on the same floor.

3. Make the column spacing narrower in one direction and so make possible a wider spacing in the other, as in the three large reading areas in Lamont with a 13 × 33-ft column spacing.

4. Hang the upper part of the building from heavy roof beams, as was done at the new John Crerar-Illinois Tech Library in Chicago.

5. Use one of the new precast-concrete methods which permit larger spans.

If a small bay size is used in a reading area and columns protrude into it, they may interfere with seating arrangements, particularly if long tables are used. Table sizes are discussed in section 11.2, but remember that if tables are 4 ft wide and 12 ft long or more, there should be an aisle between and parallel to them at least 5 ft wide, in order to give comfortable access. It is important, too, that aisles adjacent to tables and at right angles to them should not be obstructed by columns. Ingenuity in connection with layouts ordinarily can overcome most difficulties without undue loss of valuable square footage. See section 16.3 for a discussion of equipment-arrangement principles.

One of the methods noted earlier for obtaining large column-free areas may have to be used if a large auditorium is wanted. Other rooms required in a library can almost always be managed by selecting a 22½-ft or larger square bay, or by using long rectangular bays which can easily be up to 33 ft in one direction if shortened to something like 13 ft in the other, as was done in the Lamont Library reading areas.

In two public areas complications may arise. One of these is at a large service desk. Many university libraries and some colleges have circulation desks longer than the distance between columns. The size may be inconvenient if the column comes just in front of or behind the desk, as vision may be obstructed. A column dividing a desk into two is rarely satisfactory. Three comments may be useful:

1. If possible, place the desk far enough in front of or behind the column line so that neither staff or readers are bothered by it.

2. Try to plan the service so that the space

between columns will be long enough for any desk required. Many desks, if the staff is effective and makes use of good housekeeping procedures, do not need as much space as is provided between columns in a 22½-ft or larger bay. (It must be repeated that a desk should have free space behind and in front of it without column interference.)

3. Plan a curved or L-shaped desk, which will be in one bay, not in two, but thus provide the required extra length.

If no one of these methods is possible and work is so heavy that a longer desk is necessary, break the desk-work assignment in two, and use one part for the return of books and the other for charging, each in a different bay. If they are adjacent, one person may be able to service both during quiet hours.

The card-catalogue room is another public space that may cause trouble. Here an 18-ft column spacing may complicate matters. But again, a little ingenuity will generally make suitable any bay size that is likely to be adopted, although the results may not be completely satisfactory. The space lost is rarely large enough to warrant changing column spacing for the whole building.

In a very large library it may be desirable to have an entrance lobby so large that a column will fall into it, but this ordinarily should not create a problem. The same is true in large staff areas such as the catalogue department room.

Finally, stairwells should be considered. With the low ceiling heights now in use and with reasonably large bays, stairwells should not create a problem, unless they are monumental. But the complications that may arise should not be neglected.

Turning now to certain small areas, we should give some attention to: (1) walled-in areas for offices, studies, and enclosed carrels; (2) reading alcoves combining shelving and reader accommodations; and (3) individual seating, both for staff and readers. Reading alcoves present the most difficulty, but again, a little ingenuity should solve the problems. (See Fig. 7.9.)

With any of the bay sizes recommended, such as 18, 22½, 25½, or 27 ft, the chief librarian's office can be fitted in easily without column troubles. Two small offices can be placed in any of these sizes. They do not need to be square; for instance, a 9 × 12-ft office has just about as much space as one 10 ft 5 in. × 10 ft 5 in.

But here another problem arises. If these areas are adjacent to outside walls and the walls have windows, sizes must to a greater or lesser extent conform with the facade pattern. Remember that window space for offices is at a premium, and in most cases an office or study or closed carrel should use as little outside wall space as possible and reach back into the building far enough to provide the desired number of square feet.

Also remember that if the column, particularly one on an outside wall, juts into a room, it may complicate matters for an office or study, and even more for a carrel, because the column size is a greater percentage of the area under consideration.

An 18-ft bay will take care of one large office, two small ones, two adequate studies or three small ones, three good-sized closed carrels or four open ones.

A 22½-ft bay will provide outside wall space for two fine small offices or large studies, three adequate studies, four good closed carrels, and five open ones.

A 25½-ft bay will provide for two fine offices, three minimum ones, three good or four small studies, five closed carrels, and six open ones.

The extra 1½ ft provided by a 27-ft bay will not provide any more offices, studies, or carrels than 25½ ft.

Appendix B lists in tabular form recommended sizes for offices, studies, and carrels, both open and closed, and for reading alcoves.

5

Problems Relating to Height

Introduction

A separate chapter on problems relating to height may seem on first thought difficult to defend in a volume limited in size. But it should be remembered that height involves a number of basic questions that must be answered before the architect can go very far with his plans. These questions are dealt with in detail later in this chapter or elsewhere in this volume.

1. Is it better to add to an old building or to start anew? This question is discussed in section 15.1, where the author points out that modern developments in lighting, heating, and ventilation have changed the required distances from floor to floor, and that the great distances in old construction are often inconsistent with today's requirements. To match the heights used in the original construction might result in increasing the cost of an addition so much that little would be left of the savings that otherwise might result from the use of an old building. Always remember that height greater than is necessary or desirable functionally and aesthetically costs money and should be questioned. On the other hand, the floor heights in old multitier stack constructions are often so low that a modern free-standing stack with thicker floors and more flexibility cannot be installed in the same vertical space. If floor heights do not match and a few steps up or down are required in going from the old to the new areas, it becomes difficult for the persons involved; inconvenience and accidents may result, and the transportation of books may present serious problems.

2. How much clear height from floor to ceiling is desirable functionally and aesthetically in a library? That depends, of course, upon the size of the areas involved and what the space is used for. It will vary in different parts of a building, and compromises will probably be required. There is no one ideal height for all areas or functions. Section 8.1, dealing with book stacks, states that at least 7 ft 6 in. is desirable in an academic or research library with large collections. Space above that height has relatively little value for book storage but may be worth while in order to provide flexibility in stack lighting and to make the floor level useful for multiple occupancy or for other uses. The larger the open area, the greater the height desirable, and here aesthetics must not be neglected. Both the aesthetic and functional problems are discussed in detail in section 5.1.

3. How thick should floors be? This will depend (a) on bay and module sizes, which were discussed in Chapter 4; (b) on the weight to be carried and the type of construction, which is dealt with in section 10.1;[1] (c) on what a floor is to contain in the way of mechanical services between the finished ceiling below and the finished floor above; and (d) last but not least, on

[1] The following figures were provided by a structural engineer and give some indication of the factors involved. With 150 pounds per square foot loading 18-ft square bays and 14 × 18-in. columns, slab floors 8½ in. thick will support one floor on grade, plus six bearing floors and the roof. With 25 ft 6 in. square bays, 14 × 18-in. columns, a 12-in. thick grid floor will support one floor on grade, plus three bearing floors and the roof. Larger columns will, of course, support additional floor levels.

the ingenuity of the mechanical and structural engineers and the care with which they work. Points (*c*) and (*d*) are considered in section 5.3.

4. What considerations should one keep in mind in determining the preferable size and number of floor levels? The site chosen may have much to do with this, as will be seen in section 15.2, which deals with site-selection problems. The question often cannot be answered properly until the total net and gross square footage requirements of the building have been determined. These are dealt with in section 14.5, which discusses the program for the architect, and are also considered in Chapters 7 and 8, in the discussion of various library facilities from a theoretical standpoint.

5. Are mezzanines desirable? The answer to this question involves aesthetics, function, and cost. High ceilings of 30 to 50 ft are no longer required functionally. On the other hand, one should hesitate to plan a large library building today with no room in it higher than strictly functional needs demand. A mezzanine over part of a level might make up for all or a large share of the extra cost of providing an area which would give the desired effect of greater spaciousness. This problem will be discussed in more detail in section 5.2.

6. Does vertical transportation affect height problems? Of course it does. It is obvious that a twenty-story or even a five-story library without mechanical vertical transportation would be unsatisfactory. (The author of this volume worked for three years early in the century in a large college library where he was responsible for the vertical transportation of books. The building had five levels, but no book lift or elevator of any kind. All the new acquisitions came in on the lowest level.) It is well known that mechanical vertical transportation is expensive, but it is obvious that to avoid the necessity for it by constructing a large library all on one level would not be satisfactory. There are various methods of vertical transportation which may vary in cost and, depending on circumstances, in their desirability. These methods are discussed in section 6.2.

5.1 Clear Floor Heights

Questions relating to the clear height of library areas are complex. It may be functionally desirable to use one level for many different pur-

poses or for a single purpose, such as for reading accommodations, as well as for rooms that differ in size. A height that is functional and economical may not be aesthetically satisfactory. The height selected affects construction costs. Plans that make a library building satisfactory from the operational side are likely to call for areas on the same floor level which aesthetically as well as functionally may differ widely in optimum height requirements. An added complication arises from the fact that library needs may change as time goes on. Every effort should be made to provide a building in which practically all the space can be used to advantage for book storage, or for reader accommodations, or for staff. Ideally, it should have heights throughout that are usable for all of these purposes, without involving expensive building alterations when shifts are made from one function to another.

This problem of flexible space has always been difficult, but in recent years, because of high construction costs, studies of optimum heights for different purposes have been made. Early in the century when one, if not the most notable, feature of a library was a monumental reading room, that room was at least 22½ ft high in the clear, or enough for three multitier stack levels. One of the first requisites in a reading room was natural light. To provide it in an area 35 to 40 ft or more across required a room something like two-thirds as high as it was wide, with large windows going practically to the ceiling. Skylights were also often thought to be necessary, and the main reading room was therefore sometimes placed on an upper floor. Its height went a long way toward providing more or less satisfactory ventilation, at least at standing and sitting height, since hot and polluted air tends to rise without the aid of forced ventilation, which was not generally available. As already indicated, a height of 22½ ft or more made it possible to place in other parts of the same floor three levels of a multitier stack and thus avoid short flights of stairs.

As much as thirty years ago, with better artificial light and forced ventilation available, it was found that a 22½-ft ceiling height could be cut to 15 ft. This was done successfully in a large reading room at the University of Virginia Library in Charlottesville and was a surprise to many who had come to believe that the need for greater height went back primarily to a sense of proportion and not just light and ventilation.

Long before that, many libraries had experimented with a two and a half stack-level height with fairly large reading rooms, as was done at Oberlin College and elsewhere early in the century. Access from other parts of the building to the in-between stack levels was sometimes provided by ramps so steep that it was almost impossible and certainly unwise and dangerous to push a book truck over them.

But as time went on and cubic-foot building costs increased; as architects and interior decorators learned how to effect changes in impressions of height; and as lower ceilings became customary in private homes, apartment houses, and office buildings, even lower heights were experimented with for reading areas of various sizes.

The reading room on the fifth level of the Lamont Library is 131 × 31½ ft in dimensions. Since nothing but the roof is overhead, it was possible, without floor-level complications, to place the ceiling at any height which appeared aesthetically suitable. The librarian, for the sake of economy and in order to learn what he could about the problem, requested the architect to make it as low as he thought would be aesthetically desirable. The latter decided, after careful consideration, that 9½ ft in the clear would be satisfactory if the room were partially divided into three equal areas, each nearly 44 × 32 ft, by open slatted screens that were some 7 ft high and 15 ft long. This room has generally been regarded as a success, and while there are certain positions in it from which, when one looks down the full length, the ceiling seems rather low, little or no criticism or complaint has been heard.

At about the same time, the Firestone Library at Princeton was being planned, and it had been decided that a large part of its total area was to consist of three levels below the entrance floor to be used primarily for a book stack. It was important to keep down the height of these levels if they were to have outside light. This was accomplished and made easier by the downward slope of the ground to the rear of the building and the construction of a waterless moat. The desirable height was complicated by the requirement of providing, on the same levels, seminar and reading areas of at least two bays, making them 25 × 36 ft in size. A mock-up was erected with an adjustable ceiling which could be cranked up and down. "Guinea pigs," in-

cluding professors, administrators, students, and architects, as well as librarians, were assembled. They were invited to complain when the ceiling was lowered too far for comfort and appearance, and a conclusion was reached that 8 ft 4 in. in the clear would be adequate for a reading and general-purpose area as large as 25 × 36 ft. The decision made at Princeton has been accepted generally throughout the United States, and a minimum of 8 ft 4 in. has been considered standard for small reading areas, if for other reasons no greater height seems desirable or necessary.

The University of Michigan Undergraduate Library and the library at Louisiana State University are new buildings which have very large reading areas with ceilings approximately 9 ft in the clear. The planners have found that with the use of divider screens, recessed lighting, light-colored ceilings, and, when desired, space broken up by bookcases, this is satisfactory. It is suggested that librarians and architects perplexed by this problem visit libraries with low reading-area ceilings and talk with librarians and students about the results.

The above applies to the theoretical minimum satisfactory heights of fairly sizable areas for multiple human occupancy. But many libraries in recent years have found that it is desirable to scatter small groups of readers among book stacks in what are sometimes called "oases" or in alcoves or by other methods that are discussed in Chapters 7 and 8. Here ceilings of even less than 8 ft 4 in. have been found to be possible and satisfactory. One mezzanine in the Lamont Library, which measures 91 × 45 ft, proved adequate for shelving 30,000 volumes and for seating 75 readers at individual tables or tables for four. It has ceiling heights of 8 ft; another one of the same size has 7 ft 9 in. The latter height has proved adequate and satisfactory in a large mezzanine in the Georgia Institute of Technology Library. In Iowa State University in Iowa City even larger areas with an 8-ft ceiling have been provided. A height lower than 7 ft 9 in. has been widely used for many years for individual seating in carrels and faculty studies adjacent to book stacks.

The Widener stack at Harvard is just over 7 ft 2 in. in the clear, and some 400 open carrels —they are called stalls, which is perhaps a better name for them—are in use with little if any complication on account of the lack of height. The Amherst College book stacks, with a 6 ft

9 in. height, have a number of carrels. Pennsylvania State University is unfortunate enough to have stacks less than 6 ft 8 in. in height. The carrel users there are less unhappy when sitting at their desks than when walking up and down the aisles where, because the lighting fixtures take some 5 in. away from available height, there is only 6 ft 3 in. in the clear. The author disapproves of ceilings this low but remembers that he is well over 6 ft and has a 6 ft 6 in. son. There is a comparatively small inside room with no windows used by the cataloguers in the Houghton Library at Harvard in which the ceiling height is only 7 ft and a clear height under the lights just over 6 ft 6 in. The same persons have been working there for over twenty years. This height is not to be recommended for general use, but shows what is possible with air conditioning.

From the point of view of the comfort of the reader, aesthetics, and proportion, the above would seem to indicate that a large reading room need not be more than 9 ft 6 in. in height; 9 ft is possible if the room is broken up by bookcases or in other ways. A room 25 × 36 ft, which is large enough for 36 readers and 75 to 100 persons sitting in a conference is not unpleasant with an 8 ft 4 in. ceiling if ventilation is adequate. The author has sat for three days at a time in a conference in such a room. With a smaller concentration of readers, 8 ft or even 7 ft 9 in. is sufficient, and 7 ft 6 in. is enough for individual seating. To go below that to the figures that have been used in some libraries is to go below the height needed for economical book storage. It is suggested that the minimum height for any library space, except storage closets and doorways, be considered as 7 ft 6 in.

The largest use of space in most libraries, except that for reader accommodations, is for book stacks. Here two other factors come into play—the convenience of the user as he selects books and returns them to the shelves, and the book capacity made available. American users of academic and research libraries vary greatly in height, and no one stack height is ideal for everyone. As in so many other matters, compromises must be made that will not cause too much inconvenience to any considerable number. The percentage of readers under 5 ft or over 6 ft 2 in. in American academic libraries is small, and, while the number under the lower figure is larger in some other parts of the world, the short individuals can be subjected to a minor amount of inconvenience for the sake of the convenience of the vast majority and of the resulting increased book capacity. A 5-ft-tall individual can ordinarily reach a book on a shelf 6 ft 4 in. above the floor without too much trouble, but would find it difficult to go higher than that without a stool. Stools or stepladders, at least in open-access book stacks, are a menace and, to put it mildly, should be avoided because they are often tripped over. If the top shelf is 6 ft 4 in. above the floor, the finished ceiling should be not much under 7 ft 6 in. Otherwise it would be inconvenient for the very tall person and would also make it difficult to replace books without interference with the lighting fixtures. It is probably worse to bump your book, to say nothing of your head, on an electric light fixture than to have to stretch a bit to reach a shelf. So much for the convenience of readers, as far as minimum and maximum heights in a book stack are concerned.

What about book capacity, a primary requisite for book stacks? Here, of course, the height of books must be considered. This varies and probably will always do so. Part of the variation is related to the subject of the material. Books in the fine arts, largely because of illustrations, and music scores, for instance, tend to be taller than those for fiction and history. Bound volumes of newspapers belong in a category by themselves, and, as will be shown in section 8.4, special shelving can and probably should be provided for them, if they are at all numerous. On the average, a smaller percentage of public-library books will be over 10 in. high than of academic and research material. A larger percentage of older publications are outsize than of current ones. Bound periodicals are taller on the average than books.

Various studies of book sizes—that is, of heights and depths—have been made, notably by Van Hoesen of Brown[2] and Fremont Rider.[3] Mr. Rider concludes that 21 per cent of books in an academic and research library are over 10 in. high, but only 10 per cent are over 11 in. It is suggested that the 10 per cent over 11 in. should be segregated by size, in spite of the inconvenience that results. If this decision is applied to stack heights, shelves for the main collection should be 12 in. apart on centers, which, with five-eighths to three-fourths of an inch for

[2] *Library Quarterly,* 4:352–357, 1934, and 5:341–347, 1935.
[3] Fremont Rider, *Compact Storage,* Hadham Press, New York, 1949.

shelf thickness, will make it possible to place a book up to a full 11 in. high anywhere. This will mean that with a 7 ft 6 in. height in the clear and the top shelf at 6 ft 4 in., the bottom one can be 4 in. above the floor (to provide protection from water and other hazards in connection with cleaning), and each section can house seven shelves. If this desirable shelf spacing is to be kept and the ceiling height is reduced by even 1 or 2 in., the base must be lowered, which will increase the cleaning hazard and make it harder for the reader to use the bottom shelf. Not everyone has the flexibility of circus performers and, if aisles are narrow, the problem of bottom shelves close to the floor becomes increasingly serious. If a clear height of 7 ft 6 in. is reduced by even an inch or two and the base shelf remains at 4 in., the number of shelves per section in most subject classifications will be reduced to six. Seven shelves provide one-sixth larger capacity than six in the same number of 3-ft-long sections. The net increase in capacity resulting from these few additional inches over 7 ft 3 in. in height, which generally represents inexpensive cubage, will average well over 10 per cent for all stack areas, a matter of considerable importance.

In this connection, it should be noted that it is difficult if not impossible to erect a 7 ft 6 in. stack upright without a clear ceiling height of 7 ft 7 in. or 7 ft 8 in.; the exact height required will vary according to the design, but the upright can be shortened an inch or two without affecting the shelving capacity. It is suggested, therefore, that 7 ft 6 in. is the minimum ceiling height in the clear for book stacks and that the lighting equipment should be close to the ceiling.

What is the maximum desirable height for book stacks? First, remember that any additional height increases cost without materially adding to capacity. The following figures cannot be considered as definitive because conditions will vary, but it might be helpful to estimate that a 6-in. increase over a 7 ft 6 in. height, while increasing cubage by nearly 7 per cent, will probably increase the square footage cost by less than 1½ per cent. So small an increase in height will not change the cost figures for equipment, for ceilings, for floors, doors, and furniture, or for lighting, although the last of these would be affected if there were any considerable increase in height. The extra cubage, of course, adds to the cost of both exterior and interior walls, of stairs, and very slightly of heating and ventilat-

ing, although it may also be helpful by facilitating the horizontal distribution of ventilation ducts.

The question then is whether or not the additional height is worth what it will cost. If 8 ft 6 in. in the clear increases square-foot costs of the building by less than 3 per cent, 9 ft by 4 per cent, 10 ft by something like 6 or 7 per cent, and so forth, the answer will depend upon what the extra height contributes aesthetically, or in capacity, comfort, and flexibility. As far as books are concerned, nothing is gained in capacity, unless an eighth shelf is installed; this will be beyond the reach of most readers and is not recommended, except in rare instances. When it comes to flexibility, there are certain advantages resulting from the additional height. A ceiling between 8 ft 2 in. and 8 ft 6 in. or higher permits fluorescent lighting at right angles to stack aisles, thereby making it possible to shift distances between ranges of movable stacks at will, without changing the lighting. As has already been seen, a very few inches over 7 ft 6 in. makes it possible to use space for multiple occupancy by readers. How much is this flexibility worth? The room should certainly be high enough for the convenience and comfort of those who use the stack. Additional height is not required unless it is needed for light and air, or unless the rooms are so large as to make a low ceiling seem oppressive.

The aesthetic problem is hard to deal with objectively and specifically. It involves a sense of proportion. The architects' advice will be helpful here.

What about height in areas used by the staff? Staff members are likely to be in the library longer hours than readers and should have more, rather than less, comfort, but in general the same rules apply to both. Pennsylvania State University has placed its processing staff on one of the stack levels where an additional 10 in. beyond its standard of 6 ft 8 in. is provided. This is a multitier stack with the uprights every 9 ft in each direction, instead of the commoner 3 ft by 4 ft 6 in. The staff is working there without serious complaint, but the arrangement is not recommended, although 7 ft 6 in. will do, with good light and ventilation, in small areas if divided up by shelving and catalogue cases.

The greatest problem in connection with height comes when large reading areas are required on the same floor level with extensive book storage areas. If the reading room is large enough to require a 10-ft ceiling, and this adds 7 per cent to the square-footage cost of the stack portion, or, let us say in order to be specific, $1.50 a square foot, it may increase the cost of the construction of 10,000 sq ft of stack space by $15,000. This figure will, of course, vary according to local construction costs. The dilemma can sometimes be avoided to a large extent by deciding to keep large reading areas off levels with large book-storage areas, or by using mezzanine stacks where a greater height is required for the readers. This will be discussed in section 5.2.

One other point in connection with ceiling heights. If they are under 7 ft, a tall man going down staircases placed one above the other, may bump his head on the steps above. But as heights increase, stairwells take more floor space.

Advantage can sometimes be taken of different requirements for different uses on the same floor. Ventilation ducts can sometimes run under the ceiling in a book stack and leave greater heights in adjacent reading areas.

5.2   Mezzanines

If the formula used in the previous section is assumed to be correct for comparative purposes, a floor 17 ft high may cost some 20 per cent more than one of a minimum height of 7 ft 6 in. If 75 per cent of this floor has a mezzanine over it and only 25 per cent of it is the full height, the construction would add something like 5 per cent to the square-footage cost of the floor as a whole. If this floor is one of five in a building and the others have low ceilings, the increase in average square-foot cost of the whole building is cut to only 1 per cent, or $20,000, in a building costing $2,000,000. In order to obtain one spacious room, this addition might well be worth while. These cost figures, based on experience in a recently built library in the Boston area, are used simply to illustrate and clarify the problem. They are at best approximations and will differ, of course, in different places under different conditions; the architect should be asked to check them.

The chief value of a mezzanine in a library is to make it possible and reasonably economical to have a room as much as two stack levels high on part of a floor. This can give a feeling of spaciousness to the whole building without providing unnecessary cubage for the whole floor. It

also puts much of the additional cubage on the mezzanine or under it to good use for book stacks or for other purposes where great heights are not required. It has already been seen that 7 ft 6 in. is the minimum height for book stacks, and that this height is also entirely satisfactory for individual seating in carrels. A height of 8 ft 4 in. will do for rooms of fairly large size for other purposes. If the space under the mezzanine is used for offices and small reading areas and is 8 ft 4 in. in height; if the mezzanine itself is for stacks and individual seating and is 7 ft 6 in. high; and if the floor thickness can be held down to 1 ft 2 in. by keeping horizontal ventilation ducts out of the mezzanine areas, the 17-ft height mentioned earlier will be provided between the main floor and the mezzanine ceiling. The clear ceiling height of large reading areas might be reduced to 16 ft by placing ventilation ducts under the finished ceiling there.

Let us see now what would happen if, instead of using a mezzanine over part of the floor, the whole floor were made 12 ft high in the clear, one-fourth of it for a large reading area, and the remainder for services placed in the earlier plan on or under the mezzanine. The increase in the cost of the whole area—using the same formula for cost approximation for increased height as before—would be about 10 per cent, or 5 per cent more than with the mezzanine arrangement. (The cost of the furniture and equipment on the mezzanines must not be forgotten.) These percentages are simply rough estimates to illustrate the problem, but they indicate that if a mezzanine covers the major portion of a floor level and a clear height of 12 ft or more is wanted for aesthetic reasons in at least one large reading area, it is not a luxury to go up to 16 or 17 ft for the part without a mezzanine, if the area concerned is not too large. Angus MacDonald told the author that a mezzanine, to be practicable from the cost point of view, must occupy at least 60 per cent of the floor area. The general principles underlying these observations are confirmed by talks with architects and contractors.

Examples of mezzanines—they might be called galleries—have been quite numerous in recent years, and adaptations of them were not unusual in earlier periods, as in the Peabody Institute in Baltimore, the Library of Trinity College, Dublin, the old Astor Library in New York, and the Vassar College Library in Poughkeepsie. Two-level stacks or multipurpose areas adjacent to fairly large reading rooms at the Cleveland and New York Public Libraries and at Columbia's Butler Library are more recent examples. Still later ones may be found at the Linda Hall Reference Library in Kansas City and the new Hartford Public Library, where the main floor has four different areas two levels high but occupying altogether far less than one-half of the floor area. Lamont has mezzanines on two of its main floors, but they occupy at least 60 per cent of these levels. Angus MacDonald was a great advocate of mezzanines to make possible one or more high-level reading rooms at a minimum cost. They certainly should be considered, and under many circumstances can be quite useful and inexpensive and can result in a feeling of spaciousness throughout the whole building. Their use in Lamont seems to have had that effect. The average clear height of all the areas in Lamont is a little over 8 ft 6 in. With two large reading rooms with ceilings of 14 ft 7 in. and 15 ft 1 in. respectively, a two-level-high reference room and entrance lobby, the lower average height is hard to believe.

It should be noted that because lower ceiling heights have prevailed during recent years in buildings of all kinds, there may be less need for considering mezzanines than there was as recently as ten or fifteen years ago.

5.3 Floor Thickness

Bay sizes, the type of construction used, services installed in the floors, and the ingenuity of the structural engineer, all have their effect on floor thickness. Other things being equal, the larger the bay size, the heavier the floor beams or flat slabs required, and the greater the thickness of the floors. If the plans provide for floors everywhere in the building on which book stacks can be placed, something that in most libraries should be required, any bay size over 27 ft square will tend to require more steel and extra thickness, which in turn takes additional cubage. Library floors that will hold book stacks anywhere have been made, with the use of flat slab construction no more than 8 in. thick, with bays 18 ft square. With reinforced concrete slabs, they need be no more than 12 or 13 in. thick with bays up to 27 ft square if they do not have to provide space for ducts and pipes. These thicknesses are structural and do not include the finished floor or ceiling.

Space required for the services varies greatly. Plumbing and wiring require little in the way of additional thickness for floors. Air ducts for heating, ventilation, and air conditioning involve much more, although heating pipes for steam and hot water without ventilation take little space. Complications always arise when air ducts have to cross each other, and if the ventilation engineer is careless or lacks ingenuity, he may ask for a floor thickness of up to 5 ft. This may include the structural floor itself, space for ducts, for plumbing, and also for recessing the lighting fixtures into the ceiling, something that is often desirable. It can seem absurd, however, to use floors 5 ft thick, and then reduce clear ceiling heights to as little perhaps as 8 ft. Too large a proportion goes into space, most of which is not used. Vertical ventilation takes much more square footage of floor space, but it often reduces total costs, if one takes into account the additional height required by horizontal ventilation.

5.4 Size and Number of Levels

No set formula can be recommended for size and number of levels. Until comparatively recently the dimensions and shape of library buildings were determined to a considerable extent by lighting and ventilating requirements. Often the extreme limit in the depth of a building was placed at 80 ft or less so that no part of it would be more than 40 ft from windows. Skylights over the center, with a great hall below and galleries on the outside, made somewhat deeper buildings possible. The situation has now changed basically. Artificial light and ventilation can be relied on, and windows can be reduced to a minimum if desired.

Some persons with considerable knowledge of the problems involved have suggested that a library should be kept on one floor if possible, unless it is to contain more than 10,000 sq ft of gross space. If it is over 10,000 sq ft, it might well have two levels. With 20,000 sq ft, three levels, particularly if a satisfactory basement can be provided, seem reasonable in order to reduce horizontal distances and the use of ground areas. With three levels arranged in this way, few persons will regularly have to go up or down more than one floor at a time. Total square footages of wall and roof areas have considerable effect on costs. In general, the nearer square the building and the fewer the floor levels, the less the wall cost; the more levels, the less the roof cost. Curved walls and many corners and, as already noted, ceiling heights and floor thickness increase costs. Ask an architect or an estimator about the problem in your locality.

How many levels high can a library building go from a strictly functional and cost point of view? Four factors should be taken into consideration.

1. In general, the larger the square footage on each floor, the smaller the percentage of the total gross square footage that is required for stairwells, elevators, and book lifts, and the smaller the proportion of outside wall to total square footage.

2. If all parts of the building used regularly by readers are no more than two flights of stairs above or below the entrance, passenger elevator service for any but cripples and heart cases can be avoided and funds saved for other purposes. A site on a side hill with windows on one or more basement levels helps in this connection.

3. If the librarian expects to provide service and supervision on each level, the number of levels should be held to a minimum in order to reduce the number of posts to be covered by the staff.

4. It is important in many if not most libraries to have the entrance level—whether it is called the main, first, or ground floor—large enough to house the central services of the library. These include the main control and charging desks, the reference and bibliographical collections and services, the public catalogue, quarters for the members of the processing staff who are directly involved in the public catalogue, and in many libraries the current periodicals and the closed-reserve book collections. It is also desirable that as many reader seats as possible be placed on this floor. In a small research or academic library these services may require more than one-half the total net square footage. Even in a library with 100,000 volumes and seating 300 readers, this figure should probably not be reduced to under one-third. But in a university or research library with large book collections which occupy up to one-half of the total square footage, and particularly if there is a considerable percentage of the seating scattered in one way or another through the stacks, additional floors are not so serious, although the effect on the elevator problem should not be forgotten.

Tower stacks, such as those at the University of Texas and the University of Rochester libraries, have not been found satisfactory. The ones at Yale's Sterling Library and Columbia's Butler Library are large enough in area so that they are less troublesome. Harvard's Widener Library has a large enough area per floor so that its ten or more stack floor levels are not a serious inconvenience, although a user who is concerned with material in widely different fields may find that a tiresome amount of walking and stair climbing is involved. Some would suggest that stack floors as large as the A level in Princeton's Firestone Library and the largest one at the National Library of Medicine are too large for convenient use, because the traffic patterns tend to become too complicated.

If the total required floor area in a library is as large as 80,000 sq ft, four or five floors can properly be considered, and even if extra elevator service is required, it will not be unduly expensive and inconvenient. Here the value of the available ground space and the desirability of limited ground coverage come into the picture. Skyscrapers are the only economical form for construction on Wall Street. The aesthetic effect should also be considered.

The total number of square feet that can satisfactorily be included in a library building before it becomes so unwieldy as to be avoided is a problem that, with the rapid increase in the collections and the number of seating accommodations called for, will have to be faced in our larger libraries in the years directly ahead.

The above comments do little more than illustrate the problems involved. Their application may differ in a closed-access collection, such as the British Museum, the Library of Congress, or the New York Public Library, from that in an open-access academic library. Just remember that the decision on the number of floors for a library is an important one from the financial, functional, and aesthetic aspects. Keep in mind the problems of vertical transportation in cost and convenience; and consider whether an increase in the number of floors will result in more service posts to cover night and day. Consider, too, the fact that when library attendants leave their posts for another floor level, they are unavailable for service or supervision and that going from one level to another is expensive in time and time is money.

Problems in relation to vertical transportation are described in section 6.2.

6

Traffic Problems

Library buildings are designed to be used, and use obviously implies traffic. One of the essential characteristics of a functional building is the accessibility of all parts with a minimum of effort and a minimum of disturbance. If planning is to produce satisfactory traffic patterns, it must take into account problems of supervision and control of the building and its exits, facilities for communication and vertical transportation, and means of minimizing noise and other distractions. Spatial relationships are also involved.

6.1 Supervision and Control

Most librarians would rather help than supervise those who use their buildings; they have no desire to act as police officers and are eager to make controls as inconspicuous as possible if they cannot be eliminated. Fortunately, less supervision is required now than was thought necessary a generation ago. Today's students, both graduates and undergraduates, seem to be more serious than their predecessors and come to the library for study rather than for social purposes. Better acoustic materials have reduced the disturbance that results from whispering and talking. Many libraries now admit students to the stacks, where close supervision is almost impossible; consequently it is hard to justify intensive supervision of reading rooms. At least three out of four students prefer individual seating, and seating of this kind, which is being provided more and more generously, discourages conversation in reading areas and hence reduces the need for supervision. Better

traffic patterns and seating layouts, which reduce noise and confusion, help to create an atmosphere conducive to orderly behavior. Finally, there is a growing realization that the most economical and in many ways the most satisfactory location for supervision and control is at the building's exit or exits.

It should be emphasized that no one advocates supervision anywhere in a library, even at exits, if it can be eliminated without serious consequences. Unfortunately, as students grow increasingly serious and need less supervision within the building, they seem to be tempted more and more to appropriate library materials extralegally; the problem is particularly serious in the case of reserved books. Attendants at the exits cannot search everyone who leaves the building; books can be concealed in clothing, particularly during the winter. Experience indicates, however, that, if it is known that unauthorized borrowing is a serious offense punishable by dismissal or suspension, inspection at the exits can be more effective than the traditional method of reading-room supervision. Most new buildings provide either for control at the exits or for no control at all.

Control at the exits is no safeguard against theft of rare books by professional thieves; the only satisfactory procedure is to keep very valuable materials in closed stacks, supervise their use, make them available only to persons who have signed for them, and check them in immediately on their return, before the reader leaves, in order to make sure that they have not been mutilated. Exit controls can be expected, however, to prevent unauthorized borrowing by absent-minded professors and students, and to deter deliberate theft because, if an individual must conceal a book to get it past the controls, he can hardly pretend to himself or, if apprehended, to others that he has taken it thoughtlessly, rather than deliberately.

It may be suggested also that, though controls may not seem necessary at the time a building is planned, conditions may change; the building should be planned, therefore, so that exit controls can be provided at some later date without expensive alterations and without harming the appearance of lobbies.

Various methods of exit control are possible. Turnstiles were used for some years in the Widener Library at Harvard, and have been used at the New York Public Library for a long period. It should be noted that persons entering a building may also be required to pass through turnstiles, as at Princeton's Firestone Library. Either electric eyes or turnstiles can be used to count those who enter, though neither can be

relied upon for a completely accurate count, as a swinging arm may be mistaken for a person.

Velour-covered ropes or railings of some kind can be used to channel readers through a narrow lane past a desk. At the Lamont Library as many as four exit lanes can be opened at one time in the main entrance (see Fig. 6.1), and two in the secondary entrance (see Fig. 6.2), but only half of these have proved to be necessary in order to handle the traffic without forcing students to line up.

A third method, which has been used in the Widener Library since the unattractive turnstiles were removed, is to leave a passage more than 4 ft wide with a counter on the right-hand side behind which an attendant sits on a high stool (see Fig. 6.3). This has proved to be reasonably satisfactory at Widener, where most of the use is by professors and graduate students. In an undergraduate library, where there is very heavy traffic just before each class period begins, and in Widener at times of peak loads, narrow passages would be preferable, if not as pleasant.

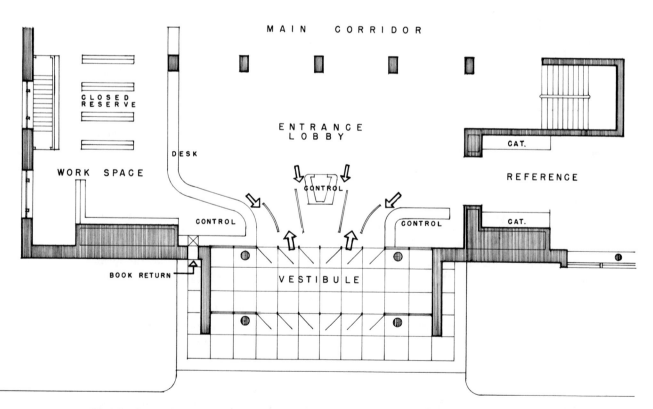

FIG. 6.1 Lamont Library, Harvard University. Main exit control. There are six doors between the vestibule and the lobby. Door handles are on the vestibule side of only the second and fifth, counting from left to right, and restrict entrance to those doors. On the inside they are labeled NO EXIT. Door 1 is always in use when the building is open. Doors 3, 4, and 6 can be used whenever necessary, as each has a control station available, but when not in use they are blocked by bars.

Control counters may also serve as information desks where the stranger can obtain directions, which are often needed in any large library. Counters are preferable to desks, because it is not convenient for readers to show books on a low surface; and height of 39 in. is suggested because some persons feel that this is high enough to lift a heavy briefcase. For use when he is not standing, the attendant should be provided with a high stool having a back and a foot-rest or a platform in the kneehole of the counter. It should be possible for the attendant to reach the outside door quickly if necessary, but it is preferable that this feature be inconspicuous.

In some cases it is possible to install a long control desk at the exit that serves also as the main circulation desk and even as the desk for service of books on closed reserve, as at Lamont. If this is possible, there are significant advantages. The noise and confusion that circulation services always entail is confined to the entrance lobby; the number of staff members who must be on duty during quiet periods is reduced, a fact which may be an important financial consideration, and the reader may avoid having his books checked twice, once when he signs up for them and again when he leaves the building.

Nothing has been said thus far of how many entrances and exits may be needed. Most libraries, of course, must have a separate shipping and receiving entrance, which may be available for use by members of the staff. Each public entrance and exit is expensive; attendants must be paid and floor space must be provided in the building plans. Moreover, the whole traffic problem within the building can be simplified if there is a single entrance and exit. In a large library, however, traffic is often so heavy and distances so great that a second controlled entrance and exit is essential. Fire laws may require it; if they do not, emergency exits with crash locks and an alarm system should be available.

Control of an additional exit may require payment of two or three salaries in a library that is open for 75 to 100 or more hours per week; moreover, a secondary exit will normally be used considerably less than the main one, and may not be a suitable place for circulation or reserved-book services; there may be a problem in keeping the attendant profitably occupied. In the Lamont Library at Harvard a portion of the

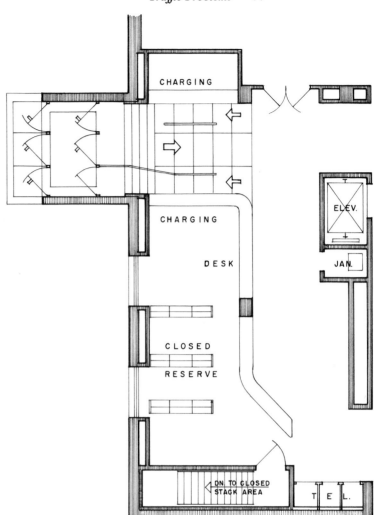

FIG. 6.2 Lamont Library, Harvard University. Secondary exit control. This is similar to the main entrance shown in Fig. 6.1, but with three doors instead of six, with the handle on the outside of the middle door only. The reader goes down five steps immediately after entering, and this descent almost automatically restricts the use of this entrance to those who plan to remain on the two lower levels. Very few will go down stairs for the sake of going up. Others prefer to take the ramp outside the building if they are going to a higher level.

reserve book collection is kept behind the desk at the secondary entrance (see Fig. 6.2), which is on a different floor level from the main entrance; those using the bottom level of the building need not climb an additional 17 ft if they come in at the side entrance, and division of the traffic load is desirable. It can be noted also that traffic is so heavy that two checking-out posts would be needed most of the time at the main entrance if another were not available elsewhere.

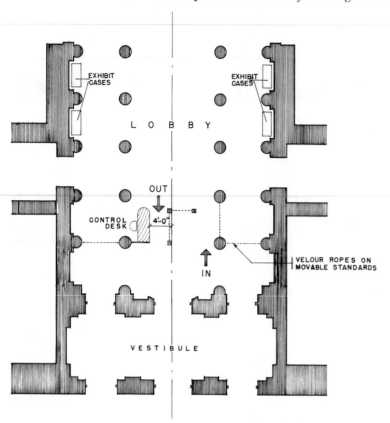

FIG. 6.3 Widener Library, Harvard University. Main exit control. Incoming traffic automatically keeps to the right. Persons leaving the building automatically keep to the right past the control desk.

In the Widener Library, the second entrance is also on a different level from the front door and controls a secondary entrance to the book stack, which is a great convenience in a ten-level stack (see Fig. 6.4). Fire regulations require that two exits be provided in both Widener and Lamont at all times when they are open; elsewhere, however, there are equally large buildings operating under regulations that call for one regular exit, supplemented by emergency exits guarded by electrical or mechanical alarms which operate automatically if the door is opened. An exit of this kind at Princeton has been the victim of unauthorized use only once in fifteen years.

A crash lock can be broken, of course, and a thief or errant student can escape unless there is an effective alarm system. If the exit door is at the end of a fairly long corridor, an electrical alarm may sound at the other end of this corridor, at the nearest service desk, and perhaps in the janitor's quarters. If the library is near a

main gate to the campus where an attendant is on duty at all times, an alarm may ring in his station.

A discussion of problems of control and supervision would be incomplete if it did not mention the difficulties that sometimes occur when there are outdoor reading terraces. These can be attractive, and some architects delight in them, but their disadvantages ought not to be overlooked. Books can be dropped from them to a waiting confederate or to the ground if a secluded spot is available. Dust and air pollution may make them unsatisfactory places for reading and, in most sections of this country, the number of dry and warm days when they can be used is discouragingly small.

Entrances and exits are where traffic patterns begin and end; the decisions made regarding them also affect the security of the library's collections and its operating costs. It is important, therefore, that entrance lobbies be designed with a view to installation of control desks in the future if not at once, with space for rush-hour traffic and provision for channeling past a desk those who are leaving.

6.2 Facilities for Communication and Vertical Transportation

Unless a library is very small or on a single level, mechanical devices for communication will probably be needed when books and people move from one floor to another. A discussion of communication and vertical transportation must consider stairs, ramps, book lifts, conveyor belts, escalators, elevators, telephones, public-address systems, telautographs, and teletypes. The uses of these varied devices will be discussed as a means of helping the librarian to decide what is needed and of indicating something of library requirements to architects and engineers.

The desirable number of stairways will depend, of course, on the amount of traffic, the size of floor levels, and, to some extent, the total square footage of the building. Local building regulations and fire codes may also impose specific requirements. They often state that no place in a building shall be more than a certain number of feet—sometimes the figure is 100—from a stairway providing direct access to an exit from the building. The codes often permit only one open stairway, that is, only one outside a fireproof enclosure with closed doors at each level. They may permit the open stairway on only one level; if it is open on the first floor, it must be enclosed at the second or the basement level. They may also determine the stair widths according to a formula or formulas based on occupancy of the floor or floors that are served.

Some buildings do not come under code restrictions, either because there is no applicable state law or local regulation or because the institution is exempt for one reason or another; sometimes a limited exemption can be obtained if sprinkler systems are installed. Fire risks are discussed in section 10.2. No building should be planned without checking the codes and regulations to which it must conform.

Architects may recommend that open stairways, often monumental ones, rise from the main floor as an architectural and aesthetic feature. A monumental stairway in a small library may be out of proportion, but it can be attractive and also functional in a large building. Contemporary fashion favors stairways as light and seemingly insubstantial as possible, apparently hanging in air and completely open except for hand railings to prevent accidents. The University of Miami Library in Coral Gables has a stairway of this kind.

The location of both main and subsidiary stairways is important; indeed, it is usually a primary factor in determining floor layouts. Stairways should be convenient for use, and reasonably conspicuous if students are to find them readily and use them instead of looking for mechanical transportation; on the other hand, they should not be allowed to obstruct the major traffic arteries on each floor.

Stairways are often placed in one or more central building cores, together with elevator shafts, toilets, and other fixed services, leaving the remainder of the building as flexible and adaptable as possible. This plan also reduces the extent of the interior walls that will be required. Another possibility is to place the main stairway immediately adjacent to the main entrance and next to an outside wall, leaving the rest of the building unobstructed by a permanent installation. As has been noted, however, fire laws and also the amount of use usually necessitate at least one secondary stairway, and large buildings require more than one; in some cases a stairway in each corner may be desirable in addition to the central stairway.

Decisions on the steepness of stairs involve questions of design, comfort, and the use of space. If a stairway ascends too gradually, space will be wasted and many persons will find it awkward to climb. If stairs are too steep, many persons will find them difficult to ascend or descend. In general, the most acceptable height for risers is no more than 7½ in., and risers of less than 6 or 6½ in. should be avoided. Treads may vary from 10½ to 12 in. Book-stack stairs may be steeper, particularly if the number of levels is limited. The following simple formulas are often used:

1. The product of the riser and the tread should be between 70 and 77 in.

2. The riser plus the tread should be from 17 to 17½ in.

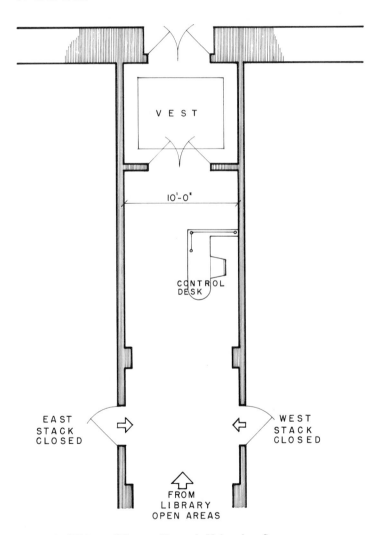

FIG. 6.4 **Widener Library, Harvard University.** Secondary exit control. Checking counter is on the right as one leaves. Secondary stack entrances a few feet from the door are controlled by push button from the desk and make the stacks available on request to the holders of permits.

3. The sum of the tread plus twice the riser should be between 20 and 25 in., preferably between 24 and 25 in.

Decisions on stair widths depend primarily on the traffic expected at times of peak load. Indeed, many decisions in library planning must be based on anticipated peak loads and, particularly in academic institutions, these normally come when classes change. Emergencies such as fire should also be kept in mind; at such times traffic can be expected to move in a single direction, making the full width available. Building codes may stipulate the minimum width, as well as the maximum width that is permissible without a hand railing down the center. Eight feet is often set as the maximum between railings. The minimum for floor-to-floor stairs is usually 3 ft 6 in. clear between rails, though narrower stairs are often considered adequate in book stacks. The legal width may depend upon the number of occupants on the other floors served. The Massachusetts regulations require 1 ft of width for each 50 persons served, with a minimum of 3 ft 6 in. in some types of buildings, and 4 ft for others. These distances are measured from wall to wall, with handrails allowed within this width with a maximum projection of 3½ in. Landing widths, which must not be forgotten if the stairs turn, must be the width of the stairs or 3 ft 8 in., whichever is the greater.

The minimum height of handrails measured at the face of the riser is 2 ft 9 in., and if the stairs go around an opening over two stories high, more than 1 ft wide, the rail must be 3 ft high. Some architects recommend railings as much as 6 in. higher.

Remember that these are Massachusetts regulations. Boston insists on a 4-ft width for landings, a 3-ft width for treads if used by more than 10 persons, plus another foot for each additional 100 persons involved. Regulations elsewhere may be quite different and should always be checked to ensure that at least minimum dimensions are met or exceeded.

If a stairway is to be a fire exit, it must lead as directly as possible to an outside door, and this door must always be made to open without a key from the inside during periods when the building is open to the public. All library stairways should have hand railings. A railing that goes a short distance beyond the bottom step will help those who are handicapped, but must be so installed that it is not a hazard for normal persons rounding the corner to go up the stairs.

Architects sometimes propose circular stairs because of their aesthetic advantages, but they are to be avoided in most cases. If the narrow edge of the circular stair tread is wide enough to be reasonably safe, considerable space must be left in the center; legal requirements often set a minimum diameter for the well. The total square footage of floor space required by an adequate circular stairwell is considerably greater than that needed for a direct stairway or for one going around one, two, or even three corners. This is particularly apparent if it is realized that the space immediately outside the circle is ordinarily useless for library purposes because of its shape. If a circular stairway is to be installed in spite of these disadvantages, it should be designed, in countries where pedestrians normally keep to the right, so that the person going downstairs on the right uses the wide end instead of the narrow end of the tread; this will reduce to some extent the dangers presented by any nonrectangular stair tread. Of course, where pedestrians keep to the left, a stairway rising counter-clockwise is indicated. It appears that in too few instances this principle has been taken into account. (See Figs. 6.5 and 6.6 for circular and rectangular stairs.)

Apropos of stairways and safety, one further warning may be offered: always avoid a flight of only two steps; a single step is even worse. In some places it is illegal to offend in this way, but the infraction cannot be excused whether it is an offense against the law or only against common sense. If a library is afflicted with such stairs, they should be properly marked and lighted. In some cases it may be possible to replace them by ramps as in the Widener Library at Harvard, where accidents had occurred on an average of once a week for thirty years.

Obviously, it should be possible to move books by truck throughout a library building with a minimum of trouble, yet architects of earlier days sometimes placed short flights of steps at a variety of points in a building. The old library at Cornell, now completely rehabilitated as the Uris Undergraduate Library, was an example of this style.

When stairs turn a corner at a landing, particularly if they are heavily used, try to arrange the landing width on the down side a full stair tread wider, as shown in Fig. 6.6.

It has been noted that the substitution of ramps for stairs helped to reduce hazards in the Widener Library, but steep ramps are to be avoided if book trucks must traverse them, and any slope greater than 5 per cent will be difficult for a person on crutches. A 5 per cent incline entails 80 ft of ramp for only 4 ft in altitude; a 10 per cent gradient takes only half this space for the same rise, and 10 per cent should be the limit even for short ramps. A nonskid surface is essential on all ramps, and handrails should also be provided. If a change in level is required at the approach to a staff elevator, a ramp is preferable to stairs, but the change in level should be avoided altogether if possible. A ramp may be the lesser evil when an addition is made to an old library and it is impossible to make floor levels match.

Escalators, which can handle a large volume of traffic and use relatively little power, can be useful in some cases. They function continually without requiring an operator. It is doubtful, however, that any library, even a very large one, can afford to install them between as many as four levels, and it is generally out of the question to go beyond three. For heavy traffic between only two levels, they may be both useful and economical, as in the new Columbia Law School Library, where every reader must go up one high-ceiling level to reach the library from the classroom floor below. In the University of Miami Library in Coral Gables escalators go from the first to the third floor, with three lifts in all, as two are used between the first and second floors. These escalators go up only.[1] Service in both directions at the same time would cost twice as much and would require twice as much space. It is estimated at Coral Gables that, though only of medium width, these escalators have a greater capacity than four elevators, and cost less for space, installation, and operation; it is exceedingly doubtful, however, that four elevators would have been necessary to handle the traffic in question.

The location of escalators calls for careful consideration, and each end should be located where it will not obstruct traffic. Particular care is necessary if more than two levels are involved. It is also essential that escalators be very carefully installed; they must be tailormade for the building if they are not to be unduly noisy. Spe-

[1] They can be reversed at closing time.

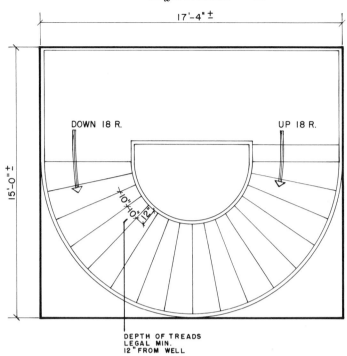

AREA USED: 17'-4" x 15'-0" = 260 SQ. FT.

FIG. 6.5 Circular stairs. The total area required for circular stairs exceeds that for rectangular stairs with landings. The space around the stairs on each floor is less usable because of its shape. They are more expensive to construct, particularly if enclosed by walls. They are dangerous because of the varying depth of each tread. If circular stairs are used, persons going downstairs should go counterclockwise, as shown in the drawing, so that when walking to the right they are on the wider part of the treads. Rails on both sides are always required on circular stairs.

cial fire-protection devices may also be required.

Book lifts, sometimes called "dumb waiters," vary widely in size; some are only large enough to hold a folio volume; others will take a loaded book truck. A few book lifts survive that must be operated manually by pulling a rope, but electric power and push-button controls now prevail. One disadvantage of any book lift is that, if no staff member is stationed at the level to which the lift is sent, the person who loads the lift must climb up or down stairs to unload it; even in a large library, where an attendant is stationed at each level, confusion may result if the attendant is temporarily absent from his post. Also, if the lift is too small to handle a truck, its use almost inevitably involves at least one or two extra handlings of each book transported. Many libraries rarely use the book lifts they have.

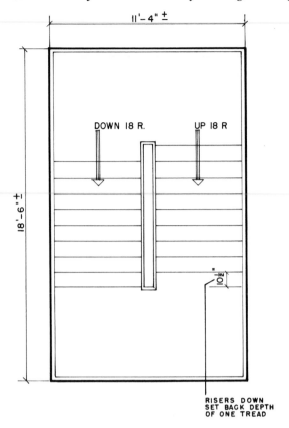

DOWN 18 R.   UP 18 R

RISERS DOWN
SET BACK DEPTH
OF ONE TREAD

AREA USED: 18'-6" x 11'-4" = 210 SQ. FT

FIG. 6.6 Normal stairs. These take less space, are safer, but in some ways not as attractive aesthetically as circular stairs. Rails on both sides are desirable.

Wear and tear in handling books is an important consideration; pages, particularly when working under pressure, are inclined to throw books into a lift. For many years at the New York Public Library thousands of books, sometimes 5,000 a day, were transported between the stacks and the main reading room by book lift, and the resultant damage to bindings was serious. Yet if a full-fledged elevator is beyond the library's means, a book lift, particularly if large enough to carry a truck, may be better than nothing. If the lift is to carry a book truck, it must, of course, open at the floor level, not at counter height. In this type of installation, building codes may require fire-resistant shafts, and insurance rates may be affected.

Elevators are clearly preferable to book lifts in every respect but one—they are more expensive. Their cost, in a small library, may represent a substantial fraction of the total expenditure

for construction. It will be affected by several factors. Is the elevator propelled by cables or by water or oil-driven pistons? What is the size of the cab? What is the maximum weight to be carried? What is the total length of the rise? What speed is stipulated? How complex are the controls required in order to provide service without an operator? Is there to be an accurate leveling device?

Electrically operated cables are always used in high buildings and often in others. Elevators propelled by water or oil-driven pistons are considerably less expensive to install and are recommended when a lift of 50 ft or less is required.[2] They are relatively slow, but may well be considered for service elevators and often for public use as well. Although they tend to be noisy, the acoustical problem can be dealt with.

The machinery for electrically operated cable elevators is usually located in a penthouse rather than in the basement; this saves in costs of installation and operation, reduces wear and tear on the machinery, and helps to minimize noise enough to obviate special acoustic treatment. When heavy loads are to be handled and speed is not important, what is known as two-to-one roping is used instead of one-to-one.

The number of passenger-elevator cabs that will be needed depends on the volume of traffic and the waiting period that will be tolerated, the capacity of the cabs, and their speed. Traffic customarily is measured by the number of persons to be transported in a five-minute peak-load period, and certain standard formulas can be used; these take into account the time required for a full-speed round trip without stops, plus time for accelerating and slowing down at each stop, time for leveling at each stop, time for opening and closing gates and doors, time for passengers to move in and out, lost time resulting from false stops, standing time at top and bottom floors, and reaction time of the operator if there is one. The wider the doors, the more rapidly passengers can move in and out; doors that open at the center of the wide side of the cab speed up operation to a considerable extent.

If wages are to be saved by eliminating operators, automatic elevators must be installed. These are of three principal types. The simplest responds to the first button pushed and does not

---

[2] Recent developments have increased the maximum figure considerably.

"remember" any other calls. The selective-collective type answers only calls in the direction in which the car is moving. Finally, a fully automatic system can be adjusted to operate in a variety of ways designed to suit traffic demands of different levels and of different times of day. The more complicated the controls, the more they cost. Small libraries are rarely justified in installing anything but the simplest type. Safety devices, however, should always be used to prevent the car from moving when doors are open. Car speed should be increased in high buildings.

Two elevators in one bank will carry more traffic without undue delay than three widely separated ones, and three together in a large building will probably be as satisfactory as five or six that are widely separated. In the Widener Library, where there are five automatic elevators averaging something like 125 ft from each other, a passenger often has to wait five minutes or more for a car; three elevators in a single bank would have given better service, though passengers on the average would have had to walk greater distances to reach them.

A major question in locating elevators is whether or not to place them in a part of the building not open to the general public or to restrict their use in other ways. Traffic may be unduly heavy if they are used unnecessarily by undergraduates going up or down only one or two floors. Use can be restricted by having elevator doors and call buttons operate only by key, and distributing keys only to members of the staff and to physically handicapped readers. Another possibility is to locate elevators behind desks where an attendant is always on duty. Control has been facilitated in several new buildings where the bank of elevators is at the rear of the circulation desk lobby or in the central core of the building. The location of stairways leading to restricted levels in similar space is an advantage. Control, it should be emphasized, may be needed for two purposes—to restrict stack access to professors, librarians, and graduate students, and to relieve the load on elevators, which are expensive to operate and maintain.

The gravity of the problem will be recognized by anyone who has waited fifteen minutes for an elevator in the University of Pittsburgh's cathedral of learning, as well as by anyone who has helped to plan an 18-story library building in which six elevators for passengers and one for freight, including space for them and for their lobbies, would cost at least $500,000. It should be added that when an automatic elevator is pushed too hard by heavy traffic its nervous system is likely to break down, and remedial treatment is costly.

One means of reducing the load on elevators is to confine the library's most heavily used facilities to the entrance level and the levels immediately above and below, which readers can be expected or required to reach by stairways. If this can be done, it will be much easier to provide satisfactory elevator service for the professors and graduate students who use the library even more intensively than undergraduates and who go to higher levels but do not rush in and out in such large numbers between classes.

In a very large university library, if the public areas available to undergraduates can be confined largely to the first and second floors and perhaps a basement level with windows, these may well be served by escalators. Passenger elevators accessible to graduate students and faculty only can then be made available for the higher levels.

A leveling device is of great importance, particularly if elevators are used for transportation of heavily laden book trucks. Without such a device, it is difficult for even a skilled operator to stop a car at exactly the right place, and a loaded truck going up and down even an inch as it enters or leaves an elevator is subjected to more wear and tear in a few seconds than during days of operation on the level; the books it carries are also likely to fall off.

If the reader is inclined to think that questions of cab size and elevator speed, or the number of cars and their location are minor matters, he is urged to reflect that a single elevator in a five-level building may cost $35,000, in addition to the cost of the space occupied by its shaft and by the lobby in front of it. This is an investment large enough to warrant careful consideration.

Conveyors should be considered if there is a fairly continuous flow of books or other library materials through a multitier building; they may provide a more satisfactory solution to book transportation problems than either book lifts or a second service elevator. An endless-belt conveyor is similar mechanically to an escalator, but it goes straight up and down. Like elevators, conveyors should be enclosed in fire-resistant shafts. Attached, usually at approximately 9-ft intervals to the chains that go up and down, are carrier prongs on which books can be placed as the prongs go past. It is desirable to provide light trays in which the books can be placed; otherwise, there is danger of books falling down the shafts. The books or trays laden with books can be placed on the conveyor at any level; they then go to the level that has been indicated by pushing a button when they were loaded. If this level is below their starting point, they first go to the top, swing around, and then come down.

It should be noted that the simplest conveyor installations have proved to be the most satisfactory; those that pick up material at any level but deposit it at only one—e.g., the reading-room level—are the least likely to get out of order. Two conveyors of this sort have been in operation at the New York Public Library for nearly forty years with very few difficulties. More complicated installations are to be found at Yale and in the old Library of Congress building where, because the stack is not directly above, below, or adjacent to the charging desk or reading room, the conveyors have to travel horizontally for a considerable distance. A central location for conveyors is highly desirable, of course; installation by a stairwell is advantageous because it may facilitate access for servicing and repair. Precautions should be taken to make conveyors as quiet as possible; many have caused trouble by creaking and groaning.

Pneumatic tubes have been used for many years to transfer call slips from circulation desks to attendants in the stacks. Propulsion is by compressed air or vacuum and slips can be delivered much more rapidly than by elevator or conveyor. Many new charging systems, however, use punched cards of one kind or another for call slips, and these cards, which should not be bent, cannot readily be inserted in the pneumatic tube containers that have been used heretofore. Larger containers present difficult but not insurmountable problems.

Much larger pneumatic tubes have been used for transporting books over considerable distances when vertical or horizontal endless-belt conveyors did not seem practicable. The connection between the Library of Congress Annex and the main building is an example; containers used there are approximately a foot in diameter and 18 in. in length. Unfortunately, they stop at their destination with an abrupt jar, and books are likely to be damaged unless they have been tightly strapped in place; moreover, of course, to strap the books tightly does them no good. Hence, there is still a question as to whether or not pneumatic tubes for transportation of books can ever be entirely satisfactory, in spite of the great advantages in speed that they offer over long horizontal distances.

The University of California at Los Angeles is putting pneumatic tubes into use this year, with material held in place by clamps instead of straps and with the speed greatly reduced at the end of the journey by going up hill sharply for a considerable distance. It is hoped that this will solve the problem. When the final section of the Australian National Library has been constructed, books may have to travel as much as 500 ft by horizontal conveyor before they reach a separate system of vertical conveyors to bring them up to readers. If they move at a rate of 80 ft per minute, which is approximately the maximum safe speed for an endless-belt conveyor, it will take them seven minutes to reach the transfer point, and the total time from stack attendant to reading-room desk will be about nine minutes—this, of course, in addition to the time taken for the call slip to reach the stacks and for the attendant to find the book and place it in the conveyor.

Telephonic, or possibly televised, communication of some kind is obviously essential in any college or university library; the large library may have its own central switchboard or even house the switchboard for its college or university. It is important to facilitate communication within the library, and money may be saved if any instrument in the building can be connected with any other there without going through the telephone company's outside switchboard.

Planners must decide how many telephones are needed and how many of these can be extensions without a separate trunk line to the outside. Location of telephones is an important matter. Unauthorized calls can be expensive—directly, in the case of toll calls, and indirectly when they waste the time of employees. Except for telephones in private offices, therefore, each instrument in the library ought to be placed where a responsible member of the staff can see and hear how it is being used; if one is located at a desk that is in use only part of the day, it should be safeguarded against misuse at other times, either by locking the dial or arranging for it to be cut off at the switchboard.

In planning the wiring conduits that are to be installed at the time the building is constructed, one should remember that installation at any later date will be much more expensive. Both extensions and regular stations are costly and should not be provided before they are needed, but it is uneconomical in the long run not to make readily available at the outset all the outlets that will eventually be wanted.

Pay telephones are usually desirable in a library, and the telephone company will gladly install as many of them as promise to be profitable. In some cases the library receives a commission on receipts, but it may be worth while to provide a pay telephone or telephones even if the institution must make up a small deficit in order to have them. They should be located where they will not disturb readers, usually in a hallway or lobby though preferably in a not too secluded place.

Other means of communication are to be found in a few large libraries. The telautograph, which may be observed in some railway terminals, enables a person to write by hand a message that is reproduced elsewhere in the same form, but its awkwardness interferes with legibility, and few libraries have found it useful. Teletype, by which a typewritten message is made available in the same form at the other end of the line, has been used at the Midwest Inter-Library Center, the Library of Congress, and elsewhere. It is expensive, particularly for intercity communication, and should not be considered unless heavy and important traffic is anticipated; for less frequent communication, long-distance telephone or commercial telegraph is cheaper. Closed-circuit television may be useful in the future.

Loudspeaker and public-address systems, as well as two-way radio installations (as in taxi-dispatching systems), have been used in some libraries, particularly for direct communication between the circulation desk and stack attendants. Care should be taken to avoid creating a disturbance either at the desk or in the stack, especially if the stack is one to which readers are admitted. In a research library particularly, complications may arise from voice communica-

tions relating to materials in foreign languages with which members of the staff are unfamiliar.

Large libraries, particularly those with open stacks, may find it difficult to notify readers of closing time in order to clear the building. Warning gongs or public-address systems may be useful. In planning stack layouts it should not be forgotten that it will be necessary in some way to make sure that all readers have left before the building is closed.

6.3 Noise and Other Distractions

In the preceding discussions of supervision and control and of communications and vertical transportation we have several times mentioned noise. Noise and other distractions are not incidental matters; they fully deserve to be considered fundamental problems in the planning of traffic and circulation patterns. Sound-absorbing materials can do much to minimize noise, but, whenever possible, prevention is better than absorption. Visual distractions are a closely related and equally important subject.

It should be conceded that certain fortunate individuals find noise and motion no problem; those who have grown up amidst large families or have worked from an early age in open offices may be nearly immune to visual and auditory distractions. Many undergraduates, however, even those who prefer to study with the radio on, are not immune, and undergraduates, as well as more advanced students, may deserve consideration in this respect. The professor can usually find a secluded corner in his own home even if he does not have a private study in the library. The graduate student in many institutions is now provided with a reasonably quiet and secluded cubicle or carrel. But for the younger student, the only alternative to a library reading room may be his own dormitory, where his roommate may operate on a different timetable and gregarious friends may be plentiful. The reading room is likely to be crowded with his contemporaries, and table space available to him there may be no more than 30 in. wide by 18 in. deep, which is not enough for spreading out books or, indeed, for opening more than one if space for taking notes is also required. The chair may be unsatisfactory; its arms may be designed for comfort, but a needlessly deep apron beneath the table may prevent the chair from being drawn close. In one large college library, two out of three readers must straddle table legs. Lighting may leave something to be desired.

Fully as serious as any of the handicaps that have been suggested is the fact that the reading room may be in almost constant turmoil; it may settle down twenty minutes after a class period begins, only to be disrupted again fifteen minutes before the period ends as students begin to leave. Afternoons and evenings may be disturbed by more continual though less concentrated coming and going. In many ways the contemporary undergraduate may be worse off than his predecessors; the great monumental reading rooms of earlier days absorbed noise and tended to engulf the reader just as a large stadium filled with a cheering crowd may leave the athlete oblivious of everything but his immediate surroundings. The newer, more intimate reading rooms are too often still surrounded by shelves holding heavily used reference books that attract steady traffic. Entrance to the room is often through a single doorway in the center of the long side or, worse still, at one end; few readers can enter or leave without going past many tables at which others are attempting to study.

The foregoing account of the undergraduate's woes may be enough to indicate why the following basic principles need to be emphasized:

1. *Noise and confusion should be kept out of reading areas insofar as possible.* Circulation and reference desks should be elsewhere, with books, walls, distance, or acoustic materials—perhaps more than one of these barriers—to separate them from readers. The public catalogue and, to a lesser extent, shelves holding reference collections are also areas of relatively heavy traffic. Use of current periodicals involves a good deal of movement. If periodicals or reference books must be in the reading area, used also for general reading, they should at least be placed at one side or one end, with adequate acoustic insulation that can be provided by walls, acoustic floors and ceilings, and books.

2. *Access to reading areas should be provided through as many well-distributed entrances as possible.* If the student can usually find a seat near the point at which he enters the room, he can be expected to leave the same way, and both visual and auditory disturbance can be kept to a minimum.

3. *Individual seating accommodations are highly desirable.* They will be most satisfactory if a barrier at the back of each individual table can be built up to a height of 52 to 54 in., which is enough to prevent the reader from seeing the head of the person in front of him. In a seat of this kind he should be able to turn slightly away from the rest of the room and obtain visual privacy if he wishes.

4. *Table surfaces should be large enough to permit the student to spread out the materials on which he is working.* Space on an individual table goes further than space on a large table; a surface measuring 22 × 33 in. is as useful on an individual table as a segment measuring 24 × 36 in. on a table that must be shared.

5. *Noise and other distractions should be kept in mind when planning traffic lanes throughout the building.* Stairs in the vicinity of reading areas should be well sealed off. Elevator lobbies should be separated from reading areas.

6. *A plan designed to avoid disturbing readers should not make a maze of the library.* Devious and complicated traffic lanes will discourage use of the building and cause frustration and wasted time.

7. *Traffic patterns in book stacks also vitally affect the welfare of readers.* The tendency is to locate a larger and larger percentage of total reading accommodations in the stacks. It is important to keep heavily used traffic arteries away from open carrels.

These are obvious principles; yet most libraries have disregarded one or more of them. Good traffic patterns, plus adequate lighting and ventilation, are essential if the library is to be a satisfactory place for study.

6.4 Spatial Relationships

Ease and convenience of use is a matter of prime importance. This is certainly true of a college library, where some of the students may never have used anything but a small public or high school library and are quite literally frightened by what may seem to them a tremendous collection of 100,000 volumes, particularly if they are given stack access. Convenience is even more important in a great university library where the necessarily large and complex areas for reading, for public service, and for book storage may seem mazelike in character. A large public building of any kind with many rooms may be difficult to find one's way about in, but an academic or research library with 1 million volumes and 30 lineal miles of shelves, and with reading accommodations for 1,500 persons, can well present an almost insurmountable problem to even an experienced advanced scholar. He generally prefers to serve himself if he can. If he can find his way through the catalogue easily, that will help, but the card catalogue as it gets larger may be very difficult to use. Few enjoy facing the 12 catalogue trays under William Shakespeare in the Widener Library or the 87 trays under the heading "United States," or the 14 trays listing the material on "Bible." Unless a reference librarian, equipped to handle the situation and available to come to the rescue, is close at hand, the undergraduate may give up in despair. Unless the scholar can find a good reference and bibliographical collection, with an experienced and helpful librarian readily available when he needs help, he will be handicapped, if not baffled, in using the library. As the library grows larger in area and collections, these problems increase in magnitude, and the climax of all is in the book stack if it seems to have no logical arrangement. There is no wonder that to many the library might be said to resemble a closed book.

There are obviously two possible approaches to a solution. The first is a straightforward simple plan with an easily understood traffic pattern. This has already been emphasized. Second and equally important is a plan by which areas frequently used in sequence by readers and staff are adjacent and readily accessible to each other whenever possible. This section deals primarily with the latter plan. It can best be described under the heading of *spatial relationships*. These relationships, which have a close connection with the organization and service pattern of the library, must be clearly stated in the program, because the architect, even if he is acquainted with library procedures, would otherwise have no way of knowing any special relationships desired by the librarian and his staff.

Discussion of the problem can well begin with the central or key services, that is, the circulation desk, the reference desk, the reference and bibliography collections, the periodical indexes, and the card catalogue—services to which the reader who does not know just how to go about his search for information will naturally turn. They should be easy to find, and the reader should be able to reach one of them that he wants quickly and easily or to go from one to the other in the pursuit of his work without having to go from one floor to another or even great distances on the same floor. Since many patrons of academic libraries come in primarily to find a place to read their own books or to obtain and read a reserve book, a general reading area and the reserve-book collection should be easily found and reached. Another large group (and from the library point of view a perhaps more important one) is represented by the reader who comes to find a particular book or a book on a particular subject in which he is interested. To find the book, its location must be ascertained. The reader may first have to obtain a reference to it in the reference or bibliography collection, but later may have to go to the catalogue to learn whether it is in the library and, if it is there, to discover its shelf mark and then its location on the shelves. As already noted, help may be required, although he may go to the shelves and help himself if he is permitted to do so, instead of asking an attendant to get it for him. When the book is found, if the reader decides to take it home with him instead of using it in the building, it must be charged out at a circulation desk. This can all be summed up by saying that if each of these central services, excluding, of course, the main book-stack collection, can be near the entrance and readily found, a large part of the battle is won.

It must be remembered that the library public-service staff must have a desk or a counter as a home base where it can be readily available to the readers. It will require quarters for its equipment, charging records, office space, and so forth. Of equal importance are the requirements for the processing staff that selects and orders the books and serials, and catalogues them. Its work is closely involved with the reference and bibliography collections and the card catalogue. If it can have quarters immediately adjacent to the catalogue and the reference collection, its work will be simplified and speeded up. Some two generations ago, when our first large modern academic and research libraries were being planned with monumental reading rooms, it became the custom to place the main reading room over the front entrance in order to find a sizable and unobstructed area. The card catalogue was generally assigned to an area near the entrance to the reading room, but too often no space was left close at hand for the staff that prepared the cards and earlier ordered the material, and it was relegated to another floor or a distant part of the same floor. As a result of this, the Library of Congress, the New York Public Library, the Harvard University Library, and others developed the practice of building up two catalogues, one for public use and the other, which was called the "official" catalogue, for the staff. This had the advantage of providing insurance, beyond that available through the shelf list, if a card disappeared from one catalogue or the other, something that did happen from time to time, because of misfiling or occasionally theft; but it also meant considerable extra expense to keep up the two catalogues. Of equal or greater importance was the fact that, even with the two catalogues, the cataloguers spent a not inconsiderable proportion of their time going from one floor to the other in order to see and check the public catalogue cards. The greatest single expense item in current library operations is in salaries. If a library can be planned so that at least the part of the processing staff that makes frequent use of the catalogue can be housed close to it, the arrangement will be a great convenience, and money will be saved for other purposes.

How can the central services, including the portion of the processing staff that uses the catalogue, be placed as close as possible to the front entrance? It should be remembered that vertical movement is normally more difficult and time-consuming than horizontal movement, and stairs are disliked. Elevators are expensive and cause delays. As a result, there has been a strong and desirable tendency in recent years to plan the central services on the entrance level of the library. Space on that level is properly considered the most valuable area in the building. Entrance lobbies are important and must be fairly large in a busy academic library, because of the movement of users in large groups between classes. Therefore, less space on the entrance floor can be left for books, readers, and services than on the other floors, and choices must be made.

One solution is to restrict the use of this floor largely to the central or key services and the above-mentioned part of the processing staff, even if this means that less reading space and less shelving for main collections are available than would have been preferred on this level.

In order to overcome the difficulty at least in part, the new Olin Library at Cornell University has a first floor more than twice the size of the levels above, which has made it possible to put all these services, as well as several special collections, on the main floor (see Fig. 2.1). In spite of this, its processing department space is already congested. But the particular point to be made at this time is that these central services should be placed as close to each other as possible, and that their relationships to each other are a matter of importance. The whole area should be planned carefully so as to leave available as much space as possible for reading accommodations and heavily used parts of the collection, but the areas assigned for lobby space and the central services should not be reduced to an extent that will cause congestion in these areas. The lobby should be especially attractive and give a feeling of spaciousness which can carry through the whole building, but an extravagant amount of space should not be assigned to it for monumental rather than functional purposes. There is no room here for space that will not be heavily used.

In a number of new libraries a great deal of space that would otherwise have been available on entrance levels, has been sacrificed by having a setback of the outside wall on one, two, or even four sides for the sake of an architectural effect. Such a setback can be very attractive. In certain circumstances there may be special reasons which make it desirable in spite of the obvious disadvantages. A good example of this situation is a proposed main library for New York University, where, because of the limited ground space available, a skyscraper building may be a necessity. It was believed that the entrance level, even if it used all the possible area the plot afforded, could not have an entrance lobby and what might be called the main distribution points, exit control, elevators, stairwells, and escalators to the basement and the second floor (which were desirable to relieve the load on the elevators) in addition to the central services. This resulted in a proposal to transfer the latter to the second floor, where these services could have the whole level and would require less space because much of the undergraduate use, which does not require these services, could be funneled off to a lower level.

In listing areas required in a library, the program should state, wherever there is preference, the areas that should be close to the one being described, specifying whether they must be immediately adjacent, or simply on the same level, or whether space immediately above or below with direct stairs or service elevator connection, or both, will be satisfactory. If elevator connection is agreed upon, it makes comparatively little difference whether they are on adjacent floors or farther apart.

There are, of course, other spatial-relationship problems than those connected with the arrangement of the central services and required square footage on the entrance level. One of them, which is too often neglected, is shelving for the main book-stack collections. It has already been noted that a large book stack—there are some today and there will be many more in the years to come—with 500,000 volumes shelved on one level may, unless special care is taken, become a maze in which it is difficult to find one's way about. Equally serious is the problem of a logical arrangement of the books on the shelves. This problem has become more complicated with the great efforts made in recent years to house readers and books in juxtaposition. Anything that tends to break up a logical arrangement of the books should be avoided if at all possible. The situation is complicated by fixed areas for stairs, elevators, toilets, special rooms of any kind, or by "oases" (as seating in the midst of a book stack is often called), or irregularities of any kind in walls or aisles; but careful study and planning can generally prevent many of the difficulties even in a very large library.

The very large A stack level at Princeton with nine main aisles (see Fig. 6.7) at right angles to the ranges, with several elevators and stairwells,

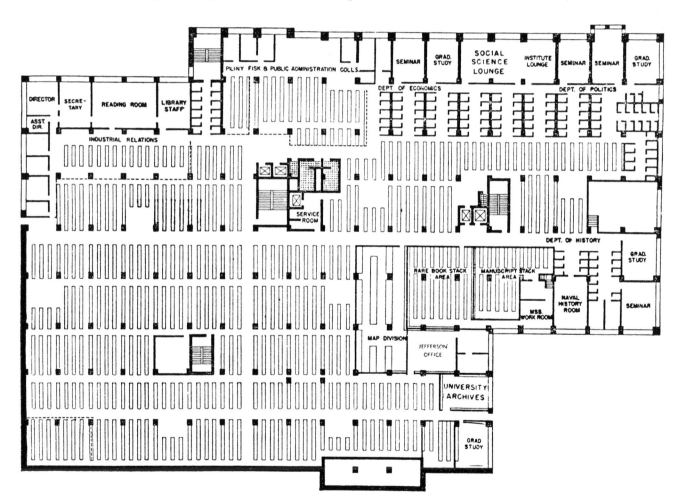

FIG. 6.7 Princeton University Library, A floor. Note the very large stack with tremendous book capacity but more complicated circulation pattern than in Fig. 6.8, there being nine main aisles, only two of which run from one end of the area to the other.

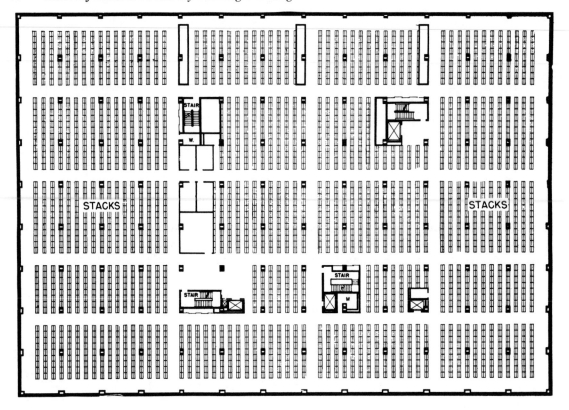

FIG. 6.8 National Library of Medicine, Bethesda, Maryland, B level. A very large stack with a simple circulation pattern. There are four cores, no one of which intrudes on a main aisle. Each of the eleven main aisles goes through from one side of the building to the other.

many special rooms, carrels and oases, illustrates the problem. The B level at the National Library of Medicine in Bethesda, Maryland, which was planned by the same competent architectural firm, represents a simpler pattern (see Fig. 6.8), and the still simpler pattern at Cornell's Olin Library (see Fig. 6.9) shows what can be done.

The plans of the Widener stack, the Widener level in the Lamont building at Harvard, the

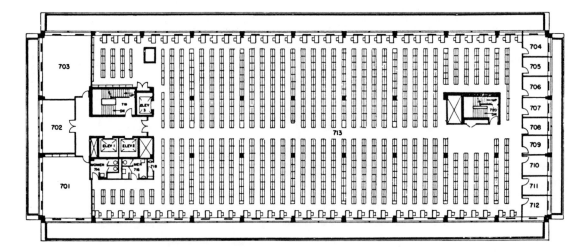

FIG. 6.9 Cornell University, Olin Library. Floor 7. Note the simple circulation pattern with the main stairs and elevators at the main entrance end of the building (see Fig. 2.1). Note also the fairly wide center aisle and the narrower side aisles with open carrels, departmental rooms at the end adjacent to the main stairs, and faculty studies at the other.

main stack at Columbia's Butler Library, and the New York Public Library main stack, shown in Figs. 6.10 to 6.13 respectively, show other simple layouts. That of the University of California at Los Angeles (see Fig. 6.14) shows in the heavy black lines the problems created by special building requirements to prevent earthquake damage and the great effort made to prevent complications which could easily have arisen.

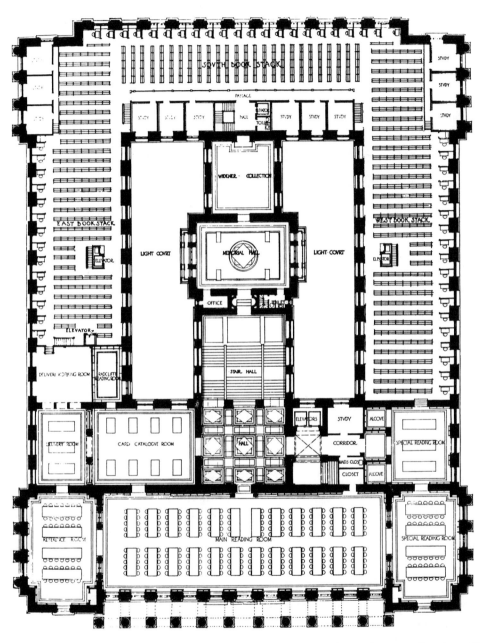

FIG. 6.10 Widener Library Stack, Harvard University. The Widener stack has ten levels surrounding three sides of the building and two courts. The traffic pattern is simple, with only one range of stacks at right angles to the main aisle. Carrels (called stalls) are on the outside walls. Faculty studies are in the outside corners and on the wall facing the courts. The ranges are 50 in. on centers with wide bases, so that the available aisle width is only 26 in. The main aisle, which is 48 in. wide, seems adequate for the heavy traffic. The aisles by the carrels are only 38 in., but with open carrels on one side and stack aisles on the other, seem wide enough.

The stack layout presents five problems: (1) The main aisle is difficult to reach from the entrance; (2) the elevators are scattered and inadequate; (3) the stack aisles are too narrow because of unnecessarily wide (24 in.) bases; (4) the distance from the entrance to the far end of the stack is over 400 ft; (5) the main entrance is reached on the eighth of ten levels after going up five steps.

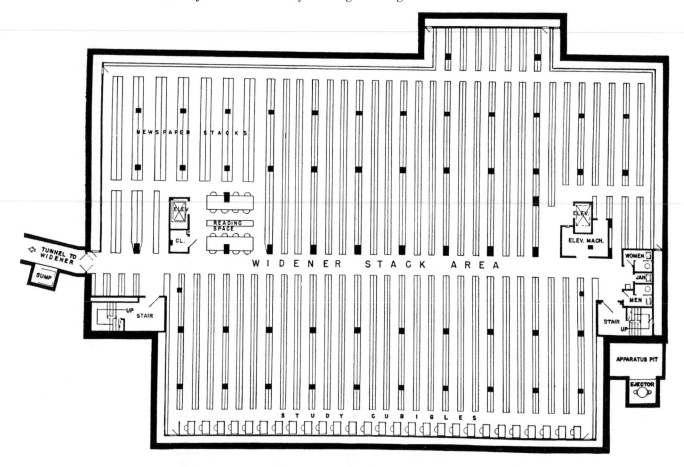

FIG. 6.11   The Lamont Library. Storage stack. This stack is connected by a tunnel with the Widener building. The circulation pattern is simple with a 51-ft long range on one side and a 42-ft range on the other side of a wide center aisle. Ranges are 52 in. on centers with 34-in. aisles. Note the newspaper shelving in the upper left corner with ranges 6 ft 6 in. on centers with 3 ft 6 in. wide aisles and with a reading area carved out of the stack.

The following suggestion may be helpful: Oversize volumes segregated on special deeper shelving with wider spacing between shelves present a special problem. Any segregation of material which takes it out of its logical location complicates matters, and the segregated material should be placed in a rather prominent location, readily accessible, probably near the stack traffic center. If the bulk is small, such material can sometimes be shelved along a wall where deeper shelving will not narrow the aisle in front of it undesirably. If there is enough material of this kind to fill one bay, it may be desirable to equip that bay with wider shelves and eliminate one stack range so as to make possible the wider aisles which are preferable with deeper shelves. The newspaper shelving at the upper left corner of the Widener level of the Lamont stack (Fig. 6.11) shows a possible solution of the problem with very large volumes.

Answers to the following questions will bring out many of the problems involved in spatial relationships. (Others will be based on local situations and details of organization, and the librarian will have to be on the lookout for them as the program is prepared.)

1. What public services should be close to the entrance lobby? At least the control, circulation, reference, and reserve-book desks, the public catalogue, reference, bibliography, and current-periodical collections, as well as stairwells and public elevators or escalators, if either or both of them are to be used, should be considered here. If something has to go because of lack of space, the reserve-book desk, particularly in a large library, might well be the first candidate for a location elsewhere, followed perhaps by the space for current periodicals.

2. Should the quarters for the processing department be on the level with the services listed

in 1 above? If the space cannot be found for all of them there, should they all be housed elsewhere, or can they be divided with accommodations for those working regularly with the catalogue on the central service level and with others elsewhere? In many libraries up to one-half of the area used by these departments is for staff members who have little to do with the catalogue. Some librarians would prefer to keep the whole processing staff together because of problems in supervision of clerical workers if they are divided. But remember that a complete or a partial duplicate catalogue will probably be demanded on a different floor and also that loss in efficiency and waste of time come when professional workers have to go from floor to floor many times a day.

3. What should be the relationship, as far as space assignments are concerned, between the shipping and receiving room and the acquisition department? If they are on different levels, should they be one above the other? It is suggested that in an academic library much less material is transported between these rooms than between the circulation desk and the stack areas, and, if the same elevator is involved in both, the convenience of the circulation staff should be given priority.

4. Should the administrative officers be on the same level with the central services? There is a great difference of opinion here. Some librarians want to be close to the central public service areas so as to be more readily available to the public. Some feel it is of first importance to be adjacent to the acquisition and catalogue departments, and some prefer to be at a distance from either of these groups to make it easier to carry on administrative and sometimes scholarly work undisturbed by routine problems.

A closely related question is whether the assistant librarians should have quarters immediately adjacent to the librarian's office in order to make consultation easier, or whether it is better for them to be close to the departments of the staff that they supervise. For instance, if an assistant librarian is in charge of public service and the librarian's suite is on the second floor, should the assistant librarian have his office next to the reference and circulation departments or on the second floor next to the librarian?

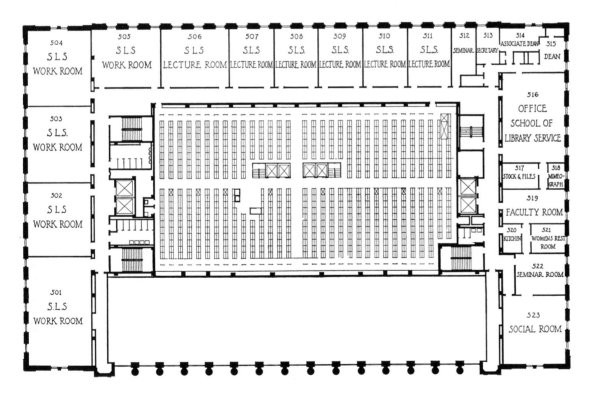

FIG. 6.12 Columbia University stack. This is one of 14 levels which vary in size, but all are in the center of the building with rooms on each of the four sides. There is only one public entrance, that through the circulation desk. This was one of the first modern stacks without ventilation slits between levels and with stairways and elevators closed off so as not to form a chimney.

5. If the library is to include an exhibition room or a rare-book room to which it wishes to attract visitors, especially friends of the library, should this be placed near the entrance so as to be readily accessible, or will quarters elsewhere in a quieter location be satisfactory? Should it consider a basement level without windows where special protection of books and manuscripts from sunlight would not be required, and where temperature, humidity control, and security might be easier to provide, or would a top floor be preferable as arranged at the new library at the University of Pennsylvania?

6. How important is it to place a large percentage of the seating accommodations on the entrance level, or, if that cannot be arranged, on levels up one or down one from the entrance to avoid unnecessarily heavy traffic on stairs or elevators? This arrangement should make for a quieter and less restless building, but at the same time it increases the difficulty of combining accommodations for books and readers, which is often desired today. The decision may be made easier if there is a separate undergraduate area with many seats and comparatively few books, which might make it possible to house this section of the library's work within one level of the entrance and make available more distant levels to graduate students and faculty who require comparatively few seats but many volumes.

These questions might be added to almost indefinitely, but it is hoped that the basic questions of most general interest have been suggested above. Others will affect comparatively few libraries, and here, as elsewhere, decisions should generally be based on local conditions. Stating the questions and in some cases suggesting possible answers is not meant to dictate decisions but to clarify the problems.

Summary

This chapter has dealt with a variety of problems, the solution of which plays a large part in the planning of a successful library building. The four sections differ widely, but it should be

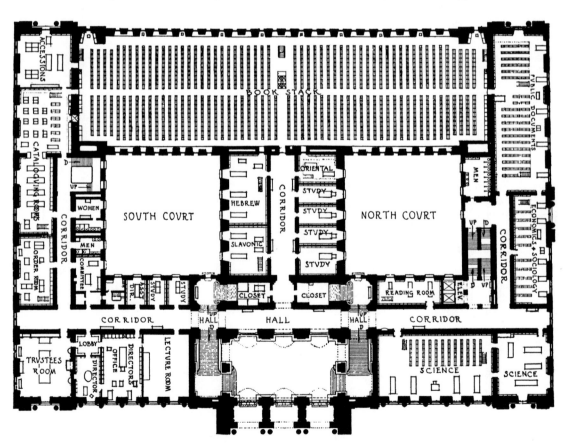

FIG. 6.13 New York Public Library stack. The stack has seven identical levels under a monumental reading room and has the simplest traffic pattern of any very large stack.

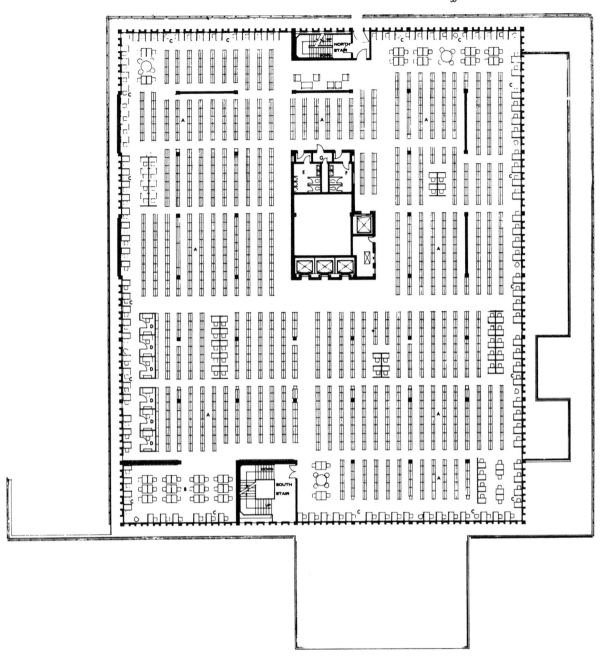

FIG. 6.14 University of California at Los Angeles. Research library. This is a typical upper floor of the first unit of a new building. The heavy lines represent earthquake reinforcements which complicate traffic patterns, but the central core and the two stairwells near the outside walls do not unduly complicate shelving arrangements.

remembered that they are all concerned with *traffic problems*. Among them, directly or indirectly, they affect all the basic elements of planning. Nothing in the design should be "frozen" until each of the four and their relations to one another have been given adequate thought and study. A successful library must have its public service, its reading accommodations, and its housing for collections and staff conveniently related to each other, to the supervision and control arrangements, and to the vertical transportation. Audible and visual distractions must be minimized so that a quiet, comfortable place for study and work will be provided. Unless these requisites are fulfilled, aesthetically pleasing exteriors and interiors and the other important features of a library will not make up for its defects. Each of them should be kept in mind, studied, and analyzed from the beginning. The traffic patterns in all their aspects should be diagrammed and tested in their relationship to other problems as the location of each area is considered. The simple and successful traffic patterns in the new Olin Library at Cornell are noteworthy. Dr. Stephen A. McCarthy, the Director of Libraries, reports: "The continuous study of traffic patterns in the Olin Library moved the entrance from the middle of the north side of the building to the west side; it moved the elevators from the center toward the west end; and this in turn dictated the location of the graduate study rooms and the conference rooms at the west end. The disposition of many of the facilities in the building flows naturally from the traffic patterns." It might be added that this was not an accident.

7

Accommodations for Readers and Staff

7.1 For Whom and for How Many?

Planning for seating accommodations for readers involves four basic questions:

1. Who are the readers? Can they and should they be divided into different groups with different types of accommodations for each group? If so, can a formula be found and used for the number of accommodations and the total square footage required for each group? These questions will be discussed in this section.

2. Should there be different rooms or areas for different subject fields, different forms of materials, or different types of use, and, if so, what fields, forms, and types should be considered? This question will be discussed in section 7.2.

3. Should different types of seating be used for different groups of readers or different reading areas? This question will be considered in section 7.3.

4. After the decisions have been reached on these three points, how many seats should be provided for each group in each area and with each type of accommodation?

College and university libraries can expect to have demands for accommodations from five distinct groups of users—undergraduates, graduate students, faculty members, visiting scholars, and others, including the general public, although not every group can be counted on in each library. These groups differ widely in the use they make of a library; in order to estimate the number of seats that ought to be provided in a new building, one should estimate the needs of each group separately and then total them.

Undergraduates. In most institutions of higher learning, though not in all, undergraduates are more numerous than the four other groups combined. Statistics reported in the January, 1960, issue of *College and Research Libraries*—the latest available in this form—show that, in 119 universities giving graduate work, the median number of undergraduates was 6,175, compared with 1,080 graduate students. In colleges and universities of other types, according to the same report, not more than 5 per cent of the students were on the graduate level, and in most cases there were very few graduate students or none at all. Undergraduates, then, represent the largest part of the clientele in academic libraries. This does not mean that their use of the library will be proportionate to their numbers or that the percentage will not change; that will depend on the character of the institution and its objectives.

No definite formula can be proposed to determine the percentage of undergraduates whom the library should be prepared to seat at one time. Institutions differ widely in the amount of use to be expected at periods of peak demands, and estimates are still more difficult to make because of uncertainty as to how much the number of undergraduates will increase during the years ahead for which the building is being planned. It is even harder to predict how much use by the undergraduates will change as the result of changed admissions regulations and new educational policies of the institution. In a word, the student group is constant neither in size nor in other characteristics. Finally, it is not easy to forecast how much a fine, new, comfortable, attractive, and adequate building will increase the demands for seating. And the effect of other possible additions to the institution's building plant should not be forgotten. A new student union, study or library rooms in residential halls, small private study accommodations connected with dormitory suites—all will have an influence on the peak loads. In spite of all these uncertainties, some estimate must be made before plans for a new library are prepared if the institution expects to provide a building large enough, but not unnecessarily large, for a reasonably long period ahead.

The author suggests that the administrative officers of the college should be responsible for an estimate of the increase in the number of students to be enrolled during the period for which the proposed building is designed to be adequate, and that they should also indicate whether plans for changes in admissions and educational policies will affect library use. If past experience gives any indication of future developments, proportionate use should increase rather than decrease, even without policy changes and in spite of the increased vogue of paperbacks owned by the students; this results from a gradual rise in the caliber of the student body and increasing demands on space in other buildings. Past experience in practically all institutions with library buildings completed since the Second World War indicates that when a well-planned, comfortable, and attractive building is provided, use will increase tremendously, sometimes even doubling or tripling if the space provided makes the increased use possible.

But other important factors may sooner or later have a bearing on this problem of the number of required seats. Is the library service to undergraduates to be centralized in the proposed enlarged or new structure? If the university is a large one with departmental libraries, how much of the service to undergraduates will be provided outside the main building? Is it a residential institution with students living in the immediate neighborhood who can be expected to use the library heavily in the evening, or does the student body largely commute, leaving the campus as soon as possible after classes are over? Are there a large number of evening students? They are often very numerous in a city institution. Generally, however, if both the day

and evening students commute, they do not use the facilities at the same time of day. Do most of the students live in dormitories on the campus? Is the university in a city, where there are many attractions outside the campus, day after day? Or is it in comparatively rural surroundings, where few outside activities attract the students, particularly during weekday evenings? Is it coeducational? Men and women tend to try to study together; coeducation increases library use if not the amount of studying accomplished.

Does the institution provide special reading rooms and library collections in the residential halls, as is done in the Yale Colleges, the Harvard Houses, and the larger dormitories in many public and private institutions today? Are the dormitories so congested and are student customs such that the dormitory rooms are not suitable for study? If so, the student who wants to work will find that he must go to the library to study any time except perhaps between 1 and 7 A.M. What are the library hours? Is it open until midnight on weekday evenings or only until 9 or 10 o'clock? If it is in a residential institution with heavy evening use, do some students spend the early evening at the library, while others go to the movies first and then to the library from 10 to 12 o'clock, reducing the percentage who can be expected at any one time? All of the foregoing questions suggest problems that ought to be considered, though they may do little to help the person drawing up the program to decide on the number of seats that should be available to undergraduate students in his particular institution.

The following additional questions should also be considered by the program writer, although, like those that have been suggested above, they have no answers that can be translated into exact figures. Does the library expect to be able to take care of the peak demands which tend to come just before and during the beginning of the examination period or during the reading period, if there is one? These are by all odds the periods of heaviest library use. They may also be those when the students are most anxious to study and when dormitory rooms may be more suitable for that purpose than at other periods. At these times students may be willing and able to study at large tables in a reading room with chairs closer together than at other times in the academic year. Is the institution prepared during peak loads to have the students use facilities outside the library, such as study halls, seminars, and classrooms, on the basis that it cannot afford to increase the size of its library by as much as 20 per cent for the convenience of its students during perhaps only 50 hours in the academic year?

Does the library encourage students to study their own books in the library on the basis that a more studious atmosphere will prevail there than elsewhere and that study with reference material immediately at hand tends to be especially advantageous?

Does the institution expect to assign seats in the library for honors students? Whenever a seat is assigned to one student exclusively and cannot be used by others, the total number of seats required is increased, because no student to whom a seat is assigned will use it during all hours of the day or even all the hours when the peak load is expected. For instance, if 25 per cent of the students are honors students and a seat is assigned for each one of them, then the remaining seats must take care of the other 75 per cent of the total student body who may study almost as much as the honors students during the peak-load periods. The author does not recommend assignment of seats to undergraduates. Very few institutions can afford to have a library large enough for this purpose. At Harvard, 60 per cent of the undergraduates go out for honors, and even more at Radcliffe; if each honors student were assigned a seat for exclusive use, the total seating accommodations now available would be completely inadequate.

Dr. W. W. Bishop, one of our wisest librarians, recommended as early as 1920 that libraries be prepared to seat one-half of the entire student body at one time, but until a few years ago the author of this volume, who had a reasonably wide acquaintance among the libraries of the country, knew of no institution that ever had a well-authenticated record of over 40 per cent of the undergraduate student body in its library or libraries at one time. However, since 1950 he has learned of a number that, on occasion, have had as many as 50 per cent. These are institutions with students of the highest quality. They are in a rural area or a small town and usually are coeducational. It is suggested that an institution with these characteristics be prepared to seat at least one-half of the undergraduate student body at one time. If such an institution is expected to grow in the years ahead for which

the library is being planned, this may mean a considerably larger percentage of the present student body. At Harvard University, with a high-grade student group in a metropolitan area, the librarian estimated some years ago that if the library provided for three out of eight of the undergraduate students at one time in either the house libraries, departmental libraries, the research library, or the undergraduate library, that should be sufficient. So far this has proved to be true, although the pressure for seating becomes unpleasantly heavy during the reading and early examination periods, and, in this widely decentralized library, since certain units are frequently inadequate, a student, in order to find a seat, may have to go to a building other than the one he would prefer.

A few years ago the author suggested at the University of Florida that at the time of the peak load up to 75 per cent of the students could be expected to be studying at one time and that one-half of this 75 per cent would, or at least could, properly use their own rooms for this purpose. This would leave 37½ per cent to be cared for elsewhere. It was then suggested that one-fifth of this number, or 7½ per cent, might well be cared for in reading or study rooms in the residential halls, and that, of the 30 per cent remaining, one-third would find their study facilities in departmental libraries, leaving 20 per cent to be cared for in the central building. In a great city university, such as New York University, with nearly 40,000 students registered altogether, but with a very considerable number of part-time and evening students, the university has been unable to provide in all of its decentralized libraries for more than 10 per cent of the total student enrollment at any one time, and 15 per cent or a little more might be adequate.

Consideration of accommodations for students in undergraduate professional schools should not be forgotten. These may include law, medicine, divinity, education, public health, dentistry, pharmacy, nursing, veterinary medicine, architecture, engineering, home economics, agriculture, and physical education, among others. Library needs of these diverse fields are by no means identical and demands for seats will vary.

Nothing has been said of departmental libraries for disciplines in the arts and sciences; i.e., the humanities, social sciences, sciences and their subdivisions. It should always be remembered that departmental libraries tend to multiply, and unless this tendency is kept under control, the cost to the institution may become very high. At Harvard University there are over 90 libraries in all, and similar situations on a smaller scale may be found in a good many of the large universities. In too many American institutions, while some of the departmental libraries are definitely recognized as part of the university library, others have simply grown up, with the university library more or less unaware of their existence. This decentralization has been carried even farther in German and Japanese universities.

A study of the circumstances should be made in each institution, and the foregoing statements can at best provide only some worth-while guide lines that may help in solving the problem. No clear rules can be suggested for determination of needs, but most of the factors involved have been outlined, and it should be emphasized that each institution must study its problems carefully, with the years ahead in mind as well as the present and the immediate future. The difficulties involved in estimating future needs make it obvious that, unless an institution is ready to start all over again with completely new library facilities every generation, its library should be planned in such a way that additions can be made without handicapping it aesthetically, functionally, or as a vital part of the educational program.

It can be suggested here that at least 25 sq ft per undergraduate student to be housed in a reading area be used in estimating preliminary space requirements and that careful planning should make that figure possible. This does not include non-assignable space outside the reading areas which is often primarily for use of undergraduates.

Graduate Students. Graduate students in arts and sciences or those working for an advanced degree in professional schools represent a somewhat different problem from undergraduates, both in respect to the square footage required per seat and the percentage of students for whom seats should be provided. Each graduate professional school is likely to have its own special departmental library, and the percentage of students requiring seating accommodations at any one time in each of these libraries may well be determined after consideration of the points

dealt with earlier in this chapter, but with a separate calculation for each professional school. In general, the percentage of seats required would tend to be larger for graduates than for undergraduates, particularly in law schools where up to 50 per cent (or in a few schools even more) may want to use the library at one time. City institutions with many part-time students are an exception to this statement. In a medical school the percentage will be considerably smaller, as so much time is required in laboratory and clinical work. Similar factors are to be considered in engineering and technological institutions. Those working in the sciences resemble the medical and engineering students; they spend so much of their time in laboratories that library demands are decreased because there are only 24 hours in the day, if for no other reason. Graduate students in arts and sciences, particularly in the humanities and social sciences, ordinarily require seats for a percentage of their number little if any less than those usually required in a law school.

Graduate students make heavier use of the library than undergraduates and, other things being equal, require more space for each student accommodated. For students working for the master's degree, some 20 per cent more space for each seat should probably be provided than for those working for the bachelor's. Thirty sq ft per seat in the reading area is proposed.

The graduate students in the humanities and social sciences working for the doctorate will make the largest proportional demands on the library in the percentage of seats required. There is ordinarily a great difference between those doing the first and second year of their work toward the Ph.D. and those who are engaged in writing their dissertations in these fields. Many institutions believe that any man or woman who is actually writing a doctoral dissertation in the humanities or social sciences should have at his disposal an assigned library seat, preferably at an individual table or in a carrel and with a bookshelf, for the full period when he is occupied with this task, and that 40 per cent more space than is provided for each undergraduate, or 35 sq ft, is none too much. Let us say, then, that in the average institution there should be a seat in the library for every man actually working full time on his dissertation in the humanities and social sciences; that for others working for the Ph.D. but not yet engaged in writing the dissertation, one seat for every two full-time students should generally be sufficient; for those working for the master's degree, a seat for 40 to 50 per cent might do in many universities, depending on local conditions. Circumstances in each institution will vary, and these estimates should not be accepted blindly. This is one of the points on which an experienced library consultant may be helpful.

The square-footage areas proposed above—25 for undergraduates, 30 for graduate students in their first year, and 35 for each one engaged in dissertation writing—are for carefully laid out, nonmonumental space, none of it in closed and locked carrels. If closed carrels are to be provided, each of them will require not less than 40 sq ft, if the adjacent aisle space is included, unless the partitions are nothing more than gratings, such as are found in the Rutgers University Library.

These figures are for the reading areas alone, and it must not be forgotten that a very considerable amount of square footage is required elsewhere in the building for other services to readers, as well as for the non-assignable space discussed in section 16.2.

Faculty. The needs of faculty members differ from those of undergraduate or graduate students, and estimating the square footage that should be provided for them is even more difficult than for the two previous groups. Customs and study habits vary a great deal between institutions. If adequate library facilities for faculty members have been provided in the past, it is probable that many faculty members in the humanities and social sciences will prefer to do much of their research and preparation for lectures in the library. In other institutions, if facilities have not been satisfactory and particularly if faculty members live close to the campus, many of them will prefer to work in their own homes, believing that they may be less likely to be disturbed there. However, as houses and apartments tend to grow smaller, they become less suitable places to study, and it should be noted that, for younger faculty members with children at home, the house may not be a satisfactory place to carry on research work. Also, a considerable percentage of these persons in many institutions are still working on their dissertations, and satisfactory quarters for research are of great importance to them. In general, there is less demand proportionately for faculty

studies in colleges than in universities. Many universities have felt that they could provide library faculty studies for senior members of the faculty only, although these men may need such accommodations less than their juniors. The institution's policy in regard to faculty offices in other buildings also affects demands for studies in the library. Many faculty members may request a study in the library, as well as an office elsewhere.

While the number of faculty members may exceed 10 per cent of the number of students in some institutions, they can probably be left out of calculation in connection with seating capacity in the regular public reading areas of the library. This is not because they do not read, but because their heaviest library use tends to be in quarters specially assigned for them when it is not in the reference room, the public catalogue, or the current periodical room, and even there they are not likely to stay for long periods of time or to add to congestion.

Instead of seating members of the faculty in the public areas, provision for their use of the library can be made in three ways: in a special faculty reading room; in faculty studies; or in the type of cubicle or carrel provided by the library for its graduate students. The dividing line between graduate students and faculty is not always clear, of course; in the case of teaching fellows, the facilities ordinarily assigned to graduate students are usually considered adequate, but the older professors are seldom satisfied with these quarters.

While it has not been unusual to provide special faculty reading rooms, their value is questionable. Faculty members doing research work or writing lectures prefer to be alone, rather than in a reading room, even if its use is restricted to their colleagues. The desirability of a small social area for use by faculty members and graduate students is worth considering.

But the great problem in connection with faculty members concerns studies. How many of them should there be, and of what size? As has already been indicated, the number to be provided will vary a great deal from institution to institution. If quarters for the faculty in the library are intended for use as studies only and not also as offices, the number and size can ordinarily be very much reduced. Most professors who are doing administrative work or who require frequent consultation with students do not like to do this in their library studies, and would prefer an office in a departmental or other building. Faculty members in the sciences are better satisfied if their studies or offices are in the buildings which they consider their headquarters. The same will be true for a certain percentage, varying in each institution, of those in the humanities and the social sciences. No attempt will be made here to suggest the percentage of the faculty members who should have studies in a central library building. This is a good problem to place before the library committee and possibly a library consultant on building planning.

Many faculty studies in many institutions are assigned to men who use them so rarely as to make them a luxury as far as the institution is concerned. Studies should be assigned for limited periods only, and assignments renewed only when the need is clearly demonstrated. On the other hand, it should not be forgotten that much of the valuable research carried on in our academic institutions is greatly facilitated by faculty studies in libraries.

But there is another problem. How large should the study be? An examination of libraries built during this century will show studies all the way from well over 200 net sq ft down to no

more than one-sixth of that figure. Other factors affecting study sizes and layouts will be dealt with elsewhere, but the program, which is discussed in section 13.1, should give some indication of the number of studies to be decided on and their average size. A preliminary estimate of 75 net sq ft each can well be used until a detailed study of requirements is made locally and the architect has offered his suggestions.

Five additional problems in connection with faculty accommodations should be kept in mind, and arrangements made to deal with them.

1. Faculty members as a group, whatever their politics or economic outlook, are ultra-conservative in their study habits and do not change them readily.

2. Few faculty members like to share a study with another, and it is much better to provide two rooms each as little as 50 to 60 sq ft in area than one twice that size with two men assigned to it. Of course, a room for two is sometimes satisfactory for men with schedules so different that they would not be using the room at the same time, and the larger study might be desirable, but this is an unusual situation. Faculty studies of different sizes from minimum to ample are shown in Fig. 7.1.

3. In a university, or a college for that matter,

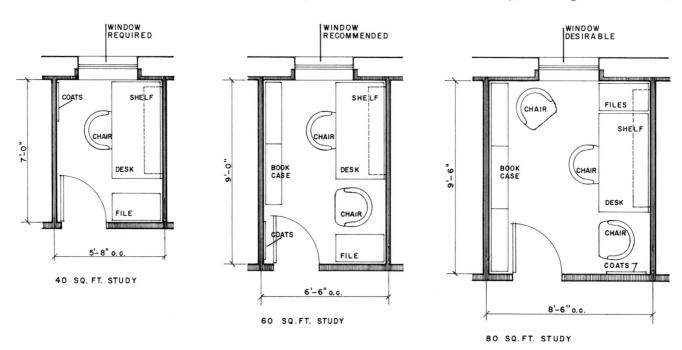

FIG. 7.1 Faculty studies of different sizes. The study at the left is minimum for a completely closed room, and a window is required. The one at the center is adequate if there is a window, but might be complained of without one. The right-hand study is generous and, while a window is desirable, it can be omitted if a clerestory window opening into a lighted book stack or other area is provided.

where research is emphasized and productive writing is an important factor for promotion, a larger number of faculty studies should be provided than in an institution which has primarily a teaching rather than a research faculty. Many college libraries find that the demand for faculty studies has been or may still be quite small, but as years go by and research is emphasized more and more, the demand for library studies will tend to increase as it will for library research collections. The author recently made a survey of libraries in the state of Maine and found a great demand for studies and research material in one institution, while in another, also with a good national reputation but with a teaching rather than a research faculty, the demand was almost nonexistent.

4. The difference between a faculty study and an office should not be forgotten. If the institution provides most faculty members with conveniently located offices on the campus, the demand for studies in the library will be greatly reduced. If faculty studies in the library must serve as offices also, the demand for them will increase, and they may prove to be a poor retreat for study and a disturbing factor for all concerned. Faculty offices, as distinct from studies, are not recommended for the library.

5. If faculty studies are not satisfactorily lighted and ventilated, complaints are sure to arise; if they contain less than 75 sq ft[1] and have no outside windows, they may present a problem for anyone with a tendency toward claustrophobia, but if a very considerable percentage of faculty members are to have studies and have them with windows, window space for other purposes may be reduced so far as to prove a serious handicap for other users. To get around this problem, studies have sometimes been placed on top floors facing light courts which go down only to that floor. One difficulty with this solution is that it houses professors at a considerable distance from the books in their subject fields.

In this connection remember that much can be done with paint (color) to cheer up inside rooms and that "borrowed" or clerestory light above the line of vision, coming perhaps from

adjacent stack areas, may help relieve the confining effect of inside studies.

Visiting Scholars. This group will be a comparatively negligible factor in a great majority of institutions, but in any one of the fifteen or twenty largest research libraries, such as those at Columbia, Harvard, Chicago, and the University of California, for instance, particularly those in large cities or on the way to and from "vacationland," it may be important. The problem of visiting scholars should be considered seriously in building planning. Dartmouth College in upper New England, with a superb college library, is another institution used heavily by visitors, particularly during the summer months. Only local experience can serve as a basis for estimating the requirements, but they should be carefully studied.

At Harvard University for a large part of the year, both summer and winter, the Widener (Central) Library could make good use of 25 studies for visiting scholars, in addition to 50 carrels. An equal number of both studies and carrels would be useful in the departmental libraries in the university. It is suggested that accommodations suitable for graduate students will be satisfactory for visiting scholars in most institutions, and square footage can be figured on the same formula used for that group.

Others, Including the General Public. Visitors who are not scholars can sometimes be ignored in estimating seating requirements but should not be forgotten because of the problem they may present. Their number is not necessarily negligible. In most college or university libraries, graduates of the institution are welcome. But high school and college students from other local institutions with poorer libraries can be expected to pour in unless they are discouraged from doing so. Here the decision as to what to do with or about them is a matter of policy for the institution's administration after the librarian has set forth in detail the effect on the library. The time when a new building is being planned is a suitable one for consideration of this problem. The 25 sq ft of space for each person to be accommodated at the time of peak load which was proposed for undergraduates should be suitable for this group.

Summary. Five different groups of readers should be kept in mind in planning seating accommodations in an academic library: undergraduates, graduate students, faculty members,

---

[1] The new Johns Hopkins Library has over 200 studies with no windows and with only 50 sq ft each. A new type of lighting fixture, good individual ventilation, careful attention to decor and equipment, and opaque glass in the door seem to make them possible.

visiting scholars, and others. Methods of determining the number of seats for each group have been discussed. The number and the percentage of possible users for whom accommodations might be required at the time of peak load have been considered. In the hope of helping the planning team and the architect, a rough net or gross square-footage requirement for each seat has been suggested for each group. But for each of these decisions, local conditions must be kept in mind, and the architect should have an opportunity to make his own suggestions. The decision reached on these points will have as much to do with the total cost of the proposed structure as any other one item, and a study of the problems involved should not be curtailed. Here, even more perhaps than in connection with any other part of the plan, advice is required from everyone concerned, and an expert library consultant may also be helpful.

7.2   Types of Areas for Readers

Many different types of accommodations are available to the present-day reader. In many of the older academic libraries all seating accommodations for readers were found in one or more large rooms, where books, except for those shelved around the walls, were brought to those who requested them. As libraries grew larger and readers increased in numbers, additional reading rooms came into use for current periodicals, for instance, or for other limited purposes such as public documents, reserve books, rare books, and manuscripts. As time went on, divisional reading rooms for groups of disciplines came into use—the humanities, social sciences, and sciences, and for more limited subjects, such as fine arts and music. In the meantime an increasing number of libraries began to open their book stacks to many if not all readers. In due course accommodations were provided in carrels adjacent to the books, and finally in recent years individual seating in larger and larger proportions has been made available throughout the library.

The different types of rooms and reading areas in common use today in academic and research libraries will be discussed in this section.

1. Reference Rooms. As will be noted in section 13.6, dealing with spatial relationships, reference rooms are preferably placed on the entrance level where space is at a premium, close to the main entrance lobby and not far from the professional staff of the processing department. If they are larger than necessary, they are likely to be used by persons simply looking for a place to read, as well as by those wanting reference information. Experience shows that the number of persons actually using reference books at any one time is comparatively small, even in very large libraries. In almost any of our older university libraries, large reference reading rooms seating hundreds of readers can be found. These have ordinarily been monumental rooms filled with large reading tables, with bookcases around the walls. One reason for making these rooms so large was to provide wall shelving for the reference collection. Wall space does not count up very fast for book capacity, particularly where there are windows coming down to the floor. (It is never difficult for a wide-awake reference staff to fill all the shelving available with reference books and then look for more.) These rooms have had the disadvantage of making it necessary for the user of the reference books to travel long distances to find the material wanted, and as a result the rooms almost always gave an impression of restlessness and tended to be noisy, although the great height of the monumental areas did a good deal to absorb sound. Their lighting was always a problem, at least after dark, and in most cases general lighting from the ceiling and skylights had to be supplemented by lighting over bookcases and by table lamps.

But to go back to the optimum size of a reference room: There is no record at Harvard University's Widener Library of as many as 50 readers using the reference collection at one time for reference purposes, and it is suggested that, unless a good reason can be found for a larger number, fewer than 100 seats are adequate for a reference room in an academic library, except in cases where it is expected to be used for other purposes as well. Obviously, a room seating no more than 50 persons, with 30 sq ft per person allowed, will not have wall space enough for the shelving required by a large reference collection. The valuable periphery of the room might therefore be used for individual seating, with seats along at least two or three of the walls, and the books might be concentrated in double-faced floor cases, either in the center of the room or at one end or side. (See Fig. 7.2.)

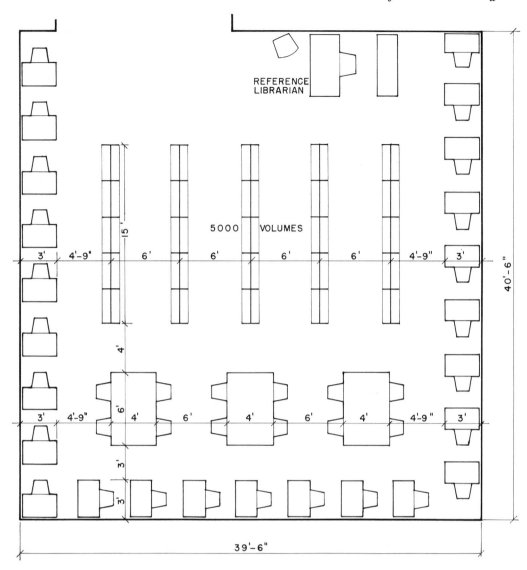

FIG. 7.2 Reference area for 5,000 volumes and 37 readers. An area of 1,600 sq ft is included here. This provides approximately 30 sq ft for each reader, 10 volumes per square foot, if figured at 100 volumes per section for the collection. This can be considered as minimal spacing.

If books are at one end or one side, and if the room is high enough, a mezzanine over the reference collection may make comparatively inexpensive additional square footage available and also absorb under it some of the inevitable noise. Careful study should be given to the spacing of the bookcases. If they are kept down in length to 15 ft, for instance, and there is a good cross aisle at each end, there seems to be no reason why reference-collection shelving should be more than 6 ft on centers, even if the shelving is made extra deep. Since reference books on the average are larger in size than others, it is quite

customary to make shelves for them up to 12 in. in depth, but this would still leave an aisle 4 ft wide, which is enough to enable two persons to pass readily on the occasions when two readers are working in the same aisle at the same time. In the Olin Library at Cornell University shelves 12 in. deep have been found to be a nuisance, because books are pushed back and become too hard to get at, particularly on lower shelves. If the aisles are dead-end, the length of the ranges should not exceed 9 to 12 ft.

Reference books are usually thicker than others as well as deeper. There is less reason to provide space for any large amount of growth in a reference collection than elsewhere, as older volumes can frequently be shifted to the stack when new ones are acquired, and it is generally feasible to estimate 100 volumes to a single-faced section, or 1,000 volumes in a double-faced range 15 ft long if the sections are full height. Some reference librarians in large research libraries would like to look forward to a reference collection of 20,000 volumes, but the author suggests that a well-selected collection of 10,000 volumes, particularly if the book stacks are open-access, is sufficient for most central reference collections in large libraries, if the bibliographical material discussed in the next section is readily accessible elsewhere. For a large university library this would mean 10 double-faced ranges 15 ft long on 6-ft centers. If seats for 50 readers in all are provided for, with 30 sq ft allowed for each, the whole room will require some 2,500 sq ft of floor space, instead of the much larger areas frequently made available in the past.

This is not to object to monumental or other large rooms, but to explain that they are not necessary in order to house a reference collection and those who use it, and that a reference room is far from being an ideal location for general reading because of its inevitable restlessness. The formula is offered only as a suggestion and a basis for discussion by the librarian and his committee. In some very large libraries the space might prove inadequate. In some small ones the figure can and should be reduced, unless the room is to include the bibliographical collection, and also magazine indexes, which should have special equipment.

Remember that the necessary conversation between library users and reference librarians tends to be disturbing, and keep this in mind in selecting the best location for the reference desk.

2. Bibliographical Collection. The situation for bibliography is very similar to that for the reference collections, but the number of readers to be accommodated and the number of bibliography volumes to be shelved can probably be cut to perhaps one-half that allowed for reference[2] in most libraries. For both reference and bibliography, at least half of the seats may be individual, the others at tables which provide more rather than less than 6 sq ft of table space per reader. Special equipment for at least part of the bibliography collection, such as the *Cumulative Book Index, United States Catalog,* and the *Library of Congress Catalog,* the catalogues of other great libraries and periodical indexes, if they are kept in this area, might well be provided. (See Fig. 7.3.) These may require several hundred additional square feet of space in a large library. It should be remembered that a large part of the consultation of bibliographical works by readers and library staff is frequently carried on at "stand-up" consultation tables. Each table of this kind may well be equipped with a high stool which can be pushed under it.

If the reference and bibliography collections are located, as they generally should be, adjacent to each other, near the public catalogue and entrance lobby, they are likely, because of the type of use, as well as their location, to have a restless atmosphere and noise will be almost inevitable. This should help to discourage their use by the general reader if he is adequately provided for elsewhere. It should be remembered that undergraduates, when looking for a place to study, will sit almost anywhere. The use of seating accommodations in a bibliography room sometimes has to be restricted to prevent their use for general reading. If these areas can also be adjacent or close to the quarters of the professional cataloguers and acquisition-department assistants, it should be possible to avoid a good deal of duplication of expensive bibliographical and reference material.

3. Current Periodicals. If the library is to encourage the use of current periodicals, as it clearly ought to do, there may well be seating

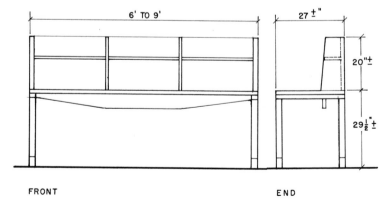

6' TO 9'   27 ± "

20" ±

29½" ±

FRONT   END

FIG. 7.3 Index table for bibliographies.

[2] The program for new quarters in a library now being planned calls for space for 60,000 volumes; it is evident that this is a controversial matter.

accommodations in a periodical room for some 3 to 5 per cent, or in some libraries even more, of the total number of readers provided for in the building. It is not unreasonable to expect one reader out of 20 or 30 in the library to be using current periodicals, but this figure will, of course, vary in different institutions. This room should also be near the entrance if that is possible, and if use of current periodicals is not sufficient to fill the seats, they are likely to be occupied by readers using their own material.

There is, of course, the problem of deciding how periodicals are to be shelved, and how many of them can be provided for within a given space. It is pleasant and often desirable to be able to place current periodicals on display cases where the cover of each one is readily in view. Special cases for this purpose are available through standard library-equipment houses or they can be built locally, but ordinarily they provide no more than five shelves to a section, and while four periodicals can be placed on some shelves, instead of three, it is not safe to count on more than 18 periodicals to a 3-ft-wide section. If the periodicals are placed flat on regular shelves 5 in. on centers and the shelves are properly labeled along the edges, it should be possible to have 14 shelves to a section, providing for 45 titles instead of 18. Many of the larger libraries with great collections of periodicals must choose between accommodating them on regular shelves or selecting the most used ones and putting them on display cases and shelving the others elsewhere, possibly in adjacent stacks. If periodicals are shelved on display cases, each square foot of floor space will provide for fewer than two—probably for no more than one and one-half titles. If they are shelved on regular shelving with 14 shelves to a section, this can be increased to as many as five per square foot. Regular shelving has less depth for a range than display shelving, and a wider aisle is not necessary. (See Fig. 8.18.)

Special provisions should be made for periodical indexes if they are to be kept in this room, instead of in the reference or bibliography rooms. If in the latter, they should be as close to the periodical room as possible. Some libraries find it possible and advisable to combine in one room the reference, bibliography, and current periodical collections.

Some libraries prefer to have the bound back files of their periodicals served by the same staff that cares for the current numbers; they are therefore shelved close at hand, on the same level (often a difficult arrangement) or perhaps on the level directly above or below with a stairway making convenient connection between the two. This can be particularly desirable for the heavily used titles recorded in the standard periodical indexes. But remember, in arranging for the seating accommodations for periodical reading, that peace and quiet and comfort are desirable, and that the readers' purpose is quite different from that of students who are consulting standard reference works.

4. Newspapers. Many libraries subscribe to only a few newspapers and keep only the current issues of most of them, discarding the others after a week or a month. They may be kept in the current periodical room, although, of course, a different type of equipment is required. Because of their size, newspapers are not easy to read. If placed on a regular library table, they tend to interfere with readers on each side and perhaps even across the table as well. A small individual table is hardly wide enough for comfortable perusal of a newspaper. If notes are required, further complications ensue. Some individuals find it convenient to read a newspaper seated in a not too large easy chair, while others prefer to read it at a stand-up counter. The various possibilities should be considered and a decision reached, so that the architect can plan the space satisfactorily. It is obvious that the area required for each reader is larger in a newspaper room than elsewhere. An area of 40 sq ft should be adequate, however. The total number of readers will rarely be large.

In a state university library, if local papers from throughout the state are made available, a considerable amount of space may be required for newspaper reading, and sometimes a special room may be provided. But it should always be remembered that additional rooms present complications, particularly if they have to have walls and doors, and that small rooms may tend to be more difficult to keep quiet and orderly than large ones. At any rate, if a library is to have current newspapers in their original form, some provision for them and those who use them is required.

Back files of newspapers are generally provided today on microfilm. For these, reading machines are required with special seating accommodations which are discussed under 12 below. If the seats can be close to the storage place for the film and other reproductions and also close to a service desk, so much the better.

Many libraries are still plagued by back files of newspapers, generally but not always bound. Those issued before the wood-pulp age (which began rather gradually about 1870 and was almost universal by 1880) are still treasured and should ordinarily be kept or transferred to a library which is ready to preserve them. Heavy use will wear them out more rapidly than books, because the strain on the paper increases geometrically rather than arithmetically as the sheet size increases. They should be given special care and should be microfilmed if heavily used. Microfilm positive copies are even more strongly recommended for wood-pulp newspapers, because the life of the original is limited at best and the cost of binding and storage space is greater than the cost of the film. Methods of microfilm storage and shelving for bound newspapers are discussed in section 8.4.

5. New Books. It is not recommended or proposed that a special room be provided, even in a very large library, for new books, but it is customary to place them in a prominent position, generally adjacent to or even in the entrance lobby, in order to call them to the attention of those interested and to make them easily available. The books are often withheld from circulation for a week after they are placed on view, but arrangements can be made to reserve them for future borrowing. A few libraries may want to provide a small amount of seating near at hand, perhaps of the lounge type. A location near the circulation desk is often suitable, particularly in a closed-shelf library, as it will provide a way for a reader to spend his time while an attendant gets the material he has requested.

6. Reserve-book Rooms. Practically all libraries in institutions of higher learning have found it necessary to provide what is known as a reserve-book section. This type of service originated in the 1870s at Harvard, largely as the result of the efforts of Henry Adams, who was then teaching there. The use of the reserve-book system has spread and increased in scope, in spite of widespread discontent with its results. Some institutions have found it possible to place all reserve books on open shelves and to rely on the students not to misuse them and to sign for them if they are taken out of the library overnight or over the weekend. Others have decided

that it is better and less troublesome to put them on restricted shelves where students have to sign for them either after helping themselves in a suitably restricted area behind the desk or by asking for the books by call slip. Many libraries divide their collection into "open reserve" for what they sometimes speak of as collateral reading and "closed reserve" for assigned reading or for books used by large classes where there are multiple copies but still not enough of them to go around during the period of peak demand. Libraries tend to shift from open to closed and closed to open reserve-book arrangements and in the percentage of material in each group. It is suggested that plans be made so that either system can be put into effect. Few institutions have been able to avoid closed reserves for long periods.

If there are to be closed reserves, a special area must be provided for shelving them. In most institutions the number of reserve books that have to be restricted at any one time can be kept to a comparatively small number, but in a few universities more than 5,000 are required at one time on closed reserve. Since these volumes can be shelved tightly together, and, in the case of multiple copies, perhaps turned on their sides, it should be possible to shelve up to 175 of them in one single-faced section of closed-access shelves, so that 15 double-faced sections should be adequate for 5,000 volumes. A smaller number will be required in most institutions, but if insufficient space is provided, results may be serious. There is a persistent tendency on the part of many faculty members to increase the number of reserve books. These books should be removed from the restricted shelves promptly when they are no longer in active use. If students can select their books at the shelves, wide aisles are desirable, but if the library attendant gets the books after a call slip is submitted, standard-width aisles are possible.

A problem that often arises is whether these books are to be used only in a special reserve-book room and taken out of it only overnight or over the weekend or whether they can be used anywhere within the library building or even elsewhere for a limited period after being signed for. The latter system has many advantages and is generally preferable, as it makes it unnecessary to provide a special reserve-book reading room, and readers are free to select the type of space and seating accommodations which they prefer. It has the disadvantage of making it easier for students to hide books for their own use or for that of a friend at a later time. Here is another decision that must be made locally. If the books are to be used within a special reserve-book room and withdrawn from it only during limited hours, the reserve-book room should in most institutions be the largest reading area in the building. It is sometimes said that well over 50 per cent of all the use of library books in most undergraduate college libraries is of reserve books. Sometimes the reserve-book room is provided with its own entrance and can be kept open after the rest of the library is closed for the night. Careful consideration should be given to planning a library so as to make this possible now or later; but students do require sleep and should generally be able to plan well enough to get through required study in regular library hours.

7. Rare Books and Special Collections. A reading room for rare books is at the opposite pole from the reserve-book room. The number of readers at any one time tends to be very small. In most institutions the books should not be on open-access shelves and should be in locked cases if housed in a reading room. The size of rare-book collections varies tremendously from one institution to another. Some, but far from all, of the very large state universities have comparatively few rare books, and are not particularly interested in them. On the other hand, some comparatively small private institutions have received, as gifts from generous friends and alumni, large collections of rare books.

Four problems of importance come up in connection with planning a rare-book room:

a. How many readers and how much space per reader should be provided for? The use of rare-book rooms in general is comparatively small. In the Houghton Library at Harvard where a considerable proportion of the rare books belonging to the university library are housed, there is a reading room approximately 30 × 55 ft, which can seat up to 35 readers. It provides within the room microfilm reading machines and "noiseless" typewriters for use by readers. When it was designed, the planners felt that it was as large a room as could be supervised from a desk at the center of one of the long sides of the room. The desk is on a raised platform, so as to provide the attendant with a better view of the readers. This room, particularly in the summer, is frequently filled to capacity, but it must be remembered that the Houghton Library has one of the great rare-book collections in the world and one that has always emphasized usefulness to scholarly research rather than the acquisition of rarities for their own sake. Only a few libraries will have to provide a reading area of this size for rare books. Remember that reading and exhibit areas should always be kept separate.

It is suggested that at least 35 and preferably 40 sq ft per reader be provided.

b. How much shelving is required? This is difficult to determine. One should probably admit from the start that few rare-book collections can hope to be shelved indefinitely within the reading area assigned to rare books; they will have to be provided for in regular or specially equipped book stacks, preferably as close as possible to the rare-book reading area. This can sometimes be done on the same floor, sometimes directly above or below, as at the National Library of Medicine, preferably with ready access for the staff between the two by stair or elevator or both. As libraries become more numerous and standard research material is in short supply, it may be necessary to transfer a larger percentage of library research collections into rare-book areas in order to protect them. It should also be remembered that the practice of giving rare books to academic libraries is something that can and should be cultivated and that first-class accommodations for rare books help to attract gifts. Rare-book collections tend to grow more rapidly than other parts of an academic or research library.

c. How should the space be arranged? Some libraries have found that having the rare-book area divided into a considerable number of separate rooms has made it easier for them to attract gifts of rare books from donors who want to have their names and their collections perpetuated. To make this possible requires special design, and if the material is to be shown as the donor undoubtedly wants it to be, supervision and control may be greatly complicated. Experience in some institutions that have faced the problem on a large scale has been that donors, when the problem is properly presented to them, come to realize that if what they are interested in is to have their collections used and their names remembered favorably, the collections should be shelved as far as possible with other similar material on the same subject, identified by a bookplate, and perhaps also by a catalogue listing the collection as a whole. Nothing is so sure as the ultimate stagnation and, to all intents and purposes, death of a collection that must be kept in a room by itself, if there is no attendant to make it readily available and no funds for enlarging it and keeping it up to date. Moreover, in an inflationary age an endowment fund tends to decrease in purchasing power.

The author remembers well in the summer of 1908 when he had charge of moving the Oberlin College Library into a new building that he finally was bold enough to ask the librarian why he placed in his new office an unimpressive old mahogany bookcase filled with a miscellaneous collection of books. He replied, "In my early years here I accepted this collection as a gift with the condition that it would always be kept together in this bookcase. The library was poor in those days and welcomed almost anything that came to it as a gift. I have been glad to have it ever since, not because of the case or its contents, but because it reminds me day by day that gifts of this kind with strings attached are undesirable and should never be accepted. With it here before me there is no danger of my making a similar mistake again."

d. What about the importance of providing the optimum atmospheric conditions for the preservation of the material? Libraries have finally learned that books deteriorate, even if they are not heavily used, particularly if they are printed on poor paper, as many of them are. One way to prolong the life and usefulness of any volume—and this is of special importance for rare books and other materials difficult or impossible to replace—is to provide an even temperature, and a relative humidity of about 50 per cent. This point will be discussed in more detail in section 9.2.

Special collections in a library generally come from gifts of friends whose collector's instincts brought them together or who acquired them in order to present them. In some cases they are purchased by the institution and are so highly regarded that they are kept together as a unit. They present the same problems as rare books. Their use will sooner or later be hampered if they are shelved out of regular subject order. To make their full research value available, they must be kept up to date by additional acquisitions, and there must be a knowledgeable at-

tendant to service them. Their housing, if they are separate and growing units, will present problems sooner or later. Do not be overly tempted by what may seem to be generous offers, and be prepared to explain in detail the problems involved. Most donors want their books to be used and their memory honored. A bookplate at the front of each volume and perhaps a separate catalogue or the name on the regular catalogue card are generally a better memorial than a dying, gradually forgotten collection.

8. Manuscripts. Manuscripts present very much the same problem as rare books and special collections. In general, they are not heavily used. Not much provision needs to be made for seating accommodations, but special supervision of the material as it stands on the shelves and as it is used is desirable. They can often be served in the rare-book room. Suitable atmospheric conditions are also important.

Storage presents a special problem because manuscripts come in all shapes and sizes, and special attention needs to be paid to accommodations for their shelving. Many libraries have found that they can be best preserved in boxes made for the purpose. These are fortunately more easily available now than ever before. A study of the design for the boxes has been made by the Library Technology Project. Shelving for manuscripts is discussed in section 8.4.

9. Archives. Archives fall into the same general category as rare books and manuscripts. Many of them are manuscript in form. If they represent primarily the archives of the institution to which the library belongs, one of the great problems is collecting them and preventing their loss through neglect in the departments where they originated. At the time of change in an institution's administration or when professors transfer to another institution, go off to Washington, to war, or elsewhere, departmental and other records tend to disappear. The administrative officers of an institution hesitate to allow what they consider confidential records to be removed from their own supervision and want to hold them in their own quarters. One hazard after another may come up.

The bulk of archival material in a great university is frightening. At Harvard in eighteen years while the author was in office there, material with bulk as great as that occupied by 350,000 average-size volumes was collected. A program for discarding, as well as collecting, is essential. But every institution should make provision somewhere for its archival material and for the proper supervision of its use by students, faculty, and others. Perhaps the most intensive use of archival and manuscript material for colleges and universities is for doctoral and master's dissertations. Special problems of literary rights are involved, and control and supervision must be provided.

Accommodations for readers of rare books, manuscripts, and archives are often and quite properly combined in one room in order to reduce overhead expenses. The same area per reader is appropriate for each group.

10. Public Documents. Many institutions provide special accommodations for the storage and use of public documents because they are unable or do not want to go to the trouble and expense of cataloguing them. At the same time, since documents are difficult to use, a trained staff to service them is often required and a special restricted reading area may be desirable. If a library attempts to collect public documents on a large scale, their bulk increases rapidly, and a good deal of shelving may need to be assigned for them. Small liberal arts colleges tend to acquire an unduly large collection of documents, partly at least because they cost little or nothing. The reading space required, on the other hand, is ordinarily not extensive, particularly if documents used for assigned or collateral reading are placed on restricted reserve-book shelves during the period when they are in demand. Special provision of some kind must be made for documents in most cases, however, unless they are catalogued in full. This is true even with American documents that can be arranged in the order followed in the Document Index. The more limited number of documents from other countries or from state and municipal governments are often even more difficult to use without help from a trained library staff. United Nations documents present problems of their own, whether in their original form or in microreproduction.

If the use of public documents is largely limited to a special reading area, its relationship to the storage area for the material may be very important. If the collection is large, it will probably have to be in the main book stack, and if the use is restricted, it may have to be in a portion of the stack that can be cut off from the rest where use is unrestricted. Document collections often include unbound material, and housekeeping will be difficult. Other things being equal, it may be desirable to avoid shelving them in a prominent location.

The square footage required for each document reader is no greater than for general reading, that is, 25 or 30 sq ft. The number to be provided for depends almost altogether on the service pattern adopted.

11. Maps. The use of a map collection in an academic or research library is ordinarily not large, although it may be important. Since map storage requires special equipment and maps are often difficult to use, a separate room is frequently provided. In an undergraduate or small college library, a map and atlas case in a reference room may suffice, and separate rooms and large collections of sheet maps may well be an unnecessary luxury. Atlas cases may be locally designed and constructed or purchased from a library-equipment firm. But many institutions, in addition to material that can be so housed, possess collections of the United States Geological Survey topographical maps. Others have large collections of historical maps in roll form that are used from time to time in classrooms. A considerable number of American institutions acquired the Army War Maps after the war, and these alone take a great deal of expensive equipment and space for housing. A careful estimate should be made of the prospective growth of the map collection and the amount of use that is to be expected, and since the transportation of sheet maps is difficult, there should be facilities for use as near as possible to their storage location. In selecting a suitable location for a map room, remember that service by staff members will probably be needed. Map-filing cases may be very heavy and often present a serious floor-load problem. It is a mistake to overeconomize in space assignments here, as shifts to provide more space at a later time may be difficult and expensive to arrange. Thirty-five and preferably up to 50 sq ft per reader is suggested, but the number of readers provided for need not be large and the total space assignment for them should be generally less than that for map storage.

12. Microreproductions. Practically all college and university libraries today are beginning to accumulate microreproductions of one kind or another on a fairly large scale, if they do not already have extensive collections of microfilm, microprint, and microcards. Each of these requires special equipment for housing, as well as for use. The one thing that can be said with reasonable certainty about them is that their use and bulk will increase more rapidly than that of most other material in a library. The amount of use and the size of the collection of microreproductions do not depend primarily on the size of the library's other collections. Indeed, some of our largest libraries have used microreproductions far less proportionately than others, because they have already acquired originals of most of the material that so far has been put onto microfilm. When the author arrived at Harvard in 1937 there were no reading machines in the central library of the university and there was apparently little or no demand for them. Now some 15 reading machines are in use in that part of the library, and certainly the end is not yet; but this figure is small in comparison with that in some of the younger universities with smaller book collections.

The new library of the Mormon Genealogical Society in Salt Lake City is providing reading machines and seating accommodations for those using them for over 600 persons. This gives some idea of prospective use of material of this kind. The problem is to decide how many seating accommodations should be provided, how they should be arranged, and the amount of space that the reproductions themselves will occupy.

It is obvious, of course, that a reading machine should not be placed so that the sun or a bright light of any kind will shine on the reading surface. On the other hand, there is no need for a darkened room, except perhaps occasionally when readers must use poor copies of difficult manuscripts. Almost any convenient space without an excess of light is satisfactory. The chief requirement is to place the reading machine where an attendant is available to thread it and help the reader who is not mechanically minded and requires assistance. Also, since the small size of the reproductions makes them easy to misplace or lose, some supervision is desirable. All this, in most cases, means that the microreproduction reading area should be near and if possible immediately adjacent to a desk where a staff member is regularly on duty. Booth or carrel arrangements with table tops up to four feet wide or in L shape will be useful. Future needs should not be underestimated. Forty sq ft per reader is suggested. At the time this is written, March, 1965, it seems probable that a reading machine suitable for use with all the main types of microreproduction, microfilm, microfiche, microprint, and microcard, will soon be available at a reasonable price. Storage for microreproductions is discussed in section 8.4. It should, of course, be as close to the seating accommodations as possible.

13. Music Rooms. Many libraries provide special accommodations for their music collections. There are a variety of reasons for this. Music material, particularly music scores and sheet music, tends to be outsize and requires special equipment. Music records used in connection with music courses can be an important part of the program of the music department, and their storage and use should be provided for somewhere in the institution. It is often thought that a collection of records can be better supervised in a library than elsewhere. Recordings of poetry should also be mentioned here, particularly recordings of poets reading their own poetry, dramatic readings, and so forth. The use of records in modern-language instruction has increased tremendously in recent years. The difficulty with material of this kind is that a certain amount of supervision is desirable, and this may require another service station, unless it can be combined with other service desks. The need for space for these purposes should not be forgotten, but the required number of seats cannot be determined accurately, because no one knows how far or how rapidly these and other audiovisual programs will expand in the next decade or two. If they expand as greatly as many persons anticipate, the space that they will require may well be so large that they should be assigned to buildings of their own. Although no serious objection can be made to housing them in a library, they can be provided for elsewhere; they are not an essential feature in all academic libraries. If a library being planned is seriously limited in area, it is suggested that the square footage for audiovisual work be restricted to easily foreseeable needs, and, if its requirements expand later, that the material then be transferred to other quarters. Seating accommodations for audiovisual purposes may call for somewhat more space than the standard library 25 sq ft per person; 35 to 40 sq ft is suggested, unless listening is carried on in groups arranged as in classrooms or auditoriums.

Seating accommodations for the use of music

books may be perhaps a little larger than for regular books, that is, up to 30 sq ft per person, because of the somewhat larger average size of the material, but this expansion is not essential.

14. Fine Arts, Picture and Print Rooms. A considerable portion of the collections for fine arts and related fields consists of large volumes with pictures and prints outsize in shape and difficult to deal with, as well as mounted photographs and slides. Each of these requires special equipment for service and for storage. In this fairly distinct and well-defined discipline, instructors tend to want a departmental library. Many of the advantages of such an arrangement can be made available in a special room in the main library, and this practice is sometimes adopted, more frequently in a large research than in a large academic library. The decision, as with music, may well depend on the size of the institution, the size of the collection, and the geography of the campus. Seating accommodations for each reader should amount to at least 35 sq ft.

15. Divisional Libraries within the Main Library. In many institutions, particularly in large universities, there is a constant and perhaps inevitable struggle between advocates of a centralized library and those who demand a large number of departmental collections, perhaps one for each discipline. Some universities have sought to compromise by establishing broad divisional collections in the central library instead of a larger number of departmental libraries. This has worked out fairly well in many of the large and middle-sized institutions. This plan and the need for a decision in connection with it are discussed in section 12.5, and the problem should be kept in mind during the planning process. If the divisional-library plan is adopted, it may completely change seating arrangements throughout the library and affect provisions for catalogues, reference books, periodicals, and shelving. It should not affect square-footage requirements for each seating accommodation, except as any subdivision results in peak loads coming in different places at different times and perhaps tends to increase total requirements.

16. Browsing Rooms. Browsing rooms have been popular in college and university libraries for many years. The earliest one, as far as the author knows, was the Farnsworth Room at Harvard, located from 1915 through 1948 in the Widener Library and since then in Lamont. In it Thomas Wolfe and others spent a large part of their Harvard years. The movement for browsing rooms spread rapidly, and they were established throughout the country, often in a room with handsomer fittings and more spacious accommodations than most others in the library, with a collection of standard volumes intended to encourage general reading. They might sometimes resemble what is called a gentleman's library. It was soon found that those which had funds available for the acquisition of new and popular books were most used. As public libraries have found, new books are, on the average, used more than older ones. Smoking, which was often permitted in these rooms though prohibited elsewhere, naturally made them popular. The Linonian and Brothers Room at Yale has been a glamorous example.

In recent years, as the book stacks have been opened in many libraries, the whole collection has been made available for browsing, and many buildings have been planned in recent years without a separate browsing room. Others have followed Princeton's example and placed in or near the entrance lobby a small collection of attractive and popular books available to those interested, almost without effort on their part. The Yale College Libraries and the Harvard House Libraries perform similar functions. A browsing room is entirely appropriate. It provides seating accommodations generally more comfortable than those in other reading areas. It can and should attract students and encourage reading of noncurricular material. If too accessible and comfortable, it will tend to fill up with those studying their own books. Some libraries have tried to prevent this, but the supervision requires an attendant. The author is reminded of an incident that happened at Harvard's Farnsworth Room many years ago. A Harvard undergraduate, now well and favorably known in educational circles, dropped off to sleep one afternoon. He was awakened by the assistant in charge shaking him and demanding, "Do you not know what this room is for?" He gasped out, "Browsing," to which the answer came in a strong voice, "Then *browse!*"

A browsing room is no longer essential, but it can be useful, if the collection is kept up to date and weeded. It costs money for books, but the space it requires may be used to good advantage if it relieves the pressure on other rooms or adds to the total use of the library. The space required for each reader tends to be larger than in other reading areas because large lounge chairs are generally provided. If supervision is supplied by checking at the building exits, the extra operating expense is nominal or nonexistent. The author has no formula to suggest for the size or the seating capacity for a browsing area.

17. Smoking Rooms. Smoking in the library is a problem. Until fairly recently it was rarely allowed, although librarians sometimes permitted themselves the luxury of smoking in their own offices, a somewhat questionable procedure if it was prohibited elsewhere in the building. There has always been a demand for smoking accommodations and, if they are not provided, students and faculty members have been inclined to break the rules, the former smoking in corridors and toilets if not in reading rooms, and the latter in their studies, thinking they would be undetected. There was a tendency for members of both groups to sneak into the stack and smoke. There are two objections to smoking in libraries: the fire hazard and the dirt which inevitably results. Books do not burn easily, but tests have shown all too often that they will burn under favorable circumstances. Fire hazards are discussed in section 10.2. Most table tops and floor coverings can be and too often are damaged and marred with cigarette ashes and live butts.

Many persons dislike studying in a room filled with smoke, yet others find it difficult to study for any considerable period of time without smoking. For years smoking in the Yale University Library was permitted only in a bare room with uncomfortable chairs, adjacent to the main toilet facilities for men. Later, when smoking areas were very much enlarged, the use of the library increased tremendously. Many libraries found that when smoking was prohibited, students stood outside the front door to smoke, leaving cigarette stubs all about and making an untidy, messy entrance. It has now become common practice to permit smoking in parts of library buildings, and it has been found that students are less likely to smoke out of bounds if an area is set aside for the purpose.

In the Lamont Library there is a smoking area on each of the five undergraduate levels. Ash trays, which are heavy and not particularly attractive, are placed in these rooms, and smoking is not a problem elsewhere, except during the Summer School, when the building is open to women who are unaccustomed to the regulations. Before Lamont was built, each of the three different student committees that were appointed, one each year during the three-year planning period, to advise on the planning of the building, voted unanimously for a smoking area on each level but was equally insistent that smoking should not be permitted in a large part of the building. It was evident that most of the Harvard students either did not want to study regularly in a room where smoking was going on or realized that many others found such an atmosphere unpleasant. On the other hand, in the Michigan Undergraduate Library smoking is permitted throughout the building.

It is suggested that, when college rules and regulations permit smoking in academic buildings, the whole problem is simplified if certain areas in the library, preferably one on each floor, are set aside for this purpose. If the building is air-conditioned or there is forced ventilation, special care should be given to the ventilation in the smoking areas. Experience in libraries indicates that, if smoking is permitted in one-third or even one-quarter or somewhat less of all the seating accommodations, this will be entirely adequate. It is suggested further that smoking can well be prohibited in most large reading areas where it is more likely to disturb readers who do not want to smoke, and that it should be prohibited in book stacks, because of fire risks and dirt; in brief, that it be restricted to comparatively small reading areas where the number of books is small and most of them are replaceable. No extra square footage per reader is required in smoking areas.

18. Conversation, Conference, or Noisy Study Rooms. Many students are gregarious by nature. The prevalence of "bull sessions" in dormitory rooms and elsewhere is generally recognized. Many students like, at least on occasion, to study with others. This may be in twos, often a girl and a boy, but also in larger groups, three to six to eight, who want to discuss their assignments together. This is especially the case in the scientific and engineering fields, and technical schools in particular have found it desirable to have in their libraries small rooms where students can talk over their work together, without disturbing others not in their group. If such rooms are provided, there is far less excuse for whispering in the reading areas.

It is suggested that every library should have

one or, in some cases, a considerable number of these rooms—if possible, at least one or more on each floor. They should seat not less than four (two can be provided for in other ways) and not more than six. Four is preferable. A larger group will not make much progress in the task before them. The rooms can be as small as 11 $\times$ 8½, even for six students. (See Fig. 7.4.) They should be equipped with one table and four to six chairs, according to size. The table need be no more than 3 ft deep instead of the 4 ft recommended for regular reading-room tables, and 2½ ft on each side per reader instead of 3 ft is adequate. The doors should have a large section of glass to permit easy supervision. The walls that adjoin other similar rooms or reading areas of any kind should be acoustically treated. If the door opens into a part of the book stack where no seats for readers are close at hand, the need for special acoustical protection will be reduced.

19. Segregated and Desegregated Reading Areas. For coeducational institutions, where boys and girls, generally by twos, are accustomed to study side by side and tend to whisper and disturb others if they are seated at a table for four or more, consideration can be given to the provision of double open carrels, on the periphery of either an open reading area or a book stack. No recommendation is made here. It should be a local policy decision. If adopted, it can help to make other reading accommodations quieter. In some institutions it is frowned upon, in others, encouraged.

A diametrically opposite possibility may deserve consideration. Some boys and girls in a coeducational institution may prefer to study in an area occupied by members of their own sex only. Why should a large library not provide an area, not necessarily with walls all around it, to which only boys are admitted and another for girls only? More and better study may well result. If smokers are segregated, why not sexes, if they prefer it?

20. Typing Accommodations. Accommodations for typing have become increasingly popular with the increased use of portable typewriters by students. There are four quite different but possible arrangements.

a. IN A REGULAR READING ROOM: In general this is not recommended, but in the Houghton Library at Harvard where rare-book material is used under supervision, the library provides typewriters of the "noiseless" variety and makes

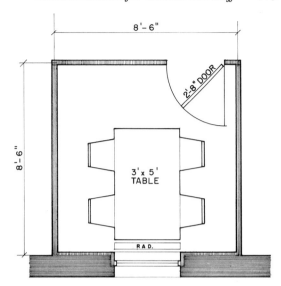

FIG. 7.4 Small conference room. Small conference rooms are popular in some institutions, particularly with students in the sciences and mathematics. (A blackboard is useful.) If used by more than four students, such rooms tend to become noisy. Rooms for more than six are not recommended. They should be acoustically protected as are typing rooms. This room (8 ft 6 in. × 8 ft 6 in. over-all) is minimal in size. If it were 2 ft 6 in. longer, it would accommodate six persons instead of four. Either size can be considered a multipurpose room suitable also for a faculty study or a "listening" room. If increased to 9 ft 6 in. × 9 ft 6 in., it would be adequate for a typing room for four. (See Fig. 7.5.)

a nominal charge for their use. (If the amount of use makes it financially profitable, commercial concerns will install coin-operated typewriters. Widener tried them, but they were later withdrawn because they were not used enough to make them worth while.)

b. TYPING ROOMS WHERE FROM TWO TO A DOZEN OR MORE STUDENTS USING TYPEWRITERS ARE SEATED: Possible arrangements for one of these rooms are shown in Fig. 7.5. Such a room concentrates and segregates the noise but necessitates walls and seclusion.

c. REGULAR CARRELS IN BOOK STACKS: This is often possible if the use of typewriters is confined to one side of one stack level, and only those who expect to use typewriters are assigned to this particular area. This plan has worked reasonably well in the Widener Library at Harvard and elsewhere.

d. SPECIAL ACOUSTICALLY PROTECTED INDIVIDUAL TYPING CUBICLES OR CARRELS. Here various arrangements are possible. In addition to quiet floors and acoustically treated ceilings, acoustic material of one kind or another is placed around the walls. These carrels do not

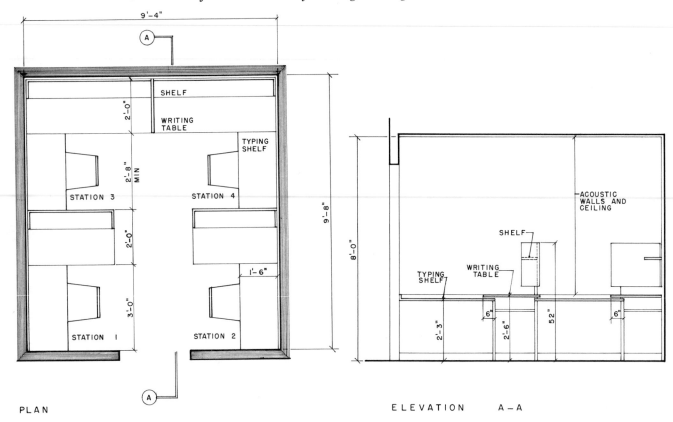

PLAN   ELEVATION   A – A

FIG. 7.5 Minimum typing room for four. Possible, but tends to become a bedlam. Individual typing carrel shown in Fig. 7.6 is preferable to any typing room for use by more than one person.

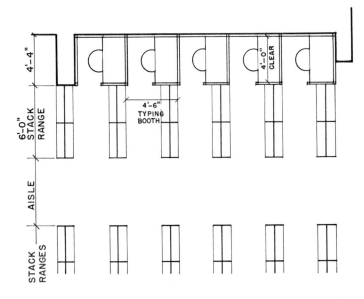

FIG. 7.6 Typing carrel at end of stack range. Carrels like these are used successfully at Wellesley with no doors. They have acoustically treated walls and ceilings.

require doors, if they are placed at the blind-alley end of a stack aisle, as they are in the Wellesley College Library with complete success. (See Fig. 7.6.) They can be held down in size and still be acceptable.

If the use of typewriters is permitted in a library, it may be convenient and desirable to have lockers where they can be stored, unless their use is in locked cubicles. Lockers of this kind are easily available with either combination or key locks. They can well be rented for a nominal fee.

21. Seating Accommodations for Study, Rather Than for Library Use. Students' rooms at home are often unsuitable for serious study, and dormitory rooms in residential halls, at least today with crowded conditions prevailing because of doubling up and with a widespread inclination to use rooms for bull sessions rather than for reading, are not conducive to study of any kind. As a result, if the institution's library is adequate in size, attractive, comfortable, convenient, and quiet, it will be heavily used by students reading their own books and papers. In many libraries this may represent half the total use of the library. To the author this use seems entirely proper and suitable. It has two major advantages. A studious atmosphere is provided, and dictionaries, encyclopedias, and other useful reference books are close at hand. The cost of providing the space is often less and rarely greater than making it available elsewhere in an institution, since the space required does not need to be individually assigned but is available for use by anyone whenever he wants it. It has the additional advantage that every time a student occupies a library chair there will be that much less congestion in the crowded dormitory rooms, and those rooms should tend to become more suitable places for study by others. One of the most serious problems in an academic institution stems from the limited number of hours when its physical facilities are used to the full. Library reading areas available to any student for long hours should tend to reduce spatial requirements elsewhere in the institution. One reading room seat for every four students, occupying 25 sq ft, goes farther toward providing suitable study facilities than an equal area added to dormitory accommodations, because the space there has to be provided for each individual not for every fourth one.

22. Overnight Study Halls. These were mentioned under 6 on reserve-book rooms. Most student and faculty members find that with a little planning ahead they can complete the work that needs to be done in the library during the fairly long hours of opening observed by their libraries. Other students—and perhaps they represent a larger percentage of the total than in earlier years—are convinced that they study better in the middle of the night than before a 10 o'clock library closing hour and are constantly advocating longer library hours. It may be claimed, and often justly, that the dormitory rooms are not suitable for study because of noise and visiting until perhaps 1 o'clock in the morning, and by that time, if there is one roommate who wants to sleep, the situation is no better unless a private study for each student is provided. Four possible solutions of this problem are suggested.

a. Library hours of opening may be extended, at least from Monday through Thursday evenings, until 11 o'clock and perhaps to midnight or even later, particularly before and during examination periods.

Many academic libraries are now open until midnight, but students seem to be as unhappy as ever. The library is faced by the problem of the cost of service for longer hours—in some states women assistants are forbidden by law to work after 11 o'clock. The cost of lighting and heating a large part of the building for longer hours piles up, and in these days of high light intensity, this may be considerable. The fact that the cleaning and maintenance staff is forced to do its work after midnight instead of before presents another difficulty.

b. Study halls may be provided in the dormitories and can be kept reasonably quiet with the aid of proctors. This represents just that much more space which is used for very short hours—one more factor in the inefficient use of academic space which is prevalent but more and more difficult to defend.

c. Dormitory rooms may be enlarged by providing individual study accommodations for each occupant or providing a larger percentage of single rooms. To do either of these for every student will, as noted earlier, cost far more than adding more library seating accommodations for use during regular library hours and will fail to provide the studious library atmosphere or reference books and other printed material that may be wanted. Some institutions have borrowed funds for dormitory construction and are paying the interest and amortization on the resulting mortgage from the returns from renting the rooms. On this basis there is a temptation to build more elaborate residential halls and restrict the number of library seating accommodations, but it is a questionable procedure.

d. A section of the library can be separated from the rest of the building and have its own entrance open after regular closing hours. A number of academic libraries have tried this solution and keep one room open for long hours or even for all twenty-four. This is the practice at Bennington College, Vermont, and elsewhere. At Bennington no library books, except perhaps a dictionary, are available, and there is no attendant of any kind. It would, of course, be possible and comparatively inexpensive in a large institution to keep a single attendant on duty to give a bare minimum of supervision and make it practicable to supply those who use the room with the library books which they are most likely to want, that is, reserve books and reference material—particularly dictionaries and encyclopedias.

The library of Amherst College, which has had an all-night study hall, at present expects to omit one from its new library building.

It is important to remember that, if an all-night room is to be provided, it should have its own entrance, arranged so that it can be cut off from the rest of the building at night when the remainder of the library is closed, but with the entrance closed in the daytime so that the room can be used without an extra control point during regular hours of opening.

23. Seating Accommodations in the Book Stack. As the years go by, a larger and larger percentage of library seating accommodations is being placed in stack areas. In some recently constructed buildings, more than half of the total seating has been in the stacks, including open and closed carrels, alcoves, "oases," as they may be called, studies for advanced students and faculty members, and so on. They will be discussed in detail in section 7.3.

24. Seminar Rooms. Most college and university libraries built before the Second World War contained a considerable number of what were called, perhaps incorrectly, seminar rooms. This practice was taken over from German university libraries. Specialized collections were kept and were made available to faculty and students in these rooms, and small advanced classes and discussion groups met in them. Oberlin, a liberal arts college, made provision for some 15 seminar rooms as early as 1908, and this was not unusual at that time. One difficulty with this arrangement comes from the fact that, if the rooms house books, the books are not available while the seminars are in progress, and the rooms are likely to contain more and more books because of the inevitably increasing pressure for shelf space. To avoid this dilemma a limited number of small rooms without shelving, in which seminars can meet, may be placed adjacent to other rooms filled with collections on limited subjects gathered together for use by advanced students. In this way collections can be made available to others when the seminars are in progress. A few seats for readers can be installed in the book-filled rooms. But even when this plan is carried out, it may involve unnecessary duplication of

little-used materials, and, in these days of open-access book stacks, it is much less defensible than in earlier times in the German universities which did not have main collections with open access. It should be possible to schedule classes in these small seminar rooms, if they are not exclusively assigned to any one discipline, for so many hours a week that they will not be an extravagance to the institution, even if they seem to be for the library. If they are placed immediately adjacent to the book stacks, so that books from the main collections are readily available, so much the better.

If, as suggested above, these rooms do not have books, they are simply small classrooms, and while it may well be useful to have a number of small rooms for this purpose in a library, they do take space, the cost of which must be figured at something like $20 a square foot and up. Unless used a considerable number of hours each week, they tend to be a luxury. There are many fewer seminar rooms being provided in American libraries built since the Second World War than are found in those planned earlier. One fairly good argument for them, however, is that they represent "expansion joints" that can be used for other library purposes later, particularly if their walls can be removed easily. One of them could be made into several small rooms for group study which may sometimes seem desirable, and they can well be planned with this possibility in mind.

General Comment. The foregoing long list of special areas in which seating accommodations can be provided has been described and discussed, not to propose that any library should make use of every one in the list, but to call attention to what has been or can be done. A warning is suggested. The architect should be informed in the program that those requested must be arranged as far as possible so that they will not require additional staff members for supervision or, for that matter, for service. Remember that a service desk is hard to defend unless the attendant can be expected to be kept reasonably busy performing his duties. Also remember that many of the areas can be separated from others by shelving instead of by either wet or dry wall partitions. This shelving should sometimes have a masonite or other simple inexpensive divider partition down the center of a double-faced case, to shut out vision. Sometimes, for acoustical purposes, glass can be placed above the top of a case running up to the ceiling. Often a number of stack ranges running parallel will provide an adequate visual and acoustic barrier. The desirability of providing multiple reading areas depends to some extent on supervision policies, which are discussed in section 6.1.

Space used by readers but without accommodations for seating is often required in libraries for special facilities. This includes (*a*) areas around service desks, beyond that required by the staff members and their equipment, that is, areas for library users waiting for service; (*b*) the public-catalogue room; and (*c*) areas for exhibitions and bulletin boards, and multipurpose corridor space. These are discussed in section 13.3, dealing with other facilities for general public use.

A library may also provide other facilities for persons entering its doors which are less closely related to book use than those listed in 1 to 24 above. They are discussed in section 16.2, on non-assignable space.

7.3 Types of Seating Arrangements and Accommodations

Section 7.1 discussed the groups of readers and the number of each for which accommodations are provided in a library. Section 7.2 dealt with special types of reading areas. This section considers nine types of seating arrangements and accommodations which should at least be kept in mind as possibilities. They will be discussed also in Chapter 11, dealing with furniture and equipment, in Chapter 13 on space requirements, in section 16.3 on layouts, and in Appendix B.

Standard Library Reading-room Tables. Until comparatively recently, practically all seating accommodations in libraries were at reading-room tables, generally in fairly large reading rooms. One of these tables accommodated from four up to perhaps twelve or even more readers. In a few libraries these tables were 4 ft across with one chair on each side every 3 ft. This was quite satisfactory. But in many college and university reading rooms, in order to increase the seating capacity, tables have been 3½ or even no more than 3 ft wide, and in a few cases even less. Too often, in order to increase capacity still further, only 2½ or even no more than 2 ft on the side was assigned for each reader. This

resulted in such crowded conditions that it was almost impossible to fill all the seats, and the total use might have been greater if more space had been allowed for each reader. To make matters worse, the tables were crowded together, sometimes several long tables in the same line without a cross aisle in between, and with an aisle no more than 3½ or 4 ft between two parallel rows. The arrangement was very unsatisfactory. When tables for multiple seating are provided in academic reading rooms, it is recommended that they be 4 ft across, if possible; that at least 3 ft be assigned along the side for each reader; and that readers never be placed at the ends of the tables. There should be at least a 5-ft aisle between two parallel tables, if more than 9 ft long, before coming to a cross aisle. An aisle 4½ ft wide is permissible if tables are only 6 ft long, but a 6-ft aisle is preferable if the tables are continuous for as much as 15 to 18 ft.

Architects often recommend round tables, but they result in accommodations of unsuitable shape and should be discouraged, except possibly in rooms for the use of current periodicals. Occasionally one may be used for what might be called aesthetic relief. On the average, they will be used less than other tables with the same number of chairs.

These comments about table sizes apply to academic and research libraries. Tables in public libraries, except in research areas, can properly provide a smaller amount of surface per reader without causing undue congestion, but greater spacing between tables may be desirable there.

Reading-room Tables with Dividing Partitions. Tables for more than one, often for a large number, with dividing partitions in front and sometimes at the side to separate the reader from his neighbors, have been common (see Fig. 7.7). Here at least a degree of privacy is obtained. It is possible to provide lights hung from the partition in front, but these tend to result in unpleasant glare. Another disadvantage lies in the fact that the student faces a blank wall; if there are side partitions on both sides, he cannot see out unless he leans back in his chair, and then his next-door neighbor is uncomfortably close at hand. In the case of tables for only four this disadvantage is partially avoided.

Slanting-top Tables. The only difference between these tables and those that have been

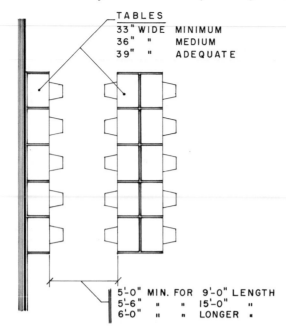

FIG. 7.7 Reading-room table with dividing partitions. Not very satisfactory if table seats more than four and reader is hemmed in on both sides. If he leans back, he is too close to his neighbor. If light is hung from the partition, it tends to cause an unpleasant glare. If partitions between readers sitting side by side are extended on both sides to provide more privacy, they become too confining.

described above is that their tops slant downward toward the reader; the slant makes it easier for him to read a volume that lies on the table without leaning forward and also helps to prevent the glare that too often reflects from the table into the eyes of the reader. If the slant is too great, the book tends to slide down into his lap, unless there is a molding or stop of some kind to prevent it, and when there is a molding some readers tend to pick at and ultimately mutilate it. A limited number of tables of this kind can be useful as at least some readers prefer to work with their books slanting slightly toward them. About 3 per cent of the seating accommodations in the Lamont Library are of this type. (See Fig. 7.8.)

Tables for Two to Six or Even More in Reading Alcoves. Tables resembling those described above may be placed in alcoves with books and shelving on at least two sides, a third side often being an outside wall with a window, and the fourth opening into a larger reading or stack area (see Fig. 7.9*A*, *B*, and *C*). There may be partitions on the tables, separating the areas available to each reader, as in reading-room tables. A nest of four individual tables in a pin-

wheel arrangement can sometimes be used to advantage with an alcove if it has inside measurements of at least 11 ft and preferably 12 ft.

The above arrangement has the advantage of placing the readers close to books. It was frequently used in alcoves adjacent to large monumental reading rooms in older buildings, with a central hall going up to the roof and one or more levels of balcony or gallery alcoves on mezzanines along the sides. While the passageways between the reader and the book shelves were generally narrow, the number of readers wanting to consult the books in any one alcove was small enough so that their movement was not too disturbing. If the alcove has the proper dimensions, this is an economical arrangement for book storage and reader accommodations as far as square footage is concerned. In recent years these alcoves have been used in the Lamont Library, where there are 36 of them in all. In Lamont there is a small table in each alcove, supposedly for two, but the tables are not as

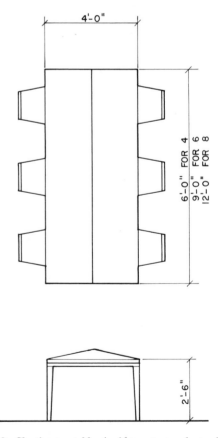

FIG. 7.8 Slanting-top table. Avoid too steep a slant, which will necessitate a molding that may damage books when pages are turned and may be picked at and mutilated.

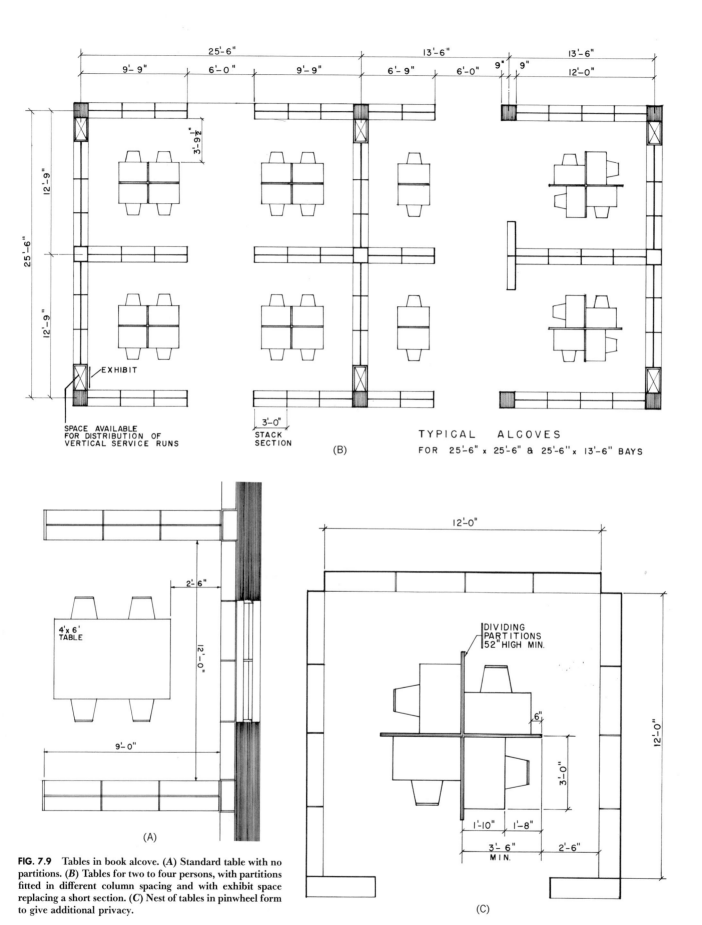

EXHIBIT

SPACE AVAILABLE
FOR DISTRIBUTION OF
VERTICAL SERVICE RUNS

STACK
SECTION

4'x 6'
TABLE

(A)

DIVIDING
PARTITIONS
52" HIGH MIN.

(C)

FIG. 7.9 Tables in book alcove. (*A*) Standard table with no partitions. (*B*) Tables for two to four persons, with partitions fitted in different column spacing and with exhibit space replacing a short section. (*C*) Nest of tables in pinwheel form to give additional privacy.

121

large as they should be. If the alcoves had been 3 ft wider, tables large enough for four could have been placed in them without difficulty.

One problem in connection with alcoves of this kind is that they have occasionally been arranged in what amounted to a maze. This happened in the original setup of the Wayne University Library, which has now been changed. Many readers do not like to sit in an inside alcove without a window if the way to and from it is complicated. It would be difficult to exaggerate the importance of the simplest possible circulation patterns throughout a library, particularly in main corridors, book stacks, and reading areas. Reading areas have often been the worst offenders.

Individual Accommodations in a Reading Room or Stack Area. These have been used in the past but were generally placed with an aisle on each side so that each table was at least 2 ft from an adjacent one. (See Fig. 7.10.) Tables so placed take somewhat more space than other arrangements, particularly if adequate aisles are provided. However, if individual tables are against a wall and at right angles to it, with an aisle on one side only—one that is required under any circumstances—square footage can

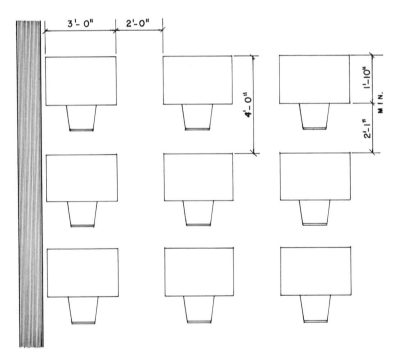

FIG. 7.10 Individual tables in reading rooms. Not recommended because of poor space utilization and because of the confusion and disturbance arising when a reader goes to or from a seat.

be saved rather than wasted. (See Fig. 7.11A to D.) In recent years the use of individual tables of the open-carrel type in reading rooms or stack areas has increased so rapidly that these now may supply up to 50 to 75 per cent of the seating capacity in an academic library. That they suit student preferences is indicated by the Stoke study of 1960.[3]

Individual tables present four problems. How large should they be? How can they best be separated from their neighbors? How much gross space do they take? What happens to the over-all cost figures when they are used?

An undergraduate student, working with one or two books only or with one book and a notebook, can manage in a pinch with a table 30 in. wide by 22 in. deep if there is no one sitting beside him. Dimensions of 33 (preferably 36) × 22 in. are better, and 42 × 23 or 24 in. is almost luxurious. Space of this character, as has been suggested earlier, can be obtained by building a partition down the center of a large table high enough to cut off the vision of the man on the other side and placing uprights between readers on the same side of the table. But the student so placed is not entirely happy because he feels too hemmed in. In the Lamont and many other recently planned libraries, individual tables of this kind are placed on a large scale at right angles to the walls of the reading areas. In Lamont they are 4 ft 4 in. on centers and attached to the walls so as to prevent their being moved. (One of the problems with a small table is that it is easily moved and an untidy appearance results.) If the tables are placed along an outside wall next to an aisle that would be there in any case, the arrangement is inexpensive in space occupied. Similar individual tables can be placed on both sides of screens and at right angles to them in a reading area. Then, with a partition the same height in front and back but an open aisle on the fourth side, practically individual accommodations are obtained and, again, no undue amount of space is used. Figure 7.11D shows that partitions at least 4 ft 4 in. high are required to prevent visual distraction. Arrangements of this kind have been used

[3] *Student Reactions to Study Facilities: With Implications for Architects and College Administrators,* a report to the Presidents of Amherst College, Mount Holyoke College, Smith College, and the University of Massachusetts (by a committee), Stuart M. Stoke, chairman, prepared under the auspices of the Committee for New College, Amherst, Mass., 1960, 60 pp.

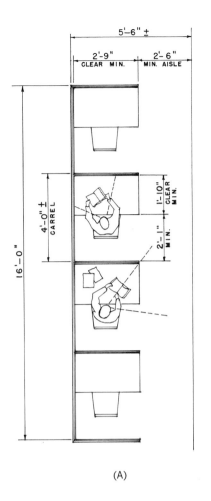

(A)

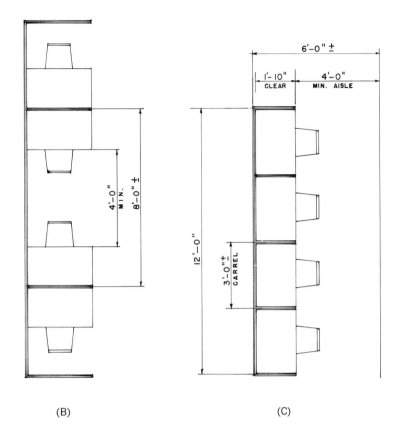

(B)   (C)

on a large scale in a number of recently constructed libraries. The University of Wisconsin Library and the Brigham Young University Library in Provo, Utah, are good examples.

Double carrels with readers facing in opposite directions are another means of providing almost individual accommodations. Carrels of this kind can be found at the Douglass College Library at Rutgers University in New Brunswick, New Jersey, and at the Uris Undergraduate Library at Cornell. If they are staggered, they give more seclusion and take very little more space. Various arrangements for double and double- or triple-staggered carrels are possible and are described in section 16.3.

Individual seating can also be provided in almost any book stack by omitting two ranges of shelving and replacing them with one double row of carrels, with a screen running between the double rows. (See Fig. 7.12*A* and *B*.) If ranges are 4 ft 6 in. on centers, the tables can be 3 ft wide, and there is still space for a 3-ft aisle on each side before coming to a bookcase. If the

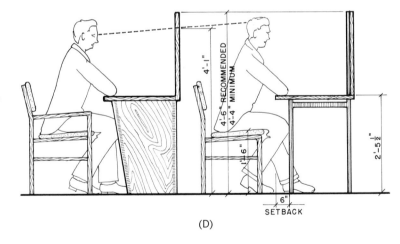

(D)

FIG. 7.11 Open carrels along a wall or a partition at least 52 in. high. (*A*) Carrels along a wall all facing the same way. (*Recommended.*) (*B*) Carrels along a wall in pairs. *Possible,* but they back up to each other unpleasantly. (*C*) Carrels facing a wall. (*Not recommended.* If there are side partitions, reader has "blinders." If he leans back, his neighbor is close at hand.) (*D*) Carrel elevation to show desirable height of partitions to prevent visual distraction. The left-hand carrel shows a rounded type of construction and the right-hand one a square type.

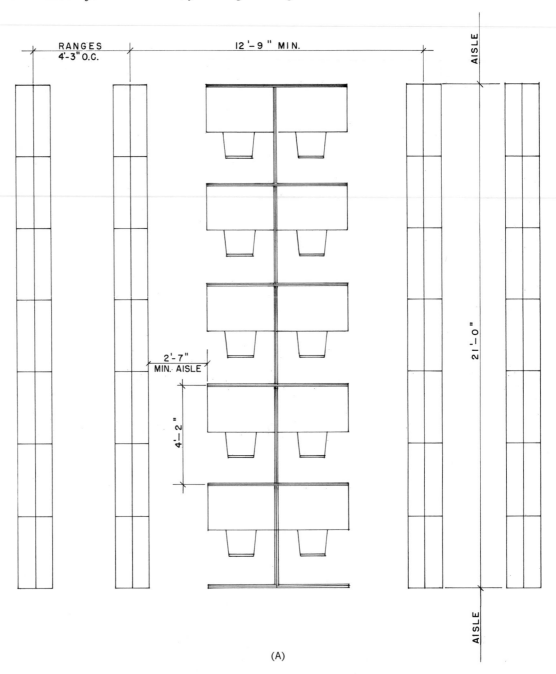

(A)

FIG. 7.12 Double rows of carrels in book stack or reading area. (*A*) Double row of carrels in book stack in place of two stack ranges. (*B*) Double row of carrels in book stack in place of two stack ranges with end pairs turned at right angles to provide adjustment to length of ranges. (*C*) Double row of carrels in reading area separated by a screen. These can be used without backs.

ranges are only 4 ft 3 in. on centers, the tables and aisles must be reduced to 34 in. While it is true that readers will occasionally come down these stack aisles to obtain books, the number of persons using any one aisle should not be great enough to cause much difficulty. There are many seats of this kind in the Louisiana State University Library in Baton Rouge, and a still greater number in the Louisiana State University Library in New Orleans. (See Fig. 2.2.) These double rows of carrels can also be placed in reading areas between parallel rows of standard reading tables. (See Fig. 7.12*C* and Fig. 16.4.)

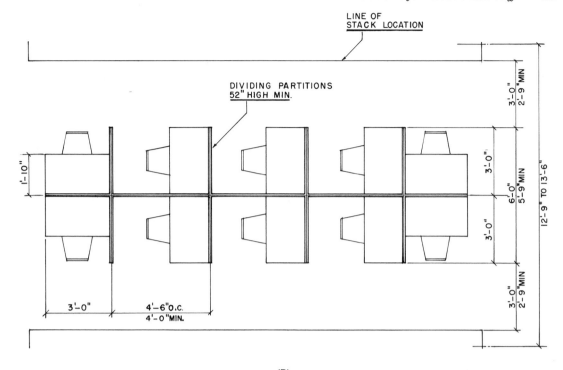

(B)

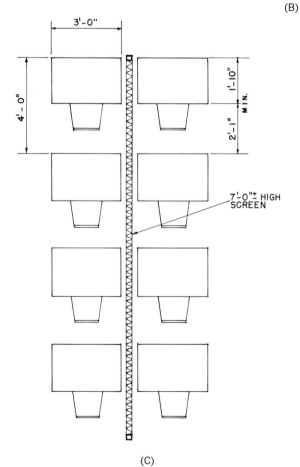

(C)

FIG. 7.12 *(continued)*

With careful planning, individual accommodations of these types can be provided in approximately the same square footage occupied by regular seating accommodations in a large reading area, and the only additional cost comes from the fact that individual tables having four legs each cost somewhat more per person than a table for four, six, or eight which has only four or six legs. Carrel and individual table arrangements are discussed again in section 16.3 on layouts.

A Tablet Armchair. Chairs of this kind (see Fig. 7.13) have been used for many years in classrooms. Thomas Jefferson designed one of these chairs for his own study, apparently finding it more convenient for certain types of work than a table and a regular chair. There is no reason why these chairs should not be used, although they are not particularly decorative and tend to result in a confused and irregular traffic pattern. The College of Agriculture Library of the University of the Philippines in Los Banos has placed them on three walls of a large reading area as close together as they can stand, just over 2 ft on centers, and the librarian reports they are heavily used.

Lounge or Semi-lounge Chairs without a Table or a Tablet Arm. Chairs of this kind are sometimes referred to as semi-lounge chairs. They are

FIG. 7.13 Tablet armchair used in place of chair and table. A much larger arm, such as Thomas Jefferson designed, would be more suitable but would take more space and might not be aesthetically pleasing.

often made too large (see Fig. 7.14*A*), particularly in browsing areas, and then take too much space, are unnecessarily expensive, and encourage the occupant to slumber and to stretch out and obstruct the aisles. A number of smaller ones can be used to advantage in current periodical rooms and in other places where not all readers are taking notes. Almost always a certain percentage of readers, if not taking notes, prefer to sit in a somewhat larger and more comfortable chair. A chair with a padded back, padded seat, and perhaps padded arms, if properly designed, may be thought to be more comfortable than a regular library chair and should not require more square footage of floor space than a chair and table. (Padded arms will ordinarily wear out before the rest of the chair.) A great many of these chairs have been used in libraries in recent years, particularly in browsing and current-periodical rooms, but, with the

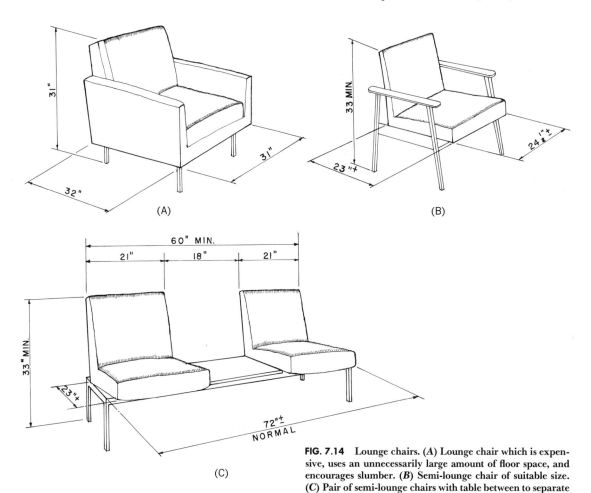

FIG. 7.14 Lounge chairs. (*A*) Lounge chair which is expensive, uses an unnecessarily large amount of floor space, and encourages slumber. (*B*) Semi-lounge chair of suitable size. (*C*) Pair of semi-lounge chairs with table between to separate readers and provide storage for books and papers. (*D*) Semi-lounge chairs replacing carrels along a wall or tables for six in a reading area to relieve monotony.

growing seriousness on the part of students, it has been found in some libraries that they are used less than ordinary chairs on the average. If 8 to 10 per cent of the total number of seating accommodations are of this kind, the number should be quite adequate in most academic libraries. They can be purchased for little more and sometimes for less than a chair and an individual table or even a chair and a section of a larger table. They are sometimes used to break up the monotony of a long row of tables or carrels (see Fig. 7.14D). They can be used successfully in pairs or even in threes all in one unit if they are separated by small tables, preferably 12 to 24 in. wide to give a place to store books and at the same time separate two readers. Because of their weight they are not likely to be moved. Small unattached tables will tend to be used as footstools.

Carrel-type Tables. This term ordinarily has been given to individual seating on the periphery of a book stack, preferably adjacent to the outside aisle or even at the end of a blind aisle along an inside or outside wall. If tables are next to a window, so much the better. Long rows of them, with a window for each, can be found in Cornell's new Olin Library and elsewhere. (See Fig. 6.9.)

In some cases carrels are completely closed in by walls of some kind; if so, they must be larger in size than would otherwise be necessary in order to prevent claustrophobia. They have seldom proved satisfactory and are rarely to be recommended. If one is open on a stack aisle, there is no need for the distance between it and the one in front of it to be longer than the distance from one stack range to another; that is, they can be between 48 to 54 in. apart. A longer distance is often used but is unnecessary. If they are as close as 48 in. on centers, the chair must be fairly small and without arms in order for a reader to get into it easily, and the table leg next to the aisle and the reader should be set in at least 6 in. toward the back of the table. This means that tables must be fastened to the wall or floor to keep them steady. With the carrels 51 to 54 in. on centers, there is plenty of room for an armchair, particularly if the table is not more than 23 in. in depth; 21 or 22 in. is possible but hardly desirable. Arrangements for carrels are discussed in the furniture and layout sections. There is no real distinction between stack and reading-room carrels.

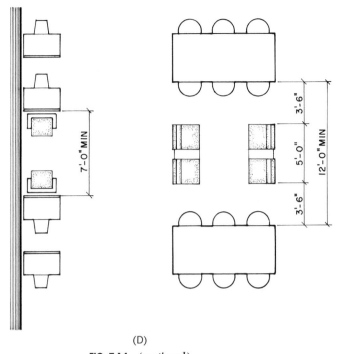

(D)

FIG. 7.14 (*continued*)

Studies of Various Sizes, Ordinarily for One or Two Persons. Most institutions feel that they should provide individual studies only for faculty members. The studies may be simply glorified open carrels with walls and a door added. In order to prevent a feeling of claustrophobia, they should be larger than a carrel that is open on one or more sides. They should also provide for extra equipment, such as a coat rack, a filing case, and a bookcase. If they have a window, they may be more easily kept down in size.

There are two major questions to be dealt with in deciding upon the type of seating accommodations.

1. What do the readers want? One can be sure that not all readers want the same thing and that a variety of reading accommodations is desirable. The problem comes in determining the number or percentage of each, and all nine types of seating should be considered.

Recent studies of student reading habits, notably that in the Stoke report, published in 1960 and referred to above, indicate that well over three-quarters of all students prefer individual accommodations. These can, of course, be provided in dormitory rooms in a residential institution, but it is usually more expensive to provide them satisfactorily for every student in a dormitory than for, let us say, every third or fourth student in the library. In addition, the average student will probably do more work in a library than in his own room where fellow students may interrupt at any time. One thing that is certain is that there has been a strong tendency toward a larger and larger percentage of individual seating in libraries in recent years, and a good many libraries are now being planned with 75 per cent or more of all the seats individual in character, that is, individual tables, or carrels, or lounge seating. Layouts for seating accommodations will be discussed in section 16.3.

2. How much space do the different types of seating accommodations take? This is a matter of considerable importance financially. If, for instance, the cost of construction, leaving out the equipment, is $20 a square foot, and a reader requires 25 sq ft, the space occupied by each reader in the reading areas alone comes to $500. This does not mean that one should attempt to economize unduly, but it is evident that, if $500 worth of space will do as well as twice that amount, it might be more useful to spend the remaining half of the money for other purposes.

This question of space requirements involves three problems. Each has been referred to already in this chapter: (1) the desirable amount of reading surface on a table; (2) the aisle space required for access to the seat; and (3) the extra space for comfort and special equipment in a closed carrel or study.

It is repeated that a large table with undergraduate readers on both sides in an academic or research library should be at least 4 ft across with 3 ft of space along each side for each reader and with no one seated at the table ends. This gives 6 sq ft of table surface and, at least at quiet times, provides room for a student to spread his material out when that seems to be a useful procedure. This much space is almost essential, at least in the United States, for male students if you expect the seats to be used—and what is the use of providing them if they are not used? Nearly everyone has seen again and again tables which are too small, with every other seat filled, and with the students getting as far away from each other as possible. It is also a common sight in a reading area with a combination of large tables and carrels, to see practically every carrel filled and only a sprinkling of students at the tables.

Four exceptions to the 6-sq-ft-table-surface rule should in fairness be noted.

a. At examination time when the urge to study is greatest, students will sit somewhat closer together if forced to do so, but it is doubtful whether they study as effectively as they would if they were not crowded.

b. Women students, perhaps because they are smaller on the average, seem to prefer chairs without arms and are more content with seating accommodations somewhat closer than those desirable for men. For them the 3 ft on a side of the table can be reduced to 2 ft 9 in.

c. As already noted, the table surface for an individual table can be as small as 21 × 33 in., or 4.8 sq ft, because there is no possibility of one's neighbor intruding on it; but even here the 6 sq ft is preferable.

d. In a reserve-book room where students will generally be referring to only one volume at a time and the motivation for study is increased at examination time, 20 × 33 in. may not be inadequate, but again the 6 sq ft is preferable.

For graduate students 2 × 3½ ft, or 7 sq ft, of table space seems desirable, and many professors and advanced students would undoubtedly be pleased and benefited by as much as 4 × 2½ ft, or 10 sq ft.

It should be remembered, however, that aisles, including those between parallel tables and at their ends, use most of the reading area, over 50 per cent on the average. A 3-ft aisle at right angles to the length of the tables will do very nicely anywhere except where the students enter and heavy traffic is found. There, at least 4 or 5 ft is more suitable.

The aisle that may involve the largest square footage and one where skimping is extremely undesirable is that between the parallel tables. The desirable width here depends on the frequency of its use, which is based on the length of the tables. If a table is 6 ft long and can be approached from an adequate cross aisle at either side, 4½ ft is enough, but one less than 5 ft wide results in congestion and interference with persons studying if three are seated on each side. If tables in a row without a cross aisle go on as much as 18 ft, that is with two 9-ft or three 6-ft tables end to end, 6 ft in between is more suitable; 5½ ft is quite possible with a 12- to 15-ft table.

It should be noted that, in the arrangements for table space, lighting should be kept in mind.

Individual and table lights in general present problems and are expensive; today they are rarely necessary or desirable. We repeat here that round tables are ordinarily far from satisfactory for study purposes, as the space available to the student cannot be used to advantage; books and papers do not fit into the area. It should suffice at this point to say that, for undergraduates, 25 sq ft for each seat in a reading area or for open carrels in a book stack should be adequate, even with a large percentage of individual accommodations, if the space is very carefully planned. But planners should be reminded that:

1. Advanced students should be given larger table surfaces and more privacy. This will require additional square footage per person. Thirty sq ft for the use of a master's candidate, 35 to 40 sq ft for one writing a doctoral dissertation, and from that up to as much as 75 sq ft or even more for a private study for a faculty member should be figured on.

2. More space should be allowed per reader in special areas, such as typing rooms, areas for using microreproductions, newspapers, archives, manuscripts, and rare books.

3. The 25 sq ft does not include space required for readers in other parts of the library, such as lobbies, public-service areas, public-catalogue rooms, toilets, corridors, stairwells, elevators, and non-assignable and architectural space in general, to say nothing of exhibition and seminar rooms, and areas used for what might be called nonlibrary purposes.

7.4 Space for the Staff and for Other Purposes

Adequate accommodations for the library staff are essential for effective service. In most institutions the space required does not loom large in proportion to space for readers and books, but in some cases—the Library of Congress, the National Library of Medicine, and perhaps a few libraries in other countries which add books rapidly and do a great deal beyond serving the public within their own walls—the staff may require more space than do the readers. If experience over the last fifty years applies today (and there is no reason to believe that it does not), it seems fair to say that in most library buildings accommodations for the staff tend to become inadequate before those for books or for readers. This may be due to modesty or timidity on the part of the librarians or to a failure to realize how much the staff may have to grow in order to process new material and provide public service. In any event, library-staff quarters all too often are congested, and the resultant crowding hinders even if it does not prevent effective work.

It is true that an overly generous supply of work space at a circulation desk has been known to "encourage" poor housekeeping, and an unnecessarily large amount of storage area for books in process has been known to slow up cataloguing by relieving pressure to push books through; but good administration should prevent both difficulties.

Space is needed for four major staff groups—administrative personnel, public-service staff, processing staff, and maintenance staff—as well as for rest rooms and lounges.

Administrative Personnel. The size of this group depends, of course, very largely upon the size of the total library operation. The chief librarian should have adequate quarters for his office work and also for meeting with members of his staff and the public with whom he deals. The space assigned to him will depend on the work required and on whether or not his office is to serve as a conference room. His office may take as little as 125 to 150 sq ft in a small library, or as much as 400 sq ft or even more in a very large library. If it is not to be used for conferences of various kinds, a room for that purpose elsewhere in the administration suite is desirable. This may also serve as a board room or for meetings of the faculty library committee, for staff conferences, and for other small groups. In larger libraries there will be one or more assistant librarians engaged in general administrative work. Their offices ordinarily will not be as large as the librarian's and might vary from 125 to 250 sq ft.

Secretarial space is normally required in all but the very smallest libraries. The secretary's office may also be a waiting room. If there are a number of administrative officers, that is, associate or assistant librarians, more than one secretary may be required. A space of 125 sq ft for each secretary, with additional space for a reception room, should ordinarily be provided. Space for filing cases and supply cupboards is essential.

A business manager or administrative assistant must also be provided for in a large library.

He should probably have an office the size of an assistant or associate librarian's because he can be expected to have business visitors with whom he must confer. Space has to be provided also for his staff, and at least 100 sq ft per person is required. A supply cupboard of some kind and shelving for office supplies will also be desirable here. A fairly large area which can be locked should be provided conveniently accessible to the administration suite for the great bulk of office and other supplies.

In large libraries separate toilet-room facilities are sometimes provided for the administrative staff or for the librarian only.

Public-service Staff. The public-service staff includes those responsible for reference and circulation work, supervision of the public, and page or messenger services. Most of this work is done from one or more desks, which take space in themselves, to say nothing of the areas required by those working at each desk and those who are served by it. In a large library, private offices will be needed for the heads of the circulation and reference departments, perhaps for interlibrary loan work, and occasionally for some other professional assistants. Anything under 125 sq ft may seem inadequate. For the other members of the staff the space required will depend largely upon the amount of equipment, but a rough estimate of 100 sq ft per person on duty at one time is not extravagant. This does not include space for the public in front of the desk. It should be emphasized that demands for service, and incidentally for a larger service staff, tend to increase year by year.

It is suggested that in a large library up to 250 sq ft of space should be available close to the circulation desk for machine charging equipment which may be wanted later if not now. This equipment can be expected to be noisy, and acoustic protection will probably be necessary.

Processing Staff. The processing staff, if the term is broadly interpreted, includes those involved in shipping and receiving, order and acquisition work of various kinds, handling gifts and exchanges, descriptive and subject cataloguing, classification, work with serials, preparation for the shelves and for binding, and the typing and clerical staffs that go with these activities.

The shipping and receiving room should ordinarily be a room by itself and should provide not only for the members of the staff but for shelving material that is arriving or leaving, with table space for sorting and packing. If too small, it quickly becomes congested. Too large a room may also be a mistake, however, because it will tend to encourage poor housekeeping. One bay will be sufficient in a small library, and few large libraries need more than two if adequate shelving space is available near at hand for storing large gifts and other shipments.

In a large library and sometimes in smaller ones, a loading dock should be provided. This is not so important as in earlier years when many shipments came in large packing cases. If possible, the dock, and, if there is no dock, the entrance should be covered so that a truck can back up to it and be unloaded in bad weather. If a truck can be garaged at the dock or immediately adjacent to it, this arrangement will be useful, but it can be urged strongly only for the largest libraries or for those with their own trucks.

Placing the shipping room on the same level as the acquisition department and close to it is a convenience. If other considerations make it preferable to place the shipping room on the floor below, for instance, a service elevator should be at hand. But do not upset more important relationships to accomplish this proximity. Remember that the cost of using an elevator and pushing a book truck 200 ft is much less than the cost of professional staff time that would be lost because of poor spatial relationships between the public catalogue and the working quarters for the professional acquisition and cataloguing personnel. Cataloguing in an academic or a research library is not a production line, as it may be in a large public library with many branches. The topography of the building site will often be a deciding factor in shipping-room location.

Order and acquisition work in small institutions may be carried on primarily by the librarian with perhaps some secretarial or clerical help. In large institutions it may be divided into as many as five groups: selection, ordering, checking in acquisitions, billing, and gift and exchange work. At least 100 and preferably 125 sq ft for each person expected to be employed on duty at one time should be provided, with an extra 25 to 50 sq ft for the person in charge.

A catalogue department may include professional members for subject-heading work, classification, and descriptive cataloguing, and also clerical assistants, filers, and typists. Members of this department are generally responsible for preparing material for the shelves, work that is carried on chiefly by clerical workers but requires space for equipment and storage of material in process. Since preparation-for-the-shelves work and typing tend to be noisy, a separate acoustically treated room will be useful.

The work of preparation for the bindery is also largely clerical in character. It may be a separate department, a section of the catalogue department, or in some cases part of the public-service department or the serials section; and as the amount of material in process tends to vary at different times of year, storage space is essential. All or part of the clerical work in processing may have to be relegated to the basement or another floor level in order to save valuable space on a main floor.

The question of providing a bindery in a library is bound to arise in many institutions. The number of library-operated binderies has tended to decrease in the United States during recent years. (They are commoner proportionately in some other countries, perhaps because commercial binderies are not as readily available.) Unionization has had something to do with this decrease, as well as the fact that bookbinding is becoming more and more mechanized and requires increasingly complicated and expensive equipment to make an economic operation possible. Comparatively few American libraries are in a position to maintain their own binderies today, in spite of the advantages which result from keeping material to be bound always under the library's own roof where it can be obtained without delay in cases of emergency. It should be added that most libraries, except very small ones, expect to do a certain amount of mending and repair within their own walls, and larger ones, when possible, do well to employ a skilled workman—perhaps an older man who is glad to get away from the rapid pace and machine work in a commercial bindery—to repair books in great demand and those so valuable that one hesitates to let them leave the building. If any provision for binding and repair work beyond the preparation for binding is to be made, space must be assigned, and the square footage required cannot be determined until the extent of the work to be undertaken has been decided. Since heavy equipment may be involved, floor loads must not be forgotten.

In recent years many large libraries have provided separate quarters and staff for the handling of serials, including in some cases ordering, checking receipts, preparing for the bindery, and even the service to the public of this important category of material. Shelf and table space for materials and equipment are essential. In recent years serial acquisitions have represented a larger and larger percentage of the average library's new material, and this trend seems likely to continue. It should be kept in mind in planning quarters.

For all these groups that can be lumped under the heading "processing," 100 sq ft per person as an absolute minimum can properly be provided for housing and equipment, plus another 25 sq ft for the section head of each section with as many as five persons. If 125 sq ft, or even 150, instead of 100 sq ft, can be made available, there will be that much more margin if the staff increases in size more rapidly than anticipated. It is possible, of course, to crowd the staff more closely together, but undue congestion prevents or at least hampers effective work.

For any processing staff of five or more, at least one office should always be available where a supervising officer can talk without interruption with a subordinate. This refers to the department as a whole but not necessarily to individual sections.

Most academic libraries make use of part-time student assistants on a fairly large scale in both public-service and processing departments. They will require locker space for wraps and at least a desk drawer in addition to work space. The total amount of square footage that should be allotted to them is difficult to determine, and the decision should be based on local conditions. The following formula may be helpful: not less than 50 sq ft in each area or staff section for each assistant who can be expected to be on duty at one time in that area or section.

Maintenance Staff. It should not be forgotten that almost any library that will be interested in this volume requires janitorial personnel who must have their own quarters. They will need a place which their members can use as a base and where they can keep supplies, brooms, mops, vacuum cleaners, and other equipment as well —supplies such as toilet paper and towels. A janitor's closet with running water and a sink and space for cleaning equipment is a requisite on each floor. Adequate supply and equipment rooms for material required for staff and public use are of great importance and in the long run will be an economy. In a very large library a separate rest room and lounge and even lunchroom facilities are sometimes provided for this group. A space of 100 to 125 sq ft for each full-time member of the maintenance staff or the equivalent should be enough to cover all these items.

Staff Rest-room and Lounge Accommodations. The staff should, if possible, be provided with a rest room, lounge space, and a kitchenette; the latter is particularly important if there are no suitable lunch facilities in the neighborhood. There should be a cot for women on the staff, in a rest room which can be used as an emergency room by the library as a whole, adequate toilet facilities for both sexes, preferably separate from those for the public, and, unless the staff is quite small, a place to eat one's lunch and to lounge during the lunch hours and morning and afternoon coffee breaks, if these are the custom. Ten to 15 gross sq ft per staff member would seem to be adequate for these combined facilities, if they are available to the library staff only. It is generally unwise to admit readers to use these facilities, and few libraries feel that it is necessary to provide public lunchrooms; they can rarely be called a legitimate function of a library. It should be remembered that any kitchen facility must be carefully controlled to make sure that vermin of one kind or another are not attracted and that noise and food odors are not spread to other areas.

The greatest problem in connection with staff accommodations is to know how many to prepare for in the years ahead. With modern modular buildings, it is fortunately easier to provide for shifting required by future growth, either within the present building or in an addition, than it was during earlier days in buildings with fixed interior bearing walls; but, as already stated, staff quarters almost invariably become inadequate before those for books or readers. Another closely related problem arises if staff growth complicates spatial relationships.

Other Space Users. So far, space for collections, seating accommodations for readers, and areas for staff use have been discussed. Two other types of space use should be kept in mind.

1. *Architectural space which is more properly called non-assignable space.* This is the difference between gross and net areas. The net is the space used for collections, readers, and staff, that is, for strictly library purposes, and the architectural space consists primarily of areas—square footage and cubic footage—occupied by inside and outside walls, stairwells and vestibules, corridors, toilets, space required for vertical transportation, mechanical rooms, etc., etc. This is space which the architect needs in order to enclose, support, and service the net usable areas. It is his responsibility to see that the amount of architectural space does not become disproportionate to that assigned to net.

2. *Space for other public facilities sometimes included in libraries, but not ordinarily used for seating accommodation of readers, for book storage, and staff quarters.* This might include space used for exhibition rooms and auditoriums, audiovisual areas, photographic laboratories, carpenter and mechanical shops, and perhaps some other areas, areas used for what are obviously nonlibrary activities, such as classrooms, offices, headquarters for other departments of the institution, etc.

In a rapidly growing library, in order to provide adequate space for a reasonably long period ahead, it is often desirable and even necessary to house nonlibrary activities at first. These activities should be selected from those that will not interfere with library service and will be easy to dispose of when the space they occupy is needed for library purposes.

Non-assignable space is discussed in more detail in section 16.3, and space for other facilities in Chapter 13. They represent a sizable percentage of the gross area in a library.

8

Housing the Collections

Introduction

This chapter on housing the collections is divided into four sections as follows:

8.1. Book-stack Shelving
8.2. Space Requirements for Book Stacks
8.3. Compact Shelving
8.4. Shelving in Reading Areas and for Non-book Materials

While in most libraries accommodations required for seating readers and for providing service areas for them and housing for the service staff make the greatest demands on library space, the square footage for housing the collections, including those shelved in reading areas and space for nonbook collections, runs a close second, and may even exceed it in a few libraries having very large research collections and limited clienteles.

The problem of shelving is important. During recent years the author has worked on quite a number of libraries that look forward to collections of several million volumes. The Library of Congress already has some 15 million volumes and pamphlets. If its very extensive collections of nonbook materials are also included, plus reasonable space for growth for the library for the next twenty years, its storage requirements will amount to space for at least 30 million volumes of average size.

If, as a rough estimate, the shelving equipment alone costs 20 to 30 cents a volume, and this equipment costs only a fraction as much as the space it occupies, the magnitude of the problem is evident. The square footage itself, with its walls, floors, ceilings, lighting, and ventilation, is the greatest single expense. To save even a small percentage in square footage used for shelving books, leaving the equipment cost out of consideration altogether, should be worth considerable time and effort.

8.1 Book-stack Shelving

Book-stack shelving involves a language of its own, which may be almost unintelligible to architects who have not had experience in planning library buildings. The same holds for administrative officials, faculty library-committee members, and even some librarians. Definitions of trade terms used in this section will be found in the Glossary (Appendix E).

Book-stack shelving will be discussed under fifteen subheadings, as follows:

1. Materials used
2. Multitier or single-tier stacks
3. Stack types
4. Stability
5. Types of shelves
6. Section lengths
7. Shelf depths
8. Aisle widths and range lengths
9. Height of shelving
10. Stack lighting
11. Color and finish
12. Finished bases, panels, and tops
13. Stack accessories
14. Vertical communications
15. Stack carrels

1. Materials Used. Stacks today are generally built of steel. In the old days many shelves were of wood, often attached to cast-iron uprights. Today very little wood is used, except occasionally for finished end panels, or in reading areas and reading rooms where there is a feeling that wood is more decorative, warm, and pleasant to the touch and sight. Wood can be said to be more flexible because it can be custom-built to the architect's design somewhat more easily than steel.

Wood shelves, particularly if they are of walnut or oak, or are painted—a Williamsburg blue, for instance—can be very handsome, but they will probably cost at least 50 per cent more than steel shelving and perhaps twice as much if they are specially designed and finished. This is not true, of course, in some countries where steel shelving has to be imported and labor costs for the construction of wood shelves are low. In India, Thailand, the Philippines, and Mexico, for instance, very handsome and well-made shelving of teak or mahogany can be obtained for considerably less than imported steel shelving, and there is less danger of rust. On the other hand, with wood, termites may be a problem, unless precautions are taken to keep them out of the building.

It should be noted also that it is possible under some circumstances to use cheap lumber and fabricate it inexpensively into fairly satisfactory shelving. This was done in the New England Deposit Library in 1941 and 1942, just as the war started and the government on three occasions took over steel shelving fabricated for the library. In order to obtain any shelving at all, wood had to be used. The builder tooled up for this shelving with gang punches that drove all the holes in an upright with one blow and made adjustable shelves possible. The shelving cost only half as much as steel would have cost at that time. It was dipped in a fireproof paint, and some of it is still standing quite satisfactorily, although steel would have been preferable if it could have been obtained. Another problem with wood is that, if the shelf length is too long, it may warp, as did the shelving in the director's office in the Widener Library at Harvard many years ago.

In spite of what has been said above, wood can still be used to advantage for small amounts of what should be considered temporary rough shelving, particularly in partially finished basements where available space is irregular because of supporting columns and foundation footings. Even here, inexpensive commercial shelving of steel should be considered, because it is less of a fire hazard and perhaps more readily available for use elsewhere later.

Before too long, plastic or glass shelving, which will be strong enough and perhaps lighter than steel and no more expensive, may be devised; but this is not yet available.

2. Multitier or Single-tier Stacks. Stacks can be multitier or single-tier, and the latter can be what is known as "free-standing" or non-free-standing. Multitier book stacks hold themselves up. Each level of stack supports the levels above, and sometimes also supports a reading room on the top floor of the building, as in the New York Public Library, and even the roof over the whole stack structure, or the glass walls enclosing the stack tower, as in the new Beinecke Library for rare books at Yale University. A multitier stack provided about as concentrated shelving space as could be found until one or another of the recently developed compact-shelving arrangements began to be used. The uprights at the ends of each section were the supporting columns for the whole structure. At one time they were made of cast iron; now they are steel. The length of the sections will be dealt with in detail later on, but in general they are 3 ft long, so that the uprights come every 3 ft in one direction and something like half as far again, or every 4½ ft, in the other direction. The companies that build multitier stacks sometimes have made them with the ceiling support coming from uprights that were 9 ft apart in each direction, giving flexibility of use for the space in between the uprights. A multitier stack still has certain advantages. Because uprights are placed fairly close together, they can be small and do not get in the way as much as larger columns do. The floors above can be thin, often no more than 2, 3, or 4 in. thick. But multitier stacks have their disadvantages also. Once installed, they are set and inflexible. You can remove the shelves, but the uprights remain 3 ft apart in one direction and up to 4½ ft in the other and cannot be shifted. On the other hand, it is amazing what can be done in a multitier book stack by removing the shelving. During the war, the sub-sub-basement of the Littauer Center Graduate School of Public Administration Library at Harvard, which was a part of a multitier book stack, was used as a radar teaching laboratory, and in it thousands of men received their training in that field. In the Lamont Library storage stack room a newspaper reading room has been provided without difficulty in a multitier stack, with supporting columns 6 ft by 8 ft 8 in. on centers (see Fig. 6.11).

Multitier stacks entail other problems. If wider shelves are wanted they can be made available only by narrowing the aisles between the ranges, which is not satisfactory, because (other things being equal) the deeper the shelf, the wider the aisle should be. In earlier days multitier book stacks were made with vertical or horizontal ventilation slots between each level. Forced ventilation and air conditioning were not available, and it was realized that books did not do well in stagnant air. These slots presented several problems. Pencils, call slips, and, all too often, books fell through them. They were and still are a serious fire hazard. The book stacks in the original Library of Congress building, the New York Public Library Central Building, and the Widener Library at Harvard, all are relatively unsafe because of these slots. A combination of multitier and single-tier stack is sometimes arranged. This plan was adopted in the Lamont Library, where every other level has a floor strong enough so that the uprights there can support a metal pan floor above together with its single-tier book stacks. The result is that a fixed stack on one level holds up a single-tier stack above it, thus giving flexibility in half the installation. Multitier stacks that are built today do not have ventilation slots. Stairwells and elevator shafts are closed in, and are hardly more of a fire hazard structurally than other parts of a library building.

Another problem in connection with multitier stacks comes from the fact that the lights are fixed. There may be no harm in this, since the stacks cannot be moved, but it is just one more element of their inflexibility.

It is generally considered that the cost of a multitier stack is less per volume housed than that for single-tier stacks, but this estimate is sometimes disputed. Multitier construction in a tower stack is undoubtedly cheaper than a long series of single-tier installations, but this would not necessarily be true with only two or three levels with a reading room above. In such a case an engineer should calculate the savings in cost that might result from the reduction in the size

of the building columns that would be made possible. Construction costs for floors and columns and ventilation arrangements must be considered in this connection.

The other basic type of stack installation is the single-tier already mentioned. This is known among many librarians as free-standing. But many stacks which librarians think and speak of as free-standing are not so regarded by the manufacturers. The latter say that a stack is not free-standing if it has to be fastened to the floor, and they also consider, with justification, that if it is not to be fastened to the floor and is to be free-standing, it must have an extra wide finished base in order to give it stability. Remember, therefore, when talking with stack manufacturers, that they assume that a free-standing stack has a broad base, with shelves above which are 2 to 4 in. or more narrower, unless the whole range has 12-in.-deep shelves and, in addition, has a finished base to provide extra stability. The manufacturers may also insist, with good reason, on special reinforcements, which will be discussed later, to provide additional stability. It is only fair to state that they were pushed into these stipulations by architects and librarians who had had experience with ranges tipping over. They tend to consider that what they call a free-standing stack with a wider base is more flexible, more easily moved, all things considered, and more satisfactory than a stack that is fastened to the floor. The author is inclined to disagree with them on this point, and in most concentrated book stacks recommends the non-free-standing single-tier type which must be fastened to the floor and often installed with the strut channels referred to later.

Almost any book stack, whether it is fastened to the floor or not, tends to damage the floor covering beneath it, whether of cork, rubber, vinyl tile, vinyl asbestos, asphalt tile, or linoleum. If the stack is moved at a later time, it will generally if not always be found that the flooring will have to be replaced or at least patched, either because of what is called the "punch" load from the uprights, which may amount to 900 pounds per square foot; the indentation made by the finished base; or the retention of color, because it has not been exposed to light. Some recently developed stacks designed to spread the load, installed with neoprene under them, are said to refute this statement. It is to be hoped that the manufacturer is right, but, even if he is, the cost of the wider base required by a free-standing stack must be kept in mind in terms of space used, as will be seen under heading 7 below. If the flooring tile has been installed around the stack and not under it, something which is seldom done, you are even worse off when you move. The cost of fastening the stacks to the floor is almost negligible, and considerable although not complete flexibility is still provided. The author is as yet unwilling to recommend any book stacks that are not fastened to the floor, even when a broad base is used, and at least a number of manufacturers concur on this point. Without the fastening, the stack can tip over, with one range falling against another and the whole group going down like a house of cards. This has happened more than once. With a narrower base, additional provision for stability is desirable and in the author's opinion necessary, as is shown later.

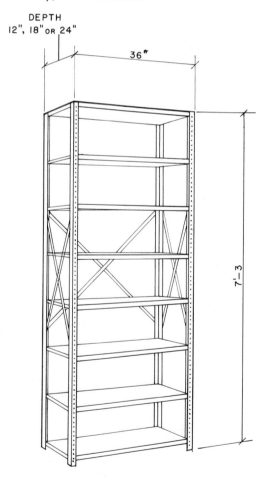

FIG. 8.1 Commercial shelving. Adjustable with use of nuts and bolts. Inexpensive. Often used for storage of little-used material for which frequent shifting is unlikely. Never to be used for valuable material.

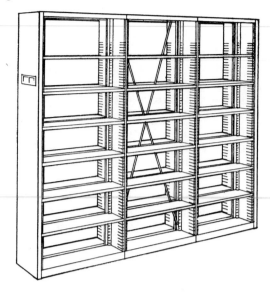

FIG. 8.2 Slotted shelving. The sway braces shown on center sections are unnecessary with finished bases, end panels, and canopy tops, or if section corners are welded.

3. Stack Types. What type of shelf is to be used after the decision in regard to multitier or single-tier has been made? There may be said to be four main types: commercial; slotted or standard; case; and bracket.

Commercial Shelving. Commercial shelving is used on a large scale in storage warehouses and elsewhere. (See Fig. 8.1.) It is plain and unadorned, adjustable only through the use of bolts and nuts, and then with some difficulty. The bolts may be a hazard to bindings. Partitions between sections are an inch wide or more, so that some 2 per cent of the lineal shelf space may be lost, but the chief objections to commercial shelving are its appearance and its lack of adjustability, which may make it unsatisfactory for use in a regular book stack. The best commercial shelving is not bad-looking, but the adjustability factor can be rather serious in a rapidly growing collection classified by subject. The cost may be no more than half as much as for other types of shelving, and commercial shelving should be seriously considered for use in warehouse storage or in basement stacks which are closed to the general public, if books are seldom moved and are shelved by size and more or less permanently in the same location.

Slotted or Standard Shelving. Slotted or standard shelving has solid end panels separating sections which are the full depth of the range, and the shelves are attached by sliding them into

FIG. 8.3 Case shelving. Doors are not necessary, but can readily be attached if desired.

slots in these panels, instead of hanging them on the uprights directly. (See Fig. 8.2.) They always have canopy tops. There usually are no backs, but backs can be installed and, when used, they add still more to the stability, which is already good. Slotted shelves are perhaps a little more difficult to adjust than the bracket type, but many persons think that they look better. They have been used in many rare-book rooms and in some reading rooms, instead of wood shelves, but the percentage installed in concentrated book stacks has been comparatively small in recent years, partly because they are somewhat more expensive. They are undoubtedly somewhat more stable in both directions and do not require all the extra bracing to provide the stability that will be discussed in 4 below. Since the weight is distributed over the full depth of the range and not concentrated at the section uprights, they are not so easy to tip into the stack aisles.

Case Shelving. Case shelving, as the name implies, is an enclosure of steel open only in front (see Fig. 8.3). It has a solid back and ends for each shelf, as well as a canopy top and base for each section. It might be said to resemble a piece of finished cabinet work. It may be less expensive than the slotted type and can be as attractive. The shelves may be a little more difficult to adjust. Many persons think case shelves are the most attractive type of steel shelving. They

have the additional advantage of being so constructed that glazed doors can be attached to them more readily than with other types of steel shelving.

If fine wood shelving is not used in rare-book areas, the case or slotted type should be considered with special attention to finishes, and an effort should be made to avoid sharp corners or places where a book can be "knifed" when shelving it. Solid backs are of prime importance in these areas to prevent loss and damage.

Bracket Shelving. Bracket shelving is at present by far the most frequently used type of library shelving; it offers the best combination now available of satisfactory performance with reasonable installation costs. A great majority of librarians seem to prefer it.

It was first used early in the century. The installation in the Oberlin College Library in 1908 was the first seen by the author. The shelf is hung on the uprights (see Figs. 8.4 and 8.5). These uprights may be tubular, cross- or star-shaped, or like an H with what are sometimes called "pigeon toes." It is possible, if one is strong, to pick up a shelf loaded with books and shift it to another section. Steel book trucks are made with end supports so designed that bracket shelves can be hung on them and six shelves

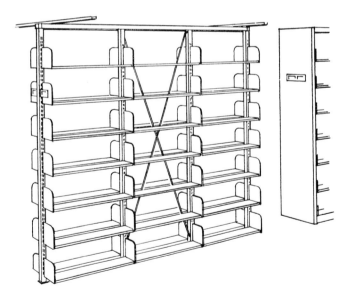

FIG. 8.4 Bracket shelving with open bases. Open bases, no end panels or canopy tops, but with sway bracing and strut channels for top bracing. Sway bracing is unnecessary if corners between uprights and top and bottom channels are welded. "Bottom spreaders" will also help stability. Range to right shows finished end panels, base, and canopy top.

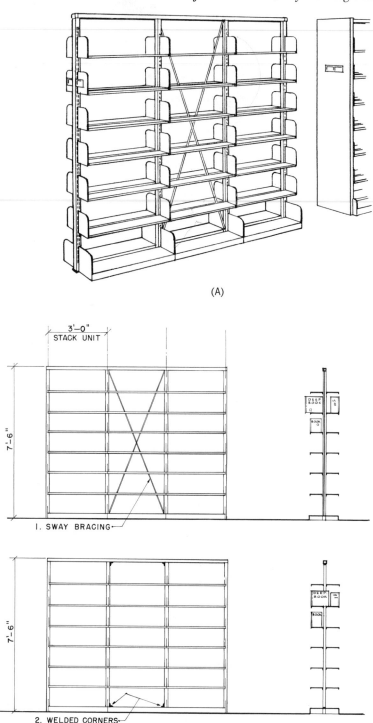

(A)

3'-0"
STACK UNIT

7'-6"

1. SWAY BRACING

7'-6"

2. WELDED CORNERS

(B)

FIG. 8.5 (*A*) Free-standing bracket shelving. Similar to Fig. 8.4 but with finished base, wide bottom shelf, and no strut channel. This is to make it free-standing, but floor attachment is always recommended. (*B*) Sway bracing and welded corners. The deep books shown at the right illustrate the advantage of welded corners over sway bracing. They make shelves 8 in. deep actual measurement possible in place of 9 in. shelves and may save up to 4 per cent of total stack area.

moved at a time from one section of a stack to another without handling a single book individually. It must be added that this is not easy to do and requires the services of a powerful man. There are two varieties of bracket shelves, one of which has hinged ends that can be folded over. These have the advantage of stacking when not in use, as the ends do not get in the way, although they still take somewhat more space than the slotted type. With the other variety, the end brackets do not fold over, although they can be detached for storage. There is little choice between the two, unless storage of surplus shelves is a matter of importance. The cost of the hinged brackets is a little greater, and they sometimes tend to flop down when one is trying to hook the shelf to the uprights. The installation charge for the unhinged ones, which must have end brackets attached in the library, usually makes up the difference in cost.

The decision as to whether to use bracket, slotted, or case shelving depends upon judgments regarding the appearance and the cost. Case or slotted shelving, as already noted, is almost always somewhat more expensive. Bracket shelving is a bit more flexible, but, as will be explained in the next section, it requires more bracing to provide suitable stability. All types are available in both multitier and freestanding installations.

The *American Library Association Bulletin,* November, 1961, pages 894–896, discussed the pros and cons of bracket versus other types of shelving on the basis of cost, appearance, flexibility, and stability. While the article is far from being comprehensive or completely satisfactory, it describes the problems faced and some librarians' opinions in regard to them.

It might be said that practically every stack manufacturer offers shelving with special features of one kind or another, for which advantages are claimed in strength, ease of installation, adjustment, and safety. Competent engineers are at work trying to improve each line. Unquestionably, progress has been made, but, as with new lines in automobiles, refrigerators, stoves, and washing machines, the cost should be kept in mind and weighed, and one should make sure that a change is a real improvement before reaching a decision to purchase.

4. Stability. Stability is a matter of great importance. Many methods can be used to make the stack more stable. One that is in common use is known as sway bracing. Heavy cross rods forming an X (see Fig. 8.5) connect the two sides of a single- or double-faced section of shelving. The results are not attractive, and a book pushed back on a shelf will run into the bracing, so that when sway bracing is used, the space between the shelves on one side of the range and those on the other is unavailable for deep books. Bracket shelving in double-faced cases generally has 2 in. between the back of the shelf on one side and that on the other side; consequently, with a shelf 7 in. deep on each side, if there is no sway bracing in the way, it is possible to house a book 9 in. deep anywhere except where there is a similarly deep book on the other side. Studies that have been made indicate that only 6 per cent of the volumes in a college or university library are as much as 9 in. deep. Of course, sway braces are not used for every section, but the manufacturers tell us that they should be used for at least one in every five, and preferably a larger percentage than that; and one cannot be sure that the unusually deep books will not come in the sections where there is sway bracing.

Sway bracing, of course, costs something to install, although it is probably the cheapest method of providing extra stability. (It has not been unknown for sway bracing to get out of order, although this is probably the fault of the person who installs it, rather than of the firm which fabricates it.)

A second method of making shelving more stable is to use a wider base. This base may be made with a "bottom spreader." Some manufacturers like to have it 20 to 22 in. wide, even if the shelving above is only 16 in. from one side of the range to the other. Of course, this improves stability and, of course, it is expensive. The bottom spreader can be a flat piece of steel fastened to the floor at the end of each section without the use of a closed base; it thus avoids narrowing the stack aisle as a finished base would do.

A third method of providing stability is by welding the corners of each section, or what is called "unitizing" the section, as is sometimes done with the chassis of an automobile. This method is fairly expensive, costing perhaps $1 or more a section. It provides practically the same strength as the sway bracing. The extra cost, it should be noted, is far less than the value of the space saved by making a narrower base available.

Another method used by at least one manufacturer is "brace-built" construction, which utilizes a channel along the base of two sections in place of sway braces and about as frequently. This helps to hold the uprights so that they cannot swing back and forth in the line of the ranges. A similar channel at the top in combination provides even greater insurance. This method might be called "standard" in most free-standing stacks.

A finished base, that is, an enclosed bottom shelf going down flush to the floor with its top 3 or 4 in. above the floor, gives extra strength in both directions and also helps to protect the books. This, of course, provides bracing for its full length and width, and also gives a more finished appearance. Since it closes the base, dust and dirt cannot get under it. (See Fig. 8.5A.) Those who have worked with the bottom shelf 3 in. above the floor know how difficult it is to clean under the shelving, although it can be done with a proper attachment on a vacuum cleaner. A closed base is, of course, an added expense. Like the other features that have been described, it is not required for stability in a multitier stack.

A finished or a canopy top (see Fig. 8.4 at the right) provides extra stability at the top and, combined with a finished base, might be said to make it practically impossible for anything to happen to the stack, except, under great provocation, for it to tip into the aisle.

Still further strengthening is provided by finished end panels. (See Fig. 8.4 at right.) These panels, like the finished bases and the canopy top, result in what appears to be a more finished job. They are often considered very desirable if not essential in reading rooms, although more than one librarian prefers book stacks without finished end panels, because more of the books, which are attractive, can be seen, and the installation gives a lighter appearance. The cost of end panels is far from negligible and should be checked. Ten per cent of the total shelving cost for steel and 20 per cent for wood is not unusual. The cost will depend on the length of the ranges as well as the width and the design of the panel.

An almost essential method of strengthening non-free-standing stacks is to use steel channels running from the channels at the top of one range to the adjacent ranges. These are called strut channels. (See Fig. 8.4 at upper left.) They may not look very well, and architects often object to them, but, if the bracing from one range to another is placed anywhere except immediately adjacent to the cross aisles, it will very rarely be noticed. The channels are comparatively inexpensive and, if carried through to some part of the building structure, are the surest method for bracing stacks against overturning. One hesitates to recommend them in reading rooms, particularly if they can be looked down on from a mezzanine above, as in the New Orleans Public Library.

The decision on bracing involves three major points: safety, cost, and appearance. No one wants the book stacks to tip over. They often have done so. The author is unwilling to recommend any free-standing stacks that are not firmly fastened to the floor; he wants to be absolutely safe. Stacks should be stable enough so that they cannot sway in any direction. All the special devices just described will help. They will all cost money, adding up sometimes to more than 25 per cent of the basic installation. The cost should not be a deterrent if it is necessary. The aesthetic factors both for and against the different methods should be considered and weighed. There is a serious objection to the indirect, rather than the direct, costs involved in broadening the base if it makes the whole case 24 in. from front to back instead of 16 or 18 in., as long as the broadening is not necessary for other reasons; an equally good installation can be less expensive and occupy less floor space.

The situation might be summed up in this way. The shelving can follow the stack manufacturers' definition of free-standing stack and have a base at least 4 to 6 in. wider than the upper shelves. Sway braces, finished bases, end panels, and canopy tops can be used. The shelving will then be safe from collapsing although it can be tipped over. The sway bracing might be said to make desirable a range 1½ in. deeper than would otherwise be necessary. The broad base and end panels deepen the range and might be said to reduce the aisle width by from 4 to 6 in. If all are used, they may add up to 5½ to 7½ in., and add 11 to 15 per cent to the stack area required to shelve a given number of books. The cost of strut channels between ranges, plus that of welding the corners of a stack section, or unitizing it, and possibly using bottom spreaders and brace-built construction, and fastening the stack firmly with bolts, screws, or whatever is used into a floor made of good quality concrete will be only a fraction as much as the value of the space saved. It will be far less than the cost

for finished end panels, bases, and canopy tops. But in any event, unless the librarian is convinced that he wants to use the broader bottom shelves for oversized books, there seems to be little excuse for the broader bases and the broader end panels and canopy tops that go with them. It is suggested that figures as definite as possible be obtained of the cost of each of the items mentioned, and that a decision be made with them in mind, never neglecting, of course, to take into account the appearance.

In all these considerations the height and length of the ranges must be kept in mind in dealing with the stability problem. Low ranges are, of course, more stable, and strut braces are impossible with them. Sway braces or something to replace them are of importance whether ranges are long or short. And do not forget the desirability of fastening any stack firmly to the floor. Otherwise it can be tipped over.

It should be emphasized that the decisions here may change the column spacing for the whole building, because this is influenced by the range spacing, as was seen in section 4.2, on the module system.

5. Types of Shelves. Shelves ordinarily come in two types—flat or bar. (See Fig. 8.6.) Bar shelving was used extensively in the past. It was supposed to be stronger, and the slots between the bars were supposed to provide for ventilation that was desirable in humid climates. Today they are not so well thought of by most librarians. They tend to damage books. A heavy volume that has rested on a bar shelf for years will often show indentations on the binding from the bars. Small and thin volumes sometimes fall between the bars. With good forced ventilation, the bars are not needed for air circulation. It is said that they have the advantage of letting the dust fall through. One may well ask, fall through to where? Why not let dust settle on a flat shelf where it will be easier to remove? Here it should be noted that the canopy top, which comes as part of the standard equipment of case-type shelving, is supposed to keep the dust from settling on the top shelf. This does not seem to be a serious problem in any case, and hardly needs be considered at all if the air is filtered by the ventilation system.

As has been noted already, bar shelves are said to be stronger than flat ones, because of the bends in the steel, which give additional strength without additional weight, just as does a corru-

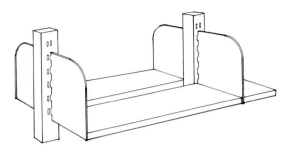

SOLID SHELVES

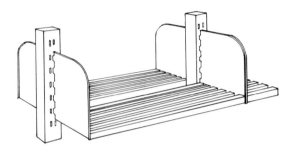

BAR SHELVES

FIG. 8.6 Bar and flat or solid shelves. Bar shelves are seldom used today because the additional strength and ventilation they provide seem unnecessary and the bars tend to damage bindings.

gated concrete ceiling. At least one stack manufacturer produces shelves with two slots running nearly the length of the shelves, forming a channel in which a special type of book support can be inserted, either suspended from the shelf above or attached below as with a regular slot support.

It is important that the gauge of steel in any shelf be heavy enough so that it will not sag or bend when heavily loaded. In general, there should be very little trouble with steel shelves warping so long as they are not more than 40 in. in length.

6. Section Lengths. Sections 36 in. long are standard in the United States. This length is gross, not net. The net is somewhere between 34 and 35½ in., depending on the type of shelving and the way the uprights are fabricated. In countries using the metric system, sections are often 1 meter long, i.e., 39³⁷⁄₁₀₀ in. Shelving that is no more than 30 in. long or even shorter is sometimes seen because it may fit into the space

available. The Boston Athenaeum has some 30 different shelf lengths in the same building, which can result in considerable inconvenience at the time of shifting the collections. The Widener Library at Harvard has 40-in. sections throughout its stacks. In places where the stack ranges are nine sections long, they have the same total capacity as ten 36-in. sections.

If a shift in the length of the sections in a modular building is decided upon, bay sizes are involved. This was discussed in Chapter 4. Since bays are ordinarily figured on multiples of 3 ft, anything that affects their size can be a matter of considerable importance. However, longer shelves should not be dismissed without further consideration. The Ames Company of San Francisco has been prepared to provide sections 48 in. long at a considerable reduction in cost per foot from the standard 36-in. sections. Six sections 48 in. long have the same capacity as eight sections 36 in. long. The Ames Company claims that reducing the number of the shelves by one-fourth and the number of uprights by two-ninths in a range 24 ft long makes it possible to reduce the total costs more than 15 per cent, even after using the heavier gauge steel which may be required for very heavy volumes because of the longer span.

The author will not venture to deny that there may be a reduction in cost, but he does not know how great it will be. He is not convinced as yet of the 15 per cent savings. He remembers that Angus MacDonald told him that the net cost with the 40-in. shelves in Widener installed in 1915 was no more than the standard 36-in. shelves would have been, but that this was the limit without a heavier gauge steel being required, which would cost more than the savings from the reduction in the number of shelves and uprights. However, what was true in 1915 when the Widener stack was installed or in 1950 when Mr. MacDonald commented on it, might not be true today. Important changes have been made in steel construction. Other equally important matters must be considered beyond the cost of the installation and the strength of the shelving.

As already noted, 4-ft sections will affect the bay size, that is, the column spacing, but it is not impossible to change the bay size if the decision on section length is not made too late, although the change can involve other new problems. The long shelves may save money, although that cannot be definitely proved until practical tests have been made with competition between different companies. For a small library, any shelf length that is not standard may be undesirable, because it may mean special tooling up if shelves are not in stock at the time they are ordered, and this may be even more of a problem at a later time if a few extra shelves are needed.

There is still another problem, on which more information is required before longer sections can be recommended, even if it can be proved that they cost less. This is the matter of inconvenience, if any, to the user. Is the human body so put together that it can use to advantage a 4-ft shelf?

In the United States, catalogue trays are arranged from top to bottom and then on to the next row to the right. This is to prevent one user from getting in the way of another any more than necessary, rather than because the arrangement is physically convenient. In some countries another method is used with the trays going from left to right on the top row and then down to the next one, and so on. One person at a very busy catalogue will tend to obstruct a considerable section of the whole alphabet from use by others. On the printed page, lines that are too long make reading difficult, and switching from one line to the next may lead to confusion and delay. Neither of these problems is completely comparable to that resulting from a long book shelf, although there is some relationship between them. It is certainly true that if shelves were 12 ft long, users might interfere with one another unduly in a busy part of the stack. When one shifted to the next shelf he might be confused just as a reader is if lines of type are too long. But the basic problem with long shelves is this: When a shelf is at eye height or immediately above or below, one can move along at least for the length of a 4-ft shelf readily, but as one gets down lower in the section, it is quite a different proposition. Even a young and agile person may find, as he searches the bottom shelf and probably the two shelves above it, that hitching along with partially bent knees, as will be required for a long shelf, will be difficult. When one gets along in his seventies and has bifocal glasses and a football knee, the situation may not be too happy. But such a person should not be considered a typical reader in an academic or any other library, and a 15 per cent reduction in cost might make inconvenience to a few seem a very minor matter.

It should also be noted that a 48-in. shelf will present problems in shelving and reshelving books. When a long row topples over, as books have a tendency to do, it will be just that much more difficult to straighten them up.

Can a satisfactory method of weighing the advantages and disadvantages of a 4-ft shelf be devised? The cost factor might be settled by a team representing perhaps three different stack manufacturers. But anyone working on this aspect of the problem should keep in mind that the cost of the book stacks probably represents not more than 20 per cent, and probably considerably less, of the total building costs involved. If the stacks cost $50 for a double-faced section, and on the average one double-faced section requires $16\frac{2}{3}$ sq ft of gross floor space, and the construction cost of that space, including floors, lighting, ventilation, and fees, is $21 a sq ft, the space costs $350 and the shelving $50, or a total of $400. A reduction in the cost of shelving of 20 per cent would be $10, or a saving of $2\frac{1}{2}$ per cent of the total. The same saving could be realized by reducing the distance between range centers by $1\frac{3}{4}$ in., or by lengthening ranges by one section.

An equally serious cost problem in connection with 48-in.-wide sections would result from the necessity of adjusting the size of the accessories, such as stack carrels, book lockers for carrel users, sloping periodical shelves, etc., unless standards for these are also changed. And do not forget the bay-size problem.

7. Shelf Depths. This problem is fully as important as the length of shelves, if not more so. Shelves which are 7 in. deep are common and can be found in many libraries through large parts of the book stacks. In this volume, in speaking of shelves, the author will refer to their actual depth unless he notes otherwise. This is 1 in. less than what the stack companies call "nominal" depth. Bracket shelving, the variety most often used today, generally has a 2-in. space between the shelves on the opposite sides of a double-faced range so that the sum of the actual depths of the shelves plus 2 in., or the sum of the nominal depths, represents the width of a range from front to back. Seven-in., 9-in., or 11-in. actual—that is, 8-in., 10-in., or 12-in. nominal—shelves are considered standard, except for the bottom ones in free-standing stacks, which are 2 in. or more wider. The shelving for atlases and for newspapers, for books in the fine arts, and for reference materials or other large-size volumes may require additional depth, and shelves varying from 11 in., the largest size noted above, to 18 in. deep are often required or desirable.

It should be repeated that bracket shelves have a 2-in. space vacant in the center of a range so that a 7-in. shelf without sway bracing can house a book 9 in. deep anywhere, unless the volume behind it is more than 7 in. deep. This will take care of about 94 per cent of all books. An 8-in.-"actual"-deep shelf will take care of a 10-in.-deep book anywhere, except where there is an unusually deep book behind it, and will be adequate for 97 per cent of all volumes. But most stack manufacturers consider an 8-in. actual—9-in. nominal—as an in-between size not generally carried. It is suggested that shelves of this depth—8 in. actual—are perhaps the best of all for most of the stacks in some universities, and there is no difficulty or undue cost involved in getting them fabricated for any but a very small order. It is to be hoped that they will become a standard stack size in the future.

The advantages of bracket shelves include the fact that they can be used with standard accessories and that shelves of different depths can be used on the same upright, something that is difficult to do with slotted and case shelves without special arrangements. But, as indicated earlier, unless the shelves are strengthened in some other way, sway braces are needed, and sway braces prevent the use of most of the 2 in. just referred to. Sway bracing may be slightly cheaper than other types of reinforcement, but the inches that it uses are so valuable that it is not recommended. The square footage occupied by book stacks is worth some six times or more what the stacks themselves cost. The space used by sway braces is an inexcusable luxury, as far as space utilization is concerned, and the braces are unattractive and a nuisance.

It has been noted that broader bottom shelves are suggested by stack manufacturers for reasons of stability. They may claim that this shelf does not interfere with the reader or the staff member as he goes up and down the stack aisles because it is at shoulder height that width is necessary. The author does not agree. He is even more interested in the width where the wheels of the book truck come. Any stack aisle that is 30 in. across is wide enough for a person to get through safely without bumping into the shelves at either side, unless he is as broad as Carver Doone was supposed to be. It is possible for most persons to squat down in a 30-in.-wide aisle. (More of this later.) The primary reason for widening an aisle beyond 30 in. is to reduce the inconvenience when two persons pass in it, and this is of less importance than some of us have been led to believe. (More of that later also.) Narrowing the ranges 6 in. from 24 to 18 by giving up the broad base increases capacity about 12 per cent without narrowing the aisles at the floor level. If one is ready to settle for ranges that are only 16 in. from front to back, as is often done, the difference may be 16 per cent. Of course, there is no reduction in the number of running feet of shelving that must be bought, but the narrower shelves should cost less per running foot. If the stack has a 24-in.-wide bottom shelf and a 30-in. clear aisle, the ranges will be 4 ft 6 in. on centers, but if it has an 18-in.-wide base with the same 30-in. aisle, the spacing may be 4 ft on centers and nine ranges can be placed in 36 ft, instead of eight, giving an increase in lineal feet of shelving of 12½ per cent in the same area.

And remember that, as indicated earlier, the cost of the total square footage occupied is the greatest expense, not the shelving itself.

In addition to the increase in stability, another argument for the wide bottom shelf is that the larger books can be concentrated there. Since the 6 or 3 per cent, respectively, of all our books that are more than 9 or 10 in. deep are concentrated very largely in a comparatively few subjects, this possibility does not help much. The oversize books can properly be segregated. Many librarians believe that it is better on the whole, less expensive, and as convenient to keep them together in one part of the stack where they can readily be found.[1]

To summarize a bit, it is suggested that book stacks, except for those in reading rooms, should always be fastened to the floor for safety's sake, that they be strengthened if necessary in other ways than by sway bracing, and that they be equipped with shelves the same width all the way up, instead of with wider bases. As to depth

---

[1] A college professor with unusual knowledge of libraries writes: "This should be emphasized even more. The practice of using bottom shelves for quartos and folios either wastes a great deal of shelf space or gets them a long distance from their proper places and makes them difficult to find. Their exact location can not be shown on a floor plan."

of shelves, it is suggested that most of them should be only 7 or 8 in. deep actual measurement, unless the bay size is such that the columns will obstruct the aisles. Seven-inch shelves save an additional 4 per cent of floor space and for storage shelving make practicable ranges 3 ft 10 in. or even less on centers. They save on the space occupied and also on the cost of the equipment. But they may be questionable for an academic library except for the literature and a few other subject groups. Eight-inch shelves actual depth will require fewer oversize books to be shelved elsewhere, are less expensive to buy and house than 9-in. shelves, and are recommended for most academic and research libraries for the bulk of the collections. They have not been considered standard by the library-equipment houses but can and should be available at less expense than deeper shelves.

In reference sections the average book is larger and deeper. Some librarians have been bothered by the size of the card catalogues in book form that have been produced by the G. K. Hall Company of Boston. They are larger than any other considerable collection of books that libraries are acquiring regularly on a large scale. They are just over 10 in. deep, and if placed on an 8-in. shelf with 2 in. available at the rear before you come to the next shelf, they will not protrude into an aisle enough to do any harm. They fit very nicely on a bracket shelf 9 in. deep actual measurement. They are ordinarily shelved in the reference room, where deeper shelving should be and generally is used. Very few reference books, except large atlases, are deeper than 10 in., and people who are acquainted with the 12-in.-deep reference shelves in the Cornell University Library and have seen how books are pushed to the rear so as to make it difficult to see their labels or withdraw them, particularly those on the bottom shelves, can understand the disadvantage in shelves that are too deep. On the other hand, if they are not deep enough, volumes will protrude into the aisles and be damaged by passing book trucks.

8. Aisle Widths and Range Lengths. Before a decision is made on shelf depths, aisle widths should be considered, as the two are closely connected in a modular building. Various factors are important, particularly the bay size available and the amount of use. Whether ac-

cess to the shelves is open or not makes a difference. The length of the ranges and the cost of space are also important. Aisles 36 in. wide are sometimes called standard for open-access stack, but every inch that this can be reduced saves something like 2 per cent of construction cost, not book-stack cost. A stack with a 1,500,000-volume capacity takes, to use a commonly accepted formula of 15 volumes a sq ft, 100,000 sq ft of floor space. If the range depth can be reduced by 2 in., it saves 4 per cent, or 4,000 sq ft of floor space, and if aisle width is reduced by 2 in. also, it saves 8 per cent, or 8,000 sq ft, which at $20 each would be $160,000. This is not to say that the saving is necessarily desirable. In many circumstances it would not be worth while and very unwise. Weigh your local situation and then decide.

To go back to the aisle widths: They should be wide enough so that the bottom shelves can be adequately lighted—more of that later; so that the user can squat down and read labels on the bottom shelf and select and remove the desired volumes; so that a book truck can get through and the attendant can take a book from the truck and reshelve it; so that two persons can pass each other without too much difficulty. The book-truck problem can be partially solved by making the trucks narrower, but their capacity is adversely affected thereby; the squatting down depends a great deal on the size and agility of the person concerned. How much should elderly, stiff, rotund faculty members with bifocal glasses and poor eyesight be catered to? Again, the decision must be made locally. How heavily is the aisle used and how long is it? The larger the book collection, other things being equal, the less any one aisle is used. The length of the aisle affects the amount of use and also affects very considerably, as will be seen later, the total stack capacity. It is suggested that aisles in a reference room or in an undergraduate open-access stack, with no more than 100,000 volumes, should not be less than 3 ft wide and ranges not more than 24 ft and preferably only 18 ft long. In a heavily used reference collection a 40- to 42-in. aisle is better still. This would also be true in a small public library open-stack collection. But in a large collection with limited use, 33- or 34-in. width for an aisle is entirely adequate; 32 in. is not impossible. In a very large library, with open access to relatively few readers, 30 in. is not too unsatisfactory. This means that in many cases with ranges 16 to 18 in. deep, a width of 48 in. on centers will do for a large, little-used collection, and 51 to 52 in. on centers can be considered standard. The effect of this on column spacing is a matter of considerable importance and has been discussed in detail in Chapter 4, dealing with the modular system. A very large library is now being planned, where a 4-ft range spacing has been adopted in place of 4 ft 6 in. A net saving of well over $1,000,000 will result. But that saving would be unwise and undesirable if the stack were open freely to a large number of readers.

The desirability of short ranges in parts of the library with very heavy use is important, as has been mentioned. But a very large, comparatively little-used collection is a different proposition. In the past a 30-ft length has generally been considered the outside limit for any library, but the new National Library of Medicine with restricted access has ranges up to 36 ft in length, without presenting a problem. The storage levels of the Lamont Library have ranges as much as 51 ft long, and this has been quite satisfactory for the use to which they have been put. If the 51-ft ranges had been divided by two cross aisles 3 ft wide or by one aisle 6 ft wide, the sections would have been reduced from 17 to 15 in each range. Seventeen is two-fifteenths, or over 13 per cent greater than 15. A national library in another country has ranges up to 60 ft in length and is not unhappy about it. If 13 per cent in capacity is gained by narrowing ranges and stack aisles and 13 per cent added to the 113 obtained by lengthening ranges, the result is a total increase of over 27 per cent. However, it would be a mistake to narrow the aisles and lengthen the ranges in this way in an open-access, heavily used stack; the increased capacity would not be worth what it costs in inconvenience. Give full consideration to the anticipated use.

The width of cross aisles is also an important factor. The difference in capacity with cross aisles 6 ft wide instead of 4½ ft is 7½ per cent with 21-ft-long ranges, and a 3-ft instead of a 6-ft aisle would add 15 per cent capacity. But, again, use should be kept in mind. Do not over-economize. You will regret it.

Cross aisles can always be inserted in a long range, if finished bases and sway braces do not intervene, by simply removing the shelves in the sections where the aisle is wanted. The reverse is also possible if the uprights are notched so that shelves can be attached.

9. Height of Shelving. Multitier stacks come with floor levels of different heights. They have often been 7 ft 6 in. on centers, i.e., 7 ft 6 in. from the first floor to the level of the second floor. If 3 in. is lost in the floor thickness, each floor is 7 ft 3 in. in the clear. Sometimes they have been only 7 ft. At least one multitier stack, that at the Pennsylvania State University in University City, Pennsylvania, is less than 6 ft 8 in. in the clear. Too often lights are so arranged that the top few inches of shelving are difficult to use. In recent years the full 7 ft 6 in. clear height has become more or less standard. It is not so high that those using the stack cannot reach it. Most people can reach up to get a book off a shelf 6 ft 4 in. from the floor, although this will be somewhat difficult for those who are only 5 ft tall (see Fig. 8.7). If the top shelf is any higher than that, it is unreachable by so many persons as to make its position inadvisable.

Studies made by Van Hoesen at Brown University and by Fremont Rider and others have shown that some 90 per cent of all books are no more than 11 in. tall. A steel shelf is not more than ¾ in. thick, and if shelves are placed 12 in. on centers, a book just over 11 in. can slide in between. With seven shelves 12 in. on centers, and with the top one at 6 ft 4 in. above the floor, giving 14 in. margin there below a 7 ft 6 in. ceiling, the top of the bottom shelf will be 4 in. above the floor, making possible a 3 or 4-in. base for protection of the books. If the distance between shelves is cut 1 in., that is, to 10¼ in. in the clear, eight shelves will still not be possible without raising the ceilings several inches, and so there is little to gain from it. The eighth shelf, if made possible by the higher ceiling, would be 6 ft 9 in. above the floor and beyond the reach of most persons shorter than 5 ft 4 in. With seven shelves, 11 in. apart on centers, the clear height from floor to ceiling could be reduced to under 7 ft, but that is rather low for comfort for a tall person. Specially designed lighting will be required, and there will then be some 11 per cent of books in an academic library, in addition to the 10 per cent that are more than 11 in. high, or 21 per cent in all, that cannot go on these shelves. This is enough to make them undesira-

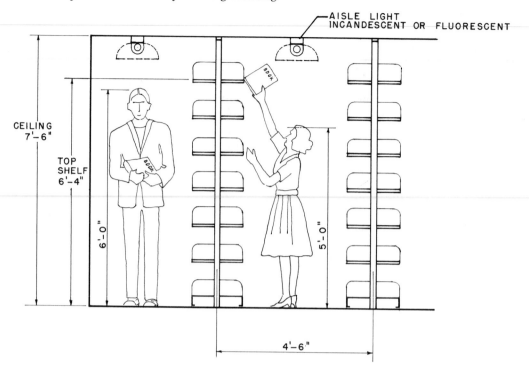

FIG. 8.7 Short reader using 7 ft 6 in. stacks. Top shelf of seven is 6 ft 4 in. high. This is the lowest possible with 4-in. base and shelves 12 in. on centers. Anything higher would require a stool. Anything lower would decrease capacity by one-seventh or require 11-in. spacing of shelves, which would provide for only 79 per cent of the books, instead of the 90 per cent which can go on shelves 12 in. on centers.

ble. All things considered, 7 ft 6 in. in the clear seems satisfactory for academic and research libraries. Do not forget that the stack uprights must be enough below 7 ft 6 in. to make it possible to install them. On the other hand, with shelves 11 in. on centers, 7 ft will be possible (questionable) in a public library, but the saving in cost will be negligible. A certain degree of flexibility will be lost. Very tall persons may be inconvenienced.

The Widener Library, with 7 ft 2 in. clear stack heights, can use only six shelves, except in the literature sections. If it could use seven, capacity would be nearly one-sixth greater, and more than 300,000 additional volumes could be stored in it, something which would be much appreciated.

If a book stack should be at least 7 ft 6 in. high, should an upper limit beyond that be considered for ceiling height? It depends on what is to be done with the extra space. The higher the ceiling, the greater the square footage cost. If there is height enough, that is, 8 ft 6 in., for an eighth shelf, it can be devoted to storage for less-used books. This would be compara-

tively inexpensive cubage, but it might also be confusing, as it would require a special ribbon arrangement for books on the eighth shelf. It is not recommended under most circumstances.

A book-stack area 7 ft 6 in. in the clear is high enough for individual accommodations for readers in carrels anywhere in the stack, and in fact is adequate and satisfactory for small groups if care is taken to place them where each person can look out in some direction for a considerable distance. In the Lamont Library there are two mezzanines 91 × 45 ft in dimensions. Each provides seats for 75 readers, who can apparently work in comfort with a 7 ft 9 in. ceiling, but each one can see out in at least one direction, although some of them are over 75 ft from any window. At Princeton 8 ft 4 in. ceilings on the stack levels permit adequate heights for rooms largely given over to human occupancy which are as much as 25 × 36 ft or even 25 × 54 ft in size.

There is no precise upper limit in stack height, except that extra height may look awkward and wasteful, that it costs more, and that the higher the lights are hung over the center of an aisle the less efficient they may be for the lower shelves. Clear floor-height problems are discussed in section 5.1.

10. Stack Lighting. The question of library lighting in its broader aspects is discussed in section 9.1. In section 4.2 it is dealt with in the consideration of bay sizes. Here the special lighting problems in relation to book stacks are considered. With relatively narrow aisles lighting has always presented a problem, particularly lighting for bottom shelves. Until well into this century in most academic and research libraries efforts were made to provide enough natural light to find books. Five factors brought about a change.

a. Constantly growing collections and tremendous accumulations of volumes in many libraries made it virtually impossible to provide natural light for any large percentage of them.

b. Better quality and less expensive artificial light became available.

c. With higher standards of lighting possible, they inevitably and properly became regarded as necessities.

d. Hours of opening were lengthened, since they were made possible by artificial light.

e. Open stack access became general.

In spite of these various developments, good stack lighting, particularly for bottom shelves, continued to be difficult and still is. Some book stacks were built with glass floors and switches arranged so that the bottom shelves could be lighted more adequately by lights from the floor below. But glass floors failed to be a conductor of static electricity and they were also vulnerable to sharp blows; at least one serious accident has resulted. The bare incandescent bulbs that were first used were unpleasant, to say the least; frosted bulbs were developed and helped but came far from providing satisfactory light. Bulb wattage was increased from 15 to 40 watts or more, and bulbs were placed closer together, but users were not happy. Bulbs were sometimes protected with wire cages and hung from cords and could be carried to the spot where better lighting was needed, particularly in little-used areas, but this method was not satisfactory because it meant that one hand was unavailable for handling books. Special fixtures with reflecting surfaces were designed to keep the light from shining in the user's eyes and at the same time to direct it toward the books. Finally, in the early 1940s, fluorescent tubes housed flush with the ceiling or suspended close to it and protected by baffles or plastic came into use and provided by far the best stack lighting up to then available. (If sunk in the ceiling, that important source of reflecting light was lost.) These tubes, however, had disadvantages of their own. If turned off and on too frequently, their length of life was shortened. They were more difficult to replace and more expensive than incandescent bulbs. Fortunately, they used approximately only 40 per cent as much current to give the same intensity of illumination, and because this illumination was spread out over the entire length of the aisle, they gave far better general light than was possible with incandescent bulbs with the most suitable fixtures. They seemed to be almost perfect for heavily used stacks, where they were required during all the time the library was open. Because of the lower cost for current, there was no need to consider installing time locks that would automatically turn them off after ten or fifteen minutes, as was sometimes done with incandescent bulbs. Students and faculty, to say nothing of stack attendants, notoriously fail to turn off lights when they are through with them. Wiring and switches were simplified and became less expensive, proportionately.

Fluorescent lights still present four problems:

a. As noted above, if they are used for short periods only and are turned on and off frequently, they burn out quickly.

b. Since the light from them does not carry out from the ends very well, a nearly continuous row is required for good stack lighting. Incandescent bulbs light well in all directions.

c. A continuous row of regular, 40-watt 4-ft tubes gives more light than some librarians believe is required. Slimline tubes requiring only one-half as much current are sometimes used but are not always available.

d. Regular wiring is fixed, and if ranges are shifted, and perhaps four instead of five ranges to a bay or six instead of five are wanted, rewiring becomes necessary.

If the ceiling height has been increased to make other space on the same floor more usable for concentration of readers, or for other reasons, it has been found that fluorescent tubes can be placed at right angles to the aisles, as noted below. This new method of stack lighting has been used in a number of libraries in recent

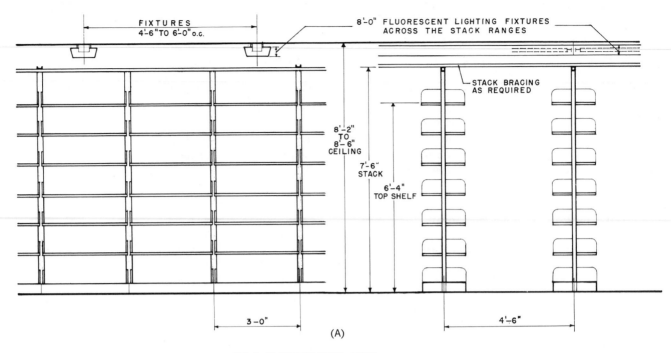

(A)

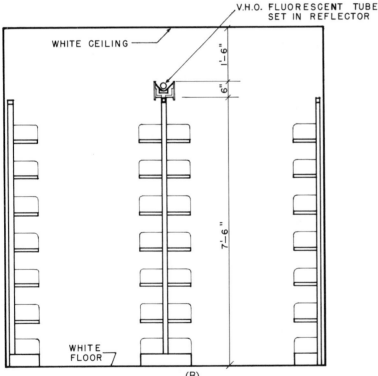

(B)

FIG. 8.8 (*A*) Lighting at right angles to ranges. Provides greater intensity on the critical lower shelves because of wider angle it makes possible. Permits shift in range spacing for free-standing stacks. Clear ceiling height must be at least 8 ft 2 in. and preferably 8 ft 6 in. to prevent heat damage of books on top shelves. The left-hand portion of the drawing shows stacks as one faces them. The right-hand portion shows the aisle with shelving at each side with the light fixtures at right angles to the ranges. (*B*) Fluorescent light on top of a stack range. A white ceiling and a white or very light floor are required with the tube set in a specially designed reflector.

years. It increases flexibility and makes it possible to shift ranges closer together or farther apart without changing the lighting fixtures. (See Fig. 8.8*A*.) Adequate lighting is still available, and the rows of lights can be up to 6 ft apart, instead of the 4 ft 6 in. or less which the standard arrangements require when they run over the center of the stack aisles, thus saving installation and upkeep costs and charges for current. If the tubes are placed at right angles and if the ranges are 7 ft 6 in. high, the ceilings should be at least 8 ft and preferably a few inches more to prevent overheating of books on the top shelf.

The narrower the ranges the more difficult it is to light the bottom shelves properly. There may be good light on the floor, but the backs of the books are at right angles and receive little light, perhaps as little as 1½ or 2 foot-candles particularly if aisles are narrow. This may seem completely inadequate, but actually it is as good stack lighting as any library had a generation ago, if not better, and few persons use bottom shelves for long consecutive periods. In an attempt to improve lighting on bottom shelves, they are sometimes tipped upward so the light will strike the back of the books at a better angle. Such shelves are costly in space, as well as in construction, and have the added disadvantage of tending to let the book slide or be shoved to the back of the shelf where it loses the advantage of the better angle and looks badly. A light-colored floor will help even more, reflecting the light to the backs of the books. Light-colored shelving is also helpful to a limited extent.[2]

The use of fluorescent lighting in book stacks gives more adequate bottom-shelf lighting than was possible with the incandescent bulbs even with special fixtures, partly at least because the light source is lengthened and the reader has less tendency to get into his own light. As has been said, fluorescent lights do not last well when they are turned on and off frequently. The question then arises, can you afford to leave them on all day? This is just one more problem that must be faced.

If the stack area has a clear height of 9 ft 6 in., what is known as the Lam fixture placed on the channel or canopy top over a range can be used and can provide completely indirect light. (See Fig. 8.8*B*.)

11. Color and Finish. Shelves used to be almost exclusively black or khaki-colored. With standard shelving, some installations had the divisions between sections and the end panels painted white, so that while they would show the dirt, they could be washed and would also brighten up the whole area. It was finally realized that the cost of other colors would not be large, and that the use of color would make shelving less monotonous and more attractive. A dozen colors are now available. A different one can be used on each stack level if desired. Some persons like intense colors; others prefer quieter tones. Of equal or greater importance, at least from the functional point of view, is the finish. The paint or enamel must be hard enough so that it will not chip easily. If it does, the underlying steel will rust with distressing results. Manufacturers may differ in the number of coats that they think are required, the amount of sanding between coats, and the temperature of the baking. Some of them prefer spraying or dipping to painting. The architect's specifications should ordinarily require the "hammer" test. These very technical questions will be dodged, except to speak of their importance and to say that too often stack installations have not been satisfactory because of poor paint jobs. It should be noted that the lighter the color of the floors and ceiling and of the shelving, particularly when it is not full, the higher is the intensity of the light made available.

[2] Since this was written, new fixtures, providing prisms which direct the light toward the lower shelves, have come on the market and should be considered.

12. Finished Bases, Panels, and Tops. Finished bases, end panels, and tops were discussed under stability. Should they be used and should they be 16, 18, or up to 24 in. deep as sometimes recommended in order to provide greater stability? They all present a more finished-looking job. There is no place under the bases for dust and dirt to collect. They are all a stabilizing factor. The cost of shelving goes up nearly 10 per cent with every 2 in. added to its depth. The cost of space is much more important than the added cost of shelving, and narrower shelves save space as well as equipment money. Each library must decide for itself what depth of shelving it prefers to have, but the facts just mentioned should be kept in mind.

Finished end panels also tend to add another 10 per cent to the cost, the exact figure varying with the panel and the length of the ranges, and the same applies to canopy tops except that the range length is not a factor. This is all for local decision.

13. Stack Accessories. Almost all book stacks require accessories, such as range labelholders, shelf labelholders, and book supports. These should not be neglected. They cost money, but will cost more later if they are ordered separately or in small quantities.

Range labelholders can be flat against range ends, stand out at right angles, or be wedge-shaped, so as to be in view as one walks down the cross aisles. If they stand out, they should be high enough so that a tall man will not bump his head or shoulder on them or put out an eye. Either variety should be large enough to contain the required information without the print or type being so small as to be difficult to read. This is particularly important with long ranges and for all open-access stacks. Standard-size range labelholders do not give space enough for all the information that some libraries wish to place on them. Labelholders are desirable at both ends of a range and one for each side of a double-face range can be useful. If of the flat type, they are more difficult to install when finished end panels are not used. (See Fig. 8.9.)

The problem with shelf labelholders is to make them easy to install but not easy to move when they ought to stay in place. (See Fig. 8.9.)

Book supports should stay put where they are wanted, yet at the same time be easily shifted; they should be so made that they will support books of various heights and will not present

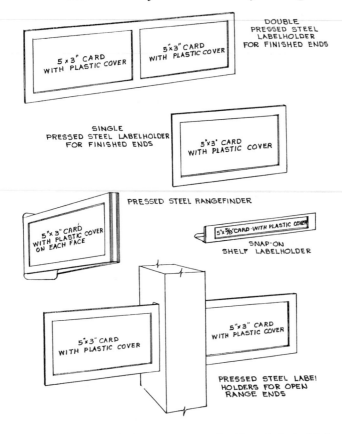

FIG. 8.9 Shelving accessories. Double and single labelholders for use on finished end panels. Range finders, protruding from range end. Labelholders for use on open-end ranges. Snap-on shelf labelholder.

thin edges which may knife a book when it is shelved. (See Fig. 8.10.) A few libraries have preferred to use bricks or concrete blocks covered with heavy brown paper or, better still, with buckram for book supports. The Houghton Library at Harvard has done this but has used decorative glass bricks in its exhibition cases. Some book supports are of wire and are suspended from the shelf above, but most are placed on the shelf with the books that are to be supported. Consider carefully the number of each accessory required. Five book supports to a single-faced section are often considered adequate, and perhaps three shelf labelholders.

14. Vertical Communications. Vertical communications in a book stack may include stairs, book lifts, elevators, pneumatic tubes, and endless-belt conveyors. Stairs take space and sometimes confuse the user if they go around several corners and land him with different orientation at different levels. They should be as simple as possible, not too wide or too narrow, not too

steep or too easy. (See Fig. 8.11*A*, *B*, and *C* for stack-stair types.) They ought not to add to fire risks by making a chimney. Stairs and other methods of vertical communication are discussed in section 6.2. Fire hazards are discussed in section 10.2. A recent book on fire hazards in a library should be useful in stack planning.[3] It is suggested that sprinklers in a book stack be avoided because water may be even more damaging than fire, but fire hazards should not be neglected in stack planning.

Book lifts must sometimes be installed because of the lack of funds for elevators, but unless there is an attendant at both ends, the book

[3] *Protecting the Library and Its Resources,* Report on a study conducted by Gage-Babcock & Associates, Inc. (LTP Publications, 7), ALA, Chicago, 1963.

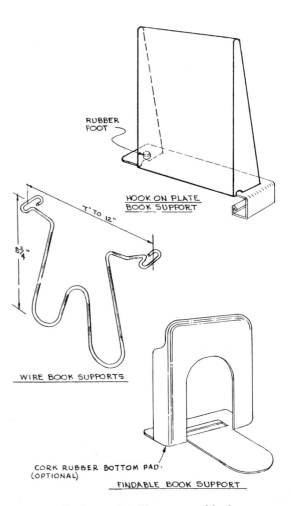

FIG. 8.10 Book supports. Three types of book supports are shown. One is attached to the shelf above, one to the shelf on which the books it supports rest, and the other is movable. Harvard has often used a brick or concrete block covered with brown paper or buckram cloth.

lift may be a snare and a delusion. The librarian will not be saved from climbing stairs, and the books will be subjected to an unnecessary handling at each end of the line. Readers are sometimes hard on books, but too often unnecessary and careless handling by the library staff does more harm to them than the readers.

An elevator, even if it is just large enough for a fairly thin attendant and a book truck will save weary hours of labor and wear and tear on books. It will also take care of a cripple or a senior faculty member with heart difficulties. Its use can be restricted by having it operated only by key.

Pneumatic tubes to carry call slips from the desk to stack stations have been used for many years. They tend to be noisy and, if call slips are in the form of punched cards that should be kept flat, they involve additional complications. At least one large university library has recently had serious difficulties. It is possible to use a telautograph or teletype or public-address system in place of pneumatic tubes. Pneumatic tubes have been used for the transfer of books over long distances, but they go so fast and stop so suddenly that they may present a serious hazard to books.

Endless-belt conveyors have been in use in libraries at least since early in the century for both vertical and horizontal transmission of books. They tend to be noisy. Too often they get out of order, generally because they are too complicated, having been made to turn too many corners, run on different planes, and receive and drop books at many stations. The more satisfactory installations have been the simplest. Of course, they are now used on a large scale in industry, and manufacturers know much more about their problems than in earlier years. As already noted, vertical communications are discussed in section 6.2.

15. Stack Carrels. Stack carrels are discussed in section 7.3, dealing with types of reader accommodations. Carrels along a stack wall can be a very economical seating arrangement, particularly if at the end of a blind aisle, and to a lesser degree if next to a cross aisle, which is required under any circumstances. In the latter case, if the wall is not interfered with by columns or heating pipes, they can be spaced as desired, even as close as 4 ft on centers if the table is held down to 22 in. and does not have a shelf which obstructs light on the table top, and if the chairs

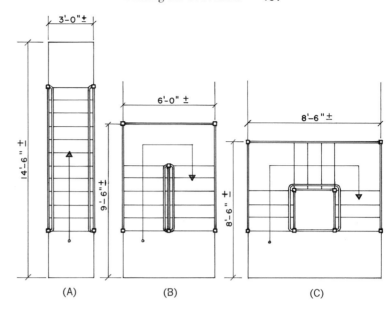

FIG. 8.11   Stack stairs. (*A*) Straight-run minimum stair. If more than two flights high, should be enclosed to avoid fire hazard. If enclosed, 15 ft length is required to provide landing at each end. Over-all width of at least 3 ft desirable. (*B*) Stair with one turn and intermediate landing. Has the advantage of same relative position and orientation on each floor. Enclosure requirements similar to those in (*A*) above. (*C*) Stair with two turns and intermediate landings.

do not have arms. Carrels which are 4½ ft on centers are almost luxurious for undergraduate use. A carrel measuring 5 ft 6 in. is very satisfactory for a student writing a thesis if the table is at least 39 in. or, better still, 42 in. wide. In many institutions carrels can well be open without doors. But all this is out of the field of this chapter.

8.2   Space Requirements for Book Stacks

This section deals with space requirements for book collections in terms of stack sections and square footage in a book stack. It will not attempt to discuss book storage in reading areas, storage of nonbook materials, or compact storage. The first two were mentioned briefly and indirectly in section 7.2 and will be dealt with again in section 8.4. Compact storage will be considered in section 8.3. This section is concerned only with books, pamphlets bound as books, and bound periodicals stored in what can be called standard book stacks.

Traditionally, libraries have run out of storage space for books before they were scheduled to do so. Crowded conditions and ineffective services have resulted. It has been difficult to obtain funds for new space, even if the old building proved to be expandable. Many of the people involved have become disgusted with libraries, which are accused of keeping quantities of useless "junk"; tempers have been shortened. Actually space for staff and readers becomes inadequate first in most libraries, but although books cannot talk and complain, lack of space for them is more evident visually and often receives greater attention. Additional seating accommodations are needed for a limited number of hours only during the year, and, if a student cannot find a seat in the library, he may go to his room or decide to do something else rather than read or study. The librarian goes on the principle that you can always find space for one more staff member and hesitates to complain. But the books, although not vocal, suffer physically; their suffering is easy to demonstrate, as is the resulting poor service.

The shortage of stack space too often may be the result of an overestimate of its capacity at the time of construction. The fault may lie with a too optimistic librarian or with an architect who has tried to crowd more capacity than is practicable into the limited space he is able to provide from the available funds, or those responsible may have failed to realize that, with a relative classification, shelves become uncomfortably crowded by the time 80 per cent of the total space is occupied and become almost unusable when 90 per cent is reached. But there are other factors.

The collections generally grow more rapidly than anticipated, geometrically, or exponentially as it might be called, rather than arithmetically. It seems to be difficult to understand in advance that faculty and students will not be content with one million volumes any more than they were earlier with half that many, and that they will continually and inevitably demand more.

There is disagreement in regard to how many volumes can be stored in a given amount of space, and the optimists who tend to overestimate the number often prevail.

Book-stack space requirements. In order to decide how much space will be needed for books in the book stack of a new building, eight basic questions should be considered.

1. What is a volume? This must be answered in order to determine how many are to be provided for or how much space a given number will require. No definition that is generally accepted has been reached up to this time. Some libraries call anything with over 50 pages or perhaps 100 pages a volume and, if it has fewer pages, a pamphlet. Some call anything that is catalogued as a separate item a volume. Some insist that a volume must have hard covers. If space requirements are to be estimated with any degree of accuracy on the basis of the number of volumes to be shelved, then a volume must be defined.

Methods of counting library holdings are far from uniform. This is not the place to attempt to summarize the lengthy debates between those who advocate counting bibliographical units and those who prefer to count physical volumes, but it should be emphasized that the rules that are used and the interpretations of these rules vary greatly in different institutions, with confusing results. Moreover, most library collections contain numerous unbound and unprocessed items that have not been counted and may be forgotten but must be housed, preferably on regular library shelving. Space requirements may be affected by an unusually large proportion of oversize volumes in such fields as music and fine arts or collections of unbound newspapers; or by a policy of binding periodicals into unusually thick volumes.

2. How tall and, even more important, how thick is an average volume?

This is as complicated as the preceding question and depends in part on the answer to that question. A figure must be determined in order to provide a basis for capacity estimates. Height and depth, as well as thickness, are involved, at least indirectly. The height and depth parts of the problem have been carefully studied by Van Hoesen and Kilpatrick as reported in the *Library Quarterly*[4] and by Fremont Rider[5] (Tables 8.1 and 8.2).

Thickness depends partly on the type of library and also on subject (see Table 8.3); partly on binding policy, particularly for periodicals; some libraries never bind a periodical in volumes more than 1½ or 2 in. thick; and partly as

[4] Henry B. Van Hoesen and Norman L. Kilpatrick, "Heights of Books in Relation to Heights of Stack Tiers," *Library Quarterly,* 4: 352–357, 1934; Henry B. Van Hoesen and Norman L. Kilpatrick, "The Heights of Three Hundred and Fifty Thousand Volumes," *Library Quarterly,* 5: 341–347, 1935.

[5] Fremont Rider, *Compact Book Storage,* Hadham Press, New York, 1949, p. 44.

Table 8.1. Measurement of Book Heights*

Group	Cm.	In.	No. of volumes	Percentage of the whole
I	Up to 20	7⅞ or less	88,582	25.0+
II	20–23	9	101,924	29.0+
III	23–25	9⅞	86,262	25.0−
IV	25–28	11	38,315	11.0−
V	28–30	11¾	14,777	4.0+
VI	30–33	13	10,348	3.0−
VII	33–40	15¾	7,268	2.0
VIII	40–45	17¾	2,377	0.6
IX	Over 45	Over 17¾	119	0.04

* Computations based on measurement of 350,000 volumes at Brown University Library.

Table 8.2. Measurement of Book Heights*

5 × 8 in. (or less)	25%
6 × 9 in.	29
7 × 10 in.	25
8 × 11 in.	11
9 × 12 in.	4
10 × 13 in.	3
Over 10 × 13 in.	3
	100%

* This table represents Rider's interpretation of Van Hoesen and Kilpatrick's compilation to include depth as well as height of books. Rider's figures for depth of books are used as a basis in the discussion of shelf depths throughout this volume.

Table 8.3. Space Requirements for Various Classifications of Books When Shelves Are Filled Solidly*

Kind of book	Volumes per foot of shelf	Volumes per single-faced section
Circulating (nonfiction)	8	168
Fiction	8	168
Economics	8	168
General literature	7	147
History	7	147
Technical and scientific	6	126
Medical	5	105
Law	4	84
Public documents	5	105
Bound periodicals	5	105
Art (not including large folios)	7	147

* This table is adapted from one in common use by stack manufacturers. It was used by Wheeler and Githens, who suggested that 125 volumes per single-faced section should be considered practical working capacity.

already noted on the policy adopted in defining a volume. It may vary from country to country, century to century, or decade to decade. The thickness of paper at different periods has its effect. There was probably a larger percentage of quarto and folio volumes in the eighteenth century than there is today. Fine-arts volumes tend to be taller if not thicker than others. If volumes are over 11 and under 13 in. high, six shelves at the most will be possible in a standard-height 7 ft 6 in. section. If they are over 13 and under 16 in. only five shelves can be used. If over 16 in. and under 20, four can be used, but extra deep shelves will be required, and it is desirable to shelve books of this size on their sides to prevent unnecessary wear and tear. The effect of tall volumes on capacity is great.

3. Is there a satisfactory formula for capacity that can be used? No. Many different formulas have been used to determine space requirements. They vary widely. The "cubook,"[6] which was proposed nearly thirty years ago by Robert W. Henderson of the New York Public Library, has frequently been used in planning; Federal government authorities based their estimates upon it in determining the book capacity of the recently completed National Library of Medicine. This formula provides for 100 "cu" or "average" size books per standard single stack section 3 ft wide and 7½ ft high; it goes one step farther and assumes that a section of this kind occupies 10 sq ft of floor space. This gives 10 volumes per sq ft of floor space in a book stack. At the other extreme, some architects, under pressure to provide more stack capacity than their clients can afford, or from lack of experience, have used estimates of as much as 175 volumes per single-face section and 20 volumes per sq ft, even when a subject classification was to be used. Collections arranged by size might fit into these estimates, as will be shown in section 8.3. Formulas for capacity are dangerous, and none of them are completely satisfactory.

4. Are the books to be shelved primarily by subject with perhaps a limited amount of segregation by size for outsize volumes, or primarily by size? (Shelving by size is discussed in some detail and its effect on capacity is indicated in section 8.3, dealing with compact storage.) This section deals with the first alternative—shelving

[6] *Library Journal*, 59: 865–868, Nov. 15, 1934; and 61: 52–54, Jan. 15, 1936.

primarily by subject, which might be said to be essential in an open-access academic library.

5. How much space is occupied by the present book collections? This question should be answered to give a firm basis on which to make further computations. It is always safer to measure the collections in terms of the number of standard 3-ft-wide, 7½-ft-high, sections that they would fill if each shelf were filled to capacity. This is not as difficult as it might seem, particularly if the shelves are well filled at present; the chief problem is to count up the vacant spaces, in terms of sections, and subtract this from the total now available. The remainder will be the desired figure. (Do not forget to include all the library's collections, not just the regularly classified ones.) It will be suggested later in more detail that if 50 per cent is added to this figure, the result will be the number of sections that the present collections would fill comfortably and leave room for reasonable growth.

6. At what rate are the collections expected to grow in the years immediately ahead?

Any formula used for this purpose must be based on (*a*) the nature of the collections; (*b*) the present rate of growth; and (*c*) changes in that rate which can properly be expected. The third is a particularly difficult problem.

In this era of rapidly advancing technology, will developments in microreproduction or electronic transmission of information enable libraries to slow up their rates of growth? The answer up to now appears to be negative, in spite of the fact that libraries have benefited greatly from microphotography in recent years. It has preserved for posterity large collections of newspapers that were on disintegrating paper stock and took a great amount of space. It has enabled libraries to acquire nearly complete collections of English books printed before 1641, American publications up to 1801, British Sessional Papers, official documents of the United States and the United Nations, and large quantities of sets of periodicals of recent vintage as well as of earlier years, to say nothing of many other volumes. These materials, if they could have been or had been obtained in the original format, would have occupied many sections of book stacks.

Nevertheless, the growth of regular stack collections in libraries has continued unabated,

and there is little indication that the rate will soon diminish, either as the result of microphotography or of interlibrary cooperation coupled with improved communication systems.

All libraries do not grow at the same rate, and they will not continue to grow at the present rate. At one extreme are the relatively new and rapidly developing institutions with libraries increasing by as much as 10 per cent or more per year; these have included in recent decades both publicly supported university libraries, such as those at the University of California at Los Angeles and the University of Florida, and private institutions, such as Brigham Young University and the Associated Colleges at Claremont. Junior college libraries have been growing on the average 7 per cent annually; so have the libraries of many other publicly supported institutions now in the process of developing graduate instruction and becoming genuine universities.

The median rate of growth for research libraries in established universities appears to have been 4.7 per cent, which is also the median for private colleges having from 500 to 1,000 students. The median for both larger and smaller private colleges (those with fewer than 500 or more than 1,000 students) has been 4.3 per cent.[7] In some "mature" liberal arts colleges the rate may be as little as 2 to 3 per cent; this is also the rate in some of the oldest and largest research collections. It should not be supposed, however, that such libraries are ceasing to grow—the Harvard University Library is increasing by only 2 or 3 per cent annually; but this means that it is adding from 140,000 to 200,000 volumes each year.

A number of factors that affect the rate of a library's growth may be noted. Increase in size of the student body has a relatively slight effect on a large university library, but may be a factor of considerable importance for a small college. The Association of College and Research Libraries Minimum Standards for College Libraries state that 50,000 carefully chosen volumes are required to support the instructional program of even a very small college and may be adequate for as many as 600 students; for each 200 beyond that number, at least 10,000 vol-

---

[7] These figures have been taken from the Association of College and Research Libraries statistics, published in the January, 1960, issue of *College and Research Libraries*.

umes should be added. It must be emphasized that these are minimum figures and that strong institutions will demand considerably larger and richer collections.

Broadening the curriculum ordinarily calls for extensive additions to a library. So does the development of honors courses for undergraduates. These facts are closely related to the adoption of more selective admission requirements and improvement in the quality of the student body. Moreover, a new, attractive building, with the improved services that it makes possible, is sure to stimulate greatly increased library use, which in turn will result in pressure for an increase in the size of the collections.

When a university undertakes advanced instruction and research in a new field, its library may be called upon to add thousands of volumes which would not otherwise be required. Meanwhile, the breadth of collecting demanded by the older fields of research continues to increase; it is no longer sufficient to buy books and periodicals from the United States and Western Europe. The Slavic nations, Africa, Asia, Australasia, and the rest of the Americas are becoming increasingly important sources of library materials as their scholarly programs multiply.

In this connection attention should be called to the fact that good research material in a library helps an institution to attract a better faculty and, in turn, a good research faculty tends to insist that a library improve and enlarge its collections.

Twenty years ago the author rashly predicted that the rate of research library growth would soon decrease.[8] He was mistaken; the rate has remained approximately the same if all American libraries are considered. He still believes that the geometrical progression will not continue indefinitely, but it does not appear that the rate will change soon enough to affect planning library buildings during the next decade or two, particularly in the case of relatively young institutions.

Estimating growth, then, is something that must be done for each library individually in the light of its present situation and its institution's

[8] Keyes D. Metcalf, "Some Trends in Research Libraries," in *William Werner Bishop, A Tribute,* 1941, edited by H. M. Lydenberg and Andrew Keogh, Yale University Press, New Haven, Conn., 1941, pp. 145–166.

plans for development. No formula can be proposed and, if any general advice is in order, it is that estimates nearly always prove to be too low rather than too high.

7. How full does the library propose to fill its shelves before the situation is considered intolerable? Librarians will not agree on the answer; some will say, "When the shelves average over 80 per cent full," because when that stage is reached a great deal of shifting is required whenever large sets or a considerable number of single volumes in a limited subject field are acquired. It is suggested as a basis for discussion here that 86 per cent be considered complete working capacity—this would leave 5 in. vacant on the average on each 36-in. (actual 35-in.) shelf. New space should be available, not just planned for, by the time that figure is reached. Certainly the cost of labor required for shifting, plus the resulting inevitable wear and tear on books, will then be so great that it will be uneconomical to permit further congestion. (If any figure other than 86 per cent is adopted, similar computations to those used below but with the different base should be made.)

If the library shelves are 70 per cent full and the collections are growing at the rate of 5 per cent a year, available capacity (86 per cent) will be reached in just over four years and two months. Four years is none too long a time in which to obtain funds, plan and build a new library or an addition, unless building funds and detailed plans are available on demand. In too many cases a considerably longer period will be required. This gives some idea of a desirable timetable, but if it cannot be carried out on schedule, shelves are bound to become overcrowded, books will be damaged, and costs for shifting will mount up rapidly. It may be necessary to place in some outside temporary storage volumes selected by subject or by the amount of use they are expected to receive. These may be difficult to select; changing their records will be expensive; and the change certainly will cause inconvenience.

Table B.12 (in Appendix B) shows the length of time required to fill shelves to comfortable capacity at different rates of growth.

8. How long should the new building be expected to be adequate before it is replaced or enlarged? This evidently must be answered in

accordance with the institution's general building and planning policies; one may suggest only that it is unwise and generally impossible to attempt to plan for long years ahead. If a new building includes satisfactory provisions for the construction of an annex or annexes when they are needed, it should not be necessary to construct extensive and expensive stack areas a great many years before they will be used. Some tax-supported institutions have been unfortunate enough to be subject to governmental regulations, made because of pressure for funds from many directions, that forbid new construction that will be sufficient for more than five years. This is undoubtedly a penny-wise and pound-foolish policy if a long-term view is taken. It should also be remembered that in such cases, if space requirements are based on the date when planning begins, and some years must elapse before the new quarters are ready for occupancy, the library will be beyond suitable capacity when the move finally takes place.

To summarize: What can be done in estimating book-stack-space requirements? Here is one possible approach in terms of a specific library, assuming that the eight questions have been answered as follows:

1. A volume is any book in or without hard covers or other material that is to be shelved in the book stacks being planned.

2. The height and thickness of volumes is such that the number now at hand fills completely the 2,000 single sections noted under 5 below.

3. No formula for a definite number of volumes in a section is selected, as the figures used in 5 below are considered more accurate. (It is desirable, however, to compare the 2,000 single sections with the count of volumes that are believed to be in the library.)

4. The books are to be shelved primarily by subject.

5. The present book collections would occupy 2,000 standard-size, single-faced sections, 3 ft wide and 7½ ft high, if the shelves were completely filled, not just filled to what might be called full working capacity.

6. The collection is expected to increase in size 5 per cent each year by geometric progression—that is, annually by 5 per cent of its size at the end of each immediately preceding year.

7. The stack is to be considered full to work-ing capacity when the shelves on the average are 86 per cent full, leaving approximately 5 in. unused space on each shelf, and additional space should be available not later than at that time.

8. It is hoped that the new building or additional stack area will be adequate for fifteen years from the date on which the estimate in 5 above was made.

Given these answers, the required stack capacity in the new building could be figured as follows:

Two thousand single-faced sections increasing geometrically at the rate of 5 per cent a year for fifteen years will fill completely 4,160 sections at the end of that time. Since the new stack is to be considered full to working capacity when the shelves on the average are 86 per cent full, the number of sections required for the new construction will be 4,880.

But another extremely important factor suggested under 7 above should be repeated here. When the shelves are 70 per cent full, which, if the estimates are correct, will be a little over four years before working capacity is reached, the next campaign for more space should begin. That will be only eleven years from the present if the space requirements are based on the space occupied by the collections at this time. If it is expected that four years will be required to prepare the new construction now planned and that the same length of time will be required the next time around, then to plan for only fifteen-years capacity beyond the present needs is probably an altogether too conservative approach, since planning for further space will have to begin only seven years after the space now being planned is available. Space for twenty-five years from the present is undoubtedly more desirable.

If the collections in question grow by 10 per cent per year instead of the 5 per cent that has been taken for purposes of illustration and if that rate continues, the date when overcrowding will be imminent would be when the shelves were no more than half full, and overcrowding would increase at an alarming pace and soon would become intolerable.

Tables in Appendix B will given an indication of the desirable schedules for planning new space when different rates of growth are used.

Square-footage Requirements. So far the discussion has dealt only with the number of standard (3-ft-wide and 7½-ft-high) sections required.

The number of these sections does not determine the number of square feet of floor space required because, as was seen in section 8.1, variations are possible in distances between range centers, which are affected in turn by shelf depths and aisle widths; variations are also possible in length of ranges between cross aisles and in the width of cross aisles. The space required for vertical communications, such as elevators, lifts, stairs, supporting columns, air ducts, and other services should not be forgotten. The "density of reader population" or the use factor is of importance here as has been noted; aisles in a relatively small stack used by many scholars need to be wider and shorter than those in a very large stack to which few persons are admitted.

The generous "cubook" formula, already referred to, with 100 volumes to a section provides 10 sq ft of floor space for each single-faced section. A much more compact arrangement is practicable if access to the stack is severely restricted, as it is at the New York Public Library or the Library of Congress. If ranges are only 4 ft on centers and 30 ft long, and 125 volumes to a section are estimated, 15 volumes per square foot or even 17 are easily possible. This can be increased to at least 20 if 150 volumes per section are estimated. The trend, however, it must always be remembered, is for increasing use of stacks by undergraduate students, and the average college or university can expect its stack population to increase rather than to diminish. The educational value of stack access is a major consideration, as is the provision of satisfactory seating accommodations and good service. Each is expensive, but is almost always worth the cost.

It is tentatively suggested, therefore, in order to provide a basis for estimates, that 10 volumes per square foot be used for small undergraduate collections of 50,000 volumes or less with completely open access. Not more than 12 volumes per square foot should be used for larger undergraduate collections of up to 100,000 volumes. Thirteen is safe for considerably larger collections and 15 for universities with great research collections and open access for graduate students and faculty only. Up to 20 can be used for a great research library with very limited stack access, narrow stack aisles, and long ranges. Section 16.3 on layouts should also be consulted as well as Appendix B.

Estimating the space requirements of a library's book collection is but one of the problems that must be faced when a new building is planned. If a completely satisfactory formula could be provided for such estimates, the task would be greatly simplified, but experience suggests, rather, that the first rule should be: *Beware of formulas.* Libraries differ, and there is no satisfactory substitute for consideration of the individual case by an expert librarian, library consultant, or architect. The figures that have been given here, if not accepted blindly, should be useful in making preliminary estimates of space for book collections, and they give at least some indication of the problems involved.

Finally, remember when in doubt another basic rule in library planning: *A healthy library tends to outgrow its book stack and its building sooner than expected.*

8.3 Compact Shelving

This section is devoted to describing methods for increasing book-stack capacity by the use of what has come to be called in recent years "compact shelving." The term will be considered here in its broadest sense as any method of shelving that increases the number of volumes that can be shelved per square foot of floor space. It is generally of interest to the large, rapidly growing research or university library, rather than to the college or public library. The subject has been discussed comprehensively by Fremont Rider, by Robert H. Muller, and by F. J. Hill. Their works are recommended reading for anyone facing a shortage in storage space.[9] This chapter attempts to supplement, rather than to replace them.

It is not easy to define precisely what a volume is or to determine the average thickness of the volumes in a library. Here, in order to simplify matters, two formulas will be taken as a base; these are arbitrary and debatable and by no means satisfactory for all institutions, but they will make it possible to compare book capacities resulting from different shelving arrangements.

The first of these formulas is that *six volumes equals the average comfortable capacity per linear foot*

[9] Fremont Rider, *Compact Book Storage*, Hadham Press, New York, 1949; Robert H. Muller, *Evaluation of Compact Book Storage Systems*, ACRL Monograph no. 11, 1954, pp. 77–93; F. J. Hill, "The Compact Storage of Books," *Journal of Documentation*, 11: 202–216, December, 1955.

of shelving if the collections are classified and space is provided throughout for growth. The matter has been discussed in section 8.2, which deals with space requirements for book stacks, and the conclusion is reached that there is no completely satisfactory formula. Nevertheless, the above formula is commonly accepted and is conservative for a college, university, or research library; it can properly be used as a basis for this discussion. It means that a standard section 3 ft wide, 7½ ft high, with seven shelves where possible, can hold 125 volumes. The figures will vary, of course, from library to library and from subject to subject within the same library; bound volumes of periodicals, for example, ordinarily take more space than monographs. Seven shelves of quarto or folio volumes cannot be provided in a section, but six volumes per linear foot is a figure conservative enough to make up for the extra space occupied by the approximately 10 per cent of the ordinary collection that is oversize and still provide a reasonable amount of space for growth. Newspapers in their original form should be dealt with as a separate and distinct group.

Other variables can modify the figure in any specific instance, and it should be added that total capacity per section is a matter of great importance in determining space requirements; possible means of inserting one additional volume or even one-half volume per linear foot of shelf should be studied and adopted unless their disadvantages outweigh the benefits. One extra volume shelved per linear foot beyond the six provided by the formula will increase capacity by 16⅔ per cent, which would provide space for an additional 167,000 volumes in a 1 million-volume stack. The construction cost for the square footage required for that many volumes may amount today to as much as $200,000.

The second arbitrary formula that will be used here provides that *15 volumes can be housed per square foot of stack-floor space.* The author dealt with this matter earlier in this chapter and will do so again in section 16.3; he will show that this figure is possible and reasonable with ranges placed 4 ft 6 in. on centers, if there is careful planning and if the average capacity per section is taken at the 125 volumes given by the first formula. Twelve or 13 volumes per square foot is a more satisfactory figure to use in an open-shelf college library.

Three basic methods can be used to increase the storage capacity per square foot of floor space. Each has its advantages and disadvantages. The total cost of housing any given number of volumes may be reduced under some circumstances, if not all, by any one of the three, and savings in space and costs may be even greater if a combination of two methods is used, or even all three. They all have disadvantages and the problem is whether or not the resulting savings make up for the inconveniences.

These three basic methods can be characterized as: (1) methods of shelving more books in the existing sections; (2) methods of devoting a larger percentage of the available floor space to standard shelving; and (3) methods of increasing the capacity of a given floor space by using special kinds of shelving.

The first two methods have been in use for many years throughout the world. The third, with minor exceptions, has been developed during recent years under the pressure of high building construction costs.

1. *Methods of Shelving More Books in the Existing Sections.* There are five subspecies to be considered under this major heading. The first of these is—

a. LESS SPACE MAY BE LEFT FOR GROWTH IN THE ESTIMATE USED: This practice has been used from the earliest times. It may take either of two quite different forms.

Under the first, books are arranged chronologically by date of receipt and shelves are filled to capacity one after another as the collection grows. This has been the traditional plan in many large libraries in other countries and often, too, in small ones; it facilitates the use of each linear foot of shelving to full capacity; once shelved, a volume need never be shifted. The chronological scheme is not an essential feature of fixed location shelving, but it is the obvious procedure. The arbitrary figure of six volumes per linear foot that has been accepted as a formula for the purposes of this discussion will fill a stack to something like three-quarters of the complete capacity that could be obtained if each shelf were completely filled. Under this system, consequently, if the formula's 125 is correct, a standard section will hold 168 volumes. But this plan should not be used with a subject arrangement.

An alternative is simply to decide that, though fixed locations are not to be adopted, a larger percentage of each shelf may be filled without too great difficulty. If seven volumes instead of six are shelved per linear foot, the shelves might still have only seven-eighths of complete capacity, yet the estimated capacity will have been increased to 147 volumes per section. There will still be room for a 14 per cent increase in the bulk of the total collection before every shelf is completely filled. Experience has shown, however, that whenever shelves are filled on the average to 80 per cent or more of capacity, a library begins to suffer from slower service. Constant shifting of books is required because of unequal growth; individual shelves and sections overflow; and space has to be found for expansion of entire subject classifications that are growing more rapidly than the collections as a whole. Bindings will be damaged by moving and pulling books from shelves filled too full.

It should be added that institutions all too rarely provide additional shelf space as soon as it is needed; often they delay until books have to be piled on the stack aisles and window ledges, a procedure which inevitably damages the books and impairs service. For this reason the author strongly recommends that, in estimating stack capacity, the conservative figure of 125 volumes per section be used. A librarian should begin to plan for more space as soon as a library stack is filled to two-thirds or, at the most, three-fourths of complete capacity, assuming, of course, that he plans to continue a classified arrangement of the books.

If a chronological arrangement is adopted, the only way to use the stacks is through consultation of the catalogue; all the advantages of classified collections must be forgone. While the reader could still be permitted open access and allowed to determine the arbitrary location from the catalogue and to go to the shelves to obtain the books he wants, he would then be acting simply as a stack attendant, and an untrained one at that; the disadvantages of open access would result without any of the manifold advantages it normally offers. There is yet another consideration. Many readers are interested in several books at once on the same or related subjects. Since these books normally were not acquired at the same time, the attendant or reader in a fixed-location stack may have to go to widely separated areas for them, taking more time than would be required under a subject-classification system. This is one of the reasons for slow service in many libraries that do not shelve their books by subject.

To be weighed against these considerations, the great advantage of the chronological arrangement is its saving in space. If a building for 1 million volumes is taken as an example, the space required for books in chronological order is at the most only three-quarters of the space a classified plan will need if moderate provision is made for growth. This alone might well save more than $335,000 in construction. But American scholars and librarians are convinced that open access and subject arrangements are of vital importance and that the cost is not unreasonable.

Do not overestimate stack capacity. This has been done altogether too often by architects and librarians.

b. BOOKS MAY BE SHELVED BY SIZE: If books are shelved by size and the system divides them into five or more groups (e.g., books less than 7 in. high, those between 7 and 8 in., 8 and 9 in., 9 and 11 in., and those over 11 in.), it should be possible to place on the average eight or nine shelves per section in a stack of the standard 7 ft 6 in. height in the clear. If the average is 8½, compared with seven shelves on the average for regular shelving, the linear footage available has been increased by approximately 20 per cent (Mr. Rider has calculated the figure at approximately 25 per cent), which would bring the average capacity per section up to 150 volumes; and if combined with the chronological arrangement described above, the figure will rise further to 200, a total increase of 60 per cent.

The Reference Department of the New York Public Library is now shelving new acquisitions in its main stack chronologically as received and by size. This has also been the arrangement for many of Harvard's books in the New England Deposit Library; other libraries following this procedure, at least in part, include the Midwest Inter-Library Center, the Hampshire Inter-library Center, and many reference and research libraries of the United Kingdom, countries on the Continent, and elsewhere. It often comes as a shock to an American librarian to discover the prevalence of shelving by size abroad; foreigners are often equally surprised to find that great American libraries shelve their books by subject.

c. FORE EDGE SHELVING: A third means of increasing the capacity of a given area is to shelve books on their fore edges as well as by size. This plan was adopted in parts of the Wesleyan University Library by Fremont Rider, and is discussed in pages 56 to 64 of his *Compact Book Storage*. It has also been adopted to some extent for infrequently used material at Yale University and elsewhere. A method of saving still more space was also proposed by Mr. Rider, when he not only placed the books on their fore edges but also sometimes cut down their margins with a power-driven paper knife and boxed them in inexpensive cardboard containers to protect them and to provide a good surface on which to inscribe call numbers.

It is estimated that fore edge shelving, if used in conjunction with arrangement by size, will increase by at least 50 per cent the capacity per section made possible by the chronological plan. It may bring capacity up to at least 250 volumes per section, an increase of 100 per cent over the subject-arrangement plan, and provide for 30 volumes per sq ft of floor space instead of 15. The procedure has all the disadvantages that have been noted above; in addition, it distresses many librarians, who observe that books are injured and their bindings weakened when they are shelved on their fore edges. If they are also cut down to reduce their size, the procedure may be likened to cutting off a man's toes so he can wear smaller shoes. In fairness to Mr. Rider it should be reported that his books were placed on their backs when boxed, so there was less danger of weakening the bindings. To double the capacity per square foot by shelving books chronologically and by size on their fore edges may save more than $650,000 in the construction of a 1-million-volume book stack if construction costs approximate $20 per square foot.

d. SHELVING TWO OR THREE DEEP: Books can be shelved two deep, that is, one row behind the other, on shelves 12 in. deep, or three deep on 18-in. shelves. Many libraries, because of lack of space, have occasionally resorted to the two-deep plan, temporarily at least. The inconvenience is extremely serious. When President Eliot proposed cooperative storage for the Boston area, which came into being forty years later as the New England Deposit Library, he suggested that the "dead books" be shelved three deep, which is even worse—two or perhaps four times as unsatisfactory as two deep. The procedure will, however, increase capacity materially. Two-deep shelving, where books are on 12-in.

shelving, with no change in aisle width, could bring the total up to 400 volumes per section or 50 per square foot, assuming that the arrangement is also chronological and by size. If the three-deep plan were adopted and the distance between range centers were increased from 4 ft 6 in. to 5 ft 6 in., as would be desirable if not necessary, capacity would rise to 600 volumes per section and, in spite of the reduced number of ranges, more than 60 volumes could be housed per square foot.

e. HIGHER SECTIONS: There is one further method of increasing capacity per square foot of floor space without abandoning standard shelving; this is to increase the height of the shelf sections. It can be done, of course, only if the stack area has ceilings higher than 7 ft 6 in. clear space between the floor and ceiling. If, as in many book stacks, there is an 8 ft 6 in. ceiling (which is lower than the ceilings in most areas of modern libraries that are used for both book storage and readers), the capacity theoretically will be increased by more than 14 per cent. This does not call for giving up a classified arrangement with open access, but it places the top shelf out of the reach of all but the tallest readers unless footstools are used. In warehouse buildings, where shelves are closed to the public, the disadvantage is much slighter. The New England Deposit Library has 8 ft 4 in. ceilings throughout.

Five methods have been described by which, without making a basic change in standard stack installations, the capacity of a given area can be increased. As has been noted, various combinations of these methods are possible; the total number of plans that might be adopted is therefore considerably greater than five. Any such method will save a large amount of money on construction and maintenance. Each institution must carefully consider its service methods and requirements before deciding to adopt one or more of these procedures. No one of the five is recommended for an open-access library, and their use in a closed-access stack for any but little-used collections is decidedly questionable. These methods should be compared with procedures of a somewhat different nature that will be described below.

2. *Methods of Devoting a Larger Percentage of the Available Floor Space to Regular Shelving*

a. SHALLOWER SHELVES: If the depth of shelves is decreased without changing aisle widths, it is possible to install more ranges in a given floor area, thereby increasing the capacity per square foot. A large percentage of all the shelving now being installed in college, university, and research libraries has ranges at least 20 in. from front to back, often with bases, bottom shelves, and finished end panels as wide as 24 in. The justification for these wide ranges is to increase stability and to provide bottom shelves on which oversize books will not project into the aisles.

It should be remembered that a large percent—94 according to Mr. Rider[10]—of all books in the college and research library measure not more than 9 in. from spine to fore edge. If shelves are made only 7 in. deep actual measurement, with a 2-in. space between those on one side and those on the other of each double-faced section, the total depth of the range will be 16 in., instead of the 20 in. or more now prevalent. One of these 7-in. shelves with 2 in. of space behind it is deep enough for a 9-in. book unless another volume exceeding the 7-in. depth happens to be immediately behind it or unless there is sway bracing in the 2-in. gap between. More space is used for aisles than for shelves, but a decrease from 16 to 20 in. in range depth increases the capacity per square foot by 8 per cent. It is possible also, of course, to use narrower shelves in conjunction with chronological and size arrangements. Further, it should be noted that shallow shelves should cost less than deep ones.

Mr. Rider has also estimated that only some 3 per cent of books in a library measure more than 10 in. from spine to fore edge.[11] Since some of the volumes that make up this 3 per cent are too large for any regular shelving, special provision will always have to be made for some portion of the collection. It is recommended that, in planning its stack, each library give serious consideration to the possibility of using a large percentage of ranges which are 16 in. or at the most no more than 18 in. deep, rather than the deeper sizes that are now so frequently used.

b. NARROWER AISLES: The standard width of aisles in research libraries varies from 30 to 36 in.; in housing infrequently used books, particularly in closed-access stacks, the width may

well be reduced considerably. When shallower shelving has also been adopted, ranges have been installed on 40-in. centers instead of 54, which increases capacity by 35 per cent. On this basis, without resorting to any of the other procedures that have been considered, capacity per square foot will become approximately 20 volumes instead of 15. It should be noted that narrow aisles increase the difficulty of lighting bottom shelves adequately.

In Dublin, the Trinity College Library uses a colonnade under its famous Long Room as a stack area, with ranges 40 in. on centers; the arrangement is by size there, with the result that some 30 volumes are housed per square foot. In the New England Deposit Library, with shelving 44 in. on centers, with aisles 26 in. wide, capacity has been increased by 23 per cent over standard shelving, in addition to the gains resulting from arrangement by size. Much of the Newberry Library stack has ranges 48 in. on centers. Widener is an open-access, heavily used stack, where books are classified by subject, with ranges 50 in. on centers.

The author suggests that aisle widths be carefully considered with present and prospective use in mind. Thirty-six in. is recommended for a heavily used stack open to a large undergraduate group; 32 to 34 in. is adequate for a collection of 500,000 volumes and over if the use is not heavily concentrated; and 30 in. is enough for a limited-access collection of over 1 million volumes. In a storage stack for less-used books, 26 in. will do, but less than 24 in. should not be tolerated. Before deciding on aisle widths, a planner should consider range lengths, which are discussed in the second paragraph below; other things being equal, the narrower the aisle, the shorter the range should be. Both factors are part of the same problem.

With shallow shelving and narrow stack aisles, special provision should be made for deeper shelving for the limited number of what may well be called oversize volumes. This can sometimes be done by placing them along end, elevator, and stair walls which are adjacent to wide aisles, or by setting aside bays where one less range than elsewhere is installed.

c. LENGTHENING RANGES AND HOLDING DOWN THE WIDTH OF CROSS AISLES: Some people have asserted that no range in an open-access stack should be more than five sections or 15 ft long. This may be valid for a public library with open

[10] Fremont Rider, *Compact Book Storage,* p. 45.

[11] A recent study of the Harvard Medical School Library by Ralph Esterquest showed that only 1½ per cent of the collection's books were over 9 in. deep.

access or even for an undergraduate collection, though it could well be disputed. But why should the rule be accepted for research library stacks open only to faculty members and advanced students? Indeed, short ranges, interrupted by cross aisles, only too often complicate shelving arrangements, particularly in a large stack area. If the ranges are properly labeled and if floor plans are readily accessible, with broad subjects or class marks clearly indicated on them, long ranges may be more satisfactory than short ones, because they may simplify traffic patterns and shelving arrangement. Ranges that extend 33 ft before a cross aisle is reached will provide 10 per cent more shelving in the same square footage than two 15-ft ranges separated by a 3-ft cross aisle. A range 36 ft long will provide 20 per cent more shelving than two 15-ft ranges with a 6-ft cross aisle between.

It is a question whether academic libraries can afford short ranges in a large book stack, particularly if they confuse those who use the stack. Does any one in a large stack experience any real inconvenience because of long ranges if the ranges are well labeled? This question should be considered and answered on the basis of local conditions, but it is obvious that shallower shelving, narrower aisles, and longer ranges can increase capacity per square foot materially without any sacrifice of the advantages of subject arrangement and restricted open access.

It is suggested that range lengths and width of cross aisles be carefully considered, again with present and prospective use in mind. Anything less than 15 ft for range lengths is extravagant in a stack area. For many heavily used, open-access book stacks a cross aisle in each bay may be indicated. But in a large library there is no reason why ranges at least 30 ft long should not be used, if they are properly labeled, and 36 to 42 ft are possible. In closed-access stacks, ranges up to 60 ft long should be considered if they can be fitted into the pattern determined largely by the column spacing.

The width of cross aisles presents similar problems. This is discussed in some detail in section 4.2, dealing with the module system. It is very often a complicating factor. Anything less than 3 ft is seldom desirable—this may be cut, however, to 34 in. by the range-end upright and a finished end panel—and should be used only

when traffic is very limited and then only when stack aisles are adjacent on both sides or a stack aisle on one side and open carrels on the other. A solid wall on one side would make a narrow cross aisle questionable.

For a main cross aisle in any but a very heavily used stack, 4½ ft is sufficient. The Widener Library aisles at Harvard are little over 4 ft. But with a module system built up from 3-ft units, 4½ ft may be difficult to arrange. A range which includes two 14- to 16-in. columns or a lectern hung on the end of a column range may help in this connection (see Figs. 4.3, 4.9, and 4.10).

3. Methods of Increasing the Capacity of a Given Floor Area by Using Special Kinds of Shelving. Several special kinds of shelving can be used with the normal subject arrangement of books or with one or more of the other plans considered above. Not all combinations are practicable. Books cannot be shelved two or three deep on any of the three kinds of special shelving that will be described below; in effect, these special shelving devices are a means of achieving the savings in space that two- and three-deep shelving provides without most of the disadvantages that are entailed if books are crowded in two or three deep on regular shelves. It should also be noted that special shelving is ordinarily designed for aisle widths and shelf depths cut almost to a minimum; hence additional space economies along these lines are impracticable. The height of ranges of special shelving should not be increased beyond the standard 7 ft 6 in., because they do not lend themselves to use with the aid of footstools. (In spite of this statement, higher than standard ranges have been used with special shelving at the University of Wisconsin Library and elsewhere.)

a. HINGED SHELVING: The hinged shelving used at the Midwest Inter-Library Center makes possible an increase in capacity per square foot of up to 75 per cent over the standard 125 volumes per section; to this can be added the savings that result from shelving by size if that procedure is also adopted. This hinged shelving was designed by that great innovator, Angus MacDonald. His proposal was accepted before the design had been completely perfected, and the shelving is not as satisfactory as it might have been if a rush order could have been avoided. This shelving consists of double-faced sections hung on each side of standard sections; each range, therefore, has what amounts to three-deep shelving on both sides. Since the hinged sections are nearly 3 ft long and are deep enough to accommodate books on both sides, the aisles had to be nearly 40 in. wide; they thereby lost part of the gain, but provided considerably larger capacity per square foot of floor space than would be available with ranges no more than 40 in. on centers.

A second type of hinged shelving is now available. It consists of swing units occupying a little less than half the length of the regular sections. These units are hung at both ends of each section; they swing out into the stack aisles and expose to view the regular shelves that are behind them when they are closed. The swing units are offered in either single- or double-faced shelving. The latter, like the installation at the Midwest Inter-Library Center, makes it possible to shelve books three deep on both sides of each range and provides access to books on the inside rows without individual handling of the books on the outer row. Since these units are only half as long as those designed by Mr. MacDonald, the aisles need not be widened; and there is less strain on the hinges.

b. DRAWER-TYPE SHELVING: Drawer-type shelving, when first introduced by the Hamilton Company of Two Rivers, Wisconsin, was called "Compo." The W. R. Ames Company of San Francisco now offers "Stor-More" book units, and shelving of this kind is also produced by Clifford Brown of Wauwatosa, Wisconsin, who designed the original "Compo" stack. The Ames units consist of double-headed drawers, approximately 6 ft in length, which can be pulled out into the aisle on either side and in this way provide extra stability but more concentrated weight. The drawers are designed to bridge alternate aisles in a stack area. They make use of existing multitier stack columns but can also be used in a free-standing arrangement.

The Hamilton "Compo" units consist of single-headed drawers, which pull out in one direction only, and are available in varying lengths from 3 to 4 ft, and in widths varying from 18 to 26 in. Each drawer can be adjusted vertically on 1-in. centers, as can adjustable shelves. If these were used to replace the 40-in. sections in the multitier stack of the Widener Library at Harvard, they would be wider than those replacing the 36-in. shelves that are to be found in most libraries; this would reduce the capacity per square foot but would make it possible to use them for relatively deep volumes. Drawer-type shelving can be installed in place of shelving in an old multitier stack or as free-standing stack in new construction only if the floors are designed to support the extra weight.

Drawer-type shelving makes it desirable or, in many cases, necessary to increase the width of stack aisles, which reduces to some extent the space they save; but, as Mr. Muller has shown, they may double the capacity per square foot, because the percentage of floor space they occupy is up to two-thirds of the total area instead of the one-third with regular book shelving with 18-in.-deep ranges and 36-in. aisles. It should be added that Mr. Muller's figures referred to capacity increases obtained by special shelving in bays 23 ft square, and might be modified considerably in a bay size specially adapted to the particular type of shelving that was to be installed in it.

c. "COMPACTUS": A third special type of shelving has gone under the name of "Compactus." It originated in Switzerland, and was apparently invented by a Zurich engineer named Hans Ingold, who has held the patent rights and manufactured the shelving. It has been used in England, Norway, the Soviet Union, Sweden, and elsewhere. It has been installed on a fairly large scale in Australia and is now available in Japan under the name of "El Ecompack." An adaptation of it can be found in the National Library at Calcutta, where Dr. Kesavan installed it in the basement and other parts of the old Viceroy's mansion in space that would otherwise have been very difficult to use to advantage for book storage. Another adaptation of it was in the Treasure Room at Harvard during the 1930s; there it was removed because the books occasionally fell and were damaged while ranges were being shifted.

Another variety, called the Rolstone Way, is available through Acrow (Canada) Ltd., in Montreal. It provides rows of mobile units installed in what would otherwise be aisle space. The particular section required for consultation is made available by the fact that the sections can be moved one at a time on tracks in a way that somewhat resembles methods used in solving Chinese puzzles.

The Aetna Steel Products Corporation of New York City, which fabricates stacks under the name of "Aetnastak," has made available still another arrangement for compact storage on wheels.

Still a different form was used many years ago in the British Museum, where wide aisles gave room for an additional range that could be pushed to the other side of the aisle.

Regular "Compactus" is made up of more or less standard stack ranges that are mounted on rails with ball-bearing wheels. These ranges can be pushed tightly together; rubber baffles on range edges are desirable to prevent them from damaging one another or the books when they are moved. Each bay or portion of the stack can be almost filled with ranges, leaving only one aisle parallel to ten or more ranges. The shelving is so heavy, when used in large blocks, that a motor must be installed to move the ranges and to open up an aisle through which one can reach the shelf desired. The weight is sufficient to require extra strong floor construction; the motor, rails, and other necessary equipment are expensive. Safety devices are required to prevent a user from being crushed by someone inadvertently starting up the motor at the wrong time. Supporting columns seem to get in the way even more than in the case of standard shelving, and this may prevent use of as large a percentage of the total floor space as might be expected.

Still, it is obvious that this type of shelving makes possible a greater book capacity per square foot than any other method yet devised. In ordinary shelving, with ranges 54 in. on centers, some two-thirds of the space is given over to aisles, and only one-third consists of shelving. With very narrow aisles, as at Trinity College in Dublin (ranges 40 in. on centers, with 24-in. aisles), the percentage of space devoted to shelving rises only to 40; with hinged or drawer-type shelving, it may vary from a little over 50 up to 66 per cent. "Compactus," however, may make it possible to fill 75 per cent or more of the total space with shelving, leaving only 20 to 25 per cent for aisles between ranges and for cross aisles; the latter are of particular importance and should be extra wide when "Compactus" is used.

Against the advantages of special types of shelving the following drawbacks must be assessed:

1. Books are not as readily available to the reader as they would be on standard shelving. Hinged shelving must be swung out into the aisle; drawers must be pulled out. The manufacturers deny that this is a problem, pointing as evidence to installations in reading rooms and open-access stacks.

2. As sections swing out or drawers are pulled out there is always some danger of books falling and becoming damaged. The extent of this danger depends on the design, and is greater with hinged shelving than with the drawer type.

3. All types of special shelving have moving parts and, unless it is as well made as the Rolls Royce engine, anything with moving parts may sooner or later come to grief. Design and quality of construction are vital considerations. As has been implied, the Midwest Inter-Library Center has encountered difficulties that can be blamed on premature fabrication before the design was perfected. The rollers and other moving parts in drawers, if well made, should be capable of standing heavy use for many years.

4. The cost per linear foot of shelf is much greater for any of these types of special shelving than for standard ranges; this is inevitable in view of the moving parts and the heavier construction required. Costs of shelving will not be discussed here, but it can be noted that Mr. Muller found that the additional cost of special shelving cancels out a large number, but not necessarily all, of the advantages resulting from increasing the capacity per square foot. As he points out, the cost per square foot of construction of the building in which a stack is to be installed is here of prime importance.

Summary. Two major questions need to be answered before one reaches a decision on whether or not to use any method of compact shelving.

1. Is the resulting inconvenience great enough to outweigh the saving in space that will be achieved? Capacity can be increased by leaving less space for growth or, if the classified arrangement is abandoned, by filling each shelf completely. Shelves or aisles or both may be narrowed. Capacity can also be increased by installing moving shelves of one kind or another. If a combination of methods is used, both savings and disadvantages are compounded. It should not be forgotten that most of the world's great libraries outside the United States arrange their books by size and use narrow shelves and aisles, and that moving shelves are in use at the Mid-

west Inter-Library Center, the University of Wisconsin, and the New York Public Library's warehouse, as well as in many smaller libraries of all kinds. It is suggested that anyone considering the use of such shelving consult libraries that have had experience with it.

2. What is the actual monetary saving that can be anticipated from adoption of any specific plan? Few persons would consider installation of expensive moving shelves in a stack built in a Nissen hut, where construction costs for the space that is saved come to perhaps $1.50 per square foot. In Wall Street, on the other hand, where ground space alone may be worth hundreds of dollars per square foot, it ought to be possible to save large sums by compact storage; a book may have to be used heavily there to earn a place on standard shelves. Most college and university libraries fall somewhere between the two extremes.

It is desirable once more to direct attention to Mr. Muller's figures, which may not now apply to any specific library, but indicate clearly the considerations that need to be weighed. They demonstrate, in particular, that any type of special shelving costs considerably more per linear foot of storage space than standard library shelving, and very much more than commercial shelving of the sort used by the New England Deposit Library. "Commercial shelving," it should be remembered, is a term used for metal shelving that can be adjusted vertically only by using a wrench for handling the nuts and bolts that hold it together. Some librarians believe that it is less inconvenient than any of the other special types of shelving that have been discussed in this section. It is used extensively in warehouse storage and often in library basements. It is available from many manufacturers, and costs perhaps no more than half as much as the more easily adjusted bracket shelving that is now standard in libraries.

Many mistakes have been made in the name of economy. There are libraries that could have used one or more of the methods of compact storage to advantage, but have failed to do so. Others have used one or more of these methods with unfortunate results.

It is not easy to estimate costs accurately; and it is difficult indeed to weigh costs against convenience. What, for instance, is the dollar value of open access and collections classified by subject? Special circumstances may also complicate

a situation. When a library is full and for one reason or another there is no immediate possibility of constructing an addition or a new building, compact shelving of one kind or another may be the only practicable solution. Even then, it is suggested that these special types of shelving be regarded as a last resort, and that the library first consider whether or not portions of its collections might be placed in a stack with narrower shelves and aisles, shelved by size, or moved out, perhaps to be transferred to a cooperative storage building like the Midwest Inter-Library Center or the New England Deposit Library. A summary of this sort can provide no one with an answer; it can only indicate the questions he ought to ask.

Microreproductions. Compact shelving should not be dismissed without pointing out that microreproduction of one kind or another is used much more extensively than all species of special types of shelving put together. This is not the place for a definitive discussion of this important development, except to say:

1. It represents greater space savings by far than any of the methods described in this chapter.

2. The inconveniences in connection with its use and the dislike that some scholars have for it must be kept in mind.

3. To replace material already in a library with microfilm may cost more than the savings in space are worth, unless it is reproduced in a fairly large edition.

4. Reading machines are expensive and involve a good deal of extra reading area.

5. Its use in one form or another will undoubtedly increase rapidly in the years ahead, but not rapidly enough to reduce present requirements for storage areas for collections. It will undoubtedly reduce the rate of growth of university and research-library collections, but can be expected to have less influence on space needs for college libraries.

8.4 Shelving in Reading Areas and for Nonbook Materials

Sections 8.1 and 8.2 have discussed "standard" book-stack shelving and stack capacity and square-footage requirements, respectively. Section 8.3 has dealt more specifically with compact storage. This section considers other storage requirements in academic and research libraries. Three main groups will be dealt with, as follows:

1. Shelving in reading areas, where what is called standard-stack shelving is not indicated.

2. Shelving for miniature books and for large folio volumes and newspapers which are not adapted for standard-stack shelving.

3. Nonbook material, for which special types of storage equipment could or should be provided.

1. *Shelving in Reading Areas.* Section 7.2 discussed 24 different types of reading areas. Many of them require book shelving on a larger or smaller scale in nonstandard sizes and with different spacing. Some of them require shelving for nonbook materials which will be considered under 3 below. Shelving in reading areas, speaking in general terms, tends to differ from regular book-stack shelving in four ways.

a. An effort may often be made to make this shelving aesthetically more pleasing than stack shelving, as it is in constant view of library users and therefore more conspicuous. This may make it desirable to use shelving of a more attractive or stimulating color than that in the main stack room; or to install case shelving instead of the bracket type if for one reason or another that is preferred; or to use wood construction. If the latter costs more than can be afforded (it may double the cost, particularly if oak or walnut or a special design is used), finished wood end panels may be used. Finished bases are in many cases found desirable, and also finished or what are sometimes called canopy tops may be called for. Each of these, in the case of metal shelving, can add some 10 per cent to the cost.

b. If floor cases are used, the spacing between them is usually and probably should be somewhat or considerably wider than that required in a book stack. Books ordinarily placed in a reading room are there because they are heavily used, and with heavy use wider aisles are advisable, the width depending upon the amount of use. A width of 3½ ft might be considered a minimum, and from there on up to 6 ft is not unusual, depending on local circumstances and the length of the ranges. If wall cases are used with adjacent tables for users, it is obvious that chairs generally should not be placed so as to back into the aisle in front of the shelving, and that the aisle should be wide enough so that the reader can consult books on the bottom shelf without obstructing the aisle. This probably means a width of at least 4 ft. (At least 5 ft is indicated if a chair on the shelving side of the table is used.)

c. The height of the shelving presents another problem. Wall shelving can go up to the standard height of 7 ft 6 in. although it may well be held down a few inches if reference books which tend to be large and heavy are to be stored. Six shelves 13 in. on centers, instead of the more common 12 in., recommended for most stack shelving, may be desirable, and with a 4-in. finished base, the top shelf will be 69 in. above the floor; it will be considerably easier for a short person to reach than one 76 in. up, as proposed in the book stack for a seventh and top shelf. The six shelves and a 2-in. molding at the top will have a total height of 84 in., and with a reading area 10 ft in height or higher, this will give at least 36 in. above the cases that can, if desired, be used for pictures or prints. It is not suggested that tops of the cases be used for plaster busts of classical and other personages, as was often done in years gone by, although this is still appropriate in some circumstances. Many architects and librarians will prefer to have wall shelving in a reading area set back into the wall, as this may give pleasing results (see Fig. 8.12). Wall shelving in a reading area is often undesirable because it makes the whole room more restless and noisy even with good acoustic protection because readers go back and forth to consult the heavily used volumes.

If floor cases are used, height is a more complicated problem. If the room is high and spacious in appearance, the same height as the wall cases—up to a little over 7 ft—may be indicated. If the shelving is reduced to approximately 6 ft in height, only five shelves instead of six will be available, but a more open feeling can be obtained. This is treading on the territory of the architect and the interior decorator and is mentioned simply because it is a question that must be decided sooner or later. But to go down to four shelves will place the finished top at about 4 ft 10 in., which will make it possible for a person of average height to look over the top, and in turn will mean that heads will be bobbing up and down as one walks through aisles, which may not be unpleasant at a reasonable distance but may be disconcerting in an adjacent aisle. The fifth shelf avoids this and increases capacity, other things being equal, by 25 per cent per square foot. Something more is said of this later.

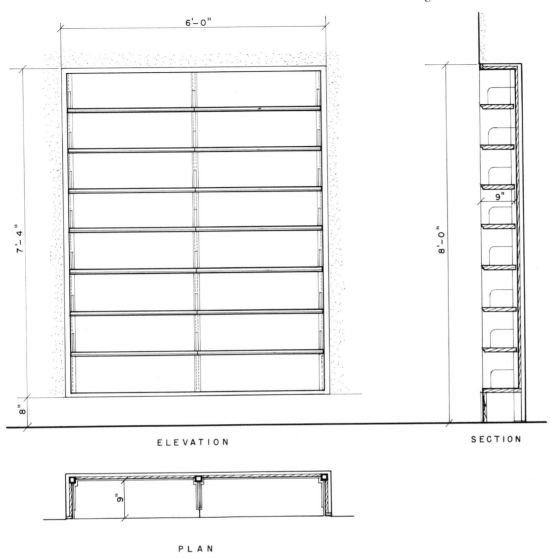

ELEVATION SECTION

PLAN

FIG. 8.12 Shelving sunk flush with wall in Littauer Library, Harvard University.

A height of three shelves will bring the finished top to a place where it can be used as a consultation table, which has definite advantages, but use of this kind will obstruct the use of the books by others and is rarely advisable in a busy area.

d. A final question deals with the depth of the shelves. As already noted, reference books tend to be thick, heavy, and tall. They also tend to be deep, and as a result many reference shelves have been built a full 12 in. deep with unfortunate results. The number of books over 10 in. deep from front to back is extremely small, except for atlases and a limited number of fine arts books, and the disadvantages resulting from overdeep shelves, particularly lower shelves, are

so great that it is suggested that free-standing reference shelves be restricted to 22 in. from front to back if they are made of wood and there is a partition down the center, and to 20 in. if metal bracket shelves are used. If a 12-in.-deep bottom shelf is used and a 7- or even an 8-in.-deep volume is shelved on it, the volume will sooner or later be pushed back and be very difficult to find and remove. This, of course, can be obviated by putting blocks at the back, but what is the use of building and paying for a deep shelf and then blocking up the back of it? As is true of regular stack shelving, if the bottom or the two bottom shelves are tilted up toward the aisle, theoretically the backs of the books will be more easily seen. (Smaller volumes may also slide back completely out of sight and bindings will not be benefited, to put it mildly.)

The above applies to reference books and bibliographical material in any reading area, with the exception of a limited number of atlases and fine arts materials, which require deeper shelving and will be dealt with later.

A word of caution in connection with the last three points made about aisle widths and height and depth of shelves should be given. Any change from the standards used for stack shelving, that is, wider aisles, deeper shelving, and reduced height, reduces the volume capacity per square foot of floor space. To this might be added the fact that reference volumes are generally thicker and so occupy more lineal footage. Fortunately, on the other hand, while reference collections are ordinarily classified and shelved by subject, it is customary and probably desirable to fill shelves fuller than those in stacks, removing old and outdated material when new books are received. (Warning should be given that reference librarians are hesitant to relegate older volumes to the stack and readily find excuses to avoid discarding from the reference collection, just as all librarians tend to find reasons for not transferring books from the main stack collection to storage.) It is suggested that 100 volumes per reference section with six shelves 3 ft long be considered full capacity, instead of the 125 figure used in regular book stacks; that this figure be reduced to no more than 85 volumes for five shelves, to 65 to 70 for four shelves, and to 50 for three shelves. When it comes to square-footage capacity, it is suggested that, with double-faced floor cases six shelves high, if the ranges are 15 ft long (with 3 ft of adjoining aisles charged against the shelving) and if the ranges are 6 ft on centers, no more than eight volumes per square foot, instead of 15 in a regular book stack, or 12 in an open-stack undergraduate library, be considered capacity.

2. *Shelving for Odd-size Books*

a. MINIATURE VOLUMES: Fortunately, miniature volumes are so few in number as to prevent their being a serious problem, but this warning seems desirable. They should not be shelved on regular stack shelving because of the danger of their being pushed behind larger books and lost for long stretches of time, if not permanently. They also are more prone to be removed from the shelves without authorization because of the ease with which they can be slipped into a pocket and the temptation they seem to present to the light-fingered. Special housing should be provided for them, probably in boxes that will hold a group of those approximately the same size. Three different-sized boxes, each 10 in. long, with one for those under 6 but over 5 in. in the largest dimension, one for those between 5 and 4 in., and a third for those with neither dimension over 4 in. would probably do very well. These boxes should not be on open shelves.

b. OVERSIZE VOLUMES NOT ADAPTED TO STANDARD SHELVING: Section 8.1 stated that 90 per cent of research and academic library volumes are no more than 11 in. high, and that with stack shelving 7 ft 6 in. high, seven shelves can be used for volumes up to that size. With the same height, six shelves, 14 in. on centers, leaving room for books up to 13 in., can be provided for, and this will care for seven of the remaining 10 per cent, leaving only 3 per cent more than 13 in. These 11- to 13-in.-high books may well be segregated and placed on deeper shelves spaced 14 in. on centers.

The author suggests that since the remaining 3 per cent are largely concentrated in a few classes and since these volumes on the whole tend to be thin in relation to their height and easily misplaced, it is desirable to segregate them on shelves where they can be laid on their sides. This will also prevent damage from warping. These shelves should be of extra depth, at least 12 and preferably 14 in. or more so as to prevent books from protruding into the aisles and being damaged. With a little ingenuity a place for this special shelving can be found. At the end of most book stacks there is a wider aisle, and the extra depth will therefore not be troublesome. Along a stairwell or elevator-shaft wall adjacent to a main cross-aisle is another possibility. It is further suggested that the deep shelves be of the cantilever type, where shelf ends will not interfere and space will be gained. A very few ranges of this kind will provide for the extra large volumes in most libraries, except for the newspapers, which are dealt with later. Elephant folios, such as the Audubon *Birds of America,* or tremendous volumes, such as the set that Napoleon sponsored about Egypt more than a century and a half ago, may require special treatment and custom-built equipment for their housing. This is one of the penalties resulting from riches of that kind; a sort of supergraduated tax.

c. NEWSPAPERS: Most American libraries, or those in other countries for that matter, do not at present preserve and bind large quantities of recent newspapers because of (1) their bulk, (2) the cost of binding, (3) the space they would occupy, (4) the fact that the paper on which they are printed is so poor that they tend to disappear almost completely in a generation or so and leave the library empty-handed, and finally because (5) most large city newspapers of importance are now available on microfilm at a cost exceeding little if any that of binding, plus the value of the space used for storage.

But there is still a large bulk of newspapers in bound form in many libraries throughout the world, and the storage problem is great enough in many cases to make special newspaper shelving desirable so as to increase the storage capacity per square foot of floor space for this material. It should be added at this point that at least a few newspapers are still issued on reasonably permanent paper and are kept by libraries because of the great demand for them.

Bound newspaper volumes, as well as unbound ones, will last longer if they are shelved flat. Most papers today are no more than 25 × 16 in. when bound, and many are in tabloid form, considerably smaller than that. Shelves 16 in. deep in actual measurement are sufficient for most. If these shelves are cantilevered out from the uprights at the end of each section, four (or more, in the case of tabloids) vertical rows lying on their sides will go in three sections, each 3 ft wide, and if ranges are placed half again as far apart as standard shelving and are made from 32 up to 36 in. from front to back, they will increase the capacity per square foot by nearly 80 per cent over that obtained when papers are shelved on standard stacks going through from front to back of a range. (See Fig. 8.13.)

A library may provide special shelving of the kind just noted if it expects to try to keep permanently any large number of bound newspapers. Roll-out shelves can be used but are very expensive. On the other hand, if a library expects to hold its newspapers unbound and discard them in a few months, special shelving is not worth while, and those that are kept can be placed on regular shelving going all the way through from front to back of a range.

There are still a few older newspapers in existence, and, indeed, a limited number still being published, which are 36 in. long and more

than 18 in. deep. They can be shelved on the type of shelving described above with the length at right angles to the range, as shown in Fig. 8.14.

d. ATLASES: Atlases represent another common type of oversize volume. Those kept in a reference collection are generally shelved in specially designed atlas cases which are made available by library-equipment-supply houses, or built locally to special order (see Figs. 8.15 and 8.16). The others that fall in this category are generally shelved in a map room, if there is one, on deep shelves made for the purpose. Newspaper shelving will often be satisfactory. Atlases, wherever possible, should be stored horizontally.

e. UNABRIDGED DICTIONARIES: Unabridged dictionaries can be used to advantage on a slanting top, standing-height consultation table, such as is shown in Fig. 8.17.

3. *Nonbook Materials Which Require Special Equipment for Storage.* Practically all libraries have greater or smaller collections of material for which special storage facilities, differing from those for books, may be desirable. They are discussed below under various headings.

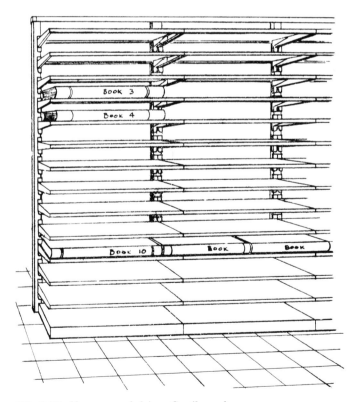

FIG. 8.13 Newspaper shelving. Cantilevered newspaper shelving with four rows possible in three sections.

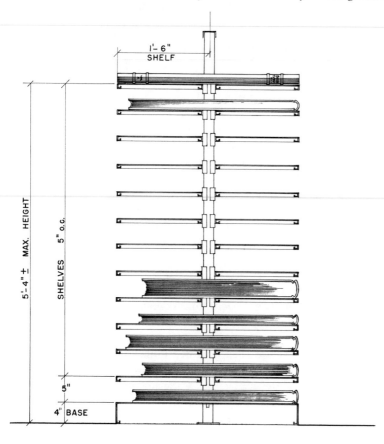

FIG. 8.14   Elephant folios on newspaper shelving.

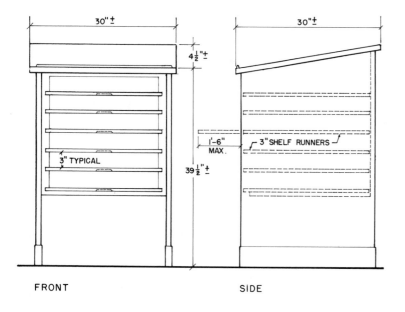

FIG. 8.15   Atlas case. Front and side elevations. Shelves constructed to pull out 1 ft 6 in. for ease of use.

a. CURRENT PERIODICALS: Current periodicals present a special shelving problem. It was considered incidentally in section 7.2. The basic decision to be made is whether to provide what is known as display shelving so arranged that the cover of the magazine can be seen and readily identified, or whether, in order to save space, the periodical is placed flat on regular library shelving, generally with the back parallel to the shelves and with the shelves fairly close together, perhaps no more than 5 in. apart on centers. Labels should, of course, be attached to the shelves so as to make it easier to find the desired title. The display cases show simply the last number, and storage for the previous numbers must be provided either in combination with the display or separately. Cases to do this are available from library-supply houses.

Illustrations of various types and arrangements are shown in Fig. 8.18. The display-case equipment is expensive and takes considerably more room, which is even more expensive. Other things being equal, the display cases are much to be preferred, but in a library with many thousands of current periodicals it may be impossible or at least undesirable to use them, because of the space they require if not because of their cost.

Another factor which should not be forgotten is the amount of use that can be expected in relation to the number of titles in the collection. Aisle width should be larger with a small collection with large proportionate use and this affects the square-footage requirements, which may vary from over 1 to ⅙ sq ft per title, according to arrangements selected.

Many large libraries accept a compromise, and use display cases for more popular material and standard shelving for the less used. This has the disadvantage of resulting in two alphabets, but faculty and students soon get used to it and, if there is an attendant to step in when help is needed, the problem will not be too serious.

A final possible variation may be considered. The popular, most-used titles may be on display racks, and the remainder of the collection on standard shelving behind a counter with an attendant to provide service. This method is expensive, but if students have to sign up for the material taken to a nearby area, loss and confused shelves can be largely avoided and at least part of the extra cost canceled. It may result in less use of closed shelf titles, for browsing—

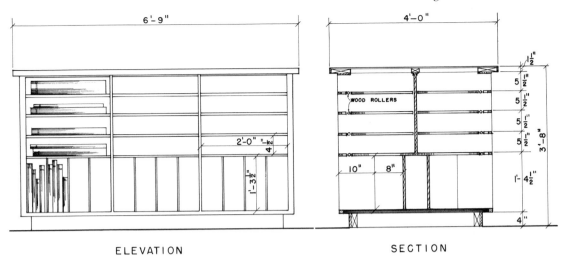

ELEVATION

SECTION

FIG. 8.16 Custom-built atlas case. This one was designed for the Lamont Library at Harvard.

something of great value with current periodicals—is seriously discouraged. In some large libraries the titles on the display racks are used so heavily that duplicates are kept behind the scenes for binding and permanent preservation.

b. MANUSCRIPTS, ARCHIVES, AND UNBOUND PAMPHLETS: Manuscripts and archives may be included in this group of nonbook materials. For them boxes of some kind will be found desirable, as it is rarely wise to bind up the loose sheets into volumes, and more protection is needed than tying up with brown paper and string and placing on standard shelves. The report of the Library Technology Project, entitled "Archival Containers," was published in 1964 and is worth careful consideration.[12] In order to make it unnecessary to fold the material, the boxes will frequently be taller than most bound books and also deeper, so that shelves must be more than 10 in. deep and there will be fewer of them per section. Estimates of the amount of this shelving will be difficult to determine because the growth of these collections is generally more uncertain than that of books.

Pamphlets are acquired on a large scale by some research libraries but to a smaller extent in most libraries. They may be kept in one of four ways:

1. In vertical filing cases preferably near the reference desk with their use restricted. Material in these files is generally kept for limited periods only and then discarded. Pamphlets

kept in this way often get hard use and tend to deteriorate.

2. Placed in inexpensive pamphlet binders, sometimes known as Gaylord binders, classified and shelved by subject in the book stack.

3. Bound in "pamphlet volumes" by broad subject and shelved in the book stacks.

4. Placed in pamphlet boxes similar to those for manuscripts and archives or of a simpler construction, and classified by subject and kept in a separate pamphlet-box file or scattered in subject locations in the stacks.

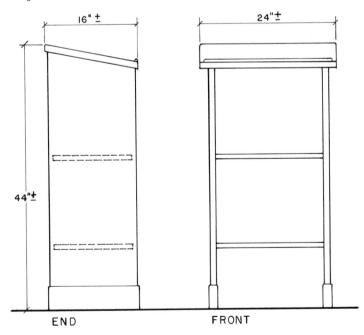

END

FRONT

FIG. 8.17 Dictionary stand. Front and side elevations. Note slant to aid use.

12 Gladys P. Piez, "Archival Containers—a Search for Safe Materials," *American Archivist,* 27: 433–438, 1964.

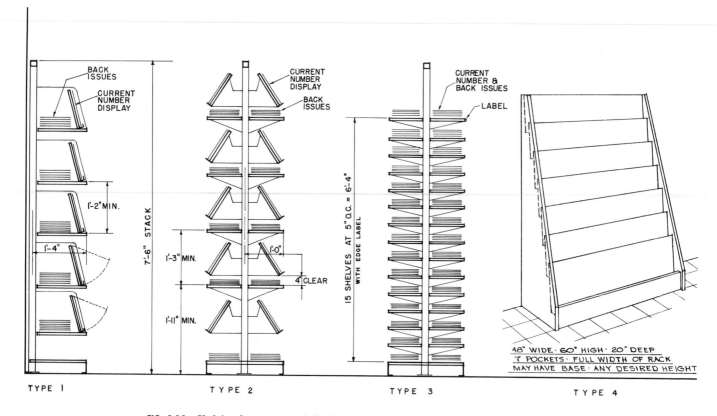

FIG. 8.18 Shelving for current periodicals. Type 1: slanting shelving hinged at the top with storage space for unbound back numbers behind. Type 2: slanting shelving with storage space for unbound back numbers below. Type 3: flat shelving with current and unbound back numbers shelved flat. Capacity is tripled, but advantage of display is lost. Type 4: display shelving with no space for back numbers.

c. PUBLIC DOCUMENTS: Some at least of the public documents in many libraries may require boxes, such as are suggested for manuscripts and archives, if they are left permanently or temporarily unbound. This is true for United States documents which come from the Government Printing Office or elsewhere, public documents from other countries, state and municipal documents, and particularly United Nations documents if acquired in their original unbound form, with binding undesirable until the volume is completed, which may be a considerable time after receipt of the first part.

d. MICROREPRODUCTIONS: Microreproductions are of five types: strip microfilm, reel microfilm, microcards, microprints, and microfiche. There are advantages in making special provision for each.

Newspaper reproductions on microfilm reels still represent and may well continue to represent the largest bulk of microreproductions in the United States if not abroad. They are gen-

erally stored in cardboard boxes 4 in. square and a little under 2 in. thick. These are often placed on shallow shelves 5 in. apart along a wall or on standard library shelving. In spite of the great reduction in space from the original form, libraries are beginning to find that microfilm reels represent storage problems. Various methods of reducing square-footage requirements are used. Library-equipment houses can supply deep metal filing drawers designed to give maximum capacity in relation to square footage of floor space occupied. These can be built so as to house provision for proper humidification, which is desirable for the preservation of film and is important if the library is not air-conditioned. These cases are expensive, and there is a question as to whether the saving in floor space that they provide is worth their cost. Another method of storage is to place the film boxes in long containers designed for the purpose that can be placed on deep shelving. For instance, the newspaper shelving described above can be useful, as it would make space for a box up to 18 in. in length. Twelve-inch deep shelving is also entirely possible for boxes up to that length. At either length the box must be strongly built so as not to collapse with the weight. A shoe box will not be strong enough for any length of time.

Microfiche film in sheet form has been less in vogue in the United States than in some European countries where it has been used on the theory that it is easier to house and that the pages wanted can be located more easily than when films are in reels. Strips are sometimes stored in filing cases with wide shallow drawers that will hold a strip 35 millimeters or about 1½ in. high and up to 8 in. long.

Warning should be given here that no library should store in its building nitrate microfilm in any form because of its explosive qualities, and that all films acquired should be examined to make sure that they are made of acetate.

It should also be remembered that acetate microfilm will dry out and become brittle and easily torn and damaged if subjected to low humidity. While it will at least partially return to its original condition when the relative humidity goes up to the desired 50 per cent, this should not be counted on, and if film is not in an air-conditioned, humidified library, special humidification should be provided.

Microcards are designed to be stored in standard catalogue trays for 3 × 5-in. (7½ × 12½-cm) cards. While these cases are expensive, 1½ cents per card stored, they are standard and house enough cards so that the cost is a comparatively minor factor. The chief problem with cards is that if available to the reader, and withdrawn for use, they are easily misplaced.

Microprint cards or sheets, which are 6 × 9 in. in size, can be placed in filing drawers designed for that size card, but they often come from the publishers in boxes designed for the purpose, and these boxes can be, and ordinarily are, stored like books on regular library shelving. The problem for all this material is how much space to provide, and that is difficult to determine at this stage in library development.

Many of the middle-sized university and research libraries with large current book appropriations have larger collections of microreproductions than some of the older and larger libraries which already have the originals of much of the material and therefore do not acquire it in the new form.

e. PHONOGRAPH RECORDS AND TAPE RECORDINGS: Phonograph records for music, drama, poetry, and language instruction are stored in special cases made for the purpose, and libraries with collections of this kind are advised to consult dealers in this material and other libraries with similar collections; no attempt will be made here to go into storage facilities for them because the situation is changing rapidly.

Tape recordings, which have come into use, are even newer, and any recommendation in regard to them might well be out of date before this volume is in print.

f. SLIDES, PHOTOGRAPHS, PRINTS: Slides, photographs, and prints are generally stored in filing cases selected for the purpose. Here the important decision relates to the suitable size of the filing drawer, and, again, if the librarian has no special knowledge of the problem, he should go to dealers and to libraries with special collections in the field that have recently installed equipment.

g. MAPS AND BROADSIDES: Sheet maps and broadsides are generally placed for protection in large sturdy folders and stored flat in drawers in cases designed for the purpose. These drawers may be as little as one inch deep on the basis that the sheets will be placed in a limited number of folders to a drawer and will be easier to handle, particularly those in the upper drawers. The author has seen these drawers in cases as much as 6 ft high, but this height is dangerous as the sheets and folders in which they are stored may be damaged as they are removed from or replaced in the cases when a drawer is so high that vision is cut off. Deeper drawers, each containing more folders, have a much larger capacity and, if built up to only 42 in. or a little higher, the case tops can be used as consultation tables and no space is lost. Reference to LeGear's volume on maps is suggested.[13]

Some companies design drawers in which folders are shelved vertically as in a filing case, but in general these have not been as satisfactory as flat drawers. Roll maps present a different problem. Libraries may have to store quantities of them for use in classrooms. They can some-

---

[13] C. E. LeGear, *Maps: Their Care, Repair and Preservation in Libraries*, Library of Congress, Washington, 1956.

times be fitted into frames that hold them in place vertically and might be said to resemble racks for garden tools.

The shelving equipment for reading areas and nonbook materials is ordinarily not large enough in quantity to affect module sizes seriously, and therefore it was not discussed in Chapter 4. However, bound newspaper collec-tions can be so large that the module size will be of importance, and it is suggested that if two ranges of newspaper-storage shelving take the place of three ranges for regular books, the stack module selected will work out to advantage. This may give an aisle a little wider than abso-lutely necessary but avoids involvement with supporting columns. (See Fig. 6.11.)

9

Lighting and Ventilating

Introduction

Architectural style, aesthetics, and interior decoration, which are dealt with in Chapter 2, are primarily the architect's responsibilities. He is the expert and, if special problems arise on which he feels he should have help, he can call in an architectural or interior-design consultant. He may in some cases have specialists in his organization for this work. Unless the architect has firm control over these matters, he can hardly provide a structure that has the desired unity.

The topics dealt with in this and the next chapter are primarily the concern of the engineers who, with the architect, work on certain phases of the planning. The architect may be an engineer himself or he may have engineers in his firm. He may go outside for engineering help, but since he is in charge, he must take the responsibility if the results are not satisfactory, and consequently must see to it that an engineer who will obtain the desired results is employed. Engineering is a specialized field, and there are various specialists within the profession—mechanical, civil, heating, acoustical, and lighting engineers, for instance. Each has his place; each should be involved early in the planning stage; and to neglect any one would be unfortunate and might even be disastrous.

The institution's administrative officers seldom have the necessary competence in the field, although in a large enterprise there should be a building specialist who knows at least enough to ask pertinent questions and to understand

whether satisfactory solutions have been reached. The librarian usually will be even further beyond his depth than he is on the aesthetic side of building planning, but he should be interested and should make every effort to see that the architect and engineers understand the engineering requirements for a satisfactory library building. These two chapters are addressed primarily to the librarian, and to a lesser extent to the librarian's building committee and his institution's administrative officers. The chapters will not encourage the librarian to interfere improperly with the architect and the engineers, but will try to state the problems in such a way that the program prepared for the architect will specify the requirements clearly. They should also help the librarian and others on the planning team to understand the language of construction well enough to make their needs intelligible to the architect and engineers. Laymen in this group too often, out of ignorance, ask for what is either impracticable or impossibly expensive.

9.1 Library Lighting

Library lighting is a complicated and sometimes controversial matter, whether approached as an engineering problem, a question of aesthetics, or a way of serving the library's readers. It is highly important from all three aspects. This section can do little more than outline the questions involved and suggest factors to be weighed before decisions are made. It cannot attempt to evaluate the merits of the different opinions held. The many problems of lighting can be classified for the purposes of this section under four headings: (1) quality, (2) aesthetics, (3) intensity, and (4) cost.

Quality. Since everyone agrees that quality of light is a basic consideration, it can properly be considered first. Quality is not easy to measure because it depends on several factors, particularly the light source, the fixtures used, and glare and contrast; moreover, it is closely related to intensity, which will be discussed later.

In consideration of quality remember that (1) it is usually desirable to provide a lighting environment in which the light sources are so unobtrusive that any fixture arrangement is bound to be aesthetically and visually satisfactory; (2) good lighting is a visual environment appropriate and comfortable for the purpose for which it is used; (3) apparent brightness is relative, depending on one's position. A room seen through an open door from the outside on a bright day seems dark. If the room is entered and the eyes are given a little time to adjust, everything looks brighter. The eye has the ability to adapt itself to the conditions to which it is subjected (see Fig. 9.1). A brightly lighted supermarket has been found to attract customers. The same may hold true for a public library at the center of a city with brightly lighted stores on all sides. The same amount of brightness need not necessarily be useful or desirable in an academic library in the midst of a college campus, but even there a change of pace, as it might be called, from room to room can be welcome.

FIG. 9.1 Lighting contrasts. Rooms seen from the outside on a bright day look dark, but a dimly lit room looks bright when it is dark outdoors. An object with low-intensity light shining directly on it shows more detail than one in the shadow with a much higher-intensity light beyond it. It is the light on the reading surface that counts in a library.

Light Sources. Until about the turn of the century the sun was the chief source of light in most libraries, and the need for making full use of sunlight was a more important consideration in library architecture than almost any other single factor. The development of the incandescent electric-light bulb finally provided a reasonably satisfactory artificial method of lighting, although the quality and intensity of early incandescent lighting would seem completely inadequate today, and the cost of electric current was relatively very high. Primitive though the fixtures were, by the end of the nineteenth century, libraries could be lighted with electricity, readers could be admitted after the sun had set, and evening hours of opening were possible throughout the year. Today most libraries have windows —many of them have too many windows—but in the United States, and to a lesser extent elsewhere, there is comparatively little dependence on natural light, which at best is difficult to control because of changes in brightness at different times of year and with different weather conditions. Artificial illumination might be said to be required throughout the whole building during approximately one-half of the hours that the average library is open for public use, and it is used, in fact, during a very much larger percentage of that period.

Even what is considered good north light on a bright winter's day may prove to be a source of discomfort if fresh snow is on the ground, unless the windows are protected from the snow glare. South light with a low winter sun can be very troublesome in northern latitudes. Western windows, late in the day, make shielding of some kind essential in all parts of the world, and in spite of wide overhangs and glare-protecting glass, expensive drapes or screening of one kind or another are desirable, and all of them have to be maintained and may have to be replaced oftener than has been generally anticipated. In spite of the architects' endeavors to utilize these corrective measures, complications continue to arise.

If costs alone were considered, and if lights are used throughout the day, it might be argued that natural light should be given up, but it is still important for psychological reasons. Yet in many libraries large areas used for reading, as well as for book storage, have no natural light today, and few people complain.

The Brigham Young University Library in

Provo, Utah, has two large floors with some 45,000 sq ft each, seating for 1,000, and no windows, but it is so well arranged and lighted that the reader soon forgets that windows are lacking. The Louisiana State University Library in Baton Rouge has a windowless lower floor with 66,000 sq ft of floor space and accommodations for many readers. Harvard's Lamont Library has a 1,500-sq ft windowless reading area adjacent to its side door, which is used as heavily as the reading areas that have natural light.

Large window areas also have the serious disadvantage of permitting cold to enter in the winter and heat in the summer. Natural light, particularly if the sun shines directly into the room, almost inevitably brings unpleasant glare and shadows in its train. But do not forget that it can be very pleasant. Natural light, as has been said, may be "for readers, not for reading," but its use is more successful if not overdone, as it has been too frequently in recent years. Windows, the problems they present, and methods to protect them are discussed in section 10.1.

Electric lamps today come in three main types: mercury, incandescent, and fluorescent. Mercury lamps have been used comparatively little during recent years, although they provide greater intensity than incandescent bulbs using an equal amount of current. They are slow in reaching their full intensity after being switched on, but the length of the delay has now been reduced, and there is a prospect of their increased use in the years ahead, often in combination with one of the other types of lamps.

Incandescent bulbs, until some twenty years ago, were standard equipment and are used today in many places. They are now available in a new form—a small tube known as an "iodine quartz lamp." An incandescent bulb concentrates the source of light into a small space, which makes it easier to remove dust and dirt but creates more filament brightness; this must be shielded to prevent glare. One should realize, however, that any unshielded light source, however much it is dispersed, results in discomfort if one looks directly at it, and should be avoided. Fluorescent tubes are a comparatively recent development. There is still disagreement as to whether fluorescent or incandescent lamps are more satisfactory in quality. Each has its place. In recent years the pendulum has been swinging in favor of fluorescent, in spite of the slight flickering and ballast noise that

are still common faults. These problems cannot be ignored, but, at a considerable increase in installation costs, modern remote ballasts can completely eliminate the humming, and the practice of using two parallel tubes in each fixture or two tubes end to end on the same ballast will largely overcome the stroboscopic effect; the use of indirect or shielded lighting will also help. Some authorities still believe that a few persons for some physiological reason are allergic to fluorescent lighting, and in a large library it may be desirable to provide for their use a limited number of seating accommodations with incandescent bulbs. One reading area in Harvard's Widener Library still has its original 1915 incandescent type of lighting, which is obviously inadequate. In spite of this it is heavily used. It is a question whether the readers are oblivious to the low intensity and substandard quality or prefer it to the fluorescent lighting elsewhere in the building. They may simply prefer the earlier lighting pattern because it is less visually distracting.

Some experts suggest that something about the quality of fluorescent light makes it desirable to use a higher intensity than is used with incandescent, but that the glare can be overcome by adding a small amount of incandescent light to the fluorescent installation. This theory has not as yet been generally accepted. At present there seems to be a slight tendency to try to improve the color effects by going back to incandescent or a combination of the two. But we might point out that while incandescent bulbs have by nature a warm color and fluorescent and mercury tubes are visually cold, the latter are now obtainable "color-corrected" to various degrees of warmth and can be further corrected by the use of colored reflectors.

Fluorescent lamps project light satisfactorily at right angles to the tubes, but their reduced efficiency beyond the ends of the tubes makes it difficult, when using direct lighting, to light shelves or individual tables along a wall at right angles to them without the installation of additional tubes parallel to the wall and fairly close to it. If the fixtures installed provide primarily indirect light, this problem may be solved. The use of fluorescent tubes is still questionable if lights are turned on and off frequently, as this use reduces their lives considerably. Although light from unprotected fluorescent tubes will fade bindings, plastic or glass covering will provide the required protection to a large extent, just as it will when the sun shines through glass windows onto books. Fluorescent lamps can provide a good over-all illumination with great flexibility and may make it easier than it is with incandescent bulbs to shift furniture and book stacks around without relocating lighting fixtures. One can choose between two basic varieties of fluorescent tubes.

1. *Cold cathode.* These are sometimes used inside exhibition cases with the electrode, which is the hottest point of any lamp, placed outside the case so that only the heat from the tube itself

is inside. (The cases must still be ventilated because these lights are not completely cold.) The tubes have a longer life than the others. (The same ones were used in the Exhibition Room cases in the Houghton Library for more than fifteen years, turned on for eight hours a day, before they were replaced, although their efficiency was greatly reduced at an earlier time.) They are difficult to replace and may not be in stock when wanted. They are somewhat less efficient than other fluorescent tubes and require more wattage to produce the same amount of intensity. They are at present out of favor,

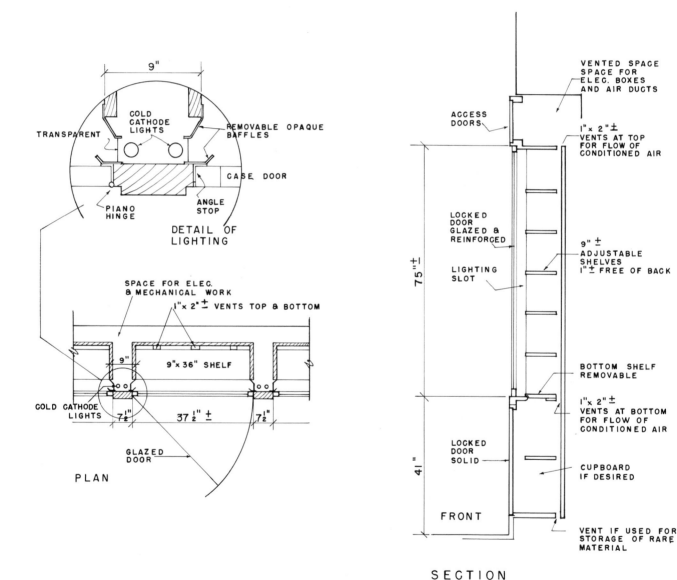

FIG. 9.2 Exhibition case with cold cathode lighting. This case used at Harvard in the Houghton and Law School Libraries is ventilated, and temperature and relative humidity are kept under control.

apparently, and little research is being done on them. They are useful where curved or bent lamps are desirable or necessary, in such places as circular coves or exhibit cases. (See Fig. 9.2.)

2. *Standard fluorescent, sometimes called hot cathode tubes.* These tubes have a variety of diameters, and each is effective for specific applications. There are many types of them: rapid-start, jumbo, slimline, HO (high output), VHO (very high output), circular, and square. Many of these and other varieties are or have been available in a wide variety of colors. By using a "lower light output ballast," 8-ft-long tubes using only 40 watts of current can be provided, thereby distributing the light obtained over a larger area than is the case with a 4-ft tube using the same wattage. These tubes are used in the book stacks, as well as in the reading areas in Lamont. Both the tubes and the ballasts are involved in the HO and VHO installations.

The advantages of fluorescent lamps can be summed up as follows: They use less than one-half of the current required by incandescent lights to obtain the same intensity and result in less than one-half of the heat, a very important consideration if high intensity and air conditioning are to be used. The Princeton University Firestone Library, built in the late 1940s, installed what at that time was considered high-intensity incandescent lighting without air conditioning, and the heat from the bulbs in the summer has presented a problem.

Fluorescent tubes have a long life, up to ten times that of incandescent lamps, particularly if not turned on and off frequently. They give greater flexibility. They have the disadvantage of higher installation and tube-replacement costs, and fixture cleaning may take more time.

If lights are required for a large percentage of the hours during which the library is open, fluorescent light is cheaper, if the long view is taken, particularly if the cost of current is high. It should be remembered in this connection that many modern libraries rely almost altogether on artificial light because of the depth of the rooms from the outside walls combined with comparatively low ceilings and often with small window areas. Lights in reading areas are commonly left on during full opening hours in the United States, in spite of efforts of instinctively thrifty administrators to prevent it.

In any closed-access book stack incandescent lights may well be used. In a very large open-access stack the use of any one aisle is often small enough so that incandescent lights may be indicated. But with a comparatively small collection and a large number of stack users, requiring light throughout the day, fluorescent lights are the more economical arrangement, and on the whole provide a more satisfactory light on the backs of the books. The type of fixture used and its position are important considerations. If the ceiling height in a book stack is 10 in. above the books on the top shelf, fluorescent lights can be placed at right angles to the ranges to advantage. They can be placed in rows up to 6 ft apart, instead of the regular 4 ft 6 in. distance between ranges and still give as good or better light on the bottom shelves, which are the critical ones, because of the wider angle made possible for the light projection. A somewhat similar result can be obtained by placing the tubes in reflecting fixtures on top of the book ranges, directing the light toward a white or nearly white ceiling. The reflected light is spread in all directions with what can be called "design integration," and the tubes do not need to be in a continuous row. A light-colored floor always helps to light the bottom shelves by reflection.

Both incandescent and fluorescent light can by one means or another be given almost any color. At one time there was a vogue for blue bulbs because they were thought to be easier on the eyes. When fluorescent tubes first came into use, their effect on the appearance of human skin, to which they gave a sickly pale green tint, was unpleasant, but experimentation and research have changed this, and at present the client can select what he wants. Attention should be paid to the color selection, particularly since the color of the light source affects the color appearance of all the materials it illuminates.

Fixtures. During the years that electric lamps have been used in libraries, there has been a continuous improvement in fixtures, as well as in the lamps themselves. In the old days when ceilings were very high, lamps were placed so high that they were seldom seen, unless one purposely looked up at them. The arrangement was essential to prevent reader discomfort. When desk lamps were used close to the reading surface, shades directed the light to the table top and at the same time prevented the reader from looking at the bulb; but this too often resulted in an unsatisfactory reduction in intensity if the material being used was moved a short distance farther from the light source, and the reader could not change position readily. Reflected glare was also a problem, particularly with glazed paper. More general lighting seemed desirable, and indirect lighting was provided by fixtures designed to direct most of the light to the ceiling. Special shades for use over bulbs in stack aisles were developed, and these helped to provide more light on lower shelves. Frosting, which relieves the strain if one looks directly at the light source, came into use for incandescent bulbs. Reflectors of various kinds were invented. Indirect light results in improved quality but may reduce the intensity derived from the same wattage, the amount of reduction depending on the reflecting surfaces of the fixtures, the ceilings and walls, and also the amount of dirt and dust on the fixtures and elsewhere. Even if the intensity is reduced, the quality may be so improved as to provide a higher degree of visual efficiency.

The first installations of new light sources and fixtures were often unsatisfactory. It seems to have been taken for granted that fluorescent lamps, since the source of light was distributed over the length of a long tube, would not require shielding. This idea did not survive very long, and the need was soon met by protecting baffles, louvres, troffers, opaque glass, and plastic coverings. Many of these are satisfactory, but the appearance of the protected installation is not always aesthetically acceptable. In reading rooms fluorescent lamps with troffers and reflectors are sometimes recessed into the ceiling, with acoustic tiles or plaster filling the space between the fixtures. The distance between the troffers depends on the intensity desired, on whether the tubes are single or multiple, and on their wattage. The fixtures and tubes do not need to be in rows. Different patterns can be used, but one must be careful to avoid what might be called a disorderly appearance, which too often results in "visual noise" or distraction.

Recently wall fixtures have been developed which are completely opaque on the room side and have reflectors on the wall side which send the light both up and down and give a different quality of lighting to the whole room. While intensity may vary in different parts of the room, the absence of glare and shadow produces a pleasing effect.

In selecting fixtures, one should keep in mind methods of cleaning. Air filtering helps because dust and dirt decrease the intensity of light. Any lamp gradually deteriorates to a point at which, even though it has not burned out, replacement becomes desirable. In rooms where scaffolding must be erected to change the light sources, it is economical to remove all the lamps at a set time before they begin to burn out and reinstall them in other parts of the building where changes can be made without ladders, thus permitting them to live out their natural lives. If the replacement of lamps is very difficult, it may be worth while to install twice as many bulbs or tubes as are required to obtain the desired intensity, arranged on two switches, used on alternate days or weeks, thus doubling the interval between changes. Fluorescent tubes should not be changed by inexperienced persons.

Glare and Contrast. Eyestrain is reduced if the surroundings provide comparatively little contrast with pages of the book that is being read. It is recommended that table tops be fairly light in color, floors not too dark, and the walls, ceilings, and woodwork on the light side. Then when the eye wanders from book to table top or to the floor or walls the pupil of the eye does not have to shift in size, an adaptation which may cause temporary discomfort. However, a glossy white table, used with direct lighting, tends to produce an excessive brightness in relation to the other surroundings. Glossy surfaces and finishes result in glare and should be avoided. In spite of what has been said, some architects and librarians feel that, even if dark surfaces in the reading room are less comfortable for the eyes and more light must be provided, they make the whole room so much more attractive that they should be used.

Good over-all shielded lighting helps to prevent glare because the light comes from all directions and uniform illumination from multiple sources bridges and overlaps, producing a relatively shadowless and glareless room.

R. G. Hopkinson's volume[1] contains objective studies of lighting problems; in its chapter entitled "For the Future" it lists "Some Principles of Good Lighting," which follow:

1. We see better the more light we have, up to a point, but this light must be free from glare.
2. We see better if the main visual task is distinguished from its surroundings by being brighter, or

[1] R. G. Hopkinson, *Lighting: Architectural Physics,* H. M. Stationery Office, London, 1963, p. 125.

more contrasting, or more colorful, or all three. It is therefore important to identify the main focal points and build up the lighting from their requirements.

3. We see better if the things we have to look at are seen in an unobtrusive and unconfusing setting, neither so bright nor so colorful that it attracts the attention away, nor so dark that work appears excessively bright with the result that the eyes are riveted on to the visual task. Good lighting therefore provides a moderate and comfortable level of general lighting, with preferential lighting on the work. This can be called "focal lighting."

4. The surroundings should be moderately bright, and this should be achieved by combination of lighting and decoration.

5. No source of light should be a source of glare discomfort. Excessively bright areas should never be visible. Windows should be provided with curtains, blinds or louvres, to be brought into use when the sky is very bright.

6. Plenty of light should reach the ceiling, in order to dispel any feeling of gloom, and to reduce glare.

7. Sources of light should be chosen to ensure that the color rendering which they give is satisfactory for the situation in which they will be found.

8. Care should be taken to eliminate any discomfort from flickering light sources.

9. A dull uniformity should at all costs be avoided. Small brilliant points of light can give sparkle to a scene without causing glare.

10. The lighting of a building should be considered always in relation to its design and in particular to the scheme of decoration to be installed. On no account should lighting be considered to be merely a matter of windows or fittings. The whole environment enters into a good lighting installation.

With indirect lighting, ceiling reflection is important. In small rooms the value of wall reflection should not be forgotten, and in larger ones the same holds for floor coverings. Other things being equal, light colors give better reflection, but glossy surfaces should be avoided.

One more comment about glare. It is important to avoid it anywhere and particularly in places where older persons are reading. The deleterious effects of glare increase considerably in middle life and later as a result of a physiological sclerosis of the lens.

Aesthetics. Too little attention may have been paid to the aesthetics of library lighting, perhaps because of the effort to improve its quality, its comfort, and its efficiency. It might be said that the initiative has passed from the hands of the architects into those of the illuminating engineers, with the result that aesthetic effect has been neglected. Whether or not this is true, the quality if not the appearance of library lighting has evidently improved tremendously in the past twenty years. A comparison of the lighting of Butler Library at Columbia[2] (thirty years ago considered a big step forward) with that of almost any library built since the Second World War gives some indication of the progress made in recent years. It is suggested that the architect be made responsible for the aesthetic effect of lighting, but that its quality and the comfort of the reader should not be neglected.

Intensity. The most desirable intensity of light on reading surfaces measured in foot-candles is an extremely controversial subject. (Intensity should always be measured in terms of "maintained" intensity, that is, the amount available after several months of use, which can be estimated at approximately one-third less than in a new installation. The exact amount may vary from 25 to 40 per cent, depending on the ballasts and fixtures used and on how much the ceiling

[2] This was described by Robert W. Jeffery in an article entitled "South Hall, an Experiment in Artificial Illumination," printed in the brochure prepared for the dedication exercises in 1934 of what is now Butler Library.

FERD'NAND ®   **By Mik**

and surroundings darken as time goes on.) Early in the century the intensity in some libraries was as little as 1 foot-candle, and 3 or 4 foot-candles were considered adequate. Since that time there has been a fairly steady geometrical increase, averaging somewhere between 5 and 10 per cent a year, compounded annually, in the number of foot-candles recommended and, in many libraries, installed. The references and comments which follow give some indication of this increase, an increase which to the writer poses a very baffling problem.

J. E. Woodwell, in "Data on Indoor Illuminations" in *Transactions of the Illuminating Engineering Society,* 1:246, 1906, says:

In the postal service, for reading addresses of mail in the endless variety of forms of pens, pencil and print with background of various color, a local illumination of from two to four foot-candles has been found by extended experiences to be required; two foot-candles is generally sufficient for desk illumination, though for work involving much detail three or even four foot-candles has not been found excessive. . . . In stores where dark goods are displayed or a brilliant effect is desired, five to ten foot-candles is not uncommon. The latter is also required for tracing, drafting, engraving and similar work.

In 1919 at the close of the First World War, the New York Public Library increased the lighting intensity in its newspaper room to 10 foot-candles because its practice of mounting its newspapers with Japanese rice paper in the hope of preserving them made them more difficult to read. The author well remembers how brilliant the lighting seemed compared with the rest of the building, where half that intensity was still regarded as adequate.

In 1925 Francis E. Cady and Henry B. Dates stated in a volume published by John Wiley & Sons, Inc., New York, entitled *Illuminating Engineering* that "under some conditions" 5 to 10 foot-candles should be used, and recommended 8. Three years later in their second edition these figures were 8 for a minimum with 12 recommended.

James T. Gerould's *College Library Building,* published in 1932 by Charles Scribner's Sons, New York, emphasized the desirability of adequate light intensity in libraries and suggested up to 10 foot-candles on reading surfaces, and 1½ in book stacks on the vertical plane, this with lower shelves in mind. His suggestions followed fairly closely the standard recommendations of lighting experts at that time.

In 1940 Eugene W. Schilling's volume on *Illumination Engineering,* published in Scranton by the International Textbook Company, proposed 20 foot-candles for reading rooms.

The next year Wheeler and Githens' *The American Public Library Building,* discussed lighting problems and intensity in detail and indicated that 9 to 13 foot-candles were adequate, although it mentioned the recommendation by certain engineers of public service companies of 30 to 50 foot-candles or even more in reading rooms. The authors then referred to a writer who, after quoting authorities advising amounts varying from 10 to 15 foot-candles, stated his conclusion that "the critical intensity of light falls considerably below ten foot-candles, probably between three and four," but he added that "ten to fifteen foot-candles of well-dispersed light should be entirely adequate for ordinary reading."[3]

The first edition of the IES (Illuminating Engineering Society) *Handbook,* published in 1947, recommended that 30 foot-candles be maintained in library reading rooms, and the Westinghouse Electric Corporation's *Lighting Handbook,* which was revised that year, made a similar recommendation. The second edition of the IES *Handbook,* published in 1952, proposed 50 foot-candles in reading rooms for "difficult seeing tasks" and 30 for "ordinary seeing tasks," while its third edition, published in 1959, which is the latest available, proposed 70 for "study and notes" and 30 for "ordinary reading."

The recommended light intensities for reading areas in European libraries today, while higher than those that were proposed in the United States before the Second World War, are no more than half what are now recommended by the Illuminating Engineering Society in this country. Many libraries in other lands, particularly those in underdeveloped countries, are fortunate if they are able to provide even the 3 or 4 foot-candles used here early in the century.

Anthony Thompson's volume, published by Butterworth & Co. (Publishers), Ltd., in London in 1963, entitled *Library Buildings of Britain and Europe,* records the brightness for library departments recommended in the 1950s by four

---

[3] M. A. Tinker, "Hygienic Library Illumination," *Library Journal,* 63: 532–534, July, 1939.

European authorities, including the British Lighting Council, which vary from 5 to 12 foot-candles for intermittent reading, and from 12 to 25 foot-candles for continuous reading at tables and in carrels. He emphasizes the three variable factors that should be considered in determining standards:

1. The human eye, which varies from person to person and also according to age in the same person.

2. The difference in the size and legibility of type, the difference in the paper used, and the contrast between the paper and the ink.

3. The intensity of the reading. Browsing and intermittent reading require less light than continuous and concentrated reading.

After discussing the position of the light sources and the types of lamps used, Mr. Thompson suggests 15 foot-candles for reading tables, 20 for the working surface in offices and workrooms, and 3 to 5 for the backs of the books on the bottom shelves.

The Hopkinson volume referred to above does not make definite recommendations in regard to intensity but states:[4]

When levels of working light fall below five lumens/sq ft most people experience some visual difficulty. Visual comfort may not be achieved unless levels are much higher. For some time it has been customary to regard a level of 10 to 15 as the minimum working light in schools or offices, with 15 to 40 lumens as the corresponding level for drawing offices, tool rooms, or other places where the visual difficulty of the work is greater.[5]

In India, Thailand, and the Philippines, where electric current is relatively more expensive than in the United States, the author has found that 3 or 4 foot-candles are still regarded as adequate on reading tables, and the users do not appear to be unhappy or uncomfortable because of the lower intensity. He has heard the dean of a professional school in the University of the Philippines say that he always works away from the windows at a table behind the book stacks where the intensity was not more than 3 or 4 foot-candles, because he dislikes the brighter light by the windows.

But, as stated above, the recommended level in the United States keeps going up. Illuminat-

ing engineers say that the 70 foot-candles proposed in 1959 is a minimum figure and that as lighting methods improve it may be increased not only to 100 but to 200 foot-candles. It is reported that in some fixture manufacturers' administrative offices 500 foot-candles are now being used. Remember in this connection that only fifteen years ago the intensity recommended by the Illuminating Engineering Society for reading areas was 30 foot-candles, and fifteen years before that 15 foot-candles was considered adequate.

Many librarians, including the author, are at a loss to know what to do about this increase and how to deal with it. They naturally tend in the United States to follow recommendations of the Illuminating Engineering Society and the lighting experts, but at the same time they deplore any unnecessary increase in lighting cost and are worried about what the future will bring. They wonder why experts in other countries recommend lower intensities. They are properly anxious to provide the most satisfactory lighting that is possible within their means and believe that the comfort of the reader and of the staff should receive very careful, and indeed first, consideration. The effect of this increased intensity on library expenditures for electricity will be dealt with below.

A considerable number of architects do not hesitate to say, in private at least, that they feel that the tendency toward very high light intensity is unfortunate and unnecessary. One of the world's best known architects told the author recently that the program for a large public building which had been submitted to him for plans specified 125 foot-candles intensity for the structure, and when he protested he was told that "the matter had been decided and he had his instructions."

Ophthalmological research specialists recommend levels well below those proposed by the engineers and fixture manufacturers. Dr. David G. Cogan, Director of the Howe Ophthalmological Laboratory, affiliated with the Harvard University Medical School and the Massachusetts Eye and Ear Infirmary in Boston, has written,

As far as health is concerned, it is a privilege and obligation of the medical profession, presumably the most qualified judge, to exercise its authority. The beliefs that relatively intense illumination is necessary for visual efficiency and that weak illumination induces

---

[4] Hopkinson, *op. cit.,* p. 114.

[5] "Lumens/sq ft," as used in this passage, indicate the same intensity as foot-candles.

organic disease of the eyes are probably the most widely held misconceptions pertaining to ophthalmology.... [Some] authors claim to have established a new science born of radically new concepts of the science of reading.

Dr. Cogan goes on to say that the recommendations of this science have come as a considerable surprise to those familiar with man's ability to adapt himself to dark and to those who are acquainted with previous reports that 10 foot-candles were adequate for ordinary purposes and that not more than 20 foot-candles were required for exceptionally fine work. He also says that intensities greater than 20 foot-candles have no practical significance. He made these statements twenty years ago, and he repeats them today on the basis that the human eye has not changed during that time.

The Ferree and Rand research team, working in the field of physiological optics, found that if light is well distributed in the field of vision and there are no extremes of surface brightness, the eye can adjust to a wide range of intensity.

It may be well to note in this connection that Dr. H. Richard Blackwell, whose 1958 studies on the effect of the quantity of illumination have been so extensively quoted by the advocates of high intensity, has clarified his position in a series of articles published in the magazine *Lighting*,[6] in which he insists that quality which is largely based on contrast is more important than intensity. He writes, "It takes a considerably smaller percentage increase in task contrast than in task illumination to bring visibility to the desired level." In a recent contribution entitled "Lighting the Library" he has said among other things,

The light intensity we require depends drastically upon the task we are to perform. The data certainly suggest that more light is needed for many tasks than for well-printed books. Illumination quality as measured by the task contrast is much more important than the illumination quantity. With the best quality light considerably lower foot-candles can be used. We can say flatly that the best lighting installation can provide visibility with less than one-fourth the light level required with the worst lighting installation.

Under these circumstances what does a library planner do? One possibility is the course that was followed in the Lamont Library. Lighting there was installed to provide from 20 to

25 foot-candles maintained, but so wired that with comparatively little expense for alterations the intensity can be doubled. There seems to have been no need for an increase in fifteen years. In this connection it should be borne in mind that fluorescent lamps have gradually increased in light efficiency in these years and, through good housekeeping and periodic replacement, the intensities available in Lamont have increased perhaps 25 per cent rather than decreased, as they might be expected to do in some installations.

It should be realized that, because desirable lighting levels are relative, when they are raised in one building in an institution, the levels in other buildings which had previously seemed satisfactory will begin to appear inadequate, and there is a constant tendency to push up levels in one area or another.

Many American academic libraries erected in the last few years have provided light intensities throughout the reading and workroom areas of something like 50 foot-candles. In a number of these libraries the results were not satisfactory. In the Wellesley College Library, for instance, where most of the fluorescent tubes were in pairs, one of them has been turned off, cutting the intensity in half, and the librarian reports an improved situation. On the other hand, it must be admitted that as the years go by higher and higher intensities are being installed; many libraries are using 75 foot-candles, and more than one within the last two years has provided more than 100 foot-candles.

In any consideration of intensity of light it should be noted again that it is maintained light—the intensity provided when the light source has had some months of use—that should be kept in mind.

The author does not claim to be a lighting expert, but he ventures to suggest that:

1. It should always be remembered that high-intensity light of poor quality is less desirable than low-intensity light of good quality.

2. Every effort within reason should be made to improve the quality of visual atmosphere. The comfort of the readers and the aesthetic results are of first importance.

3. An intensity of 50 foot-candles on the reading surface should be satisfactory for all but the most exacting reading tasks in a library, for persons with normal or close to normal vision.

4. Twenty-five to 30 foot-candles should be

---

[6] *Lighting*, vols. 78–81, July, 1963–February, 1965.

sufficient in most library reading areas so long as 50 are readily available in some areas and 75 in a very few places for those who have impaired or defective vision or who are using difficult-to-read manuscripts or other material. Fifty foot-candles might be provided in large sections of the processing rooms where staff members are working long hours, frequently with difficult material, and in small parts, perhaps 25 per cent, of the public reading areas. Different persons prefer different types of seating accommodations, different temperatures, and also different light intensities. In a large library it should be possible to provide what each one prefers, instead of making everything uniform, representing a compromise with mediocre results.

5. The reading areas with an intensity of light higher than 30 foot-candles should be further from the entrance than the less brightly lighted areas, in order to avoid causing the reader's eyes to become adjusted on the way to his seat to a higher intensity than he will find when he reaches it. (This suggestion is questioned by at least one expert.)

6. Light intensities in lobbies, corridors, smoking and lounge rooms, stairwells, and toilets can be kept down to between 10 and 20 foot-candles, which is entirely adequate, except for concentrated reading and study. Then when the reading and work areas are entered they will seem bright.

The wiring throughout the building should be heavy enough so that future changes made in fixtures in order to improve the quality, which may necessitate the use of higher-wattage light sources, will be possible without expensive rewiring.

Costs. Lighting expenditures fall into three groups.

1. Installation costs, which include wiring, switches, fixtures, lamps, and the construction costs that are derived from lighting and also those required in order to dispose of the heat generated by lighting. This last may be very considerable and should not be forgotten if high-intensity light is to be used.

2. The cost of maintenance and upkeep, which includes the repair and cleaning of the fixtures, and the replacement of lamps. Careful planning will help here.

3. The cost of electric current, which depends primarily, after the installation has been made, on cost of current per kilowatthour (KWH) and

the number of hours in a year that the lights are on, as well as the intensity provided, the efficiency of the lights, the type of fixtures used, and the ceiling heights. Current costs vary a great deal from place to place, but large users generally pay a lower rate. For many institutions 2 cents per kilowatthour will include the cost of current, plus the maintenance and repair of the installation and lamp replacement. The figures used in the following paragraphs are based on that rate.

It should be repeated and emphasized that a library is not satisfactory unless it is lighted well enough to enable the reader to work in comfort and without unnecessary fatigue. Costs should not be overemphasized, but disagreement on the desirable quality and intensity complicates the problem. Too often librarians, and other administrative officers for that matter, have given little thought to lighting costs because these have not been included in the library budget but have been paid directly by the institution. The author recently talked with a librarian in a fine new library with attractive lighting, giving unusually high intensity even for the present time—over 100 foot-candles—and asked what the lighting bill came to. The reply was, "We don't know yet, but it has been suggested that it would come to some $400 a month." A little figuring, carried out by multiplying the wattage used in each bay by the number of bays, the hours of opening a week, and the cost per kilowatthour of current used, indicated that $4,000 a month would be closer to the mark. Whether or not this would be serious for the university, which was endowed, is another matter, but because the building was almost a glass box, this intensity might be said to be necessary or at least desirable in order to avoid too great a contrast with the excessive natural light resulting from the glass walls.

There are approximately 150 university (as distinguished from college) libraries in this country. The median of these libraries has a collection of 450,000 volumes and a student body of 7,500. Such a library, if we use generally accepted formulas, which are discussed in detail elsewhere in this volume, will require at least 100,000 sq ft of floor space today without making provision for future growth. (This figure for space needs can be expected to increase at the rate of at least 5 per cent a year because of increasing collections and the growth in the number of students.) Illuminating engineers report that 1½ watts of light per sq ft of floor space should provide 25 foot-candles in a typical installation today. The 100,000 sq ft in the median university library would use 150,000 watts or 150 kilowatts an hour in order to obtain 25 foot-candles throughout the building, and this, at 2 cents a kilowatthour, would cost $3 an hour. If the average university library is open for public use 4,000 hours a year, this would mean $12,000 a year for lighting. This figure does not include after-hour cleaning time. It can be reduced, however, to $10,000 because hallways may properly have a lower intensity, and processing quarters, which are used for shorter hours, more than cancel out the cleaning time. Stack-lighting intensities are generally less but require nearly as much wattage per square foot, and in most libraries with open-access stacks, lights are kept on all day long. If the library uses 100 foot-candles, which is the level that can apparently be expected to be recommended within a few years, and if the above calculation is correct, lighting will cost $40,000 a year for the 100,000 sq ft of floor space, or $30,000 more than for 25 foot-candles, even if the square footage used does not increase, as it undoubtedly will. These figures are presented simply to give some indication of the amount of money involved and, even if the extra cost is only $10,000 or $20,000 a year instead of $30,000, it is extra.

Conclusions. The question that administrative officers must answer is whether it is more important to spend the money for better quality or for increased intensity of light or for something else—books and service, for instance. What is reasonable? The author suggests that:

1. Whatever the cost, the lighting should be of a quality that will attract, not discourage use, and that will not be tiring to the reader.

2. Institutions should always watch for opportunities to improve the physical conditions provided for their students and staff, just as they should seek to improve the quality of the education that they provide. They should not be content with the present on the basis that what was good enough for the preceding generation is good enough for the generations to come.

3. There seems to be no evidence that, in earlier years when lower light intensities were customary, there was more defective vision than at present or that reading speed and comprehension were less than they are now.

4. The judgment of qualified medical eye specialists is of more importance and probably more impartial in determining the optimum intensity to be used than that of engineers, lamp and fixture manufacturers, and public utilities companies.

5. The importance of the architectural effects of the lighting should not be forgotten or neglected.

6. The importance of the quality of the light and, in particular, the efficiency of the illuminant and fixture should be kept in mind. A low-efficiency fixture may require double the wattage to attain a specified light intensity but at the same time may improve the quality of the light made available. Talk the problem over with the architect and the illuminating engineer, and make sure that everyone involved understands the situation and the financial implications.

7. Remember that the higher the intensity, other things being equal, the greater the glare problem and the greater the undesirable heat generated in warm weather; this is expensive to remove and uncomfortable to endure.

With these seven points in mind, it is suggested, as noted in the section on intensity, that a new library be wired so that 50 foot-candles of light intensity on reading surfaces can be made available anywhere without complete rewiring, that it be provided in a few public rooms and in one-half of the staff work areas, and that in the rest of the building where reading is carried on, including the book stack, from 25 to 30 foot-candles be installed. It should be noted that the book-stack intensity refers to reading surfaces 30 in. above the floor and not to the backs of the books on lower shelves. The high-intensity reading areas should include those for manuscripts, archives, and rare books and the space set aside for use by persons with defective vision. In all cases the installation should be so designed that by changing the ballasts for fluorescent tubes double the intensity can be provided, thus making it possible later on at a reasonable cost to increase the quantity or to install new fixtures which would improve the quality with or without reducing intensity. It should be remembered that very small egg-crate fixtures can reduce intensity by perhaps 50 per cent, but may improve quality and give better aesthetic effects.

Twenty to 25 foot-candles were provided in 1949 for the Lamont Library, and this intensity can be doubled by adjusting the ballasts; but doubling would bring the intensity to little more than half what is apparently to be proposed in the near future. If the recommended intensity doubles again in the next ten or fifteen years, as there seems to be every prospect that it will, judging from past experience, the annual cost of lighting will also increase, although less rapidly than the intensity used because lamps should continue to become more efficient. (This statement assumes a stable price level.)

It is evident that, if as much as 100 foot-candles are used, the heat generated, even with fluorescent tubes, will become so great as to place additional loads on air-conditioning equipment, if it is used, or to make buildings almost impossibly hot in summer months if air conditioning is not available. The costs involved here are difficult to predict but will be considerable.

Several other comments are pertinent.

1. If the higher intensities are deemed desirable, ways and means should be worked out so that during the winter the buildings can be heated as far as possible with the heat resulting from the lighting. This is done now in some office buildings. It does not, however, relieve the overheating during the summer, although progress is being made in solving that problem.

2. The author wishes to repeat and emphasize that if comparatively low intensities are used in most of a library's reading areas, it is desirable —one is tempted to say essential—to provide higher intensities in one or more readily accessible areas for use by those who prefer more light, who have defective vision, or who are working with small print or hard-to-read manuscripts, carbon copies, penciled notes, and other difficult material. He suggests that these reading areas should not be too readily accessible or in view from the rest of the building, as the higher intensity, when seen, will reduce pupil size, and when one looks back at his own table with lower intensity he will tend to believe that he has inadequate light.

3. If high intensity has been installed, particularly with tubes in pairs, it is possible to arrange light switches so that the right-hand tubes can be used one week and the left-hand ones the next (or some similar arrangement). This practice is in vogue in the Lamont Library main-entrance lobby. There the use of one-half of the tubes at a time practically doubles their life, a matter of some importance, because a scaffolding is required when they are changed. There is the added advantage that when the reader goes from the entrance lobby to the reading areas he finds higher intensity but still only 25 to 30 foot-candles, and he seems to be satisfied.

The importance of the relation between the intensity in different locations in the same building is great. At the Air Force Academy near Colorado Springs some of the rooms used by the processing staff have no windows. While theoretically they are adequately lighted, the staff is unhappy because they enter their quarters from much more brightly illuminated parts of the building where the glass outside walls in the Colorado sunlight have intensified the light far beyond any normal artificial illumination.

4. Remember that the narrower the stack aisles, the more difficult it will be to light the lower shelves, but that in these cases, if the ceiling is high enough—8 ft 4 in. is adequate— to permit installation of fluorescent lights at right angles to the ranges, intensities on lower shelves will be increased. If the ceiling is 9 ft 6 in. high, indirect lighting installed on top of the ranges can be considered.

5. Do not forget the great aid that good reflecting surfaces can provide. A light ceiling, light walls, shelves, and floors, particularly in book stacks where lower shelves are a problem, will help. Avoid glare, and do not neglect the importance of the aesthetic effect of lighting.

6. Remember that if the lights are to be left on all day in the reading areas and throughout the book stacks, the wiring and switches can be greatly simplified and installation costs reduced. Switches should be controlled by the staff and should be inaccessible to readers.

7. Do not sacrifice quality to obtain quantity.

In connection with the foregoing comments questioning high intensities, the author freely admits that he is not convinced that anything over 25 to 30 foot-candles is required, except in limited areas. In fact, if the quality of the light is good and a person enters a reading room from an area where the intensity is 5 foot-candles or less and settles down to read, he doubts if one person in a hundred can tell, even after an hour of reading, whether the intensity available to him is 10, 25, 50, or 100 foot-candles. He suggests that this test be tried under strictly controlled conditions where the situation is not complicated by excessive natural light.

But it is only fair to call attention to the following:

1. The recommended standards of the Illu-

minating Engineering Society which are available in its 1959 *Handbook,* section 9, page 80; and the pages on "Library Lighting," section 12-21 to 12-27.

2. The statement of Miss Edna Voigt of Remington Rand, an expert in library and equipment problems, emphasizing the aesthetic advantage of dark furniture in spite of its effect on light intensity.

3. A long list of studies made by scientists which seem to prove that higher intensities improve the speed and accuracy of reading and the understanding of what is read. (A selection from these is listed in the Selective Annotated Bibliography, Appendix D.)

4. The series of articles in the *Architectural Record,* June, July, and October, 1960, by William M. C. Lam, entitled "Lighting for Architecture," which emphasize the architectural aspects of lighting.

5. The volume written by Faber Birren, entitled *New Horizons in Color,* published by the Reinhold Publishing Corporation of New York in 1955.

6. Leslie Larson's volume on *Lighting and Its Design,* published by Whitney Publications of New York in 1964, which vigorously attacks the current high intensity recommendations of illuminating engineers.

It is suggested that Dr. Cogan's comment quoted in this section be kept in mind, as well as those of the advocates of high intensity, that a visit be made to libraries using low as well as high intensity, and that librarians and users be questioned in regard to their opinions.

The conclusion reached by the Tufts-Harvard study of eye fatigue may be pertinent here.[7] This detailed study might be summed up by saying that in the early 1940s, when money went farther than it does today, Harvard students could use the microfilm reading machines then available for six hours at a stretch with no measurable sign of eye fatigue, eye damage, or effect on their speed of reading or appreciation of what they read so long as they were paid 75 cents an hour for their work. The bibliography in this volume includes 409 items. Chapter 5, pages 126 to 147, summarizes the literature on the subject on intensity of illumination up to the date of publication. It notes the striking difference of opinion

between experts and arrives at the conclusion that an intensity of 16 foot-candles is a satisfactory base for a detailed scientific study of eye fatigue. This statement was made eighteen years ago, and many new studies have been made since that time, but it seems doubtful to the author that the human eye has changed since 1947, and the conclusion reached that the fatigue from reading for long periods is not important with 16-foot-candle intensity seems to be still valid, particularly since it coincides with the opinion of competent medical authorities.

A few final suggestions are in order. Lighting design can, should, and will change as the years go by. Mistakes can be and often have been serious. Proper and understandable fear of the new can often be overcome by "mock-ups." Do not forget the potential of indirect lighting coordinated with such daylight as is or can be made available.

Always remember that quality is much more important than intensity. Quality means enough light, control of contrasts, absence of direct or indirect glare and unpleasant shadows, and no exposed units with which the eye has to deal. High intensity without quality will never be as satisfactory as what today is considered low intensity with quality lighting. Martin Jay in an article on lighting in the September-October, 1963, number of the periodical *Interior Design* stated it very well when he wrote, "Illumination levels are not everything and 15 lumens/sq. ft. without glare may well give better lighting conditions than 150 lumens/sq. ft. provided by fittings that are excessively bright."

But remember also that the surroundings become of special importance if the intensity is unnecessarily high or undesirably low.

9.2   Heating, Ventilating, and Air Conditioning

Each of these three—heating, ventilating, and air conditioning—presents complicated and highly technical engineering problems. They are dealt with in detail in the American Society of Heating, Refrigerating, and Air Conditioning Engineers' *Guide and Data Book,* New York, 1962. A competent heating engineer, working closely with the architect, should design the systems and select the equipment. Tables and formulas for his use are readily available. This section is not for engineers, but for the laymen, the ad-

---

[7] Leonard Carmichael and Walter F. Dearborn, *Reading and Visual Fatigue,* Houghton Mifflin Company, Boston, 1947.

ministrative authorities of the institution, the building-planning committees, the business manager, and the librarian. It will attempt to present the problems which the architects and engineers must solve and also to indicate the types of installation from which the institution can select. Some oversimplified comments on desirable requirements and costs will be given, with only enough detail to explain and outline the various facets of the problem and make it possible to prepare a program statement to guide the architect in regard to the library's requirements.

In some parts of the world climatic conditions make heating of any kind unnecessary, and in other parts the need for heat is so slight that it is uneconomical to provide a central heating system, and it is customary to get along with local units of one kind or another. In other areas the cost of central heating has in the past been large enough to make it impossible to consider. As a result, various emergency devices have been used.

The great monumental library at the University of Tokyo until recently had a few areas with general heating, but on the whole relied on old-fashioned stoves with chimney pipes going out through windows in the outside walls. In climates where heating is unnecessary or a questionable luxury, two other problems may loom even larger—high temperature and humidity. Both can be combated by planning that makes it possible to take advantage of cooling breezes and that may keep the humidity from rising and mold from developing. Most academic and research libraries in India are planned on this basis, following specifications worked out by Dr. Ranganathan. There the square footage used for readers and books is much larger than would be required in the United States, but construction costs are low. Natural ventilation is a basic requirement, since the apparatus for artificial cooling is more expensive than it is here and often, because of governmental regulations, cannot be considered. In an industrially underdeveloped country where cooling apparatus has to be imported, it costs more than in the United States and Western Europe and very much more in relation to other construction costs. The problem, while great enough in the United States, may be even more serious elsewhere.

In libraries in the United States, with the possible exception of Hawaii, heating of some kind is taken for granted. The same is true for most Western European countries now and in many other parts of the world, although in the tropics, where the outside temperature rarely falls much below 60°F, the problem can be ignored without any great consequent discomfort. But, as already indicated, in many libraries in many countries general central heating has been omitted and, one might say, sometimes neglected. Certain rooms have been heated only by one kind of device or another, going all the way from electric heaters to kerosene stoves. Many scholars who have worked in older libraries in Europe have suffered from the lack of adequate provision for heating.

It must be admitted that heating is expensive to install, operate, and keep up and that the lack of it does not in itself harm books. The paper in books stored in unheated or poorly heated rooms is often in better condition than that in many of our overheated American libraries. One of our paper experts is inclined to believe that a temperature not much above the freezing point may extend the life of paper. Further studies, it is hoped, will extend our knowledge in the near future. If temperatures too low for human comfort are proved to be desirable for book storage, nonheated book stacks might solve the problem, but the need for heating parts of a library used for continuous human occupancy will not be affected. It would be difficult to imagine a library kept at 40° for the sake of paper preservation, with readers and staff wrapped up in overcoats and perhaps only their faces and a few fingers exposed.[8] If cold book stacks are found to be desirable, book-storage arrangements may have to be replanned and books and readers housed in separate quarters; this solution seems doubtful at present.

But if a library is to be heated, how and how much? Most Americans believe that comfort requires a temperature in cold weather of not less than 70°, although some of them and a considerably larger percentage of persons in other English-speaking countries would be content with 65° with reasonably high relative humidity in a draft-free room. On the other hand, there is a tendency on the part of Americans engaged in sedentary pursuits to prefer 72 to 75° or even more on a cold winter day.

---

[8] When a figure for the degree of temperature is given without being followed by F or C, it means Fahrenheit.

Henry Wright, an architectural consultant from New York, stated in a paper at the Summer Workshop Council for the Advancement of Small Colleges at the Massachusetts Institute of Technology in August, 1962, that "the emergence of air conditioning has tended to underscore the fact that given the standards of clothing, activity, and diet current in our (American) culture, the indoor temperature level that is actually widely preferred is about 75 degrees Fahrenheit and differs only slightly in winter and summer." He goes on to state, "For average sedentary activities almost everyone finds a temperature range between 73 and 79 degrees comfortable. Contrary to a good deal of highly respected opinion, relative humidity will be found to have little to do with the lower limit of this range; the point at which we begin to feel cold. On the other hand, relative humidity has a great deal to do with the upper limit; the point where we begin to feel hot." When we do not remain happy within this range, he says, "it is likely to be due to: (1) higher or lower activity levels; (2) heavier or lighter-than-normal clothing; (3) too much air movement—especially of the air somewhat below the average room temperature; or (4) exceptional radiant gains from the sun or the electric lighting system, or exceptional radiant losses due to cold wall or window areas."

Each institution must decide for itself the desired temperature for the winter months. It is suggested that in many parts of the world outside the United States if 68 to 72° can be maintained, by shifting the thermostat controls, that will be adequate, but that in the United States at least 75° as a high is not unreasonable.[9]

[9] Anthony Thompson says in *Library Buildings of Britain and Europe*, Butterworth & Co. (Publishers), Ltd., London, 1963, p. 31, "The temperature accepted in this country as comfortable for clerical and light work indoors is between 60° and 70°F (about 16–21°C). For sedentary work about 65°F is accepted, and for light physical work involving body movement, such as is done in library stack rooms, about 60°F." Bleton, the French specialist on library building planning, suggests 64–68°F, and Piasecki of Poland, 64°F. Thompson goes on to say, "The conclusion from this is that a range of 65–70°F is the right temperature for libraries, although storage libraries may safely economize on fuel by allowing the temperature to drop to about 55°F." Gerould in his *The College Library Building*, Charles Scribner's Sons, New York, 1932, p. 106, dodges the question of a definite recommendation, but comments as follows: "It is a matter of common experience that in spring and early fall, when there is no artificial heating, people will sit comfortably in a room at 60°, or even

This temperature is understandable perhaps when one considers modern clothing fashions. It must be admitted that no one temperature suits everyone in all countries or even in the same country. We have all seen some students in a library reading room in their shirtsleeves while others in the same room are wrapped up with heavy coats, sometimes with scarves around their necks. This is one of the problems resulting from a concentration of human beings almost anywhere, a concentration which in itself raises the temperature level because of body heat. It must be realized, however, that the architect and engineer must receive instruction as to the desired temperature if the results are to be satisfactory. And in these days when a larger proportion of readers are seated in the book stack, it is unwise to say that the stack can be kept down to 50° or 60° or even 65°, while the rest of the library is at 70 to 75°, to say nothing of Mr. Wright's 73 to 79°, which to the author seems unnecessarily if not unreasonably high for the cooler months. Exceptions to a uniform rule throughout the building might be made by suggesting that the entrance lobby can be a few degrees cooler without any discomfort because persons using it, including those at control desks, keep active. The same might be said for the shipping and receiving rooms, just as for stores and factories. If the temperature here is to be lowered, every effort must be made to avoid drafts. It may be that as time goes on large libraries will provide certain areas with higher temperatures than others, just as in the preceding section it was suggested that higher light intensities be provided in certain areas. This possibility should receive serious consideration.

Comfort and book-preservation problems, as far as atmospheric conditions are concerned, can properly be broken down into six headings. Each of them will be dealt with, not in great detail, but sufficiently, it is hoped, to show their relationship to the comfort of readers and staff and to the preservation of books, and also to indicate the financial problems they present. There is no need to point out to the architect the engineering and architectural problems with

below, but will complain bitterly of the cold should the temperature fall to anything like this during the winter months." Wheeler and Githens in *The American Public Library Building*, Charles Scribner's Sons, 1941, propose 70° in winter and up to 80° in summer.

which he is already acquainted, but he should be aware of the special problems that are faced by the library and the institution with which he is dealing. The six headings are heating, cooling, humidifying, dehumidifying, filtering, and ventilating.

Heating. Heating, as already noted, varies from place to place. In most of the United States, Canada, and Western Europe, it is considered a necessity, although in Florida, the Gulf in general, and Southern California it may be needed for comparatively short periods. In parts of the world where the average temperature day and night may be below 55° or 60° for weeks at a time, central heating is certainly indicated and can generally be found. In a library in such a climate, whether the heat is derived from warm or hot air, through registers or by radiators of one kind or another, or by radiant heat, it should provide along the outside walls, particularly near the windows, a curtain of warm air to prevent drafts that can easily make this space uncomfortable and too often uninhabitable. Methods of providing the heat as well as the fuel to be used—gas, oil, coal, wood, electricity—will vary according to locality.

Heating arrangements should not interfere with library activities and usable space. These facilities may occupy floor space, that is, square footage, and reduce the space available for other purposes by just so much. The problems will vary considerably. Vertical heating ducts take the most square footage and radiant heat the least. Horizontal ducts use cubage, sometimes on a large scale. It must be realized that the space used by the heating plant and the total cost of installation and operation will vary also. Each of these items can be important, and unless the librarian and the officers of his institution understand the problem and insist on a satisfactory and reasonably economical solution, the results can be unfortunate.

Two other problems in connection with heating frequently make difficulties.

1. Undesirable and unnecessary variations in temperatures from one part of the building to another—one side of a reading room, the north side of the building as a whole, for instance. A good installation should and can avoid variations by the use of thermostats, proper insulation, and adequate zoning of ducts and piping. Thermostats, except those in private offices, should be designed so that they cannot be adjusted by members of the public or, for that matter, anyone but a properly authorized member of the staff.

2. Difficulty in reducing the quantity of heat provided on a warm day or increasing it on a cold one. The person or persons responsible for the decision should study the problem and discuss it with the institution's administrative officers, maintenance staff, library-building committees, and (of equal importance) with the architects and engineers. They should learn the possibilities and costs involved, should understand what different heating methods will do, and should know their flexibility under different conditions in providing the desired temperature. The author's suggestions are: Make sure that rooms with reasonably uniform temperature are provided and that they are not 60° beside the windows with a strong draft, while 70 to 75° elsewhere; that they do not have cold floors; that the heating does not provide a blast that is unpleasant to feel and noisy to hear. Make sure that the heating engineers and architects have considered the heat loss through floors, walls, windows, unheated attics; that each room is a unit that has been figured separately; and that the pressure coming from heated air in a duct installation is sufficient to prevent cold air infiltrating through windows and door cracks, and so forth. The heating-plant capacity should be equal to its task in severe weather, that is, the heat load it provides for should be capable of equaling the heat loss through conduction, radiation, and infiltration. Careful calculation of the heat load is required because if the plant is too small and pushed beyond capacity, results will be unsatisfactory, but if it is too large, the installation cost will be unnecessarily high. Normally a heating system is designed to meet a specific theoretical "low" temperature, and when this "low" is exceeded, the designed room temperature will drop. In Boston the design is quite generally for 0°F. In Nashville, Tennessee, for instance, it is for plus 3°F.[10]

Heating is ordinarily by one or more of three methods, combinations often being used:

1. Warm air, with heat supplied by bringing in air above room temperatures, to a degree

---

[10] American Society of Heating, Refrigerating and Air Conditioning Engineers, *Building Guide*, 1962, vol. 2, *Fundamentals and Equipment*.

sufficient to counteract the heat losses. Warm-air systems today generally have fans to propel the air, instead of depending on gravity. Air is ordinarily discharged at a temperature of 90 to 100°F or, with certain types of installation, up to 135°F, because at lower temperatures the room will feel drafty as the air comes into a cooler space. It should be so arranged as to blow a curtain of warm air across cold or exposed walls and windows, from grilles not too far above the floor, because warm air tends to rise to the ceiling, and the cooler air from the floor should be used for recirculation. A certain amount of fresh outside air is included. The velocity of the air is important. If too low, the ducts must be very large. If too high, the system will be noisy and the rooms drafty. As has already been indicated, the heating engineers will use detailed formulas which involve all the pertinent factors. With proper system design and thermostatic controls, it is not difficult to provide a satisfactory range of temperature.

2. Hot water or steam, with the heat coming to the rooms through pipes and radiators. Hot water is ordinarily pushed along by a circulation pump as warm air is pushed by an air fan. Gravity systems have been used for both in the past, and in certain cases may even find limited uses today. The pump in hot-water systems is to provide greater flexibility in design and to speed up response to changed requirements. The forced circulation makes possible smaller pipes and more sensitive control. Expansion tanks are a necessary adjunct, as well as properly located vents. The librarian and the officers of his institution should remember that these take space for housing, as does the other mechanical equipment. Enough area must be provided for this functional necessity, which all too frequently is crowded into too small a space for efficient operation by the seemingly more demanding needs of the library. Always remember that a properly planned and organized mechanical plant requires space for operation, maintenance, and possible later expansion.

3. Panel or radiant heating consisting of warm coils in the floor, ceiling, or walls, provided with warm air, warm water, or electric-resistant heating elements. Radiant systems require different formulas for figuring the amount of heat required.

In this connection the amount of heat—British Thermal Units or "BTUs" as they are called—required to keep the temperature at the desired level can be determined by standard formulas. The formulas are based not only on the number of cubic feet of space to be heated, but also on the heat loss and gain resulting from:

1. The number of persons occupying the space. People produce heat, the amount depending on whether they are active or in sedentary work.

2. The heat provided by the lighting equipment. This may amount to far more than anticipated, particularly if the high lighting intensities that are now popular are used. Some buildings today, even in cold weather, can be warmed almost entirely by heat produced by the lighting installation. (The two foregoing factors should not be left out of consideration when selecting equipment for cooling.)

3. The heat loss or gain through floors, walls, and ceilings. In a library this comes chiefly from outside walls and windows, to some extent from the roof if there is no attic, and more and more often from the floors.

Cold coming through the floors results primarily from a cold unheated basement or from an overhang resulting from a floor cantilevered out over the great outdoors, as in the University of Chicago Law Library. In these cases, unless heat is provided in the floor, or unless at least proper insulation is applied to the underside of the slab, the area around the periphery of the building may become almost uninhabitable in severe weather.

The amount of the heat gained or lost through the ceiling will depend partly on the type of roof insulation, particularly in the ceiling of the top floor of the building.

But the great problem is in the outside walls. There the heat loss or gain depends on the construction of the walls, the insulation used, and the amount of window space, together with the kind of windows and the kind of glass used.

Some will remember the metal frame casement windows in older libraries, such as the New York Public Library Central Building at 42d Street and Fifth Avenue, where the cold air has tended to come in around the frames because they are not quite tight. Metal sash loses heat more readily than wood sash through the frame itself. Casement windows present a problem, particularly with poor-fitting metal sash. Weather stripping can be useful. Leaky windows present a condensation problem also. Fixed sash is often used today in air-conditioned buildings and largely eliminates the leakage problem. It should be remembered, however, that with fixed windows the operation of the building is at the mercy of the air-conditioning system. If the unit breaks down in hot summer weather, the building can become unusable, with no relief available from open windows. If the system relied upon is prone to break down and particularly if a good repair mechanic is not always available —something which is not unusual in rural areas and sometimes even in large cities—the use of fixed windows may be questionable.

Too many modern buildings with their walls made up very largely of glass lose more heat than would be the case with a masonry wall. Glass is made today that, it is claimed, will reduce heat loss from the cold, or heat gain from the sun for that matter, but it is rarely if ever completely satisfactory. Double glass provides an air space between the two layers. Quiet air is perhaps the best of all insulation materials, and double glass reduces condensation of water on windows if the room is humidified in cold weather.

The architectural program should indicate the temperature to be maintained in the building and in the different parts if there is to be a variation within it. The institution's representatives should keep in mind the effect of different types of walls on the cost of heating and should certainly talk the problem over with the architect before plans are approved, in order to avoid misunderstanding. If the building is to be humidified, the walls should have a vapor barrier. The question of windows will be discussed in more detail in section 10.1.

The possibility and desirability of installing heating pipes to melt snow on sidewalks at the entrance or on roofs and gutters should be kept in mind in planning heat installation.

Cooling or Air Conditioning. Cooling is only a part of air conditioning, but the term is too often used loosely as though it were in itself all that there is to air conditioning. Cooling consists of reducing or removing unwanted heat by supplying cool air. An excess of heat, at times when a building is not heated artificially, results from heat transmitted to the space under consideration through the walls, windows, ceiling, and floors, directly or indirectly, by radiation from the sun, plus the heat generated in the library from lights, people, electrical and gas appli-

ances, and outside air brought in for ventilation purposes.

The total heat load, that is, the load imposed by transmitted plus internally generated heat, must be determined to decide on the size of the cooling plant required. The temperature to be obtained by the cooling must be agreed upon. A larger plant will, of course, be required to provide for 60°F than is required for 75°F. Again, formulas are available for use by the engineers. A total cooling load is divided into two parts— sensible heat that shows on a dry-bulb thermometer and comes from the sources listed in the preceding paragraph, and the latent load, which is the cooling required to remove unwanted moisture from the air-conditioned space.

For comfort, cooling a room to 80° dry-bulb and 50 per cent relative humidity is under some circumstances acceptable. If the outside temperature is 95°, to cool to 70° would be unduly expensive and actually would provide too great a contrast for comfort. Some quite satisfactory installations are made with a capacity to keep the temperature no more than 10° lower than it is outside. Always remember that not only the outside temperature is involved. People, particularly if they are active, generate heat. Artificial lighting, especially that with high intensities, complicates matters considerably, varying with the type of the light source. Incandescent lights use more current to produce the same amount of light than fluorescent and therefore generate much more heat for the same lighting intensity, perhaps 2½ times as much. Even with fluorescent tubes, the very high intensity now sometimes used may be sufficient to heat a building in all but the very coldest weather without any other source. If persons are to remain in a room for long periods of hot weather, a lower temperature may be desirable than if they are coming and going at short intervals. As was indicated earlier, the architects and engineers must be told the desired temperature to be maintained. It is suggested, at least as a basis for discussion, that in hot weather there never be more than 15° difference between inside and outside temperature in the shade and that 72° be considered satisfactory until outside temperature gets above 82°. When the temperature goes above 82° outside, the inside temperature can properly go up at least 2° for each 3° increase outside. It is suggested that from 72 to 75°F for inside temperature might be planned for, and in very hot weather that it be permitted to rise higher simply because the installation will not accomplish anything more.

As already noted, it may be found that lower temperatures are desirable for book storage. These temperatures are not too difficult to maintain in many places if the stacks are in well-insulated locations, such as below-surface basements, where the ground temperature is between 45 and 60° the year around, as it is in most of the United States.

Humidification and Dehumidification. The third and fourth factors are humidification and dehumidification. Many persons have failed to understand or to realize that heating systems in places where there is severe winter weather, which may lower the outside temperature to as much as 20 to 30° below zero, will reduce the relative humidity in a room heated to 70° or more to a point where it is no more than 10 per cent and is as dry as the Sahara Desert or drier. What are the results? Most persons will quickly become accustomed to it; the skin and the mucous membranes dry out and may feel unpleasant; respiratory ailments may tend to increase; but we have always lived that way. Alas, however, bindings and paper under these conditions dry out also. Some of us have seen old pigskin bindings that, after having survived in English manor houses without central heat for hundreds of years undamaged, warp in a short time under American library conditions, so that the cover leather binding has actually pulled off the boards. Paper, particularly our modern wood-pulp or other paper with a large percentage of chemical residue left in it, will not only dry out quickly but disintegrate altogether. Chemicals, activated by the heat and the dryness, literally burn up the paper. The larger the amount of acid in the paper, the more rapid this action. Present-day newspapers, indeed almost all newspapers dating back to the beginning of the wood-pulp era in the 1870s, have a short life at best, and in an overheated library that life will be greatly reduced, often to less than twenty-five years if the use is more than negligible. Mr. Barrow of the Virginia State Library tells us that some 80 per cent of twentieth-century American books are doomed within two generations or less. The author suggests that the useful life span might well be doubled if the relative humidity in the rooms where they are stored is kept up to between 45 and 55 per cent in the heating season. Fortunately, this is not too difficult, although it may be expensive to accomplish satisfactorily. With warm-air-heating installations moisture can be sprayed into the air as it enters the heating system. Three problems must be met, however:

1. The moisture must be controlled, as it may rust out the ducts as it settles on metal surfaces.

2. The water must be filtered; otherwise, when it evaporates it may leave a residue of solids which settles in the form of dust on books and elsewhere. Dust is a serious enemy to books, not only because of the dirt, but because, however fine it may be, it is an abrasive.

3. In severe winter weather, when air with a relative humidity that is satisfactory strikes the cold surface of a glass window or any other cold substance, the moisture tends to condense and will run down the window or the wall with possibly serious results.

The author has had some very unpleasant experiences in trying to humidify rooms that were constructed years ago with no thought of later winter humidification. Double glass, Thermopane, for instance, will prevent condensation, but it is, of course, expensive, particularly in our modern "glass-box" buildings. Satisfactory insulation of walls and inclusion of a vapor barrier will help solve the problem if there is not too much glass. But the three traps noted above which may waylay the unwary should be kept in mind.

If severe winter weather is of short duration, the condensation problem can sometimes be avoided without double glass by permitting the percentage of relative humidity to drop for a few hours. The moisture held in the books and bindings will help temporarily, but the period must not be prolonged more than perhaps 48 hours at the most or damage will result.

Winter humidification can be produced by adding moisture to the air brought into the building in connection with its heating. But remember that a rapid drop in outside temperature will bring condensation on walls and particularly windows and the duct work, and that, since all building materials are porous, condensation of moisture in the walls may freeze in severe weather conditions; the expansion that comes from freezing may then cause structural cracks and severe damage in concrete or cinder blocks. As previously mentioned, a vapor barrier is required.

Dehumidification is in most ways and in many locations as serious a problem as humidification. This is particularly true in our coastal areas in climates where there are prolonged hot and humid spells. At least from Philadelphia on the East Coast to the south and west until the dry Southwest is reached, as well as in sections of the Middle West, the normal summer temperature stands in the eighties with long periods of high humidity. Under such conditions mold spores, which are always present, begin to grow. This happens frequently even in New England and all through the Northern and Central states, particularly if wet basements result from rains and floods during a humid hot spell. It is difficult and expensive to remove moisture from the air. Four methods are used:

1. Condensing machinery in connection with the ventilation installation. This is expensive to install and to maintain and, like most apparatus with moving parts, can be expected to wear out in due course. Twenty years might be considered a normal satisfactory lifetime for most installations.

2. Chemical moisture absorbers. With these the air is passed through or over moisture-absorbing chemicals.

3. Local portable unit dehumidifiers. These are sometimes installed in damp basements. They may resemble in shape the old-fashioned oil heaters. No expensive ducts are required, but the moisture they remove must either be carried out of the building by hand at comparatively short intervals during very humid weather, or the unit must be provided with a drain connection that will result in the condensed water running outside.

4. A fourth method sometimes used is to exhaust the hot humid air with fans during the hours when the outside air is cooler than that inside but not too humid. The library is kept closed up in the daytime, with window shades lowered so as to prevent overheating from radiation from the sun, and then late at night, when the outside temperature is at its lowest point, an exhaust fan is set in motion, and the previous day's hot air is removed and replaced by the cool night air. Unfortunately, in very humid weather, it sometimes happens that the night air brought in is very close to the dewpoint and, if the daytime temperature does not go up, condensation inside may result and mold spores may grow. If a humidistat is placed in the intake

and adjusted to stop the change in air when the relative humidity outside is too high, this difficulty can be largely obviated.

Filtering. All ventilation installations should, if possible, include filtering units. Removal of dust from the air results in a healthier atmosphere and lower maintenance costs for cleaning; it also prevents cooling and heating coils and ducts from becoming blocked, and, perhaps of even greater importance, prevents damage to books. All of us have seen accumulations of dust and dirt near air intakes and realize that air passing through a library can be dirty. A good look at a used filter shows that it has been useful. Filters may be of a throwaway or a cleanable type. In earlier days air was passed through a water spray to remove the dust, and oil filters were sometimes used. Among the more effective filters are the electrostatic ones which may be used in connection with other types. The electrostatic process removes smaller particles and is useful, particularly for rare-book collections, where dirt may be as serious an enemy as unsatisfactory humidity and temperature. What is known as the Cambridge Aerosole filter has come into use recently. It is a mechanical filter and, if used in connection with the electrostatic process, will prevent the serious damage which has sometimes resulted when the latter breaks down and the ventilation fans continue to operate. The two in combination should provide desired insurance for a very valuable rare-book collection because, if the electrostatic filter breaks down and the dust that has been collected is pushed on through the ducts, it will be caught by the mechanical filter. The use of the better grade of Cambridge filter without the electrostatic filter should be seriously considered in locations where there is little danger from sulfur from industrial waste in the atmosphere. The maintenance cost of the electrostatic filter is quite expensive and upkeep is too often neglected on that account with serious consequences.

The location of the air intake is important. If it is close to the ground, it may take into the air-supply system the chemical and exhaust pollutions which unfortunately abound, particularly in urban areas.

One of the factors of great importance in filtering is the removal of industrial chemical pollution from the air which in our large cities, particularly, tends to include a considerable amount of sulfur dioxide. This, combined with the chemical residues left in a large proportion of our modern paper, hastens its deterioration and in fact gradually permits it to burn up with the distressing results which we have all seen in an extreme form in late nineteenth- and twentieth-century newspapers.

Ventilation. Heating, cooling, humidification, dehumidification, and filtering by themselves will not provide completely satisfactory atmospheric conditions. Ventilation must come with them. It requires a change of air rapid enough to counteract odors and pollution of any kind. Building codes and local rules govern minimum standards. In most places with limited occupancy ventilation is provided for through the heating system in cold weather or through leakage of air or open windows in hot weather or by "gravity" circulation caused by the weight difference of hot and cold air. A ventilation system may be called a dilution process, by which odor or heat removed is equal to that generated on the premises. It is particularly useful in windowless or below-grade areas, where, without a change in air, a stale or musty odor may result. The amount of fresh air that should be brought in will depend on the total cubic footage of the area and the amount of heat, moisture, and odor generated in it, which in turn will be largely affected by the number of persons occupying the premises and their activities. The amount of fresh air in terms of cubic footage per person required in a theater where the occupants are sitting quietly may be no more than 10 per cent as much as is desirable in a gymnasium. Many ventilation systems are unsatisfactory primarily because they do not provide adequate changes of air.

Summary. Air-conditioning and ventilation systems in libraries today are generally part of what are known as central-heating systems that cover the building as a whole. Indeed, in many academic institutions a single system may serve the whole institution, but to be satisfactory, even with a perfect installation, there must be local thermostats or controls. The demands on the system will vary with the number of occupants, the direction of the wind, the amount of sunshine. No installation without local controls can be completely satisfactory, but local controls, of course, add to the cost.

In some buildings the whole system is based on local units, one for each room or section of the building, and makes use of room or unit conditioners which have become fairly common in recent years in single rooms in private houses, apartments, and offices. The Grinnell College Library has used this method. The use of local units to this extent is generally frowned on by mechanical engineers and maintenance personnel. Decentralized maintenance arrangements present complications, and the provision of satisfactory "comfort" cooling or heating within a reasonable degree of engineering standards is lost. On the other hand, there is less likelihood of the building becoming completely uninhabitable because of mechanical breakdown.

One other note: Air conditioning requires not only machinery, electric current, and the availability of an expert mechanic, but also an adequate water supply. Be sure that each of these is or can be made available. Each is expensive. If an adequate water supply is not available at a reasonable cost from local governmental or private agencies or perhaps from a well driven for the purpose, a cooling tower or, in small installations, an evaporative condenser will help. Remember that there may be local restrictions against "waste water" used in air-conditioning systems and that wells have been known to run dry.

Whether or not a new library should provide for full air conditioning, that is, not only heating, but cooling, humidification, dehumidification, and filtering, as well as a satisfactory change of air, will depend on local conditions and funds available. The decision will be difficult to make because the costs involved are considerable; not the least of them is the cubic footage of the space required for the mechanical installations. Ducts and mechanical rooms occupy space, and it is cubic and square footage that are the basic costs in a new building. Space for the mechanical room and perhaps for a water tower can sometimes be found in an unused basement area or on the roof of an adjacent building, thereby saving valuable square footage in the new structure. This was done in Widener at Harvard for the mechanical equipment and cooling towers for Houghton and Lamont, and in Langdell Hall for the International Legal Studies building. Many institutions will feel that complete air conditioning is unnecessary. If an institution has no summer school and is located in a section of the country where the number of days with the temperature rising above 85° is limited, exhaust fans for use at night in all but very humid weather may solve the problem with reasonable satisfaction. The deciding factor may not be the comfort of the readers and the staff but the value of the collections. If so, a solution may possibly be found by segregating the rare and irreplaceable books and manuscripts and providing humidification and dehumidification for them but not for the building as a whole. A generation ago comparatively few libraries were air-conditioned; indeed, satisfactory air conditioning had not been evolved. Theoretically, the Widener Library, built in 1915, was air-conditioned, but the system was so expensive and the results were so unsatisfactory that within a few months after the opening of the building it was given up and never used again.

In the winter of 1941–1942, when the Houghton Rare Book Library at Harvard was put into use, it had a complete air-conditioning installation which was very satisfactory until twenty years later, when the refrigerant condensing apparatus wore out and it became difficult to maintain the desired relative humidity. This condensing-equipment installation has been replaced. The air conditioning in the Lamont Undergraduate Library is not quite as elaborate as that in Houghton, but has proved to be satisfactory. It has had occasional lapses. It naturally took some months to get the air conditioning properly adjusted when the building was first opened. The inexperienced librarian expects to walk into his newly completed building and to be able to have the air-conditioning system operate in accordance with the design criteria set up by the architects and engineers; but unfortunately, all air-conditioning systems are fairly complicated and require a "shake-down cruise" of at least one year during which (1) the controls, air flow, fan speed, valves, etc., are adjusted for maximum results, and (2) the best method of operation is learned by the personnel who are responsible, a method which often is quite different from those with which they have previously been acquainted.

One of the great advantages of Lamont's air-conditioning system has been the fact that it has been an important, perhaps the most important, factor in making possible a rapid increase in the size of Harvard's Summer School. As many as 17 classes can be held in the library at one time, and it has become the center of summer-school activities.

Less than fifteen years ago states as far south as North Carolina refused to install air conditioning in their state-supported academic buildings because of the expense. It is often found that if one building in an institution is air-conditioned, the demand for similar installations in other buildings is greatly increased. New York City held off for many years on air conditioning its public buildings and refused to provide such an installation in any building occupied by workers paid with city funds. It was said at that time that to air-condition all space occupied by New York City employees would cost a billion dollars. North Carolina and New York City rules in this connection have now broken down. A large percentage of new libraries throughout the country are using air conditioning. In some cases, in order to save funds, unsatisfactory installations have been made. In others the air-conditioning ducts have been installed with the hope that the mechanisms involved would be acquired at a later time, but unfortunately when this has been done the ducts have not always been adequate in size, and when the air conditioning has been finally installed it has proved to be inadequate.

The author is not prepared to recommend complete air conditioning for all new library buildings. Undoubtedly there are libraries where, because of climatic conditions, comparatively small summer use, or lack of funds to provide for other equally or more important requirements, air conditioning is not essential; but it might not be an exaggeration to say that in many and probably a majority of cases in the United States a new library without air conditioning is obviously obsolete at the time its doors are opened.

From time to time the question of air conditioning an old library building comes up. Often it can be arranged, but the installation tends to be more expensive than in a new building because holes for the ducts must be opened up in walls and floor; it is difficult to conceal the ducts satisfactorily, and too often the results have not been up to standard. An example of a good installation of this kind is at the Newberry Library in Chicago. Sometimes it is possible and less expensive in an old building to provide local air conditioning for parts of the structure or to use small high-velocity ducts with sound absorbers, as was done at the Chinese-Japanese Library of Harvard. Top-floor rooms, where the attic can be used for the apparatus, or first-floor rooms adjacent to basements where there is unused space or space unusable for other purposes are possibilities. Window air conditioners are another, but they do not add to the attractiveness of a facade and are not satisfactory in other ways.

Remember when considering the air-conditioning and ventilation problem that there are at least five alternatives, as follows:

1. *Heating only.* This is not recommended in most libraries.

2. *Minimum recommended installation.* Heating and ventilating with air filtration.

3. *Comfort installation.* Heating, ventilation, air filtration, and cooling. This is recommended if the library is open to the public during long hot and humid periods.

4. *Conditioned installation.* Heating, ventilation, air filtration, cooling, and humidity control. This is recommended for situations noted in 3 if the collections have rare and irreplaceable books and manuscripts.

5. *The ideal installation.* Heating, ventilation, air filtration, cooling, and humidity control, all within certain specified narrow limits in order to maintain ideal conditions of temperature and humidity the year around, regardless of outside conditions.

Of course, the cost of installation and operation increases with each step. If a library adopts the minimum procedure, it may be desirable to size the duct work and equipment space so that the comfort and conditioning installations can be added in the future without undue cost.

Remember also the desirability of filtering (one might almost say the necessity of filtering) if any system that brings outside air into the library is used.

Remember that if air cooling for the building as a whole is not possible because of the cost and if use of the library during the unpleasantly hot months is limited, it may be desirable to install local room units in working areas and possibly in one reading area.

One final word of warning about air conditioning. It is a comparatively exact science, and an installation should be designed by a reliable and competent architect and engineer.

Perhaps the best advice in regard to heating and ventilating, as in regard to lighting and acoustic problems, is to say that the ideal is to provide physical conditions that make one completely unaware of them when one is reading or studying. Such conditions would, of course, become monotonous in time, and some change may be desirable in different parts of the building. It is to be hoped that most physically active people can get out of doors from time to time in both summer and winter and find different temperatures, different intensity of light, and different acoustical conditions and that they will continue to enjoy the changes that are available between day and night and summer and winter.

The cost of heating, ventilation, and air conditioning depends primarily on three factors: the availability and the cost of (1) the heating agent, generally coal, oil or gas, or exhaust steam from an electric generating plant; (2) the cooling agent, generally water; and (3) electric current to provide the power required. These costs vary considerably in different parts of the United States and in other countries and even from year to year in the same place. Many heating installations today are so designed that a shift from coal to gas or oil can be made fairly readily and inexpensively.

There is a tremendous variation in water costs. Occasionally enough water at a desirable temperature can be provided by a well on the premises. As we have already advised, be wary of well water. Wells are notoriously unreliable. Often water costs are high enough so that a water-cooling tower will pay for itself; it may be required by law. It is desirable and economical to recirculate the water used for condensing the refrigerant.

The cost of electric current varies also. And do not forget in figuring costs that the intensity of artificial light and the heat gain and loss resulting from too much natural light or poor insulation in walls and roofs may be a large factor. On the other hand, satisfactory physical conditions are bound to promote the use of the library and are well worth paying for.

Do not forget that air conditioning may present acoustic problems, a satisfactory answer to which may require the use of an acoustic engineer. These problems may arise from:

1. Compressors or transformers immediately above, below, or beside a reading or workroom area.

2. Fan noise transmitted through walls or duct work.

3. Air movement at too rapid a pace through supply or exhaust duct work.

4. Motor noise, particularly through walls or duct work.

5. Cooling-tower fans, a noise usually more disturbing outside than inside the building and a serious matter when the building is near dormitories or residences, particularly at night when the noise seems to be amplified by the quiet prevailing elsewhere. This problem has been too often neglected.

In connection with the sections on lighting, heating, and ventilating, the possibility of the use of central power plants for the services required by a library should be mentioned. Central electric-generating plants, either available at a price from commercial companies or operated by the institution, are almost universal. Central steam generators are quite common and are generally available in larger institutions. Central refrigerant generators, however, are comparatively new and seem to be the next step. The use of a centrally controlled electrical panel for heating and ventilation may also be indicated in a large operation in order to reduce personnel overhead in buildings unoccupied at night, on Sundays, and on holidays.[11]

[11] Smith College in Northampton, Massachusetts, is now planning central refrigeration, and Harvard University is planning central control panels.

Other Mechanical and Construction Problems

10.1 Basic Construction Problems

Problems dealt with in this section may be even more technical than those considered in the preceding ones, and will be discussed in an even more superficial fashion. The author will attempt only to list the problems, define a few terms with which the librarian should be acquainted, and state some of the requirements that the building should meet to be functionally satisfactory. Lighting and ventilating have been discussed in Chapter 9.

Construction problems include:

1. Soil mechanics and foundation problems
2. Building materials of all kinds
3. The calculation of stresses and strains, loads and wind pressures, and the problems of beams, trusses, columns, arches, and domes, which must be solved in order to design satisfactorily and safely
4. Other basic problems more or less closely connected with the foregoing, which must be dealt with by the architects and builders, such as the question of steel, masonry construction, wood framing, windows of all kinds, exterior and interior walls, doors, laths, plumbing, hardware, floors, roofs, ceiling coverings, water permeability, and many others
5. Vertical transportation, which was discussed in section 6.2
6. The problem of estimating and costs, which has been considered in Chapter 3
7. The question of drawings, specifications, and contracts, which is dealt with in section 16.4

The librarian must leave the very technical problems to the specialists, although he should try to understand them and the solutions which are selected. If the architect is competent, he will understand the problems, although he in turn may have to call on engineers for help on various details.

Soil Mechanics and Foundation Problems. A firm foundation is essential for any building. Because of the weight of books, if nothing else, libraries place a heavier load on their foundations than many other structures. These loads must be carried with a reasonable margin of safety. To oversimplify, the "static" or "dead" load is the weight added to the structure by its contents. In libraries, the latter consist primarily of the furniture and equipment, the book collections, and persons using them. There is no need here to discuss what are known as repeated loads, impact loads, and a number of other kinds, including those that come from wind, weight of snow on the roof, etc. These are of importance to the architect and engineer and must be provided for in the structure, but are outside the field of this volume. Except for book stacks, map cases, and a few other pieces of heavy equipment, it is fair to say that in general 60 pounds per square foot for reading areas is considered sufficient as far as live load is concerned. But 100 pounds should ordinarily be provided for corridors, 150 is standard for stack rooms, and up to 175 may be required for compact storage areas and map cases. As much as 200 pounds may be required for garages with heavy trucks, and 250 pounds per square foot for vaults.

Today it has become customary, and on the whole wisely so, to construct all library floors strong enough to carry a live load of up to 150 pounds per square foot. Such strength will make it safe to install book stacks anywhere, to change internal arrangements freely, and to place practically any equipment wherever it is wanted. In many older libraries, which were not so constructed, it has often been found unsafe to place book stacks in reading areas, for instance. This limitation has complicated matters when additions were being planned or changes were made in space assignments.

Buildings are supported by columns or bearing walls or a combination of the two. Bearing outside walls do not present a problem, except that they may be very much in the way if an addition is made to an old building, because they may restrict connections between the old and new anywhere except where there has been a door, window, or other opening. This should be kept in mind if an addition is anticipated later in a building now being planned, or if plans are now being made for an addition to an old building. Internal bearing walls present more of a problem, as they complicate any alteration or shifts within a structure and, if a flexible building is desired, they should be avoided, except perhaps around fixed features, such as stairwells, elevators, and toilet rooms. Remember that interior bearing walls are not the same as nonbearing wet walls. The latter are inflexible only in that they are difficult and messy to remove; but removal of a bearing wall requires a structural change in what might be called the building's skeleton.

Adequate footings under both columns and bearing walls must be provided so that no part of the building will sink. Section 15.2, on site selection, discusses this problem. Sometimes deep piles are required and may prove to be very expensive. If the piles are of wood, they must not be allowed to dry out, or they will rapidly deteriorate. Sometimes it is desirable to sink caissons because of soft soil conditions. Sometimes the whole building must be supported by or floated on a concrete slab, so as to spread the weight and avoid the possible shifting of the soil beneath if there is quicksand or slippery clay. Sometimes soil must be removed to a considerable depth to lessen the ground load before the new building is constructed. Sometimes the problem is expensive excavation of solid rock by blasting, which can be difficult and annoying, if not dangerous.

Always be sure that soil conditions are known before a site is irrevocably selected, and, if a later addition is anticipated, remember that it should be arranged without interfering with the footings in the original structure. This can sometimes be managed through cantilevering out beyond supporting columns or load-bearing walls in the new part of the structure. If the addition or the old structure is floated on a concrete slab, very careful calculation will be necessary to avoid having the addition sink too far or not far enough and so leave a step up or down between the two. Do not forget the danger that a floating building or one with unstable foundations may tip slightly to one side or the other, as happened to the Leaning Tower of Pisa.

Steel or Masonry Framing. Construction above the foundations, whether supported by columns or bearing walls, is ordinarily, except in a few quite small libraries, of masonry, concrete or steel. In some locations local sand for use in concrete may be unsuitable and present a problem, as in certain parts of upstate New York. Careful estimates of the comparative costs of concrete and steel should be made. The latter may amount to considerably more than the former, but if it makes possible smaller columns, particularly in the book stack, the saving in space may make up for the additional cost.

Walls. Interior walls present other problems. Great efforts have been made in recent years in many libraries to avoid wet walls—those that cannot be removed without breaking them up. In their place it is possible to use book shelving or dry walls, which in nontechnical terms are simply movable partitions, often of steel. Shelving can often be satisfactory and, if it is freestanding, is more flexible than anything else, but it may involve acoustical problems if noise carried over from one area to another is not to be tolerated. Metal and glass partitions, as well as folding partitions, are also too often unsatisfactory acoustically. They must be fitted tightly to floor and ceiling with no gaps through which noise can penetrate. Movable steel partitions for offices and faculty studies are often considerably more expensive than wet walls. However, if moving is necessary as often as twice in ten years, it will probably be less expensive to provide steel partitions than to demolish and re-erect wet walls.

Dry partitions of Transite with metal studs are being used extensively in other types of structures and can well be considered for library interior walls, as they are comparable in price to unplastered cinder or concrete block walls. But, again, in any type of interior walls, keep in mind acoustical problems. These problems can be solved, but the solutions may cost money. Cinder and concrete block walls, particularly for inside walls, have been used much more in recent years than earlier. They may present a difficult problem when used for outside walls because of cracking, and waterproofing may be necessary if they are to be exposed to the elements. Another block used today is pumice. It is often left unpainted, as in the Harvard Divinity School Library, because of its pleasant natural color. No doubt in other parts of the world other types of block are available.

Section 3.3 states that the outside walls of the building represent approximately 10 per cent of the total cost of the finished structure, and describes different types of masonry walls and their relative costs. It goes on to consider the effect on costs of the ratio of the length of the exterior walls to the inside area. Other things being equal, the larger the building, the smaller the amount of outside wall per square foot of enclosed space. But as the enclosed square footage on each floor is increased, the roof, which is another expensive part of the building, becomes larger also. A curved wall is always more expensive than a straight one, although it surrounds more square footage of area per length of wall. A wall with a good many jogs in it will, of course, increase the amount of outside wall space while decreasing the enclosed area, and a square or rectangular building may enclose considerably more square footage in relation to the length of the wall and also reduce distances to be traveled within the structure. The preceding statements should not be taken to mean that every library should be a cube with only four corners on the outside walls, but the cost of different arrangements for outside walls may well be kept in mind.

Remember that cost figures may differ because of variations in wage rates and the distance from the source of supply for materials. Construction magazines carry monthly countrywide tabulations of relative building costs which might indicate, for example, that those in Nashville, Tennessee, are 10 per cent less than in Boston. These tabulations are affected by time as well as by place. But remember also that important considerations from the librarian's and the institution's point of view are to obtain a building, within the means available, which is aesthetically satisfactory, will last more or less indefinitely with low maintenance costs, and at the same time will enable its administrators to give the best possible library service. All this should be made clear to the architect, and he should be permitted to go ahead with his planning with no more interference on the part of the client than is required to bring about the desired functional results.

It is important for the architect to keep up to date with innovations in construction which are developing rapidly throughout the world. A new type of steel beam has been introduced recently which is claimed to be cheaper and stronger than beams used in the past. Can it be used to advantage in your building? Will prestressed or precast concrete make possible the effects desired and still save funds for other purposes? Will lift-slab construction be useful or the long spans that can be provided by prestressed beams? Some of these may be functional but not particularly satisfactory aesthetically.

It is not easy, perhaps not possible, for anyone but an expert in the particular branch of the construction field to decide on the suitability of new methods or units for incorporation in a building. A great danger in the use of new materials and methods is their lack of time testing. This can sometimes be provided only by experiments which require considerable technical equipment and involve considerable expense. Unfortunately, changes in the quality of products, both new and old, occur frequently with what may be unfortunate results. Examples of this kind will be found in the discussion on flooring later in this section. Sometimes new materials and new methods are difficult to make use of because of labor restrictions of one kind or another.

Windows. Windows are of many varieties: They may have wood or metal frames, be double hung or casement or have other arrangements for opening; they may be of different shapes and sizes; they may be made of large or small panes of clear, opaque, or colored glass, to say nothing of glass blocks. The window pattern can take innumerable forms, and the resulting facade is of first importance aesthetically. The librarian should give particular attention to the effect of windows on library functions. There are physiological, psychological, and perhaps sociological factors. Windows provide light and ventilation; and human reactions are aroused by their presence or absence.

Other things being equal, the closer the windows are placed to the ceiling, the higher the intensity of light admitted. But if the windows are above the eye level, nothing can be seen out of them, except possibly sky, tall trees, other buildings, or another part of the same building. There is some truth in the objection that any window through which you can see anything may be a distraction and will interfere with reading; on this basis one can advocate a completely windowless library. Many people today spend much of their working lives in windowless areas. On the other hand, comparatively few people are ready to recommend that a library be completely windowless, particularly in its reading areas and in areas occupied by the staff.

Halls, corridors, and stairwells do not need to rely on outside light and probably should be provided with at least low-intensity artificial lighting during all the hours the library is open. In all other areas, even if they are well supplied with windows, artificial light is required in most libraries today for approximately half of the hours of opening. In general, library users, at least in the United States, do not depend on natural light completely, and reading areas are artificially lighted throughout the day. It is a question whether this is necessary, but it generally happens and, if natural light is not depended upon, it is possible to plan a building with large sections far away from natural light. It should also be noted that books are harmed by direct sunlight because of the ultraviolet rays that come with it, rays which fade bindings and hasten paper deterioration.

One of the important decisions in connection with windows concerns the percentage of the outside wall which should be of glass. In some states there are regulations for schools and some other public buildings, specifying at least 20 per cent glass, but these regulations are falling more and more into disuse with the improvements in artificial lighting and ventilation. Many persons are ready to say that windows and natural light are for readers, not for reading. That means that they are for psychological not physiological effect. On the other hand, in recent

years the "all-glass box" style of building has come to the fore. This too can present physiological, psychological, and also functional problems. If any area in a library has an all-glass facade, it will be practically impossible to store books near the outside walls without harming them, unless, of course, the glass is completely covered up and protected. Young women with short skirts will hesitate to sit near windows if the windows go down to the floor. If the windows are on the west, or, in the North Temperate Zone, on the south, much of the space, if it is not shaded in some way, will be practically unusable for reading during parts of bright days because of unpleasant intensity, unless suitable protection of some kind is available. Leaving out for the time being the question of the sun's effect on heating and ventilation problems, we may find it easy to overdo the use of glass as far as reading is concerned because of the resulting glare. On the other hand, it would be a shame in many locations to prevent the users of a library from looking out on a handsome lawn, trees, and distant hills. However, Mr. Pecksniff in Dickens's *Martin Chuzzlewit* was probably on the right track when he spoke of the desirability of "moderation in all things." The author remembers some years ago recommending large windows in every bay on one side of the Bennington College Library where there was a fine mountain view available, and Dean Pietro Belluschi saying, "This view will be appreciated more if there isn't too much glass."

Of course, sunlight can be prevented from interfering with readers or damaging books by covering the glass on the inside or out. On the inside, old-fashioned window shades which shut out the light almost altogether are possible. If they are made so that they can be drawn down from the top and up from the bottom, they can take care of the light under different conditions at different times of day, but, of course, constant adjustment is necessary.

Both horizontal and vertical venetian blinds are also possibilities. The horizontal ones have been used for many years. Their cords tend to wear out, and they may present a cleaning problem, but if they are used carefully, if they are not so large as to be difficult to manipulate, and if the outside air that comes in is filtered, they will last a great many years with little cleaning or repair. In recent years vertical venetian blinds have come into use, and are in some ways more effective, but they present the same problems, and in addition, if the room is high and the blinds are long, they tend to get out of order quickly.

Drapes of various materials are also used extensively. They can be very decorative. The Georgia Institute of Technology has a tremendous quantity of specially designed, made-to-order draperies which add a great deal to the decor of the building. Unfortunately, because the bright Georgia sunlight fades them rapidly and because it is expensive to replace them, the librarian, who had been enthusiastic about them, now issues a warning about their use. At the Massachusetts Institute of Technology, where the large windows on the south wall of the reading rooms look out over a very handsome view of the Charles River and the Boston skyline beyond, the draperies have presented similar difficulties. They burn out rapidly and, in addition, are so large and heavy that they are difficult to move. At the Air Force Academy a tremendous expanse of glass has been covered by draperies so extensive in size that it has been found necessary to operate them with motors, and if the motors break down while the drapes are drawn, they cannot be opened, or, if open, they cannot be drawn, and a good part of the reading area becomes uninhabitable.

The Educational Facilities Laboratories College News Letter 5, November, 1964, reported that a polyester plastic sheeting coated on one side with microscopic metal particles and fixed with an adhesive to the inside of the window will reflect up to 80 to 85 per cent of solar energy and make it impossible for the glass to become hot enough to produce excessive reradiation. It is recommended for use in overheated rooms designed with huge expanses of glass.

Windows can also be protected from the outside in a number of ways:

1. With large vertical metal fins a foot or so wide which can be adjusted by a crank operated from inside the building, or by automatic equipment that turns them with the sun. Because they are outdoors and have movable parts, they tend to get out of order and to become noisy in a high wind. It is suggested that persons who have had experience with them be consulted before they are adopted.

2. With screens of one kind or another parallel to the walls and windows, and a few feet away from them. These have been used for hundreds of years in India, and have been introduced on a large scale in recent years in the United States by Edward Stone, Marcel Breuer, and other architects. They may be of metal or of concrete, or they may be of hollow tiles of various depths, shapes, and sizes, through which comparatively little direct sunlight comes, except for a few minutes a few days in the year. They can be decorative and pleasing aesthetically. They are not inexpensive, and they may present a serious cleaning problem and become a nesting place for birds.

3. With a horizontal projecting shelf reaching out from the building at the level of the floor above. Such shelves may extend out 10 or 12 ft or even more, and on the south and west sides, where the sun may be a particularly difficult problem, will almost completely shut out the direct sunlight. The lower western sun in late afternoon may make trouble, but on lower floors at least, trees and shrubs should prevent difficulty. But if shelves project too far, they shut out a good deal of light and may make the use of artificial light necessary throughout the day except during bright sunlight periods. There may be a temptation to use these projections as porches for strolling, or as outdoor reading areas, but this involves various hazards; readers inside may be distracted and books may be passed from porches to the ground without proper authorization. On the whole, because of the limited number of days during the academic year when the weather and the sun make them satisfactory for use, outdoor reading areas in most of the Temperate Zone are seldom worth what they cost. This situation may change as summer schools become more common, and they may prove very useful in the Tropics and the parts of the Temperate Zones nearby.

The difficulty with all of these methods of screening from the inside or the out is that they are expensive and their total cost, added to that of the glass itself, tends to be greater per square foot than a good masonry wall. They may also let in so much light as to make higher intensities of artificial light desirable. They can, however, contribute considerably to the decoration of the building. Always remember that covering large areas with a few folds of cloth—light colored glass-fiber curtains, for instance—is functional in preventing glare and also has aesthetic advantages both day and night, but especially at night for the reader, when curtains cover the hard, unpleasant, reflective surface of the glass; they also might be said to humanize the space enclosed. Lighting to a low intensity the area outside will also help.

But windows, particularly very large windows, also make it more difficult to heat and cool the building properly. Single glass does not keep out the cold or the heat as well as a masonry wall, particularly if the latter is satisfactorily insulated. Closely related to this objection are several other facts. If the building has winter humidification, water will condense and run down the windows when the outside temperature falls below the freezing point. If windows are sealed shut and the air conditioning breaks down, a serious situation develops; yet, unless the windows are sealed shut, someone sooner or later will open them, and the effectiveness of the air conditioning will be ruined. It might be added that with air conditioning in an area where the electricity is likely to break down and where repairmen are difficult to reach, it may be unwise to seal the windows. In a great city where such mishaps are less likely and where competent repairmen may be readily available, windows can be sealed without fear of serious consequences. A limited number of them should be openable by a key so that one can use them to get out onto a porch roof or elsewhere outside the building. It must be remembered that sealed windows must be cleaned from the outside, and the necessity may present a serious problem. Double-glazed windows are nearly always sealed and, as already indicated, they are practically necessary if the humidity in the winter is to be kept up above the middle thirties when the outside temperature falls below the freezing mark.

In the section on seating the author suggested that an economical arrangement is to place tables at right angles to a wall, glass, plaster, or masonry, beside an aisle that is required under any conditions. If this seating can be adjacent to a window, even a small one, it is attractive, although this arrangement is not necessary for an open carrel. A small closed carrel, without a window, will rarely be popular. The same holds true even for a larger faculty study. Any room with much less than 60 sq ft that is completely closed and has no windows will be objectionable to many persons. Glass in the door through which the occupant can look down a stack aisle or into an area with outside light will help, as

will a clerestory window near the ceiling. The use of bright colors will also be helpful. With even a small window, 40 to 50 sq ft may be adequate for a completely closed room. If the area is completely open, except for a front and back partition high enough so that the top of the head of the person in front cannot be seen, a carrel 3 ft wide and 4 ft on centers may be entirely satisfactory without windows. "Stall" may be a better term for a carrel of this size. It is worth repeating here that with the use of color and with seating arranged so that the reader does not face blank walls on both sides, as well as in front of him, most persons will very soon forget about the lack of windows. This has been proved in many recently built university libraries.

Doors. Doors serve to bar or permit entrance and exit to a building and to bar or connect interior spaces in the structure; on occasion they are useful also for acoustic purposes and to prevent the spread of fire. Each of these functions should be kept in mind, as well as the cost of doors, their psychological effect, and their effect on architectural harmony and ornamentation. They may be hinged at the top or side. They may slide horizontally or vertically, or revolve. If they are hinged, it must be remembered that they can swing a full 180° only when the hinge is on the side of the opening where the full swing is expected and where there is wall space available. Door closers may also prevent it. If the door is hinged so that it can go in both directions, it can with difficulty be made tight enough to avoid drafts and the transfer of sounds to the other side. It is important to place each door with traffic patterns and circulation definitely in mind. Fig. 10.1 shows how the door at the main entrance of the Widener book stack, until a recent change was made, led everyone directly past the stack reading areas when it would have been possible to have the entrance adjacent to the main aisle that is 30 ft away from the carrels.

Fig. 10.2 shows a door placed improperly and seriously complicating the use of a small area.

Double or French doors, one opening to the right and the other to the left, with no upright between, are unfortunate, particularly if there is much traffic and if the doors are heavy, because a person coming from the outside and pulling the right-hand door toward him tends to swing in front of the left-hand door, and if a person is coming out at the same time unnecessary complications arise. Where there are pairs of doors

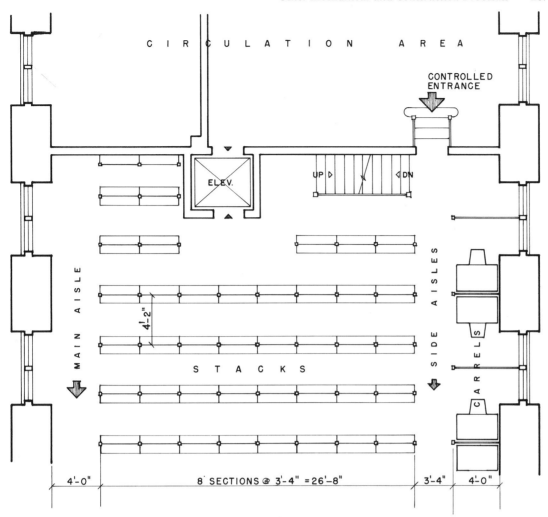

FIG. 10.1 Main entrance to Widener Library stack. The entrance leads directly to a secondary aisle which passes carrels. If it had been placed at the upper left of the drawing, it would have saved 60 ft of walking for most users and made the carrel area quieter and less restless.

at a busy entrance, both should be hinged on either the right or the left. (See Fig. 10.3.)

Ellison doors, which are hinged some 6 in. from the side of the door, may be useful for doors 4 ft wide or more, as they are easier to open. They may be dangerous when used by children; they are more expensive and are not desirable for narrow doors.

Doors in a library should almost always have a glass panel at eye height, large enough to enable both short and tall persons to see through them so as to prevent accidents, as well as to make supervision possible, even if supervision is not ordinarily required.

Folding doors are sometimes used to divide areas temporarily; for instance, to make a small classroom into two seminars, or to break up the

staff lounge so that part of it can be used for other purposes. These doors may be wide enough so that they become partitions, in fact if not in name. They may be collapsible or of the hinged type. The chief problem in connection with them is that they are seldom sufficiently soundproof. The door itself may have all the required attributes, but the sliding mechanism at both top and bottom has gaps through which the sound is carried. If this is a serious matter, two folding doors parallel to each other can be installed with an air space in between—a method which is expensive. The great virtue of the folding door is the flexible division of space which it provides and the fact that it is easier to operate and install than is a sliding door panel.

Hardware. The selection of the hardware to

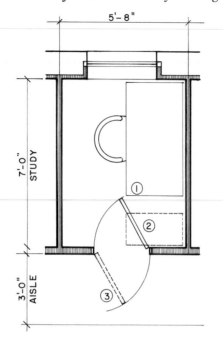

DOOR SWING

1. OBSTRUCTED BY FURNITURE
2. DISPLACES FURNITURE
3. OBSTRUCTS AISLE

FIG. 10.2 **Poorly placed door. This door interferes seriously with the use of the room. If the door had been placed farther to the left and hinged on the left, it could swing inward without difficulty.**

be used in a library is important enough to require the attention of both the librarian and the building maintenance department, as well as that of the architect. The better the quality, the lower the maintenance and replacement needs in the future. The importance of quality in hardware cannot be overstressed.

Door hardware that contains moving parts, such as a latch, if it is installed where it will be continuously turned and operated by the general public, will require considerable upkeep no matter how good the quality. Thus, it is advisable to have most, if not all, of the heavily used doors operate on the "push-and-pull" principle and confine the use of latches and similar hardware to the staff areas of the library.

Push-and-pull doors require mechanical closing devices. These may be installed at the top of the door, incorporated in the hinges of the door itself, or recessed in the floor. The third method results in the best appearance but needs considerable maintenance and is more expensive than either of the other two. The self-closing device located at the top of the door has generally proved to be the most satisfactory method from the over-all point of view. In addition, modern hardware designers have considerably improved its appearance and, with only a small

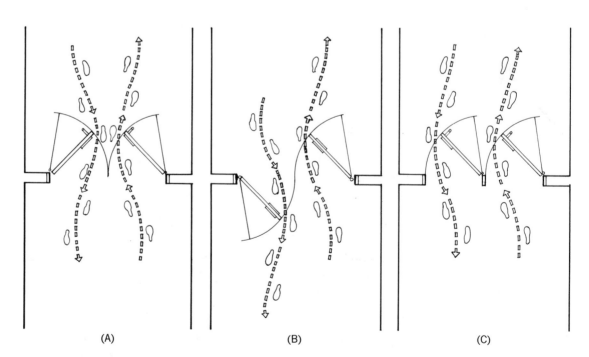

(A)   (B)   (C)

FIG. 10.3 **Double-door problems.** (*A*) Doors opening one way only with danger of collision when used from opposite directions at the same time. Not recommended. (*B*) Doors opening both ways used from opposite directions at same time present less danger of collision, but if they are outside doors with uneven air pressure, they may be difficult to keep closed when not in use. Possible. (*C*) Doors opening one way only, but each hinged on left-hand upright. No danger of collision. Recommended.

sacrifice in durability and some increase in cost, have produced devices that may be concealed either within the door or in the frame above. The devices often called "bomber hinges" are most frequently used today on desk-counter gates, rather than on full-size doors.

Self-closing doors are usually required for public safety at the entrances to stairs and other fire-protected shafts and spaces. They are necessary, in any case, on outside and vestibule doors if the air pressure, temperature, or humidity conditions within the library are to be maintained at levels different from those outside.

Sometimes, because of pressure difference, if outside doors are large and heavy they become difficult to open, and automatic opening devices by means of "magic carpets" or "electric eyes" are useful, but they are expensive to install and require continuous maintenance. "Assist" hardware is also available which helps or assists once a person has pushed against the device, and which decreases somewhat the cost of maintenance. There is also a mechanical device already referred to, called the "Ellison hinge," which decreases the area of the door that one pulls open without decreasing the usable width of the opening. It is considerably more expensive than the normal hardware. Its action is peculiar and feels strange to the user until he becomes accustomed to it. Although helpful on wide doors, it definitely seems to interfere with comfortable passage through a narrow door and may be dangerous when used by children.

Double doors should also be avoided if possible, especially if they need to be locked. It is better to install two single doors side by side than a double door. Then the two traffic lanes which the double door is intended to serve can be separated from each other rather than brought together, and the problems of hardware and locking have been simplified.

If turning knobs and latches are used, it is wise, from a maintenance point of view, to have the hardware devices incorporated into a large "escutcheon" plate rather than individually mounted in or on the door. This strengthens the entire assembly and enables it to take more abuse from the users.

Locks are most important hardware items, and most large institutions have standardized the locking system they use in all their buildings. This standardization frequently restricts the choice of hardware and limits the price advantage of competitive bidding for the supply.

This need no longer be so, because of the invention of removable "key-way" devices which enable any type of keying to be inserted easily into any lock. In the end, the decision on this matter of locks should be determined by the policy of the institution rather than by the librarian, the architect, or the planning team.

The method of keying, on the other hand, is in the province of the librarian, and he should determine which areas he would like to have locked and who should have keys for them. From this determination, a system of master and submaster keys will be developed to suit the needs of the library. A locksmith can, without too much difficulty, change the keying of any particular lock after it has been installed. This change is made even more rapidly and easily if the removable key-way device referred to above is installed.

The locking of exit doors is usually a special problem, as public safety requires that in any emergency these doors should be capable of being opened from the inside without the use of a key. This requirement introduces two difficulties:

First, if the exit door is in an unsupervised area, it may be used by a reader to leave the library without passing a control point. This defect can be largely overcome by installing on the door a mechanical or electric alarm, which goes off if the door is opened, and also by requiring glass or other breakable material to be broken to open the door.

Second, if the operation of the exit door is push-and-pull and it is to be locked from outside use, some method of releasing the lock from the inside must be installed. The device usually employed is a "panic bar" or "handle," which releases the locking mechanism when pushed. However, the public safety laws frequently allow the use of small knob turns on the locking device if no considerable number of people will be in the building when it is locked.

Roofs. Roofs may be flat or they may be sloped, or pitched, as the inclination is sometimes called. A sloped roof has the advantage of letting water run off and consequently is easier to keep waterproofed. Heavy snow will tend to slide off, but the live load from wind will be increased. It may also provide inexpensive mechanical space in the attic, if that is desired. But the greater its slope, the larger its square-foot area and cost.

A flat roof is always difficult to make watertight. It must be custom-built in a single unit and seamless. With either a flat or a sloping roof, insulation should be used to reduce the heat loss in winter and the gain in summer. Flashing problems should not be forgotten. Do not try to economize here, as a leaky building—walls as well as roofs can be involved—is almost impossible to correct after the construction is finished without completely rebuilding the affected area. Projections of any kind introduce a potential leak and make it more difficult to waterproof successfully. The base around a chimney presents a hazard of this kind, as do skylights. Some architects tend to recommend skylights, particularly for the lighting of large reading areas, and sometimes over courts in the center of a building where there is an opening to the roof. Skylights are still being installed, although a good many academic and other institutions have given them up because of the danger of leaking. It is suggested that they always be challenged and not accepted without the approval of all concerned.

Skydomes and similar prefabricated roof-lighting devices come with flashing rings to mount on roof curbs and when properly installed have proved to be much more satisfactory than the skylight built on the job.

Ceilings. Ceilings are of interest from a number of points of view. They are important in connection with lighting and acoustics, as was seen in the sections of the previous chapters on the subject. The clear height of ceilings above the floor is dealt with in section 5.1. The upkeep of ceilings is often difficult because scaffolding must be erected. Ceilings should not be forgotten in connection with fire protection, as the use of combustible material there tends to spread fire rapidly.

Furred-in or false ceilings are often used to conceal air-conditioning ducts, to provide a radiant heating surface, or to make it possible to install lighting flush with the false ceiling. Ducts, of course, can be exposed, but they do not give so finished an appearance and tend to be dust and dirt collectors. Some architects prefer to have all the ceilings on one level of the building at the same height above the floor, while others believe that a shift as one passes from one room to another is unobjectionable. It is suggested that when one part of a floor is occupied chiefly by book stacks, where a lower ceiling is more acceptable than elsewhere, the ducts can

sometimes be confined to this section and greater height thereby made available in the reading areas.

Floors and Floor Coverings. The base for library floors may be of concrete, terrazzo, marble, ceramic tile, or wood; glass has sometimes been used in book stacks. Concrete is often left uncovered in little-used basements or even in book stacks, but should be treated with a filler and then painted in order to prevent dust from becoming troublesome. Terrazzo is often used in entrance lobbies and toilet rooms, but it may be slippery and dangerous when wet. Marble floors are expensive, and any but very hard marble, particularly if used on stairs and in heavily traveled areas, will wear down; marble stairs may eventually become dangerous.

Ceramic tile is long-wearing and can be considered in heavily used corridors where noise is not a problem. Wooden floors, particularly of hard wood, can be handsome and long-wearing, but require considerable care to keep them in good condition. They have the advantage of permitting refinishing. Soft wood floors do not wear so long but can be suitable in certain areas. Glass floors, used in book stacks originally with the idea of letting light through from the floor below to light the bottom shelves, are little used now. They tend to produce static in cold, dry winter weather, and in time they lose strength and can be broken by a sharp blow with disastrous results.

Most concrete library floors today, except those mentioned above, have a covering of one kind or another. These coverings may come in tile form with tiles generally 9 or 12 in. square, or even 12 × 24 in. They may come in different patterns. Many of them are available in sheet form. These tiles include rubber, linoleum, cork, asphalt, and vinyls of various kinds. Each has its advantages and disadvantages. Cork, for instance, has high sound absorption and resilience, qualities which make it suitable for libraries, but it is difficult to maintain. The wear and the maintenance costs can be reduced by coating the tiles with a penetrating sealer and wax or some other recommended coating, such as varnish or lacquer. Cork should not be used for on- or below-grade concrete floors which have not been adequately waterproofed. It is particularly important to have it laid on a good, dry, level, rigid, and clean subfloor. The quality of cork available in the American market has fallen off in recent years. Cork can still be found in some of the older libraries that has not had particularly good care and is in good condition after fifty years, but much of the cork that has been installed since the Second World War has not lasted. Some institutions have found that Spanish cork is more satisfactory and long-wearing than the cork tile manufactured in this country.

Rubber floor coverings in general have good resistance to wear and residual indentation, and they are resilient and make a comfortable floor. They are generally not satisfactory on concrete floors in direct contact with the ground, unless the concrete slab has been waterproofed.

Linoleum, either in tile or sheet form, is less expensive than rubber tile. It has been on the market for many years and has had a good record. Its resistance to wear is satisfactory. It should not be installed on floors in direct contact with the ground. Heavy battleship linoleum has in the past made a particularly satisfactory library floor, but it is difficult or impossible today to find a good quality linoleum without importing it.

Vinyl floor coverings have come onto the market in recent years. They tend to be less expensive than cork, rubber, and linoleum. Their surface is generally somewhat harder and, as a result, noisier, although the noise can be reduced by the use of a felt base. Vinyl asbestos has some advantages over regular vinyl.

Asphalt tile is one of the least expensive of floor coverings. It is one of the few types that can be satisfactorily installed on a below-grade concrete floor subjected to appreciable moisture from the ground, but it is not as resistant to wear and indentation as the other floors. In heavily used areas it will not last many years, but it has often been found satisfactory in restricted stack areas. It is considerably noisier than most of the other coverings.

Carpets. Within the past ten years carpets, which had been used in libraries previously only in prestige areas and perhaps in the librarian's office or the board room and not often there, have been installed on a large scale in a constantly growing number of libraries throughout the United States and elsewhere. The areas chosen for carpeting have varied considerably. In some libraries it has been installed in reading rooms only; in others throughout the building, except perhaps in little-used book stacks. Some libraries have used it in the entrance lobby, on the basis that it was a first-class shoe cleaner and reduced maintenance requirements throughout the rest of the building; others have left it out of the lobby because it would wear out so quickly there.

The basic problems to be decided in connection with carpet might be said to be six in number, as follows:

1. What type and quality of carpeting should be purchased? The generally agreed-upon conclusion is that a carpet of first-class quality is justified because it will wear so much longer. There may be some dispute about which type is the best in this respect. In general a dense, closely packed pile will keep its looks and texture. Tightly twisted yarns can be expected to wear better than loosely twisted ones.

The sharp heels on women's shoes endanger the person wearing them and damage the carpet; in fact they shorten the life of any floor covering. Any carpet that becomes heavily soiled will tend to mat and will be difficult to clean. Wool has always made a fine carpet, having natural resiliency and ability to recover from crushing, but good nylons and acrylics do well in this respect also. It seems fair to say that the way the carpet is made is as important as the type of fiber used.

Durability of colors is also a matter of importance. Watch out for fading, which may make it difficult to patch or to match the carpet at a later time. Some shades tend to fade more rapidly than others. Some have superior qualities in concealing soiling. Light colors quite naturally show soil most and combinations least. Soil resistance and easy cleaning are quite different matters.

2. How does the original cost of installation compare with that of other possible floor coverings? It does not pay to order any but high-quality carpet, and the cost of any quality carpet is without doubt considerably greater than that of the most expensive cork, rubber, or vinyl tile or sheet covering that might be used as an alternative.

3. How do the wearing qualities compare with other possible coverings? Although the best modern carpet has first-class wearing qualities, the carpet manufacturers do not claim that it will wear as long as the best-quality vinyl, rubber, and cork tile.

4. What about the upkeep? This question of

maintenance is a debatable feature. The carpet manufacturers claim that vacuum cleaning at frequent intervals will cost considerably less than the cleaning, buffing, and waxing which is advisable for other coverings, and that this factor will more than make up for the extra cost of the original installation and also for the cost of replacement if it is found that the carpet will not wear as long as another covering that might have been selected. This claim is based on the experience of hotels and to some extent upon schools that have used carpet in recent years. The decision on this point may well turn on the question of the level of maintenance that the institution is accustomed to provide for its floor coverings. A first-class hotel vacuum-cleans its carpets every day, but how often do other floor coverings anywhere in a college or university, including the library, receive anything more than a quick sweeping with a brush-broom? How often are floors buffed and waxed, a procedure which, it must be admitted, is time-taking and expensive? Many libraries economize in maintenance, and many buff floors only semioccasionally and wax them perhaps once or twice a year if they are the type that need waxing. Check with your maintenance department on this point before making your decision. Be sure you are comparing like with like.

5. Does carpet have other advantages in addition to a possible saving in maintenance cost? Here there can be no question. Carpets have first-class acoustical properties, good enough so that costs for other acoustical installations may be reduced. In some places acoustical tile in the ceilings will be unnecessary with carpets on the floor. Sometimes, where there is a special acoustical problem, carpets will save money. In recent years, with low ceilings and intensive space utilization, libraries have too often presented very unsatisfactory acoustic conditions. Carpets are pleasant to stand on, as well as quiet to walk on. There is no other floor covering, not even the best quality of rubber tile or cork, which will be as comfortable for a library attendant to stand on for hours at a time as a good carpet.

A less definite but not to be forgotten advantage of carpets is the effect on the behavior of the users of the library. In schools it has been found that children seem almost automatically to behave better with carpets. Rooms are quieter; the whole aspect and atmosphere changes; and everyone is more likely to conduct himself as he should. This has undoubtedly been the experience in the few years that carpeting has been used in schools. How long this will last is hard to say.

6. What about patching or repair when the covering is damaged? One of the problems with the maintenance of all floors comes from the danger of scorching from cigarettes, from staining through careless use of ink, and so on. The carpet manufacturers insist that while a live cigarette may damage a carpet just as it will other floor coverings, or table tops for that matter, it is possible to cut out a small section and patch it just as easily or more easily than with tile, and certainly more easily than with sheet material of one kind or another. Ink stains, if gotten at promptly, can be cleaned or in the case of an emergency can be patched. There probably has not been enough experience as yet to give a definite answer as to the cost.

Carpets certainly should be seriously considered for fairly large sections in new libraries. Libraries that have used carpets should be questioned about their experiences. The Undergraduate Library at the University of South Carolina and the library of Carleton University in Ottawa, Canada, were among the first to install them and have the longest experience on a large scale, but by the time this volume is published, literally dozens of libraries throughout the country will have used carpets to a greater or lesser extent. It is suggested that you check with them in regard to their experience. Do what you can to figure out the total long-run cost, which should take into account the original installation, maintenance, and the frequency of replacement. You will have to decide for yourself the value of the undoubted advantages that carpet has. The author hopes that carpet will prove to be satisfactory from the economic standpoint because of its other advantages, but he doubts if the question has as yet been answered with complete satisfaction.

If you decide to install carpets in your library, you have four decisions to make in selecting them. What color do you want? What texture and pattern? What quality will you choose? How much are you prepared to pay? Then keep three other points in mind:

1. The padding or underlay on which the carpet is placed should not be neglected. A good base will lengthen the life of the carpet.

2. Remember that book trucks are used in libraries, that their wheels must be adapted to carpets, and that carpets should be of a type that will not present too much of a problem to the book truck.

3. Be sure to realize that, if you use carpet in areas with very heavy traffic such as stairs and main traffic arteries, this is the place for the best quality so as to prevent too rapid wear.

Plumbing. The problems of plumbing are many and specialized. To solve the mechanical ones, it is usual to employ a sanitary engineer to be responsible for the layout, the operations, and the legality of the installation. However, a number of questions ought to come to the attention of the planning team before they are answered. They are concerned mainly with the problems of (1) location, (2) noise, and (3) maintenance.

Location. Toilet facilities should be located in the library so that they are adjacent and convenient to the main traffic arteries and also so that both the visual and audible disturbances attendant upon their use will be isolated from the reading areas. The practical requirements of plumbing must also be kept in mind. Plumbing code regulations have not yet been standardized and vary considerably from place to place, but all of them require each toilet fixture to be equipped with a "soil" and a "vent," the first a pipe which leads down to the basement and the sewer, the second a pipe which leads up to the roof and the atmosphere. Fixtures may be arranged in batteries, either horizontally or vertically, and their respective soils and vents may be combined. Naturally the more this combined piping principle is applied, the less expensive is the installation. Thus the grouping of toilets and other plumbing facilities adjacent to one another in plan and above one another in section is economical and desirable.

Sometimes the bottom floors of a library are below the level of the sewer to which the plumbing fixtures are to connect. In this case, fixtures on these levels should be reduced to a minimum, as they will have to be drained through an ejector which will pump their sewage up to the sewer above. A large installation of this sort is expensive to install, occupies space, and must be maintained. Its use should be avoided wherever practicable.

In locating plumbing facilities, one must also remember that they form inflexible elements in the plan. The piping connections, the toilet stalls, the fixtures and the marble and tile finishes generally used in connection with fixtures all combine to make these elements almost as permanent as stair and elevator wells. In any case, they are expensive to change and difficult to move. For these reasons, toilets are often grouped with the stairs and elevators and vent shafts in such a manner that they interfere as little as possible with the flexibility of the spaces for readers and books, which form the bulk of the library.

The number of toilet fixtures required in any library varies with the number of reader accommodations provided. Often this number is regulated by law. It may be affected by the proximity or remoteness of the dormitory or other similar facilities. The number of seats provided in the library is, except under unusual circumstances, in excess of the number of readers present at any time. For this reason, it is acceptable and usual library practice to provide at least one plumbing fixture for each 35 seating accommodations in anticipation that this fixture normally can be expected to serve 25 readers. In tabulating fixtures in proportion to reader seats, urinals and water closets but not lavatories are counted. The total number of fixtures required should then be distributed in one or more toilet rooms for each sex so that they are as convenient as practicable to the readers. Often separate facilities are provided for both staff and building help.

In all toilet rooms in a library it is wise to install shelves for the depositing of books and other papers while the facility is used. This is not only a convenience for readers but also a protection for the library materials.

Other plumbing fixtures, in addition to toilets, are required, such as janitors' and work sinks, wash basins in work areas, kitchenettes, and drinking fountains. All of these, except the last, should be inaccessible to the public. Drinking fountains present a hazard if they are located in the vicinity of book shelves. They should be isolated so that no water damage to books, except those carried by the users, can be expected. These other plumbing fixtures should also be grouped with the toilets if the maximum economy of installation is to be realized.

Noise. The problem most frequently neglected in connection with plumbing fixtures is the noise resulting from their use. This is important in a modern library if the toilet facility is adjacent to reader and book-storage areas. Unfortunately, the most efficient and easily maintained fixtures seem to be the noisiest. When this is coupled with the fact that the hard washable finishes used in toilet rooms are anything but sound absorbing, the noise of a flushed water closet can create a din which can easily penetrate beyond the walls of the toilet, unless special precautions are taken.

Be sure that the sanitary engineer has selected the quietest fixtures consistent with ease of maintenance and efficiency of operation. This applies to water closets and also to urinals and lavatories.

Do not accede to a ventilation requirement for an air supply through the doorways to the facility. This is an economical solution, but it leaves openings through which the sounds can escape into adjacent areas. It is better to soundproof the doors by weatherstripping and provide a self-contained ventilation system. In any case, all openings through the toilet-room walls should be protected with sound-absorbing boxes, and the walls themselves should be built so as to provide a reasonable amount of sound isolation.

The incidence of sound within the toilet room can be reduced by the use of an acoustical ceiling. This will soften the sounds within the room itself, will make it a much more habitable place, and at the same time will reduce the volume of sound that may be transmitted to the adjacent spaces through the walls and doors.

Maintenance. The best-quality plumbing fixtures and accessories are the most economical in the end, because the cost of their maintenance will be considerably reduced. In any public facility, the abuse given to both fixtures and accessories is considerable and must be offset by a first-class installation of the best and strongest available.

Fixtures that are mounted off the floor will make cleaning easier. Modern water closets are made for wall mounting, as are lavatories and urinals. When these are combined with ceiling and wall-mounted stall divisions, the floor of a modern toilet room can be kept free of obstruction to the cleaning process. When fixtures are wall-mounted, the fastenings must be strong enough to resist the pressures imposed by a person leaning his entire weight on the front edge. This is particularly true of lavatories. Usually

they are installed with large metal brackets embedded in the wall and floor, called "chair carriers," which receive and resist pressures imposed on the fixtures.

Often a floor drain is installed in the toilet room in order to help the cleaning up or hosing-out process. If one is installed, mopping or hosing must be done regularly; otherwise the trap, or the water seal that prevents the escape of sewer gases through the fixture, will dry out.

The arrangement of fixtures within the toilet room is important, both for appearance and privacy. An open space immediately inside the entrance to the lavatory area makes a better impression, and the use of screens beside the urinals, as well as stalls around the water closets, contributes to privacy. It is always desirable to enter large toilet rooms through vestibules, and the rooms themselves should allow space for traffic and waiting.

The floors and walls of a toilet room should be of a hard solid material easily cleaned. Marble, tile, and terrazzo are usually used. The setting of these materials on the floor generally requires a "bed," and the structural floor must be recessed in order to accommodate it; otherwise the floor of the toilet room would be higher than the surrounding areas. This recessing adds to the cost of construction, as it interferes with the rapidity of execution desired during the rough construction period. Today, fortunately, adhesives are made which can successfully fasten tile to a concrete floor without the use of a bed.

The type of plumbing that has been discussed above is termed "sanitary." The soil piping from the fixtures leads to a sanitary sewer and a disposal plant. Frequently, plumbing must be installed also to drain off the "storm" water both from the roofs and the grounds around the building. Since the introduction of storm water into the sanitary sewer is likely to overtax the disposal facilities and piping, the storm-water piping is generally connected to a storm sewer with independent and less elaborate methods of dispersal. Interior storm-water conductors, which run horizontally, should be insulated. Otherwise the cold rain water in the conductor will cause condensation.

In connection with construction materials and mechanical installations of all kinds, two final points should be made.

1. Very rapid changes are being made in materials available and in their design. Older materials that were once standard may no longer be on the market. It is difficult, for instance, if not impossible today to purchase battleship linoleum or cork tiles equal to those available a generation ago. The cold cathode lighting tubes that were quite popular at one time are now difficult to procure.

The physiological, psychological, and even sociological effects of new developments should not be forgotten. Some persons object strenuously to, and are unhappy with, air conditioning of any kind. The same holds true for fluorescent lighting. Some insist on natural light throughout daylight hours. In this latter connection, the architect should be sure to know something about climatic conditions, including temperature, humidity, rain, wind, and solar radiation for the particular location under consideration. Local customs and habits should be kept in mind. Temperatures that are entirely satisfactory in England may be completely unacceptable in the United States. These conditions require special attention and discussion between the architect and his client so as to prevent any possible misunderstanding.

Buildings are still known to collapse because of faulty construction, faulty engineering techniques, materials, or sometimes earthquakes, unprecedented floods, and hurricanes. In most areas building codes are in force to minimize such hazards. They should, of course, be observed. It should also be noted that building codes may be out of date and require what are obviously unnecessary precautions and expense. This is a problem that may be outside the province of the librarian, but certainly his institution should be in a position to speak up and try to obtain suitable changes.

10.2 Fire and Other Hazards

This section will deal with hazards of all kinds. Proper attention to them and to their causes during the planning process can reduce or avoid them altogether. They may be grouped as follows: (1) fire, (2) water, (3) acts of God, (4) insects and mold, (5) theft, vandalism, and mutilation, and (6) injury to handicapped persons.

These headings overlap to some extent. Water damage, for instance, may and frequently does result indirectly from fire. Earthquakes, which come under the heading of "acts of God," can bring destructive fires in their train. Insect infestation and mold may stem from humid conditions which in turn are the result of dampness. All six will be dealt with here. The first is covered in much greater detail in a volume entitled *Protecting the Library and Its Resources: A Guide to Physical Protection and Insurance,* a report on a study conducted by Gage-Babcock and Associates, Inc., and published in 1963 by the Library Technology Project of the American Library Association. The volume should be examined with care by one or more members of any library building planning team to make sure that proper use is made of the information found therein.

Fire Hazards. Fire hazards in a library stem in almost all cases from one of four sources:

1. The heating plant, where there may be defective or overheated chimneys or equipment, hot ashes and coals, or escaping gas

2. Wiring used for lighting, heating, electrical devices and appliances

3. Careless housekeeping and smoking habits and use of matches, the storage of combustibles near heaters, and spontaneous combustion

4. What might be called outside intervention, such as lightning, earthquakes, arson or fire originating elsewhere, or fires resulting from the use of welding and cutting torches by maintenance and other workers

Each of these sources has been responsible for a considerable number of library fires, and the danger is likely to continue. The third and fourth sources might be said to fall outside the scope of this volume, except as good construction can prevent the spread of fire, if careless housekeeping or smoking habits have started it, and should also tend to lessen the risks from lightning or earthquakes by providing a structure and equipment which will result in minimizing the hazards.

Since approximately one-fourth of library fires have their source in defects in the heating plant, it is evident that all parts of the heating installation that could become overheated to the point where fire might result should be designed and installed so as to prevent the possibility of fire. The same holds true for the electrical services. The engineers designing them should be competent and should pay proper attention to the related building codes, which have been prepared to reduce risks and hazards of all kinds. The workers who install the heating plants should, of course, be competent also, and their work should be checked by experienced and knowledgeable inspectors. United States National Codes of both the Electrical and the Heating, Ventilating, and Air Conditioning Societies should be used as a minimum standard.

But with the best of care, even if the construction itself is satisfactory, accidents may happen, although the better the quality of construction, the less chance there will be of fire starting. There are five major types of construction. They are listed below in order of cost, from the cheapest to the most expensive. The fire risks decrease as the more expensive types are used.

1. Wood-frame construction, in which the structural members are wood.

2. Ordinary construction, in which the supporting walls are brick, the floors are wooden joists, the interior finish too often conceals space in which fire can spread, and there is little protection for the stair shafts. This was a common type of construction in older libraries. It can be used, however, with protection for the stair shafts by isolating them with brick walls and self-closing fire doors. The wooden floor and roof joists can be and often are protected with fireproof plaster, and the concealed spaces can be fire-stopped. If these three steps are taken, the risks are greatly diminished. If they are not, this construction is little better than the wood-frame type. Consequently, construction of this kind is of three grades: (*a*) where no attempt to protect from fire is made; (*b*) partially fire-protected with fireproof floors but with a roof with wooden rafters; and (*c*) fire-protected.

3. Noncombustible construction of steel or steel and masonry with exposed structural members. Exposed structural members do not necessarily mean exposed *to view*, but exposed *to fire*, that is, not protected from contact with a fire if it should start.

4. Mill construction, which is sometimes called "slow-burning," with thick brick walls, floors of 3- or 4-in. planks, or 8- to 12-in. posts and girders of wood, and no concealed places behind interior finish. This is desirable construction for many buildings and is used especially in factories and warehouses.

To the layman, the exposed steel and masonry construction in 3 might seem safer and more fire-resistant than the wooden mill type. But remember that when steel is exposed to fire it will quickly buckle and collapse. Mill construction uses structural members of wood at least 3 in. in thickness. When they are exposed to fire, they will, of course, burn, but, because of size, so slowly that they will remain intact through a serious blaze, usually until the fire can be controlled.

5. Fire-resistive construction, more commonly called fireproof construction. It is usually of reinforced concrete or steel and masonry with steel structural members encased in concrete, or other fire-resistant material. This type is recommended for academic and research libraries whenever possible.

The removal or lessening of hazards will not stop fires altogether. The question of fire detection, alarm, and extinguishing must be considered.

Insurance companies tend to insist that the solution of the problem in libraries is the installation of a sprinkler system. An examination of the Library Technology Project volume referred to above shows that there are various types of sprinklers available which should be considered, but also indicates that the majority of libraries—and the author agrees—believe that the risk of water damage from sprinklers is greater than the risk of fire in most areas in a properly designed modern library building, if construction and housekeeping are up to standard. The engineers report that properly designed library stack areas are not especially hazardous and that if the eight following conditions prevail in the library, the need for introducing an additional hazard by the installation of an automatic sprinkler system throughout the whole building and particularly in the stacks would seem to be eliminated:

1. A building of fire-resistive or fireproof construction in a location with good public fire protection.

2. Division of the building into fire areas by the use of fire walls and fire doors. These areas may be as large as 15,000 sq ft and in some cases even more. Fire codes may specify the size allowed, in order to limit the spread of fire to a predetermined area. The smaller the area, the smaller the spread of fire. This problem may have to be taken up with the fire authorities or

the insurance companies. Many large areas without fire walls have been built and approved in recent years.

3. Elimination of vertical draft conditions and prevention of propagation of fire upward by means of horizontal barriers, such as fire-resistive continuous floors, enclosure of stairways and elevator shafts, and "fire-stopping" vertical mechanical shaftways.

4. A minimum use of easily combustible materials in interior finish and furnishings, through which fire spreads rapidly and poisonous gases may be generated.

5. The installation of a good detection and alarm system, properly supervised and maintained in good working order.

6. Installation of protective devices, such as automatic closing of fire doors, or the use of self-closing fire doors, cutoff of air circulation ducts, and first-aid fire-fighting equipment kept in good working order.

Automatic fire doors may lead to disaster by leaving personnel on the wrong side. The self-closing doors may not be quite so satisfactory in preventing the spread of fire, but they can be opened from either side and might be said to be more considerate of human life if not of property. Some experts in the field suggest that fire walls and fire doors are old-fashioned and out of date, going back to 1890 building codes and insurance company standards, adopted when construction methods resulted in much greater hazards than are involved in good mid-twentieth-century buildings. But always remember that unless modern construction is used, special protection, such as a sprinkler system, should be installed, and that, even with modern construction, areas containing materials or use conducive to the incidence of fire should be isolated and sprinklers should be used.

7. Careful supervision of library operations, including good housekeeping practices and also control of smoking.

8. An effective system of periodic inspection of the entire premises for unsafe fire conditions, such as defective electrical wiring, or deficiencies in the air-conditioning or heating system.

It should be added, however, that the following kinds of building situations call for serious consideration of sprinkler protection:

1. Library buildings of wooden frame construction.

2. Libraries in areas not protected by an or-

ganized fire department or more than five miles from the nearest fire department station. In the few cases that fall in this category, the use of walls to prevent the spread of flames might be preferable to sprinklers.

3. Library buildings with highly combustible interior finishes and equipment. These hazards should not be permitted to continue, and if finishes or equipment of this kind have been installed, they should be replaced rather than sprinklered.

4. Libraries located in basements or other building areas to which access for effective fire fighting is difficult.

5. Library buildings of combustible construction in areas subject to high incidence of arson. Depending upon circumstances, a fire-detection system alone might be acceptable in buildings of noncombustible construction.

6. Those rooms or areas in libraries presenting greater than ordinary hazards, such as storage and work areas, carpenter shops, paint shops, printing shops, bookmobile storage rooms, and servicing rooms, garages, and so forth.

Special attention is called to the building or the areas in buildings noted in items 1 and 6 above. It may well be that sprinklers should be installed in them, but the author ventures to suggest that for categories 2 to 5 every attempt be made to reduce the hazard and that sprinklers be used only as a last resort.

It is only fair to consider at this time the key advantages of sprinkler systems. These include proved capability on a 24-hour basis to detect, control, and, in many cases, extinguish fires before they have caused extensive damage. In addition, sprinkler systems may discharge less water in extinguishing a fire than might otherwise be used. This is because the particular sprinkler heads that open are immediately above the fire; they discharge water only into the actual combustion zone. The 15 to 20 gallons of water per minute normally discharged from a single sprinkler head can often do a far more effective extinguishing job than 250 gallons per minute discharged in a hit-and-miss manner from fire hoses.

Sprinkler systems are not generally required or installed in space occupied by offices, even though there may be furniture of wood, combustible floor coverings, and wooden wall paneling, as well as much paper in the open or stored in steel or wooden files. The fire hazard in ordinary offices is considered to be low. It would appear that sprinklers should not be required in those areas of libraries with comparable fire risks.

If the sprinkler system is not to be used, other types of fire detection and arrangements for fire extinguishing should be considered. These are described in detail in Chapter 4 of the LTP volume, and only methods of fire extinguishing with portable equipment will be discussed here. To be useful, fire extinguishers should meet four fundamental requirements:

1. They must be located properly; at least one not more than 100 ft from any person, no matter where he is; one for every 2,500 sq ft in most library areas, according to the hazards in that particular area; and at least one on each floor and one at the approach to each exit.

2. They must be in good mechanical condition, which means inspection at least annually by a competent person.

3. They must be appropriate for library use and not too large for use by staff members.

4. All staff members should be acquainted with their location and the way to use them.

The problem of fire extinguishers is complicated by the fact that there are different classes of fire—wood and paper, inflammable liquids, and those with the hazard of electrical shock. The various types of extinguishers include soda acid, water under high pressure, dry chemicals, and carbon dioxide. The soda-acid type is very effective with wood and paper fires, but may damage the books. High-pressure water is easily controlled and generally preferred to soda acid. Carbon dioxide is useful for small fires and often recommended, but is extremely dangerous to persons if used in large quantities. It is recommended especially for rare-book collections as being less damaging to books. Water under pressure under complete control so as to avoid unnecessary water damage should be considered. New types of dry chemicals recently developed may prove satisfactory. Always remember that reignition, after a fire is apparently suppressed, is a serious danger.

Smoke damage should not be forgotten. It can result from fire in a room and also from smoke coming through heating ducts. These ducts should have shutoff valves that will close automatically when smoke appears, or, if they must be closed manually, the valves should be readily accessible. The risk of fire in connection with burning grease in a kitchenette should be kept in mind, and a different type of extinguisher considered.

Special problems and their possible solution should be considered.

The building should be placed, if possible, where risk of fire from outside is small. The taller the building and the larger the area on any one floor, the greater the fire risk, other things being equal. If areas are large and there are no internal walls, risk is increased.

Danger may come from interior finishes and from open spaces with vertical drafts.

Hazardous areas should be segregated and protected with sprinklers or possibly with fire walls. These may include garage areas for bookmobiles and other library vehicles, storage for gasoline-powered lawn mowers and for flammable fuels, lubricants and paints, shipping and receiving areas, miscellaneous storage areas for recent gifts, binderies, carpenter, electrical, and print shops, heating plant, and maybe a kitchen or kitchenette.

There is danger that air-circulating-system ducts can permit the spread of fire, as well as smoke. Dampers with fusible links should be required at points at which the ducts pass through fire walls and floor. However, dampers are not a safe substitute for fan cutoff devices because they do not operate rapidly enough. Fan motors should be connected with a fire-detection system. The shutdown action is then immediate and automatic. The use of a smoke-detection device in the air-circulation system will help. Thermostats are sometimes installed in the circulating ducts to shut off the motors, but this is not recommended because damage can occur before the ducts are hot enough to actuate the thermostats. Whether or not automatic protection is provided, there should always be a conveniently located station from which the circulating system may be manually shut down by the librarian or members of the staff. Many libraries lack such manual trip stations. Others have all such controls located in the building utility areas where they are readily accessible only to the maintenance personnel.

Smoke spreading throughout a building makes evacuation of personnel more difficult. Smoke also makes it difficult to determine the exact location of the fire itself. Air-circulating systems should therefore be capable of being shut down quickly in an emergency.

Electrical services should have ample capacity for the addition of new circuits and other safety factors. When fluorescent lighting is used, each ballast should be individually fused. Protection against circuit overloading should be provided by circuit breakers as opposed to simple fuses. Special emergency circuits supplied directly from the electrical service entrance points should be used for fire detection, alarm purposes, exit lights, and exit lighting. If it appears, as is very often the case, that additional lighting is needed for exits, emergency power arrangements supplied by batteries or a stand-by generator might be considered.

Noncombustible acoustical materials should be used.

While one mezzanine stack tier produces no special hazards, a series of one above another, which was often used in the last century, does.

In spite of fire experience, too many new libraries are being constructed with open stairways running between more than two floors, often for purely aesthetic rather than functional reasons. From the standpoint of safety, proper enclosures provide safer methods of exit and also prevent the open spaces from serving as flues for fire, smoke, and toxic gases.

A building planned with few or no windows means that emergency access in case of fire may be a matter of special significance.

If the design of a new building calls for large open areas without fire walls, the over-all fire safety measures taken must compensate for the increase in the single fire risk thus presented.

Load-bearing steel retains its full strength under high temperature conditions only if it is insulated by encasement in concrete or other materials having equivalent resistance to fire and heat.

Fire-risk consultants are sometimes recommended, but be careful not to choose one who is primarily a salesman for some special piece of equipment. The right person will be hard to find. To some candidates a remote possibility becomes an immediate hazard, and neither the laws of probability nor the value, or lack of it, of the material protected has any place in his analysis. Some large institutions that are self-insured and are particularly anxious to avoid

losses but at the same time are watching their expenditures carefully, employ fire-prevention experts who may well give sounder advice than those with a different motivation.

Consider the possibility of special protection —a vault, for instance—for a shelf list or a microfilm copy of a card catalogue as insurance against total loss of the record of the library's holdings.

And, finally, always keep in mind the desirability of constant inspection to make sure that good housekeeping is observed. This is a matter of fundamental importance.

Water Hazards. Many librarians are much more worried, and properly so, about damage from water than from fire. As already noted, one source of this damage could be from sprinklers. Other obvious sources are floods from heavy rains or melting snow, water from broken pipes, faulty drains, inadequate waterproofing, and leaky roofs. If there are drains under or in the basement floor, they should be arranged so that they can be cut off in case of floods when the water level rises to a point where water could back up through them into the building. Backwater valves should always be installed.

Broken or defective water, steam, and drain pipes present special problems in libraries because of the possibility of water damage to books. In planning a new library, the architect should locate water pipes so that in case of failure they can be gotten at easily and also so that books will not be exposed to damage. At least one library, the Houghton at Harvard, has a protective apron under all water pipes, which will collect water from a leak, carry it to a safe place, and set off an alarm.

Condensation on cold-water pipes and roof conductors can be as serious as a leak and is often mistaken for one. This can be prevented by insulating the pipes, usually for economy reasons on the horizontal runs only.

Mold from too high humidity, particularly during hot weather, is another serious hazard in many areas. This is discussed in section 9.2 under heating, ventilating, and air conditioning.

Acts of God. These include primarily lightning, earthquakes, and wind. Modern library buildings have rarely been struck by lightning, and unless the building construction creates a higher than average susceptibility, this should not present a problem today.

Earthquakes are another matter. Local building codes in regions where earthquakes are prevalent have introduced design and construction requirements which greatly reduce the probability of damage from earthquakes. If your library is in an earthquake zone, be sure that proper precautions for extra strength are used, following the provisions in the California Building Codes. These sometimes present a functional problem, as they result in solid structural walls in places where a main traffic artery would be placed under normal conditions, and special care in planning circulation patterns must be taken so as to avoid complications. (See Fig. 6.14.)

Wind damage should not be a problem with a properly designed structure, but if the panes of glass are too large and the wind is very severe, glass breakage and its results may be serious. With the recent tendency toward the construction of "glass boxes," this has become a matter for concern in more than one library, particularly if the glass used is too thin and set too tight. In this connection, it should be noted that vertical fins that are used for sun protection required by too much glass tend to become noisy in a high wind and after exposure to weather may become immovable. Their design should be carefully considered.

Insects and Other Animal Life. Damage from insects, bookworms, silver fish, cockroaches, etc., has not been a significant problem in American libraries in recent years, but it has been very serious in tropical countries. Most insects dislike light. General cleanliness and good housekeeping do not please them. Ventilation and temperature control within the limits of human comfort do not satisfy them. In spite of this, various precautions should be taken. Termites in northern parts of this country, and more frequently in the South, have tended during recent years to be a problem in any wooden structure or in any part of a building where wood comes in direct or fairly close contact with the earth. They have done considerable damage in some libraries, eating out floor beams and dropping equipment and furniture to the floor below. Some major libraries, in which books are acquired from tropical countries and others where modern construction is not in vogue, may have trouble with bookworms of one type or another. If your library acquires books on a large scale from all over the world, a small fumigation chamber for the treatment of book shipments will not be out of place. It should be remembered that bookworms and other insects may be very fond of leather, wood, parchment, and glue, as well as paper, and great damage may result from their depredations.

One final point in this connection. If food is to be served in the library, the greatest care must be taken to provide for proper housekeeping, as cockroaches and mice tend to appear wherever there are food operations. This is one of the greatest objections to installation of snack bars and food-dispensing operations in a library.

Mold will develop whenever and wherever high humidity is present at the same time as high temperature. The mold spores seem to be ever present, waiting for suitable conditions to arise. Air conditioning with humidity control will solve the problem, but without it mold may grow almost anywhere in the Temperate Zone and is still more prevalent in the tropics. It is a serious problem throughout the southern United States and up the East Coast as far as New England and in the more humid sections of the Middle West. If humidity control is not possible, keep the air moving and avoid dead air pockets in basements and elsewhere, particularly during the summer dog days and after heavy rains when basements may have taken in some water.

Theft, Vandalism, and Mutilation. These are of interest in connection with library design chiefly because they can be reduced but not completely avoided by proper exit controls and supervision. Very valuable books should perhaps be kept under lock and key, although it can be remembered that unique material and volumes with the greatest value are ordinarily not salable, particularly if they have concealed library marks. Consequently, many of our great libraries with millions of dollars' worth of irreplaceable books have had no difficulties.

The best method to prevent theft of irreplaceable material is to place it on closed-access shelves. If the material must be stored in a reading area open to the public, it should be protected by locked doors on the bookcases. These books should be made available only on signature from known reliable persons, and the call slips should be kept in a safe place until the books have been returned and been examined to show that they have not been damaged.

Roland Baughman of Columbia University

writes in *Protecting the Library and Its Resources,* page 265, "In a case of a rare book collection the present insurance value would represent only the merest fraction of the probable cost of bringing together a great collection. For such libraries the only true insurance lies in the provision of maximum physical protection." This statement applies to any research collection with difficult to replace material, as well as to rare books.

For less important books which are kept on open shelves, the best protection is examination of the holdings of all readers as they leave the building.

The question of vandalism and mutilation is a much more serious one, as there is no way to prevent it when students and others have free access to book stacks and cannot always be under supervision. There is little that can be done in library planning to minimize this problem. From time to time (fortunately comparatively rarely) college students have been known to destroy books just for the sake of being destructive. The most difficult problem is mutilation, where a student cuts out a page so that he can use it elsewhere at his convenience or where he underlines what he considers the more important parts of the text. The latter has sometimes been encouraged unwittingly by professors who have forgotten that if they suggest that students do it with their own books, they are likely to do it with library books. Mutilation can be minimized if a Xerox 914 or a Docustat is available for copying at a reasonable cost.

Injury to Handicapped Persons. It is desirable to take into account the special problems of those persons who are handicapped by being confined to wheel chairs, who require crutches, who are blind or have other sight impairment, who have hearing disabilities, or who have faulty coordination due to brain, spinal, or other nerve injury, or those whose age has reduced mobility, flexibility, coordination, and perceptiveness.

Special consideration to problems of such persons should be given in planning a building. Planning should start from the outside, perhaps beginning with a parking area so designed that it will not be too difficult for a person on crutches or in a wheel chair to leave the car. Curbs and distances to the entrance may make a problem. Walks to the library should be at least 4 ft wide, should not have a grade greater than 5 per cent,

and should not be interrupted by steps. This should make it easier for a handicapped person to approach the building. At least one building entrance should be reached without going up steps, with a ramp available if necessary. The ramp should have a slope not greater than a 1-ft rise in 12 ft, or approximately 8 per cent. On at least one side and preferably on both sides a ramp should have handrails 32 in. in height and extending 1 ft beyond the top and the bottom. The ends of the handrail should not become a hazard; they will not if they are on the side of a wall; curved rather than sharp ends will help. Ramps should have a level platform before a door is reached.

Doors should have a clear opening of not less than 32 in. The door itself will have to be 34 in. This applies to both exterior and interior doors. Doors with two leaves should be avoided, unless each provides a 32-in. clear opening. This is required for wheel chairs, as well as for persons using crutches. Standard wheel chairs are 25 in. wide and cannot easily be turned in a space smaller than 63×56 in.

For the sake of occupants of wheel chairs, there should be an elevator, if the building has more than one level, with a door at least 32 in. in the clear so that a wheel chair can enter it. Stairs should have handrails 32 in. above the tread at the face of the riser. Stairs with abrupt or square nosings should be avoided, as they present a hazard for persons with restriction in knee, ankle, or hip movements. Main stairs should have risers that do not exceed 7 in., unless an elevator is available. Stairs are ordinarily something like 7½ in. high.

Slippery floors are dangerous and should be avoided throughout the library. There should be a common level throughout each floor of a building. A step up or down going from a corridor to a toilet room, for instance, should be avoided, as should door sills.

Every library should provide at least a few chairs with arms, as some persons can get up from a chair only by using the arms for support.

At least in a large library, special facilities should be provided in toilet rooms.

Detailed specifications can be found in the *American Standard Specifications for Making Buildings and Facilities Accessible to and Usable by the Physically Handicapped.* These are standards approved by the American Standards Association on October 31, 1961, and are available from the

Association at 10 East 40th Street, New York 16, N. Y. The Federal government has specifications on the subject which must be followed on Federal building projects.

Other facilities that should be watched out for in order to make them accessible to the handicapped include water fountains and a public telephone with a shelf low enough so that a person in a wheel chair can roll up to it and reach the dial. Easily approached elevators and electrical switches of all kinds are also of importance. Hazards such as low-hanging signs and ceiling lights were mentioned elsewhere. A minimum height of 6 ft 6 in. to 7 ft from the floor is recommended in order to avoid the possibility of complications.

11

Furniture and Equipment

Introduction

Furniture and equipment can be divided for many purposes into three main groups, which in government circles are often referred to as follows:

1. Fixed or built-in equipment. This would certainly include multitier book stacks, catalogue cases which are custom-built into space available in a wall (these are not recommended), and many circulation counters; it could include any book shelving fastened to the floor, carrels attached to a wall or constructed as integral part of a fixed-stack installation, etc. This equipment is customarily included in the general building contract.

2. Loose or movable equipment which might be considered reasonably permanent, such as chairs, tables, desks of some kinds, catalogue and filing cases, unattached carrels, and perhaps some audio and microfilm equipment. This is ordinarily purchased separately outside the general contract.

3. Equipment which has a limited life and must be replaced in a comparatively few years, such as typewriters.

No fixed line need be drawn, but it should be noted that shelving in book stacks and in reading areas, as well as that specially designed for the storage of nonbook material, will not be dealt with here. Reading tables are discussed in section 7.3, on types of accommodations, as well as in this chapter and elsewhere in this volume.

Appendix B, "Formulas and Tables," includes them also.

Remember that built-in equipment becomes part of the structure and is generally difficult and expensive to remove. Unless its design is good aesthetically and functionally, it may be extremely unfortunate for all concerned. Remember also that the results obtained are much more important than the classification of furniture and equipment into the three definitive mutually exclusive groups. The classification referred to above can be changed unless government policies prohibit. One well-known library-equipment firm suggests that instead of the division proposed here the most favorable prices on quality equipment might be obtained with the following grouping:

1. Steel book stacks
2. Technical library equipment
3. Occasional and decorator equipment
4. Office furniture
5. Machines
6. Carpets and draperies

Section 11.1 will take up general policies in regard to furniture and equipment, including the question of who is responsible for design and selection, whether the furniture should be stock or custom-built, contemporary or traditional, together with a discussion of quality, upkeep costs, finishes, and so on, and its relation to interior decoration. It will then go on to the problem of specifications and bidding procedures. Section 11.2 will consider special library equipment, such as card-catalogue cases, book trucks, and control and service desks.

Furniture is no less important than the topics dealt with in the ten preceding chapters and is affected by decisions in regard to most of them. It involves aesthetics, construction and functional problems, as well as costs. Furniture should be designed to fit into the module size selected for the building if good space utilization is to be obtained. Heights of ceilings must often be kept in mind as furniture is chosen. Furniture provides accommodations for readers and the housing for the collections; it has a close relationship to the other space uses in a library; and its arrangement must be carefully considered in connection with the lighting, ventilation, and mechanical and construction problems which were dealt with in Chapters 9 and 10.

Furniture is certainly such an important feature in a library that policy decisions in regard to it should not be left to the last moment. If they are delayed, the furniture and equipment selected may turn out to be unsatisfactory because they were hastily chosen. Too often the occupancy of a new building has been held up because furniture delivery was not possible, although everything else was finished and ready. Remember, then, that furniture and equipment are important and an integral part of a new library building. Particularly in a modern library with large areas undivided by partitions, the furniture often sets up the special divisions and creates the atmosphere that surrounds the readers, in addition to fulfilling its more normal functional and aesthetic purposes.

11.1 General Policies

Fairly early in the planning process general policies in regard to furniture and equipment should be agreed upon, but the time for this consensus is after the planning team is ready to go into action and not before. The matter concerns all the groups and individuals involved. Each should have an opportunity to express an opinion, even if a complete agreement for the whole group cannot be obtained. The planning team, as will be seen in Chapter 12, should consist of one or more members of the institution's administration, someone involved in building maintenance, a building planning committee representing other interested groups, including, in an academic institution, the faculty and stu-

dents, the librarian, of course, and the library or architectural building consultant, or both (if it has been decided to have them), and in some cases an interior designer in addition to the architect. The consultants, because of their experience, can be very useful.

An important policy decision regarding furniture and equipment must settle the question of who is responsible for their design and selection. The architect can properly be asked to assume direct control. He will generally want to do so, as he is the person who can expect to be blamed if the results are not satisfactory. If he is given the responsibility, he must, of course, be paid for it directly or indirectly, although not always on the same percentage basis as that for the building-construction planning. The amount may vary according to whether the architect actually designs the furniture himself or selects it from manufacturer's stock which is available. He may fall back completely on a manufacturer's consultant, keeping just enough control to make sure that the selections made fit into the whole scheme. In this event his fee should be smaller than if he does the designing. A manufacturer's consultant may take the assignment with the understanding that his firm's percentage or fixed fee for the work will be canceled if its equipment is selected. Although architects are inclined to object, the better-known library-equipment houses are prepared to accept assignments on this basis if stock material is to be selected. Some of them do not limit their work to prospects wanting stock materials.

The selection of any consultant, whether the representative of a manufacturer, an interior decorator or designer, or a librarian, should be based on his reputation for integrity, ability, and professional competence. If he has talent in design, if he has accumulated through long experience first-hand knowledge of solutions to library problems in other institutions, and if he has information on construction problems which is backed perhaps by an engineering department that can test new ideas and thereby save the library costly mistakes, he should be extremely useful. As is true of a library consultant, he can be more helpful if he is engaged while plans are still fluid. Tasks which can be assigned to him and which should be kept in mind in determining his fee may include:

1. Visits to the library's present quarters for

direct observation of the operation and for a note of existing materials.

2. Checking possible space assignments for capacity. This may involve the development and drawing of equipment layouts.

3. Offering solutions for housing special types of materials.

4. Furnishing budget estimates on equipment, even if it may not turn out to be his own, if he is a manufacturer's consultant.

5. Attending library building planning conferences and institutes.

6. Writing specifications for equipment.

7. Rendering interior-decorating service.

8. Producing special designs for equipment if they are wanted.

9. Assisting in the evaluation of equipment samples and bids.

Sometimes the architect will select an expert cabinetmaker and work with him, designing the furniture with satisfactory results. If this method is used, the institution must be sure that the furniture will be handsome and fit in the building, that it will be sturdy, comfortable, and functional, with a satisfactory finish, and that the cost is not out of line.

If an interior decorator is employed, he may make no direct charge and may simply act as a salesman and receive a commission from the manufacturer. He may sometimes have access to types of furniture not otherwise readily available. He should be selected with great care, as should the architect or any other consultant, particularly if he is inexperienced in library operations. What may be an exciting design is not always satisfactory functionally, and in too many instances equipment has not been sound in its construction.

A number of American architects who have had considerable library building planning experience have designed satisfactory carrels, with special features to fit the decor of the building as a whole. Some of them have designed chairs as well, but unless they are experts in work of this kind or have expert help, the results have not always been sturdy, convenient, and comfortable, even if they are aesthetically pleasing.

Another method frequently used in recent years is to employ an independent interior designer who is a specialist in the field and have him select and sometimes design the equipment. Specialists in the field have spoken at the Ameri-

can Library Association Building Institutes on a number of occasions, and it is evident that they can properly be considered for such an assignment. Methods of determining the fees of an interior-design consultant are discussed in section 12.2. But if it is decided to have a furniture specialist or interior designer on the planning team, the architect and his final responsibility should not be forgotten.

Whatever course of action is decided upon, be sure that the results will not look as though the architect and the furniture dealer were not on speaking terms, and that neither of them had talked with the librarian or the library consultant about the use of space. Too often results such as were found in the Widener Library at Harvard have occurred. The mammoth catalogue cases there, with 520 drawers each, were placed in a room where the two large windows had no relation to the cases and where the dimensions of the whole room were such that at least 15 per cent of the potential card capacity for an area of its size was lost. The same situation held in the Widener Main Reading Room, where each of the eleven pairs of adjacent tables lined up in a different way with the windows and the walls between the windows. In both cases the rooms, although magnificent architecturally, looked to some persons as though the furniture had simply been dropped haphazardly into them.

Stock or Custom-built. Two of the first questions to be answered in connection with the selection of furniture and equipment are whether they should be stock or custom-built, contemporary or traditional. A small library can rarely afford to consider the purchase of anything except stock furniture. To have it specially designed and built to order would be too expensive in all but exceptional cases. This situation may well be different for a very large building. If the number of chairs to be purchased runs into four figures, it may well be that a special design can be afforded, and in many cases the chairs can be less expensive than those from a standard library-equipment house with its necessarily large overhead for selling and service. The danger arises from the fact that specially designed furniture does not always stand the test of time and is less likely to be well designed structurally.

A compromise between stock and custom-built furniture was used in connection with the selection of the chairs for the Lamont building at Harvard. This was in 1947, soon after the war, when furniture stocks were depleted and the types of chairs available were limited. However, some forty samples were found. The architect and the librarian, with advice from many others, selected the three that seemed closest to what they wanted. They then called in the manufacturers and asked whether they would make certain changes in the design and what the cost would be. One of the three was chosen. The manufacturer made the alterations requested after a number of different samples were submitted. The chairs have been satisfactory in every respect except for the finish. (The finishes available at that time were not as good as they are today.) Only one chair in 1,100 has broken in sixteen years, despite the use and abuse that are inevitable in a busy undergraduate library. But this procedure could not have been carried out without the aid of an architect who was interested and knowledgeable and a manufacturer who was ready to make use of his wide experience and also work closely with the institution. Given these conditions, custom-built furniture is profitable and, as has been said, may be a money saver; but a risk is involved.

Any one of the standard library-equipment houses has the knowledge and experience to produce first-class library furniture, and their better lines will generally fulfill the requirements. Competition is keen enough to keep prices within reason. The manufacturer's special knowledge of library problems can also be used to good effect, particularly if a library consultant is not on the planning team. Once more, this is a matter for local decision after all the arguments for and against have been considered, and the local situation may well affect the choice made.

A library in a city where library equipment and furniture are manufactured can sometimes obtain considerable discounts from regular prices. A cabinet-making firm, if controlled by men belonging to the same religious group that sponsors the institution seeking equipment, may make special discounts. Much can be said for the use of furniture from manufacturers other than those who specialize in library equipment, as the furniture, especially the lounge chairs, may have aesthetic advantages. But make sure that it is sturdy and will stand the wear and tear of library use.

Contemporary or Traditional. The question of contemporary or traditional design is another perplexing one to which the author cannot provide a definite answer any more than he can say that the architectural style of the structure itself should be Gothic, Renaissance, Georgian, colonial, or modern and contemporary. Simple lines, good proportions, and carefully selected, properly cured, and well-finished wood are the primary essentials, but unfortunately they are likely to be expensive and difficult to obtain. Keep these points in mind:

1. The functional aspects, in the broad meaning of the term, which will be discussed in more detail later in this chapter, must be satisfactory. Sturdiness, comfort, appearance, and a reasonable cost are all possible with both traditional and contemporary furniture. They should come first.

2. Furniture should not be so extreme in its design that it will be dated, so that in 1970 it will be referred to, perhaps contemptuously, as obviously 1965.

Quality, Upkeep, Finishes, Cost, Function. No attempt will be made here to go into detail regarding these five points. The first four are closely related. Quality is not good if upkeep is high or if frequent refinishing is necessary. The cost should have a definite relationship to quality and should generally be considered in connection with the expected length of useful life. On certain occasions consideration might properly be given to an inexpensive contemporary model with the idea of replacing it after a few years and before it is completely outdated.

Function is not unrelated to the first four. In addition to fulfilling the functions assigned to it, furniture should be attractive, sturdy, and comfortable. Sturdiness depends to a large extent on design and materials used. Good engineering involves a practical knowledge of factory procedures and also ingenuity. The Lamont chair, which has stood up so well, has already been mentioned. Elsewhere at Harvard are large numbers of chairs of another type that can be called standard and are attractive but that are much more vulnerable. The maintenance department has in the past budgeted $1.50 a year per chair to keep them in repair and has devoted a special room in its maintenance shop for parts used as replacements. A sturdy chair and table and other pieces of furniture can be said almost to pay for themselves in a relatively few years if no repairs are required.

The back of a chair may often come in contact with a wall or, in a carrel, with the upright of the carrel behind it. A chair rail around the wall or a strip of leather or rubber attached to the back of the chair may save damage and expense.

If a chair is designed so that it is not comfortable when one tips back in it, this will relieve it of much of the severe strain that comes at the critical junction point where the back and the seat meet. Splaying the back legs will do much in this direction, although it must be admitted that young college students today will have an even greater tendency than before to put their feet on the table if they cannot tip back, and one may have to choose between two evils. Arms on the chair will also help to strengthen the above-mentioned joint. Experience at Harvard has indicated that a large majority of the men prefer armchairs, while a similar percentage of the women prefer chairs without arms. This may be just as well, as the men obviously tend to put a greater strain on the chair. But what do you do when both sexes use the same area?

No one chair will be equally comfortable for all persons. The height and depth of the seat are important, and since they are directly related to the length of the legs, both upper and lower, of the occupant, they should be considered here. The height of the back is another critical point, and in this respect many chairs, both contemporary and traditional in model, are inexcusably unsatisfactory. Be careful to make the back high enough.

Persons sitting in a chair studying intensively for a long period will find that the design of seat will have much to do with their comfort. If it is hollowed out properly, its design will go a long way toward improving the situation. A padded seat and back will help, of course, as may, to a lesser extent, pads on the arms, but the latter are seldom requested except for "occasional" chairs. All of them naturally add to the cost, not only the original purchase price but the cost of keeping the chair in repair. They can also add color and be an important part of the interior decoration. The selection of covering for the padding is another matter for consideration. Leather of good quality has in the past been better than anything else but has also been more expensive, and women are inclined to dislike its coldness. Various plastics have been used in recent years to replace leather; their quality can

be expected to improve and perhaps to equal that of leather in due course; and they should prove to be less expensive. Leather, if of good quality and properly installed, should last on the average twenty years under heavy use, depending partly on humidity control. The plastics will sometimes do well also, but a deep scratch will be somewhat more likely to start a tear, and cigarette burns, cold, and sharp blows are also hazards. Both leather and plastic can be cleaned, but light-colored plastics present a problem. Fabrics tend to become stained and unattractive, particularly if hair comes in contact with a high back, but they are now available with protective finishes. Some modern synthetic fabrics are getting to be the equal of synthetic leathers, but they are still usually more expensive. A good maintenance program with vacuum cleaning perhaps once a week will help.

Before any covering for a chair is selected, consideration should be given to all the points and to the costs of each. Don't overeconomize and be penny-wise and pound-foolish, but keep the injunction in mind that you cannot spend the same dollar twice.

Furniture and Equipment and Their Relation to Interior Decoration. Furniture and equipment are an integral part of the decor of a library. If the results are to be satisfactory and effective aesthetically, they and the structure must be planned as a single unit, not as separate entities. This does not mean that because the style of the building as a whole is, for instance, ultramodern, everything in it must be the same. It is possible to install a traditional rare-book room in an ultramodern building, just as it was possible a few years ago to add with complete success a contemporary wing to the classical Wellesley College Library. But to accomplish it, the colors and proportions in the facade must not clash, and where the break between the two styles inside is considerable, it may be wise to have a closed door.

A good architect by himself or a good architect working with his own or another interior designer can bring about the desired results, although it must be realized that in a matter of taste architects and designers do not always agree. On the whole, however, controversies are more likely to involve other members of the building team and later on, alumni and the general public, which frequently include vocal extremists representing widely different points of view. Fortunately, as time goes on, temper and violent opinions tend to tone down. Persons become accustomed to changes, just as they do to modern music and indeed modern art, and if the results are in good taste, there is little likelihood of a permanent problem arising, unless the construction has gone to extremes in one direction or another more for the sake of being different than of being effective functionally.

The Problem of Specifications and Bidding Procedures and the Selection of Bidders. These problems lie outside the scope of the book, except in very general terms. If the institution is compelled by law, as are many tax-supported organizations, to accept the lowest bid that meets specifications, these specifications must be as detailed and specific as possible to ensure the desired results from fabricators who may be unscrupulous and try to get by and make a greater profit, or who, in order to obtain the contract, have bid too low and feel that they must find some way to retrieve their losses. It must be remembered that it is fully as difficult to provide foolproof specifications for furniture and equipment as for any other part of a building. A good clerk of works—that is, the institution's watchman on a construction job—can watch the concrete mixture and keep it up to standard. He can see to it that proper waterproofing is provided in the structure. But it is more difficult to keep track of what is going on in a furniture factory. It is of first importance to have samples submitted and to insist that the finished product match the samples, which should be retained to make comparison possible. The specifications should read that "it must match a specific standard piece of furniture or be its equal," but this can be a source of difficulty. Too often disagreements occur.

The furniture may, to advantage, be included in the general contract; an ample allowance may be made for it, with the understanding that it will be selected by the architect or a representative of the institution and paid for from the allowance.

The American Library Association's Library Technology Project is sponsoring a volume on furniture specifications which will discuss construction, finishes, and aesthetic aspects; it should provide much more useful information on these matters than this chapter can attempt to do. But remember that the specifications they propose will almost have to be minimal and, if

awards must go to the lowest bidder, minimal quality may have to be accepted.

Lists of dealers who advertise furniture and equipment in library periodicals can be found regularly in the *American Library Association Bulletin* and the *Library Journal.*

11.2   Special Library Equipment

Library Tables and Chairs. These require little further discussion beyond that given in Chapter 7 and earlier in this chapter, except to reemphasize that they should be functional, comfortable, sturdy, attractive, and not unduly expensive, and that the size of each item is of importance. If their dimensions are too small, they will not be satisfactory. If larger than necessary, they will be more expensive and will occupy more space. The total square-footage requirement for seating accommodations is dealt with in section 14.5. Their arrangement, which is a matter of vital importance, is discussed in section 16.3, dealing with layouts. Appendix B includes tables dealing with square-footage requirements.

Lounge chairs fall into a special category in this group. Remember that they are acquired because they are supposed to be more comfortable. Make sure that they are. Make sure also that they are not so large that they will take more space than is necessary and will encourage their occupants to sprawl. They should generally be semi-lounge not lounge chairs. Added size, particularly if combined with quality, costs money. Semi-lounge chairs can be very useful; but do not have too many of them. Some libraries in recent years have found that they are not used as much as others. Probably no more than 8 to 10 per cent of the total number of chairs can profitably fall into this group in most libraries, and very rarely as many as 12 to 15 per cent. A large share of those used should be in the current periodical and browsing rooms and areas where persons sit temporarily to provide "a change of pace" when they are not taking notes. It will be found that their use will be increased if a small table can be placed beside them to hold books. This table between two lounge chairs separates them and makes each a more satisfactory place to sit. Chairs can be bought in units of two seats with an attached table between them; they have the advantage of being heavier and more difficult to move around.

Carrels. Carrels are sometimes called "cubicles." At Harvard they are referred to as "stalls," which at least has the advantage of one instead of two or three syllables. Their origin can be traced to the time of the early Christian monasteries. Open carrels are separated from each other by partitions on one or more sides to provide at least a certain amount of visual privacy. Closed carrels are simply small study rooms, and should provide a high degree of auditory as well as visual privacy. Each one accommodates at least one chair, a table, generally a book shelf, and perhaps a wastebasket, a coat rack, or as a substitute, a hook on one of the walls. It may have a door that can be locked. If it does, the door should be of glass or mesh wire for the sake of supervision. The latter will not break or require cleaning. A small window or even a clerestory window may make it possible to reduce the net size to a minimum of 25 sq ft or a little less of enclosed area.

For our purpose here carrels are considered to be open if without a door. An open carrel can have walls on all four sides, except for the opening for access on one side or it can be closed visually on three sides, or only two, the front and back, for instance. (If shielded on two sides only, it can be part of a table for multiple seating.) The carrel partitions, whatever the number, as well as the table itself, can be of metal or wood, or in part at least of glass or one of the plastics.

Carrels in American university libraries began to be used on a large scale as far back as 1915, when 300 of them were installed in the Widener building at Harvard. There they are used chiefly along the outside walls of the book stacks, as far as possible adjacent to a window. There is generally an aisle next to them parallel with the outside wall, and then beyond the aisle the stack ranges at right angles to the outside wall. In installations in other libraries the aisle is sometimes left out, and the carrels simply take the place of the last stack section and are at the end of blind-alley stack aisles, with or without an adjacent window. Standard spacing of stack ranges, that is, 4 ft 3 in. to 4 ft 6 in. on centers, has proved to be adequate, particularly for open carrels where the occupant can look down the stack aisles with his table occupying the space corresponding to that of the book ranges. Four ft as a minimum is possible for the spacing of carrels. The critical factors in carrel sizes are that the table should have a large enough surface for satisfactory work and that the space between the table top and the next carrel should be large enough so that the user can get into his chair without difficulty.

Beginning after the Second World War, carrels began to be placed along reading-room walls, partly as space-saving devices, when it was found that individual seating was desirable. They are used frequently along walls with large window areas which do not provide a large capacity for books. Still later, double rows of carrels were placed in reading rooms away from the walls with screens or partitions between them. (These were used on a small scale as early as 1912 when the new New York State Library in Albany was constructed.) Double rows of carrels with partitions between each pair, as well as in front of each one, are used in stack rooms in place of two stack ranges, as in the Louisiana State University Library in Baton Rouge and elsewhere. (See Fig. 7.12.)

In the years after the Second World War, nests of four carrels were provided, dropped down sometimes too casually in reading areas. They can also be placed to advantage in reading alcoves. Double carrels, with two persons facing each other with a partition in between, were often used in the late fifties, but have the disadvantage that when placed in long rows close together two readers find themselves back to back in close proximity. (See Fig. 7.11*B*.) In the early 1960s at Douglass College and later at the Cornell University Uris Undergraduate Library, double carrels side by side with partitions between and the readers facing in opposite directions came into use, and still later double- and triple-staggered carrels were designed in order to provide visual privacy and make it a little easier to enter the inside one (see Fig. 16.10).

The open carrels that have been discussed here are available through library-equipment houses. They are quite expensive, but can be very useful. If desired in large numbers, they can sometimes be custom-built for less than standard prices for stock units. Carrels of all types are discussed in section 7.3, and are dealt with again in section 16.3, on layouts.

Card-catalogue Cabinets. Information in regard to card-catalogue cases or cabinets and their arrangement should be made available to the architect after being considered and approved by the librarian. It should cover eight points, as follows:

1. An estimate of the largest number of cards to be housed during the life of the building, and a definite statement as to the number when it is first occupied

2. An estimate of the largest number of readers and staff expected to use the catalogue at any one time now and later

3. The over-all height permissible for the cases

4. The width of the cases and the number of rows of trays that is required to fit the width

5. The over-all depth of the cases

6. The question of reference shelves and consultation tables

7. Suggestions about the preferred arrangement of the cases and the aisle space required between them

8. An estimate of the total area required to house the catalogue and those who are using it

Each of these is important and will be discussed with pertinent suggestions for alternatives in section 16.3.

Decision on each of these problems may affect the design of the catalogue cases. The over-all height, width, and depth of each individual case, its total bulk, the base on which it stands, and the methods used for labeling it, as well as its aesthetic features and functional requirements, should be kept in mind, as should its relationship with the other cases in the installation.

In an effort to find catalogue cases more attractive than the standard ones which have been in use in the United States for many years, cases with new designs have recently been imported from Europe. Those in the United Nations Library in New York were built in Sweden and might have been a success but for the fact that the clear height of the space in each tray, while high enough for 3×5-in. ($7\frac{1}{2} \times 12\frac{1}{2}$-cm) cards, is not high enough for standard guide cards, and these are bent over and soon broken as the trays are drawn in and out.

The Harvard Divinity School card cabinets were made in Germany. They are handsome and a welcome change, but are not as well built as they should have been and will not stand up under heavy use. They have slanted fronts, which make it possible to withdraw them and return them to their places without the use of the customary handles, and this leaves space for larger labelholders, which are welcome. But the slanted front is larger than necessary, and each

tray takes over 5 in., instead of 4 to $4\frac{1}{4}$ in. of vertical height, so that a 10-tray-high case is higher than a 12-tray standard one. This design can be corrected.

If cases with new designs are considered, it is suggested that specifications be used that will avoid the problems mentioned in the two preceding paragraphs. It should be added that the construction of catalogue cases is the most difficult cabinet work that can be found in a library. The wood used must be kiln-dried to prevent later disastrous shrinking and warping, and the joints must be carefully fitted. The trays receive severe strain as they are used. Only the best-quality wood is satisfactory. For many years the finest-quality, close-grained, quartered white oak was standard. This is no longer available, and present-day oak tends to splinter, or to be damaged in other ways when dropped. Black walnut, if available, is sometimes used, as is imported wood of quality. Teak cabinets have been used frequently in recent years. Between the trays, maple and birch uprights that have been given a treatment called densification have been found satisfactory. The catalogue cases in the Widener Library, going well back into the nineteenth century and coming on up to the present, represent a history of catalogue-card cabinets of wood from the time when Ezra Abbot, the Assistant Librarian in the Harvard College Library, "invented" them for 2×5-in. cards in 1863.

It should be mentioned that in the past (and it can still be done if wanted) tremendously large cases—12, 13, 14 trays high and as much as 14 ft long, with a similar row backing up to them, all in one great unit, housing altogether over 500 trays—were not unusual in large libraries. They are unwieldy, of course, inflexible, and almost immovable, as well as expensive. Too frequently they have become white elephants. They are not recommended.

Many libraries which have acquired comparatively low cases permit readers to use their tops for consulting the cards. Others have installed reference or sliding shelves, which are often placed halfway up in the catalogue case, so that the reader standing at the catalogue can conveniently use the trays from the lower or upper part of the case without moving away from it. If no sliding shelf is provided, the tray should be withdrawn and used at a consultation table elsewhere. Consultation tables should, of course, be placed conveniently close to the catalogue. They may be simply a shelf fastened between two cases or they may stand independently between two parallel rows of cases.

A final design problem comes in regard to the arrangement of the catalogue cases within the space assigned to them. In many libraries they have been placed along a wall, sometimes recessed in it. The latter may give a very satisfactory appearance, but it more or less arbitrarily limits the growth of the catalogue in the years ahead and also means that the cases must be custom-built, which usually makes them more expensive. In a few instances the catalogue has been used as part or all of a wall between the public-catalogue room and the cataloguers' quarters, with the drawers so designed that they can be pulled out from either side. This has certain advantages, but may have disconcerting results when a tray is pulled away just as one starts to reach for it; it may even be dangerous if one's finger is caught in the handle. Special hardware is required on the staff side to prevent a reader pushing a tray completely through the case.

Anthony Thompson recommends, on page 43 of his volume on *Library Buildings,* bases 30 in. high and six or at most seven drawers high. This brings the top of the case to the height of 54 in., but he says nothing of a consultation table. Heights of this size have been widely used in Australia and elsewhere. Mr. Thompson gives wise specifications for construction, suggesting that the cases should not be built in and that they should be of hard wood; he comments critically on the disastrous results of the use of soft wood cases at the UNESCO Library in Paris. He proposes, among other things, that rods should have a release catch and not a screw. It has been found that the cases fabricated in many countries were not of high quality but that the higher cost of American and British cases represented a serious problem.

In many parts of the world steel cases, which cost considerably less than well-made ones of wood, have come into use because of their lower price. They have two serious handicaps. They are noisy, and the gauge of steel used is light enough so that the drawers tend to become bent and difficult to use if wear and tear is heavy.

It is only fair to add, however, that a very large number of substandard cases of wood that stick in damp weather and pull apart at the poorly fabricated joints have been acquired in this and other countries. Cases should not be bought from an inexperienced or unreliable manufacturer just because they are cheaper.

What are known as sheaf catalogues, which are in loose-leaf binders, are used in many other countries, but rarely in the United States. They have the advantage of taking less space and can be used with regular library shelving, but their adoption in the United States seems unlikely. It is much more probable that libraries will go back to book-form catalogues printed by offset, perhaps from IBM or other punched cards, supplemented by card catalogues and brought up to date by reprinting in book form at regular intervals. If this takes place, a considerable number of copies should be made available and even if less space is required to store the catalogue, the space for those using it will not be reduced, and there will be little difficulty in making use of the areas assigned for the public catalogue.

This discussion of catalogue cabinets has tried to list the theoretical problems in connection with them but has not dealt with space required and detailed arrangements. The program statement on catalogue cases in Chapter 13 should be based on information given in this section. The discussion of catalogue-case arrangements in section 16.3, on layout, will go into more specific details in regard to space requirements, and the tables in Appendix B should also be useful.

Book Trucks. Book trucks, which in other parts of the English-speaking world are called book trolleys, are essential in a library of any size. They are used for horizontal transportation of books on wheels. They should also be made, if possible, so that they can be used in connection with vertical transportation by running them into service or passenger elevators, or what are known in some countries as goods or passenger lifts.

Book trucks are expensive pieces of equipment. The wheels, which may be from three to six in number, are the most expensive and critical parts. They must be so arranged that they can be easily swung around corners within a short axis, because stack aisles where they are used are frequently narrow.

They can be made with only three wheels, two at one end and one at the other, but are likely to be unstable and to tip over easily, unless

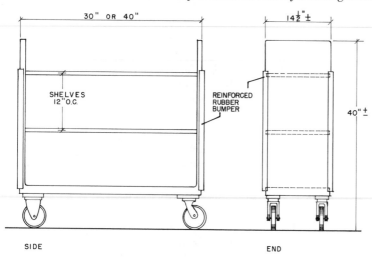

FIG. 11.1   Book truck. Length depends on aisle widths and type of use. Width of 14 in. minimum desirable to make possible shelving on each side. Width of 18 in. is safer but may present difficulty in narrow aisle. Note rubber bumpers on corners.

they are very low-slung. The single wheel should be on a pivot and well out in front, but then the truck will be easy to trip over.

Four-wheel trucks can have two at one end and two at the other, with one or both pairs on pivots. Unless the wheels are widely spaced, perhaps projecting beyond the sides, the truck will be none too stable. Pivot wheels may help to make trucks easier to turn in close quarters, but if one of a pair swings in one direction and the other in a different one, they are inclined to be balky. Four-wheel trucks are sometimes built with two wheels in the center and one at each end, the end ones being on pivots, and for the sake of stability well out toward the end or beyond it.

In a very large library with generous main and cross-stack aisles, large trucks are sometimes used with six wheels, with the center pair reaching down a little farther from the bottom shelf on the truck than the end pairs, so that by bearing down at the rear of the truck and pushing it, the front wheels are freed from the floor and it is easy to turn. Trucks of this kind at the New York Public Library Reference Department were built 4 ft long and wide enough for two deep rows of books on each of three shelves, providing for 24 lineal feet in a full load or more than will go on a standard 3-ft-wide single stack section when it is completely filled.

Be sure that the wheels, whether pivot or sta-

tionary, are first-class, so that they will not bind. If possible, they should be made with ball bearings, should not have to be oiled, and should not squeak. A squeaking truck in a book stack or a catalogue room, to say nothing of a reading room, can be very distressing.

The larger the wheels are in diameter, the more easily they will push, but large wheels raise the center of gravity and affect stability or must be fastened at the sides of the truck where they are in the way and can be tripped over by attendants or will bump into furniture, stacks, or books. Even if the wheels do not project, there is always danger of a truck body bumping stacks and books if they protrude, and the corner uprights and perhaps the sides of the book-truck shelves should be bound with strips of leather or rubber (see Fig. 11.1).

Watch for the distance between shelves when selecting trucks, so that books will seldom have to be turned down on their fore edges, with the danger of weakening their bindings. A distance of 12 in. on centers is suitable, providing for books 11 in. high. Watch the width of the shelves, so that two rows of good-size books can be carried on each shelf without danger of their falling off; but remember that a wide truck in a narrow aisle may make it impossible for a reader or a staff member to pass or for a staff member to withdraw books for shelving. At least 14 in. is advisable, and 16 in. or even 18 in. is better if aisles are wide. Trucks come all the way from 22 in. long to the 48 in. mentioned above. They are generally from 39 to 45 in. in over-all height.

New trucks should not be acquired without bearing in mind the "bottlenecks" that they must go through in the building being planned, that is, the narrow aisles and sharp corners. An end-loading book truck, which has been designed for narrow aisles, is shown in Fig. 11.2. If carpets are to be used on the floor, be sure that the wheels selected are suitable. The American Library Association Library Technology Project report, on page 787 of the September, 1963, *ALA Bulletin*, should be useful in this connection. It can be summarized as follows: Hard rubber or plastic wheels perform best on carpeted floors. For a book truck carrying a 200-pound load, a 5-in. wheel with a 1- to 1½-in. tread width should be selected. For larger trucks carrying a 400- to 500-pound load, a 6-in. wheel with a tread width of 1½ in. appears to be significantly better.

One final warning that will not make the author popular with many librarians: most cataloguers, one might say most librarians, find book trucks altogether too convenient storage places and, if not watched, will tend to use them by their desks in place of book cases. Because of the cost of their wheels, they are too expensive for use in this way; if kept standing while heavily loaded, the wheels will deteriorate, and, to be cynical about it, they are also an aid to poor housekeeping and procrastination.

Service Desks or Counters. Service desks include three basic types:

1. Circulation or charging desks from which books are borrowed for use within or outside the library and to which they are later returned. They are also called delivery desks.

2. Reference desks, sometimes called information or inquiry desks, from which readers are helped in the use of library collections.

3. Control desks for reading areas or entrances and exits.

There may be one or more of each of these types of desks in a library; but on occasion in a small library any two of them or all three can be combined into one. This combination may also be used in a special-subject reading room. Their size and design will, of course, be determined largely by the way they are to be used and the amount of use. Each type will be discussed in turn.

Circulation Desks. The basic essentials for a circulation desk are:

1. Enough length for the staff which is required to provide good service at the time of peak load and to work comfortably together.

2. A place where the reader may charge his books and may return them after use. If the desk is a busy one, the return-book area should be separated from the charging-out area to prevent the unnecessary crossing of traffic lines. The returned books can be placed on top of the desk; the space should be large enough so that confusion will not result, but not so large that the books will be ignored until they pile up, become unsightly, and give the impression of poor housekeeping. A large pile of returned books in sight of the public will result in their challenging the accuracy of the library's records, and the accusation will be difficult to deal with.

Some libraries have a return-book slot below the surface of the desk through which the books can be slid into a waiting box on wheels which

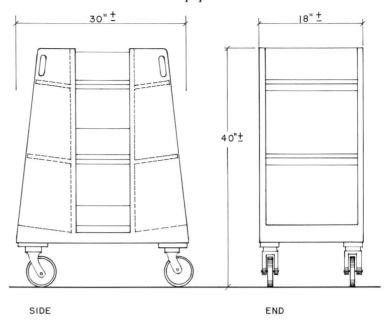

FIG. 11.2 End-loading book truck for narrow aisles.

can be removed when full. This slot and the box should be carefully designed to prevent damage to the books by rapid movement, too great a fall, and one volume knifing another. Another box can be placed next to a return-book slot in an outside wall for use after library hours. Some students like to study after the library closes, late in the night, and return the books before going to bed in order to avoid early rising. Boxes with false bottoms over a heavy spring which are available from library-equipment houses will help. The Lamont Library has one which is equipped with an electric eye. When the eye sees a book, a motor starts and drops the false bottom just far enough so that the next volume will not fall too far but will not jam into the preceding ones.

3. A place adjacent to or in the circulation desk for the storage of books returned from use.

4. A place in the desk or adjacent to it for the equipment in constant use and for circulation records.

5. Working space adjacent to the desk for staff members doing record work; in a large library, for an office for a circulation librarian and, in addition, space for installation of mechanical equipment (IBM, for instance) if there is prospect for its use. This should be looked into carefully. Such a room may require an area of up to 250 sq ft. Since the IBM installation will be noisy, it must be protected acoustically and,

since it will not operate well without temperature and humidity control, complete air conditioning, perhaps with local units if the building as a whole is not air-conditioned, will be required.

6. If the desk is to serve reserved books, adequate shelving for them and extra staff-work space should be provided as close by as possible.

Library supply houses have available stock units of various sizes and designs for circulation desks which can be combined to suit the customer. They are expensive, but are well made and designed by experts who understand library needs. They may include among other things space sunk in the surface to house circulation-card file trays, as well as cubbyholes, drawers, shelves, locked cupboards, and so forth. It is often possible to have a desk specially designed to the librarian's specifications and custom-built by the library-equipment house. Sometimes a local cabinetmaker can build one to specifications at a lower price. They represent less of a construction problem than catalogue cases, and a good cabinetmaker should be able to build a suitable desk successfully.

Special care should be taken in the design. A toe hole at the bottom, both in front of the desk and behind it, will make its use more comfortable for the readers and for the staff members who work at the desk while standing. A staff member who expects to sit at least part of the time should be provided with a kneehole at least 2 ft wide at the proper spot.

Four other points in the design of the desk should be considered: the length, the shape, the width, and the height. As already noted, the length should not be so great as to discourage good housekeeping or to make it necessary for the staff member to walk greater distances than necessary, but it should be long enough. Some desks, particularly in large university libraries, have been too long. The desk can be curved to present a greater length to the reader than to the staff. A curved desk costs more than a straight one foot by foot, and the staff, being on the shorter side, may not have the space within the desk that is required; but, with only one or two on duty at a time, the curved desk may be useful and in some cases have an advantage aesthetically. If the desk is more than one bay long and in the column line in a modular library, the column in it may prove inconvenient by cutting off the view between readers and

staff. Many desks turn one or two corners of 45 or 90°, making them the shape of an L or two or three sides of an octagon, or may be curved to form part of a circle or a flat-bottom U. A turned corner or a column in the center of the desk may make a desirable division between charging and return, or the side of the desk beyond the corner may make possible by careful planning a satisfactory, easily controlled, narrow lane, leading to the book stack or other restricted areas.

The width of the top of the desk can be a controversial matter. If it is too far through from front to back, the staff member and the reader are too far apart and may have difficulty passing books back and forth. A few desks are as much as 3 ft wide, and many are 2 ft 6 in. or more. The wider they are, the greater the storage space on top for circulation records and for returned books below, although if the shelves are too deep, the returned books are likely to be piled up like cordwood two or more deep and be difficult to remove. A width of 22 to 24 in. is generally enough, but the depth should be sufficient so that the reader and the staff member will not, when leaning forward, bump noses. If the desk is high enough, the encounter is much less likely.

The standard height for desks—it is preferable to call them counters—which once was as low as 33 or 36 in. and has been in recent years 39 in., has tended to go higher, and 40 to 42 in. is not uncommon. The latter is a good height, particularly in an institution in the United States where males predominate. In countries where the average height of readers is less than in the United States, 39 in. may be enough. But keep in mind that if the staff member behind the desk is to sit during a large part of the time, a high stool will be necessary for comfort, and the sitting height of the high stool should bring the attendant's eye level to approximately that of the reader for the sake of the comfort of each.

One other warning about circulation desks, or any desks for that matter where the reader may have to stand for a few minutes or more. They are often paneled for the sake of appearance. Panels are expensive and apt to be damaged and hard to repair. One solution is the use of half-rounds on the front of desks in the Lamont Library (see Fig. 11.3), where the damaged portion can easily be removed and replaced by a new one.

Reference, Information, Inquiry, and Reader's Adviser's Desks. These are all desks where information about the library and its use and its collections is provided by a staff member, where readers are assisted, and where such reference work as is provided has its headquarters. Very large libraries, such as the New York Public Library, may have an inquiry desk in a monumental entrance lobby to enable the reader who is overwhelmed by the magnitude of the building to get started in the right direction. At any reference or inquiry desk immediately adjacent to the entrance or elsewhere, there should be at least a limited number of what might be called quick reference works, which will enable a good many readers to find the answer to their questions without going farther into the library. This is also a suitable place for the display and perhaps the distribution by sale or otherwise of library publications of one kind or another.

A regular reference desk will ordinarily have in or adjacent to it a larger number of quick reference books than an inquiry desk, including those which require some restriction in their use in order to keep them from disappearing. This desk should, of course, be placed as close as possible to the main reference and bibliography collections and also to the card catalogue, which may be used by the reference librarians as much as the reference books. Again, the question of size comes up as with the circulation desk. Ordinarily it does not need to be as long as the circulation desk. Many librarians like to have a regular office-type desk, 30 in. or a little less in height, with a chair adjacent for the reader to sit down and talk over his problems with the librarian. This can be very satisfactory, particularly if what has come to be known as reader's advisory service is given; but it can also result in serious abuse. The average librarian can serve satisfactorily twice as many readers if the reader is standing. On the other hand, both persons will find it undesirable for the reader to stand while the librarian is sitting down and looking up at him. It is suggested on this account that a reference desk be a counter rather than a desk, and that it be at least 42 in. or perhaps preferably a little higher, with the librarian sitting on a comfortable high stool with a high back, with a ring on the stool for a footrest, and a kneehole in the counter with a platform in it for the feet. Even a short librarian with a stool adjusted to proper height can then sit comfortably with eye level approximately that of the reader, and everyone concerned will be happier, and more business will be transacted. Sometimes the librarian will want two desks, one with a sit-down and the other with a stand-up height.

If it is the policy of the library to have the attendants do a great deal of reference work for the readers, the staff must, of course, be larger than would otherwise be the case. Office space, or at least desk space, in addition to and behind the reference counter should generally be provided where the librarian can work on difficult problems, answer reference letters, and consult with inquirers who can then sit down and be dealt with on a basis different from that at what might be called the "front" desk. This is a matter for local decision, but it does have a good deal to do with the area required for the reference

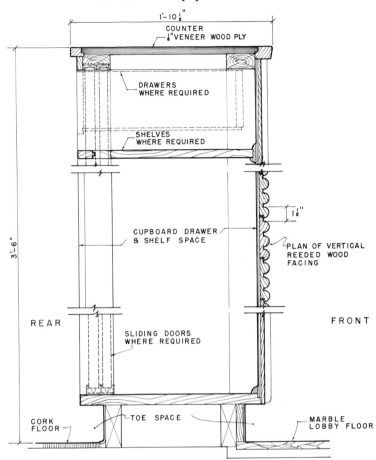

FIG. 11.3 Lamont Library charging desk faced with half rounds instead of panels. The half rounds which are indicated in the drawing as vertical reeded wood facing can be replaced individually if damaged. Note the toe space on each side, the 42 in. height, and the 22½ in. width, which might be called substandard but which has proved adequate.

staff and incidentally with the cost of the service. Almost any large library should provide one and sometimes a number of offices for reference workers, and a very large library may use 1,000 sq ft or more for this purpose.

In this connection, it should be noted that a good many different reference "desks" may be set up in one library. The New York Public Library Reference Department not only has its information desk on the top floor in the public-catalogue room, but has some fourteen subject reading rooms, each with its own reference desk and reference workers. In recent years many academic libraries have adopted the divisional system with three, four, or five departments, each with its own reference staff and perhaps with its own catalogue. Reference desks and space for the reference workers and for the readers consulting them must be provided in each of these. Ordinarily, they will not have to be as large as the main central reference desk in a large library. Any reference desk should have in or adjacent to it space for the reference tools required and should be designed with this in mind.

Control Desks. Control desks to maintain discipline or to prevent unauthorized removal of books are not a recent innovation. In earlier days in reference, academic, and public librar-ies, each reading room had a control desk, or at least a desk from which supervision was provided and from which, if need be, both circulation and reference service might be given. In recent years in academic libraries, reading-area supervision has been pretty well given up, and in many of them the only real control point is at the entrance or perhaps it is better to say the exit lobby or lobbies. There, specially designed desks should be available. Again, as with circulation desks, the problem of the preferable length, depth, and height comes up. If the traffic load is so great that more than one person has to be assigned to the control task at one time, it may be better to have two or even up to four or six separate desks in a very large library rather than one long desk with a number of attendants working at it. There will be less chance for confusion. If there is more than one control desk in the same lobby, lanes, defined either by cords or dividing lines of one kind or another, can lead past the desks to the exit door or doors. A library large enough to require a number of control desks should have a number of exit doors leading into one vestibule, or in some cases where fire laws necessitate it, into two or more separate ones. Some libraries have used turnstiles, but they are to be avoided if possible, because they give an appearance of regimentation.

part 2

The Planning Process

12

Planning Preliminaries

12.1 Preparing for the Task

Planning a new library building is an expensive and complicated matter and should not be undertaken without proper preparation. Part 1 of this volume has attempted to provide much of the background information that should be available to those who are to work on the task. The persons requiring this information will include the librarian and almost always a number of others who cannot or should not avoid responsibility for planning. This chapter will deal with additional sources of information and with methods of organizing the work of planning.

Study of the Literature. Few librarians and even fewer university and college presidents, deans, business managers, and building-maintenance officers have had any direct and practical experience with special problems involved in planning a library building. Yet knowledge of these problems might be said to be a prerequisite for writing the program, to say nothing of helping in the actual planning after the program has been given to the architect.

One way of obtaining the required information is by studying the literature on the subject. Although this literature is extensive, it is not well organized for the purpose. This volume is not intended to make further reading unnecessary, and it includes, as Appendix D, a Selective Annotated Bibliography, which should help the inquirer to find his way through the maze of material. It is suggested that those involved in the planning should begin by more or less casu-

ally examining Part 1 of this volume in order to orient themselves and to see what they can expect to find here, as well as what additional information they think would be useful. Then, after perusing the bibliography, and more thoroughly studying the remainder of this volume, they should be prepared, without too much waste of time, to do the additional reading that seems desirable. They will find that neither this volume nor other available literature will make their decisions for them. As a result of their reading, however, they should be aware of the preliminary information on which decisions should be based. The literature should help, but the decisions should be determined by the local situation. In the meantime, through their reading and with the aid of the Glossary in Appendix E, they should become acquainted with the vocabulary of building planning, which will be useful in writing the program and later in dealing with the architect and the builder.

Who should become acquainted with the literature? Probably it ought to be kept in mind that "a little knowledge is a dangerous thing." If the study is too casual, and if the reader tends to consider everything he reads as gospel truth, he will be bound to come to grief and have to relearn some things. It is suggested that the librarian, in addition to absorbing as far as possible what is pertinent in this volume, try to become well acquainted with the more important materials in the selective bibliography, and be prepared to turn to other material as he feels the need for it. It is further suggested that this volume be placed at the disposal of the others involved in the program writing and that their attention be called to the parts of it that fall within their special fields of activity, as well as to the pertinent material listed in the bibliography. It is repeated for emphasis that the purpose of the study of the literature, and of this volume as a whole, is primarily not to solve the problems but to call attention to them, to explain them, and to outline the different possible courses of action which must be dealt with on the basis of the local situation.

If the institution's president expects to take an active part in the program writing, his attention should be called to the literature and its possible usefulness. The same holds true for any other senior administrative officer who is involved, such as the administrative vice-president, the provost, the deans, the business manager, the maintenance officers, the chairman of the library building committee, and later the architect and the architectural and engineering consultants, if one or more of them are appointed.

The Planning Team. When those primarily involved have acquired sufficient knowledge, through the examination of the literature of library planning, to take the next step, it is time for them to consider the desirability of appointing planning committees representing the different groups involved, of calling in one or more consultants, and of organizing what is often called the planning team.

Planning Committees. The following planning committees might be considered, though it would be unusual and probably needlessly complicated to use in any one institution all of those suggested in the following paragraphs.

A trustees' building committee may be desirable, particularly if the trustees expect to keep a tight rein on building planning. Often trustees may find that they can control the situation satisfactorily by asking the president to represent them in the planning, but with the understanding that final policy decisions, especially those which involve financial matters and public relations, will be referred to them before action is taken. Sometimes one or more members of the board of trustees having special interest, knowledge, and competence in the building planning field can be asked to serve on a committee made up of representatives of the other interested groups.

A committee representing the institution's administrative officers is a second possibility. The president himself may want to be a member or even the chairman, but often it is enough if he is represented by an administrative assistant in whom he has confidence. Other members may include the treasurer, the business manager, the head of the building-and-maintenance department, and the vice-president in charge of educational policy. To these might be added other officers, such as the provost and one or more deans.

A faculty committee to ensure that faculty and educational interests receive proper consideration is certainly not out of place. This committee might well include men and women who are known to have special interest in the library and preferably those with some practical knowledge and imagination. They should represent each of the major fields—science, social sciences, and the humanities.

A student committee can sometimes be useful in enlisting student interest and cooperation in the project. If there is a strong student council, it might be asked to appoint this committee. If not, the dean who deals most intimately with the students should select its members.

A library staff committee should not be ruled out. In a large institution such a committee can properly be appointed, often with the librarian as chairman, but sometimes with a senior staff member who has special knowledge of planning problems in charge.

The librarian should be a member of all of these committees as a coordinating officer, if nothing else.

Often no one of these committees or combination of them, for that matter, may be of much direct help. The problems involved may not be understood by the committee members. Committee work is difficult, and time for it is hard to find. But it should be remembered that each group is deeply involved in the results. Frequently important help can come from one or all of the groups, and to include representatives of each in the planning process is a matter of first importance to the institution, if only to prevent unnecessary and destructive criticism of the building when it is finally erected. If one or more of the committees are not appointed, the librarian or some other officers might be assigned the responsibility of keeping in touch with all the groups concerned to make sure that their different attitudes and points of view receive full consideration by the architect and librarian as planning proceeds.

The Question of Outside Help. This problem is a complex one. Often the first question is whether or not an architectural firm or an individual architect should be employed to make a master plan for the development of the campus as a whole, including the selection of the site for the library.

A master plan is certainly desirable and too often is not available, but if the governing board approves the site chosen by the master planner, the architect, when selected, may for some good reason feel that a better site could be found and may properly recommend it. If such a suggestion is made, the procedure to be followed is perhaps out of the province of this book, but the author suggests that the librarian also be given an opportunity to express his opinion on this important problem to the campus planning group and to the architect.

The institution may have a regular supervising architect whose approval is required for all new construction and who is involved before the library architect is chosen. His relationship to the latter should be carefully defined in order to avoid misunderstanding. Instances could be cited where disagreements between supervising architect or campus planner and the library architect have caused serious difficulties.

Should one or more consultants from outside the institution be selected before or, perhaps, after the architect? In general, with the exception of the library building consultant, such appointments might follow the selection of the architect, who should have an opportunity at least to express his preference in connection with them. Indeed, sometimes he will select and appoint the consultants himself, and they will be working for and paid by him. Sometimes the institution will want help from a consultant in selecting the architect. As usual, circumstances alter cases.

Probably the most important consultant, so far as concerns problems considered in this volume, is one who has special knowledge and experience in library building planning, and who is called in to advise and work with the architect. He may be a librarian with experience in building planning or an architect with experience in the library field. Whether he is appointed in advance or only after consultation with the architect will depend on local circumstances.

Sometimes the architect will be selected with full knowledge on the part of the institution that he has had little or no experience in library planning and will be appointed with the understanding that he will work with a library or architectural consultant. If the librarian has had some planning experience and the architect little or none with libraries, an architectural consultant with library planning experience should perhaps be appointed. If, on the other hand, the architect has had library planning experience and the librarian has had little or none, it may be better to appoint a librarian experienced in library building planning as a consultant. It sometimes happens, however, that a good architect, inexperienced in library building planning, and a librarian without experience in library planning will be involved. If the enterprise is very large, running into millions of dollars, it may be worth while under these circumstances to have both an architectural and a library consultant. Yet if only one is needed, other things being equal, a library consultant will probably be more useful, as he can keep the architect informed on special library functions and problems. Fortunately, today, quite a number of architects have planned a considerable number of library buildings and are ready to serve as consultants to other architects who will have the responsibility for the detailed planning, and a number of library consultants are available, as will be seen in section 12.2.

Briefing and Coordination of Efforts. Whether or not all the individuals, groups, and committees mentioned above who will be involved in the planning are asked to become acquainted with the literature, they should at least be briefed by their librarian or perhaps better by the president or by someone whom he designates on the basic financial and educational problems that the institution faces in undertaking the planning of a new library building and on the "ground rules" which are to be used in dealing with them. They should be told about what is going on, and their help should be solicited. It is undoubtedly true that, when a large group is given an opportunity to comment, the floodgates may be opened to unnecessary and perhaps undesirable criticism but, if carefully handled, this procedure should make everyone involved feel that he has had a part in the proceedings, and hence he will be less likely to criticize the results than if he had not participated. The publicity obtained should also help directly or indirectly in fund raising, if that is an essential part of the situation.

Of course, if all these individuals and groups are involved, special care must be taken to see that their efforts are coordinated, that each one understands what is and what is not expected of him, and that their activities do not come into conflict with each other—something that could very readily happen. This, a matter of first importance, is too often neglected by the institution's administrative officers.

By the time the administrative officers and others who are to have a part in the planning have become acquainted with the literature and have been briefed on planning problems to be faced, the advisory committees that are to be selected should be appointed, and agreement should be reached as to the relationships and responsibilities of each group.

Visiting Other Library Buildings. There is no better way to obtain an insight into library building problems than to visit other libraries. Few persons have imagination enough to picture what these problems are without seeing examples of them, and a careful examination of the literature of the subject by itself is not sufficient. This topic might well have been placed earlier in this chapter, or perhaps, in order to make sure that the architect takes part in the visiting, after section 12.3 below, which deals with the selection of an architect. His training and experience have prepared him to understand better than the layman the problems to be faced, but he still needs to examine some concrete examples of recently constructed libraries.

In spite of the value of visiting, too much of it is perhaps as bad as none at all. Saturation sets in, and one's head may well get into a whirl and all impressions become indistinct. Ordinarily not more than six or eight libraries at the most need be visited by any one person, but those selected should be examined carefully enough to make the enterprise worth while.

What libraries should be selected? They should include both good and bad examples. One can learn almost as much from an unsuccessful solution of a library building problem as from a good one. This of course brings up the question of what is a good or what is an unsuccessful solution. The author cannot attempt to present specific answers to that question. Even the experts will often disagree among themselves

and will emphasize different points. It is to be hoped that persons who study this volume and learn about the variety of possible solutions of their particular planning problems will have fairly definite ideas about their basic objectives for the building which is being planned, and will know what they want to look for.

Be sure to choose the libraries of several institutions that are similar in character to your own (that is, in the number of students, the size of the collections, and in general outlook) because such institutions are more likely to have dealt with problems that resemble yours. On the other hand, do not hesitate to go to larger or to smaller libraries if they have something special to present.

Among the things worth noting when one visits libraries are first impressions, general appearance, traffic patterns and spatial relationships, table sizes, dimensions of individual seating arrangements, aisle widths and shelf depths, coatrooms, drinking fountains, arrangements for smoking, heating and ventilating installations, lighting, and ceiling heights.

After an examination of the literature on library building planning, the prospective visitor might well put down a list of the things that he feels should be noted in the program and of which he would like to see examples before making his decisions.

What procedure should be followed when the libraries to be visited have been designated? One method is to have the librarian go first by himself to one or two libraries and to suggest to the architect that he do likewise. Then a joint expedition is desirable, perhaps including a member of the faculty library committee and a representative of the institution's maintenance department. Probably not more than five should join in a visit. A larger number cannot easily keep together and see things that should be seen, and the librarian of the institution being visited is likely to be overwhelmed.

If it has been decided to employ a library consultant, his presence as a visitor may be helpful, for he is in a better position than others to point out both satisfactory solutions of problems and failures. He will undoubtedly want to warn in advance the library that is to be visited.

Ordinarily, half a day, except in a very large library, is enough for one building, although a large university building might require a full day. Be sure to reserve time after the visit to talk it over and to prepare a written report. This will help to organize the information gathered and make it available to others. If the librarian of the building visited can be persuaded to comment on its good and bad points, his remarks should be illuminating.

Some three libraries of the same type as your own should probably be included in the list, and at least three others of other sizes and types, with two from each group selected because you understand that they are good examples of what might be done, and one because it is not believed to be satisfactory. Not more than three consecutive days should be spent in visiting. A list of questions to which answers are wanted might well be prepared in advance. If a camera can be taken along to take pictures of significant points, the photographs can be useful, although occasionally so much time may be spent in taking pictures that full advantage of the visit is lost.

The following are examples of things that might be looked for. Many academic libraries have tables for six that are 7 ft 6 in. long and only 3 ft wide. If you find a table like this, the chances are that it will not have more than two or at the most three readers sitting at it, even at busy times of day. What do you want for your library? Examine the width of stack aisles. You can find them all the way from 26 to 40 in. There is no definite rule as to the proper width. It depends upon circumstances, but seeing different widths with your own situation in mind should help you to decide on the proper width or widths for your building. The same holds for the depth of shelves and the length of ranges. Keep a good lookout for individual seating arrangements. They may present a special problem because of space used. Watch for traffic patterns. What has been done to make it easy to find your way about and not disturb others? Is the air conditioning satisfactory? Is it noisy? Can the windows be opened, and, if so, are the results good or bad? What floor coverings are used? Is the lighting good? Is the supervision satisfactory? How many public exits are there, and how are they controlled? Do any parts of the building seem unduly congested? What about ceiling heights? Did you detect waste space? Did you like the arrangements for coats, other wraps, and other possessions? If there are faculty studies, are they too large or too small? This list could be extended indefinitely.

If you have made proper preparation for your visits by studying the literature of library planning and have made note of the points you want to include in your program, your list of questions on which you want to obtain information or of which you want to see visual demonstrations should be reasonably complete. There is such a thing as getting too involved in details and losing out on basic principles, but visits should be a fascinating task and very useful for you and your library.

12.2 Consultants

Library Building Consultants. Five questions should be answered in connection with library building consultants.

1. Why have a consultant?
2. How should he be selected?
3. At what stage in the planning should he be selected?
4. What should he be paid?
5. What should he do?

Why Have a Consultant? A consultant is ordinarily appointed because the institution that employs him realizes that without a consultant it will have no one available, including the architect, who has had the desired experience in planning a library building. In spite of the large number of libraries that have been planned and constructed since the war, the average librarian rarely has an opportunity to participate in the planning of more than one building during his career, and until very recent years, comparatively few architects had specialized in library planning. An institution then may well believe that a consultant should be appointed in order to place at the disposal of its planning team knowledge and experience that would not otherwise be available.

The institution often has one or more special planning problems which make a consultant particularly desirable. There may be a trustee who wants what his grandfather wanted, and only a monumental or a Gothic building will satisfy him. There may be a dean who thinks that audiovisual work is more important than a library. There may be a professor with a continental background who believes in excessive decentralization of library facilities or in seminar rooms for his advanced classes in which the basic collections in his special field are shelved. There may be a science professor who is convinced that no library, as we now think of it, is going to be needed in the future because of technological developments. There may be a librarian who refuses to use new "mechanized gadgets." There may be other special problems too numerous to mention, and the institution's representatives who have the over-all responsibility for the building may very often believe that an outsider could provide a needed balance wheel. "A prophet is not without honor save in his own country."

But in most cases a consultant is wanted because of the realization that special knowledge is not locally available; that the cost of a library building is great—it sometimes doubles the institution's investment in its library, amounting to as much as twenty times the annual budget—and that mistakes would be extremely serious. This is an age of experts, and it is not strange that library building consultants should have been more and more in demand during the last twenty years. Before that time, when libraries were planned, the librarian generally had comparatively little to say about the details. There were exceptions, of course. But too often the architect went ahead without knowing library problems, and, since he was primarily interested in the aesthetic side of the matter, the results were not satisfactory functionally.

The chief reason for a library building consultant, then, is to make available special knowledge of the functional needs and requirements in a library building, and to make sure that an effective advocate will speak for these needs as planning proceeds.

How Should a Consultant Be Selected? Experience is a most important consideration. Ralph Ellsworth advises against taking a man who has not already had at least three assignments of this kind.[1] This is easier said than done. There are not enough experienced library building consultants to go around. And how does a new consultant get started? The requirement resembles those of trade unions that do not want to admit newcomers; but experience for newcomers is obviously desirable. It is important for the experienced consultants to bring in younger men to help them. There is a similar situation in administrative work of any kind. One of the most important things that a head librarian can do is

to train others to take his own administrative position or another; and the best way of training people is to see to it that in some way they get experience.

Select a consultant with experience. Investigate and find out about the results of work that he has done elsewhere. Keep in mind, of course, his knowledge of building planning, and also his ability to influence persons with whom he deals and make them understand the basic problems involved. An expert in library building planning who cannot get his ideas across to the architect, to the other members of the planning team, and to the institution's administration may be pretty useless, however much he knows.

The consultant should have the ability to explain the reasons for his point of view and to persuade those with whom he deals of the importance of carrying out his suggestions. He must be a good salesman. He must not be over-dogmatic. He should be fearless in expressing his views. He must avoid undue aggressiveness. He must understand the local situation.

While he should not be expected to be an architect and an engineer and he should not become too deeply involved in the problems of those professions, he must understand them well enough to avoid unsuitable and impracticable suggestions. He must realize that planning a library building involves not only functional but architectural and engineering problems. He must also keep in mind both the present situation and prospective library developments.

The desirability of picking the right consultant cannot be overemphasized. He should be the right person for the particular job at hand. A man under consideration may be suitable for one institution and not for another. Circumstances alter cases again and again in this world.

The qualifications for a good librarian do not necessarily make a good library building consultant. Just because a man is eminent in the library profession does not mean that he has had experience in planning buildings. You should not pick a building consultant because he is the successful administrator of a large library. Neither should you do so just because he is in the same city or state. The fact that he may have worked successfully on a public library building does not necessarily mean that he can do the same on a college library or vice versa. Problems of college library building planning and university library building planning differ con-

---

[1] Ralph E. Ellsworth, "Consultants for College and University Library Building Planning," *College and Research Libraries*, 21: 263–268, 1960.

siderably, and so on. Pick a man who seems to have the knowledge, the experience, and the broad-gauge mind that will enable him to understand your particular problem and to help you in the places where you need help. If you need someone to influence your governing board, library committee, or administrative officers, rather than to help with the details of the building planning, pick someone who, in your opinion, can be persuasive. A poor selection may be worse than none at all.

At What Stage in the Planning Should a Consultant Be Selected? If you are going to have a consultant, select him just as soon as possible. He can be of use in deciding whether you should build a new building or add to an old one. He can help to select the site. He can properly give advice on the selection of an architect. Normally he should not recommend a specific firm, but he can offer suggestions regarding the qualifications that should be met. If the consultant can be appointed early enough, before important decisions have been made which it will be impossible or embarrassing or expensive to change, he may prevent these mistakes. Too often he is not called in until decisions that are difficult to alter have been made by the institution and the architect and it is too late to get started with the right foot forward. This does not mean that it is unwise to have a consultant unless he is chosen at the beginning. A situation may often develop which makes the appointment imperative; better late than never.

What Should a Consultant Be Paid? There is no accepted schedule of payments for library consultants as there is for architects. The latter are almost always employed on a percentage basis, the percentage varying with the type of building and its location. As yet library building consultants are not in an organized and accepted profession, and they may never be. It is hoped that they will not base their charges primarily on what the traffic will bear.

Three fairly definite methods are used in charging. One is on a percentage basis, the percentage varying according to what the consultant is expected to do. Is he to follow the procedures through from beginning to end, as the architect does, being on call during the construction as well as during the preliminary planning, and the working-drawings and specifications stage, or will his assignment be completed when working drawings are authorized? The

answer, of course, makes a difference in the percentage.

The second method is an agreement by which the work will be done for a definite sum, or at least an amount not exceeding that figure, with consideration given, as the plans develop, to the amount of time spent. Ralph Ellsworth very modestly suggests, in his *College and Research Libraries* article, that for a $1,500,000 college library, 0.1 per cent or $1,500 may be budgeted for the consultant. He adds that it may not all be used, and he goes into some detail about how many days may be required. If this method is adopted, Ellsworth's computations can form a basis for calculations,[2] if one keeps in mind that the size of the project and the experience of the consultant may well affect the percentage figure used.

The third method is for the consultant simply to say that his charges will be so much a day, plus expenses. The per diem may vary from $50 up, according to the experience and, you might say, the prestige of the consultant and the job at hand. A small college library or a branch library costing $200,000 might need a consultant, but 0.1 per cent of the total or $200 would not be adequate, even if only a few days were involved.

A man with a great deal of experience may feel that in a situation where he is likely to run into complications of one kind or another the $150 a day which Mr. Ellsworth suggests as a standard rate for an experienced person is not adequate and that $200 or more is not unreasonable. A team of consultants, working together and contributing between them expert knowledge in various fields, may require altogether a larger percentage of the total cost but perhaps less per day per person, and so on.

This work is not sufficiently well organized or set in its ways at present so that a definite scale for any of these methods can or should be proposed. Some consultants, particularly those working with institutions in which they are personally interested for one reason or another, do a great deal without charge except for expenses.

The author makes two definite suggestions in connection with charges. The institution should not base its selection primarily on the cost but on the person whom it wants. The consultant should not try to bargain and charge as much as

[2] *Ibid.,* p. 265.

traffic will bear but should set his rate for the particular job and let the institution take it or leave it.

What Should the Consultant Do? The consultant should do everything that he can to plan the best possible building, making available to those concerned his knowledge and experience, using the best judgment that he has as to when to push and when perhaps to hold back temporarily or permanently, if he believes that someone else's voice on a particular point at a particular time can be more valuable. He should refrain from getting into arguments for the sake of argument or to show off his knowledge. He should defer to the specialist in a field for which he is not particularly qualified, although if he has a definite opinion based on good authority, he should state his case as quietly and persuasively as he can. He should not be underhanded in his work, but should avoid butting his head against a stone wall if there is a good way around it.

To be more specific, if the consultant is called on at the very beginning, he should as his first task go over the whole situation in general terms, so as to obtain a firm grasp of it. He should try to learn enough about the institution, its history, its background, and its objectives, so that the framework of the library's requirements becomes reasonably clear. He should then translate these requirements, in his own mind if not for publication, into square footage, with the realization, of course, that the results will be only an approximation. A consultant may have basic formulas for use in this way. Different formulas are required for different types of institutions. For a small academic library, for instance, something like the following might help: Ten to twelve volumes can be shelved in 1 sq ft of gross floor space. In a larger library up to fifteen may be a safe figure. Fifty sq ft or a little more will accommodate a reader. This 50 sq ft will provide not only for reading-room space but for the staff to serve the readers, the processing work space, and the non-assignable space for the whole building as well. The two added together, that is, the space for books and for readers and services to readers, will give the gross square feet if no unusual special facilities are required, such as an auditorium, audiovisual areas, an exhibition room beyond normal lobby space, classrooms, more than a limited number of seminars or faculty studies, and special lounges. These are extras and must be added to the previous figure.

With a very rough total of space requirements available, the present building should be carefully investigated. The question should be answered as to whether, with rearrangements within that building, the space required for a few years more can be provided, or whether a wing could be added without leaving the building in an undesirable position aesthetically or functionally. The possibility and advisability of an addition should always be considered, so that no interested person can say that such an alternative has been left out of consideration.

At this stage, of course, it is desirable to reach a decision as to the time ahead for which plans are to be made, for not only the present but the future requirements are of interest.

When a conclusion has been reached as to the total space requirements, the problem of a site should be settled. Do not permit the decision on that point to be frozen until you know what is needed and can be sure that a satisfactory building of the size required can be placed on the plot selected. If the long view is to be taken, be sure that thought is given to the next stage when the new building will be outgrown.

It will now be time to consider in detail the program for the architect and make sure that it is complete. It should provide, if not the exact size of each area, an indication of the required size in terms of readers, staff, and collections to be housed and the desired spatial relationships between the different areas. The role of the "program" is discussed in section 12.4, and Chapters 13 and 14 are devoted to what it should include.

This problem of the program is a matter of greatest importance. As often as practicable the program should be written locally by the librarian or his building committee or by someone on the scene who is skilled in a task of this sort. It is almost impossible for an outsider to obtain the required information in a short time. But the consultant can and generally should take a vital part in the program preparation, primarily by asking the questions that should be answered and by making sure that important points are not omitted. In other words, he should be the guide and critic, rather than the author. Sometimes he will think that he could do it better and more easily by himself, and perhaps he could; but on the whole, if the program is written by those who have to live with the results, it should be more satisfactory. The building committee and the librarian, for instance, will understand the program better if they have written it or taken pretty direct responsibility for it. They will then be able to explain it more successfully to the faculty and students or the governing boards and the public in general, than if it is written by the consultant.

The part of the program dealing with spatial relationships within the building is of first importance, and will have much to do with the success of the building. Other important factors to be kept in mind are the special features that the institution wants to incorporate, such as all-night study areas, open or closed stack access, seminars and studies, smoking rooms, lounges, exit controls, auditoriums, exhibition areas, special rooms of any kind, etc.

Help in selecting the architect, either after or before the program has been completed, can in many cases be provided by the consultant. But, as has been already noted, he must do this carefully, preferably confining himself to suggestions on the type and characteristics of the architect to be selected rather than recommending a particular firm.

The consultant, or the librarian for that matter, should ordinarily not prepare schematic drawings or preliminary sketches for the architect beyond those which indicate desired spatial relationships. It is important, however, for the consultant to see and discuss with those concerned the drawings that the architect makes, particularly those that have to do with spatial relationships and function. He should also comment on the adequacy of the space assignments proposed and on their capacity to fulfill the program requirements. He certainly should be involved with equipment layouts and traffic patterns, floor loads, floor coverings, lighting, acoustic problems, ventilation, and so forth. He should study all the architect's proposals. Furniture design is within his province, particularly sizes, and, to a limited extent, color and finish.

If, during the planning stage, the architects and one or more members of the planning team visit other libraries to learn how to solve planning problems and, of equal importance, how not to solve them, this can often be done under the sponsorship and direction of the consultant, who can suggest libraries to be visited and points to be kept in mind during the visits. If he goes along—which is sometimes desirable—he can call attention to important features.

He should be available by telephone and by letter as questions and problems arise, through-out the working-drawings stage and preferably during construction as well, even if he does not appear on the scene himself.

It should be noted that it is always dangerous to attempt to give advice without knowing fairly intimately the local situation, including the climate, the terrain, the campus and its master plan, if any, as well as the general spirit and atmosphere, philosophy, and objectives of the institution. It is difficult to get acquainted with these without being on the spot. Consulting "in absentia," either here or abroad, is not effective.

A final question, and perhaps the most difficult of all, in connection with "What should the consultant do?" lies in how far he should insist that the architect and the institution follow his recommendations. For instance, should he withdraw if his suggestions are not followed? Should the institution be asked to agree that it will not proceed without the written approval and the consent of its consultant? If a prospective consultant believes that the answer to these questions is "yes," as some consultants have proposed, this should be specified and approved by both parties before the work is undertaken. The author, who learned many years ago that ultimatums are dangerous, that few persons are infallible, and that "circumstances alter cases," suggests that a "yes" answer to these questions is too drastic. A consultant can always withdraw and refuse to have his name associated with the project, but experience with some two hundred planning enterprises suggests that a procedure of this kind is seldom if ever necessary or justified. Architects, in the author's experience, as well as librarians and academic administrators, tend to be reasonable men. They are all seeking the best possible results with the funds available. Agreement cannot always be reached, but why add fuel to the flame by ultimatums, threatenings, and quarrels? Talk over the problems. State the case clearly. Lay all the cards on the table, and then accept the results, stating the reservations when they exist.

Interior-design Consultants. Possible need for other consultants should not be forgotten. The institution or the architect who has been selected may ask for an architectural consultant or adviser or associate. One or both may want help from an interior designer. There are consultants in both of these fields who have had wide experience in library planning. The only warning in this connection holds for library building consultants also. Their assignments should be well defined. All concerned should know whether the consultants are working for the architect or the institution and who is financing their operations.

Interior designing is certainly within the accepted province of the architect, since it involves the design and purchase of furniture and equipment. Sometimes it is taken out of his hands and turned over to the purchasing agent of the institution, on the basis that the architect's commission, which may run, for this particular type of work, up to 10 per cent of the total, will be saved. However, if the furniture does not fit into the structure, the effects may be unfortunate. The library building consultant has the functional arrangements as his primary responsibility and can rarely, if ever, be counted on to give satisfactory advice in connection with the aesthetic side of the problem. Since library furniture and equipment is a special field in itself, an interior designer who specializes in library work is sometimes called in as a consultant. If this is done, he should, of course, work very closely with the architect and with the library consultant, if there is one, so as to avoid any conflict in interest. An interior designer can be a very useful person. The problem will immediately arise as to the cost of his services. Since the work to be done will vary widely from one building to another, it is difficult and probably unwise to propose a definite formula. One of the foremost interior planning consultants and designers who has specialized in library work has prepared the following statement.

This work may entail critique of architect's preliminaries to equipment layouts, color schemes, furniture selection, the writing of detailed construction specifications, including "conditions to bidders," aid in assessing alternate proposals—this is most important—and final inspection of the installation. There are several different methods of charging.

One is a percentage of the overall cost of furnishings and equipment; normally this is ten per cent, although the size of the project can affect this. Another is a percentage of the overall building and furnishing budget, with one per cent being a common base. Again, the one per cent figure can be unfair. On one project recently the budget was approximately two million, yet a survey of the program made it clear that a twenty thousand dollar fee was considerably too high.

Of the two methods stated above, the percentage of overall budget has the advantage of immediately clarifying the approximate amount the fee will come to, since this budget is normally a known factor. On the other hand, a percentage of furniture cost alone can be greatly altered as the job proceeds:

1. The original furnishing budget might prove to be entirely unrealistic and require revision.

2. The cost of the building itself might force a drastic cut in final furniture allowances—not a happy thought, but it does happen. In such an event, I have found a reverse ratio occurring: my fee is thereby cut, but my required time and energy to cope with a greatly reduced budget is expanded.

3. Steel stacks are sometimes included in the furnishing budget, sometimes in that of the architectural work. Since the cost of stacks is high, this matter must be clarified before arriving at a fair percentage fee.

4. In some instances a library will require a time-consuming survey of existing furniture to determine what might be re-used in non-public areas. This, too, must be determined since the use of existing furniture reduces expenditure and thus the fee.

In brief, I have had some clients question a percentage of furniture costs by saying: "But we must have some idea what we will actually pay you." (In one case which I won't mention by name, I contracted with a Board on a percentage of furniture basis, and only after my contract was signed did they inform me of anticipated reductions, additional surveys and studies that were necessary, and planned use of considerable existing furniture. That job was a source of loss as well as bitterness, I must admit.)

A third method of charging is of course a flat fee, in which a study of the program is made and a definite dollars-and-cents amount quoted.

Rather than complicate matters I usually work out a fee arrangement to include travel, with a stipulated number of trips this is to include. Six seems to be an average in my case.

There are two additional points which might require comment: sometimes it is necessary or advantageous for one reason or another to place the interior designer's contract under the architect's. Often when this is done it is because the Authority refuses to hire such a consultant—who perhaps is wanted by the librarian—but is agreeable to extending that of the architect to include interior matters. The second point has to do with consolidating consultants into a single contract—that of the library buildings consultant and the interior planner. I have started doing this in some cases. Under this method I will accept an entire contract to cover the entire scope of consultation with the agreement that I will in turn retain a competent library consultant, paid from my fee, to round the "Team." This is done because some Boards resist the hiring of one consultant after another, becoming confused by the multiple advisory "needs" requested.

Other Consultants. Many competent architects do not have on their staff engineers who are capable of designing difficult foundations, heating, air conditioning, plumbing, and electric-lighting installations for a large and complicated library building. In some cases they will, as part of their assignment, call in one or more consulting engineers for the work. Sometimes the institution may ask the architect to select the engineering consultant or ask him to work with a man selected by it in order to ensure the desired results. If the initiative is taken by the institution, it must expect to pay for the additional cost but, whatever arrangements are made, the financial implications should be examined, and agreements should be reached.

An architect's contract ordinarily includes the foundation, structural, heating, air conditioning, plumbing, and electrical parts of the work. If he does not have in his own organization men who can supply these services, he will engage engineers at his own expense. Engineering consultants, under these circumstances, are ordinarily employed only when an unusual problem is encountered. Then they are often engaged for special services either by the architect or the owner. Such services as soil and foundation investigation, acoustical engineering, and lighting design are specific and common examples.

12.3 The Selection of the Architect

One thing that college and university administrative officers can be sure of is that the selection of a good architect is essential if a well-planned library building is to come into being. This chapter cannot give full specifications, but it suggests that the following characteristics are essential.

1. The architect must be professionally competent.

2. He must be able and prepared to interpret the needs of his client. (A client's wishes may be and often are quite different from his needs, and he requires help in reconciling them.)

3. He must have the imagination and creative ability to produce satisfactory results if given a good and intelligible program.

4. He must be a good listener, with a clear mind, but must also have the ability to explain clearly his own point of view.

5. He must understand the institution for which he is working, its problems, and its educational objectives.

6. He must realize that the functions required by his client's problems, rather than his own inclinations, should dictate his architectural answers. If his client's wishes and needs do not coincide, he is free to try to persuade the client of that fact, but his primary task is to answer his client's needs functionally and aesthetically.

7. He must, of course, have good taste and a feeling for what is appropriate and must be prepared to plan a building so that the functional requirements of the inside are integrated and in harmony with the outside; he must have a full understanding of the importance and weight of both function and appearance.

8. He must know the costs of constructing the building that he plans and must not underestimate them, while on the other hand he must not overestimate so much that the client does not obtain as good a building as he should from the available funds.

9. He must have on his own staff or readily available engineering competence, which is highly important in producing good plans today. Without this help he cannot produce a good building.

10. He must be prepared to get help, when he needs it, from an architectural, engineering, or library consultant.

11. He must have a staff proportionate to the task he is working on, so as to be able to produce the working drawings and specifications in reasonable time.

12. He must have almost infinite patience, but if his client demands changes so late in the planning process that they cannot be carried through without extra cost, he must in due course say firmly that no more changes are possible.

13. He must not insist that he knows more about his client's requirements than the client himself, but he must have the tact and ability to get his ideas across.

14. He must always be ready to learn. No one knows everything.

15. He must realize that genius alone, admitting that he has it, is not enough.

16. He must be prepared to admit to himself and his client that a distinguished building that is not functionally sound will not be satisfactory.

17. And in addition to all these, he must be a man of integrity.

Beyond these seventeen characteristics, other matters must be considered. If a competent local architect can be found, certain advantages will undoubtedly result. The cost, other things being equal, may be less. His knowledge of building materials locally available, of building codes, construction firms, labor, and special community problems, should be valuable. He will be available when wanted; the client will not have to wait for a week or more when it is necessary to deal with him. His services will also be more readily available during construction. It is of first importance for the architect to keep track of what is going on during that period.

An architect supplies supervision of a job under construction as part of his normal services. If an architect from a distance is selected, he should have a local representative during construction, in order to avoid complications.

It should be emphasized again that the architect must be honest with his client and himself and must be sure what can be built with the funds available. If the cost is underestimated, unfortunate compromises will generally have to be made, or perhaps the whole campus building program may be jeopardized. Too often the architect fails to face up to the real cost until so late that embarrassing situations result. It is suggested that an architect should not be selected until the institution has consulted some of his former clients on this and other points.

Another problem that should be kept in mind is whether the architect should be an expert in library building planning. This is less important than his skill, competence, and imagination, his willingness to listen, and his honesty in facing building costs. Ordinarily of course, an experienced library architect should be selected. If the architect selected has not had experience in library building planning, and particularly if the librarian has never been through the mill of planning a library, it is of the utmost importance that consultants be called in. The question of consultants has been dealt with in section 12.2 above. The architect's assignments and fees were discussed in Chapter 3 under financial problems.

The importance of good architecture and the selection of a good architect cannot be overestimated. The architect's role is not a simple one. His tasks are varied. He should have an opportunity to influence the building program if he finds flaws or omissions in it. He must be an artist and designer, who can bring together the complex elements that make up a building in such a way that it is efficient, workable, and pleasing. He must have the requisite technical knowledge of materials and of structural and mechanical systems. He must also have competence as a supervisor and coordinator.

The American Institute of Architects, with its national headquarters at 1735 New York Avenue, N.W., Washington, D.C., and its chapters and state organizations, as well as similar organizations in other countries, distribute pamphlets which should be useful in selecting an architect or architectural firm. The following titles indicate their scope: *The Role of the Architect, a Brief Outline; Facts about Your Architect and His Work; Architectural Services and Compensations.* Do not hesitate to write to Washington or your local AIA chapter for information. The series of articles in *The Architectural Forum* beginning in July, 1963, called "What It Takes to Be a Client," with individual titles as follows, "How to Pick an Architect"; "What Architects Do and How to Pay Them"; "How to Turn a Problem into a Set of Building Plans"; "How to Go from Concept to Construction"; and "How to Turn a Set of Plans into a Building," should be useful in selecting and dealing with an architect.

Architectural Competitions. Early in the century architectural competitions were not unusual for a library, particularly in the case of large buildings. This device is still used occasionally in the United States and more frequently abroad. Theoretically, it has several advantages. If a number of architects attack a specific building problem, results should be better than if one of them is chosen in advance and told to do the best he can. A competition calls attention to the building and provides publicity that may make fund raising easier. It may allay criticism after the building is built; people will feel that every effort has been made to obtain the best possible plan. Often these arguments for an architectural competition are more theoretical than practical. It should generally be possible to select a competent architect and to work with him closely enough so that a good building will result without a competition, which in itself is bound to be expensive and take time.

Possible objections to a competition are the fact that the winner may have presented a plan that is exciting and sensational, but unfortunately is not particularly functional, and it is difficult to make changes after he is selected. The architect may claim that he won the competition because of certain proposals in his plan and may be unwilling to alter them. Competitions take extra time—sometimes six months or more. They are costly because of prize giving and other inevitable expenses. The first prize, which goes to the winner, is considered part of the regular fee, if the building is constructed. But the other prizes and the expenses of the competition are all extras. Competitions are not judged by the client but by a group of judges, the majority of whom are architects who may be more interested in architectural features than library function. Many of the better architects hesitate to compete because of the work involved and fear that their reputations will be damaged if they do not win.

There are two main kinds of architectural competition: (1) limited competitions open only to a selected group of architects invited to participate, and (2) open competitions to which one and all are invited. These may be national or international in scope.

Attention is called to three recent library building competitions, one in the United States and two abroad. The American one was for the recently completed Washington University Library. The original structures on the campus of that university were built largely to provide quarters for the St. Louis Exposition of 1904. Buildings added later followed the general architectural style of the exposition. Criticism was sure to arise if changes were made for new construction. There was a limited competition in which three local and three nationally known architects were invited to participate. All the plans presented were for exciting buildings. The winner was a local architect, and the building which has now been completed is without doubt one of our better university libraries. More than one of the other plans submitted, while good from the architectural point of view, would have been disastrous functionally and perhaps financially.

Trinity College, Dublin, in 1960 and 1961 had a competition for an addition to supplement its great early-eighteenth-century building, which is one of the finest libraries architecturally to be found anywhere in the world. It was believed there that the publicity that would come from a competition would be useful in raising funds and that, while there was danger of serious criticism of any plan selected, this danger would be less if it could be selected from a large number. There were 218 submissions,

and it is interesting to note that most of those that received prizes or honorable mention were, taken as a whole, functionally satisfactory.

The third competition was for a new national library for Argentina, which will serve also as a library for the University of Buenos Aires. There were a large number of entries. The winner presented a plan which might be called completely unorthodox but which, considering all of the circumstances, may with no basic changes turn out to be a good functional library building.

Architectural competitions should always be conducted under the direction of the local Institute of Architects or, in the case of international competitions, of the International Institute of Architects, which has its headquarters in Paris. There are accepted rules and regulations for these competitions, which are distributed by the various institutes of architects.

12.4   The Question of a Program

Before the task of preparing a program is undertaken, three points should be considered: What is the purpose of a program? Should there be one? Who should write it?

What Is the Purpose of a Program? It is sufficient to summarize the reasons for a program as follows:

1. The preparation of a program is the best way that has been found for the librarian, his staff, and the institution's administration to determine the essential needs of the library and to make all concerned face up to them.

2. It provides the librarian with an opportunity to point out to the institution's administrative officers and the faculty the physical and, to a lesser extent, the other requirements of the library and to obtain formal approval of this estimate of requirements and of methods to be used in dealing with them. This approval is a matter of first importance.

3. It forms the basis on which the architect can plan a satisfactory building. Much of this volume deals with this third purpose and the things that develop in connection with it, but the first two reasons should be emphasized and not forgotten as the program is prepared.

Should There Be a Program? When the time came to plan the Lamont Undergraduate Library at Harvard, the author knew that building programs were sometimes written, although before the Second World War it had been unusual for librarians to prepare them. But he did not feel competent to write one, in spite of the fact that he thought he knew pretty well what he wanted. Fortunately, he had dealt with his architect on other occasions. He was sure that he could work with him and that a program could be evolved between them as time went on and plans developed, without setting it down formally. These circumstances may have been rather unusual but, fortunately, the plan worked reasonably well with Lamont. A written program is strongly recommended, however. Without one, the advantages that can and should come from points 1 and 2 above will be lost, the architect will be too much on his own without guidelines, and it will be difficult for the librarian and his institution to bring their influence and ideas to bear on those who design the library.

Who Should Write the Program? Theoretically, at least, the librarian should write the program, if he is capable of doing so, because he should and generally does know more about the requirements than anyone else. But there are competent librarians who are not equipped with sufficient background for the preparation of a program, although some of them could with time and effort acquire it. The literature on the subject is considerable. A selection from it is listed in the Selective Annotated Bibliography in Appendix D. It is hoped that this volume will provide a substantial addition to that literature.

As just noted, certain librarians are not suitable candidates for the task of program writing and should not undertake it, either because of lack of native ability, because their time could be spent to better advantage in other ways, or because of the availability of a better person to undertake it. In any case, the librarian should be closely in touch with the preparation of the program, and, for his own protection and that of others concerned, should pass on it before it is turned over to the architect.

In a large library there will sometimes be a senior assistant to whom the main responsibility for the task can be assigned. This person may be either a man or a woman, though sometimes it is easier for a man to obtain the required information. The program writer should talk over certain problems with the institution's building-maintenance force; he might find it useful to discuss matters with builders and architects of his acquaintance, with administrative officers of the institution, and with others. Often these conversations can be carried on more successfully by a man than a woman. It should be stated, however, that the author has worked with a number of women college librarians who have written first-class programs and seem to understand the problems involved better than many men with whom he has dealt.

In some colleges and universities there is a building expert or administrative officer to whom the task might well be assigned by the president or trustees, but, if this is done, the person selected should work very closely with the librarian and his staff to make sure that use is made of their special knowledge of the needs. The program writing in most cases should not be a one-man affair. It should be a compilation of the best information that the institution can gather together on the subject, and the one primarily responsible for preparing it should not hesitate to call for help from others. An experienced library consultant may be as useful here as at other stages in the building planning proceedings. Sometimes, but only as a last resort, the consultant is asked to write the program. The outsider can help and be very useful, but he can rarely know and understand the institution as well as the program writer should, and in order to do a first-class job, he must learn more about it than he can be expected to do in the time available. Whoever writes the program, engineering and technical help from the staff of the institution or from outside should be made available, because any statements dealing with engineering problems such as construction, plumbing, heating, ventilating, air conditioning, lighting, etc., should be examined and approved by someone who has more than a layman's knowledge of what is involved.

Who Should Pass on the Program? When the program has been completed who should pass on it? If the architect is to pay proper attention to it, he must be made to realize that it records more than the hastily prepared ideas of the librarian or an outside consultant. It is to be considered an official document of the institution and its administration. The program should, therefore, be approved by the library committee of the faculty, by the administrative officers, including the president, and, finally, perhaps, by the governing board. After emphasizing the necessity of these formalities, we should add that architects should be told that the program is not a Bible or the "laws of the Medes and the Persians that cannot be changed" as planning proceeds, and that mutually agreed-upon alterations are to be permitted and encouraged if they represent improvements.

The architect might prefer to consider the program unchangeable in order to prevent his client, too late in the planning process, from altering the ground rules. There should be a definite understanding that up to an agreed-upon point in the planning process both sides are free to question the program and propose changes if they believe that a better building will result. But there should also be an understanding that the time must come when further changes cannot be made without an addition to the architect's fees, just as there should be an understanding that the plans submitted by the architect must be satisfactory to the institution and represent a building that can be built with the funds which he has been told are available. If the architect is commissioned to plan a building before the funds are available, there should be an understanding as to his fees if the building is not constructed. All this may be outside the province of a librarian, but it should be part of the contract between the institution and the architect which will be signed by both before the work is undertaken. The matter is mentioned here simply to call attention to the business details that should be settled in advance in order to avoid later misunderstanding and unpleasantness.

12.5 Decisions on Basic Problems before Detailed Planning Begins

At least nine major policy decisions should be agreed upon before the writing of the program for a library building plan is completed. These policy decisions, which may affect the whole enterprise, should answer the following questions:

1. Can or should a new building be avoided by undertaking alterations, additions, decentralization, or by other means? This is discussed in section 15.1.

2. What is the plan for supervision? Will efforts be made to supervise each room or simply the exits? In this connection, reference to section 6.1 is suggested.

3. Will nonlibrary facilities be housed in the building temporarily or permanently? This possibility is discussed in section 13.5 and also in this chapter.

4. Are the book stacks to be closed- or open-access?

5. What percentage of individual accommodations for readers is desired?

6. What is the understanding about smoking in the library?

7. Is the divisional plan of service to be used?

8. What provision is to be made for future growth when the new building is full?

9. Where will the structure be placed? While thought will undoubtedly be given to the site selection long before this stage is reached, it is well to review it at this time in the light of the answers to the eight questions above and after the selection of the architects and the consultants (if any). The question of site selection is discussed in section 15.2.

Exit Controls. Many libraries, particularly smaller ones and those in rural areas, with high-quality students, may feel that there is no need of exit control of any kind either to the book stacks or the building itself; that the students are honest, that books will not be taken out without authorization, and that one can just forget about controlling the exits because there are practically no disciplinary problems.

The author must confess that, with such knowledge of human nature as he has accumulated in the past sixty years in library work, he is inclined to feel that any new library should be planned so that exits can be controlled easily without adding unreasonably to the cost of the operation of the library. Some libraries provide for this by narrowing the exit lanes, so that attendants have no difficulty in checking everyone who leaves the building. In others, turnstiles are installed as an aid. Some librarians object violently, not only to turnstiles, but to checking of any kind, considering it an insult to those who are checked. But too many libraries have found to their regret that books were disappearing wholesale and that checking at the exits is a deterrent. The books that seem most likely to take flight are those for assigned reading. Usually they come back when the student is through with them, but meanwhile they are not available when other students need them. Libraries with a collection of rare and irreplaceable books have often found that it is desirable to segregate them and give them out only after a call slip has been signed so that it is known at all times who has any one of the books that is not in its place on the shelves.

The Lamont Library at Harvard was so planned that at least during quiet times of the day the attendant at the desk where books are regularly charged can also check any volume, library or personal, that a student wants to take from the building. This saves staff, and in many cases saves a double check, one at the charging desk and one at the exit.

If academic libraries were never used by any-one except persons directly connected with the institution, the controls discussed in this section could often be omitted, but it should always be remembered that, particularly in urban areas, there may well be an influx of high school students, students from other institutions, and the general public, to say nothing of professional book thieves, who sooner or later may well descend on any institution which has valuable holdings.

In any case, exit controls constitute a policy problem that should be decided before the program is sent to the architect, because they should be taken into account in planning the structure.

Nonlibrary Facilities. Since libraries tend to grow very rapidly, particularly in newer institutions that are gathering collections for use by large numbers of students, it is often desirable to construct a building considerably larger than will be necessary for the first five years or more; the additional space will inevitably be needed later. But any new institution that is growing rapidly will almost always have greater space demands than can be readily met. It has become not unusual, therefore, to use part of the library building for other than library purposes during the first years after its construction. These other purposes may be of almost any kind. The space has often been used for the general administrative quarters of the institution. Classrooms have often been placed in a library, with the idea that they would be removed later as the demands for space on the part of the library increased and a new separate classroom building could be made available. Audiovisual departments, which are growing rapidly, have sometimes been assigned library space, with the understanding that they would have quarters of their own at a later time.

Two points should be made in connection with the proposal for use of library space for other than library purposes. The first is that if the library exits are to be controlled and if books and papers carried by the users of the library are to be checked at the exits, it is desirable and almost obligatory to have a separate exit and entrance for the parts of the building used for nonlibrary purposes. With modern flexible construction, this is comparatively easy.

It is sometimes irritating to the user of the other part of the building who would like to come directly into the library without going outdoors, to have to walk around the building and then come into the same structure again, but it is strongly advised that when nonlibrary activities are assigned to a library they be given a separate entrance and exit, if the arrangement is in any way feasible. Another possibility is illustrated by the Lamont Library at Harvard. There, access to the ten classrooms in the building is through the entrance lobby and then by stairwells that are cut off acoustically from the parts of the building used for library purposes. This works out well, although it does necessitate checking the students who have attended classes and are leaving the building, just as though they had been using the library and library books. (See Fig. 13.4*A–C*.)

The second problem, equally serious, and one emphasized by many librarians, is that when extraneous services are permitted in the library it is almost impossible to get rid of them, even when the library is in desperate need of space. The institution's administrative staff often find the library one of the most attractive buildings on the campus. They hate to ask for other space, knowing the needs of other parts of the institution, and tend to stick to their quarters in spite of the fact that they are no longer welcome. Classrooms are almost always in great demand, and the library will find it hard to remove them once they are installed.

The attitude of the author is that when an institution is pressed for space, the librarian, if he is to obtain additional space within his building or by the construction of an addition or a new building, must be able to prove that his need is greater than that of others, and that giving the library additional space will be better policy for the institution educationally than making any other arrangement. In other words, the librarian must take his turn with the others, and must prove his case. There will undoubtedly be occasions when he will suffer, but it will not add to his prestige or his popularity with the administrative officers or with the institution as a whole, if, like a dog in a manger, he holds space that he does not need for even a few years for the sake of having it later when it is desirable.

Open or Closed Stack Access. While in most libraries, there has been since time immemorial a certain amount of access to the main book collections by a limited number of readers, on the whole until the past generation the book stacks have generally been closed to the public in academic libraries. In some medieval libraries books were chained to their cases, so that they could not be taken away. In many of the libraries constructed during the nineteenth century, the books were stored to a large extent in one tier after another of alcoves surrounding a great hall. Users of the library were admitted to these alcoves, sometimes freely, sometimes under restriction, but a certain amount of supervision was possible. In the later years of the century, when the accumulation of books became so great that the only way to store them seemed to be in large multitier stack rooms, with parallel ranges close together so as to increase the capacity, stacks were generally closed to the public. In academic institutions it became customary, however, to admit members of the teaching staff. Then graduate students were admitted, and later more and more of the smaller academic libraries opened up the book stack freely to the other students and the whole clientele of the library. As time went on it became more and more customary to provide for seating in the book stack, so as to make it convenient, particularly for an advanced scholar, to obtain the books he required in his work and often to reserve them in a carrel to which he was assigned. The above statement has nothing new in it, but it must not be forgotten as it is an important part of the background of library planning.

One might say, what does this have to do with the basic planning of a library? The answer is simply this: If the use of the stack is to be very much restricted, the entrances and exits to it must be controlled. If the stack is to be completely wide open and the readers admitted anywhere, there is no problem about control of the stack, but any control provided must be shifted to the exits. In a large building, particularly, this problem may become one of considerable complexity and may well affect the basic plan. The ten-story Widener Library stack at Harvard, to which faculty and graduate students have almost completely free access but to which access by undergraduates is limited, has some 31 different doors. It is wrapped around three sides of the building. Obviously, there cannot be 31 exit controls. There are doors at each of these exits which can be locked. It has been customary to give to faculty members keys that will fit the stack doors—but not the outside doors of the building; students, however, can go in and out any one of the three entrances, two controlled by one desk and the third by another. Both control desks are manned by persons to whom other duties are assigned. Fortunately, these desks are so placed that stack access is not too inconvenient for the student. This is simply one way that has been found of controlling a large book stack. Serious construction problems may arise unless the decision as to what is to be done is made very early in the planning. If the public entrance to the stack is at one place and one only, it is comparatively easy to place that entrance at a service desk where an attendant is always on duty while the building is open. But it can readily be seen that, if the stack is an extensive one, spreading over a number of floors and opening into public rooms or corridors on those floors, a serious problem is presented. The best solution is obviously to plan the building so that the stack entrance can be controlled, preferably at one place only, and that any other exits required by fire regulations will be emergency exits, perhaps with crash locks.

Individual Seating. Until comparatively recently the general practice was to seat readers in libraries at large tables. Often, in order to increase the capacity, less than 3 running feet was assigned for each reader at the side of a table. As readers enter a large reading room, they almost automatically space themselves out as far as possible from each other until the number in the room makes it necessary for them to sit closer together. But reading rooms were often not large enough, and large tables seemed to be the way to provide the largest number of seats in a given number of square feet.

However, the custom gradually developed of placing carrels along one or more sides of book stacks, thus providing for individual seating close to the books. This was first done on a large scale in the Widener Library, where in 1915 nearly 300 carrels were installed. Libraries in due course began to place individual tables wherever they could in buildings, sometimes in carrel form, sometimes simply small individual tables. It was evident that students were glad to have these individual accommodations and that in almost all cases they were the first seats in a building to be used. In the past fifteen years the percentage of individual accommodations in libraries throughout the world has been increasing rapidly. This problem was discussed in more detail in section 7.3. Some may say that this is simply a temporary trend, and that there will be a change as time goes on. Some will say that the expense of providing individual seating is prohibitive because it will take more square footage per person and will cost more. On the other hand, it can be said with justification that individual accommodations properly arranged will tend to keep the library quieter, will help to solve disciplinary problems, and do not necessarily take more space.

Section 16.3 on layouts will indicate different methods of individual seating. It must be admitted that the peak load in libraries comes at examination time when students will study almost anywhere and that during the rest of the year when the library is only partially full, the students will scatter around the tables and keep as far away from each other as possible. At any rate, it is evident that a decision should be made, and the program for the architect should state the type of reader accommodations desired, if a large percentage of individual accommodations are to be provided, because it may have a considerable effect on the basic plan of the proposed building.

Smoking. Smoking involves another policy decision that should be made before a building is planned, because of the effect on ventilation and, incidentally, on the comfort of both the smoker and the nonsmoker. It has been dealt with in section 7.2. Until comparatively recent years, smoking was prohibited altogether in almost all libraries. As the practice of smoking increased, there was a gradual change in the attitude toward it. Some of the graduate departmental libraries in the large universities permitted smoking, while the main library did not. Special smoking areas were sometimes set aside. But four problems remained: the fire risk, the effect of smoking on ventilation, the dirt which is bound to follow the use of tobacco, and finally the inconvenience and sometimes dismay caused

to the reader who dislikes studying in a smoke-filled room.

The recent study on protecting the library indicated that one-sixth of library fires had their origin in smoking.[3] The fire hazard was particularly great in the old-fashioned book stack, with ventilation slits which made the whole area a chimney. The question of fire risks has been discussed in section 10.2.

The problem of the dirt has been ignored in some libraries by simply saying that they would not worry about it, and smoking is permitted anywhere in the reading areas. An alternative is recommended: to provide special smoking areas in the building to which the student or faculty member must go when he wants to smoke. Some libraries have found that when only one room in a library was provided for smoking, the traffic back and forth to that room became a disturbing factor. When the Lamont Library at Harvard was planned, a smoking area was provided on each of the five undergraduate levels of the building. At something like one-third of all the seats in Lamont smoking is allowed, and this fact is made evident by placing large and not particularly attractive ash trays at frequent intervals in smoking areas, but smoking is not permitted in the book stacks or in the three large reading rooms. It seems fair to say that the amount of space where smoking is permitted could have been reduced somewhat without causing any particular inconvenience. It must also be admitted that smoking habits may change in the years ahead, and the number of seats where it is sanctioned should be accordingly increased or decreased.

The final problem in connection with smoking deals with ventilation. When smoking is permitted in a large reading room the atmosphere tends to become pretty thick. A frequent change of air will help a great deal. A large percentage of new library buildings today are being air-conditioned for the sake of the books, if not for the readers. If there is air conditioning or forced ventilation, it should be remembered that a certain amount of the air is generally recirculated in order to hold down costs. Arrangements are sometimes made to confine the smoking to a limited number of bays in one corner of the

[3] *Protecting the Library and Its Resources,* LTP Publications, no. 7, American Library Association, Chicago, 1963, p. 7.

building and to have the air exhausted from that area, not recirculated. In the Lamont Library there are three air-conditioning units, one for the two levels of storage book stack in the basement which have nothing to do with the undergraduates and where because of the comparatively small use and the good insulation—this area is completely underground—the air-conditioning problem is comparatively simple. A second covers a part of the building, including the stack areas and the large reading rooms where smoking is not permitted, which is on a separate unit; and the third, the smaller area, where smoking is permitted. In this particular case it might be noted that because of uncertainty as to the extent of smoking areas that would be desired, the ventilation unit for the section where smoking is permitted was made large enough so that additional space in the building could be shifted to it from the second area.

Divisional Plan. During the past twenty years a considerable number of the larger academic libraries have adopted the divisional plan of library service. The commonest form is to have three divisions, one for the humanities, one for social sciences, and one for sciences. This might be said to divide the service of the library into three main groups in separate quarters. At the University of Nebraska, for instance, this plan has been carried to its logical conclusion, and each of the divisions has its own collections and its own reference staff of specialists in the fields covered, and also does its own book selection, ordering, and cataloguing. This is not the place to argue for or against this plan or to make comments on the basic plan or the number of divisions. Many libraries have a separate division for general reference material and one for periodicals; some have one for public documents, and so on. But it is evident that when the collections are to be divided, and particularly if the reading areas are to be divided, the plan of the whole building is affected. It is sometimes possible to adapt an old building to the divisional plan if there are a number of large reading rooms, but in general if the subject-division plan is to be adopted, it is easier to put into effect in connection with a new building.

We might outline here some of the difficulties arising from the divisional plan, not in order to criticize but simply to state the problem. The more services are divided, the more the cost rises, if service for the full opening hours of the library is to be provided in each division. The larger the number of units, the more difficult it is to determine the space requirements for each division. Estimating space requirements for a whole library is difficult enough, but a fair guess can be made. When the space is to be divided up, the possibility of, and particularly the percentage of, miscalculation for any one section is likely to be very largely increased.

On the other hand, no one can deny that having specialists to select, to catalogue, and to serve books in a general subject field should be a very great advantage. The point to be made here is that if there is any thought that a divisional plan is to be adopted, it should be in the program for the new building, and final decision in connection with it should be made in advance if complications are to be avoided.

Provision for Growth. As has been indicated elsewhere in this volume, one thing that a library can be sure of is that its space needs will increase as the years go by. Even if the number of students does not increase, and we know all too well that in general it will, the book collections will tend to grow. About the only exception to this situation that can be thought of occurs when a college for one reason or another absolutely refuses to permit the number of students to increase, deciding that quality counts rather than quantity, and when it then at the same time takes the attitude that its book collection can be continually weeded out and does not have to go beyond the number that can be housed in its present building. A few college librarians and more academic administrators have said there is no need for the library ever to go beyond a certain figure. This figure may be 50,000, 100,000, 250,000, or 500,000. The same situation holds in universities, but the figures for the maximum size of collections are much larger. It is well to keep in mind three points: (1) The quality of the students tends to increase if their number does not, their use of the library increases, and enlarged seating accommodations become essential; (2) curriculum changes and a shift from textbook to other types of instruction are tending to increase demands for both seating space and enlarged collections; and (3) no one has as yet been able to find a satisfactory way of holding down the size of collections when the maximum agreed upon earlier in good faith and after earnest consideration is reached.

At the time a new building is planned, it is suggested that even if an agreement restricting the ultimate size of the collections has been reached, a way out be provided. It is evidently very important to plan almost all new libraries so that they can be added to, unless it is admitted and agreed that you cannot plan anything today to last more than a limited number of years and that at the end of twenty-five years or some other definite period, the building can be discarded as a library, if not for all purposes, and replaced.

Two other possibilities can be mentioned, however, particularly in a university. It can say, as a number of large universities have done in recent years, that when the present building is outgrown, the collections can be decentralized. If this is to be done, one method is to develop a research library for the institution and a separate undergraduate library, using either the present building or the new one for one group or the other. Or the library can make arrange-

ments for more compact storage of the collections, either by shifting ranges closer together (this will be possible only if the bay size permits it and multitier stacks have not been used) or by the installation of some one of the types of compact storage discussed in section 8.3.

But, as has been said above, before the building is planned some decision should be reached as to what is to be done about additional space needs when the proposed building becomes inadequate. While it cannot be guaranteed that the course of action decided upon today will be taken a generation from now, at least retreat would not be cut off. And almost always a site should be selected with space for a satisfactory addition, and the internal planning should be so arranged that traffic patterns in and to the addition will be simple, floor heights will not be complicated, and the building with its addition will be functional and handsome.

The program should state clearly the desired answers to each of these problems, and they should be kept in mind in connection with the sections of this volume that follow.

The Program for Assignable Space Requirements

Introduction

Chapter 12 has discussed the preliminary steps that should be taken before a program for a new library building can be written satisfactorily. This chapter deals with the program itself. As an integral part of it but as an introduction, the objectives of the institution and its library should be described, in order to provide the planning team and later the architect with what might be called the atmosphere and philosophical background on which to base his plans. This is an important feature of the program and should help the architect and the consultant, if there is one, to understand the more specific requests. It should present the institution's wishes and attitude in regard to fundamental policy and requirements concerning which there might be questions. It should set the tone for the whole project.

In an institution where the librarian is a comparative newcomer or for some other reason is not well qualified to write this part of the program, there may be someone else to whom the task should be assigned—a professor, an administrative officer, a senior library committee member, or in some cases the president himself. Often it would be easy to write a long dissertation on the subject, but a short concise statement, only a few pages long at most, will be equally useful and less confusing to the architect and others concerned. The statement should be detailed enough, however, to tell what the institution is trying to accomplish and the role that the library is expected to play in its educational program. It should not deal with the present situation only; the future is an even more important factor in planning a new building. Any prospective changes in the educational program and curriculum that would affect the library should be noted, as well as anticipated changes in the size, character, or intellectual level of the student body or in the percentage of those doing graduate work. Appendix A includes sample statements of objectives that may suggest points to be covered, but each library differs from every other, needs its own statement, and should not copy one prepared for another.

After the objectives of the institution and the library have been stated, the program should indicate to the architect the facilities required in the proposed structure. This should be done in terms of sizes, quantity, quality, and such other attributes as the planning committee agrees upon.

There should always be a careful statement of spatial relationships between the different services, and somewhere in the document should be a description of how the library operates and is administered. The program should also give as accurate information as possible about plans for the future, when the building is outgrown, so that the architect can prepare a design to which a later addition is practicable. In many libraries special facilities that are not necessary adjuncts to the library should be listed and described if they are to be included.

The statements for reader accommodations and shelving should be first of all quantitative in character, specifying the number of persons to be cared for at one time and the number of volumes to be housed, but they should go well beyond this, because the library will expect to provide a variety of different accommodations for readers, and it will house not only monographs and bound volumes of serials, but other materials as well. Unless each group is recorded and described, the architect will be at a loss to know what to provide for and what equipment will be required. He must also be given some idea as to how the space is to be divided. Are there to be separate rooms for reference books or for periodicals, for instance? How many volumes and readers are to be accommodated in each of a large number of separate areas? It is probably dangerous and unwise to try to tell the architect exactly how many square feet will be required in the reference and other rooms, but the program can properly specify that the reference room should house, for instance, 3,000 volumes and 50 readers. Moreover, it may not be improper to suggest in the program that it should be possible to provide suitable accommodations for undergraduate readers in 25 or 30, or some other specified number of square feet per reader, or that 12 or 15 or some other number of volumes can be stored in a square foot of stack floor space. This will give the architect some idea of the problem that he is facing, if he is not acquainted with library planning. It can also call to the attention of those concerned any differences of opinion in regard to square footage requirements before serious misunderstandings develop.

The program must then indicate what is desired, quantitatively, but the architect should always have an opportunity to make proposals of his own on the planning and design of the square footage needed to fill the requirements.

The program should rarely dictate in detail the type of heating, ventilation, and air conditioning, but it can properly say, for instance, that a ventilation system should be provided which will include filtering and humidification in the winter but not cooling in the summer, if that is what has been decided upon. The quality and intensity of lighting desired is important. A statement that tables should be finished well enough so that they do not have to be refinished at frequent intervals is an example of a com-

paratively minor consideration that might properly be included. All of these and many other matters will be dealt with in some detail in the sections that follow in this chapter and in Chapter 14. Background theoretical information in regard to them was included in Chapters 7 to 11.

The program, stated in the simplest possible terms, should provide answers to the questions on which the architect will need information in order to design the building. He must be told the number of seating accommodations wanted and the amount of shelving to be provided. The other facilities that will be required must be made known to him. The number of square feet that these accommodations will use depends in part on the plans he must make but cannot be completely dictated by him. The problem of the square footage per reader and volume capacity per foot is basic; it must ultimately be determined, and an agreement on space and equipment-layout arrangements must be reached by the architect in close collaboration with the institution's representatives. The librarian should know what he requires. The architect should tell him how to get it, and what the total space requirements will be. Neither one should dictate to the other in an arbitrary fashion.

This question of total square-footage requirements is taken up in more detail in section 14.5.

One way to clarify the program problem is to put down the various questions to which the architect should provide answers. Some of them will be stated in this and the next chapter, much as the architect might put them before the institution's representatives if a program were not provided. These questions, with commentary on them, will be asked for each of the main categories of space needs.

13.1 Accommodations for Readers

The program should answer the following questions in regard to reader accommodations:

1. How many seats altogether should be provided in the building for each of the following groups: undergraduates, graduate students, faculty, visiting scholars, and others who will use it; the last of these groups may include alumni, local adult residents, high school students, and casual visitors. The basic problems that arise in determining the number of accommodations required for each group are discussed from the

theoretical point of view in section 7.1. In the program the answers must be worked out with the present and future situation in mind.

2. How many seats should be in each area where readers are to be housed? Twenty-four possible areas, discussed theoretically in section 7.2, should be kept in mind.

3. What types of seating accommodations should be provided in each of the areas specified in 2 above? This problem and the space that each type of accommodation might occupy are discussed in section 7.3. The different types include primarily upholstered seating or what might be called lounge chairs, tables for one and other individual accommodations, tables of various kinds for two or more, as well as open and closed carrels and faculty studies.

It is obvious that to answer the three foregoing questions can be an exceedingly complicated task, requiring a large amount of detailed recording of requirements. It should not be improper to suggest to the architect and to specify in the program that he should have some leeway in allotting the number of seats and the types of accommodations in each of the areas for general reading, so long as the total number for each group is met by the building as a whole; that is, if he finds that he can readily provide more seats than the number specified in the reserve-book room and fewer in the general reading room, for instance, this might be satisfactory. Most areas, of course, will not be reserved completely for the use of one particular group of readers.

Appendix A, entitled "Program Examples," and Appendix B, "Formulas and Tables," should be consulted in this connection.

13.2 Accommodations for the Collections

1. What is the present count of volumes in the main stack collection?

The answer, or perhaps it is better to say the answers, to this question should include all printed materials, monographs, periodicals, public documents, etc., which are shelved as books. The significance of this figure is questionable because, as is noted in section 8.2, libraries have been unable to agree among themselves on a basis for counting, and even if they did agree, the average size of volumes in different libraries may vary as much as 20 per cent or more. In an attempt to simplify matters, stack manufacturers and librarians have from time to time worked out formulas for the number of volumes that can be shelved per lineal foot of stack space, varying the figures according to the subject of the books, using one formula for fiction, another for history and economics, and still others for science, law, medicine, and periodicals, etc. These are recorded in Appendix B, Table 11. But even if formulas are agreed upon, this is only a start, as will be seen by the questions that follow.

2. If the present collections included in question 1 above were shelved without vacant space for growth, how many standard single-faced sections, 3 ft wide and 7½ ft high, would be completely filled? This can be determined fairly precisely and without too great difficulty by a careful measurement of the collections, and the answer is generally more accurate and useful as a basis for computation for future requirements than any that can be obtained by the count of volumes or pieces proposed in question 1.

It is suggested that if 50 per cent is added to the answer to question 2, it will give the space now required for comfortable housing of collections in the average library using a subject classification. Although this result will be more accurate than one based on a count of volumes, it is often desirable at this point to check and compare the answer to question 2, plus 50 per cent, with the figure obtained when the answer to question 1 is divided by 125—this on the presumption that 125 average volumes will fill a section to comfortable working capacity.

3. What is the anticipated rate of growth of the collections in the years ahead? Is it expected to be arithmetical in character (i.e., an increase in numbers for the coming year approximately the same as in the years that follow it) or geometrical, with each year's growth being a fixed percentage of the number at the end of the immediately preceding year, by what might be called compound interest or geometric progression?

If each year's additions amount to 4 per cent of the present collection, it will take twenty-five years for space needs to double. On the other hand, a rate of 4 per cent per year compounded will double the collection in approximately eighteen years. Appendix B, Table 12 shows, for instance, that if the collections fill the shelves two-thirds full and are growing at the rate of 4 per cent annually by geometric progression, in six years the shelves will be 86 per cent full and, if the vacant space is equally distributed, there will be only 5 in. of vacant space for each shelf and the library will be in serious condition. If the collection is growing at the rate of 6 per cent a year, the crisis will come 4 years after the shelves are two-thirds full on the average.

4. How much on the average is the library prepared to place on its shelves before it regards them as filled to capacity?

In an attempt to answer this question, to simplify the problem, and to provide a firm basis on which to make estimates, computations might well be based on a standard library book section 36 in. long (it should be realized that shelves may vary from 34½ in. to 35½ in. with different types of shelving) and 90 in. high.

Librarians like to consider, as is indicated in 2 above, that when two-thirds of the space on each shelf is filled, the library has a comfortable working capacity. (Whether this will provide for 125 volumes to a standard section or a smaller or larger number will depend, as has been noted, on the subject field, the type of library, binding practices, and counting procedures.) They could, with considerable justification, say that shelves have reached full working capacity when on the average 75 per cent of the 36 in., or 27 in., are occupied. It must be kept in mind that, with books arranged by subject, as they almost invariably are in American libraries, growth is very irregular in any one subject, and additions may come rapidly, perhaps in the form of multivolume sets. The time comes when the cost of shifting and the damage done to bindings by shifting is so great that the provision of additional shelving is financially desirable. It probably should be admitted that shelves can be 86 per cent filled before a serious crisis arises, but by that time additional shelving should be available and not just in the planning stages.

It is evident in any case that plans for more shelving should be made a considerable time before it is an absolute necessity. Some will say that libraries have found that there is at least a grain of truth in the old saying, "There is always room for one more," but this, unfortunately, is too often counted on to the extent that the collection and the services are permitted to deteriorate while waiting for additional space.

5. How many years ahead are to be provided for at this time?

It is suggested that if an institution now has available funds for new construction but the requirements have not yet been given to an architect, the library cannot expect to occupy new space in less than two years, and that four years would be a safer figure to use. The problem is how many years beyond these two to four are to be planned for. While the answers to the questions set forth above make it easier to plan for the space required immediately and in a definite number of future years, it should always be realized that the best-laid plans may go awry. It is suggested as a basis for discussion by the planning team that a new library should provide space for twenty years after it is completed.

6. If the questions asked in 1 to 5 above do not apply to special collections of various kinds, reference, bibliography, and other collections in reading areas, nonbook collections, and other material not considered part of the main stack collection, what is the situation for each of these groups of materials?

It is suggested that housing for the reference and bibliographical collections, the current periodicals, rare books, archives, maps, pictorial materials, slides, and special collections of various kinds, perhaps music, fine arts, and public documents not shelved in the main collection, always including those that are now on hand and are expected to be on hand later, be considered separately. If there are to be special rooms, which were dealt with in section 7.2 above, what should their shelf capacity be? Would overflow from them be provided for in the stack? Storage facilities for uncatalogued materials waiting for cataloguing, materials being processed and on workroom shelving, unbound serials awaiting processing, materials on the way to the bindery, etc., should not be forgotten.

For each of these special groups different formulas for space occupied by the present collections and for the anticipated rate of growth should be made as far as possible with the realization that they probably cannot be as accurate as for the main-stack collection. And do not forget that if overflow from any of them is to be shelved in the main-stack areas, this overflow must be provided for.

Before the program requirements can be determined, answers to the six questions listed above should be prepared. A study of Appendix A, "Program Examples," and Appendix B, "Formulas and Tables," as well as Chapter 8, "Housing the Collections," should be useful at this point.

13.3 Other Facilities Generally Required for Public Use

Public Catalogue. The problems here are quite similar in character to those relating to accommodations for readers and collections. How many cards should be provided for? How many inches of filing space will they occupy now and later? How many filing trays will be needed and how many square feet will be required to take care of the number of cards and trays that are expected? How many persons will be using the catalogue at the time of peak loads? Space for them as well as for the card cabinets must be provided. All these matters are mentioned in section 11.2, dealing with library-furniture problems, and are discussed in detail in section 16.3.

The number of cards will depend upon the number and character of catalogued titles the library expects to include at the end of the period for which the space is planned to be adequate, and the library's policy in regard to cataloguing. For some libraries, 2½ cards per volume or 4 per title will be sufficient,[1] while for others the figure may be somewhat larger. Remember in the estimates the difference between volumes and titles and remember that if bound volumes of periodicals are included, as well as multivolume monographs, the number of titles in some libraries may be little if any more than half the number of volumes. Every title should, of course, have its main entry. The number of cards per title is affected by the number of added entries for editors, compilers, and joint authors; the cross references that are made; the extent to which title cards are included; the amount of analytical work carried on; the length of entries, which may result in more than one card for a title; and, most important of all, the number of subject cards used. This number varies tremendously in different libraries; the Library of Congress uses a great many more than some other large libraries, such as the Harvard College Library. If the number of volumes or titles now in the library is known with a fair degree of accuracy and the number of cards now in the catalogue can be estimated,

and if no change in cataloguing or acquisition policy is expected in the years ahead, a fairly accurate estimate can be made of the number of cards that should be provided for during the period for which the library is being constructed.

The next problem deals with the number of cards that can be suitably housed in an inch of filing space. This, of course, depends on the thickness of the cards; those used early in the century were much thicker than the new cards that are standard today. But it must also be remembered that cards tend to become thicker as the result of use. Eighty cards to an inch was a good basis for estimates fifty years ago. The Library of Congress cards and cards available for sale from other organizations have tended to become thinner year by year. New cards may run to as high as 110 to 120 to an inch when filed closely together. It is probably safer to figure on no more than 100 to an inch of net usable filing space in making provision for a catalogue. In order to give space for consultation and also to allow for irregular growth and the cost of shifting, net filing space should be estimated at approximately 70 per cent of the total inside measurements of the drawers between the front and back blocks.

The next question dealing with the amount of square footage required will depend primarily on the catalogue cases used and their arrangement in the room assigned to them. Space for cases will be based primarily on depth of trays and the number of trays in each vertical row in the installation selected. Their arrangement is discussed in detail in section 16.3.

The number of users of the catalogue, as well as its size, must be taken into account in the arrangement. In libraries with small collections, serving large numbers of readers, the problem is to provide space for the user, rather than for the cards. In a great research library with a comparatively small clientele, the opposite holds. In general terms, it can be said that a small collection with many readers can properly use fairly low cases and short trays, while a large collection with few readers should use higher cases and longer trays.

But the program itself should answer the following questions:

1. How many cards must be provided for?

2. How many trays should the height of the catalogue cases provide?

3. What length of tray is recommended?

---

[1] A volume is one physical unit. A title may include many volumes; for instance, Toynbee's *Study of History* has 12, the *Encyclopaedia Britannica* has 24, and the current volume of the *Atlantic Monthly* is no. 214.

4. How heavy is the use that is expected at the time of peak demand?

The answers can well be prepared after a study of section 11.2, on catalogue cases, section 16.3, and Appendix B.

Service Desks of All Kinds. Decisions regarding control stations, circulation, information, and reference desks are important. They may affect costs of library operation even more than they affect construction costs, because they are one of the basic factors that determine the size of the public-service staff. Each desk requires space for itself and for the library staff members who provide the service, plus an equal or greater amount of square footage adjacent to it for the library's clientele. Each desk also requires continuing expenditures to pay the salaries of the assistants stationed there, generally for many hours each week.

The Widener Library at Harvard can be open evenings and give service with only four desks manned, the circulation desk, the reference desk, and, because fire regulations require two exits, the two exit-control desks. For the Lamont Library, the figure can be reduced to three, as the circulation desks are combined with the two exit-control desks. At the same time many a comparatively small university library may, because of its organization, require service at a reference desk, a reserve-book desk, a periodical room, a circulation desk, and, if the divisional plan is used, several more reading-room desks, in addition to exit-control stations.

The program should answer the following questions or at least explain them in such a way that the architect can prepare answers:

1. What desks are to be provided and for what purpose?

2. How many staff members will be working at each desk at times of peak load?

3. How much work area for these members is required in the immediate vicinity or elsewhere?

4. How much space for readers is required adjacent to each desk?

The areas around service desks should be large enough to prevent congestion during times of peak loads. (Readers should not have to queue up unnecessarily at the circulation desk.) Seating accommodations, not in a regular reading area, should be provided in an adjacent space for those waiting for books to be brought from the stacks; these persons will include those who do not have stack access and those who

have been unable to find the volumes desired. These seats can properly be close to shelves provided for new books.

Readers should not have to line up at the reference desk, except very occasionally and then for limited periods, and a few chairs—perhaps those used also for the circulation desk if the two are adjacent to each other—should provide a satisfactory waiting space. It is suggested that readers in general should rarely be asked to sit while consulting a reference librarian, as they will tend to take twice as much time as necessary; but if the consultation is one where it is obvious that the time required is more than a few minutes, they should be invited into the reference librarian's office and provided with a chair, but not at the reference desk in view of others who may be waiting.

Ordinarily, readers should not have to line up for more than a very brief period at an exit-control desk. This means that in a busy library the lobby must be large enough to provide several check-out points for use during rush hours. It is suggested, as a basis for discussion, that one point should be adequate for a building with seating accommodations for 300 or less. Two might be required for from 300 to 800 seats; three for 800 to 1,500; four for 1,500 to 2,400; five for 2,400 to 3,500; and six for over 3,500 readers, the exact number depending on the number of students leaving the building in any five-minute period and the type of check-out required. The larger the number of readers, other things being equal, the larger the number one attendant can deal with, because the peak loads tend to be rounded off. The care with which a student's books are checked also affects the number of desks required. The suggestions proposed above should be carefully checked with the local situation in mind.

13.4 Staff Facilities

Basic theoretical problems of planning for staff facilities are covered in section 7.4. Staff demands for space may vary greatly between libraries, even among those with collections and clientele of the same size. Do not forget that staff areas have almost always tended to become inadequate sooner than those for other purposes. Staff areas required today may not reliably indicate tomorrow's requirements. There are five purposes for which space must be provided

—administrative offices, public-service staff, processing staff, maintenance staff, rest rooms and lounge accommodations. Each will vary in rate of growth from year to year.

The administrative group may change area requirements less than the others, unless it is affected by an alteration in the general organization. If, for instance, accounting and other business procedures are transferred to general university offices, the needs might decrease. If, because of growth of staff as a whole, a personnel officer with assistants is required, or if two or more assistant librarians instead of one are appointed, the total area required may be increased even disproportionately to that for other staff units.

The requirements for public or reader services depend largely on two factors: (1) the organization of the service and the planning of the building as a whole, which determines the number of desks that must be manned during all library hours, and (2) the amount and quality of service given—reference, circulation, and control—which stem from basic library policy and philosophy. High-quality service breeds greater demands, as does an increase in the number of students and their intellectual level. Whether students are commuters or whether dormitory provisions are suitable for study are also important factors. The educational policies of the institution as they affect the curriculum and the demands made on the library should not be forgotten. Remember also that a new and comfortable building will attract more students and that the same holds for improvements in the quality and size of the collections. Each of these affects the desirable size of the public-service staff and its space requirements.

The required size of the processing staff will depend primarily on (1) the rate of acquisition; (2) the total size of the collection—it generally takes more time to add a volume to a 1 million-volume library than to one with 100,000 volumes; and (3) cataloguing practices and policies, including the percentage of acquisitions catalogued with Library of Congress cards, and the use of mechanical methods for reproducing cards. In the past, processing staffs have tended to grow much more rapidly than expected, and quarters have become congested in altogether too short a time after entering a new building. The new Olin Libraries at Cornell and at Washington University, respectively, are examples.

Congestion is almost sure to affect efficiency.

Another feature which should not be forgotten is the question of a bindery. If the library is to have one, quarters must be made available and a considerable area is required.

The space required for the maintenance staff will, of course, depend on the total square footage to be cared for and the quality of the structure as far as it affects maintenance. Tables and chairs should be so planned as to make cleaning around them easy. Floor coverings vary in their upkeep needs and affect the square footage one janitor can deal with in a given period. The quality of maintenance to be provided will also affect the size of the staff. But do not reduce the space for the staff on the basis that the quality of maintenance will not need to be high. Do not forget the desirability of providing at least one janitor's closet with slop sink on each floor level and the need for adequate space in a convenient location for janitor's supplies. The institution's maintenance department should be useful in preparing this part of the program, but its proposals should not be accepted unquestioningly without investigation of any unusual requirements which may be suggested.

Staff rest rooms, lounge and locker accommodations will be based first on the total size of the staff but will be affected also by the availability of suitable lunchrooms in the immediate vicinity of the library, to say nothing of the institution's policy about coffee breaks, the hours of opening, etc.

In determining areas for the various staff groups, the program makers must estimate the number of persons to be provided for in each of the groups discussed above after careful study and discussion with those concerned, always keeping in mind future as well as present needs. Staff areas are often more difficult to add to than quarters for books and readers, when conditions change or additions are planned. No two libraries are alike in their present, to say nothing of their prospective, requirements. It is suggested, however, as a basis for consideration, that an assignment of not less than 100 sq ft (and preferably 125 sq ft) for each person and his equipment should be provided in the work areas, and then there should be added to the total the following:

1. A suitable amount for a conference room for library staff meetings. This may be part of the librarian's office or a separate room.

2. Twenty-five to 50 sq ft for each staff member who is assigned a private office. It is suggested that 25 is enough for section or department heads with no more than 5 persons reporting to them, 50 for those with from 6 to 15, and 75 for larger groups.

3. At least 100 sq ft, and in a large library up to 500, for receiving and shipping, plus space for the shelving required for large gifts.

4. At least 50 sq ft for each staff member who is engaged in binding-preparation work and as much space for a bindery as it is decided to have after consultation with an experienced binder who is acquainted with binding requirements.

5. For the staff locker, rest, toilet, lounge, and lunch rooms, 15 sq ft per person for the first 50 staff members and at least 10 sq ft for each beyond that number is suggested. Do not forget to decide whether separate rest rooms and lunch facilities are to be provided for the maintenance staff in a large library.

The number of persons on duty at one time is a factor, but extra space in a convenient location for a locker for personal belongings should be assigned for each part-time employee or student assistant. These figures for staff housing do not include areas for readers waiting for service.

Keep the future in mind. It should be repeated that staff space tends to give out before space for readers and books. Librarians in the past at least have been unduly modest in their demands for space for their own use.

Remember that the space requirements suggested above are minimal and in many libraries should be greatly increased; they should be increased in almost every library for rooms where working equipment is bulky.

The program should answer the following questions in regard to staff facilities:

1. What is the basic square footage to be provided for each staff member and his personal equipment whether in a workroom or a separate office?

2. In what areas and for what persons is space beyond the basic allowance to be provided and in each case how much extra?

3. How many staff members will be on duty at one time in each room or area at the time of peak load?

4. What rest rooms and lounge facilities are to be provided?

5. What special architectural, aesthetic, or functional requirements should the architect know in order to draw up satisfactory plans? For instance, should the librarian's office or the conference room have special equipment or finishes?

Do not forget the space requirements for part-time assistants or for storage areas for supplies. Do not forget and do not permit the architect to forget problems presented by bulky equipment, such as shelf lists and filing cases, shelving for reserve books and materials being processed or awaiting processing. Remember that, while the architect will try to provide for needs that he knows about, he is not a library specialist and should have help and at least a listing of requirements.

13.5   Other Space Users

Libraries differ from one another in their operation, their needs, and special requirements; they differ in the square footage of space for each group of facilities discussed in the four preceding sections. Few of them require all types of shelving, or areas for all types of the reader accommodations that were considered, or all the varieties of staff quarters discussed, but practically all require shelving, seating accommodations, public-service areas, and staff accommodations of some kind.

Space for still other facilities may be provided in some library buildings. These can be divided into two groups: (1) those directly or indirectly for library purposes; and (2) those for nonlibrary functions. The latter may be assigned permanently to the building or may be housed in it while the space is not needed for the library.

Space for what, by a broad interpretation of the term, could be related to library purposes might include one or more of the following: exhibition areas, photographic laboratories, audiovisual facilities, electrical and carpenter shops for building maintenance, and library schools. The requirements for these, if it is decided to provide for them, will vary according to the local situation, and it would be impossible for anyone without knowledge of the local situation to make specific suggestions in regard to them. However, the following comments may be pertinent.

Exhibition Rooms. Exhibition areas, unless unusually extensive, can often be housed in the entrance lobby or in long corridors that have been made a little wider than would otherwise be necessary, thus giving a feeling of spaciousness for the whole building but still not making undue demands on square footage. Exhibitions take time to prepare, and time is hard to find and costs money. Unless they are changed frequently, a relatively stable group of readers, such as is found in an academic library, will pay little attention to them. Do not make these areas too extensive.

Photographic Rooms. If a library plans to do photographic work for itself or for readers, it may require a photographic laboratory. The square footage will depend, of course, upon the extent to which this work is to be developed. The Library of Congress does photographic work on a tremendous scale, approaching one-half million dollars annually. The New York Public Library photographic work has a staff of over 40 persons. It is suggested that a subcommittee of the planning team be assigned to the problem of determining needs for this space and consult experts from other institutions that have good modern laboratories. The two libraries just mentioned have used basement space that was not originally planned for the purpose. The same holds true for Harvard and most institutions that occupy old buildings. If an opportunity is presented to design space especially for photographic purposes, every effort should be made to make it more suitable than basement space which was not intended for the purpose. Special wiring and plumbing are generally needed, and often a room with a higher ceiling than is normal in many library areas today.

Do not forget that most libraries today require or would at least find use for one or more of the new copying machines, such as the Xerox 914 or the Docustat, and space near a public-service area would be useful for this purpose.

Library School Quarters. There are some 35 accredited library schools in the United States and a larger number of unaccredited ones; many of the latter group train teachers for school library work. They are all affiliated with academic institutions, and most of them are housed partially if not entirely in the central library building of the institution. More schools are likely to be organized. All of them have housing problems. It is natural and proper, though not imperative, for a library school to have its headquarters in a library. Its accommodation there

may make it unnecessary in some cases for the school to have a special library collection and a librarian of its own. If the school is in the library building, the students are close to the general library collections which serve as their laboratory. This position is not essential, any more than having all science classes in the laboratory building, but it is recommended that a library school be placed in the library when possible. Remember that the school is a space user which in an emergency can be moved out of the library and that its quarters can be considered one more possible "expansion joint."

Library school quarters require offices for the administrative and technical staff, classrooms of various kinds and sizes, housing for the collections, and most important of all, perhaps, from the space standpoint, a desk for each student as the home base from which to operate. Altogether a very considerable amount of space is required. More than a whole floor in the Columbia University Butler Library is given over to the library school. If an institution is considering housing its library school in a new library, it is suggested that talks with the deans of other schools and visits to them be arranged and that advice and suggestions regarding the problem be requested. Fig. 13.1 shows part of the quarters planned for the purpose for Columbia University. The remainder are shown in Fig. 6.12. The Louisiana State University Library School is shown in Fig. 13.2.

Audiovisual Work. Audiovisual work is a comparatively new development and as such often has no building of its own and is looking for quarters. To those in charge of a library, particularly a new one, this work may seem more suitable than classrooms for space not yet needed for library purposes. Some librarians, however, object to providing space for audiovisual work on the basis that it has little or nothing to do with library work, which they think of as the use of printed or manuscript material. They anticipate that it is bound to grow and grow, that it will tend as time goes on to take over more space required for library purposes rather than less, and that it will be hard to eject at a later time. Others welcome it on the basis that it enhances their position and shows that they are alert to modern developments.

Few will deny today that audiovisual work has a place somewhere in institutions of higher

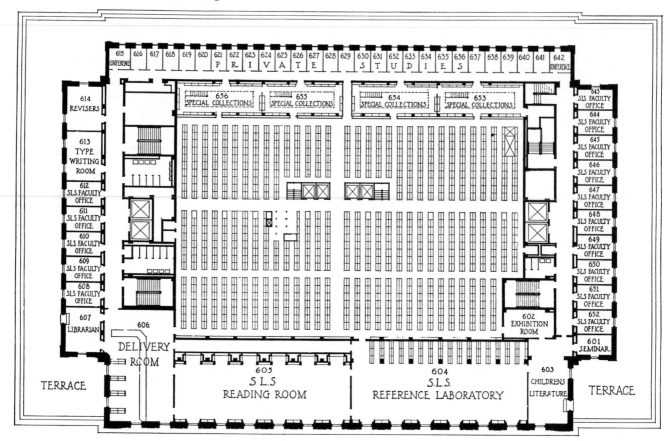

FIG. 13.1   Columbia University Library, School of Library Service headquarters on sixth floor. The school also occupies most of the fifth floor, which was shown in Fig. 6.12.

learning and that its space needs in the future are indefinite and may expand tremendously. If such an extensive development comes, audio-visual work will need a building of its own in due course, and this may solve the problem more or less automatically.

One way of facing the situation is to suggest that, if funds for extra areas are available, the department be offered space on a temporary basis when a new building is planned, with the understanding that the assignment cannot be enlarged. A special committee might well be appointed in this connection. Certainly, a high-level decision should be made as to how far this work will be allowed to develop in the library. It might "snowball" and in due course occupy as much space as the whole library. But it may be suitable use of space, temporarily or even permanently.

Carpenter and Mechanical Shops. Carpenter and mechanical shops were often assigned basement space in older buildings, and this still may be desirable in a new large reference or research

library when the library represents the main activity of the institution. In academic libraries it is generally possible to have the university maintenance shops care for this type of space, except that reserving a cupboard or two for equipment may be desirable. If these shops are included, they should use the service entrance, and the fire hazard which they present should be kept in mind and guarded against.

Other Facilities. The use of library space for purposes that have no direct relation to library activities should always be seriously questioned. It is evident, however, that libraries must envisage future growth and that needs for space in other parts of almost all institutions exceed that available. One could hardly defend a policy, in an institution which is perhaps doubling its space needs in twenty-five years, by which a library, in order to obtain a building large enough to last for a generation, goes into a new building with twice the area required at the time of its completion and leaves much of it unoccupied. It may well be desirable to use a portion of the building for other purposes, but this use of library space should cease when the library needs to expand into it. This, of course, will require special planning. Heating and lighting requirements for the alternate purposes must be made available. In most instances a separate entrance for the nonlibrary activities should be provided so that hours of opening can differ in the two areas without complications. The interior walls separating the two groups of activities should be so constructed that they can be moved, perhaps gradually over a period of years, without extensive or expensive alterations, as the library expands into the extra space.

It is not necessary to describe in detail the different requirements for the second group, the nonlibrary activities that might temporarily occupy space in a library. If unnecessary expense is to be avoided, they should be those which can suitably be housed in areas with ceiling heights that are satisfactory for library purposes, and the stairwells and other fixed areas should be appropriate for library use.

A few of the uses most often assigned to library areas are discussed here to indicate some of the problems that may be involved.

Meeting or Assembly Rooms. There is often a demand for the installation of a meeting or assembly room in a library. This is sometimes promoted by the librarian who wants a place where his staff can gather together, where classes in the use of the library can be held conveniently, where "Friends of the Library" can meet, and so on. Under these circumstances, there may be some justification for it. Others question the need for this type of accommodation in a library, particularly because they realize that an auditorium of more than medium

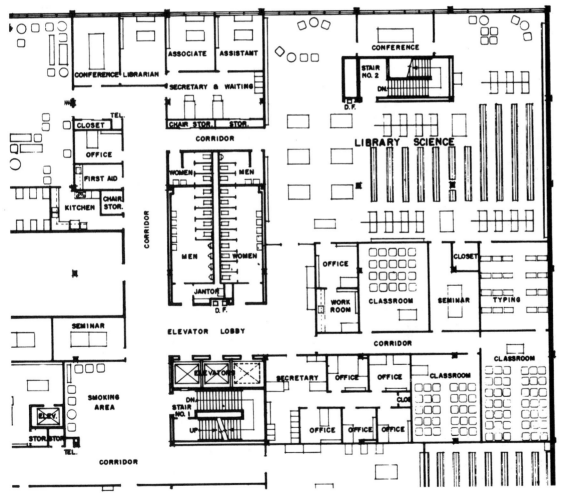

FIG. 13.2 Louisiana State University Library School quarters. The school occupies fifteen bays in the northeast corner of the second floor.

size will probably make necessary a two-level room, and so might be said—although this is not quite accurate—to occupy twice the square footage of floor space otherwise required. A conference room, with perhaps 300 to 600, or even twice that number of square feet, or a staff lounge of the same size might take care of the need for a meeting room for library purposes. Most colleges and universities have a considerable number of large classrooms and auditoriums which can be made available on occasion. Again, each institution must solve the problem for itself, but would be well advised to avoid in a library an auditorium with a sloping floor which necessitates space on two floor levels and will be seldom used. If you cannot have both, which is more important for the library—a 1,000-sq-ft auditorium seating up to 100 persons or shelving for 15,000 additional volumes or accommodations for 40 more readers?

Classrooms. Classrooms are similar to seminars, which are discussed in section 7.2, in the problems they present, except that they are larger in size and are ordinarily not used for housing books. They take space and may be hard to get rid of when the library needs to expand. But when it is possible and desirable to build a new library (or an addition to an old one) much larger than is required for the first years of its life in order to be adequate for a longer period in the future, it may be wise to include classrooms initially but not permanently. They can involve four definite problems, beyond those for seminars, that should be kept in mind during the planning process.

1. If access to classrooms is to be through the regular library entrance, they bring unwanted and undesirable noise or disturbance into the library, and in any event they should be provided with special acoustical protection.

2. They may complicate exit controls.

3. If they are used at hours that differ from regular library hours, the control problem is increased.

4. They may require greater ceiling heights than would otherwise be necessary.

It is suggested that classrooms be included in a library only after thorough discussion with the library faculty committee and the institution's administrative authorities, and then with as definite as possible an understanding that they will be removed when the library needs the space. If it is decided to include classrooms, they should in most instances be placed so as to have an entrance of their own, thereby avoiding some of the difficulties just mentioned. This has been done quite successfully in the Princeton Theological Seminary Library (see Fig. 13.3). At Lamont (see Fig. 13.4), however, the ten classrooms in the building have no separate entrance but access to them, although they are on four different levels, is through stairwells and corridors so placed that their use does not disturb students in reading areas. Lamont's exits are controlled, and the classrooms are heavily used; it is necessary on occasion to have multiple exit-control points in operation when class periods change.

But the most important and difficult problem in connection with classrooms in a library is how to dispose of them when the library is full and needs more space for readers. At such a time additional classroom space is generally required for the institution also. Yet pressure for classroom space and library space at the same time may increase the pressure for a new classroom building and make its provision less difficult. At any rate, it is well, as has already been noted, to have as definite an agreement as possible that the classrooms will be removed when the librarian and his committee agree that the library needs the space they occupy.

One final word of warning in this connection. Classrooms in a library should always be planned so that the space they occupy can be used to advantage for library purposes when the time comes.

Offices. Other facilities sometimes placed in temporarily unused library space may include the institution's main administrative offices, that is, those for the president, vice-presidents, and deans. These officials are often attracted by quarters in a library, as it may be the handsomest, largest, and most central of the academic buildings. If a separate entrance is provided to prevent after-hours complications, this arrangement can be quite satisfactory, as it should make it easier for the librarian to call to the attention of the administrative officers his financial, space, and other problems. The most frequent complication arises from the librarian's hesitation to push the administration out when additional library space is required, and a modest president hesitates to ask for new quarters for himself when he realizes and appreciates better than anyone else the other space needs of his institution.

Many professors would like nothing better than to have their offices in the library, but librarians are warned that, while faculty studies properly belong in the library if they are used as "hideouts" and research headquarters, offices within the library's doors for any except the library staff tend to bring unnecessary and undesirable traffic into study areas that should be quiet. It is suggested and strongly urged that faculty offices, particularly those for professors with administrative duties, should be avoided in a library at all costs. The same policy should hold for academic post offices, university-press headquarters, and other facilities that will bring in nonlibrary activities which are bound to cause noise and confusion, and, in the case of the two activities just mentioned, shipping and receiving problems.

As was noted earlier, most new libraries, if adequate for as much as twenty to twenty-five years ahead, will have extra space for a limited period that could be used for other than library purposes. The author, who disagrees with many of his colleagues, is inclined to believe that the librarian's willingness to help out others when he can without too great inconvenience should enhance his standing with the institution's administration and in the long run should make it possible for him to obtain required space when he really needs it, rather than leave him in a predicament when he needs the space temporarily assigned to others.

If it is decided to bring into a new library building any of the nonlibrary activities just discussed or any others, the building program should answer in some detail these questions: What other facilities are to be provided for, where are they to be placed, how much space will they occupy, what special requirements do they present, and what will be done with them when the library needs the space that they occupy on a temporary basis?

Non-assignable or Building and Architectural Space. There are demands for square footage in a library other than those already mentioned. The most important is for what is known as architectural or preferably non-assignable

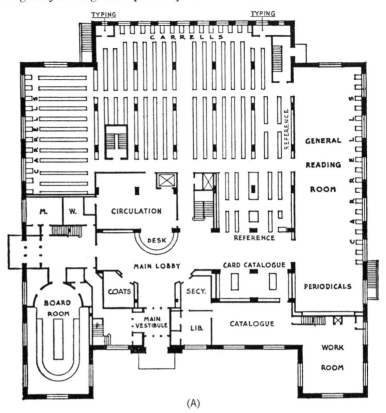

(A)

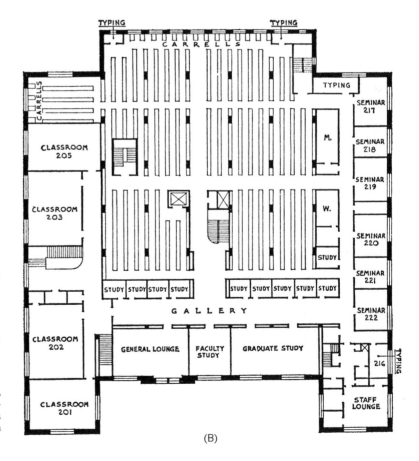

(B)

FIG. 13.3 Princeton Theological Seminary Library, (A) first and (B) second floor. Classrooms are on the left-hand side of second floor, with their own stairways, and a separate entrance on the first floor. Doors between classroom wing and library on both floors are kept locked.

space. This usually takes from one-fourth to one-third of the total building area, the figure varying according to the method used for its computation, the ingenuity of the architect, and the areas used for architectural rather than functional purposes. The architect is primarily responsible for non-assignable space, but the architect, the librarian, and the institution's other representatives on the planning team should watch carefully to see that it is held down as far as possible without spoiling the architectural or aesthetic effects of the building or interfering with its functional aspects. Architectural space is dealt with in more detail in section 16.2.

13.6   Spatial Relationships

Section 6.4 discusses the problem of spatial relationships on a theoretical basis and lists questions in this connection to which the architect should have answers before he can present satisfactory diagrammatic, to say nothing of preliminary, sketches. The answers to these questions should be prepared by the librarian and his staff because they are most intimately connected with the operation of the library. Because of the importance of the answers, they should be approved by the planning committee.

This is the time to reconsider the library's

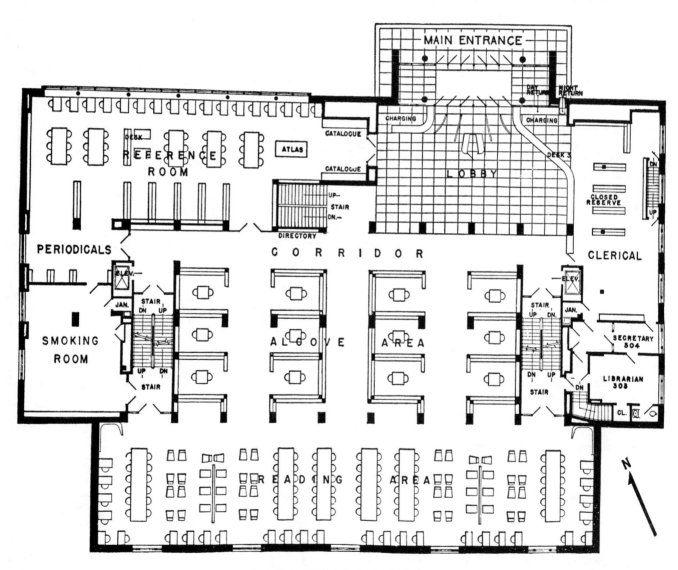

LAMONT LIBRARY, THIRD LEVEL

FIG. 13.4   Lamont Library, Harvard University. Rooms for conferences or small classes on second and sixth levels. Rooms are reached directly from third-level lobby by stairways that are cut off from reading areas.

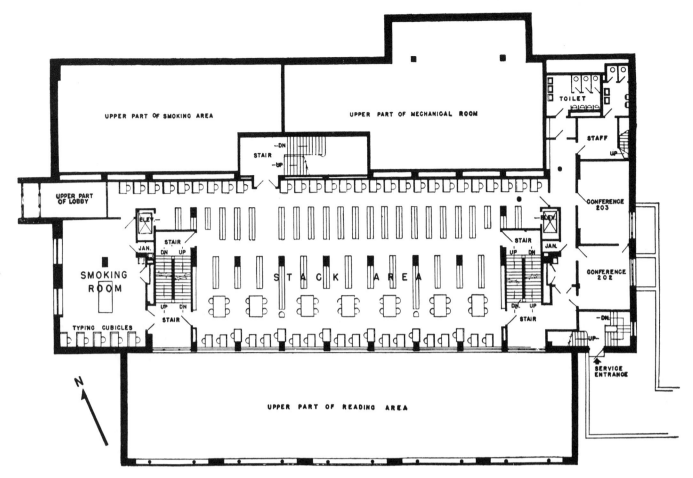

LAMONT LIBRARY, SECOND LEVEL

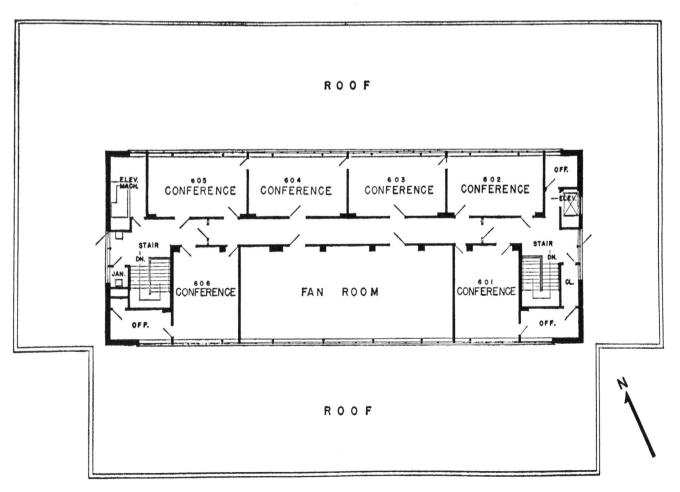

LAMONT LIBRARY, SIXTH LEVEL

FIG. 13.4 (*continued*)

organization and operation. Just because work has been handled in a certain way in the past does not necessarily mean that the old practices should be continued. Here is an opportunity to study the problems involved. The convenience of faculty, students, and staff should be kept in mind and also the cost of the services rendered. The arrangements decided upon may have a great effect on operating costs both for service and processing additions to the collections. Other things being equal, the fewer service desks that have to be manned for full hours, the better. The shorter the distances the staff members have to travel vertically or horizontally at frequent intervals, the better also; but do not go too far in inconveniencing the readers and reducing the quality of service rendered for the sake of the staff.

Spatial relationships start with the location of the entrance or entrances, the lobby or lobbies, and the exit or exits. In arranging for them, keep in mind the various uses made of the library by the students and faculty, which include the following: study hall for reading; reserve books for use in the library or outside; general recreational and collateral reading, the latter in connection with course work, preparation of reports of various kinds, and research work; use of current periodicals and newspapers, manuscripts, maps, and microreproductions; and listening to records. To these should be added searches for reference and bibliographical information and consultation of the catalogue. For the last three of these activities appeals for help from the staff are frequent.

There are, of course, other uses. For all of them the shorter the distances to be traveled by everyone concerned, the better. Even walking on the level through reading areas is likely to be disturbing, and traffic up and down stairs can be noisy. Visual and auditory distraction of readers should be avoided as far as possible. Do not forget that going to smoking rooms and toilet facilities and returning to reading areas is part of the whole problem.

The staff side of the picture is also important. Spatial relationships have a great deal to do with staff effectiveness. Salaries are the largest single expenditure in most libraries, and if in a large library a number of staff members have to walk 100 feet thirty times a day or go up and down stairs twenty times that could have been avoided by more careful planning, the extra

time consumed counts up. Once or twice a day might not be serious; it is the total amount of travel that counts. Pushing one truck loaded with books each day from the shipping room to the acquisition department is not serious, even if the distance involved is 100 ft, but if the circulation desk is adjacent to the entrance and the service elevator or lifts are 100 ft away and 10 truckloads of books must go back and forth each day, the situation may be serious.

No one can lay down definite rules for spatial relationships for libraries in general, except to emphasize their importance, particularly for what are known as the central services, but they should be studied *de novo* for each institution. The program should show what is wanted. Answering the six questions listed in section 6.4 is one way to provide the desired information. References to the problems will be found in the program examples in Appendix A.

13.7 Provision for Growth

No program for a new library building can properly be called complete unless it states the institution's desires in regard to the difficult problem of providing for the future enlargement of the prospective building, or at least suggests a course of action when additional space is required. One of the basic characteristics of libraries is their tendency to grow—even, the apparent inevitability of their growth. This has been emphasized throughout the volume, beginning in Chapter 1, "Looking Ahead." It has been discussed in some detail in section 12.5, as one of the basic problems to be settled before detailed planning takes place. If a new building is to be satisfactory, plans for future needs must be kept constantly in mind.

Books record the accumulated knowledge of what has happened in the past and what mankind has learned, in addition to the products of its imagination. Few libraries, if any, in this day attempt to be all-inclusive because of the profusion of books. "Of the making of books there is no end." Few, if any, attempt to be complete in even extremely limited fields, and in most fields they must be selective. But with the steady increase in the printed word in the fields in which libraries collect, even the most selective libraries—even those willing and able to carry on a constant program of weeding and discarding—tend to grow and, unless some new and potent factors come into the picture, they must grow to keep alive and be as useful tomorrow as they were yesterday.

A library strictly for undergraduates which attempts to limit its collections to a definite figure soon finds it tends to become at least a little larger year by year, because some of the older books are standard and classic and never get out of date, and the number of volumes of this kind increases as the years go by. The number of new worth-while books published year by year does not decrease. Meanwhile serials, which make up a larger and larger percentage of new publications, cannot always be discarded when they are, let us say, five or twenty-five years old.

Of course it must be remembered that new technical developments, such as the photostat, microreproductions of one kind or another, automation and retrieval systems, facsimile reproduction sent over the air, added to the increasing use of interlibrary loans and other forms of interlibrary cooperation, may help to limit space requirements. But there is no sign at present that any one or all of these put together will reduce in bulk even the limited collections gathered for younger scholars. These developments have undoubtedly slowed up the physical growth of academic and research collections, but they have not stopped it. If new methods and practices can prevent geometrical growth and make it arithmetical instead, that is about all that can be expected.

But collections still occupy little, if any, more than one-third of the total area in a typical academic or research library and, even if collection growth were successfully halted, space for reader and staff needs might still continue to rise. Reader accommodations for those using microreproductions take more space than for those using books in their original printed forms. Readers using typewriters—and their number increases steadily—use more square feet per person. Those using voice recordings of various kinds in listening rooms need much more rather than less space. When the percentage of graduate students increases, as it seems bound to do in the years ahead, the demand for closed carrels which, as was seen in Chapter 7, may take more space for each accommodation provided, will increase, particularly if they are assigned to individuals. A somewhat similar situation holds for service areas. The total number of librarians, even without an increase in the number of stu-

dents, tends to go up and so does the demand placed on service areas; to complicate matters further, the number of students can be expected to continue to grow.

Staff space has always in the past tended to be the first to become inadequate because increased demands make a larger staff desirable, and equipment that staff members use, even in this day of mechanization, does not seem to take less space. Photographic laboratories become more common, and the same holds for other special services. It is true that binderies at present seem to be on the way out in even large libraries because of the more expensive equipment they require and the higher efficiency obtained in large commercial operations.

Altogether it is clear that almost every library will require more space in the years ahead than at present, and when it is remembered that a large percentage of our libraries are increasing the size of their collections rapidly enough today so that they will double in considerably less than twenty years, and as the number of students in most institutions of higher learning is today increasing at a comparable rate, the importance of providing for growth in buildings planned at this time is self-evident.

In this connection, it should be noted that the interest in higher education and research throughout the world today is so great that it makes increases in appropriations for collections, reader accommodations, staff, services, and also for new library buildings more readily available than ever before in history.

The required additional capacity that will be needed later can be provided for in a library building in several ways:

1. By bringing stack ranges closer together, by installing compact shelving of some kind, by removing less-used books for storage elsewhere, by discarding outdated and obsolete materials, by using microreproductions in place of originals, by crowding accommodations for staff and readers closer together at the risk of discouraging use and making service less effective, by using corridors and even exhibition areas for other purposes, by moving out nonlibrary facilities, and by decentralization of library activities.

2. By providing enough space in a new library when it is built to last for as long a period as possible. The space can be used at first by spreading out the library over the whole building or by using part of it for other academic or

administrative use, as has been discussed in section 13.5.

3. By providing an easy way to add to the structure now being planned without undue extra cost and inconvenience. What seems to be the obvious way decided upon when the plans are made may not always be the one selected, but it should be available. Additions can be horizontal or vertical. If horizontal, they will ordinarily be immediately adjacent, in which case care must be taken to make them possible without interfering with footings. Cantilevering out from the last column in both the old and the new buildings may help. Curtain walls, which are easily removed, may be useful in this connection; but many of them have not been waterproof, with disastrous results. Lawrence Thompson of the University of Kentucky has offered his new library as an example of what not to do in that connection. If the old structure is floated on a concrete slab which has settled, it may be difficult to add a wing which will settle to the same extent and not involve problems where the structures join. Floor-level heights may also present a problem in connection with a new wing, and too often in the past have added unnecessarily to the cost of new construction or have made an addition practically impossible. Although additions can also be built connected to the old structure by a bridge, circulation patterns are often complicated by this method.

Vertical growth also presents problems, both architecturally and from an engineering standpoint. The columns in the first stage must be heavy enough to carry the load of the extra floors above that are to be added later, and this costs money. It is difficult to remove a roof and replace it without great inconvenience to the occupants and risk of water damage during the process. Unless a building is planned with vertical growth in mind, it may present almost insuperable problems. But some method of enlargement should always be planned for, unless the institution is content to face one of the following alternatives:

1. Starting over again in a limited number of years, and either tearing the old building down or using it for other purposes. With modern flexible construction, the latter plan is more possible than it used to be.

2. Admitting that growth within the building is limited and that an addition at a later time should not be contemplated; simply deciding that further growth will be impossible and that decentralization with all its disadvantages and expenses will have to take place.

The above makes several points clear:

1. Plans for growth should be made at the time when the site is selected, and the site chosen should be one that will make additions practicable when the time comes.

2. It should be kept in mind that in many institutions finding funds for an addition may be more difficult than raising money for a new structure. A donor or donors may hesitate to provide funds for a new wing for a building named for someone else.

3. Remember that alumni, from whom funds in private institutions and sometimes in public ones must be obtained, can tend to be sentimental about old structures and will not want to alter them, to say nothing of tearing them down to be replaced by a new building.

The above do not represent reasons why a building built today cannot be useful for many years to come so far as its basic construction is concerned. Plan flexibly and in a way that will make additions inexpensive and easy to carry out.

The program should state what the basic needs for the future are expected to be, and the architect should be requested to propose practical methods for providing for them and to show where and how he can make the space available without becoming involved in aesthetic or functional atrocities. And, finally, the proposals for an addition should be placed prominently in the record so that they will not be forgotten.

It seems well to state here again, as has been stated in Chapter 2, that some architects feel that the structures they plan are so perfect that they should never under any circumstances be added to and may even refuse to accept an assignment where the program asks for a statement of ways and means for enlargement; or they may simply ignore the problem and go ahead and provide a building that cannot be added to; the client may not realize that his wishes have been circumvented. The institution, through its administrative officers, the librarian, and the library consultant, if there is one, should not forget this hazard and should take steps to overcome it.

In spite of the best-laid plans, it may turn out that when a structure is no longer adequate for library purposes, but while it is still structurally worth preserving, it is desirable for one reason or another to discard it as a library and start over again. This may be because of changes in the basic situation, such as a shift in the center of the campus; it may result from poor planning in the original structure, which makes it impossible or unduly expensive to add to it; it may be due to poor campus planning, which has permitted the obvious area for an addition to be used for other purposes. But if the old building is sound structurally and reasonably flexible, it can sometimes be adapted for use for nonlibrary purposes for less cost than would be incurred by incorporating it in an enlarged satisfactory and adequate library. It is surprising what an ingenious architect can do in altering the functions of an old library building at reasonable cost in spite of the fact that alterations too often prove to be more expensive than anticipated. The old Carnegie Library at Grinnell, built in the first decade of the century, obviously had to be discarded as a library; it has been altered into a good classroom and office building; providing the same amount of space for these purposes in new construction would have cost far more.

This, it is fair to say, has resulted in a considerable reduction in the net cost of Grinnell's new library. The old library at Baker University, Baldwin, Kansas, has also been used successfully for classrooms and offices. Often the book stacks, particularly if they are of the multitier type, will present the greatest problem, and in such cases it is sometimes desirable to keep them unchanged and use them for storage of less-used library collections or for other storage purposes. Sometimes it may be worth while simply to dismantle them and use the space in other ways.

But always remember that if the building is to be enlarged either vertically or horizontally the original structure should be planned with that in mind and the site selected must be one that makes the enlargement practicable and aesthetically satisfactory. And, of course, the architect must be told, preferably in the program, what the institution's plans and expectations are in this connection.

Problems to be faced in adding to an old building are discussed in some detail in section 15.1, which deals with alternatives to new construction.

14

The Program for Mechanical Facilities, Comfort, and Other Requirements

Introduction

Chapter 13 dealt with the space requirements for a library primarily on the basis of square-footage needs. The program for them is largely the responsibility of the academic members of the planning team.

This chapter deals with the parts of the program which concern the construction, the equipment, and the other physical requirements of a library building. For them the academic members of the building team cannot be expected to be experts, and the solution of the problems involved must be in the hands of the architect and his engineers, with suggestions from the institution's buildings-and-grounds representative, who will be responsible for the maintenance and operation of its physical plant.

Representatives of the institution, however, should know enough about the problems so that they can explain what they want, and then count on the architect, with the aid of experts in the various fields if he does not have them on his staff, to prepare the plans that will provide the desired results. The architect should, of course, propose the solutions, obtain approval, and accept responsibility for the results. These problems will inevitably include, among others, the style of architecture and aesthetics. However, section 14.1 will deal primarily with requirements, beginning with foundations, framing, plumbing, hardware, windows, walls, ceilings and roofs, and floor coverings. Section 14.2 will

take up hazards of various kinds, mechanical facilities, safety and comfort requirements. Section 14.3 will discuss column spacing, room heights, and floor areas, including mechanical transportation and communications. Section 14.4 considers furniture and equipment. And finally section 14.5 goes into the all-important problem of the determination of the total square-footage requirements.

The architect should be given fairly wide latitude in these matters. The program should express in general terms the wishes and desires of the institution in connection with these items and many more minor ones. It is unwise to try to state them too specifically, although sooner or later specific decisions must be made, but they should be postponed until the architect has had an opportunity to explain the problems involved and has made sure that they are understood.

It should be emphasized that while this part of the program can and should be prepared before the architect begins his planning, it cannot be considered final until the assignable or net space requirements are determined and the site selected, matters which are discussed in section 14.5 and in section 15.2, because they may well affect some of the decisions.

Aesthetic Problems

A major aesthetic problem is the architectural style of the building as a whole. The institution's representatives on the planning team may or may not have definite opinions on this matter, but if they intend to insist on or to prefer a traditional building, the program should so indicate, and the architect should be selected with this style in mind. Some architects are not prepared to do work of that kind. An architect in most cases should be selected who customarily works in the building styles desired. If the institution is ready to have a contemporary building, its preference should be noted, but, of course, the architect should have an opportunity to present his point of view. The specific questions to be answered might include the following:

Are there any instructions or suggestions for the architect in connection with the architectural style? Should it, for instance, be traditional or contemporary? The architect can frequently learn more from what the client does not like aesthetically than from what he does. This approach is generally better than to have him dictate the desired style. Is the first emphasis to be on function or aesthetics? This is the place for the institution to make its wishes known. If the financial limitations are great, function may have to come first. What are the financial requirements and to what extent can or should they be subordinated to the aesthetic side? Can a definite sum be budgeted to make possible special architectural and aesthetic features, including perhaps murals and sculpture?

These aesthetic problems are discussed in Chapter 2.

14.1   Construction Requirements

Foundations. If a good solid foundation base is not available, should the building be floated on a concrete slab, or should it rest on caissons or piles? Should the foundation go down to solid rock, or is there sand, clay, or gravel which will provide a satisfactory base without going so deep? How deep below the surface will it be safe and economical to go for the lowest floor level of the building? Have arrangements been made for trial borings or test pits? One or the other is almost always desirable. Their cost will generally be a separately budgeted item for which the institution is responsible. The answers to these questions are the engineer's province. He can properly suggest alternatives and their financial and other implications. Some institutions retain a soil-mechanics consultant to work with the foundation engineer.

The depth of the lowest level will, of course, be influenced by the slope of the ground and the institution's desire or willingness to have one or more basements without any windows or with windows on only one, two, or three sides. A properly insulated basement with or without windows may often provide square footage that is even cheaper than space aboveground to construct, maintain, and operate, because walls can be less expensive, and heating and cooling may be simplified.

Framing. Should the building framing be of wood, steel, steel protected by concrete, reinforced concrete, or precast or prestressed concrete, and should the floors be flat concrete slabs or of beam construction? Should the walls be of the bearing type? Wood is often the cheapest framing, but since it may be a fire hazard, it is seldom used except in a very small library. Steel, unless covered with concrete, succumbs readily to fire if one is started. Reinforced concrete brings with it fire resistance. Steel covered with concrete may be more expensive than reinforced concrete but may make smaller columns possible. It is fire-resistant and may be not only desirable but necessary if columns are to be kept to no more than the width of the stack ranges so as not to interfere with stack aisles. If precast concrete is used, care must be taken to make sure that joints are tight. Decisions on framing should seldom appear in the program except to indicate column-dimension requirements.

It may be well to obtain cost estimates for the different types of framing. Unless there is an expert on the planning team, decisions on these matters should certainly be left to the architect and his staff of structural engineers. If bearing walls are used, remember that they limit to certain locations, or at least make more expensive, openings required later on when an addition is placed beside the first stage of the building, but they may in some cases be economical.

Plumbing and Hardware. Plumbing and hardware are grouped simply for convenience and because they both involve fixtures. Since they are largely outside the field of the academic members of the library planning team, the team should not be expected to select the fixtures. They can properly specify that the plumbing be sufficiently silent and so placed that it will not be disturbing and embarrassing to those outside the toilet rooms and that it will be of a good enough quality so that the maintenance cost will not be high.

The location and the capacity of the public rest rooms and toilet facilities for each sex are important. If they can be provided on each floor—with the exception perhaps of the main floor or entrance level—it will considerably reduce disturbing traffic through the building. If they can be fairly centrally located—particularly if the square footage per floor level is large (over 25,000 sq ft)—the same results will follow. If they are placed in the same area on each floor, they will be easier to find, and installation costs will be reduced. The provision of an adequate number of fixtures, wash basins, water closets, and urinals is a matter of importance. A minimum of one water closet or urinal is suggested for every 35 seating accommodations in most libraries. The optimum number may be affected by the provisions in adjacent buildings, the number of commuting students, and the proximity of residential halls. There may be building or sanitary-code regulations in this regard, and they should be checked and followed.

Good-quality hardware should be used. This applies particularly to door fixtures and locks. These items are expensive to change, and sturdiness and appearance are both of importance. In many cases the institution will have already adopted standards in connection with both plumbing and hardware which should, more or less automatically, be accepted for the library, but in all cases a representative of its buildings-and-grounds staff who preferably should be on the planning team, should watch out for these matters.

Discussion of plumbing and hardware is included in section 10.1. The program should include any directions the institution wishes to give the architect in regard to them.

Windows. The planning team should hesitate to dictate details in connection with the library's facade, but it can properly state in the program that the building should not be a glass box, if it has so decided. The effect of glass on heating, cooling, and lighting should be kept in mind; glass on the west and south must always be protected in some way, and to a lesser extent that on the east. Even a northern exposure in the Northern Hemisphere presents glare problems, particularly on a sunny day after fresh snow. Possible methods for protection are discussed in section 10.1. It is the finished structure and its functional success and the comfort of its occupants in which the institution is interested and, if the architect is given general directions, he

should be able to bring about the desired results. He was appointed because it was believed that he had the ability to find satisfactory solutions to the problems involved.

If the library does not want windows to come down below table height in reading areas and book stacks because it considers safety and comfort important, it should say so in the program, so that the architect can provide another solution and will not have to change plans after he has made them. The same holds for the types of windows to be used. Should it be possible to open them or should they be sealed shut? The question as to whether they should be gray glass, heat-absorbing, antiglare, Thermopane, and so forth, should be talked over with the architect, if not specified in the program, in order to guide him in his proposals.

The problem of having windows sealed shut is particularly difficult; if the ventilation system breaks down, the building may become uninhabitable in hot weather. But if they can be opened they will be considerably more expensive, and you can be sure they will be opened sooner or later and that this will interfere with the satisfactory working of any air-conditioning system. In some places the only solution seems to be to have them locked so that they can be opened in case of emergency. Certainly, in an area where there is likely to be a breakdown in the electric current from time to time and competent repairmen are not readily available, there should be some way to get fresh air into the building.

Walls, Ceilings, and Roofs. These are even less in the province of the laymen on the library planning team than the questions dealt with in the paragraphs above, although the walls and ceilings have functional as well as aesthetic aspects. Whether the roof is flat or sloping or gabled may be of importance to the institution if it is trying to provide unity in its campus. Whether it is covered with slate or some other roofing material should certainly be considered from the point of view of maintenance, fire protection, and aesthetics. Remember that if a flat roof is recommended in the program, it may afford no place for ventilation apparatus that might cost less and be more efficient if it were placed there; that some place must be found for the elevator penthouse; and that a flat roof, particularly if the building is low and large, may present aesthetic problems. The author knows of libraries where elevators do not reach to the two upper stack levels so as to prevent a penthouse showing on the roof. One can easily understand the inconvenience that results. The aesthetic aspects may be understandable, but this is a place where function is of first importance. Remember that climatic conditions must be considered in connection with roof design. A leaky roof cannot be tolerated. If skylights are used, don't forget their weakness in this respect, and see that special precautions are used. Plastic domes may be preferred, as they are generally easier to keep tight. Valleys resulting from gables or irregular construction can be a special hazard, as are gutters in an area with heavy snow and frequent freezing and melting. Roof insulation, to prevent overheating of the top floor and thereby adding to the ventilation problem, may be important.

Walls present similar problems. They must not leak around the windows or anywhere else. They should be well insulated. They have much to do with obtaining a satisfactory aesthetic effect, and care in the selection of brick or stone or other wall materials is required.

Desirable ceiling qualities resemble those for roofs in most ways. Heat and cold and noise must not penetrate unduly from floor to floor. Well-designed ceilings should have satisfactory acoustic properties. Areas where quiet is a functional requirement should be specified. Whether or not ceilings should be furred and hung affects the decor and decides other problems, such as providing space for horizontal mechanical air distribution below the floor construction. Today most libraries are lighted from ceiling fixtures, either from those flush with the ceiling or hung from it. Do not forget the possible difficulties in changing lighting sources—bulbs and tubes—when they are in or near the ceilings. Radiant heating is sometimes successfully placed in the ceiling.

The planning team should study the architect's proposals for walls, ceilings, and roofs. The architect should initiate them, but should be informed of the institution's previous experience and its wishes.

Floor Coverings. Selection of a floor covering involves the comfort of the occupants in connection with its acoustic properties and in other ways. Cost of maintenance and length of useful life, as well as installation costs, are also factors for consideration. It is doubtful whether the program given to the architect should be specific in its recommendations because costs and available materials vary from time to time and place to place, but a general statement in regard to preferences and quality is desirable.

Wall-to-wall carpets of good quality are probably the most satisfactory of all types of floor covering as far as comfort and acoustic properties and perhaps even maintenance costs are concerned if properly selected, but they do not last as long as other standard floor coverings. The cost of installation and replacement, as well as of maintenance, is the crux of the problem. It may come down to a question of what can be afforded. If the institution is prepared to provide the highest quality of maintenance, such as is available in a first-class hotel, and to face the extra costs involved in installation and replacement, carpets may be indicated. It might afford carpets in reading areas if it is prepared to economize elsewhere, in basement storage areas, for instance, by using concrete which has been painted after the application of a good filler so as to keep down the dirt and reduce cleaning costs; and in little-used stack levels where noise will be of little significance, by using asphalt tile or vinyl asbestos which have a good life expectancy. Possibilities like these should be considered. But if carpet is selected, be sure that it is installed over a good base and, if it is used on stairs, be careful about its selection and installation. Instruct the architect or the interior designer that the pattern selected be such that invisible patching can be inserted to replace ink stains and cigarette burns. Remember that if carpets fade from exposure to the sun, a patch may be more conspicuous than are new tiles that vary in color from the rest of the surface. If carpets are used on main traffic arteries, a different pattern or quality may be desirable there as these places will tend to wear out first and their replacement should not necessitate replacement of adjacent carpet. What about carpets for entrance lobbies? How about stack floors between ranges? The latter question is complicated by the current practice of combining reading areas and book stacks.

And do not forget to consider other types of floor coverings, rubber tile, for instance, or battleship linoleum and cork. The latter two may have to be imported in order to find high quality, such as was readily available here before the Second World War, or new types may come onto the market at any time. The American Library Association Library Technology Project has a study of floor coverings in process which should be useful.

All of these are matters for the designer or architect. As was indicated earlier, it is doubtful whether they should be covered by set instructions in the program. But be sure that the problem is discussed before a decision is reached. To put it differently, if the floor covering to be used is not specified in the program, see to it that those who are to make the decision do not make it before the planning team is apprised of it and given an opportunity to veto the proposal if it cares to do so. It is also suggested that the best possible cost estimates for installation and maintenance for different possibilities be presented.

14.2 Protection against Hazards; Mechanical Facilities; Safety and Comfort Requirements

Fire Hazards. The fire-hazard problem is important from at least four points of view:

1. The safety of the occupants with all its direct and indirect implications

2. The cost of suitable installations to reduce the hazards and also the extra cost of insurance if a reasonably fireproof structure is not specified

3. The protection of the collections which may be irreplaceable

4. The peace of mind of those responsible for the building

In almost all cases fire-resistive construction of reinforced concrete or steel and masonry, with steel structural members encased in concrete or other fire-resistant material is indicated. Certainly, if rare books are involved, this is essential. A small building all on the ground level with many ways of egress might be an exception if the collections are not of importance. Be sure that suitable fire extinguishers are available and inspected regularly so as to be effective. Sprinklers are not recommended, except for limited areas, such as those for miscellaneous storage, carpenter and repair shops, and so forth. But, if sprinklers are not used, be sure that you can make your peace with the fire insurance companies. The reader is again referred to the American Library Association's Library Technology Project Publications number 7, *Protecting the Library and Its Resources,* published in 1963. A study of section 10.2 above

should provide the information required for this part of the building program.

Provision for the Handicapped. Section 10.2 explains the problems involved and lists possible steps to be taken to aid the handicapped in using the library. Almost any library can expect sooner or later to have handicapped persons among its clientele. Certainly a large institution should consider them and perhaps adopt all the measures outlined in the section mentioned. It will never be less expensive than at the time of original installation. But some of the provisions may be very expensive, and the institution must decide how much it is prepared to invest in them. Usually it is better to be on the safe side. But, again, the program should state the wishes of the institution, unless it is ready to leave the matter completely in the hands of the architect.

Lighting. Should the lighting be with mercury, fluorescent, or incandescent lamps, or a combination of them? If they are to be fluorescent, should cold cathode, slimline, jumbo, or one of the other types of tubes be used? Should there be a second, a third, a fourth, or more tubes in each fixture? What kind of fixture or fixtures should be used and should they protect the light sources by baffles, plastic coverings, or reflectors? Should they be hung, ceiling-mounted, semirecessed, or recessed? With some types the fixture can be adapted to any one of these four mountings. Can the lighting be largely indirect so as to avoid the need for protection?

What intensity is wanted in reading areas on a reading surface, and should it vary in different parts of the library? What intensity is wanted in offices, in the stacks, on the lower shelves, where light is a critical matter? Remember that, other things being equal, 100 foot-candles on a table top will cost twice what 50 and four times what 25 will cost. (Intensity should always be measured by maintained intensity, not by the original brightness when new lamps are first installed.)

In book stacks, if fluorescent tubes are used, should the lighting be at right angles to the ranges, down the center of the aisles, or with indirect lighting hung on top of the ranges? What kind of ballasts should be used? Can the light be kept from being unpleasantly noisy, and what can be done about flickering?

Should the light switches be available to the public or only by key in the hands of an authorized person? Can the expense of separate switches at each end of each stack aisle be avoided on the basis that lights will all be on throughout hours of opening, or should time switches be installed to reduce the use of current? (Time switches are not satisfactory with fluorescent light because turning off and on shortens the lives of the tubes.) Is it worth while to have reading-room lights on perhaps three separate circuits, one for the inner third of the room, one for the middle third, and one for the outer third, so that they can be turned on as needed?

Should the lighting, in a high room where lamps cannot be changed without scaffolding, be installed and wired so that half of the lamps are used one week and the other half the next week, so as to lengthen the period between replacements? If this arrangement is made, replacements should be on schedule, with all tubes removed at the same time, regardless of condition and those still good used again in more accessible places.

Remember in connection with lighting that the areas of window space may affect the intensity required. Large window areas may make it unnecessary to use lights near windows during a large share of daylight hours, but in the United States they probably will be used in spite of this. And remember also that if natural light provides very high intensity near the windows, it will make desirable higher intensity for the artificial light in the rest of the building during daylight hours and, as a result, in the evening as well. Should there be individual table lights, which some persons seem to prefer but which are expensive to install and likely to be abused, or is over-all lighting to be preferred? The cost per kilowatt of current used by a particular institution may help to provide the answer for a number of these questions.

Should there be emergency or night lights with current from a separate source, such as batteries, in order to provide insurance against breakdown? They are often required by law.

These and other questions must be answered by the program, unless the institution is prepared to leave the answers to the architect and his lighting engineer. This can be and often is done, but it may be desirable to give at least general directions. Section 9.1 deals with lighting on a theoretical basis and discusses the problems involved in some detail. Remember that considerable sums of money for the original

installation, maintenance, and operation are involved. But also remember that good lighting has much to do with the comfort of the readers and staff members, that quality is more important than intensity, and that completely uniform lighting throughout a building is not attractive aesthetically or desirable functionally.

Ventilation. The architect and his heating and ventilating engineer should have directions in connection with the heating and ventilating system desired; but do not tie their hands completely. Remember that six different factors are involved: heating, cooling, humidification, dehumidification, ventilation, and air filtering. The decisions reached should be based on the climate in the location where the building is to be constructed, the amount of use during periods with extreme weather conditions, the importance of the collections, the incidence of pollution and dust in the air, as well as the costs of the various types of installations available for use. The maximum and minimum desired temperatures and the relative humidity to be maintained, during the winter and, if air conditioning is used, during the summer, are factors in the design. Obviously in some libraries, because of local atmospheric conditions and financial problems, little can be done about ventilation except to provide construction which will minimize the importance of doing anything; just as in other libraries the best possible installations affecting each of the six factors noted are indicated. It may be well to remember that here, as with all other arrangements, the building is for use not in 1900 and not only in 1965, but it is to be hoped for many years to come. No library should make a fetish of "keeping up with the Joneses," but as a new building costs money, the expenditure is justified largely by the amount of use it will be given and being unduly Spartan will not solve the problem of use.

It is suggested that section 9.2 be studied, the problem be discussed by the institution's representatives, bearing in mind the five different levels of heating and ventilating outlined in that section, and then, with a tentative program at hand, that it be considered in detail with the architect and his heating and ventilating engineers and the costs involved in the different possible decisions be determined as closely as possible. All too often costs for both installation and operation are underestimated.

In addition to a decision on the six factors and

the five levels, specifications must sooner or later be provided by someone in regard to the temperature and relative humidity to be maintained, including the permissible variations and the requirements in different parts of the building and at different times in the year.

14.3 Column Spacing, Room Heights, Floor Areas, and Mechanical Transportation

Column Spacing and Module Sizes. The first decision is whether to make use of the module system. Its advantages and disadvantages have been spelled out in section 4.1, and need not be repeated here. The institution should hesitate to give definite instructions to the architect, unless there is some special reason for it. Usually, if the module system is to be used, the architect should propose the dimensions and say whether or not the bays should be square. The program, however, can properly provide suggestions on the following points after making it clear that the architect should not hesitate to make counter-suggestions if he believes that there are adequate reasons for doing so.

1. The columns should, if possible, be kept down to 14 in. in diameter if they are round and 14 in. in the line of the ranges and 16 to 18 in. in the other direction, if these dimensions can be used without raising other problems. The columns should not interfere with stack aisles, and in a long stack range two columns should occupy the space of no more than one standard 3-ft section. If the columns are to carry ducts alongside the structural support and all the stack ranges are to run in the same direction, the columns can be up to 16 to 18 in. in size at right angles to the ranges and up to 32 in. in the other direction.

2. If the columns are to be square or round, the distances between them in line with the ranges should be multiples of 3 ft, plus 4 to 6 in. for the stack uprights, and the columns should come in exact sizes, so that full advantage can be taken of the space available.

3. In the direction at right angles to the ranges, the distance between column centers should be an exact multiple of the preferred distance between range centers for the main stack collection (see 4 below).

4. With collections of less than 500,000 volumes anticipated during the life of the building and with students having free access, it is suggested that range spacing can well be 4 ft 6 in. on centers, with 4 ft 3 in. for a minimum if the institution is pinched for funds. If a collection of over 500,000 volumes is anticipated or if, with a smaller collection, there is to be restricted stack access, the 4 ft 6 in. can readily be reduced to 4 ft 3 in., and perhaps as low as 4 ft 2 in., according to the peak load and the amount of student use anticipated. Remember in this connection that if, during the earlier years when the collection is smaller, the column spacing brings the ranges closer together than would be desired, this can be partially counteracted if shorter ranges are provided by the use of cross aisles, which can later be eliminated.

5. If the stack can be so laid out that most of the heavy through traffic is cared for by a generous main center aisle, that aisle in a stack with over 100,000 volumes on one level can well be up to 6 ft wide, although 4 ft, 4 ft 6 in., and 5 ft are possible and will increase capacity. For a smaller stack, 4 ft 6 in. should be entirely adequate, unless the use is very great. It is difficult to arrange for a 4 ft 6 in. aisle, or anything between 6 ft and 3 ft, when the stacks are planned on the basis of 3-ft sections, and the distances between columns are multiples of 3 ft. Methods of solving this problem were discussed in section 4.2.

Secondary cross aisles along the ends of stack ranges used only for local traffic or to reach adjacent carrels can be as narrow as 3 ft, less the inch or two projection into the aisle of the end stack uprights. If adjacent carrel tables are over 3 ft wide, adjustments may have to be made in this aisle width; but try to avoid anything less than 33 in. in the clear, even in a little-used stack.

6. If square bays can be worked out, they are preferable as they give more flexibility, and ranges can be turned at right angles at a later time more easily. If the columns are to be 14 in. or less and the ranges are to be 4 ft 6 in. on centers, the only possible square bays are 13 ft 6 in., which is too small, 22 ft 6 in., which is generally acceptable, and 31 ft 6 in., which is so large that it will probably be unduly expensive and will result in oversize columns which get in the way.

7. There are three possible rectangular instead of square bays which give flexibility if the columns are to be small enough so that two of them can take the space of one stack section and if the parallel ranges are to be 4 ft 6 in. on cen-

ters: 13 ft 6 in. by 22 ft 6 in.; 13 ft 6 in. by 31 ft 6 in.; and 22 ft 6 in. by 31 ft 6 in. If columns are to be rectangular and take the place of a full instead of a half section, 18-ft or 27-ft square bays are possible. If range spacing other than 4 ft 6 in. is agreed upon, there are many other square and rectangular bays to be considered. A square bay 25 ft 6 in., with ranges 4 ft 3 in. on centers is possible, for instance. See Appendix B for other possibilities.

8. The larger the over-all size of bays can be, the more flexibility they provide, but, of course, the cost of thicker floors and heavier beams required must be kept in mind.

9. In general, bay sizes and column spacing are less important in nonstack than in stack areas, particularly if no large reading areas are proposed. Try to keep columns out of the center of reading rooms. Unless there is special reason for using columns for decoration, keep them hidden as far as possible. If a bay dimension can be divided into two, three, four, five, or six equal parts, each with a window, that match desirable sizes of offices, studies, or carrels, and if these parts when on an outside wall can be so arranged as not to interfere with the facade design, the arrangement will help functionally and aesthetically.

10. The width of the stack range has a major effect on the desirable distance between range centers and must not be neglected.

Reference to Chapter 4 on the module system and to Appendix B on space-requirement formulas is again suggested.

Room Heights and Floor Areas. Again, definite or specific directions to the architect are undesirable, but suggestions may be in order. If the site selected and other considerations will permit an entrance at the ground level with no more than one step up and with a ramp in place of that step at one side, the results will be worth while. If the site is such that a good basement with windows on at least one side is available, the clear height on a basement level can be held down to 8 ft 6 in., 8 ft 4 in., or even a little lower, according to the uses to be made of the space. If a basement with only two levels above it will provide the requisite square footage, traffic will be simplified, and a three-level structure can generally be recommended, unless the total area required is more than 50,000 gross sq ft. If no more than two levels above the entrance, plus

one or more basement levels are required to provide the square footage needed, student use of elevators can be avoided or greatly restricted. If a very large percentage of all the seating accommodations can be provided within two levels up or down from the entrance and even better on only one, it will be advantageous. With very large collections, particularly if large portions of them have comparatively little use, a higher building can be tolerated more easily but, other things being equal, buildings with more than five or six levels should be avoided.

Unless 9 ft 6 in. to 11 ft in the clear for the entrance floor level satisfies the architect and the planning team, consideration should be given to a height of something like 17 ft for that level, with a mezzanine over as large a portion of it as possible. If the mezzanine can cover at least 60 per cent of the floor area, it will not be uneconomical financially. Only rarely is there a functional need for upper floor levels exceeding a clear height of 9 ft to 9 ft 6 in., if they are largely occupied by book stacks and contain no very large rooms. As low as 8 ft 4 in. to 8 ft 6 in., suggested for basements, should be adequate in many cases for the upper floors with no rooms larger than two bays or modules. Floor thicknesses should be watched and engineers requested to hold them down as far as is consistent with satisfactory structural and mechanical arrangements in order to save height of stairs and the cost of the additional cubage involved. The program can properly make suggestions along these lines to the architect.

Mechanical Transportation and Communications. A service elevator or at least a book lift should always be provided if a building has more than one level. (Book lifts are seldom satisfactory.) It is not desirable to carry books up or downstairs in bulk by hand. Stairs should be carefully placed so that they can be easily found and will not be in the way of local traffic patterns. They should be arranged so that their use can be restricted if desired at any time. Elevators should be so placed or equipped as to make it possible to restrict their use to authorized persons. Escalators can properly be considered but are rarely practicable. If other methods of mechanical transportation or if communication devices such as telephones, public-address systems, or class bells are desired, they should be specified in the program. Methods used for vertical transportation and communication are discussed in more detail on a theoretical basis in section 6.2.

14.4 Furniture and Equipment

The program should answer the following questions in regard to the furniture for a new building:

1. To what extent, if any, will the furniture in the old building, if there is one, be used? The use of old equipment should be avoided as far as possible if the equipment can be used satisfactorily elsewhere in the institution, and particularly if it is of poor quality or does not fit the decor of the new structure. Sometimes, of course, a considerable amount of furniture in the old library may have been purchased in recent years with the new building in mind and will be entirely suitable. Sometimes it may be necessary, for financial reasons, to move old furniture into a new building. But completely new furniture will generally have a much more satisfactory psychological effect on the occupants. They will take better care of it and start off with better habits and behavior than if unsuitable old furniture is transferred.

2. If new furniture is to be purchased, who is responsible for its selection? Section 11.1 deals with this question. The architect should certainly have a hand in it. If there is an interior-design consultant, he must work closely with the architect. In too many cases, in a proper effort to save money for the institution, furniture is selected without reference to the architect, to the serious detriment of the decor of the building. The purchasing agent may in some cases be able to buy less expensively, but the task should not be left in his hands without guidance, and he should keep in touch with the architect if he receives the assignment to be sure that he and the architect do not work at cross purposes.

3. Should contemporary or traditional furniture be selected? This must be, in the final analysis, the institution's decision, but the interior and exterior design must not be forgotten. Other suggestions are to emphasize the importance of sturdiness and comfort and the avoidance of extremes that will soon be dated, if not obsolete, and to remember that cost is, of course, also important.

4. Should furniture be stock or specially de-

signed custom-built? The answer is closely related to the points made in the preceding paragraph. Custom-built furniture purchased in quantity may cost less than standard stock material purchased from a manufacturer that specializes in library equipment, but if custom-built furniture is considered, the price should be compared with other possibilities, and the importance of sturdiness, comfort, and design, as well as the cost, should be kept in mind. If the quantities to be purchased are small and if there is doubt in regard to the decision, it may well be wise to purchase the standard stock equipment. The program probably should not go beyond general terms.

5. What percentage of individual seating accommodations should be provided, and how many and what types of lounge chairs should be selected? The planning team should give reasonably specific directions to the architect or the interior designer. Remember the Hampshire Report[1] and the experience of libraries in recent years indicating that at least 75 per cent of students prefer individual accommodations, and that more study will result if they are provided. Lounge chairs can be attractive and useful, but they should be held down in size and in number to 8 or 10 per cent of the total, except in unusual circumstances, and should not be concentrated in special areas with two possible exceptions—lounges and the room for current periodicals. A few, scattered around through reading areas, will break up the monotony and relax the institutional aspect of the installation.

The question of whether regular library chairs should have arms should be faced. If armchairs are used, the tables must be so designed that the arms do not run into the table aprons. Arms, other things being equal, will strengthen a chair and prolong its life, and in general are preferred by men but not by women. They cost more. Why not some of each? The reader is referred again to Chapter 11, in connection with furniture selection.

6. What should be the dimensions of the various types of furniture used?

The program can very properly go into the question of the dimensions of tables and special library equipment, such as service desks, cata-

---

[1] *Student Reactions to Study Facilities with Implications for Architects and College Administrators,* The Committee for New College, Amherst, Mass., 1960, 60 pp.

logue cases, and book trucks. Remember, for instance, that it is unusual to find six college or university students who are prepared to sit at a table 3 or even 3½ × 7½ ft, and that, although a table 4 × 9 ft takes more floor space and inevitably involves more adjacent aisle space, it is worth it if the result is a higher ratio of use per seat supplied instead of a higher theoretical capacity. Give at least some directions to the person who selects furniture in regard to counter heights, book-truck sizes, catalogue-case dimensions, and so forth.

Shelving. The shelving is generally the most expensive single item of library equipment, and certainly occupies the largest amount of square footage, which, it should be remembered, represents the major cost of a building. On this account, if for no other reason, it should be selected with the greatest care on the basis of function, and space utilization, as well as cost. Do not try to save money on it if the results will not be functional. You could purchase double-faced stack shelving only 12 in. from front to back. It would save money and space, but it would rarely be functional or desirable, as there would be too many books that could not be shelved on it satisfactorily. You could buy ranges 24 in. from front to back on which you could shelve 99 per cent of all your books, with the exception of newspapers. The cost would be greater, of course, but the additional cost would be far less than the value of the unnecessary extra area such ranges occupy, and they are not recommended even from the functional point of view, because books shelved on them would be bound to get pushed back, where they would not look well and would be difficult to find. Section 8.1 discusses the problem of shelving in detail and should be useful in preparing the program, which should answer, among other things, the following questions:

1. What types of shelving—standard, case, bracket, cantilever, or commercial—should be purchased, and how much of each? Remember that it is not absolutely necessary to fill in all the space at once if the shelving will not be needed for some years to come and that different types can be used in different parts of the library.

2. Should there be finished bases, finished end panels, and canopy tops? You can select any one or all of these for the sake of appearance, but they are not necessary functionally, except that they provide additional stability and that

finished bases may simplify cleaning and maintenance problems.

3. Should the shelving be of the multitier variety, free-standing with a wide base, or the type of free-standing that is generally not so designated by the manufacturer because for stability it must be securely fastened to the floor, although it can be moved by withdrawing the nails or screws which attach it? This type of free-standing stack must be braced in one or more ways in both directions, but it need be no more than 16 to 18 in. deep even at the bottom for a double-faced range, and this depth will more than cancel out the cost of extra bracing because it reduces the total area used to shelve a given number of volumes. Sixteen-in.-deep ranges give 16 per cent larger capacity than 24-in. ones without affecting the aisle width at the floor level.

4. What other stabilizing factors should be used, such as fastening to the floor, sway bracing, welding, unitizing, and so forth? Be sure that the results are safe.

5. What and how many accessories, such as book supports, shelf labelholders, and range finders should be provided? Careful estimates are desirable. Often too many supports and shelf labelholders are ordered.

6. What width and length of shelves are wanted and what are the decisions in regard to both stack and cross-aisle widths and range lengths? These have much to do with space utilization, and in turn are affected directly or indirectly by the decisions in regard to column spacing, which are discussed in section 4.2.

7. How high should the shelving be? Height enough for seven shelves with the top one not more than 6 ft 4 in. above the floor is suggested, if they are to be arranged 12 in. on centers. With a 4-in. base, this means approximately 7 ft 6 in. over-all.

These seven questions apply primarily to stack shelving. Similar questions must be answered in regard to shelving in reading areas, where the installation may be of wood instead of steel and where the height of the ranges, the depth of the shelving, and the width of the aisles may differ widely from those in the main stack. It may also vary in different reading areas. Many of these questions are also pertinent in connection with the special equipment for housing collections that is discussed in section 8.4.

The best general advice that the author can

provide in connection with furniture and equipment is that the institution wants a good functional installation that is convenient to use, that utilizes space to the greatest possible advantage, and that still avoids undue congestion and an unattractive appearance.

For all the topics discussed in this chapter, it should be noted again that while the decisions reached are of importance to the function of a library, they are largely technical in character. The architect, engineer, and interior designer concerned should have basic general instructions and a statement of the wishes of the institution, but the experts employed to plan the building should be asked to make specific recommendations and then talk them over with the representatives of the institution before the final decisions are reached. The decisions should be the result of a meeting of minds. The institution's representatives may have the final responsibility, but the decisions should be based on the recommendations of the technical experts. They must have their day in court, and their proposals should receive full consideration. These experts are responsible for the soundness of the structure and the operation of the plant. Remember again that it is misunderstandings that cause most of the troubles and disagreements.

14.5   Determination of Total Square-footage Requirements

This section deals with another basic problem in library building planning, the determination of square-footage requirements. Until a reasonably good estimate is available, it is unwise (1) to make a final decision on whether to construct an entirely new building, or to make changes in the present quarters, or to solve the space problem by construction of an addition; (2) to select the site if the decision is for a new building, because, without a knowledge of the square-footage requirements, it is difficult to know whether a site that might otherwise be suitable is adequate.

These questions are discussed in sections 15.1 and 15.2.

This section discusses the space requirements of the five categories dealt with in sections 13.1 to 13.5: reader accommodations; accommodations for the collections; facilities for general public use; staff quarters; and other facilities

not always required, to which should be added a sixth, preferably by the architect after consultation with his client: the required non-assignable or the architectural space which will not be available for seating accommodations, book storage, and staff quarters, and which is considered in more detail in section 16.2. This sixth category of space uses cannot be accurately estimated until the requirements discussed in sections 14.1 to 14.4 have been dealt with.

Reading Accommodations for Library Users. Consideration will be given here only to seating accommodations in space set aside especially for the purpose in regular reading areas or in book stacks. (The public service and other special public facilities will be dealt with in later parts of this section. These include among others much of the non-assignable or architectural space, lobbies, corridors, stairs, lifts, and toilets.) As is true of all space requirements, three primary problems appear in connection with accommodations for readers:

1. How many readers should be provided for?

2. How much space will each reader take?

3. How should the readers be seated so as to utilize the space to advantage?

The first question is in many ways the most difficult to answer because one cannot foretell accurately the needs for reader space that will come in the years ahead, whether enough of it will be available and whether it will be attractive and convenient. Even if today's requirements can be estimated with reasonable success, what will the future bring? Educational programs and policies change, as do those for admission. Each institution, in this country at least, goes its own way to a large extent, and a suitable formula for one will not do for another.

The one thing that can be looked forward to with some degree of assurance is that the total number of college and university students seems likely at least to double in the next fifteen or twenty years if not sooner. The question is how much of that growth will come to your institution. Most colleges and universities have adopted a policy on enrollment growth, but there are almost as many policies as institutions. Some plan to hold the line at the present number, come what will, hoping as a result to be able to improve the quality of the students admitted and provide them with a better education. But in spite of this, a large number of endowed institutions, which can claim with justification that each student costs them many hundreds of dollars more than the tuition he pays, are for one reason or another gradually increasing their enrollment. There are also struggling private colleges seeking more students in order to increase their tuition income. Many of the publicly supported institutions, which are bound by custom and sometimes by law to admit any high school graduate within their district, may be the largest single group so far as student numbers and the rate of growth are concerned. Finally, many new institutions will undoubtedly be organized, and it is difficult to assess their effect on the number and the quality of the students in the older ones.

Admission authorities of all institutions must, if they make any pretense of planning for the future and are not just drifting, make estimates of the number of students they plan to provide for during the period of time they expect a new library building to be adequate. This figure should be broken down into the different groups of students, as the library needs of one group may well differ from those of others. This problem is dealt with in section 7.1 on a theoretical basis and again in section 13.1 dealing with a program for a specific library. The following ground rules, however, might well be kept in mind. Graduate students now and later will tend to use the library more than undergraduates. Students in the sciences, either graduate or undergraduate and in professional schools other than those for the study of law, use it somewhat less. But law students, particularly those in graduate law schools, and graduate students in the humanities and social sciences use it more heavily than any other group. Even more important than the field in which a student is working, however, is the type of institution which is under consideration, its location, and its other facilities. These things largely determine the percentage of students that can be expected to use the library seating accommodations at one time, which is the point at issue here. But this is not the place to repeat the theoretical discussion of the number of seating accommodations to be provided, except to remind those interested that there will be a great variation between institutions and that an estimate for their own institution must be made.

The second problem about space requirements for readers is the amount of space to be scheduled for each reader to be accommodated. Here different institutions will differ in what they may wish or are able to provide. The architect and the librarian, working together and using the answers to the questions given in section 13.1, can determine with fair accuracy the total square-footage requirements for readers in each specified reading area and for each type of reader accommodation. If 25 sq ft for each undergraduate student, 30 sq ft for each beginning graduate student, 35 to 40 sq ft for a graduate student working on his dissertation, and 50 to 100 sq ft for each faculty study is used, the calculation will give at least a rough estimate. In order to be safe, it might be worth while to add 5 sq ft to the above for each reader.

To cite an example, if the program calls for seats for 500 undergraduates, 50 beginning graduate students, 25 doctoral candidates, and 40 faculty studies, the total could come to:

Square Feet

$500 \times 25 =$	12,500	for undergraduates
$50 \times 30 =$	1,500	for beginning graduate students
$25 \times 40 =$	1,000	for doctoral candidates
$40 \times 75 =$	3,000	for faculty studies
615	18,000 sq ft	

If 5 sq ft per reader is added, that is, 615×5, or 3,075 sq ft, it will bring the total to 21,075 sq ft for reading accommodations. But it should be repeated that each institution must make its own decision, and more generous provision may seem to be desirable. (This is all on the basis of net square feet with no space for corridors, stairs, toilets, and walls included.)

The third problem, and an important one in connection with total space requirements for readers, relates to the arrangement of the seating accommodations. This question has been neglected too often and, when the layouts for equipment are prepared, it may be found that the expected number of seats cannot be provided for without creating congestion. This may be the result of (1) an unfortunate bay size, which makes it difficult if not impossible to utilize to advantage the square footage available; (2) poor planning of aisles, which results in their being used from one instead of both sides; or (3) unnecessarily and undesirably large chairs and tables. Chapter 4, dealing with module sizes, attempt to show how to prevent or minimize the effect of the first factor, and a good consultant working with the architect and librarian should be able to help with this as well as with the second and third problems listed. The estimates used above are reasonably adequate and have been used again and again for reading areas which appear spacious.

It should always be remembered that these figures for space requirements in reading areas do not include space used for readers in the third category, which is discussed on page 292.

Accommodations for the Collections. The theoretical discussion of accommodations for the collections found in Chapter 8 and the answers to the questions proposed in section 13.2 should provide a basis here. The librarian must determine whether he will base his decisions on a count of the number of volumes now in the library or on an estimate of the number of standard 3-ft-wide and 7½-ft-high sections which the present collection will fill completely with no room for additions. The latter is generally safer. If the former method is used, an estimate of 125 volumes to a standard section should be reasonably safe for the present needs. If the latter is used, 50 per cent should be added to it to provide comfortably for present needs. The answers to questions 3 to 5 in section 13.2 are now required. They were: What is the anticipated rate of growth of the collection during the years ahead? Is it expected to be arithmetical or geometrical in character? How full is the library prepared to fill its shelves before it considers full working capacity has been reached, and how many years ahead does it hope to provide for in the new quarters?

By applying the answers to the present requirements, those for the new quarters can at least be estimated. If, for instance, the count of the present collections is 125,000 volumes, they can probably be stored comfortably in 1,000 standard sections at present, or, if the actual space used by the present collections is 667 sections and 50 per cent is added to this to provide reasonably for present needs, the figure is again 1,000 sections. If growth is to be provided for twenty-five years and the rate is estimated at 4 per cent per annum compounded, the 2,000-sections requirement will be reached in some seventeen instead of twenty-five years.

If 2,000 standard sections for present needs and future growth are the number required, how much square footage will they occupy? As shown in Chapter 4 on the module system and in Chapter 8 on the housing of the collections,

this will depend on the utilization of space; the module size selected is important, and the shelf depth, stack and cross-aisle widths, and range lengths are all factors. Section 16.3 on layouts and the formulas in Appendix B will help here. If ranges are 30 ft long, spaced at 4 ft 6 in. on centers, and normal width cross aisles are used, a figure of 8⅓ sq ft for each single-faced section will be adequate unless an unusually large amount of space is used for aisles. Stairs and lifts are not included, as they come under nonassignable space, which is dealt with later on. Two thousand sections can then be estimated at 16,667 sq ft for a collection of 250,000 volumes or 15 volumes a square foot.

If the ranges are placed 49 in. on centers instead of 54 in., the 8⅓ sq-ft requirement for a standard section can be reduced to as low as 7½ sq ft per section in a very large library where the stack is little used. It may be desirable to increase the requirement to 10 sq ft per section in a very heavily used stack with wider range spacing and shorter ranges. Some persons would go so far as to suggest 10 volumes per square foot for such a library, but, while that is a good figure for a small undergraduate stack area, it is too generous elsewhere. Twelve should be adequate in any large university library, however heavily it is used, if the use of space is carefully planned. Do not become confused between square-foot requirements for standard-sized single-faced sections and volume capacity per square foot. The tables in Appendix B should be helpful in this connection.

It should be remembered that the above applies only to the book collections in the main stack, not to nonbook material, which must be figured separately, with answers based, if possible, on the present situation for these collections and the best available estimates for their development. Neither does it apply to the collections housed in what are primarily reading areas, for instance those for reference and bibliographical material, current periodicals, and perhaps for rare books and special collections, which may be shelved separately and include a large percentage of odd-sized materials. The same uncertainty holds for manuscripts, archives, maps and atlases, pictorial material, slides, music, and the fine-arts collections, if not shelved in the main stack. Storage shelving for uncatalogued collections, for those being processed, for volumes waiting for the bindery, etc., must also be provided. Separate estimates, if not a formula, must be worked out for each of these groups, based on its present requirements and the expected annual growth.

When these various estimates have been made and added to the main-stack requirements, the total will include all the collections, but, if the special groups are to be provided for in separate areas, it is desirable to specify the needs of those areas individually, always keeping in mind the needs for reader and staff accommodations in them, as well as those for storage.

In connection with the space requirements for reference and bibliographical collections shelved in reading areas, it must be remembered that, if the shelving is of less than standard height or if it is placed wider apart on centers than 4 ft 6 in., the number of sections and also the number of square feet required per section will be proportionately increased. The type of shelving used for periodicals will, of course, have its effect. If they are on display shelving with five shelves to a section and three periodicals to a shelf, there will be only 15 to a section, while 15 shelves 5 in. on centers with periodicals lying flat will provide for 45 of them, or three times as many, but may not be as satisfactory. If floor shelving is used with the ranges 6 ft 9 in. on centers to provide wide aisles, the capacity will be only two-thirds as much as it would be if the ranges were 4 ft 6 in. on centers.

The architect must sooner or later be provided with the information as to what is wanted. The librarian may not be prepared to give definite figures and specifications in the program but must be prepared to discuss the problem intelligently with the architect. He may prefer simply to say, among other things, that the reference and periodical shelving should be placed with generous aisles and the periodicals be suitably spaced in display cases.

Again, as was the case with seating accommodations, the layout of the stacks and the space utilization is a matter of importance, and three factors quite similar to those noted in connection with seating apply: The length of the ranges, the depth of shelving, and the width of the cross aisles determine the requirements in terms of square feet. Avoid congestion but use the space available to full advantage.

Other Facilities for General Public Use. Areas involved here are those for (1) space adjacent to but not within public-service desks (control, circulation, reserve-book, and reference), including those in special reading areas; the desk requirements are discussed below when staff facilities are dealt with; and (2) the public-catalogue room.

Section 13.3 considers these problems in detail. If students have to wait for services at any desk, something that cannot always be completely avoided because students' timetables are not so staggered that demands are spread evenly throughout the day, there should be adequate space for those waiting. They pass through exit controls in large numbers as they leave the library to go to classes, or just before closing time if large groups stay in the library to the end of the library's hours of opening. A somewhat similar situation may be found at a reserve-book desk or at a regular circulation desk, although it is not likely to be as extreme as at the exit-control point. The reference desk may have some congestion, but a skillful reference worker can help the situation by making suggestions to a questioner that will keep him busy in a profitable manner while she deals with another reader. The larger the demands, the greater the waiting area required, but the increase in space should not be proportionate to the increase in the demands. It is suggested that if the control, circulation, and reserve desks can be in or at one side of the entrance lobby, the space there should be adequate for the needs of those waiting. This arrangement is often feasible. The entrance-lobby requirements are dealt with below in the section on non-assignable space.

The reference-desk problem is difficult, and no definite formula is suggested. The architect might well be asked to try to lay out the area with 25 sq ft extra allowed for each full-time member of the reference staff beyond the 100 or 125 sq ft provided by the formula used for other workers and their equipment. Public-service desks in special reading areas might be figured on the same basis as reference desks, except that the 25 sq ft extra should be allotted for each full-time worker who meets the public, plus 25 for the first one at each desk. The total number of square feet involved here is not great, and much of the requirements will depend on the general layout of the area and on whether some of the needs can be provided for from the non-assignable space that, as will be seen below, is a necessity.

The space requirements for the public catalogue are not easy to estimate. The determining factors are the number of cards to be housed and the number of persons consulting the catalogue at the time of heaviest demand. With a very large catalogue and a limited number of readers, over 1 million cards can be housed in 225 sq ft of floor space if one-third more, or 75 sq ft, is added for aisle space to approach it. This means a total of 300 sq ft, or 3,333 cards for each gross square foot involved. The figure can be increased in an emergency to more than 4,000 cards per square foot, but this is not recommended under normal conditions.

The provision for readers using the catalogue is of great importance. The more readers using the library at one time, the larger the space required around the catalogue, and if consultation tables are to be used heavily from both sides, the tables should be wide. In order to relieve congestion if the reader use is exceedingly heavy, the rows of drawers should not be more than perhaps 8 high, instead of a maximum of 12 to 15, and cabinets should be arranged in parallel rows, instead of in alcoves. On this basis, the catalogue capacity could be figured anywhere from as low as 1,000 cards to a square foot up to 4,000.

Section 16.3 on layouts will illustrate different possibilities, and each library after careful consideration should make its decision and propose it to the architect either in the program or by word of mouth. But do not forget that catalogues grow with the book collections and that difficulties arise if space gives out.

Staff Facilities. Section 13.4 spells out in detail staff requirements for space. If the total staff members, figured on a full-time basis, with one added for each 35 to 40 hours per week of student assistance, are multiplied by not less than 125 sq ft, and preferably by 150 or in some cases by 175 sq ft, this calculation should provide for the working quarters and equipment. It should take care of the private offices for the senior members of the staff, the rest- and workroom facilities, as well as the shipping and receiving room and binding-preparation room, but would not include special storage areas for materials awaiting handling beyond those actually being processed. If a staff consists of 25 full-time workers, plus 175 hours a week of student work, figured as 5 more, making 30 in all, the suggested allotment would be not less than

30 × 125 sq ft, or 3,750 net sq ft, or preferably, 30 × 150 sq ft, making 4,500 net sq ft, or in some cases 30 × 175 sq ft, or 5,250 net sq ft in all. Always remember that the staff requirements tend to grow more rapidly than those for other parts of a library.

Special Facilities Not Always Required. No detailed suggestions will be made here. Section 13.5 states the problems involved. When the high-level decision has been made as to what special facilities to include in the library, enough square feet to provide for these facilities should be added. This amount will, of course, vary tremendously from library to library. One added word of caution: Be sure that the space allowed for these special facilities is space that can later be adapted to library purposes.

Non-assignable Space. Non-assignable or architectural space is mentioned in section 13.5, and is dealt with in more detail in section 16.2. It includes space required for construction, stairs, elevators, corridors, toilets, and mechanical and building-maintenance services. This is primarily in the field of the architect, but should be watched carefully by the owner's representatives and the planning team as a whole.

The total requirements are often estimated at the start by adding a certain percentage to the building's net space, which in turn is the sum of the requirements mentioned in the discussions above, to provide for the non-assignable space. The percentage to be added will depend, of course, on various items, including:

1. The type of building. If it is monumental in character, the percentage for non-assignable space will be greater.

2. The amount of space required for the mechanical installations. This will vary from institution to institution, and will also be affected by the type of installation used. If there is a central heating and ventilating plant for the institution as a whole, a lower percentage of space would be required for the library. If most of the ventilation ducts are vertical rather than horizontal, a somewhat larger percentage of square footage but a smaller percentage of total cubage will be required.

3. The third variable depends upon the care with which the layouts are made and the space utilization. Lobby and corridor sizes, the number and size of stairways and toilets are significant items here as well as aisle width and equipment.

The total gross square-footage requirements may then be estimated by adding to the total of the five categories for assignable space the percentage that the architect, after consultation with the planning team, finds necessary. This is discussed in considerable detail in section 16.2; today it will rarely amount to less than one-third, often at least 40 per cent and unfortunately sometimes 60 per cent. It is desirable in most cases to do the best that can be done, with the understanding, however, that as space utilization is improved, the cost per square foot of the building generally goes up slightly but not proportionately.

Sample computations for an imaginary small university library on a reasonably generous basis follow:

CATEGORY 1. *Reading Accommodations*

Square feet

500 undergraduates	at 25 sq ft..	12,500
50 graduate student carrels	at 30 sq ft..	1,500
25 doctoral candidate carrels	at 40 sq ft..	1,000
40 faculty studies	at 75 sq ft..	3,000

Total 615 18,000

CATEGORY 2. *Housing for the Collections*
2000 single sections for 250,000 volumes at 9 sq ft per section 18,000

CATEGORY 3. *Other Facilities for General Public Use*
Space around service desks, for the public catalogue, and for extra square footage for collections in public-service areas (reference, bibliography, and current periodicals) because of more generous spacing 5,000

CATEGORY 4. *Staff Facilities*
24 at 150 sq ft each 3,600

CATEGORY 5. *Special Facilities*

Assembly room	1,500
Photographic department	500
Audiovisual facilities	500
Seminars (2)	500

Total 3,000

Total Net 47,600

CATEGORY 6. *Non-assignable Space*
47 per cent of categories 1–5 22,372

Total 69,972

If the 47 per cent non-assignable space could be reduced to 40 per cent, it would reduce it 3,332 sq ft to 19,040 and at $15 a square foot might save up to $50,000 of the construction cost of something over $1,000,000.

None of the figures in the above estimates should be taken as anything more than approximations, but they should give some indication of a method that can be used to approach the problem of determining total space requirements. Again it should be emphasized that every library differs from every other.

15

First Steps in Planning

Introduction

Long before the program for a new library building has been completed and turned over to the architect a study should have been made of possible alternatives to a new building and consideration should have been given to the selection of a site for an addition or a new structure. In spite of this, after the program for the requirements, which have been discussed in the two preceding chapters, has been prepared, it is desirable to restudy and reconsider both these decisions so as to be sure that the best possible solution to the library's problems is selected. For this reason this chapter has been placed here instead of earlier in the volume. Final decision on alternatives to new construction and on the site should not be made until the requirements have been determined.

15.1 Alternatives to a New Library Building

The price tag for a new library building in these days of high construction costs often comes to twenty times the library's annual budget, or even more. This being the case, alternatives to new construction ought to be considered. Buildings may become inadequate for a variety of reasons; they do not usually wear out, but fashions, standards, and needs change. Inadequate size, however, is usually the most urgent consideration when replacement of a college or university library building is advocated, and it

may be appropriate, therefore, to begin by saying something of growth and space.

Library collections grow. New acquisitions for the most part do not replace the books that are already available. There are additions, but normally very few subtractions. The staff of a library also grows as the collection becomes larger and more complex and as use increases. Increased use requires increased space for readers. Changes in teaching methods in many institutions often result in larger demands on the library, and no end to this tendency seems to be in sight.

The factors of growth that have been mentioned must be taken into account, even if the institution intends to maintain a student body and faculty of constant size. Libraries grow, and most American colleges and universities are growing rapidly in nearly every respect and expect still further growth.

In spite of the apparent inevitability of library growth, the librarian will certainly be in a better position to support a request for new construction if he has considered and studied carefully all the possible alternatives. This section will try to deal at least briefly with these alternatives and will start by considering additional space needs for books, for readers, and for staff.

Space for Books. Obviously, a library ought not to add books indiscriminately. It is rare, indeed, for acquisition funds to be so plentiful that large quantities of useless material are purchased, but some libraries have made the mistake of accepting practically everything that has been offered to them by gift or exchange. The need for improved selection policies is generally recognized; but, in a well-administered library, more rigorous selection promises to improve the quality of what is added rather than to reduce the quantity.

Discarding is often a more promising method of reducing growth, because not all books that are added to a collection remain useful indefinitely. The problem is to identify those that are no longer worth the space they occupy. Almost any volume may conceivably be useful to someone's research some day. It is difficult and expensive to select material for discard; the mistakes made in the process are more likely to be discovered and to be criticized than those that are made in choosing additions to the collections. It is also expensive to cancel catalogue records as books are withdrawn.

A librarian is conscious of his responsibility to scholarship generally. Even if a volume will almost certainly never be used in his own institution, he feels, quite properly, that he ought to try to find a home for it where it will be useful; but intelligent relocation of such material is a difficult task and is also costly.

Problems of this kind are being investigated at Yale, Harvard, Chicago, and other institutions. Adequate treatment of them would require a book, rather than part of a single section. It need only be emphasized here that, before he attempts to obtain more shelf space, a librarian ought to satisfy himself that judicious weeding would not free the shelves that he needs nor perhaps even make his collections more readily usable.

Space for Readers. Since increasing use is one of the best evidences of a library's good health, it may seem paradoxical to suggest the desirability of considering methods of solving space problems by decreasing use. It will certainly not be suggested that use be discouraged by permitting collections or services to deteriorate. But many college and university libraries—particularly those with strong collections in the large metropolitan areas—are heavily used by students and professors from other institutions. This is not the place to advocate that they give such service freely, that they charge for it, or that they refuse to give it at all; but something ought to be said of the building costs that are entailed by that use. In most libraries the readers and reader services occupy far more space than books. A fair generalization, based on formulas that have been described in this volume, is that

25 sq ft in a reading room, plus 25 sq ft elsewhere in the building, are required for each reader and the services he needs. This total of 50 sq ft may well cost something like $1,250 for construction and equipment at today's prices. When the demands on a library approach the limit of its capacity, the student or professor from another institution who uses it does not simply occupy space that would otherwise be unused; he hastens the day when a new building will be necessary. This point should not be overemphasized, but in a number of our metropolitan institutions it is pertinent.

Space for Staff. In most college and university libraries space for staff becomes inadequate before space for books or readers. Staff needs are often neglected because it may be possible to find a corner for one more desk without realizing the loss in efficiency and in productive labor that results from overcrowding. However, a careful rearrangement of workrooms can often provide for additional staff members without decreasing their effectiveness.

More Efficient Use of Space. If a crowded library has few books that ought to be discarded and is serving only readers whom it ought to serve, there may still remain a possibility that, by making better use of the space it occupies, it can at least postpone the date at which additional space will be essential. Difficult and complex problems can be expected, and it may turn out that costs of rearrangements, alterations, and rehabilitation will be greater than can be justified. It is not easy to assess or describe all the factors that ought to be taken into account. Before a decision is made, possibilities in at least six areas should be considered.

1. Provision of shelving for additional books may be practicable. Compact storage of one kind or another may increase the capacity of a stack by 50 per cent or more, even if the stack is of the self-supporting, multitier variety. This is likely, however, to be an expensive installation. If reading areas are larger than necessary, as they may be in an old building, it may be possible to place additional shelving at one end of a reading room. Extra sections of shelving can usually be inserted in one place or another.

2. Additional seats for readers can often be provided by rearrangement of tables and chairs. This may be neither convenient nor aesthetically desirable; many reading rooms are so crowded that it is almost impossible for readers to get to and from the seats, and in many cases

the table space for each reader is inadequate for serious study. There are monumental reading rooms, however, with needlessly wide aisles and spaces between tables. It might be pointed out here that the secret of providing as many seats as possible is to make all aisle space do double duty. Twelve or 13 sq ft will normally suffice for a reader's table space and chair. An additional area of about the same size ought to be enough for aisle space, but it is often increased and even doubled if aisles are used which serve seats or shelving on one side only.

3. As already noted, one more desk can usually be squeezed in for one more staff member; the problem is to determine the point at which this addition creates overcrowding which in turn reduces efficiency. In academic libraries overcrowding usually occurs first in the space assigned for staff use because the librarian at the time of construction was too modest in his request, failed to understand the prospective needs, or at least did not convince the authorities that the staff would grow as time went on.

4. It may be possible to make use of halls, lobbies, and what has been considered non-assignable or architectural space—that is, space that has not hitherto been assigned for library purposes. An unused basement might be utilized. One difficulty in making better use of basements is that they are often damp, if not wet, and it is expensive to rehabilitate them. Monumental corridors can also be used for exhibits, which may enable the library to devote its former exhibition room to readers of books, to shelving, or to staff.

5. A mezzanine can sometimes be installed over part of a reading room that is two or more stack stories high. The cost of doing this, particularly if it must include air conditioning, may be too great, but the possibility is worth keeping in mind.

6. Many libraries house nonlibrary facilities, such as classrooms or administrative offices. Whether or not this use of space has been desirable, it is obvious that when the library needs more space for books, readers, and staff, the librarian ought to be prepared to explain why more of the space within the building should be made available to the library.

The best way to determine probable costs when considering any or all of these six possibilities is to have the structure carefully examined by a reliable builder and to obtain an estimate from him after consultation with an architect.

Let us take a hypothetical example. A library finds that the stack capacity of its building can be increased by 100,000 volumes if compact shelving is installed in an unused basement. This would postpone the need for a new building for an additional ten years, but it would require the installation of a new stairway, the discarding of old furniture, and the removal of an unused coalbin. Old heating and water pipes that are no longer useful would have to be torn out; a cement floor would need to be replaced and a new floor covering provided for; new lighting would have to be installed; and the ceiling would need refinishing and repainting. The cost of these alterations, plus the new shelves might, because of the difficult problems involved, amount to $150,000, or as much as it would cost to build an addition to the library large enough to house the same number of volumes. An addition might be preferable.

However, other factors may need to be considered. It may be easier to obtain funds for renovation than for new construction, although this is not always true. Possibly only a small addition to the building is practicable at the present time and a larger one will be more feasible at some later date. Temporary expedients may be worth while.

On the other hand, providing for 100,000 volumes in the old basement may take care of only a fraction of the total needs for space that can be foreseen in the near future; a new building may be the only real solution, and, if so, renovation of the basement may be an expensive way of providing space that will become nearly if not completely useless as soon as a new building is constructed. Yet if the new building will cost $1,500,000, each year that its construction is postponed might be regarded as saving the income on that sum. This income, at 5 per cent, is $75,000, which means that renovation of the basement at the cost of $150,000, if it enables the library to postpone construction for more than two years, may be an economical course of action. Prospective increases in building costs and business cycles should not be forgotten. Finally, however, a good new building ought to enable a library to provide better services than are possible in an old one. It is difficult indeed to estimate how much this improvement is worth to the institution.

Many a librarian may be sure, both before and after he reads the above paragraphs, that only a new building or an addition can provide space of the kind he needs and in sufficient quantity. But his position will be stronger if, before he asks for new construction, he has carefully investigated the alternatives, instead of waiting for others to do it for him. He ought to be prepared to demonstrate that he has considered them and that they will not be satisfactory. He ought to be able to show that the space now available is not being wasted and that the cost of continuing to live in the present building, including the cost of required rehabilitation work and the impaired efficiency in services, is greater than the cost of new construction. In the course of examining all the possibilities, he may discover means of postponing such construction; if not, his examination ought to have provided him with convincing arguments for it.

Storage and Decentralization. Even if it is proved to the satisfaction of all that a library needs more space, it does not necessarily follow that a completely new central building is imperative. An addition or annex of some kind may be practicable. Problems involved in construction of this sort will be discussed later. First, however, it is desirable to consider whether or not the useful life of a building can be prolonged without altering it, by storing a part of the library's collections, or by detaching portions of its services and collections and housing them separately. Expedients of this sort should be regarded as forms of decentralization.

Storage should always be considered when a library has many books that are used infrequently but seem to be worth keeping. Such books can be housed more inexpensively in a structure designed for them than in a central library building that occupies expensive quarters.

Cooperative storage with other libraries offers further advantages if it promises to develop a common pool of resources and to eliminate needless duplication. Three quite different organizations have been pioneering in this field in the past twenty-five years: the New England Deposit Library, the Hampshire Interlibrary Center, and the Midwest Inter-Library Center. Other libraries have made arrangements for their own storage buildings. These include the University of Michigan, the New York Public Library, the Iowa State University Library. The Bowdoin College Library has used a chapel basement for local storage, and Iowa State a Nissen hut. By making its own arrangements for storage, a library can avoid the complications of

cooperation, though it must also forgo the advantages. If a new building for other purposes is to be constructed near a library, it may be possible to plan its basement as a storage area. In this way the Harvard Law School Library acquired space for 500,000 books beneath the Harvard Graduate Center at a total additional cost for excavation, construction, and equipment of less than 25 cents per volume. The large mature library is more likely to find storage advantageous than the rapidly growing young institution that normally has not yet acquired an extensive body of infrequently used materials.

Most university libraries are decentralized to some extent, with libraries for professional schools, such as law and medicine, housed separately from the central collection. Other subjects may also be detached. The sciences may develop their libraries near laboratories and museums. It is preferable in most cases to establish a central science library, rather than one for each subject. The humanities and social sciences are more resistant to separation from the main collection, but music, fine arts, Far Eastern language materials, and Slavic literatures are among the subjects that in some large universities have been housed in separate libraries.

Decentralization of this sort has both advantages and disadvantages. It is clearly undesirable when the units are too small to warrant a staff that can provide service during full library hours. Some of the financial considerations that may need to be weighed can be suggested by the situation at Harvard, where replacement of the central library building, the Widener Library, would require $30,000,000, if the additional cost of the upkeep of the new building were capitalized and added to the cost of construction. Hence, each year that decentralization enables the university to continue to use Widener might be said to represent a saving of $1,500,000, which can provide a considerable book fund and useful library service.

As has been noted, subject decentralization is common in university libraries. In addition, Harvard has adopted another form of decentralization, within the central library itself, with infrequently used materials in storage at the New England Deposit Library and in basements throughout the university, and with special provision for rare books and manuscripts in the Houghton Library building and for undergraduates in the Lamont building. In this way books have been sorted out and housed appropriately, the infrequently used materials in inexpensive storage, the rare books and manuscripts in nearly ideal atmospheric conditions in a building designed to facilitate careful supervision, the books most frequently needed by undergraduates in a selected collection to which they have free access. Removal of undergraduate services from the Widener building has made it a better place for research, and its stacks are open to those who need access to them, including many undergraduates.

Decentralization of this kind is by no means confined to Harvard. At Michigan the Clements Library houses many of the rare books, and there is also an undergraduate library, as well as a storage building. Yale has built a separate rare-book library, and is prepared to place large quantities of material in either regional or local storage. Cornell has constructed a new central research library and has rehabilitated its old building for use as an undergraduate library. The University of California at Los Angeles has followed a somewhat similar procedure, as have the University of South Carolina and other institutions.

Annexes and Additions. If a library must have more space and if storage or other forms of decentralization will not take care of the situation, an alternative to the construction of a new building may still remain—an addition to the existing structure. This is rarely an easy way out, but it may be desirable. Planning a satisfactory addition to an old library building is usually more difficult than designing a completely new one. But since it promises to call for only as much new construction as is required by growth, it often appears to be a much more economical solution than a whole new building, and it deserves to be investigated.

The apparent savings, in particular, call for scrutiny. They may turn out to be much smaller than they seem or may even prove to be non-existent. A hypothetical, but by no means impossible, example may illustrate this. Let us say that a library occupies 50,000 sq ft of gross space in an area where new construction, including architects' fees but omitting equipment, can be estimated to cost $20 per square foot. This would seem to mean that providing the same space in a new building will cost $1,000,000, and that this amount might be saved if construction of an addition would enable the library to continue to occupy its present quarters. Further analysis,

however, might demonstrate that this estimate is far from sound.

It should be said, to start with, that an architect, a reliable builder, or an experienced library consultant should be consulted on the problem. The following paragraphs indicate why, in some cases, the addition might not turn out to be a wise investment.

1. The gross square footage in the present building may include an unreasonably low percentage of useful space. Analysis might show, for instance, that 50 per cent of the total square footage consists of what can be called architectural, monumental or non-assignable space. The space includes such things as lobbies, stairways, corridors, and walls, as well as unusable attics and basements. It is impossible to avoid a substantial percentage of such space, but 25 to 35 per cent has proved to be sufficient in many recent library buildings. A new building should always prove to be more efficient and useful. It may, therefore, be possible to demonstrate that 40,000 sq ft in a new building could provide as much useful space as the old one does with 50,000. If so, the $1,000,000 shrinks to $800,000.

2. It may be necessary to sacrifice space in the present building or in the addition or in both if satisfactory connections are to be provided between the two. If this loss amounts to a total of 5,000 sq ft, it will reduce the value of the new space by $100,000 and reduce the $800,000 to $700,000.

3. Because the old building has reading rooms 14 ft high, it might seem necessary, in order to avoid irregular floor levels, to build higher and therefore more expensive reading rooms in the annex than would otherwise be needed. This may well mean an expenditure of an extra $100,000, which must be subtracted, and the $700,000 becomes $600,000.

4. It might be impossible to fit new stack heights for full capacity into the old pattern or, if they have to be multitier like the old, desirable flexibility will be sacrificed. This may decrease values by $75,000, thus reducing the $600,000 to $525,000.

5. The cost of breaking through walls of the old building to make connections with the annex may be estimated at $25,000, which will bring the net gain down to $500,000.

6. The old building with an addition might not be so easy to operate as a new one and would require for good service one additional staff

member at $5,000 a year, or the income on $100,000, thus reducing the net advantage of the annex to $400,000.

7. The location of the old building may be such that with an addition a second entrance will be required, which will have to be manned at all times when the building is open. If a completely new building could be so located and planned that two public entrances would be unnecessary, it would save $10,000 per year, or the interest of a capital sum of $200,000, which ought to be deducted from what would be saved by continuing to occupy the old building. This would reduce the $400,000 to $200,000.

8. There may be serious long-range considerations. The present building, though centrally located in the campus when it was built, may no longer be so, because of new construction for classroom buildings. Or the addition may fill up all the available space that remains, making any further construction impossible; yet the institution may be growing so rapidly that still more space will be needed within a comparatively few years. This means that an addition now will still entail a completely new structure in the near future. It is difficult to make any monetary appraisal of these disadvantages, but if the poor location is a $100,000 handicap and if the fact that the original building, plus the annex, can be expected to be useful as a library for only ten years is also assessed as a $100,000 disadvantage, the saving from using an addition instead of new construction, which started as $1,000,000, has changed to no saving at all.

9. The cost of rehabilitation of the old building to make it suitable for today's requirements may also be considerable. If there is need for air conditioning for the sake of the preservation of valuable and irreplaceable material, its cost should not be forgotten.

10. Finally, the *coup de grâce* may be provided by consideration of other needs within the institution. The university's fine arts department may badly need a new building that would cost $500,000. It may be ready to accept the old library, which is handsome and monumental and could be adapted to serve its purposes. The cost of alterations for this purpose may be little more than would have to be paid for the rehabilitation that would be needed in any case if the building continued to house the library.

This hypothetical illustration is not necessarily typical; all the disadvantageous circumstances that were enumerated would not always

occur. Each situation should be examined to determine which of these factors or others are present. The decision should not be reached without consultation with an architect and perhaps with an experienced builder and possibly with a library consultant. An addition can be an economical solution and can be entirely satisfactory from the standpoint of the library. This is demonstrated by some of the specific cases that follow.

Wellesley College offers an excellent example of a successful addition to a building, although the original library was nearly fifty years old and was in an architectural style that was impracticable to duplicate. The old building was ideally located, well constructed, and attractive. The architects found a reasonably satisfactory solution to the extremely difficult problem of floor levels. Available floor space was more than doubled by the addition, which cost considerably less than a completely new building, and it is generally agreed to have been a good solution. The building is now more satisfactory functionally than it was before the addition.

Smith College successfully added a large new wing to a fifty-year-old building about a decade ago and has now added two more additions. Both are relatively small and involved few complications. A third and considerably larger addition can be made later if needed. The library is fortunate in its floor levels, and circulation patterns throughout the original structure and the additions can be kept simple without undue construction costs or waste of space.

Vassar College recently solved its library-space problems for a number of years by filling in the two courts around which its building was constructed. The additions, together with the rehabilitation of the old building, improved the structure functionally but were at least as expensive as an exterior addition would have been.

Amherst College, though it has a sturdily constructed building that is not as old as Wellesley's or Smith's, was confronted by very difficult problems in attempting to plan an addition, because its present multitier stack has only 6 ft 9 in. in the clear throughout most of its area, and no way has been found to provide direct corridors from the present building to any addition except through the stack. As a result, it has a new building under construction.

The University of Connecticut Library is only twenty years old, but was expensive to construct and wasteful in the use of space. Satisfactory additions are difficult because any new reading areas directly connected with the present building would have to have unduly high ceilings. Stack levels are too low to match new ones, and it will be hard indeed to provide a good circulation pattern. In spite of these problems, the university has gone ahead with an addition.

The University of Michigan enlarged its library more than forty years ago by wrapping a new structure around the old one. This proved to be reasonably successful. Thirty years later, however, when plans were considered for wrapping a third building around the second, it was decided that the complications would be too great, and the present undergraduate library was built instead. An addition to the old building may still be worked out later.

The Library of Congress managed to get along in its building for longer than could have been expected in view of its rapid growth from 1900 to 1935, because it could fill in all or part of three of the four large courts around which it was built.

The University of South Carolina found it unwise a few years ago to add to a twenty-year old structure, though adjacent space was available; the existing building was too inflexible and was cut into rooms too small for satisfactory use, by internal walls that would have been very difficult and expensive to remove.

The University of Alberta, finding its library building overcrowded at the early age of nine years, was faced by great difficulties in building an addition. Stack floors were of unequal heights; connecting corridors were lacking; and monumental construction proved to be a very costly handicap.

This list could be enlarged almost indefinitely, and any library contemplating an addition might be well advised to study the problems involved at a number of the institutions considered in the preceding paragraphs.

There are relatively few cases in which it is now possible to build a satisfactory and economical large addition to a library that is more than fifty years old. The reasons for this, which have already been suggested, may be summarized here.

1. Modern lighting and ventilation have radically changed requirements for floor heights, and it is generally uneconomical to plan new construction that will match the old.

2. The older architectural styles, Gothic, Renaissance, classical, and to a lesser extent, Georgian (particularly if it has a pitched roof), are often too costly to duplicate; if an addition departs radically from the style of the original building, aesthetic difficulties may be almost insurmountable.

3. The cost of tearing out old walls may be excessive, unless the existing building was planned with a view to facilitating access to new wings.

4. The location of many library buildings has become unsatisfactory for library purposes because of shifts in the position of other activities in the institution.

5. Many a building was planned as a complete architectural unit by an architect who did not want to have his "gem" modified or damaged aesthetically by future generations.

This last point calls for further comment. More than one architect has said that he would refuse a commission if his instructions included a requirement that the building be planned in such a way that additions would be readily practicable without impairing it functionally. It would be rash to propose a universal rule that no library building should be planned without a suitable addition in mind, but the presidents and governing boards of colleges and universities ought to realize that most academic and research libraries, unless they are much more mature than most of those in this country, still grow at a rate that doubles their space requirements every twenty years or less—every ten years in some cases. Unless the institution is prepared to provide completely new housing for its library at frequent intervals, perhaps every ten or twenty years, it ought to arrange for expansion at a later time.

The exceptions should not be overlooked. Certain mature institutions have acquired their basic research materials and have library collections growing at the rate of only 2 per cent each year, instead of the prevailing 5 to 10 per cent. If such an institution also has a student body reasonably static in size (an unusual situation at present), it may hope to get along without additions to its central library building for many years, if the building is reasonably adequate now and if the library will make the most of savings in space that are possible by means of microfilming, discarding, storage, and other forms of decentralization. It is recommended that all other institutions deliberate very carefully before they employ an architect who insists that no additions be made to his building.

A number of questions need to be answered before plans are made for an addition.

1. When the present building was planned, was an addition contemplated? If so, were drawings for it then made? Are they available and still suitable? Many architects fortunately have realized that an addition would be needed and have proceeded accordingly. The plan of the main library building of the University of Illinois may be regarded as standard in this connection. Repeated additions have been made, and still more are practicable. There is room at the rear for almost indefinite expansion of stack and reading areas. The limitations of the Illinois plan are that additional cubicles in the stack are available only in places where there is no outside light; new space for readers and stack may not be in a satisfactory proportion in each addition; and, finally, it is not easy to provide for new staff housing. It may also be noted that the magnificent monumental reading room over the front entrance does not in 1965 seem so attractive functionally as it did fifty years ago, and this valuable and extensive space in the building cannot be used to best advantage.

The Walter Library at the University of Minnesota, with much the same basic floor plan as the University of Illinois Library, is cut off from a similar solution to its space problem by its geographical position. It is backed up against a main traffic artery which cannot well be moved and across which are fairly new, large, and expensive buildings which again would prevent expansion for the library.

2. Is it possible when adding to a library building to obtain an easy and satisfactory circulation pattern with direct access to the new part of the structure? The University of Florida Library at Gainesville, which was built in 1929 and has already had two additions, is an example of a building that is still in good physical condition but is hard to enlarge because difficult circulation patterns would result and would require the sacrifice of valuable space; moreover, sufficient additional space to provide for a considerable period ahead is not available on the site in any direction.

3. Do floor levels in the present building make efficient use difficult? It was not unusual during the past century and, alas, even later, to plan a library in which it was impossible on any level, even the main one, to go from one end of the building to the other without ascending or descending a few stairs along the way. American technology has not yet devised a satisfactory and inexpensive method of taking a loaded book truck up and down short flights of stairs. Additional elevators may help, but they are expensive, particularly if their mechanism must be capable of making frequent stops a few feet apart. The old Cornell University Library, dating back to the 1890s, is a good example of what ought not to be done. Shifting of books from one part of the building to another was seriously complicated by the numerous short flights of stairs, many of them without elevator connection. There is also the danger that the users of the building will fall on unexpected stairs.[1] In the Widener building at Harvard, where there were two steps and then a landing just before the main stairway to the reading room began, someone fell every week on the average for thirty years. The two steps were finally replaced by an unattractive ramp, which has now saved countless sprains and breaks, to say nothing of bruises. It is recommended that short stairs, primarily for architectural purposes, be avoided wherever possible in library buildings.

4. How large an addition will be required? It is one thing to add a small stack or a small wing for reading areas, increasing the size of an old building by 20 to 25 per cent. It is quite a different matter to build an addition that is larger than the original building, something that is often required in these days of rapid growth. The small addition, if it will provide satisfactory space and will not crowd other buildings or encounter other complications, is often desirable. The large addition is more likely to result in problems because it tends to perpetuate any unfortunate features of the old building, making the tail wag the dog.

5. How long can the proposed addition, plus the present building, be expected to provide adequate space, and what can be done at the end of this period? Will still another addition then be practicable, or will this one be the last? Are the institution and the space needs of its library growing so rapidly that a much larger building will be needed within twenty years? If so, it may well be uneconomical to enlarge now

[1] It should be noted, however, that in spite of the stairs, this building has with great ingenuity been rehabilitated and made into the University's extremely successful Uris Undergraduate Library.

instead of starting over. In a privately endowed, liberal arts college, such as Smith, an addition may be desirable, even if the existing building is fifty years old. Smith does not expect to increase its student body to any considerable extent. Its library collections are mature enough to be growing not more than 3 per cent a year, and the Hampshire Interlibrary Center is available to house and supply infrequently used materials.

But tremendous physical expansion of its library must be expected by a tax-supported state university if it now has 5,000 students but plans to have 15,000 within a generation; if its collections, now no larger than Smith's 450,000 volumes, are growing at the rate of 10 per cent a year; and if it expects to support advanced research in an increasing number of fields. Money may well be saved in this case by replacing a building that is only twenty years old or even less as at the University of Alberta. Each institution has its own problems that must be examined before an intelligent decision can be reached.

6. Are there serious aesthetic obstacles to an addition? Following the style of an older structure is likely to be prohibitively expensive, but building a contemporary wing on a collegiate Gothic, classical, or Georgian building may be very difficult. Even if it is done to the satisfaction of many persons with good taste, it may arouse violent alumni criticism. It has been done successfully—the 1958 addition at Wellesley is an example—but there have been many failures.

7. Are strategic financial or other considerations to be weighed? Sometimes the donor of a building or members of the donor's family will give funds for an addition but will not contribute to a new structure. The sentimental value of an old building may be so great that it would be unwise to discard it or use it for other purposes. The library of Delaware State College in Dover has occupied the oldest building on the campus for many years—a building that was once the chapel of the slave plantation on which the college developed after the Civil War; students and faculty regard it with great affection as the heart of the institution. The college was fortunate in being able, without materially changing the character of this building, to enlarge it and continue to use it for its library.

Despite all difficulties, the possibilities of an addition ought to be examined before a decision

is made to give up an old building. It will often be desirable to call in an architect, a builder, or a library consultant, or all three to make sure that an addition is practicable. The costs ought to be estimated as carefully as possible and the advantages and disadvantages assessed. No simple formula will take the place of thoughtful study in light of the library's future and the institution's educational program.

15.2 The Selection of a Library Site

It might be supposed that the logical order of procedure would be to decide that a new library building is needed, then to decide what sort of building it ought to be and the architectural style to be used, and finally to decide where it should be placed. Unfortunately, however, the situation is practically never so simple as this. The availability or nonavailability of a satisfactory site is one of the factors that affect the decision on whether or not to build; this was true at Harvard when replacement of the central library building was given up twenty-five years ago.[2]

One can hardly determine how much space is necessary for an adequate site, unless one has studied the objectives of the library and projected its future growth and its space needs. One can hardly judge whether or not a particular location will be reasonably convenient for those who use the library, unless one can predict the extent and direction of future physical growth of the institution served by the library. If the institution is in its infancy and there is ample room, it may be wise to select the library site first and to plan the future building program for the whole college or university around it. More often, however, the problem is one of fitting a large building into an existing pattern that may have made no provision for it.

It should be emphasized also that one cannot design a satisfactory building and then look about for a vacant space in which to park it that is large and convenient enough. Instead, many features of a good building are determined by

[2] The only available site for a new central library at Harvard was more than a quarter of a mile off center. This was not the only reason for the decision not to build; tremendous costs were involved, and a building large enough to provide for another generation would have had to be so large that professors and graduate students, to say nothing of undergraduates, would have found it difficult to use.

its site. In order to compare the advantages of two sites, one must compare the two somewhat different buildings that could be erected on them.

The problems that have been outlined in the preceding paragraphs indicate that the selection of a library site is so important for an institution as a whole that it should be preceded in many instances, if not most, by the preparation of a master plan for physical development of the campus. Master planning is a problem for the institution as a whole, not just for the library. This master plan should consider among other things the following:

1. The objectives of the institution

2. The estimated prospective size of the student body and faculty, including separate figures for graduate and undergraduate students and professional schools, if there are or are to be any

3. The size of the physical plant that will be required in the next generation, and, if possible, for a longer period

4. The parking facilities required for faculty, staff, and students

5. The general landscaping and servicing plan for the campus

6. Policy decisions in regard to the type and architectural style of the buildings to be erected

Without a master plan for development of the institution's physical plant, the difficulties of selecting a satisfactory site for a new library will be greatly increased. It should be noted that certain architects and landscape architects make a specialty of preparing master plans for the development of colleges and universities.

Five major factors should be taken into account in evaluating a site for a library. First, is its size adequate? Second, what is its relation to neighboring buildings and to the whole population distribution and traffic flow of the institution? Third, what orientation is possible for a library building erected on it? Fourth, are there advantages or disadvantages in the slope of the land? Finally, what complications will arise from the nature of the ground beneath the building?

It may be, of course, that only one site will be available that is large enough and in an acceptable location. Even so, the other factors should be examined to determine how they will affect the proposed building. How, in other words, can it be designed to make the most of favorable circumstances and to overcome the difficulties presented by this site?

Size. A new building ought, if possible, to provide for present collections, staff, and readers, plus anticipated growth for at least twenty-five years to come, and preferably, with later additions, for twice that period. There may be cases where for one reason or another it is impossible to build a new library large enough to be adequate for even twenty-five years. The State of California planning authorities, because of the tremendous demands for additional space in the tax-supported institutions of higher learning in that state, have in certain instances ruled that new buildings constructed at this time should be large enough for five years only, after which a second stage of their construction should be proposed. In many rapidly growing state universities throughout the country the size of an addition to an old building or of the first stage of a new building is determined by the size of the appropriations that the university administration is able to obtain from the state's fiscal authorities, rather than by prospective needs during a specified number of years ahead. In private institutions also the sums that can be made available, rather than the needs, are too often the determining factor. This question of total space needs is dealt with in section 14.5; but two points should be emphasized here.

1. If a new library or an addition to an old one is inadequate for space requirements for the next twenty-five years, obvious disadvantages will result, which should not be overlooked. Another new building or addition will be required before that time. It will probably be more difficult to obtain funds then, when the old one has proved to be inadequate so quickly, than if a longer period had elapsed. If the present or about-to-be-built structure is named for the donor or in honor of a friend or benefactor of the institution, to have to give it up so soon might cause dissatisfaction and make future money raising a problem. The cost of planning and moving into a new building every twenty-five years is a matter of importance, as is the dislocation of the staff and the service which is inevitable.

2. The site selected, wherever it is, should be large enough for additions that will extend the useful life of the building until it is outmoded functionally or in other ways. Even when the desirable square footage has been determined for a building and its prospective additions, there is, alas, no definite formula that will translate these figures into the minimum dimensions

for the site. A building does not look well if it fills a plot too full. Spacing of buildings is an aesthetic problem, and is affected by what has been done already on a campus or is planned for the future. Proper landscaping can often help to make space go farther than might be expected, and its possible usefulness in this connection should not be neglected.

It may not be out of place to remind librarians, administrative officers of educational institutions, and even, in a few cases, architects, that a college or a university that prides itself on providing its students with a good liberal education should appreciate the fact that a handsome, comfortable, and functional library building may have an important contribution to make in bringing about the desired results of the whole educational process. A library should not be a monument; it should not be wasteful of space; it should be economical in construction; its planners should always take the long view and keep in mind the cost of maintenance, as well as the original building costs; but it also should provide an atmosphere that encourages profitable and satisfactory use by students and faculty.

The size of the plot also depends on the height of the building, which involves functional as well as aesthetic considerations. The number of floors that will be satisfactory from the functional standpoint cannot be determined without taking account of the total square footage, the type of library, its collections, and use. These matters are treated in some detail in section 5.4; but a few general observations may be made here.

A library requiring 10,000 sq ft or less, and often one considerably larger, will usually be more satisfactory functionally if it is all on one floor. In larger libraries it is often desirable that the entrance level and the one above, plus the one below, particularly if it has windows[3] be large enough among them to house the central services[4] and provide seating for at least 75 per

cent of the readers—particularly those who come and go at short intervals. If this is practicable, there will usually be no serious problems with public elevators. As far as possible, the most heavily used books ought to be shelved comparatively close to the entrance.

Sometimes a site will prove to be large enough for a building and its additions only if expansion takes the form of additional floors. This is expensive and inconvenient, but, even so, may be preferable to any other alternative. At the Louisiana State University in Baton Rouge and also at the New Orleans campus, the libraries have a central location in the heart of the campus, and fill the available plot almost completely. This was realized and accepted when the buildings were planned, and the architects provided for construction that will make it possible to add two more floors when they are needed.

The total height of a building above ground is determined by four factors: the percentage of the building that is below ground level, the number of levels above ground, and their height, the thickness of the floors between finished ceilings and finished floors above, and the type of roof used. If a large part of a building can go below the main entrance level, as at the Princeton University Library, the University of Cincinnati Library, and the Lamont Library of Harvard, which in some ways resemble an iceberg with the major fraction of their square footage in their basement floors, the total apparent height can be correspondingly reduced. It should be noted that the percentage of space required for stairs and elevators generally, although not necessarily, increases with each level that is added. Also, three levels with 8-ft ceiling heights require no more height than two with 12-ft ceilings, except for the thickness of one additional floor. In buildings with as many as five floors above ground, the thickness of floors is an important factor in the total height; if each one, for instance is 5 ft thick instead of 2 ft, the five would take 5×5, or 25 ft, instead of 5×2, or 10 ft, making a difference of 15 ft, or almost enough space to provide two additional stack levels. Thick floors make it easy to plan ducts and services that can be run almost anywhere,

---

[3] The question of windows was discussed in section 10.1. It is suggested here simply that their importance is primarily for readers, not for reading, and is chiefly psychological.

[4] The central services referred to here are generally considered to include the circulation and reference desks, with the offices and service areas that go with them, the bibliography and reference collections, with such reading space as they require, the public catalogue, and in many cases the current-periodical collections, with an attached reading area, and also accommodations for the use and storage of microreproductions if they are to be serviced from one of the service desks mentioned above. To this should be added at least the work

areas housing those members of the processing staff (particularly acquisition and cataloguing) who have frequent need for using the catalogue and the reference and bibliography collections.

but it is more economical, at least in gross cubage, to run services vertically rather than horizontally in so far as possible.[5]

Central or Eccentric? The library has often been called the heart of the university; it is visited frequently by nearly everyone in the institution and, if a good library, will be used at least as much as any other building on the campus. Obviously, its location ought to be convenient. Does this mean near the dormitories, the classroom buildings, the laboratories, the student union, or the athletic field?

No one answer is correct for all institutions. If most students commute to the campus, it may be best to place the library near the transportation center, enabling the student to return books on his way to classes and borrow others as he is leaving for home. The location of lockers for commuting students may also be an important consideration.

A location near the classroom center is usually preferable to one near the dormitory center; to lengthen the walk to the library between classes by two minutes is more disadvantageous than to lengthen by five minutes the time required to reach the library in the evenings from dormitories.[6] If there are dormitories on opposite sides of the campus, as in many coeducational institutions, a location near classroom buildings may be approximately equidistant from the dormitories. If a choice must be made, it is preferable to place the library near classrooms for the humanities and social sciences, rather than near those for the sciences. If it is much easier, either in the daytime or evening, to reach the student center than the library, a temptation to defer study has been left in the student's path.

Convenience evidently implies a central location, but it is possible for a site to be too central. Some campuses still have a large unoccupied space in their central squares, and this might at first glance seem to be an ideal site for a new library. In fact, however, there are usually serious drawbacks.

First, because the space is so centrally located and conspicuous, the donor and, less frequently, the officers of the college and even the architect may be tempted to decide that it is the place for the single monumental building on the campus.

To be sure, it is possible for a good library to be monumental, but it is less likely to be a good functional library if it is planned primarily as a monument. The successful combination is rare. Moreover, a monumental building usually costs much more than one that is primarily functional. If funds available for library construction are limited, it may be impossible to pay for the space that is needed if this space has to be housed in a building that is to be the showpiece of the campus.

Second, if a library is in the center of the campus, with students approaching it from all directions, there will be inevitable demands for public entrances on all sides. One objection to this is that each entrance, with the lobby attached to it and the corridors leading from it to the circulation desk and other central services, takes valuable space. If, for example, an extra entrance requires a vestibule of only 100 sq ft, plus a small inside lobby of 500 sq ft, plus a corridor (otherwise unnecessary) 100 ft long and 10 ft wide, there is a total of 1,600 sq ft that adds nothing to the building's seating or shelf capacity, may interfere, sometimes seriously, with its functional properties, and cost perhaps $30,000. This is only 3 per cent of the total in a $1,000,000 building, but it would provide space for shelving 25,000 volumes or, used as endowment, would bring in an income of $1,500 per year for books or services.

The extra entrance will prove to be still more expensive if the library decides, as more and more libraries have done, that the cheapest and most effective way to supervise the building is not to have an attendant in each reading area, but to check all readers at the exits as a means of discouraging unauthorized borrowing. If this is done in a building open 80 hours per week, a very modest number of hours today when student and faculty pressure is for a midnight or later closing time, each exit may increase the payroll by $4,000 to $6,000 annually. It will be hard to resist the demand for one or more additional entrances and exits if the building is too centrally located; students and professors do not like to walk around a building and then have to return part of the way as soon as they enter. (The question of supervision is given further attention in section 6.1.)

Third, and, in many ways, the most serious objection of all to a location at the center of the campus is that it increases the difficulties of making an addition to the building that will be

---

[5] This problem is discussed in more detail in section 5.3.

[6] Some librarians disagree with this argument, on the basis that evening study is on the whole more important and that the library should be as close to the dormitories as possible.

aesthetically and functionally satisfactory. Often, indeed, it makes an appropriate addition not only difficult but almost impossible. A centrally placed building tends to be symmetrical, and an addition usually threatens to destroy this symmetry. If it is also monumental, the cost of an addition will be greatly increased. It should be emphasized once more that most library buildings, if they continue to serve the purpose for which they were designed, have to be enlarged sooner or later, and ought to be planned with this in mind.

A final and not unimportant objection to a too central location is that it may occupy space that is very precious particularly in an urban area, and should be used for an attractive lawn and planting.

What is wanted, then, is a convenient location, but not one so central that it calls for an unreasonably expensive, monumental, and unfunctional structure. Figs. 15.1 and 15.2 illustrate some of the points that have been made.

Orientation. No single orientation is ideal for all seasons, climates, and other conditions; but orientation is a factor to be considered, particularly in areas where extremes of heat or cold, strong winds, or intense sunlight may be expected. Near the tropics the sun shines in east and west more than in south windows. As one goes farther north, the southern sun becomes more and more of a problem; the situation is reversed, of course, south of the equator.

The extent to which the sun penetrates into rooms at the hottest time of day is a matter of some importance in most areas. The problem is minimized if it is usually cloudy, and, in a country where central heating is not customary, the winter sun may be a useful source of heat. More commonly, however, when direct sunlight streams into a building it creates glare and overheating and is bad for the books; if there is air conditioning, it adds to costs. An architect should be able to provide drawings showing the penetration of the sun into a room at any latitude during any month of the year for any proposed orientation of a building.[7]

The amount of direct sunlight, as well as heat and cold, that enters a room depends also, of

[7] An apparatus called a "solarscope" has been constructed in Australia which, when placed beside a properly sized building model, will show graphically sun penetration at any time of day on any day in the year. It must, of course, be adjusted for latitude. Graphic drawings give the same information but may not be so dramatic or persuasive.

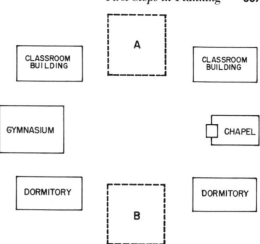

FIG. 15.1 Library site selection in relation to other academic buildings. (*A*) Suitable site for library because of nearness to classroom buildings, but limited in expansion possibilities. (*B*) Possible site for library, but one closer to classroom buildings is preferable, other things being equal.

course, on the height of windows, the percentage of wall space that they occupy, and the depth of the room from windows to inner walls. Prevailing winds and extremes of heat and cold should also be taken into account; double windows and certain special kinds of glass may do much to counteract unfavorable conditions, but they are expensive and sometimes, if broken, are

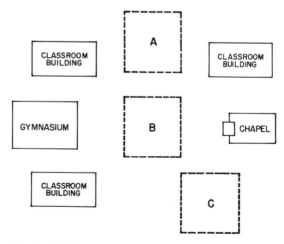

FIG. 15.2 Library site selection. (*A*) This is too small an area, and possibilities for an addition are limited. (*B*) This would be difficult if not impossible to expand and would encourage demands for entrances on all sides, which would be difficult and expensive to control and would reduce assignable areas on the critical entrance level. Its central location would increase the temptation to erect a monumental structure. A shipping entrance would present problems. (*C*) Apparently the most desirable location for the library since expansion possibilities are unlimited and problems presented by (*B*) are lacking.

difficult to replace. Outside concrete, tile, brick, wood, or metal screens have been developed in recent years to reduce the problems resulting from excess sunlight.

In most parts of the United States the western sun is the most difficult to control. The eastern sun generally presents much less of a problem because it is rarely so hot, and the sun is ordinarily higher above the horizon and penetrates a room a shorter distance by the time the library is open in the morning or is heavily used. The southern sun becomes more of a problem as distance north from the equator increases. Sun rarely causes trouble in northern windows in this hemisphere, as it occurs only in early mornings and late afternoons in midsummer. The sunshine and its glare can be kept out during these periods by relatively inexpensive landscaping because the sun is low in the sky.

The use of special glass and screens of one kind or another some distance beyond the outside walls has already been mentioned as a means of protection from glare and heat. These screens may be placed a few feet beyond the outside wall and protect windows from direct sunlight except, possibly, for a few minutes at the end of the day on a western exposure. Examples of such screens can be found in the undergraduate library of the University of South Carolina, the new University of Southern Florida in Tampa, and the New Orleans Public Library, to mention only a few. In place of any of these, awnings or wide shelves projecting horizontally from the building above windows, or metal vertical venetian blinds outside the building can be used. Inside the windows, venetian blinds (vertical or horizontal), curtains, or drapes will help. The inside and outside types sometimes tend to interfere with the circulation of air in an unexpected fashion, if there is no air conditioning. Each means expense and often a good deal to construct or install and replace when required. An engineer should be asked to supply estimates for the specific locality.

The window problem is discussed in more detail in section 10.1, but it should not be forgotten that a reduction in the percentage of glass in the walls will reduce considerably the heat and cold that is transmitted to the inside. Some architects prefer all-glass buildings, which can be very effective aesthetically. Others prefer to have no windows at all, or very few, with a wall pattern to provide the architectural effects

desired. Though small window areas produce savings over large ones in heating and air conditioning, they may require artificial lighting over a longer period, but the additional resulting cost is rarely great. A library open for 14 hours a day in a climate with an average amount of sunlight will require artificial lighting for reading approximately half the time it is open, even if it has large windows, and, while some readers feel a great need for windows and tend to have claustrophobia without them and many others prefer them, it should be remembered that the "light that comes from windows is not for reading but for readers," that is, for psychological purposes.

The western sun is the most objectionable throughout most of the United States. It follows that a rectangular building with long north and south sides and short east and west walls is to be preferred if practicable in other respects. If the long axis runs directly east and west, objectionable effects of sunlight will be minimized. If a building faces to the southwest or southeast, it will usually suffer from both the south and west sun even more than if it faces straight south. In addition, the east side will be more troublesome, and in late afternoon the sun will come in on the northwest side. In other words, a building that is placed at a 45° angle from north to south tends to have greater difficulty from excess sunlight than one that has its main axis straight east and west.

If the north side of a building is the best area for reading, it will be preferable, other things being equal, to have the main entrance on the south, leaving the entire north side free for reading space. Furthermore, if the stronger winds and storms usually come from the north and west, an entrance on the south or east is preferable and may require a smaller entrance vestibule than would otherwise be needed.

It should be kept in mind that direct sunlight, with its ultraviolet rays, is harmful to book bindings and paper. Book ranges should not extend to a wall where the sun can come through windows between them; if ranges extend to any wall, they should do so only on the north. As far as possible the ranges should be at right angles to walls that have windows; if they parallel such walls, the full force of the sun will strike the volumes in the first range.

It is obvious, however, that the ideal for most of the United States—a library with its entrance on the south and its long axis running directly east and west—may be impracticable in many cases because of other considerations. A convenient location is more important than an ideal orientation; but orientation is a factor to be considered, and its effects on building costs should not be overlooked. If other factors dictate a particularly undesirable orientation, special attention should be given to avoiding the complications that would arise from large areas of unprotected glass and to the corrective measures that should be taken.

The Slope of the Land. If a campus is flat, as many are, one site is like another as far as slope is concerned. Otherwise, however, the extent to which the ground slopes and the direction of the incline may be important considerations.

A flat site is not always ideal; it has distinct disadvantages. If the main entrance is to be at ground level or only one step up, it will probably be difficult, but not impossible, to have windows in the basement. This may not be of too great importance, but even with the best of air conditioning and lighting, some persons are inclined to think that reading and staff accommodations without any outside light are substandard. This is particularly likely to be true if the rooms also have low ceilings, as they often do in basements. A basement is not essential, and may be impractical because of ground and soil conditions; but a basement can often provide a large amount of useful library space comparatively inexpensively and conveniently located a short distance from the entrance level. With central-heating and air-conditioning plants for whole campuses, basement space may not be needed for mechanical rooms, and there may be as many square feet to be assigned to readers, staff, or books in the basement as on any other floor—more, usually, than on the main floor, where a large entrance lobby is almost always required. If the basement has windows, this space may be highly attractive, and it has the great advantage of being only a short flight of steps from the entrance level. It may also make possible a separate entrance and, if so, can house facilities that are open at times when the rest of the building is closed. Modern basements can be very different from those of an earlier period.

It should be noted that a short flight of steps leading to the entrance on the main floor may make it possible to have a basement with windows all around, but it should be remembered that a building without such steps, entered directly from the grade level, is in many ways more inviting. Areaway windows can sometimes provide nearly as much light as those completely above ground, but they entail problems of landscaping and drainage. If the first floor is approximately 30 in. above ground level on a flat site, a loading platform at the rear is automatically available; this is not essential, but it is a convenience even today, when most shipments reach a library in small parcels rather than in the tremendous packing cases that used to prevail. Shipments leave the library also, it should be remembered.

One further observation on flat sites may be made. If soil conditions permit, modern earth-moving machinery can change ground levels a few feet at small expense, and, with adequate landscaping, the results may be excellent. It may thus be possible to have a front entrance at ground level, but with a loading platform at the rear.

A considerable slope may be a distinct advantage or disadvantage, depending on its relationship to the main entrance. At a given site, there is usually one side where the main entrance ought obviously to be—a point at which traffic to the library naturally converges. If there is a fairly steep downward slope from this entrance to the rear of the building, it should be possible to have windows in the basement—possibly on as many as three sides and even part or all of the fourth. Indeed, if the slope is sharp enough, there may also be windows in a subbasement or, as it is sometimes called, the minus-2 level. At Princeton and the University of Cincinnati Libraries, even the minus-3 levels have windows on one or more sides. A slope of this kind offers the further possible advantage of reducing the height of the building above the entrance level on the most prominent facade. One may enter a building with five floors at the middle of its five levels; this may make it possible to dispense with a public elevator if there is a service elevator for the transfer of books and for persons who cannot climb stairs.

In order to avail themselves of a minus-1 level with windows, some libraries have an entrance set back from the top of a hill and approached by a bridge, as at the Carleton College Library in Northfield, Minnesota, Douglass College in New Brunswick, New Jersey, and the University of Pennsylvania in Philadelphia. Construction of a short ramp up to the front entrance can serve the same purpose. At the Grinnell College Library there is a ramp and then a bridge to the entrance; the result is that, though the campus is relatively flat, windows can be provided wherever wanted in the basement.

On the other hand, if there is a sharp upward slope toward the rear of a building, the back of the first floor may have to be sunk into the ground; windows may not be possible on one or more of its sides and there will be none at all in the basement. This may be a disadvantage if natural lighting is desired and may also involve difficult drainage problems.

If the ground falls off to one side of an entrance and rises on the other side, the slope may facilitate basement fenestration on one side but make it impossible to provide windows on the other side of the main floor. It will probably complicate the landscaping and make architectural planning of the building more difficult. It may also seriously complicate plans for a subsequent addition.

In general, then, a site is to be avoided if the ground slopes upward from the entrance or if it slopes from one side of the entrance to the other. A flat site is to be preferred to one that slopes objectionably; but it is better yet if the ground slopes from the entrance downward toward the back of the building. No one of these factors is of first importance. But, other things being equal, they may prove to be the deciding considerations in site selection.

Soil and Ground Conditions. A site for a library should never be selected without some knowledge of ground conditions. When information on this subject is not available, at least one or two and in some cases a considerably larger number of preliminary borings should be made. This may be expensive, but it will ordinarily cost hundreds rather than thousands of dollars and will be well worth the cost if it prevents great unanticipated expenses for excavation and foundations—misfortunes that have been much too common in library building. One university library had spent more than $60,000 on its plans before it realized that foundations alone for its library would cost approximately $500,000 extra because of ground conditions.

Since this volume is not an engineering treatise, it should suffice to give a brief summary of the points that ought to be considered.

If the foundation runs into ledge or boulders over ½ cubic yard in size, there may be substantial additional costs for removing this material. The extra costs which would result from placing a building in this type of soil should be carefully estimated by a qualified professional estimator or a contractor familiar with this kind of work. On the other hand, it should be kept in mind that solid rock makes a fine foundation for a library; books are heavy, and stack areas in particular need a firm foundation. In excavating for the Lamont Library at Harvard, shale was reached before the foundation was excavated to the proper depth, but practically all of it was friable enough to be handled by a power shovel, and, as it was removed, an excellent foundation of harder rock was exposed for the footings.

If loose, fine sand, soft clay, silt, or peaty materials are encountered, piles or caissons may have to be driven down great distances in order to provide an adequate foundation. Along the Charles River in Cambridge and in the Back Bay section of Boston, Massachusetts, (areas that once were tidal swamps) it may be necessary to go 200 ft or more below the surface to reach a solid bottom, and the cost of driving piles or sinking caissons to this depth is great. Under certain conditions it is possible to pour a concrete mat on which the building will "float." The Library of the Massachusetts Institute of Technology is floated in this way, but adoption of this method dictated the construction of the building around a large court in order to spread the weight, and this resulted in a disadvantageous circulation pattern. The Yale University Library is built over quicksand on which a concrete slab was poured, but conditions were such that it was possible to build a tower stack, despite the great weight of such a structure.

There are problems in connection with floating a building on a concrete slab or mat. It may sink quite a number of inches. This may not be too serious in itself, but if the sinking is greater on one side than another, it may be a serious matter. Also, if an addition is to be constructed later, the problem may arise again.

In many sections of the country there are numerous springs, subsurface ground-water flow, or other water conditions to complicate the construction of foundations. It is possible to excavate for a foundation, keep the water pumped out, and waterproof the building either outside or in; but these undertakings are expensive and, unless the construction is of highest quality, difficulties will arise sooner or later. During flash floods, the water table around the Widener Library at Harvard occasionally rises above the subbasement floor; twice during nearly fifty years, water has come up through the concrete slab in small sections of the floor.

Another problem sometimes occurs on hill-sides, which have been particularly recommended as building sites if they slope the right way. In certain ground formations the whole side of the hill may begin to slide in wet weather, as has happened from time to time in canyons of the Los Angeles region.

The Louisiana State University Library in Baton Rouge is built on Mississippi River delta land that can carry only a limited weight per square foot of surface. It was necessary to reduce the pressure on the bearing strata by removing the overburden. This made it necessary to include a basement in the building, and consequently a drainage problem was involved. The basement and the drainage difficulties could have been avoided if the site had not been so small that it was necessary to plan for what will ultimately become a five-level building.

A specific example illustrating some of the considerations involved in the selection of a site may be provided by the Lamont Library at Harvard. This site was selected from four possibilities after some weeks of discussion and the preparation of rough sketches of a suitable building in each location. Its position in the southeast corner of the Harvard Yard was chosen because:

1. It was the only remaining available site in the Yard large enough for a building of the desired size. Its location in the Yard close to the two other central library buildings, Widener and Houghton, to which it could be connected by tunnel, was an important factor.

2. It was so placed that the freshmen passed its front entrance six times a day going to and from their meals in the Freshmen Union. It was near a main walk between the houses where the upperclassmen lived and the classrooms, and closer to the latter.

3. It had a long east-west axis, giving the desirable long north and south exposures for the reading areas.

4. The ground slope was such that two levels with windows below the main entrance, which was only one short step up, were possible, with two more without windows below them. It was possible to have above the entrance level a mezzanine, a full second floor, and a penthouse with a good deal of useful space in it, and still have the latter closer to the ground than the main reading room in Widener.

5. Policy decisions on the part of the university, limiting the number of undergraduate students, and on the part of the library authorities, limiting the size of the undergraduate book collection, indicated that provision did not have to be made for a future extension.

Summary. To recapitulate, the site should be large enough to provide for the building and for projected additions, and it should be in as convenient a location as possible. This does not mean that it ought to be in the exact center of the campus; but it ought to be readily accessible from classroom buildings, particularly those for the humanities and social sciences. The orientation, ideally, should be on a long axis running directly east and west, with the entrance on the south. A site that slopes downward from the entrance to the rear may be advantageous. Costs of construction may be greatly increased if ground conditions are unsatisfactory. Parking and delivery problems should not be forgotten. Since a site will rarely be found that is ideal in every respect, careful assessment of the advantages and disadvantages of each possible site is called for before a decision is made.

16

The Final Plan

Introduction

The final plan should be based on:

1. The program as discussed in Chapters 13 and 14, which dealt with assignable space requirements, construction problems of all kinds, mechanical facilities and comfort requirements, shelving, furniture, and other equipment.

2. The decisions discussed in Chapter 15, in regard to possible alternatives to a new building, and the selection of a site.

3. The specifications agreed upon for spatial relationships, which were discussed in Chapter 6 and again in section 13.6.

4. The architect's proposals for non-assignable space, which will be discussed in more detail in section 16.2.

5. Layouts for furniture and equipment and, if it proves to be desirable, mock-ups prepared for visual demonstration of controversial aspects of the construction. These are dealt with in section 16.3.

6. The contract and legal papers, including the specifications and the working drawings and supplementary documents discussed in section 16.4.

7. Decisions reached by the architect, the librarian, and the planning team working together during the planning period.

16.1 The Architect, the Librarian, and the Planning Team during the Planning Process

The matter of the relationship of the architect, the librarian, and the planning team has been dealt with indirectly in Chapter 2 in the discussion of aesthetic problems, and in Chapter 12, where the selection of the architect was discussed. This relationship, from the time when the architect is selected, during the planning process, and until the building is completed, is of primary importance. If the architect was selected without the approval of the librarian, the whole planning process may have gotten off on the wrong foot. If, on the other hand, the architect knows that the librarian had an important part in his selection, the good rapport between the two may be a great help. The first talk between them may be crucial, and every effort should be made by the institution's administration to see that a good start is made. If the president, in notifying the architect of his selection, is able to, and does, say that he has great confidence in the librarian and hopes that the architect will work closely with him and give due consideration to his suggestions in regard to functional matters, his statement will go a long way toward ensuring a successful building. The writer knows of one case where the librarian had recommended the architect who was selected, and the president said to him, "Since you have recommended the architect, you should notify him of the selection." This took place, and an important step toward the success of the building was taken.

If the librarian has had a major part in the preparation of a good building program and the architect realizes it, and if the librarian appreciates and understands what his part in the planning process should be and understands that the architect is not just to follow out detailed instructions, but is to produce a first-class building that will be aesthetically satisfactory and also functional, a good atmosphere is created. The librarian must, of course, be prepared to answer questions, and he and the architect should reach a mutual understanding of the part each is to play.

The architect and librarian must understand that, carefully as the program may have been worked out, it is not like the laws of the Medes and the Persians that cannot be changed. At the same time, the librarian must realize that he cannot go on indefinitely making suggestions and changes.

The architect must realize that the librarian's province is to provide readers' services conveniently, efficiently, and economically, and that he or his adviser or consultant is the expert for these matters on the planning team. The librarian, on his part, should understand that he is not the designer, the planner, or the builder, and that the institution has placed the responsibility for these matters in the hands of the architect. The architect is equipped and trained to analyze and interpret functional needs spatially and to translate this interpretation into bricks and mortar.

If the librarian presents to the architect his functional problems and requirements and if the architect then studies them seriously and solves them, each of these important members of the planning team is fulfilling his proper role. Sometimes the librarian has contributions to offer in the architect's province and vice versa; but only if a clear understanding as to the ultimate responsibilities of each one is reached will a completely harmonious relationship exist.

In many large architectural firms, the principal architect or head of the firm is not the one who works directly with the librarian; this duty is turned over to one of his partners or associates. The architectural decisions mutually reached should, of course, be reviewed by the principal architect prior to their submission to the institution for approval. The closest possible rapport is important.

All this can be summarized by saying that misunderstandings between the architect and the librarian must not be permitted. The same holds true for the other representatives of the institution. The librarian, the administrative officers, and the planning committee members, individually and as a group, must also have an agreement on the place of each person concerned in the planning process. They should never be played off one against another.

The planning period should not be extended indefinitely. Neither should it be hurried too much; under pressure the best of architects and librarians will miss important factors. It is very rare for a satisfactory building to be planned and working drawings completed in less than a full year. Lamont took more than a year and a half to plan, in spite of the fact that the librarian and the architect had already been considering possibilities and thinking about the building for six or seven years in advance.

The planning process can be extended too far until all concerned become stale and unwittingly careless of important details. It is often desirable to have a definite timetable worked out in advance, and both the architect and the institution should be expected to keep to schedule.

Be sure, to start with, that the contract with the architect is signed and agreement reached in regard to payments. The agreement should consider what will happen if for one reason or another, such as the lack of funds or disagreement on the proposed plans, the building is never constructed.

After the program has been submitted to the architect and he has had an opportunity to study it carefully, he should be prepared to discuss with representatives of the institution points that he does not understand, that he questions, that he would like to have covered by more specific instructions, or that he thinks are too specific, and on which he would like to propose changes. This is the time when most of the uncertainties should be resolved and definite decisions reached, if possible. The architect needs a clear understanding before he prepares sketches for preliminary plans or sets his draftsmen to work on details that might have to be changed because of previous failure to understand each other's wishes. Most difficulties come from a failure on someone's part to make himself clear and to explain his reason for wanting what he requests. If neither party has had experience in library building planning, it is easy to see why neither one understands the technical language to which the other is accustomed in his own profession. Preconceived notions of what is right and essential become all too easily so deeply entrenched that they are hard to change.

It is very important for the success of the enterprise that all members of the library planning team keep in close touch with each other and with the progress of the architect after he tackles the problem and begins to prepare sketches indicating the proposed spatial relationships and space assignments.

As definite a timetable as possible should be worked out. It may well include a time when the preliminary sketches should be approved and the architect should be authorized to prepare working drawings and specifications; the time when drawings and specifications are to be ready and bids called for; and the date when construction should begin. Do not try to push the preliminary stages too fast, particularly if for any reason frequent conferences between the two groups cannot be scheduled. The time required for preparing working drawings and specifications will depend largely on the size of the architect's staff and the other work on which it is engaged. Not less than six months is perhaps a good average for a large building. The taking of bids and the assignment of the contract may require two months or more, and the construction for a building of 20,000 sq ft at least a year and for larger buildings as much as eighteen months or even two or more years, depending on geographical location and local labor conditions. Try to plan so that the completion of the building will come at a time when it is possible to take advantage of it. A large university library should, if possible, be finished early enough in the summer so that the shift to it can be carried out without too much pressure during the summer months, and leave a shakedown period before the university opens in the autumn. A smaller institution might attempt to move in during the Christmas holidays or the Easter vacation, but if the winter climate is severe, this may be difficult or impossible. Problems in connection with the moving are discussed in section 17.3.

Definite agreement must be reached on the site. It is evident that nothing more than the most preliminary plans can be made before the site is selected. As early as possible, but not too early, the module sizes, if the modular system is to be used, and the column sizes should be agreed upon. This cannot be done, however, until decision has been reached on the size and number of floor levels and perhaps on whether a central utility and vertical communication core is to be used or whether these facilities are to be scattered. Make as sure as possible that in either case the core or cores do not interfere with present or prospective horizontal circulation patterns.

The architect must constantly keep in mind the total cost of the project, remembering that over-all costs include equipment, fees, and landscaping, as well as net or gross square-footage construction costs. He must not permit a misunderstanding with the library's representatives in the matter of cost.

Planning of the heating and ventilation system must not be forgotten. It may have been assigned to an outside ventilating engineer if the architect does not have one on his staff. A similar assignment may have been made to an electrical and illumination engineer. Work on the plans for these services must not be delayed because they may take much more square footage than anticipated and reduce what is available for library purposes, thus complicating the plans in other ways.

Before working drawings are begun, it should be clearly understood just how frequently and on what basis consultation between the groups in the planning team will be arranged. The institution should not abrogate its rights for further consideration at this time. Neither should it expect to interfere continually with progress. Authorization for working drawings means that the basic plans are agreed upon, but there are still what may seem like minor matters where the librarian's opinion should be given consideration. These will include, for instance, the location of doors and door handles and the direction in which the doors swing. The placing of light switches is another example, as may be the selection of hardware and plumbing fixtures. As the working drawings are prepared, it may be found from time to time that an unexpected 6-in. or 1-ft difference in space available will require decisions regarding how the space is to be used or how to deal with the lack of it.

Meanwhile the furniture and equipment should not be forgotten or neglected. Too often decisions on these matters are delayed, with the result that the design and selection process is hurried, and in too many cases the equipment is not available when the structure is ready for it. What part of the equipment will be in the general building contract? What are the architect's responsibilities for the furniture design and selection? Be sure that whoever has the responsibility understands the timetable so that construction will be completed and shipments can be made at the proper time and will not interfere with the building construction or involve storage problems, and yet not delay the opening of the structure. If, by any chance, construction is delayed beyond the date set, agreement should have been reached either for storage of equipment if it arrives on time or for the manufacturer to be ready to hold it and deliver it later than originally proposed.

16.2 Non-assignable Space

An oversimplified definition of non-assignable space for libraries might state that it is the difference between gross, which is the total area in a structure, and net, which is that part of the total area which can be assigned for strictly library purposes, that is, for readers' accommodations, library services to readers, and storage of the collections. "Non-assignable space" is a term that is preferred to the frequently used "architectural space." It now generally occupies a smaller percentage of the square footage than it did in the past and an even smaller percentage of the cubic contents of the building.

Gross square footage of floor space is the total amount for all floors, including the outside walls, whether they are bearing or curtain walls. The area under a colonnade, if it can be walked on, is generally figured at one-half full square footage in estimating costs. Gross cubage is the gross square footage as figured above, multiplied by the distance from one foot below the lowest floor, in order to include a proper amount for the foundations, up to the top of the roof, including mechanical roof housing for fans, elevators, penthouses, and so forth, less the space not enclosed because of sloped roofs, but plus the cube for parapets and any walls projecting above the roof. A colonnade, or any porch that can be walked on, if covered by a canopy or overhang, is ordinarily figured at one-half in cubic or in square footage.

Net or assignable square footage is that directly useful for regular library purposes. It ordinarily includes space for readers and reading areas, stack space for collections and other storage, space for staff and for services to readers, including public-service desks, the public-catalogue area, and so forth. To repeat, non-assignable space is the difference between the gross and net described above. Exterior walls, to say nothing of interior ones, are no longer built 3 ft or more thick, as they were in the New York Public Library at 42nd Street and Fifth Avenue, and the Widener Library building at Harvard. There are fewer monumental stairs and lobbies

and corridors. Clear ceiling heights have been greatly reduced because, with modern lighting and ventilation, very high rooms are no longer necessary. But non-assignable space is still a very large user of both square footage and cubage, the amount depending on the precise definition of the term, the type of building, and the planning. It is regularly considered to include the following: walls, columns, entrances, vestibules, lobbies, corridors, stairwells, and other spaces used for vertical communication and transportation, toilet facilities, unusable attic space under a sloping roof, and finally mechanical spaces and shafts throughout the building. There is some question about corridors and lobbies which may be multipurpose areas and about some other areas which will be mentioned later.

In the early part of this century non-assignable space frequently equaled 50 per cent of the total square footage. Even since the war it has sometimes equaled one-half the total, but 30 per cent to one-third is more normal. The last of these figures would mean that, when assignable space for collections, readers, and service to readers and staff has been determined, the architect will have to add 50 per cent to obtain the gross. To be a little more specific, a library with 100,000 sq ft of gross space might use 30,000 sq ft for a collection of 400,000 volumes; 30,000 more sq ft would take care of 1,000 readers in reading areas; 6,700 sq ft would house a staff of 50; and the remaining 33,300 sq ft would be used for non-assignable space. Something on this order can be called typical. This is a great improvement over older buildings where assignable space might be less than 50 per cent of the total, and the non-assignable or architectural space would require all the rest.

Recent careful planning has increased considerably the efficiency of space use. The elimination of some corridors or their use for exhibition space and book storage, as well as for traffic circulation, and the elimination of, or reduction in, the area used for monumental features have enabled the architect in some circumstances to reduce the architectural space to between 25 and 30 per cent of the total gross area. After computing the assignable areas, the architect has to add as little as one-third of that net square footage or a little more for the non-assignable space in order to determine the gross. This may be possible, particularly if much of the area formerly used for mechanical space is eliminated by housing central-heating and ventilation installations for the whole institution in another building. On the other hand, if a new building is air-conditioned and the apparatus for this is in the library, the space so used may be considerable, and will increase the percentage of non-assignable space accordingly. To prevent misunderstanding in this connection, it is important for all concerned to have an agreement as to just what is included in non-assignable or architectural space. Some librarians and architects have claimed that the non-assignable areas have been reduced to as little as 20 per cent of the gross, but that undoubtedly means including the borderline areas as assignable space.

This topic is not a new problem for architects and engineers. It is understood by many others who have had previous experience with building planning. Indeed, persons whose work has been largely with monumental buildings and academic construction more than twenty years old may have a somewhat exaggerated idea of the amount of such space required in a modern building. But librarians and faculty committee members and others without building planning experience have been known to make the mistake of ignoring or forgetting that there must be a large amount of both square and cubic footage in a library which is not usable for the seating accommodations, for the housing of the collections, for working quarters for the staff or for direct service to readers, but for which it is necessary to plan and to pay.

As already indicated, the problem may arise as to just what is included in the term non-assignable space. What about arcades and ornamental columns, balustrades, areaways, tunnels, or covered walks connecting the building with other parts of the institution, and unused basement and attic areas? This is not the place to give a definitive statement regarding what should or should not be included; but be sure, if the matter comes up for discussion within the planning team or with outsiders, during or after the planning, that those concerned are comparing apples with apples and not apples with pears.

The reduction in non-assignable architectural space in recently constructed buildings results from (1) a decrease in wall thickness; (2) planning which has avoided monumental lobbies and corridors; and (3) gains through better layouts, which are discussed in section 16.3. But please remember (and this is emphasized)

that corridors should not be reduced to a point where traffic will be congested, and that, to save square footage, layouts should not result in rooms that lack all feeling of spaciousness. A considerable percentage of non-assignable square footage and cubage will always be required, but the average ceiling height can be greatly reduced, and the percentage of non-assignable space, in a few cases, as already stated, can be as little as 25 per cent of the total without aesthetic loss or discomfort. One-third should be a safe figure to use in preliminary space calculations, even if the final plans work out more efficiently, but if a degree of monumentality is desired, non-assignable areas may still require more than that. One-third means that one-half of the net assignable space must be added to obtain the gross square footage.

The cubic footage is affected also, of course, by room height and floor thickness.

While it is generally true in a library building, as elsewhere, that you get what you pay for, it is still a fact that good planning can increase the percentage of usable space very considerably without affecting the results aesthetically or functionally. Much of this volume represents an effort to accomplish this combination of aims. These additional comments may be pertinent:

In recent construction, walls, particularly interior ones, are seldom bearing walls. The building is held up by columns and by beams or flat slab construction for the floors between the columns. Nonbearing walls are thinner and occupy less square footage than those that support the building. But columns can get in the way if there is not careful planning, and they tend to make it difficult to use efficiently the space adjacent to them. Some architects like to use them to make the structure visible as part of the architectural concept, but this can be a serious handicap to space utilization. Others prefer to have them hidden as far as possible. Many buildings today are supported by columns which are practically unseen. In the reading rooms they can be along the periphery of the room. In the book stacks they can be literally buried in the ranges. As already noted, one of the chief problems in connection with columns is the fact that they must be watched or there may be a good deal of unusable space on all sides of them. (See Fig. 16.1.)

Vestibules and entrance lobbies are generally considered non-assignable or architectural space. They are used primarily to enable one to

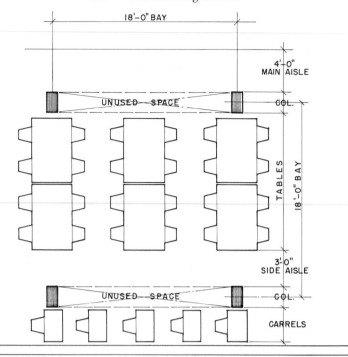

18'-0" BAY

4'-0" MAIN AISLE

UNUSED SPACE COL.

TABLES

18'-0" BAY

3'-0" SIDE AISLE

UNUSED SPACE COL.

CARRELS

FIG. 16.1 Columns placed so unused space results. This shows the result when equipment sizes and arrangement do not fit column spacing.

adjust to being indoors, as a place to shake off snow and wet and dirt from shoes, to check readers in or out, and as a distribution point for readers and others. Very often in recent years, however, the lobbies house the main circulation desk and sometimes the reference desk as well. This makes it difficult to determine whether they are assignable or non-assignable areas. They naturally tend to be noisy and cannot well be used for study purposes. Unless there has been careful planning, they may also be drafty, and, therefore, not particularly satisfactory for staff members who have to work in them. Because they are noisy it is desirable to have them screened from reading areas. Some architects suggest an entrance lobby two levels high for the feeling of spaciousness it provides. It can be very attractive, and, as is shown in section 5.2, which deals with mezzanines, it need not be overly expensive in relation to its advantages. But remember, if this plan is used, that the space on the mezzanines around the double-height area will tend to be noisy and not suitable for reading accommodations, in spite of the attractive views into the lobby which it may command. Some librarians may prefer to keep the lobby low and provide two-level heights in adjoining

reading areas, which will be quiet and make the mezzanines above them more suitable for readers on one to all four sides.

Corridors are almost always necessary. Libraries today are often large buildings, and outside windows are not used as much for light and ventilation as in earlier years, but the distance between opposite sides may be so great that corridors may have become even more necessary than in the past to carry traffic without disturbing readers.

Very few inside walls may be needed in many libraries, except those around plumbing and vertical transportation areas. Corridor partitions may consist of shelving, and in order to avoid auditory and visual distraction in adjacent reading areas, a divider of some kind can run down the center of the stack ranges, and glass going up to the ceiling can be used above them. Or a corridor may be a wide stack aisle with ranges at right angles on each side.

Stairwells and vertical transportation arrangements of all kinds, such as elevators, lifts, and escalators, are considered non-assignable space. Elevators are expensive, and two of them naturally cost more than one. Two elevators placed side by side will provide transportation with less delay than three widely separated ones. On the other hand, to go from one level to another by elevator one may have to walk farther. There are often specifications in building codes regulating the size and capacity of elevators. Their location, number, and size are important matters. Stairwells should rarely be put together in banks, as has just been advocated for elevators, although a main stair is often split at the landing halfway to the next floor or is placed in the center of a large area with space left for traffic on all sides. Although this arrangement may be effective architecturally, it is space-consuming (see Fig. 16.2).

Ducts for ventilation may take a great deal of square footage and also cubage. They are included in non-assignable space. If the ducts are largely vertical, they take more square footage, of course. If they are largely horizontal, they use more cubage directly or indirectly, particularly if they are to be concealed above a false ceiling. Horizontal ducts one foot thick sometimes make necessary the addition of one foot to the height of a whole floor, and so add as many cubic feet of space as there are square feet in each floor. Sometimes they are hung exposed from the ceil-

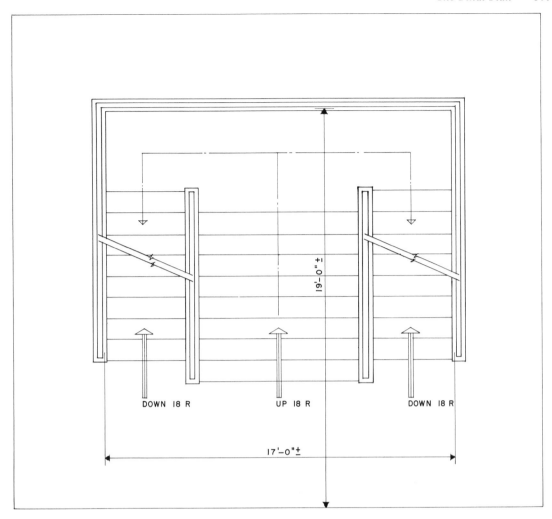

FIG. 16.2 Split stairs. Frequently used for architectural effect. Tend to be space-consuming if they require traffic corridors on more than two sides of the floor levels which they connect.

ings and leave extra height for most of the floor, but they then present a less finished appearance and may be dust collectors.

Toilets and rest rooms are considered non-assignable areas. They are important, and their size and location should be very carefully worked out. Some librarians feel that toilet facilities should never be placed on an entrance level, for fear they will attract people to the building to use them instead of for library purposes. They also take up extremely valuable floor space on an entrance level. If they can be made available on all floors of the building, with perhaps the exception of the entrance level, traffic will be reduced back and forth from one level to another. If they can be placed in the same location, in the center or in the same corner of each floor, they will be more easily

found and the cost of the plumbing will be reduced. They are discussed in more detail in section 10.1.

If the entrance lobby should be large for other reasons, it may contain suitable exhibition space. Wide corridors can often be used for this purpose. In the Lamont Library at Harvard the fifth-level corridor, 9 ft wide and 100 ft long, with exhibition cases running the full length on one side, except for doors, and with open reserve collections for history on the other side (see Fig. 16.3), gives a feeling of spaciousness to the whole floor, and the wide triple-purpose corridor might be said to be less expensive in square footage than many corridors one-half as wide which would result in crowding and congestion. Corridors used in this way can hardly be called non-assignable space.

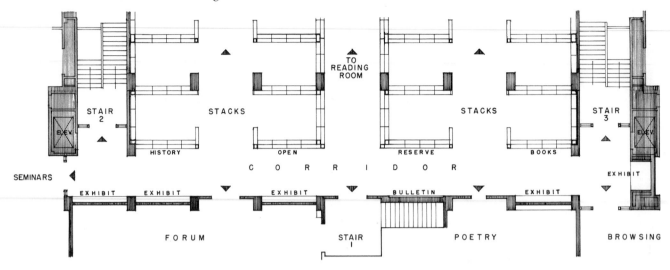

FIG. 16.3 Lamont Library fifth-level corridor. The corridor is 9 ft wide. It provides the main traffic artery for a level accommodating well over 400 persons. It also houses an important bulletin board, nearly 50 running feet of exhibition cases, and the open-reserve books in the popular field of history, each of which would require considerable space to avoid congestion. It represents a multipurpose area, and is used enough so that it is not an extravagance and does much to provide a feeling of spaciousness to the floor as a whole.

This section on non-assignable space might well be summed up as follows: Non-assignable space is essential. There is no satisfactory way of avoiding it completely. It may add very considerably to the spaciousness of the building, the importance of which should not be minimized. On the other hand, it can and should be kept under control. If the percentage of non-assignable areas can be reduced from 40 to 30 per cent, or occasionally to as little as 28 or even 25 per cent, it may be possible to provide for more students and larger collections. The librarian should have frequent consultations with the architect about this space, but with the full realization that it is the architect's special concern and responsibility.

In connection with the discussion of space within the building's four walls that is not available for strictly library purposes, it should be noted that classrooms, auditoriums, audiovisual space, exhibition areas, and other non-library areas must be considered and watched. They may be important to the institution. The librarian himself may be very much interested in them, but they take space and cost money, and, if they are permitted to be extended, the areas left for strictly library purposes may be greatly reduced.

The important thing for the librarian and his institution to keep in mind is that the non-assignable space and areas provided for non-library purposes must not be forgotten, but should be watched and reduced as far as practicable without affecting the building aesthetically or functionally.

16.3   Layouts, Mock-ups, and Space Utilization

Libraries are planned to provide satisfactory housing. To oversimplify, this involves aesthetics, physical comfort, and convenience. The first, aesthetics, has been commented on incidentally throughout the volume, and Chapter 2 is devoted to it. Aesthetics is primarily the architect's province, although the institution can properly indicate its wishes. The second, physical comfort, lies largely in the province of the engineers working under the direction of the architect, but in accordance with the program proposed by the institution. It is discussed in Chapters 9 and 10 on a theoretical basis, and again in Chapter 14 in connection with a specific library that is being planned. The third, convenience, includes the spatial relationships of the rooms, areas, and services and the arrangement of the equipment. It is more directly the responsibility of the librarian, working very closely, of course, with the architect, who, because of his wider experience, can explain the problems to be solved. This section is devoted to the last of these, the arrangement of the equipment.

Equipment layouts cannot be completed until the large-scale spatial relationships and the quantitative requirements in terms of the number of units of seating accommodations, volumes to be stored, and other space users have been agreed upon. Aesthetics and physical comfort should not be forgotten. Both are an important part of the scene here as elsewhere. Equipment layouts should look well. The results should be both comfortable and convenient. To look well they must be well designed. The same holds for comfort and, for that matter, convenience. A handsome, overstuffed, large chair may be very comfortable, but in most cases would not be a convenient place for research work that requires note taking and reference to a number of items at one time.

A satisfactory layout must be based on properly designed, comfortable furniture of the right size for the task at hand, so arranged that it is easily accessible and provides the desired work space without undue interference from or to others. This section will deal with general principles for satisfactory layouts for seating accommodations, shelving, and card-catalogue cases. Between them they involve most of the basic problems which must be met. Seating accommodations, except for the possible use of book shelves, chiefly involve two planes, as far as space utilization is concerned, aisle space and working-surface areas. Shelving, whether cases are only 3 or up to 9 shelves high, one above the other, involves, as far as storage capacity is concerned, both height and cubage, in addition to square footage, and, to perhaps an even greater extent, the requirements for adjacent aisle space. Card-catalogue-case arrangements involve problems similar to those for shelving, but the capacity for cards per square foot of floor space may vary even more than that for books, as cases may have trays in rows up to 15 or more in height, and the use of the aisle space tends to be much more concentrated than that for shelving or seating.

The architect, with the program submitted by the institution as a guide, will in due course prepare schematic drawings or preliminary sketch plans which he will show to the library's representatives. The first ones will probably do little more than indicate spatial relationships. Later the square footage of the different areas will be included, but in rough terms. Later still, proposed equipment layouts should be shown. This can sometimes be arranged by drawing in the equipment with the sizes that have been agreed upon. It can be done to advantage by using templates of paper, cardboard, or metal drawn to scale. These have the advantage of making it possible without erasure to shift the templates and find the most suitable arrangements. Making the drawing on crosshatched paper, with each square, for instance, representing one foot, may ease the task. If crosshatched paper is not used, it is particularly desirable to have a large-scale drawing, so that it will be easier to move the templates around. A scale of 1 in. to 4 ft is suggested, unless a very large area is to be covered. Special boards fitted up with magnets which hold a metal template in place are sometimes used. In all this it must be remembered that many laymen find it difficult to picture from a drawing just what the finished results will look like and to decide whether a 3-ft aisle between tables, for instance, is adequate, whether a 3×5-ft or a 4×6-ft reading-room table is preferable for four persons, or whether a shelf 7 in. deep will give space enough for books. The architect, who is more experienced and adept with tasks of this kind, may be able to give satisfactory answers to questions, but in some cases a visual demonstration will be desirable.

One method is to go to a library or to libraries where tables, shelving, catalogue cases, and other equipment of different sizes can be seen in their proper setting. A demonstration with furniture in one's own house might help, but a library with rooms approximately the size planned in the new building would do better. An experienced library consultant can probably suggest libraries to visit. In almost any large city or metropolitan area it is possible to find examples of arrangements that would be useful. The author has on scores of occasions taken visiting librarians, architects, library committee members, and others through libraries in the Boston area and elsewhere in order to show good and poor solutions of layout problems. The Harvard University Library, with its 90 separate collections, can demonstrate most of the problems and possible or attempted solutions to many of them.

If new types of equipment or methods of construction are to be used, there may be occasions when a mock-up on a larger or smaller scale will be advisable. When Princeton's Firestone

Library was being planned soon after the Second World War, the architects arranged for the construction of a four-bay mock-up. In two of the bays sample book stacks of various types were installed. The other two were used for the layout of other accommodations. A false adjustable ceiling that could be cranked up and down was installed to test out ceiling heights. Sample lighting and other equipment were made available. Those interested had an almost ideal visual demonstration of problems for which solutions were desired.

When Lamont was under construction and plans were made for a larger number of open carrels than had ever been used before in a library, sample carrels with tables of different sizes, with and without shelves, with backs of different heights, and with other variations were built and carefully studied.

Library plans should never be accepted before an agreement has been reached on the furniture layout, to make sure that the seating and book capacity is satisfactory, and that the results will not be too crowded and congested, and those responsible should, if at all possible, have had a demonstration, on paper or in some other way, of what the proposed layouts will look like. Appendix B of this volume gives tables listing sizes of furniture of various types, aisle widths, the resulting capacity for books and readers, and other items of interest. If these tables are used in combination with library visits and suitable drawings, the results should be satisfactory.

It should always be remembered that in furniture layouts, as in other things, circumstances alter cases. The interior-decoration scheme may help to make a room look larger and more spacious, just as it may make it look more crowded and congested.

In this same connection, if a visual demonstration of the results of the lighting installations, both in the reading areas and the book stacks, can be provided, it will be useful, and it must be remembered that the window areas and the intensity of the light coming in from the outside at different times of day have an effect on the desired and required intensity of the light within the building as well as on its quality.

Satisfactory layouts may be products of an exact science, but often they are achieved only by trial and error. The following general principles are suggested:

1. The optimum size of the proposed equipment should be agreed upon. Should a table for four be 3 × 5 ft, or would 4 × 6 ft be more satisfactory, although it takes more space?

2. Aisles occupy more space than equipment, and every aisle, to be economical in space utilization, should be used on both sides.

3. An aisle that has chairs backing into it should be wider than one used even more heavily as a main traffic artery, but without seating.

4. Visual and auditory distractions should be kept in mind.

5. A wall on one side and, to a greater extent, walls on both sides of an aisle or corridor make it seem narrower. A 3-ft corridor with walls on both sides reaching above eye level appears very narrow. A 3-ft corridor with an open carrel on one side and the ends of book ranges on the other will seem quite adequate visually and, when two persons pass in it, one of them can slip into the stack aisle or the space in front of an unoccupied carrel table while the other goes by. A room with no obstructions above table height, that is, 30 in. plus or minus, seems open. Partitions 4 ft 6 in. in height on three sides of carrels do not take much away from a feeling of openness for a person who is standing, and one sitting and studying is generally not interested in openness and enjoys being partially shut off from neighbors so long as light and ventilation are good, and he can look out in at least one direction. Most persons will feel that floor cases in a reading room up to 5 ft 6 in. high, which permit five shelves of books, will give a surprisingly open feeling to one going down a 4- or 4½-ft-wide aisle at right angles to the ranges, particularly if the ceiling is 8 ft high or more.

6. Main traffic arteries in a straight line are preferable, unless they are at least 100 ft or more long. If they have to turn corners and pass obstructions that are above eye level in height, a hemmed-in feeling and confusion may result.

7. A great reading room with row after row of tables parallel to each other gives an unpleasantly regimented effect, which screens 6-ft high or more placed at intervals may help to eliminate.

8. A long row of open carrels along a wall on one or more sides of a room with table backs 4 ft 6 in. high will not be nearly so monotonous as an equally long row of carrels placed between two ranges in a book stack. A break in a long

row of carrels or tables, used for lounge chairs or other seating arrangements, may relieve the situation. (See Fig. 16.4.)

9. Wall shelves in a large reading area are seldom desirable, as they require wide aisles in front of them. Shelving can be placed more economically on ranges with shelving on both sides, as the aisle then receives full use.

10. Shelves along a reading-room wall have the additional disadvantage of increasing the distances involved in using the collections and of creating visual and auditory distraction. Reference and other heavily used materials should be concentrated as far as possible, with accommodations for readers who will be using them adjacent on one or all sides.

11. The use of curved walls or those with angles that are not 90° should always be questioned, as good space utilization will be difficult and never completely successful. Curved bay windows in their proper place can be attractive aesthetically, but are expensive to construct, and furniture and equipment are seldom designed to fit them. Radial stacks planned on the basis that they permit better supervision may be useful under some conditions in public libraries, but square footage varying from 10 per cent up is lost, and some congestion inevitably results when ranges approach each other near the center where traffic is heaviest; it is invariably difficult to use the periphery to advantage. If radial stacks are used in very large areas, some-

what better space utilization becomes possible, but most readers will find it difficult to keep properly oriented and will often have to come back to the center and take extra steps before going to another section. Circular arrangements for shelving and seating have been tried again and again in the past, and as far as the author has been able to learn have never proved to be completely satisfactory.

Seating Accommodations. As an aid in planning layouts, suggestions are presented for arrangements for seating accommodations in reading areas and book stacks. They are based on the theoretical discussion of seating arrangements in section 7.3. Remember that academic and research (not public) libraries are under consideration, and the sizes and arrangements suggested are for academic and research use.

1. Single open carrels with the long axis of the table tops at right angles to a wall. These may be in reading areas, or in book stacks with walls on one side, a subsidiary cross aisle on the other, with the end of stack ranges beyond the aisle, or they may take the place of the last stack section in a range. Single carrels should preferably be fastened to the wall or floor in some way so as not to get out of position. (See Fig. 16.5*A* and *B*.)

The suggested minimum size for the table tops, without book shelf or shelves above, is 20 × 33 in.; medium size 22 × 36 in.; generous 24 × 42 in. Shelves are rarely recommended

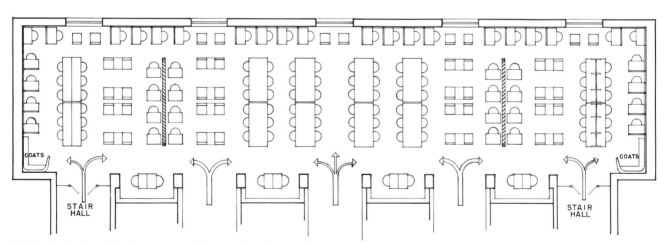

FIG. 16.4 A variety of seating accommodations used in a large reading area. Students do not all want the same kind of accommodations. The use of a variety relieves monotony. There are too many large tables here, but comfortable semi-lounge chairs scattered about diminish the rigidity. Slanting-top tables, partitions on long tables, individual tables separated by screens, double carrels facing each other in shallow alcoves, all help. Note also the five entrances that reduce distances to be traveled to reach the seats, and the inconspicuous coat racks in two corners in sight of many readers. This plan is adapted from the Lamont reading rooms. The room is not congested and has one chair for every 25 sq ft.

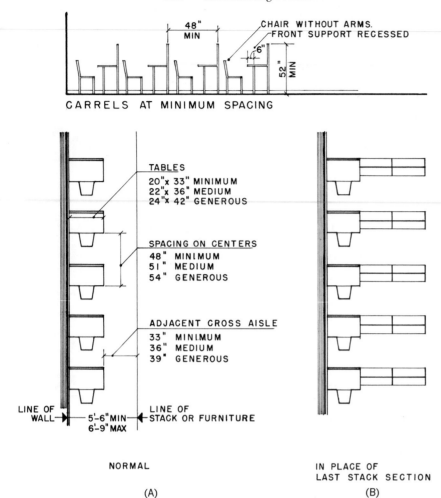

CARRELS AT MINIMUM SPACING

TABLES
20"x 33" MINIMUM
22"x 36" MEDIUM
24"x 42" GENEROUS

SPACING ON CENTERS
48" MINIMUM
51" MEDIUM
54" GENEROUS

ADJACENT CROSS AISLE
33" MINIMUM
36" MEDIUM
39" GENEROUS

NORMAL

(A)

IN PLACE OF
LAST STACK SECTION

(B)

FIG. 16.5 Carrels at right angles to a wall. (*A*) Suggests sizes and spacing and shows elevations. (*B*) Carrel in place of last stack section next to a wall. The working surface of the carrel should be in line with the stack range instead of the aisle, in order to make it easier to get into the chair.

for undergraduate work. If they are used, 5 in. should be added to the depth of the table top. A preferable size is 27 × 42 in. For a carrel for a graduate student writing a dissertation, a table top 27 × up to 48 in. may be useful. Anything larger might be called extravagant. If the table in the book-stack installations can be placed in a line with the stack ranges, the reader is in a better position to look out when he wants to.

If the stack ranges are only 4 ft on centers and the tables are to have the same spacing, a table that is more than 22 in. deep will leave the student less than 26 in. to get in and out of his seat. An armchair then becomes questionable, and the table leg under the corner where he enters should preferably be set back at least 6 in. Stack ranges 4 ft 6 in. on centers will be possible on the

same terms for a 27-in.-deep table, with a shelf provided above. Ranges 4 ft 3 in. on centers with a 23-in. table give 28 in. behind the table, minus the thickness of the back of the table. The carrels, of course, do not have to match the stack ranges in spacing, and for graduate carrels it may be desirable to provide greater distances on centers in spite of the resulting irregularity. Here the question of windows and the facade should be considered. Fig. 6.9 shows single open carrels as they are found at Cornell's Olin Library.

Single carrels similar to those just described but with shelves to one side are sometimes used. If space between carrel centers is at a premium, these may be useful. If the shelving faces the aisle, it can be more extensive, going down to the floor, and can at the same time provide additional privacy. (See Fig. 16.6*A*, *B*, and *C*.)

2. Single closed carrels along a book-stack wall and opening into a subsidiary stack aisle. These are quite similar to the open carrels described above, but have partitions and a door and, unless considerably larger, they may be difficult to ventilate and to light and tend to cause claustrophobia. Partitions to the ceiling are not recommended for undergraduates, but if the area, including the adjacent aisle, is at least as much as 5 ft × 6 ft 8 in., it can be used for graduate students if there is glass in the door. Light from an outside window will help. Fig. 16.7*B* shows a closed carrel with a door.

3. Single carrels in place of a stack section at the end of a book range. (See Fig. 16.5*B*.) As far as space use is concerned, this is the most economical way to provide a seating accommodation, and it gives a great deal of seclusion, which many readers want. It presents four problems, however, as follows:

a. The space from front to back is limited to the distance between range centers, which in some cases is minimal.

b. Unless the table top is specially designed to occupy the full depth of the double-faced range, as shown in Fig. 16.5*B*, it may be difficult to get into the chair because the table top will jut out into the aisle.

c. Some readers, particularly if there is no adjacent outside window, will feel too shut in for comfort.

d. Since the seat is at the end of a blind aisle, the length of the range should not be more than half that of a range with cross aisles at both ends.

If acoustic walls are installed on all sides ex-

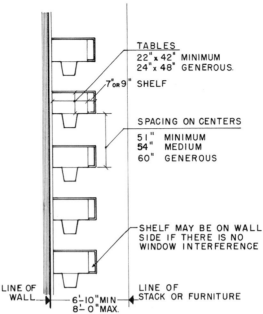

TABLES
22"x 42" MINIMUM
24"x 48" GENEROUS.

7"OR9" SHELF

SPACING ON CENTERS
51" MINIMUM
54" MEDIUM
60" GENEROUS

SHELF MAY BE ON WALL
SIDE IF THERE IS NO
WINDOW INTERFERENCE

LINE OF
WALL

LINE OF
STACK OR FURNITURE

6'-10" MIN
8'-0" MAX.

WITH 7"-9" DEEP
BOOK SHELF AT SIDE

(B)

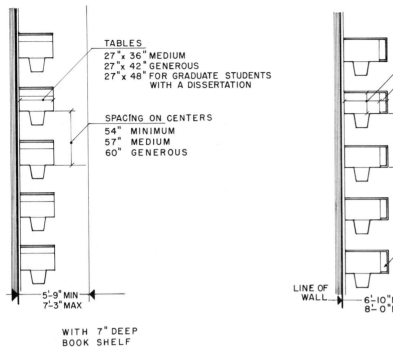

TABLES
27"x 36" MEDIUM
27"x 42" GENEROUS
27"x 48" FOR GRADUATE STUDENTS
WITH A DISSERTATION

SPACING ON CENTERS
54" MINIMUM
57" MEDIUM
60" GENEROUS

5'-9" MIN
7'-3" MAX

WITH 7" DEEP
BOOK SHELF

(A)

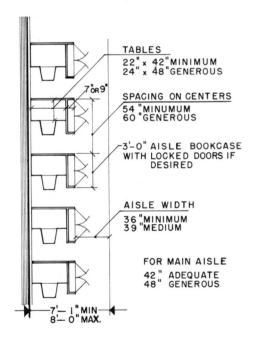

TABLES
22" x 42" MINIMUM
24" x 48" GENEROUS

SPACING ON CENTERS
54" MINUMUM
60" GENEROUS

3'-0" AISLE BOOKCASE
WITH LOCKED DOORS IF
DESIRED

AISLE WIDTH
36" MINIMUM
39" MEDIUM

FOR MAIN AISLE
42" ADEQUATE
48" GENEROUS

7'-1" MIN
8'-0" MAX.

WITH 7"-9" DEEP
40"-52" HIGH BOOKCASE AT SIDE

(C)

FIG. 16.6 Carrels with shelves. (*A*) Shelf in front of reader. The table should be 5 in. deeper than one without a shelf, and adequate spacing between carrels may be difficult to arrange. (*B*) Shelf at one side instead of in front. (It can be at either side.) This requires more width but less depth. (*C*) Shelf at one side facing the aisle. This can provide more shelf capacity and greater privacy; it also demands greater total width.

cept at the stack aisle, such a carrel will be satisfactory for typing and no door will be required. (See Fig. 16.7*A*.) The table top for typing should be at least 3 ft 6 in. wide by at least 20 in. deep and 27 in. above the floor, instead of a standard 29½ to 30 in. If used in this way as a typing carrel, with no door provided, the insertion of Celotex or other similar material between the front and back of the adjacent double-faced ranges will help, and the books themselves have good acoustical properties.

4. Single seats facing a reading room or stack wall or a high partition down the center of a regular reading room table, sometimes with a high partition at the sides projecting 6 in. beyond the table top into the aisle, to cut one off from his neighbors. There is no place to look out, except directly at the neighbor to the right or left when leaning back in the chair. These have been used in long rows at Bryn Mawr College, Cornell University, the Library on the undergraduate campus at the University of Tokyo, and elsewhere. They are not recommended, except in an open area in groups of four where the reader can look out in at least one direction, because few students enjoy facing a blank wall, unless they can look out at least a

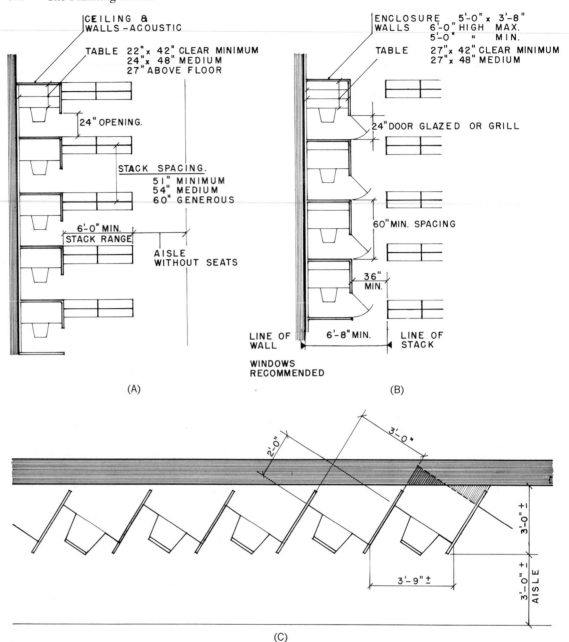

FIG. 16.7 Other types of single carrels. (*A*) Partly open typing carrel in place of last stack section with acoustically protected walls and ceiling aided by adjacent books. Absence of other seating close at hand makes doors unnecessary. (*B*) Closed carrel with door and shelf. If there is no window, wider spacing is desirable to prevent claustrophobia. Ventilation and lighting will present problems. (*C*) A dog-leg carrel is a compromise for one facing a wall, which is disliked by many, if partitions are extended enough to provide seclusion. The carrel is open on one side.

few feet on one side without seeing a neighbor close at hand. (See Fig. 7.7.)

The new Notre Dame University Library has single carrels in a sawtooth, or what is known as a dog-leg arrangement, shown in Fig. 16.7*C*, which is popular in Sweden and elsewhere. They are preferable to those directly facing a wall, as the reader can look out on one side and

still is protected from his neighbors. They require no additional space.

5. Double carrels in rows in a reading room separated by partitions which are at least 52 in. in height in the front and on one side of the working area. Working-surface sizes proposed for 1 above are adequate. Partitions in front can be held down to no more than 3 to 10 in. above

the table top because a full view of one's neighbor all the time is less distracting than a head bobbing up and down occasionally; but 52 in. above the floor is preferable. (Fig. 7.11*D*.) In some places two rows of individual tables separated by a screen as in Fig. 7.12*C* may be useful.

6. Double carrels in rows in place of two stack ranges. A size of 33 × 22 in. can be used in place of two stack ranges when ranges are 4 ft 3 in. on centers. A size of 36 × 22 in. can be used comfortably with ranges 4 ft 6 in. on centers. By placing one or both end pairs at right angles to the others, the carrel range and the stack range length can be made to match with table tops and distances between centers of standard size. (See Fig. 7.12*A* and *B*.)

7. Double carrels at right angles to a wall, as at Douglass College, Rutgers, the Uris Undergraduate Library at Cornell, and at Brandeis, with partitions on two sides and with two readers facing in opposite directions or the same way. The partitions should be at least 52 in. above the floor to prevent visual distraction. Table tops of the same sizes as in 1 above are recommended. A distance of 4½ ft on centers represents a minimum, with 5 ft on centers preferred. These are possible but not recommended, because the readers are sitting side by side even when facing in opposite directions. (See Figs. 16.8 and 16.9.) Those described in the next three paragraphs are preferred.

8. Double-staggered carrels with the adjacent table tops overlapping by one-half their depth, the same sizes as in 1 above, placed along walls, with 4½ ft minimum on centers and 5 ft preferred. Pairs of them on each side of a screen or low partition are quite possible, if the back of the inside carrel is kept low. (See Fig. 16.10*A* and *B*.)

9. Triple-staggered carrels in a reading area, preferably 5 ft on centers with table tops of the sizes proposed for others. If the center carrel in each group of three is thought to be too confined, the partition at the back of the table can be left out altogether, or preferably held down in height to from 3 to 10 in. above the table top to give some privacy. These can be separated from another set of three by an aisle at least 3 ft wide; preferably one 3½ ft to 4 ft wide should be used. A series of them, or of double-staggered carrels as proposed in the preceding paragraph, on each side of a partition might be considered in some cases, if a very large seating capacity is

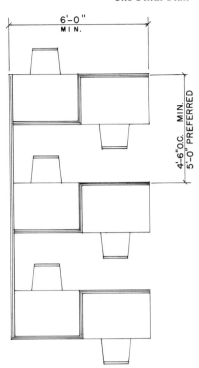

FIG. 16.8 Double carrels with readers facing in different directions. Used at Douglass College and Uris Undergraduate Library at Cornell. These are quite possible, but those shown in Fig. 16.10 are recommended.

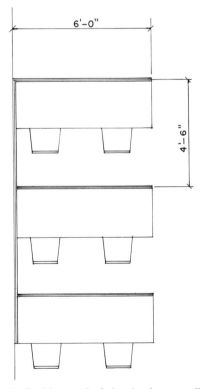

FIG. 16.9 Double carrels facing in the same direction. Adaptation of those used at Brandeis. These are not recommended except possibly for coeducational study.

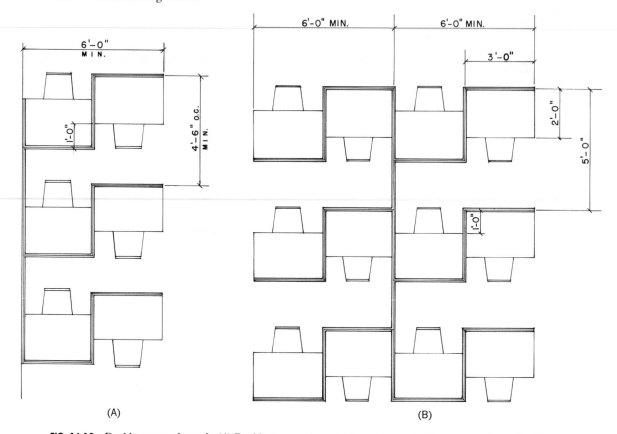

FIG. 16.10   Double-staggered carrels. (*A*) Double-staggered carrel adjacent to a wall. The carrel by the wall will be helped by a window. Partitions should be 52 in. high or higher. Recommended. (*B*) Double-staggered carrels on each side of a screen or partition. A space saver, but recommended only when necessary to provide required seating capacity. The backs of the inside carrels should be no more than 40 in. high.

required with a small collection of books. It might be set up in a city university in a large study hall in order to increase capacity or used in place of three stack ranges. (See Fig. 16.11.)

10. "Pinwheel" groups of four carrels, preferably in a reading alcove. If the alcove is 12 × 12 ft in the clear, table tops 22 × 36 in. are recommended, with partitions at least 52 in. in height, which extend 6 in. beyond the end of each table. Shelves are ordinarily not recommended for these cases, particularly if the table top is less than 27 in. deep.

This arrangement fits perfectly in a 27-ft column spacing with two alcoves to a bay. If the module size is 25 ft 6 in., the space in each alcove will be reduced a total of 9 in., and one of the shelf sections will be only 27 in. It can be used for shorter shelves or set up as wall space for a bulletin board or for a picture or other decoration.

If ventilation is adequate, alcoves can be partially closed in on the fourth side by a single

or double-faced book section, which may help to use space to advantage and make possible the best utilization of the available bay size. The main aisle between double rows of alcoves can be as narrow as 4½ ft. (See Figs. 7.9*B* and *C* and 16.12.)

These pinwheel groups have been successful in large reading areas, but they tend to give an impression of disorderliness when not in an alcove.

11. Carrels in alcoves with tables for four installed with 52-in.-high partitions in each direction. These alcoves may be as little as 9 ft deep and 11 ft 3 in. to 12 ft wide in the clear. With a 25 ft 6 in. bay and 4 ft 6 in. main aisle, an unusually large capacity is possible. (See Figs. 16.12 and 7.9*B* and *C*.) With a 27-ft bay, the space utilization is still good, and the main aisle can be widened to 6 ft.

12. Individual semi-lounge chairs to break the monotony of a long row of carrels or tables, as shown in Fig. 7.14*D*.

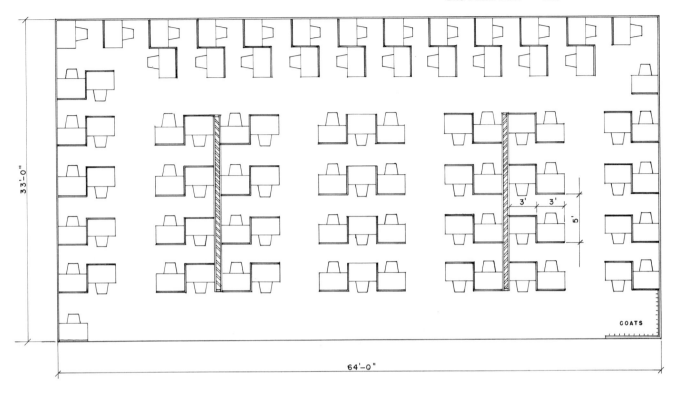

33' x 64' STUDY HALL (2112 SQ. FT)
88 SEATS

FIG. 16.11 Triple-staggered carrels. Can be used in large reading area in conjunction with double-staggered carrels or other arrangements, or in place of three stack ranges which are 4 ft on centers. If the top of the partition at the back of the center carrel is held to no more than 40 in., the occupant will feel less hemmed in.

13. Pairs or trios of semi-lounge chairs in units with low tables, which are at least 1 ft wide (preferably 1½ to 2 ft) and of seat height, between each pair. These can be purchased in units and may be preferable to single chairs, which are more likely to be pushed out of position. They can be used in place of two single carrels if they take less than 9 ft in length or in pairs or trios between rows of carrels or tables in a large reading area.

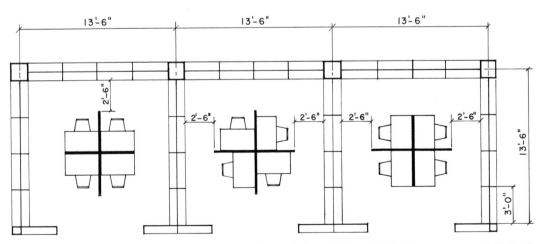

FIG. 16.12 Carrels in alcoves. Pinwheel arrangement is suitable if alcove is 12 × 12 ft inside measurement. Table for four with partitions possible in a 12 × 9 ft alcove.

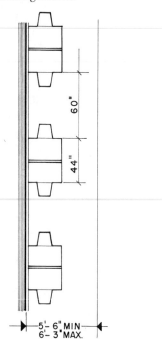

60"

44"

5'- 6" MIN
6'- 3" MAX.

FIG. 16.13 Carrels back to back. These are often proposed by architects but are not recommended because the reader at one's back is as close behind as in a reading room with rows of parallel tables. See also Fig. 7.11*B*.

Many of these arrangements for individual seating accommodations in semi-lounge chairs or in carrels can be placed in between rows of standard library tables in a large reading area. (See Fig. 16.4.) They can also be placed, preferably in bay-size groups interspersed with carrels, in a large book stack. (See Fig. 16.14*A* and *B*.) Small groups, sometimes called oases, such as are used at Princeton, are not so desirable because they tend to complicate shelving arrangements and to become noisy. (See Fig. 16.15.) The larger groups can be made quite attractive by changes in the lighting and floor covering; these breaks in the monotony of a very large stack are often a relief.

Book-stack Arrangements. The following principles should be kept in mind in connection with book-stack layouts.

1. Other things being equal, traffic patterns should be kept as simple as possible, particularly if open access is provided, so that the uninitiated or infrequent user can easily find the material he wants.

2. If there is more than one main aisle in a stack, finding books becomes more difficult, but, of course, not impossibly so.

3. Blind corners or pockets, which result

from stairwells and elevators, should be avoided if possible. If for any reason they seem necessary, it is suggested that they be used for purposes other than housing parts of the main collection where there should be a simple and logical sequence of classes. (See Fig. 16.16.)

4. Every aisle, as in reading areas, should be useful to the space on both sides of it. This can sometimes be accomplished by placing carrels, studies, small conference or other rooms, such as seminars, on one side of an aisle, with book ranges on the other. (See Fig. 6.9.) Book ranges can run to a wall with no cross aisle beyond it, or to a carrel at the wall end in place of the last section or sections of stacks, as shown in Fig. 16.5*B*. It should be repeated that a blind aisle between stack ranges should not be more than one-half the length agreed upon as the maximum suitable for a range with aisles at each end.

5. A book-stack arrangement which is a simple rectangle with no more than one center and two side aisles is desirable, other things being equal, but is not always practicable, particularly in a very large stack. If more aisles are required, be sure to keep the traffic pattern as simple as possible. (See Fig. 6.13.)

6. All stacks should have prominently displayed on each level in at least one place, and preferably in more than one, a chart showing the arrangements of the books on the shelves. The chart should always be oriented so that the reader will see it with the top of the chart in the direction that he faces. Too often this orientation has been neglected, with confusing results.

7. Stairs and elevators should be enclosed so as to reduce fire risks. There should be adequate lobby space by any elevator door so that passengers (staff or public) and book trucks can get in and out without difficulty, and the same is even more necessary for the stairs if they have doors that open into stack aisles. Three types of stack stairs are shown with dimensions in Fig. 8.11.

8. If the module system is used and there are columns within the stack area, be sure they are in the stack ranges and not in either stack or cross aisles and, as far as possible, are not wider than the ranges. (See Figs. 4.5 and 4.8.)

9. Avoid odd-length sections as far as possible, and, if only a few might be required (these few should be in the column ranges), try to replace them with lecterns or shelves, at counter height, for short-time book consultation. (See Figs. 4.9 and 4.10.)

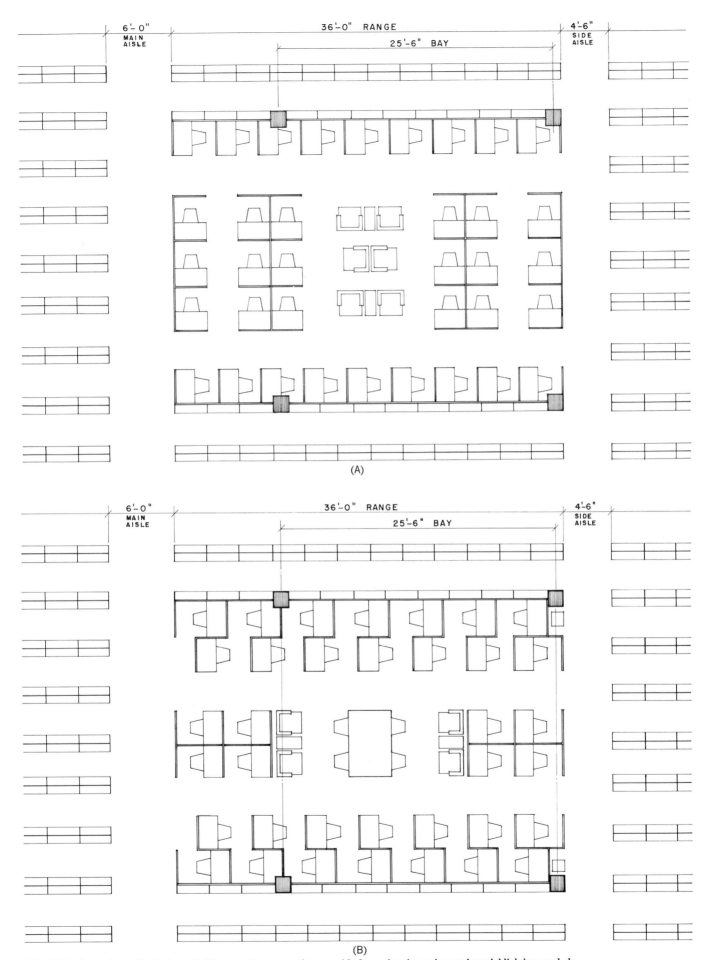

FIG. 16.14 Large "oases" in book stack. These are large enough to provide for variety in seating, and special lighting can help to overcome the monotony of a large book stack. Less than 25 sq ft per person is required with individual accommodations. If desired, either oasis shown can be reduced to one full bay in size without causing complications.

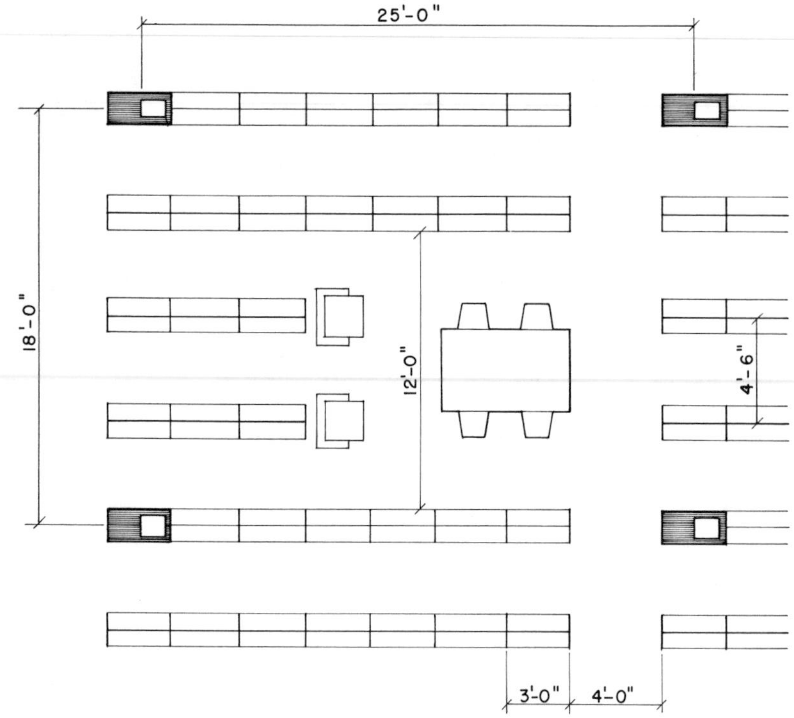

25'-0"

18'-0"

12'-0"

4'-6"

3'-0"   4'-0"

FIG. 16.15   Small oases in book stack. These tend to disrupt shelving arrangements and to promote undesirable sociability; they become noisy unless occupied completely by individual seating with readers well protected from one another.

10. A multiple of the space between stack-range centers should equal space between column centers, and the column spacing should, therefore, as far as possible, be based on the desired range spacing.

11. The total stack capacity depends primarily on the number of stack sections, single or double-faced, that are installed in the area available, and, if the problems stemming from column sizes and column spacing are left out of consideration, this will be based on: (*a*) the width and number of main and subsidiary cross aisles, (*b*) the length of ranges, and (*c*) range spacing on centers, which in turn must be affected by stack-aisle widths and shelf depths.

a. Width and Number of Main and Subsidiary Cross Aisles. The width of aisles should depend primarily on the amount of traffic expected. If side aisles are used primarily for access around the ends of ranges or to reach carrels along the walls, 3 ft minus the width of stack uprights and finished end panels is sufficient, and as little as 33 in. is possible; but up to 42 in. is to be preferred if the stack is large and large book trucks are to be used. Traffic on side aisles next to a row of

carrels can be reduced by extending one range in each bay across the aisle to the adjacent carrel. (See Fig. 16.17.) The book sequence will be complicated unless the arrangement starts in the upper left of the drawing.

Center or main aisles used as main traffic arteries should preferably be not less than 4 or 4½ ft wide. If they are wider than the subsidiary or side aisles, they should almost automatically attract traffic, but either of these widths is difficult to arrange if bay sizes are based on multiples of 3 ft. In a very infrequently used storage stack these aisles can, if necessary, be narrower; but keep in mind the problem of maneuvering book trucks. A width of 5 to 6 ft for a main aisle is extravagant, unless there is only one main aisle and the stacks are very large—that is, over 150,000 volumes on one level—and ranges are 30 ft long or over on both sides of it.

b. Length of Ranges. The length of ranges

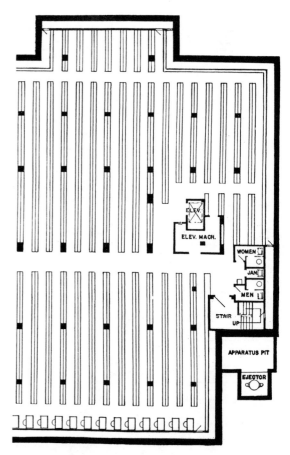

FIG. 16.16   Blind corners and pockets in book stack. The shelving above the long secondary cross aisle at top and that to the right of the elevator represent pockets unsuitable for the main collection, which should be arranged in a simple and logical sequence. These pockets are often unavoidable.

should depend primarily on the amount of use, the width of the stack aisles, and whether there is a cross—side or main—aisle at each end. Fifteen feet should be the maximum for a dead-end aisle, except in a little-used or closed-access stack, where on occasion it might be increased to as much as 18 ft to 21 ft. Fifteen feet may be long enough also for heavily used open-stack undergraduate collections limited in size, even with 36-in.-wide aisles between ranges and wide cross aisles at each end. Stack aisles up to 42 in. may sometimes be desirable for very heavily used stack areas or for deep folio shelves. As the collection becomes larger and the use of each aisle is smaller, ranges can probably be increased to 30 ft in length with the aisles decreasing to 33 in. in width, with collections of perhaps 100,000 volumes on one stack level. In the case of a great university library with collections including millions of volumes and with use restricted to advanced students, range lengths of 36 ft, or even 42 ft, with a 33-in. aisle between them can be used. A closed-access stack in a great national library can manage with ranges up to 60 ft in length, and the aisles can then be as little as 30 in. in width. If extra-wide shelves are used in certain bays so that stack aisles are narrowed by 2 to 6 in., the maximum stack range lengths should be reduced to counteract the effect, and in some cases different range spacing will be required.

c. Range Spacing on Centers. As already noted, range spacing is bound to be affected by the column spacing. The column spacings generally recommended in academic libraries are 22½, 25½, or 27 ft. Ranges 4 ft 6 in. on centers are suggested for 22½ and 27 ft; ranges 4 ft 3 in. are suggested for 25½ ft—all with 8-in. actual, 9-in. nominal depth shelves for nine-tenths of the stack, and 9 in. actual, 10 in. nominal, for the rest, except for newspaper shelving, where ranges should be 6 ft 4½ in. or 6 ft on centers and with 16-in. or 18-in.-deep shelves. If 7-in. actual depth shelves are used for the main installation, a larger percentage of deeper shelves will be required for the remainder. In a closed-access stack in a very large library, 4 ft on centers for fairly long ranges, 7-in. or 8-in. actual depth shelves, and 24-ft column spacing are suggested. Shelves of 8 in. actual or 9 in. nominal depth have not always been standard, but in large installations can be made available without increasing costs over the next larger size, and it is

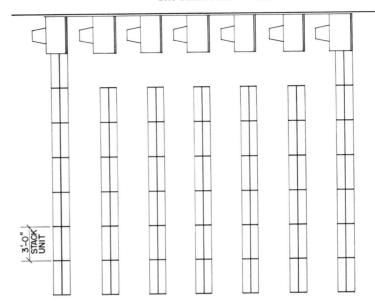

FIG. 16.17 Aisle traffic adjacent to carrels. Heavy use of aisles between open carrels and book-stack ranges is disturbing; it can be reduced by extending one stack range in each bay to the adjoining carrel. In the illustration shown here, the classification sequence would have to run from left to right; otherwise it will be interrupted where the ranges extend to carrels.

hoped that they will be made standard in the future.

If portions of stacks have restricted access and are seldom used, one more range to a bay should be considered there. These will give 3 ft 9 in., 3 ft 7⅗ in., and 3 ft 10⅔ in., respectively, for the three bay sizes proposed above. For this arrangement ranges over 18 in. from front to back would be questionable but not impossible.

Do not forget the effect of both shelf depth and aisle width on the desired range spacing. Also remember that all these figures are on the basis of stack ranges the same depth at the bottom as at the upper levels, and that if broad bases are used, aisle widths at the floor level and lower shelves, which are the critical points, will be reduced. But if ranges are narrow at the base, they must be stabilized by fastening them to the floor and by cross struts firmly attached at one or more places to a fixed point, such as a wall or a supporting column that cannot give way. This matter was discussed in detail in section 8.1.

12. If there is a good possibility that stack ranges will be shifted later to provide different range spacing, that process will be simplified by installing fluorescent lighting fixtures at right angles to the ranges. This will give better and more intense light on the lower shelves, which

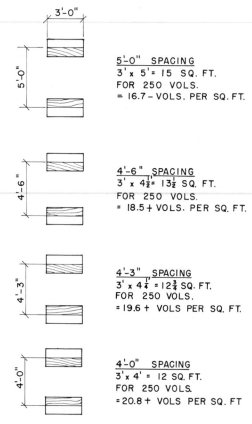

5'-0" SPACING
3' x 5' = 15 SQ. FT.
FOR 250 VOLS.
= 16.7 – VOLS. PER SQ. FT.

4'-6" SPACING
3' x 4½' = 13½ SQ. FT.
FOR 250 VOLS.
= 18.5 + VOLS. PER SQ. FT.

4'-3" SPACING
3' x 4¼' = 12¾ SQ. FT.
FOR 250 VOLS.
= 19.6 + VOLS PER SQ. FT.

4'-0" SPACING
3' x 4' = 12 SQ. FT.
FOR 250 VOLS.
= 20.8 + VOLS PER SQ. FT

FIG. 16.18 Stack capacity with different range spacing. No allowance is included here for cross aisles. See Figs. 16.19–16.23 for their effect. Stack capacities used in Figs. 16.18–16.22 are on the basis of 125 volumes to each single-faced section.

are the critical points. To install the lighting a ceiling at least 8 ft high in the clear will be necessary if lights are flush with the ceiling; if they are hung, 8 ft 4 in. should be available. If the lighting is indirect, with the fixture fastened to the range instead of over the aisles, and if the ceilings are as much as 9 ft high, the lights can be shifted with the stacks.

13. If stack lights are expected to be on whenever public access is permitted, wiring can be simplified and reduced in cost by elimination of switches at range ends.

14. If stacks may be shifted later, do not count on the floor covering beneath them to escape unscathed from the pressure of the stack ranges.

15. As was noted earlier, total stack capacity will, of course, depend on the number of stack sections that can be placed in the area available and the number of volumes that can be expected to be shelved comfortably in the average single or double-faced section. This was discussed theoretically in section 8.2. The tables in Appendix B will give figures in this connection.

Figs. 16.18 to 16.23 show actual layouts and capacities estimated at an average of 125 volumes for each standard section 3 ft wide and 7 ft 6 in. high. Areas required for stairwells and elevator shafts have been omitted on the basis that they should be charged against non-assign-

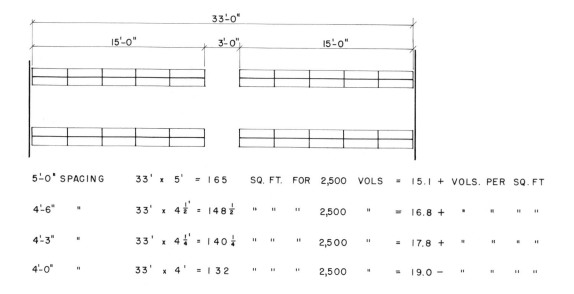

5'-0" SPACING   33' x 5' = 165   SQ. FT. FOR 2,500 VOLS = 15.1 + VOLS. PER SQ. FT

4'-6"   "   33' x 4½' = 148½   "   "   "   2,500   "   = 16.8 +   "   "   "   "

4'-3"   "   33' x 4¼' = 140¼   "   "   "   2,500   "   = 17.8 +   "   "   "   "

4'-0"   "   33' x 4' = 132   "   "   "   2,500   "   = 19.0 –   "   "   "   "

CROSS AISLES = 1/11 AREA

FIG. 16.19 Stack capacity with different range spacing and minimum cross aisle.

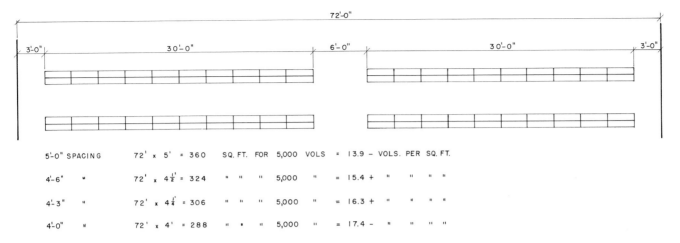

5'-0" SPACING   72' x 5' = 360   SQ. FT. FOR   5,000   VOLS   = 13.9 – VOLS. PER SQ. FT.

4'-6"   "   72' x 4½' = 324   "   "   "   5,000   "   = 15.4 +   "   "   "   "

4'-3"   "   72' x 4¼' = 306   "   "   "   5,000   "   = 16.3 +   "   "   "   "

4'-0"   "   72' x 4' = 288   "   •   "   5,000   "   = 17.4 –   "   "   "   "

CROSS AISLES = ⅙ AREA

FIG. 16.20 Stack capacity with different range spacing and generous cross aisle. In some cases main aisle might be narrowed and side aisles widened.

able space and should be planned by the architect.

The space occupied by columns is not shown in the drawings because it will vary with different bay and column sizes and complicate the estimates tremendously. It may reduce the capacity by up to 2 per cent of the total. Figs. 16.21 and 16.22 show carrels along the walls at right angles to the ranges and indicate that if carrels are charged with half of the adjacent aisle space, utilization is improved.

Catalogue Cases. Theoretical problems in regard to the design of catalogue cases are dis-

cussed in section 11.2. Space requirements will be discussed here in terms of card trays and floor areas and also in Appendix B, item V. In arranging catalogue cases, planners should remember that the number of readers and staff members expected to use the catalogue at one time is as important as the number of cards to be housed.

The use of the catalogue will depend not only on the size of the student body and the faculty, but also on the ease with which the library's clientele can use the books directly from the shelves, avoiding to a large extent the use of the

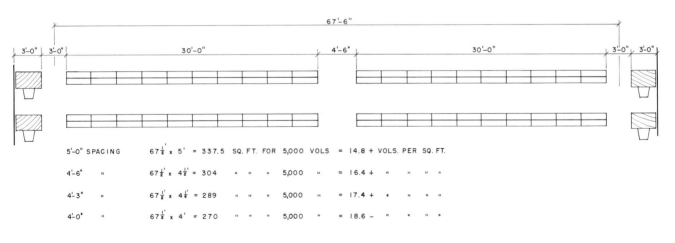

5'-0" SPACING   67½' x 5' = 337.5 SQ. FT. FOR 5,000 VOLS = 14.8 + VOLS. PER SQ. FT.

4'-6"   "   67½' x 4½' = 304   "   "   "   5,000   "   = 16.4 +   "   "   "   "

4'-3"   "   67½' x 4¼' = 289   "   "   "   5,000   "   = 17.4 +   •   "   "   "

4'-0"   "   67½' x 4' = 270   "   "   "   5,000   "   = 18.6 –   "   •   "   "

CROSS AISLES = ¹/₁₀ AREA · HALF OF SIDE AISLE CHARGED TO CARRELS

FIG. 16.21 Stack capacity with different range spacing and with carrels along walls on both sides. If one-half of the area of the side aisles is charged against the carrels, stack capacity per square foot is increased. Compare with Fig. 16.20.

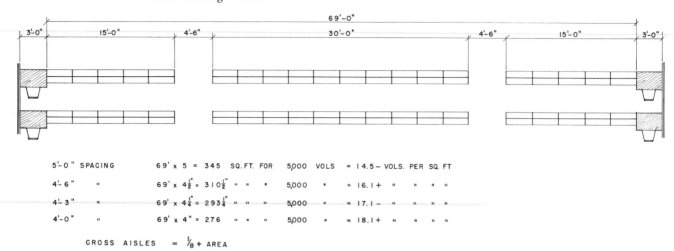

5'-0" SPACING   69' x 5 = 345   SQ.FT. FOR   5,000 VOLS = 14.5 — VOLS. PER SQ. FT

4'-6"   "   69' x 4½" = 310½" "   "   "   5,000   "   = 16.1 +   "   "   "

4'-3"   "   69' x 4¼" = 293¾" "   "   "   5,000   "   = 17.1 —   "   "   "

4'-0"   "   69' x 4" = 276   "   "   "   5,000   "   = 18.1 +   "   "   "

CROSS AISLES   = ⅛ + AREA

FIG. 16.22 Stack capacity with different range spacing and with carrels at end of blind aisles. Length of ranges with blind aisles should not be more than half as long as those with cross aisles at each end. If one-half of each cross aisle is charged against the carrels, the stack capacity per square foot is increased.

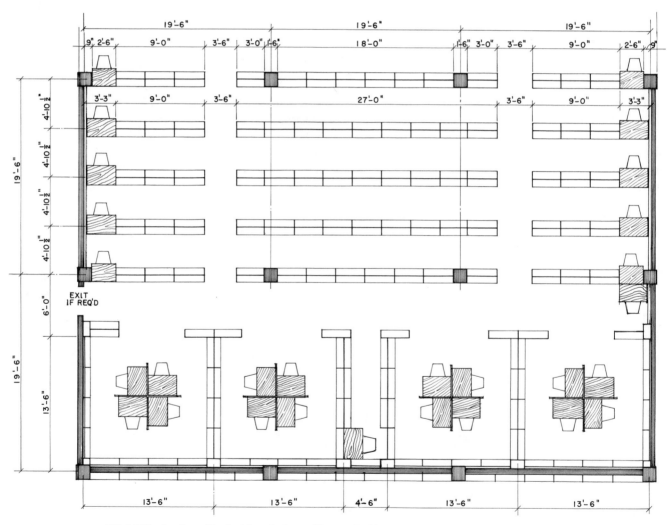

FIG. 16.23 Stack combined with stack alcoves. Nonstandard bay sizes can sometimes be used to advantage without seriously affecting capacity per square foot.

catalogue. In the Lamont Library, where the number of students is large and the collection is limited, the catalogue is used comparatively little. On the other hand, if stack access is forbidden or severely limited, the use of the catalogue will be greatly increased. If use of the catalogue is to be very heavy in relation to its size, the problem is to prevent the readers from getting in each other's way, and it may be well to spread the trays out in a ribbon arrangement with cases housing only a few trays in a vertical row and taking a great deal more floor space than would otherwise be required.

How many trays high can the catalogue be without making it too inconvenient for users to reach the top or bottom trays, and without causing them to interfere with one another? A large percentage of cases provided by library-equipment houses are 10 drawers high. This is certainly suitable in some libraries. But it should be remembered that as the library grows, the catalogue grows, and sooner or later space for it may be at a premium. There is no reason why adults cannot reach considerably higher than is required for 10 trays. Twelve is not at all unusual today, and is becoming standard in academic libraries. This may bring the top drawer no more than 68 in. above the floor if a 16-in. base is used. Some years ago in the Smith College Library, where space for card cases was at a premium, cases 15 trays high with a very low base were installed, and in spite of the fact that women on the average are several inches shorter than men, the results are reported to be satisfactory. Many academic libraries are now using cases 13 to 16 trays high.

Several possibilities are available. If the academic librarian is convinced that there will never be a shortage of storage space, it is suggested that cases 10 or 12 trays high be used. Twelve will give 20 per cent greater capacity than 10. If the librarian is worried about the future, one cabinet seven trays high might be used on top of another, giving 14 in all. With a 12-in. base, which is a standard height, this would bring the top tray to no more than 6 ft, which is possible for a person 5 ft tall to reach, although it may not be convenient or easy. A third possibility is to acquire cabinets 10 trays high, with a 26-in. base and to plan to place a unit three to five trays high on top at a later time, and reduce the height of the base. This will be easy to do if open bases with plain legs

of wood are used, but the special cases to fit at the top may prove to be unduly expensive and may not be aesthetically pleasing.

The total height of cases is of importance in several ways. If the top trays are too high, it is difficult for a short person to pull them out and bring them down to a consultation table, particularly if they are full. If the bottom trays are too low, it is difficult to lean down and pull out a tray, particularly for an old, rotund, and stiff person and, even in the absence of these handicaps, the aisle may be temporarily obstructed. A third problem of equal importance is that the labels on the top and bottom trays will be difficult to read if they are too far above or below eye level. In an effort to solve this particular problem, the fronts of the top trays are sometimes slanted downward and the bottom ones upward to make it easier to read the labels.

This brings up the whole problem of labeling. The larger the label that can be used, other things being equal, the easier it will be to make it legible. Sometimes labels are printed in large letters. If this is too expensive, large typewriter type can be used. If a skilled letterer is available, hand-lettering with India ink will help. Labelholders that provide space for a tray number help to keep the trays from being misplaced, and sometimes special symbols or colors are used for the same purpose. It must be remembered that the larger the labelholder, the more the hardware costs, and that it may interfere with the rod. The type of handle used is also important. Some drawers have almost closed ring-type handles into which a finger can be inserted. This makes it more difficult to drop a tray. Libraries are advised to consider all the possibilities in connection with catalogue tray hardware and to consult with manufacturers about the advantages and disadvantages of different types.

What about the width of the cases? The standard in the United States today is six trays with over-all width of about 40 in. They can be built five trays wide or just over 33 in. A case five trays wide and 12 to 14 high is in itself a bit too narrow to be aesthetically pleasing, but as part of a series it avoids this handicap. It has the advantage of fitting between the uprights of a standard shelf section 3 ft wide and may also be useful in connection with the wider units if available space, because of bay sizes, cannot be used to advantage with one width only. See Fig. 16.24*A* and *B*. But the narrower cases, as

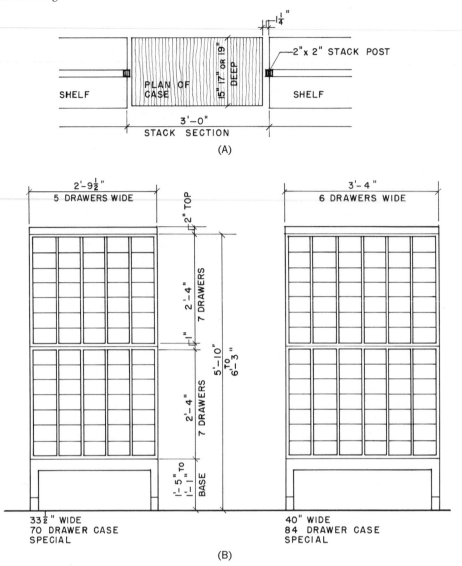

FIG. 16.24   Width of catalogue cases. (*A*) Cases which are five trays wide can be fitted into a standard 3-ft-wide book section, an arrangement which is sometimes useful. (*B*) The right-hand case is a standard six-tray width; both cases are in two parts, each seven trays high for additional capacity. Additional horizontal support provided by thicker cross pieces (not shown) will be required in each part.

well as the higher ones, are considered special today and will cost more per inch of filing space, unless a manufacturer can be convinced that something like 10,000 trays can be sold annually and will make them a stock item.

What about the depth and capacity of catalogue trays? As stated in section 13.3 in more detail, it is suggested that 1,000 cards for a 17-in. case be considered capacity, and 1,150 for a 19-in. case, because cabinets should never be filled to maximum capacity, any more than should book shelves; growth is uneven and it is expensive to shift cards. Even when trays are as

full as has been suggested, filers may object to their weight. Readers may be unhappy, particularly when pulling out a full upper tray. On the other hand, it may be desirable, under some circumstances, to install the deeper trays and the higher cabinets so as to ensure the maximum of capacity at a later time. A cabinet 19 in. deep, with trays 15 high, will provide 17,250 cards in one row, while with 17-in. cabinets, 10 high, only 10,000 can be housed. This represents an increase for the longer trays and higher rows of 72½ per cent. Here is another matter for local consideration and decision, keeping in mind the disadvantages of the extra height and weight. In general, the longer and higher cases are recommended for libraries that anticipate very large collections and are more worried about space for card storage than for readers using the cards. It should still be remembered, however, that heavier trays may be dropped more frequently than lighter ones and consequently damaged.

The next problem deals with the use of reference or sliding shelves, which are often built in halfway up in the case so that the reader standing at the catalogue can conveniently use the trays from above or below without moving to an adjacent consultation table. Obstruction by users is a great inconvenience with a busy catalogue (see Fig. 16.25), and it is suggested that, in general, sliding shelves should not be installed in an academic installation. You may be sure that, if they are, they will be used. If no sliding shelf is provided, consultation tables should be installed close by. They may be simply a shelf fastened between two cases or may stand independently. Figs. 16.26, 16.27, and 16.28 show different possible arrangements; Fig. 16.26*A* depicts dimensions and accessories. The distance between the consultation table and the catalogue case is of importance. It the catalogue is heavily used and tables are too close, it will be difficult for the users to pass each other. If they are too far away, the filers and readers will complain that they have to carry the trays too great a distance and will demand a sliding shelf in the case or will rest the tray they are consulting on another that is pulled out partway. Either plan will obstruct the passageway, and the latter procedure tends to damage the guide cards.

Two other problems arise in connection with consultation tables. How high should they be and how wide? The decisions must be a compromise. The users will differ in height. A height of 42 in. or at least 40 in., rather than the earlier 39-in. standard, is suggested. The amount of use is a factor in the width, which should depend on whether the use is large enough so that a number of readers can be expected to be working on each side at the same time. If this is the case, the table can be 3 ft across, but that is very unusual. Generally, 24 in. is adequate, and often 18 to 20 in. is considered sufficient, depending on the length of the trays and the pressure for space.

How should the cases be arranged? If they

are not backed up against a wall, which tends to limit flexibility, they are generally placed in double-faced rows parallel to each other, at suitable distances apart, so spaced that it is possible to go around either end of each row to reach the next one. As catalogues become larger, it may be desirable and perhaps necessary to fill in one of the ends, making an alcove closed on three sides. (See Fig. 16.26.) This may add to the capacity of the area by as much as 50 per cent, but it must be remembered that, if corners are tight together, there is danger of bruised knuckles when a tray from the row next to the corner is pulled out. A 4 to 6-in. break, preferably covered with a filler, is desirable on each side of the corner. A double row of alcoves with a corridor in between, perhaps 6 ft wide, as shown in Fig. 16.32, may give the largest possible capacity in a given area.

The Princeton University Library arrangement, shown in Fig. 16.27, is another possibility, but it requires a reader either to carry the drawer a considerable distance or to use it at the catalogue to the inconvenience of others, with possible damage to the cards if there are no sliding shelves.

Suggested layouts for four libraries, each representing a different situation as far as size and use are concerned, are shown in Figs. 16.29 to 16.32.

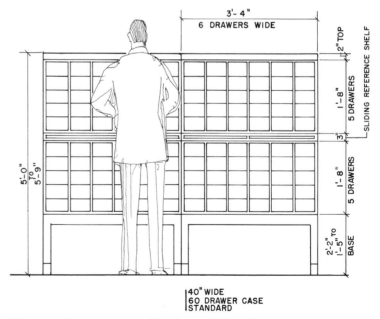

FIG. 16.25 Catalogue cases with reference shelves. These are not recommended in a busy academic library because the user obstructs the use of many trays by others. Consultation tables should almost always be substituted.

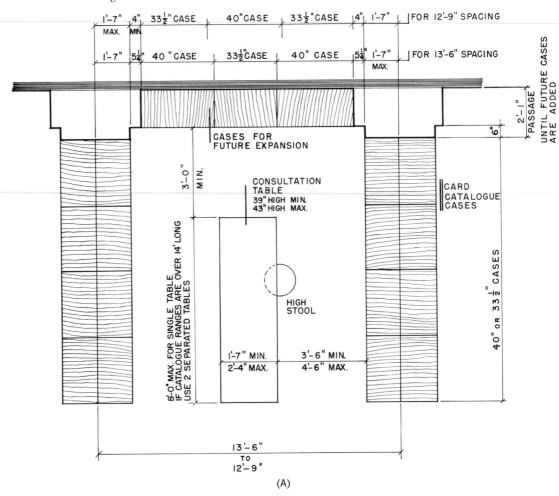

(A)

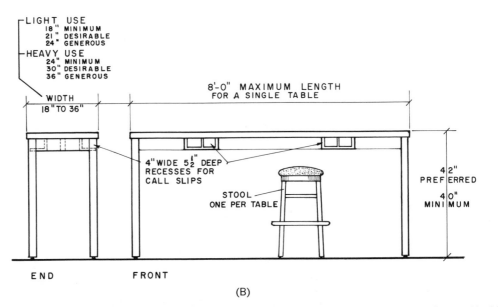

(B)

FIG. 16.26   Consultation table adjacent to catalogue cases. (*A*) If the table is placed between parallel rows of cases with aisles of suitable width, it will prevent obstruction and not require the trays to be carried uncomfortably long distances. (*B*) This shows an end and front elevation of a consultation table indicating possible widths and heights and accessories.

16.4 The Contract Documents, Specifications, and Working Drawings

After the program has been written and analyzed, after the conferences of the planning team have been completed, after space and locations have been assigned to library functions, after the aesthetics have been determined and the budget allocated, it then becomes the province of the architect to translate all the diverse and interrelated agreements and decisions into such a form that the building contractor can estimate his costs, make his bid, and with his workmen transfer the completed plan into a reality in brick and mortar, a reality that will be satisfactory functionally and aesthetically and will also be structurally sound and easily serviced.

The tools through which the architect accomplishes this important task are termed "the contract documents" and may be divided into five parts: (1) plans, (2) elevations, (3) sections, (4) schedules, and (5) specifications. The first three of these are explained by drawings, the last two by writing. To the uninitiated, these are often difficult to read and understand, since the drawings are diagrams drawn "to scale," the writing is technical, and both are replete with conventions and abbreviations—a language understood by both architect and contractor, but

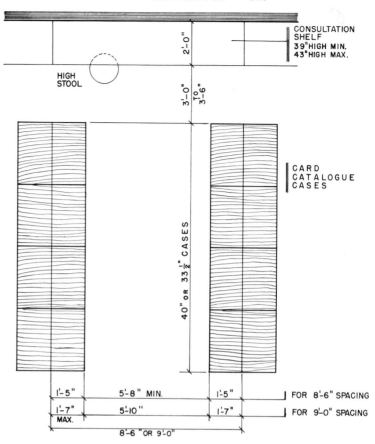

FIG. 16.27 Consultation table along a wall at right angles to catalogue cases. With this arrangement, cases can be placed closer together but trays must be carried considerably farther, and there will be a tendency to try to consult cards without removing trays. Congestion and damage to cards may result.

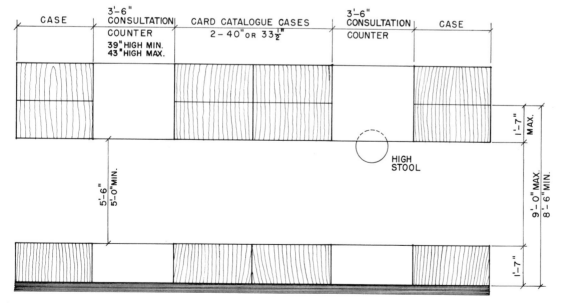

FIG. 16.28 Consultation tables in line with and between catalogue cases. Consultation tables arranged in this way save steps but partially obstruct use of adjacent trays.

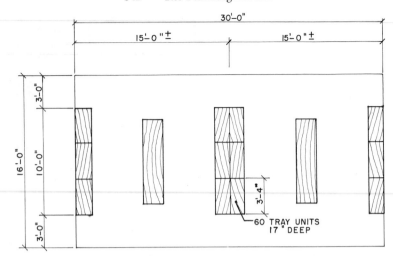

FIG. 16.29 Catalogue for a small library. With 3-ft-wide aisles at end of each row of standard cases six trays wide and ten high, 720,000 cards can be housed in 480 sq ft, giving 1,500 to a square foot. This is adequate spacing for a library with 300 seats.

hard for the layman to translate. Only a brief explanation of these tools can be attempted here in the hope of doing little more than acquaint the reader with their appearance and purpose. No library planning team should be considered complete if it does not include at least one member representing the institution who has had previous experience with and understanding of these contract documents.

Plans. There should be an architectural plan showing each floor level of the building. It will illustrate this floor diagrammatically as if the roof or floor above had been removed, exposing the shape and size of all rooms and spaces and the location of all the doors, windows, columns, walls, stairs, elevators, and vertical shaftways for distribution of mechanical services. In addition, all fixtures and furnishings built into or attached to the building, such as washroom fixtures and book stacks, will be shown. The locations of loose furniture may also be indicated, as this will help materially to clarify the objectives of the plan. Such locations are usually indicated with dotted lines, as movable equipment is rarely the responsibility of the building contractor, who uses the drawing in estimating and constructing the library. Dotted lines contrasting with the solid lines of the main parts of the plan indicate that the object or space so presented is not part of the work expected from the contractor. They are frequently marked with the initials NIC (Not in Contract).

These plans must be dimensioned in feet and inches, or meters and centimeters, and drawn to scale. In other words, they must be exact and

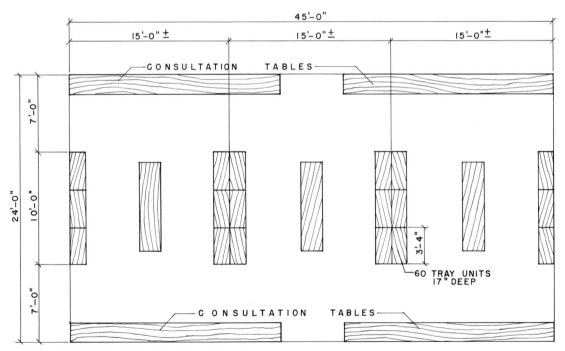

FIG. 16.30 Catalogue room for a small university library with 1,000 seats. A larger proportion of the area is required for consultation tables and only 1,000 cards per square foot of floor space is provided.

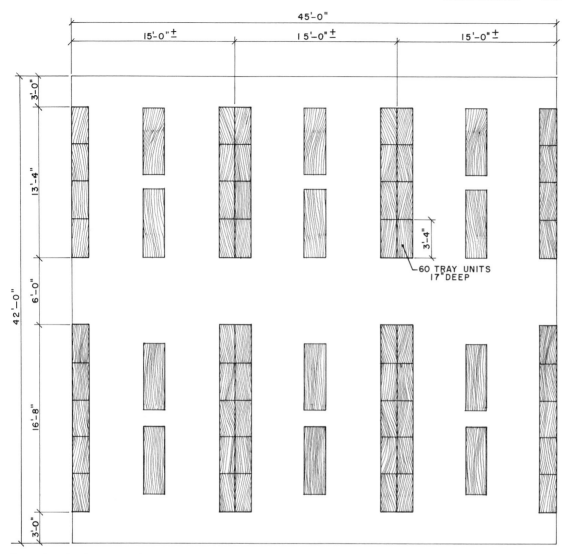

FIG. 16.31 Catalogue room for typical large university library. Provision is made for 1,500 cards per square foot of area with adequate space at tables for readers consulting them.

proportionately reduced from the actual or "full" size desired in the completed building so that any desired dimension can be determined by measuring it on the drawing and multiplying that measurement by the amount of reduction employed. Architects and engineers use rulers that have this multiplication factor incorporated in their markings and which can then be read directly in feet and inches or meters and centimeters. These rules are called "architect's" or "engineer's scales," and the act of using them is "scaling." The scale, or the amount of proportional reduction used, should clearly be stated on each plan. In the United States the term "architectural scale" is usually given to one expressing a foot by $\frac{1}{16}$, $\frac{1}{8}$, $\frac{1}{4}$, $\frac{3}{8}$, $\frac{1}{2}$, $\frac{3}{4}$, or 1 in.;

the term "engineer's scale" to one expressing a foot by $\frac{1}{200}$, $\frac{1}{100}$, $\frac{1}{50}$, $\frac{1}{40}$, $\frac{1}{20}$, or $\frac{1}{10}$ in. The usual architectural scales employed on plans are $\frac{1}{16}$ in. = 1 ft or $\frac{1}{8}$ in. = 1 ft or $\frac{1}{4}$ in. = 1 ft. If a more detailed plan explanation is required, larger scales ($\frac{3}{8}$ in., $\frac{1}{2}$ in., $\frac{3}{4}$ in., and 1 in. to 1 ft) are used, but these are more frequently employed for sections.

In addition to the floors, plans of the roof and the plot are needed. These are sometimes combined on one drawing and usually use an engineer's scale, particularly if the building is a large one. However, architectural scales of $\frac{1}{16}$ in., $\frac{1}{32}$ in., or even $\frac{1}{64}$ in. are sometimes employed. The roof plan is required to show the pitch, or direction of slope, the method of drainage on the

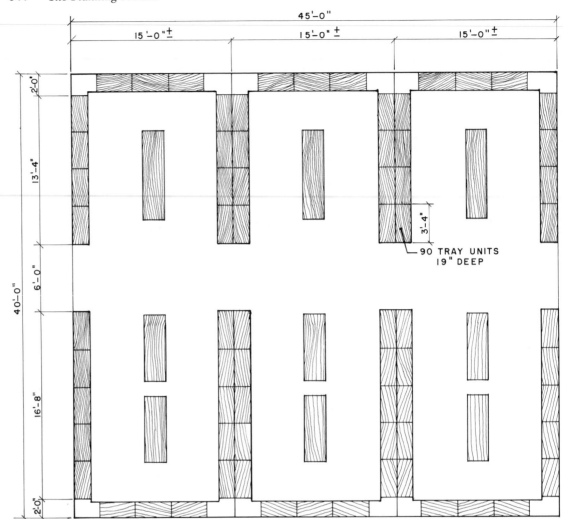

FIG. 16.32 Catalogue arrangement proposed for very large library with limited space available. This shows what can be done by placing cases on the third side of each bay and using units fifteen trays high and 19 in. deep, thereby housing 4,000 cards to each square foot.

roofs, and the location, housing, and size of mechanical services which must project above the roof levels. Usually safety regulations require door access or window access from the building to all flat roofs, a provision which is also an aid to maintenance and which generally should be shown on the roof plan.

If a great deal of mechanical equipment is on the roof, rather than within the building, a roof plan at an architectural scale may be required in order to illustrate properly the sizes and locations. The increasing importance and amount of mechanical work in modern buildings has led to such an extensive use of the roof for elevator equipment, fans, cooling towers, and related ductwork and piping that there is a tendency to enclose all of it on a separate floor or roof house

of its own or to contain it within a barrier or fence built on the roof so as to screen the usually untidy appearance of this heterogeneous assembly of mechanical equipment. This problem is less acute in libraries than in laboratories or similar buildings requiring a high concentration of mechanical equipment, but it is present, particularly if the library is air-conditioned.

The plot plan illustrates the location of the building relative to adjacent structures and the ground. It shows the source and direction of all services which must be brought into the building from outside and locates all walks, roads, parking areas, and planting beds and grass required as part of the completed building. If the site has trees, planting, walks, roads, or buildings, the plan should show them so that they may be properly protected during construction or removed as part of the contract. Frequently, the land made available for the use of the contractor during the construction period must be restricted and protected so that the operations of both the institution and the contractors may be conducted without undue interference with each other. The limitation of the areas assigned to the contractor and to be protected by him should be shown on the plot plan. In determining their size the architect must remember that space is required not only for the storage and receiving of equipment and building materials, but also for construction shanties, workmen's facilities, and parking. A site difficult of access will increase the building costs and the hardships placed on the contractor, and will be reflected in the construction cost.

The plot plan shows the relationship of the building to the ground by elevations or grades which indicate the number of feet, or meters, any particular spot is above sea level or some other predetermined point which will remain undisturbed during construction. These grades are based upon a survey of the site, usually made by a professional surveyor. The main floor of the building should be given a grade, and the elevations of the new grounds and walks should be indicated either by spot grades or by grade lines, which represent the cut which would result if all the ground above any particular elevation were removed.

In the United States, grade elevations are usually indicated in feet and tenths of a foot (261.25), rather than in feet and inches (261'-3"), just as plot plans are usually at engineers' rather than architects' scales.

Elevations. The plans of the architect are supplemented by the elevations. Whereas the plan is a horizontal graphic representation of the library to a scale, the elevation is its vertical representation to a scale. Like the building plans, this scale is almost always an architectural one. The elevations show the building heights and the location in the vertical plans of the doors, windows, and columns or supports on the various facades, and the materials from which they and the walls are built. Thus it also illustrates the appearance of the building. Since it is a graphic representation, there is no attempt at perspective, and the most distant facade is drawn to the same scale as the closest. For each elevation, a "picture" plane is chosen, usually parallel to the facade which is represented, and nothing is illustrated on that elevation which is not reached by a line drawn perpendicular to that chosen plane. Thus a rectangular building can be fully illustrated by four direct elevations, one taken parallel to each of its four sides. The elevation of one of these sides shows no part of any other.

This would not be true of another building shape; at least one of its facades would be shown foreshortened on one of the "picture" planes parallel to the other sides, since it can be reached by lines drawn perpendicular to that plane. A circular, or curved, shape results in a gradual increase in this foreshortening in proportion as the curve recedes away from the "picture" plane.

The foreshortened part of an elevation always shows the actual scale of the vertical dimensions, but the horizontal scale is reduced in accordance with the degree at which the plan slopes away from the picture plane.

An elevation is drawn to give information necessary in the construction of a building. The location of floors, roofs, and other objects hidden by the facade that is being illustrated is shown by dotted lines. The design of features, such as windows and doors, can be drawn carefully once and repeated elsewhere only in outline. The indication of materials is stylized and usually confined to one end of the elevation.

It can be seen, as a result, that an elevation "drawing" frequently gives a very inadequate idea of the aesthetic appearance of the building. Such drawings are often used, however, as the base for an elevation "rendering," which represents in different colors or values the materials and openings of the building and which often ranks among the most interesting and artistic products from an architect's office.

To the layman, however, the stylization required in an elevation and its lack of perspective make this type of rendering somewhat difficult to visualize. As a result, many architects furnish their clients with rendered perspective drawings or models, both of which illustrate the aesthetic appearance of the building with more natural realism and are generally better understood.

Sections. To illustrate a building completely, the plans and elevations are supplemented by one or more "sections." A plan is a horizontal cut through a chosen level of the building. A section, similarly, is a vertical cut through a chosen part of the building and exposes the elevations and vertical relationships of the spaces through which it is cut. It shows ceiling heights, construction methods, stair details, and interior design, and furnishes an excellent visual picture of the spatial relationships in the building, which can only be deduced from the plans and elevations.

Illustrative sections are usually drawn to the architectural scale used for the plans or elevations. However, one of the most frequent uses of sections is to detail specific objects or features in the building, in which case they are drawn to a much larger architectural scale, usually ¾ in. or 3 in., but sometimes as large as one-half or actual full size. Detail sections of this nature may be cut either vertically or horizontally and are used to explain the construction details and shapes of walls, windows, toilets, stairs, and any other architectural feature which needs such careful illustration in order to ensure that the required soundness and appearance will be incorporated into the building.

A plan, elevation, or section is said to be "reflected" when the surfaces it illustrates are behind or above, rather than before or below the chosen plane or cut being used on the particular drawing in question.

Since plans, elevations, and sections for a building are drawings to a scale, a desired size or dimension can be ascertained from the drawings by the use of a rule or scale. In addition, important dimensions which cannot be left subject to the small inaccuracies attendant upon scaling are written on these drawings. Notes explaining the construction or specifying the finish or materials that are being illustrated supplement the drafted information. The extent of the written dimensions and the items noted are indicated with arrows or dots at the end of light connecting lines.

Schedules. Drawings can no longer contain sufficient information to enable a contractor to estimate and build a satisfactory building. They must be supplemented with written directions. Most of these are incorporated into schedules which may either be included on the drawings or bound in the specifications. Such schedules are usually keyed by symbols, numbers, or letters to those parts of the drawings to which they apply.

Schedules are most frequently used in the following ways:

1. *Room or Finish Schedules.* These schedules tabulate the materials which will form the finished surfaces of the walls, floors, ceilings, base, and dado, and verbally point out any special feature which may be required in a particular room. In order to key a room or finish schedule to the plans, each room is given a name, space, or number on both the plan and schedule. The finish schedule then tabulates the finishes after each space designation.

2. *Door Schedules.* The doors or openings inside the building may be of different widths, heights, design, and material. They may be solid or may contain glass panels. They may be flush wood or paneled metal. They may be hung in wood frames or metal bucks, which in turn may have sidelights or transoms. Ventilation requirements may call for the use of louvers in the doors or for leaving a specified amount of clear space between the bottom and the floor. Sound or temperature insulation may require soundproofing or weatherstripping.

The individual requirements for doors may be, and usually are, many and varied. As a result, each door or opening in the building is given a symbol which refers directly to the schedule, where the size and other characteristics can immediately be determined. This schedule is usually accompanied by scale elevations showing the main type of door designs which are being described.

3. *Hardware Schedules, Painting Schedules, Furniture Schedules, and Stack Schedules.* These relate to or supplement the finish and door schedules. These supplementary schedules are often compiled during, rather than prior to the construction of the building, but should be completed in time to have the materials and work based on them ready for installation and performance without delaying the progress of the job.

4. *Mechanical Schedules.* Schedules for the finished materials required for the mechanical trades are important items in the appearance of the building. Electrical, plumbing, and heating fixtures have a functional purpose, and also a conspicuous and extensive aesthetic effect. Their location and use are generally keyed into the mechanical plans by schedules, and an adequate understanding of the completed library cannot be reached without carefully consulting these schedules.

5. *Engineering Schedules.* The structural engineering also needs to be supplemented by sched-

ules which indicate to the builder the size and strength of columns, beams, and floor slabs. If they are of steel, the size and weight must be given; if of concrete, the dimensions, the amount of reinforcing, and the strength of the mix.

Specifications. The drawings and the schedules explain and illustrate the size, shape, finish, and relationship of all the spaces, walls, and materials contained in the building. They do not specify the quality of the materials or the level of the workmanship. These are described and enumerated in a written specification which accompanies and complements the drawings. In their modern form in the United States, specifications group under the various trades or suppliers all the work in the building which each will perform or furnish. The required quality is carefully explained and the expected performance of all materials specified. The method of workmanship is described and procedures explained. The control of materials and workmanship explained in a carefully written specification can aid materially in accomplishing a satisfactory result both aesthetically and functionally.

Often the desired result or quality can best be attained by specifying one particular material or manufacturer. It may well be decided that the granite or limestone from a predetermined quarry is necessary for the proper appearance of the building, or that a particular stack or elevator manufacturer can best satisfy the functional requirements of the library. If so, only that material or manufacturer should be specified. In buildings for private institutions, this can be done directly by name or carried in the contract documents as an allowance of the amount of money determined as necessary for its purchase or installation. If, however, other materials or manufacturers are considered as equals, the specifications will also name them. For public institutions, the general requirement is that at least three manufacturers or suppliers be named, and the naming of only one is not allowed, except under unusual circumstances. If allowances are permitted in public work, they, too, must be let competitively.

Specifications often describe in detail the material or manufactured items desired and allow any supplier or manufacturer who is able to satisfy the specifications to furnish the required items. If one or more names are specified, they are often accompanied by the phrase "or equal,"

which means that any manufacturer or supplier who can show that his product is equal in every respect to those that are named will be acceptable.

The sectional division into trades and suppliers most frequently used in specifications today is as follows: site work; excavation and grading; concrete work; masonry; waterproofing; roofing; structural steel; miscellaneous metal work; doors, windows, and frames; carpentry; lathing and plastering; tile work; flooring; painting; glass and glazing; and the "mechanical trades," i.e., plumbing; heating, ventilating, and air conditioning; and electrical work.

Four other factors assist or supplement the five contract documents just discussed:

1. *Mechanical.* The last three sectional divisions of the specifications listed immediately above were devoted to trades which are grouped under the term "mechanical trades." In the preparation of the architect's working drawings and specifications, the organization of the work of these trades has become more important in recent years. For instance, in 1900, in a good many library buildings which are still in use today, the work assigned to the mechanical trades was no more than 15 per cent of the total construction cost of the job. Today, it is rarely less than 35 per cent and, if the library is air-conditioned, may run as high as 45 per cent.

As the importance of the mechanical trades in building construction has increased, so has the complexity of the installations. Electrical and pneumatic controls, transformers, motors, fans, pumps, switchboards, valves, contactors, to name the more usual devices hidden from view in panels, closets, and mechanical rooms, multiply with every added mechanical comfort; space is required to house them, and new building laws or regulations must be satisfied in order to ensure that any possible faulty operation will not create a hazard to the occupants or contents of the building. Just as the modern architect usually engages structural engineers to prepare structural drawings and specifications and to assure him that the strength of the floors, walls, and columns will be adequate to support the loads expected to be imposed on them by the building, its contents, and its occupants, he also engages mechanical engineers who are responsible to him for the proper installation and operation of the mechanical systems. To accomplish this, these engineers prepare special plans devoted entirely to illustrating the work of the mechanical trades, write their sections of the specifications, and compile any schedules pertaining to these specifications and drawings.

The architect may employ one engineer to prepare the drawings and specifications for all the mechanical work or one or more separate specialists in the engineering work required for each of the three trades—a heating, ventilating, and air-conditioning engineer; an electrical and lighting engineer; and a sanitary and plumbing engineer.

These engineers are responsible to the architect for the preparation of drawings illustrating the installation and operation of the work assigned to their respective trades. It should be remembered that these installations will occupy space and affect the appearance of the building, and that their operation will be accompanied by a certain amount of noise and will affect the comfort of the occupants. In order to ensure that the satisfactory operation of the mechanical plant will not adversely affect either the aesthetics or the function of the library, the engineering drawings and specifications prepared to illustrate the mechanical trades must be coordinated with the architectural drawings and specifications prepared to illustrate the space relationships, sizes, finishes, and structure.

This coordination between the mechanical trades, the structure, the architecture, and the furnishings is difficult at best and can be only partially accomplished if the drawings ensure space enough in plan and elevation for the equipment, ductwork, and piping and if they assign proper locations in the library areas for the visible parts of the installations; every detail must be consonant with comfort and aesthetics and must not allow the work of one trade to conflict with that of another. In addition to this coordination on the drawings, the specifications require coordination on the job between trades; they state which trade will have precedence in the choice of the space available; and they indicate that the mechanical drawings are, of necessity, largely diagrammatic, so that the actual job installation must be made to fit precisely into the space assigned to it on the drawing or available for it on the job.

2. *Addenda and Shop and Detail Drawings.* The architect has three other tools which are employed during the bidding and construction periods to ensure the completeness and proper interpretation of the working drawings and specifications.

The first of these is the addendum, which is a written amplification of the contract documents distributed after they have been issued to the bidders but before the bids have been received. It is the result of a careful review of the drawings and specifications by the architect and his engineers and the institution, a review which is conducted during the bidding period and which should correct any discrepancies, conflicts, errors, omissions, or misunderstandings which may have crept into these documents during their preparation. Since these addenda have been prepared and issued prior to the award of a contract, they become part of the contract documents and are just as binding on the building contractor as the basic drawings and specifications.

The second and third of these other tools are produced during the construction period. The architect, during this period, may issue explanatory "detail drawings," which will enlarge and clarify sections of his original drawings so that the parts in question may be manufactured and installed in exact accordance with the functional and aesthetic requirements.

Much the same objective is also attained by "shop drawings." The difference between a shop drawing and a "detail drawing" is that, whereas the latter is produced by the architect and permitted by the specifications, the former is required by the specifications and produced by the contractor and approved by the architect. Both are valuable tools, and both may make as important a contribution to the success of the work as do the supervision of construction and the written directives of the architect.

3. *Reproduction.* The drawings, specifications, and schedules produced by the architect, his engineers, and the building contractor must be reproduced in quantity in order to satisfy the requirements of bidding and construction.

One of the usual methods of multiple reproduction, such as printing or mimeographing, is generally used for the written specifications and schedules. The drawings, however, are too large for economical use of these methods. They are therefore drawn on "tracing" paper or cloth, which is semitransparent and which owes its name to the fact that originally architectural drawings were produced on regular drawing paper and reproduced for distribution by being manually "traced" on transparent paper, the process being repeated for each reproduction desired.

Today, however, the initial drawing is produced directly on the transparent paper. This transparent drawing is then mechanically reproduced by being "blueprinted" or "lineprinted." These terms are applied to the result of the contact of the architectural drawing with a paper chemically treated so that exposure to light will change its color. The lines of the drawing prevent the light from reaching the surface of the treated paper, so that they are exactly reproduced on its surface. The reproduction is then "fixed" to prevent further changes in color, and it is distributed for use in bidding or construction. Originally the source of light was the sun, and the chemically treated paper changed from white to a dark blue, hence the name "blueprint." The reproduction was a negative of the original since the light penetrated the transparent areas of the tracing paper, turning the white chemically treated paper blue in these areas, and leaving white the lines of black pencil or ink in the original. Today this reproduction process is often done by machines specially designed for the purpose, which reproduce not only blueprints, but line-prints, or positive reproductions, in either black or blue lines.

4. *Legal Documents and Bidding.* Normally, written specifications are accompanied by a preface or introduction which describes in detail (*a*) the "general conditions," or the legal contract terms under which the construction of the building is undertaken, and (*b*) the "instructions to bidders," or the methods which will be used to arrive at and ensure the performance of these contract terms.

Since the first part of this preface, "general conditions," is basically a legal document, standard forms are available which have had incorporated into them the past experience of actual court or arbitration proceedings in connection with construction contracts. In the United States, these standard forms of the general conditions of the contract for the construction of buildings are prepared and distributed by the American Institute of Architects and are regularly revised in order to incorporate or recognize the most up-to-date procedures. The architectural organizations of other countries have similar forms. Public authorities and governments who are responsible for directing a large amount of construction work frequently have prepared their own standard form of general conditions. Sometimes a lawyer may be engaged to draw up one for an individual project. Most frequently, however, the standard form is used, and its terms or procedures are adjusted to the local custom and law by means of a supplement. This supplement describes the modifications and additions to the standard form that may be desired or required on the particular project for which it is written.

The general conditions define the rights, duties, and responsibilities of the institution, the architect, the contractor, and his subcontractors, in the mutual undertaking and determine or direct ownership, protection, inspection, changes, claims, termination, payments, insurance, bonds, liens, and other general procedures.

The second part of the preface, "instructions to bidders," as its title implies, instructs all prospective contractors, who are planning to bid or present proposals to the institution for constructing the building, on the methods they must follow and the obligations they must assume in their submission. These instructions are often accompanied by forms which are prescribed for the contractor's use (*a*) in submitting his proposal, or tender, (*b*) in providing for any required bonds or guarantees, and (*c*) in signing an agreement with the institution.

The instructions to bidders should document for the contractor the intentions of the institution and the architect relative to the scope of the work, the bidding procedure, and the method of contract award.

The scope of the work is a term used to designate a general description of the work to be done by the contractor, the premises upon which this work is to be constructed, and the contract documents in which it is specifically defined. It should point out any difficulties the contractor might be expected to encounter during his conduct of the job because of the requirements and operations of the library or any other department of the institution. If it is planned to have him work with other contractors engaged by the institution under separate contracts or if he will operate in the same building jointly with the library, the full implications of his required cooperation and coordination should be expressed.

Bidding procedures need to be defined so that the bidder may know the proper channels to follow in order to obtain bidding documents, to request and receive interpretations and clarifications of them, and to submit his bid in proper form.

Bids may be received in several forms, the most common of which is the "lump sum." This term is used to indicate a proposal on the part of the contractor agreeing to provide all labor and materials required for completion of the project as specified and drawn for a stated sum of money. On occasion, the contractor may be requested to submit only an estimate of the construction cost and the amount of his proposed fee for conducting and directing the building operation. Sometimes, in this instance, he is expected to guarantee that the final construction cost will not exceed the total amount of his estimated cost.

The bidder is frequently required to state alternate prices which may be added to or deducted from his base price, either lump sum or estimated cost, for increasing the scope of the work or for omitting or changing some part of the specified scope or quality.

In most cases, but not all, the type of bid received determines the method of contract award. Thus a lump-sum bid usually results in a lump-sum contract, an estimated cost-plus-fee bid, in a cost-plus-fee contract, and a guaranteed-maximum estimate, in a guaranteed-maximum-cost contract. Public authorities are usually required to let all building contracts on a lump-sum basis. The advantages of this type of contract are several. The cost of construction can be budgeted at a specific amount, and all risks of actual costs greater than those estimated are assumed by the contractor. On the open, highly competitive construction market, lower bids are apt to be realized than by any other method. Of particular importance to the public authorities is the fact that such bidding eliminates the possibility of favoritism if the award is made to the lowest responsible bidder. Frequently, on private work, the bidders are limited to an invited or previously approved group of contractors whose former work has been proved satisfactory to the institution and the architect. In this case, also, the award is usually made to the lowest bidder. The institution, however, in both public and private work, retains the right to reject any and all bids, if it is in their or the public's interest legally to do so.

The lowest bid does not always provide the best building. If time of completion is a factor, if the quality of construction desired is unusually high, if the project requires an extraordinary approach to the design and methods of erection, or if the proper determination of the full scope of the work by means of drawings and specifications is difficult, the fee type of contract is frequently used.

This type of contract is usually negotiated directly with a chosen contractor of predetermined competence and ability, but the selection is sometimes the result of competitive bidding between two or more. The final choice between them can be based either on the fee requested, the amount of the estimated cost, the time required for completion, or on any combination of the three. This type of contract has every advantage except that of predetermined minimal cost. Because of the careful selection of bidders, the choice of a contractor may be made and construction begun before the drawings and specifications are fully finished. Thus months may be cut from the schedule for completion of construction. The contractor is one selected on the basis of ability rather than of minimal cost, and the institution and architect have much greater control over his procedures and his purchases. The advice, experience, and cooperation of the contractor are made available during the determination of building procedures and costs rather than afterwards. In any case, when the plans and specifications have been prepared, the bids have been received, and the contract has been let, a new member of the planning team has been chosen. The contractor enters the picture, and actual construction begins. He is essential, and he is important to the success of the project, perhaps at this stage the most important member of the team, for upon his shoulders rests the responsibility to construct what has earlier been only a concept drawn from the minds of architects, librarians, and engineers and set down in diagrams and words on paper.

The Formal Contract. After the contractor has been selected, whether through competitive bidding or invitation, a period of negotiation frequently intervenes between his selection and the signing of the formal contract.

This negotiation can take two forms: (1) a change in the proposed construction cost, and (2) a change in the proposed subcontractors.

The first, a change in cost, if a decrease, may have been made necessary by budget limitations, especially if the selected bid is in excess of the sum originally anticipated. In the much rarer instances when the cost is less than was anticipated, an increase in the work scope may be arranged.

In contracts which involve public funds, it is generally required, and in all competitive bidding it is wise, to limit any change in contract scope after receipt of bids to a small percentage of the total proposed construction cost, generally 5 per cent. Thus a proposed construction bid of $1,000,000 can be legally and properly negotiated up to $1,050,000 or down to $950,000, by changing the scope of the work after consultation with the contractor. If, however, the desired change in proposed construction cost is greater than 5 per cent, some amount of competitive rebidding is generally advisable from the point of view of the institution and is more considerate to the bidders.

This rebidding may be confined to the three or four lowest original general contract bidders, and even to certain subcontract bidders, such as those for heating and ventilating, electrical, or plumbing work, if the increase or decrease in the scope of work is to be confined to one or more of these trades.

The second form of negotiation—for a change in proposed subcontractors—may result in the employment by the successful general contractor of subcontractors who are, for one reason or another, more acceptable to the institution or the architect. In any case, a list of the principal subcontractors which the general contractor proposes to use should be reviewed and agreed upon. Sometimes a change in subcontractors may be negotiated without change in the proposed cost, but more frequently a small increase is required in order to effect such changes.

In public bidding for states and cities in the United States, the principal subcontractors may be required by law to submit "filed" bids, that is, bids the amounts of which are public knowledge, or even to submit the separate bids directly to the awarding authorities.

In private work in the United States the general contractors are sometimes required to name the principal subcontractors and their respective costs in the bid proposal, but separate bids are rarely taken on any subcontract. If closer control of the subcontractor selection is desired, the "allowance" method is usually employed.

In work requiring funds from the United States Federal government, the naming of subcontractors or the filing of their bids is usually omitted and sometimes forbidden under present construction procedures. The omission of this requirement from the bidding rules generally results in a lower total construction bid.

When the subcontractors' bids are filed, or recorded, a change from one subcontractor to another may be made by adding, or, rarely, deducting the recorded difference in bids to or from the total proposed cost. Under most public bidding laws, the contractor is not restricted in his choice of subbidders, but the institution is required to accept the lowest responsible subbidder. In private institutional work, no such restriction exists, and a discreet review of the subcontractors who will be employed on the work may be an advantageous procedure.

After these negotiations, if required, have been completed, or even during the negotiation period, general contractors may be willing to commence construction upon receipt of a "letter of intent." Such a letter, sent to the contractor by an authorized officer of the institution or by the architect, states the conditions under which it is the intent to award the contract. Work may then be commenced, pending the preparation, approval, and signing of the formal contractual documents.

The Construction Period and the Final Stages

17.1 Time Schedule

The contract may deal with the question of when the finished building will be turned over to the institution and made available for installing the movable furniture and equipment that is not included in the basic contract, in one of four ways, as follows:

1. It may make no mention of time.

2. It may state an estimated time for completion (usually based on calendar days).

3. It may state an agreed-upon time for completion.

4. It may state an agreed-upon time for completion with penalty and benefit payments if time is delayed or bettered.

If either 3 or 4 is to be used, it should be included in the bid form or the negotiations; 4 is rarely used in institutional work, since its chief application is to business which can make or lose money through early or late completion dates. While 3 is a little more forceful than 2, it is impossible to enforce if the agreement is not met, and means little more than 2. Either 2 or 3 is quite common in institutional work, but both generally represent optimistic estimates on the part of the contractor, and the inevitable and usually excusable delays sometimes postpone completion quite seriously.

It should be kept in mind that union rules may not permit the installation of movable equipment during construction, but that sometimes carrels that are attached to walls or floors and book stacks, even if called "free-standing," can become and be considered part of the build-ing, thus avoiding complications. If they are considered part of the building, they may become part of the general contract, or a separate contract can be arranged. The difference between the two procedures may be important. By making them part of the general contract, the institution can often avoid trouble because the primary responsibility for the complete installation is that of the general contractor who is building the structure as a whole. On the other hand, by placing them under a separate contract, the institution can make its own purchases, and, unless it is under governmental regulations forbidding this procedure, can select the manufacturer and weigh the quality and functional requirements against cost, rather than depend on the contractor's purchase of a specified quality. (No matter how carefully described, a quality is open to varied interpretations when a manufactured item such as book stacks is to be acquired.) This problem can sometimes be solved by specifying a single manufacturer, but the cost advantage of competition is lost. It should also be remembered that a separate contract might lead to union trouble if one or the other, that is, the general contractor or the manufacturer, is nonunion, as there are always likely to be difficulties when there are divided responsibilities and two prime contractors are working in the same building at once.

In any case, if the institution decides to enter into "separate contracts," this decision should be stated in the specifications or in the agreement with the general contractor, because coordination of two or more contracts may impose certain hardships and entail added work and cost for him and perhaps for the architect and the institution. Sometimes the advantages of both plans can be realized by carrying the equipment in the general contract documents as an "allowance." This means that the contractor is required to include in his contract bid an amount previously determined, a specified sum to be set aside for the purchase of this equipment or material desired, and the final selection of the manufacturer or supplier and the cost will remain in the control of the architect or the institution. When they have reached a final decision on this matter, the contractor assumes the contractual obligations negotiated by the institution, and his total contract amount is adjusted up or down, in accordance with the difference between the final cost of the equipment or material and the specified sum previously set aside as an allowance.

Allowances are frequently carried for such items as book stacks, hardware, elevators, special built-in equipment, and landscape planting. They are sometimes, but less frequently, used to purchase movable equipment such as furniture and drapes.

Allowances are generally not permitted in public work for municipal, state, or Federal governments, which usually require that the "lowest responsible bidder" be awarded a contract and which look on allowances as a means of avoiding the democratic method of selecting a manufacturer and regard the open-bidding procedure as a safeguard against political favoritism in the selection of a successful bidder. Separate contracts are generally permitted, however, and the Federal agencies will often accept allowances, provided that the final award is made to the lowest responsible bidder.

There may be deviations from these rules in the case of very specialized equipment for medical and scientific research, for instance.

The following factors may affect the building structure and, therefore, the completion date.

1. The start of construction may be delayed. There are a variety of possible causes.

   a. The working drawings, plans, and specifications may be delayed because the architect fails to complete his task on schedule. He may have been delayed by the institution's constantly holding up decisions on vital points, by a shortage of help, or inability to get the details from the engineers who are doing the mechanical-services planning.

   b. The time when the plans and specifications are ready may not be propitious for taking bids. An economic boom with great building activity may result in bids 10 per cent higher than if they could have been taken earlier, and perhaps a delay may result in lower bids.

   c. Plans and specifications may be ready for the taking of bids during a strike. This might mean that an increase in wages may result in higher prices, and contractors are cautious on making close bids. Frequently there is an anticipated and sometimes a previously agreed-upon wage-rate increase which affects bidding, as the bidders are well aware that the increase will come or is due to come. It does not necessarily have to be accompanied by a strike. A strike itself is no more likely to affect bidding than the anticipation of one. A strike during construction will delay completion but may not materially affect the cost, unless the contract contains some form of negotiated cost-plus agreements.

   d. Weather conditions may be unfavorable. In many areas a late spring, for instance, may delay the start of work for two or three weeks. Frozen ground, a late heavy snow, an early beginning of the rainy period, and so on, are all possible delaying factors.

2. Local labor conditions may affect the situation. The contractor is anxious to carry on the work at a pace that will enable him to make the largest possible profit. He does not want to have to import labor from outside the area at extra cost. On the other hand, the longer he has to keep his team in operation, the lower his profit tends to be.

3. Weather and other unforeseen conditions may slow down construction. Unexpected wet spells or a very severe winter may bring about delays as may other unforeseen problems during construction, such as faulty or unfortunate test borings that have failed to discover ledge rock, pockets of quicksand or peat, or other soil conditions affecting the building's foundation. If much of the material for use within the structure is brought in from a distance, there is always a possibility of delay, first at the point where it is fabricated, and second in transportation to the site.

Labor may not be available at the required time. Strikes, for instance, may interfere, or a building boom in a nearby city may attract labor away from the job. A poor foreman may be unable to get the work properly coordinated, and considerable delay in finishing the task may result, or the contractor may become engrossed in more profitable work elsewhere and not push the library.

It can be seen from the above that "there is many a slip 'twixt the cup and the lip"; but at any rate, the time schedule should be given careful consideration, and the contractor should be requested to notify the institution as promptly as possible if any delay is anticipated in the completion date so that the institution can alter its plans. This may be of very great importance if the old building is to be used for other purposes and it cannot be vacated at the expected time.

17.2 Relations between the Institution, the Architect, and the Contractor during Construction

The institution and its planning team will find, if they did not realize it in advance, that their tasks have not been completed when the building contract is signed, the time schedule set, and the construction begun. Many decisions will have to be faced as the building work proceeds. The librarian can, of course, remove himself from the picture completely, and the architect and contractor in many cases might prefer it that way, as a librarian may make a great nuisance of himself on matters that are quite outside his province.

In this connection it should be made clear that the librarian should not have direct contact with the contractor, except in response to a request through the architect, as confusion will result if the builder and his men have more than one source of information and direction. If there are two sources, conflicting directions inevitably result. The librarian should, of course, be interested and also watchful, but his dealings must all be through the architect, or, if this has been agreed upon, through the clerk of works, who is the institution's representative at the construction site.

The building contract and agreements between institution and architects may provide for a clerk of works, representing the institution, whose duties are to see that the construction matches the working drawings and specifica-

tions, to keep track of the innumerable details, and to call the contractor's and architect's attention to discrepancies. The architect, as part of his contract, must supervise construction along the same lines. The differences between the supervision provided by the architect and the clerk of works are two:

1. The clerk's supervision is continuous and the architect's periodic, generally no more than once a week, unless at critical times and on a very large enterprise.

2. The architect can interpret and direct procedures and initiate required changes in structure or design, while the clerk's duty is to see that the requirements of the contract drawings and specifications are fulfilled by the contractor and his workmen.

Too often careless workmen may seriously lower standards. Too often a contractor may hope to save money and increase his profit by skimping on the concrete mix, or finishings of all kinds, or providing slightly inferior quality material which could escape detection if not watched. It is to be hoped that a reliable and honest contractor has the assignment and can be trusted, but, particularly in government jobs where the "lowest responsible bidder" must be assigned the contract, if the bid has been figured too closely and there is danger of loss, very careful supervision must be provided. It is very difficult to prove that a bidder is irresponsible if he is able to get himself "bonded" by an insurance company; and not all insurance companies have as high standards for contractors' qualifications as might be desired. A first-class clerk of works representing the institution and the architect is, therefore, of great value. The clerk of works must, of course, be acceptable to both the institution and the architect. He can be employed by either but is not part of the usual architectural services. The working drawings and specifications can be of great help in this connection. If they are very clear and specific, it is hard to find a loophole in them. Their clarity can help also in the bidding. If the contractor's responsibilities are spelled out so well that he knows just what he is supposed to do, he can bid much closer to the actual cost than if they are indefinite and he must provide a greater margin for discrepancies.

Change Orders. Change orders present difficult problems which involve reversal of earlier decisions or take care of previous omissions on the part of the planning team, the architect, and possibly the engineers involved. Change orders may also and frequently do reinstate items or work previously omitted in the interest of economy, particularly if a more favorable bid than had been expected has been received or additional funds are made available.

The contractor can, of course, take advantage of change orders to increase his contracted-for cost unduly. The librarian's view tends to be that this increase is unwarranted, but in the contractor's defense, it should be pointed out that he would generally prefer that *no* changes be made during the progress of the work. Any change, no matter how small, may upset his schedule and his procedures to some extent and will cost him money, just because it is a change. That is why he does not allow full value for work omitted and charges more than normal rates for work added.

There are, it must be admitted, legally minded contractors who comb the specifications and drawings for omissions and discrepancies on which extra charges can be based, but in general the contractor is eager for the sake of his reputation, if nothing else, to provide a complete and acceptable job to the institution. The institution will almost always enjoy the services of a satisfactory contractor if it has a free hand in the selection of bidders.

If change orders add to the cost of the building and to the sum that must be made available, a problem arises unless there is a contingency figure in the original budget, part of which was left over after the contract was signed. There should always be a sum for contingencies in the budget both before and after the signing of the contract or contracts. This figure can vary from as much as 12½ per cent at preliminary stages of the planning to as little as 2½ per cent after the award of the contract. The usual figure is 10 per cent preliminary, 7½ per cent after quantity survey estimates, or 5 per cent after award of the contract. The economic climate at the time of planning may properly affect the percentages; in periods of inflation they may need to be made greater than at other times.

To have a good margin is always desirable because the winning bid may be higher than was expected, and also because of the possibility of the need for change orders. It is generally much cheaper and more suitable to place change orders if it is evident that they are desirable than to wait and make alterations after construction is finished. These change orders may be very simple, such as adding or subtracting a door, or putting the hardware on the other side of it, or they may be much more complicated, such as putting in a new partition or making a major variation in the electric light switch pattern, or even adding to the scope of the whole job.

One important precaution, if trouble is to be avoided, is an agreement on procedures to be followed in any changes made in the working drawings and specifications. This agreement is part of the AIA (American Institute of Architects) general conditions of the contract.

Temporary Heat. In cold climates, construction in the winter months is complicated by the need to provide temporary heat, in order to prevent the freezing of building materials that initially contain moisture, such as concrete, mortar, plaster, adhesives, and paint, to dry out the building so that moisture damage to the finished materials may be avoided, and to eliminate the danger of "freeze-ups" in the mechanical and sanitary installations.

Temporary heat may be provided in many ways. In the open, concrete is usually poured only at above freezing temperatures, and it is then protected with straw covering until it has dried out or "cured." Otherwise, this work is done under tarpaulins or similar tent coverings and kept above freezing by space heaters. Antifreeze "admixtures" are beginning to be used in the concrete mix, but at the present time many engineers object to their use because of the effect they may have on the ultimate strength and durability of the mix.

When the building's structural frame is in position, it may be completely or partially covered with a temporary skin of tarpaulins or plastic, often transparent, and the enclosed portions heated with space heaters. If the exterior walls are complete, only the window and door areas need this temporary protection in order to enclose the building.

The types of space heaters employed for temporary heat vary, depending upon whether gas, coal, oil, or electricity is used. The most commonly used types in very cold climates are charcoal braziers and oil-fired unit heaters, which are frequently equipped with electrically operated blowers.

When the heating system for the building has been installed and all window and door openings have been either permanently or temporarily closed against the weather, the contractor is frequently allowed to use the heating system for supplying his temporary heat, provided always that he allows no permanent damage to the system to result.

In institutions which are equipped with central heating plants, the steam may be either sold to the contractor or provided free of charge if the quality of his weather protection and the amount of his heating requirements can be controlled.

In any case, all construction contracts for buildings in climates susceptible to subfreezing temperatures during the construction period should contain specified requirements for temporary heat, generally entirely at the expense of the contractor, who is responsible for closing in the construction and for maintaining and providing the labor, equipment, and fuel necessary to keep the closed-in space at several degrees above freezing temperatures. When the installation of finished woodwork, flooring, or painting is in progress, the required minimum temperature should be raised.

Payments. Payments to the general contractor on account and to his subcontractors are usually made monthly and cover the cost of all labor and materials incorporated in the construction and all materials on the site at the time the application for the payment is made. This application is itemized and prepared about ten days before each monthly payment is due. It is submitted to the architect for his approval and may be required to be supported by receipts or vouchers for material, labor, or subcontractor payments.

If a clerk of the works or resident engineer is employed on the job, his approval of the contractor's application for payment is generally made a prerequisite to final approval by the architect. When the application for payment is approved, the architect issues to the institution a certificate for payment to the contractor for such amount of the application as he decides is properly due at the time. The requisition should then be honored by the institution.

Payments to the contractor may be withheld by the architect if defective work is not remedied or if the contractor fails to make proper payments to subcontractors for material and labor, or for other actions detrimental to the interests of the institution, but payment must be made once these grounds for withholding it are removed.

Payments made to the contractor by the institution do not indicate acceptance of any work or material that is not in accordance with the terms of the contract.

After final payment, the contractor binds himself to remedy any defects due to faulty materials or workmanship which appear within a period of one year after the date of occupancy by the owner or of substantial completion of the building. Before final payment, he should supply the owner with evidence and affidavits that all his obligations for material and labor entailed as a result of the contract have been paid.

In order to ensure such payments and to facilitate completion of the work if the contractor should default before it is completed, it is usually the custom for the institution to retain 10 per cent of the funds applied for by the contractor during the progress of the work. This retained percentage is insurance that the contractor will fulfill his financial obligations before it is paid. If he fails to do so, the institution may then pay these obligations directly with the retained percentage.

Frequently, on large buildings which require a large sum of money and a long construction period, this 10 per cent retainage becomes quite considerable by the time the building is well along, and the continued withholding by the institution creates a financial hardship on the contractor. For this reason, either through prior arrangement or in consideration of this hardship, the institution frequently rewards the contractor for his acceptable execution of the contract by reducing the retained percentage in proportion to the amount of work remaining to be done.

Before final payment, the architect, the institution, and the contractor should jointly prepare a check list which itemizes all the noticeable defects, deficiencies, and omissions which remain to be corrected or completed on the job before the contractual obligations can be considered to have been fulfilled.

17.3 Preparation for Occupancy, Moving In, and Shaking Down

During the time of construction, the librarian must be alert to possible changes in the working drawings, plans, and specifications, and must be prepared to step in when new decisions are required. But there are other tasks waiting to be dealt with. If the library is being constructed for a new institution, he will have the task of building up a staff to provide services in the new building and an equally difficult task of acquiring and cataloguing a book collection suitable to serve the students when the doors are opened. If the new building is intended for undergraduates and supplements an already existing general library and if a new collection must be built up from scratch or by the transfer of material from other parts of the institution or by both methods, there is much work to be done. This is not the place to describe in detail the problems involved in what is at best no mean task.

The end is not yet, as anyone who has been responsible for moving into a new building can testify. The actual labor of moving is bad enough, but first the task should be worked out in great detail in advance in order to save time and confusion while the moving is taking place. Subsidiary problems in connection with the moving should not be forgotten. Will the physical plant be ready when the move is scheduled? Will the approach walks and driveways to the building be completed? Will the equipment and the furniture arrive and will it have been installed? Will the light, the heat, and the elevators all be in operation so that the building will be habitable? What is to be done about library service during the move? Will it be continuous or will it be shut down for a few days or even a few weeks? What extra help must be employed? Will the move be made at a suitable time of year when the service load is low? Is there money and help available for preparation for moving and the shift itself? The equipment to be used in connection with the moving must be ready and available. The containers in which the books are to be packed may have to be designed and constructed, and this may take time, or they may be rented. Ways and means of removing the material from the old building and taking it to the new in the least expensive and most expeditious manner must be decided. But keep in mind that neither safety of the material nor the avoidance of wear and tear on it is a minor matter. The location of each book and each piece of equipment that is to be moved must be determined. This includes office equipment, files, pictures, the card catalogue, pamph-

let files, current periodicals, and so forth. Do not overlook the special types of materials that are not included in the main collection, such as the rare books, manuscripts, anything that goes into a vault, if one has been provided, the duplicates that have not been disposed of, the uncatalogued material and that which is in process, the unbound periodicals, and material waiting for binding. Be sure that a place is ready for each of these and that you know just where it is going.

The largest task, of course, is the decision on the location of each book in the new quarters. The more definite the decision can be the better. This means that measurements of books in each class must be made so that no unfortunate surprise comes to light during the moving and that as far as possible material has to be moved only once; if a second move is necessary, it should not be more than a few feet, so that books will not have to go on to book trucks or into boxes a second time.

The moving can be done by contract or by the library staff or by the institution's maintenance department or even by the students on a volunteer basis. See the Selective Annotated Bibliography in Appendix D under the heading "Moving," for different methods that have been used. The well-planned move that is carried out successfully can be one of the most pleasant experiences that a librarian will ever have, but an ill-planned one can be a catastrophe and is to be avoided at all costs. Whoever does the moving, each large group of material should be measured and its location decided upon. It will help if each range in the new structure can be numbered and labeled in some way so that it is easy to find, with a card attached to it, perhaps with scotch tape, showing just what is to be placed in each section and with a duplicate of that card placed with the material in the old library. Decisions will have to be made as to how full the shelves are to be, how much space is to be left in each section or each shelf, and whether the top shelves and the bottom shelves are to be used to start with or left vacant.

The method of the shifting itself must be determined. Should it be done by hand, by hand cart, by an endless chain of students or others passing the books from one to another, or by book trucks? If the last method is selected, can the trucks be pushed out of one building and into the other without difficulty? Should dolly trucks with boxes piled on them be used, or will a motor truck be required? How do you get from one floor to another in the old and in the new building? The speed of moving may depend on the number of elevators available in both buildings. If elevators are inadequate, it may help to arrange shifts so that books going to a level where an elevator will not be needed can be in the moving process at the same time as those that will require an elevator. Will a book chute or a ramp carry books from the older building to the ground floor or outside? Will it be worth while with a very large collection to install a temporary endless-belt conveyor? Two points are obvious. There must be detailed labeling. There must be a foreman in charge who enjoys coordinating and getting people to work smoothly and rapidly. A major problem is to keep everyone busy but not too busy. It may well be that one person can plan the job and do the measuring and labeling, but that a very different person should be in charge of the actual shift itself.

If the books are to be moved in boxes, should they be one- or two-man boxes, boxes where books can be placed in single or in double rows? They may be 36 in. long with a single row, or 18 in. square for double rows. They may be of heavy cardboard, or wood, or papier-mâché. They should be deep enough so that for all the books that are less than 11¼ in. high, the boxes can be stacked one on top of another. If books are placed loose on ordinary library book trucks, there is always danger of their falling off. Boxes are safer if there are any hazards in connection with the move. Boxes can be stored on book trucks if the book trucks are of the right dimensions, but dolly trucks that are up to 2 ft wide and a little over 3 ft long may be more suitable. They should be narrow enough so that they can go down a stack aisle and long enough to hold a 36-in. box or two 18-in. boxes. If proper arrangements are made, the boxes can be placed on the dolly, filled from the shelves, and the individual books not handled again until they are taken out of the boxes at the other end. The boxes can be three deep on the dolly at the time it is moved, the second and top ones being placed above the others before they are filled. If this is done, the dolly should have ends that rise far enough so that the boxes cannot fall off, and the ends can be used for pushing and pulling.

If the books are to be shifted with dolly trucks

transported in motor trucks, a satisfactory loading dock should, of course, be available as it is impossible to push a loaded dolly truck from the ground up into a motor truck. This is perhaps enough to indicate the problems, and a study of the literature of the subject may indicate the best solution for your particular library.

Do not forget or ignore the fact that last-minute delays in completing the construction, resulting from strikes or miscalculations on the part of the contractor, may mean that the building is not ready at the expected time. In most cases if the move can be scheduled for as early as possible in the long summer vacation, the worst risks can be avoided. Even this may not give a sufficient margin. The librarian in one large university, planning to move into its new building during the Christmas holidays, realized in time that the building would not be ready and relaxed the pressure on the contractor, with the result that the building was barely completed in time to move in at the end of the next summer. Some librarians have absolutely refused to attempt to move during the regular academic year, although Cornell managed successfully to complete its shift in midwinter just in time for the second semester, in spite of the upstate New York severe weather. This was made possible by the tunnel which connected the old with the new building. But comparatively few libraries enjoy such an advantage. The major part of the move of the 75,000 volumes from Widener to the Lamont Undergraduate Library took place in four hours on a Sunday morning during the Christmas holidays with the aid of forty staff members who volunteered to help, working with four elevators in the old building, with book trucks going through the tunnel connecting the two buildings to two elevators in the new one. This move, which brought five loaded book trucks every three minutes to Lamont, was a good example of careful planning worked out in the greatest detail by the staff members responsible.

Unexpected delays that make postponement of moving necessary often come from delays in arrival of equipment, rather than from slowness of construction. Here the trouble may stem from the supplier, but in too many cases it results from delay on the part of the institution in selecting and ordering the equipment. Too many librarians, and even too many business managers, fail to realize that an order of anything but stock furniture takes time to design, to produce, and to ship, and in the case of book stacks, to install. Even stock furniture is often out of stock, particularly if ordered in large quantities, and will have to be fabricated after it is ordered. It is of the utmost importance to order furniture in time.

Here is a list of questions on which decisions may be required in connection with moving into a new library building.

Is the move to be made by hand, endless chain of students or others, endless-belt conveyors, book truck, "dolly" truck, handcart, or by motor truck, or in some other way, or by a combination of two or more of these?

Can the books be removed from the old building by a chute?

Should a hole be cut in the wall of the old building to get the books out?

Will the books be placed in boxes before loading on a dolly truck or motor truck so as to avoid unnecessary handling of individual books?

Are loading docks available or needed at one or both ends of the move?

Will the work be done by the library staff, by the building-maintenance department, or by outsiders employed for the purpose; on an hourly basis, or by a lump-sum contract?

Are the books to be cleaned and fumigated at the time of moving before going into the new building?

Have they been measured accurately so that it is known just how they will fit into the new structure, and have all the details of their placement been worked out?

What can be done to keep them from being disarranged in the course of moving?

Is there a problem in connection with bad weather during the moving and how can it be dealt with?

What about the timing of the start of the moving, and how long will it take?

What about the wages of the movers and the cost of mix-ups in the books, or damage to them through careless handling? Where will the money come from?

Are you sure that the importance of team work and coordination in connection with the moving has been kept in mind and planned for adequately?

Shaking Down. A sometimes neglected point should not be forgotten. Before the day of opening arrives, it is well to give the staff a full week to settle down in the new surroundings; to read the shelves and make sure the books are in order; to become acquainted with the location of materials and the traffic patterns, so as to make it easy to direct the students and faculty. It will help to have floor plans installed in prominent places throughout the building, always so placed and lettered that one does not have to stand on his head or turn his head at an angle of 90° to read them or to orient himself. If these plans can indicate not only service desks, reading areas, and toilet facilities, but the location of each main classification of books, so much the better. The plans can and often are prepared especially for this purpose by the architect as an *extra* service.

It is suggested that on the opening day and during the weeks immediately ahead, if a public-service staff somewhat larger than will be required later can be on duty, a favorable impression will be made which will carry over almost indefinitely. If the ventilation can be properly adjusted, criticisms that may continue, whether or not justified later, can be avoided. If the students can be given the impression from the start that the new building is primarily for them, rather than for the library staff, half the battle will be won almost before it is started; the old saying, "Well begun is half done," is very pertinent.

Sometimes the librarian has failed to realize in the wild rush of planning the building, carrying on during the moving process, and getting started with the new services, that the demands made on the library in the past may very well be doubled or even tripled with the new more comfortable and attractive quarters. The results in terms of the number of reference questions and size of book circulation (involving charging, discharging, and reshelving) may be frightening and monumental in character. In spite of the best of planning which makes possible more effective work than in the past, the staff as a whole may be swamped and almost buried in the additional routine work. It is to be hoped that this will have been anticipated by the librarian and, of equal importance, by the administration of the institution, and that a staff adequate for the task it faces will have been provided. To spoil the impact of a fine new library on the whole program of the institution because of a staff which is inadequate in size or quality or both would be exceedingly unfortunate.

17.4 Dedication and Other Ceremonies

It is customary to have a ceremony of some kind at the beginning of or during construction. This may be completely informal or may be accompanied by speeches. It may come when the excavation starts. There may be a cornerstone laying, with the insertion in a cornerstone of documents appropriate to the occasion and dealing with the institution's history, the donor or other matters; the stone may be placed with the aid of a senior representative of the institution or the donor himself.

Long before the new building is completed, moved into, and opened to the public, it is to be hoped that the institution and the librarian will have been making plans for a dedication or other ceremony to celebrate the completion of the new building. This can take place before the occupancy, as happened at the National Library of Medicine, but it is generally preferable to schedule it after the library is in full operation,

so that those interested can observe the results which have stemmed from the new building. Each institution must decide for itself what it wants to do at this ceremony or dedication and what it hopes to accomplish by doing it.

Often a donor should be honored, and care should be taken to pay tribute to him fittingly. If the building is as good as it should be, the architect should have his day in court. The librarian should receive any credit that is his due, as should those with whom he worked during the planning.

Without being dogmatic in this connection, the author might suggest that the dedication itself should be reasonably brief, that honor be bestowed on those deserving it, and that an address be made by someone who has something to say on a topic related to the occasion and knows how to say it effectively. The place of the library in the institution's educational program and what can be expected of the new building and the service that it provides is a suitable topic.

ACKNOWLEDGMENTS

Architect:
ROWLEY, PAYER, HUFFMAN & LEITHOLD, INC.

Library Design Consultant:
KEYES D. METCALF

Sculptor:
WILLIAM M. McVEY

Interior Design:
ERNST PAYER

Furnishings Coordinator:
JORDAN A. TRUTHAN

General Contractor:
ALBERT M. HIGLEY

75th Anniversary Year

JC

Expanding the Circle of Knowledge
1886-1961

Dedication
GRASSELLI LIBRARY
JOHN CARROLL UNIVERSITY
December 1, 1961

2:00 P.M.   ACADEMIC PROCESSION

NATIONAL ANTHEM

INVOCATION . . . . Most Reverend John F. Whealon
Auxiliary Bishop of Cleveland

PRESENTATION OF PROCLAMATION . . . . Anthony J. Celebrezze
Mayor, City of Cleveland

REMARKS . . . . The Very Reverend Hugh E. Dunn, S.J.
President, John Carroll University

ADDRESS . . . . The Very Reverend Paul C. Reinert, S.J.
President, St. Louis University

MUSIC . . . . John Carroll Glee Club
Jack T. Hearns, Director

CONFERRING OF DEGREES . . Reverend William C. Millor, S.J.
Executive Dean, John Carroll University

BENEDICTION . . . . . Right Rev. Monsignor Lawrence P. Cahill
President, St. John College

PROCESSIONAL (Organ Music)

3:00 P.M.   INSPECTION OF GRASSELLI LIBRARY

GRASSELLI LIBRARY OPEN HOUSE
3:00 - 5:00 P.M. — ON
FRI., DEC. 1 — DEDICATION GUESTS
SAT., DEC. 2 — NEIGHBORHOOD DAY
SUN., DEC. 3 — ALUMNI AND PARENTS DAY

FIG. 17.1 John Carroll University, Grasselli Library dedication program.

Conference Program

"New Directions for the University Library"

Tuesday, October 9

9:00 a.m.   CONFERENCE REGISTRATION: Olin Library
Lobby
Tours of the Library Buildings

* Coffee served in Olin Library Lounges, 9:30 a.m. to 11 a.m.

11:00 a.m.   OPENING SESSION: Olin Library Lounges

Presiding: SANFORD S. ATWOOD, Provost
Cornell University

"The Cornell Library System"
S. A. McCARTHY, Director of Libraries
Cornell University

"The Central Library Buildings"
CHARLES H. WARNER, JR., Architect
Warner, Burns, Toan & Lunde

12:30 p.m.   LUNCHEON: Memorial Room, Willard Straight
Hall

Presiding: J. L. ZWINGLE, Vice President
Cornell University

Remarks: DEANE W. MALOTT, President
Cornell University

2:30 p.m.   SECOND SESSION: Alice Statler Auditorium

Presiding: G. F. SHEPHERD, JR.
Assistant Director of Libraries
Cornell University

Wednesday, October 10

9:30 a.m.   THIRD SESSION: Alice Statler Auditorium

"THE RESEARCH LIBRARY AND
INTERNATIONAL AFFAIRS"

"Shrunken Globe, Swollen Curriculum"
STEVEN MULLER, Professor of
Government and Director, Center for
International Studies, Cornell University

"The Research Library and International
Affairs Programs"
WILLIAM S. DIX, Librarian
Princeton University

"International Values in American
Librarianship"
RAYNARD C. SWANK, Dean, School of
Librarianship, University of California,
Berkeley

"THE LIBRARY AND HIGHER EDUCATION"

"The True University of These Days is a
Collection of Books"
W. R. KEAST, Dean, College of Arts
and Sciences, Cornell University

"The Scholar's Caution and the Scholar's
Courage"
LIONEL TRILLING, Professor of English
Columbia University

"Libraries, Students and Faculty"
RALPH E. ELLSWORTH, Director of
Libraries, University of Colorado

4:00–5:00 p.m.   TOURS OF LIBRARY BUILDINGS

5:15 p.m.   COCKTAILS: Foyer of Alice Statler Auditorium

6:00 p.m.   DINNER: Statler Ballroom

Presiding: PRESIDENT MALOTT

"Yes, But What Does a Curator Do?"
GEORGE H. HEALEY, Professor of
English and Curator of Rare Books
Cornell University

8:15 p.m.   BAILEY HALL
Beethoven Concert in honor of the Dedication
of the Libraries

The Philadelphia Orchestra and the Cornell
Glee Club and Chorus
EUGENE ORMANDY, Conducting

Dedication Program

Wednesday, October 10

12:30 p.m.   DEDICATION LUNCHEON: Statler Ballroom
Honoring the Donors to the Cornell University
Central Libraries

Presiding: DEANE W. MALOTT, President
Cornell University

Cornell Glee Club
THOMAS A. SOKOL, Director

2:00 p.m.   DEDICATION PROGRAM: Alice Statler
Auditorium

Presiding: DEANE W. MALOTT, President
Cornell University

"Let the Past and Future Fire Thy Brain"
SIR FRANK FRANCIS, Director
and Principal Librarian
British Museum

Dedicatory Remarks
ARTHUR H. DEAN, Chairman
Cornell Board of Trustees;
U. S. Ambassador, Geneva
Disarmament Conference;
Member, U. S. Delegation
to the United Nations
General Assembly

3:30–5:00 p.m.   RECEPTION BY THE LIBRARY STAFF:
Gallery, John M. Olin Library

FIG. 17.2   Program of the conference and dedication of the John M. Olin and the Uris Libraries, Cornell University.

It may be worth while to emphasize the different problems that must be solved if the building is to fulfill expectations. A discussion of the library's program and needs might be desirable. This may be a golden opportunity to promote interest in the library and to stimulate gifts in money and in kind. Remember that with the improved facilities now available, the demands made upon the library for service and materials will take a leap forward, and to have to reduce hours of service, as has been known to happen for financial reasons, would be a serious blow to the prestige of the library and the sponsoring institution. In too many instances the use of funds to construct the library has left the institution unable to provide full services for the long hours desired by the students or to staff the reference desk in the evening, or even to pay for light and heat during certain hours. If problems of this kind have arisen or are likely to arise, here is a chance to publicize the needs and perhaps to bring in the funds required.

This may be a time to conduct a symposium on some problem of interest to libraries all over the country and to present a group of competent speakers to take part in it. This may be profitable to the institution and its staff and to the library world in general.

The occasion is generally accompanied by a luncheon, tea, or perhaps a banquet to which the distinguished guests are invited.

Finally, it is to be hoped that guided tours of the building will be made available to those interested, the friends whose interest and support is essential, as well as the students and faculty who may well need help of this kind before they can take full advantage of the improved physical resources.

Successful dedications require, in addition to a good program, much additional planning. Who is to be invited? Is there, for instance, a problem in connection with the housing and transportation of out-of-town guests? Four typical programs are appended, not to be copied but to stimulate imagination for your particular situation.[1] (See Figs. 17.1 to 17.4.)

---

[1] Note that the architect is, in each case, recognized in some way on the program.

PROGRAM

Thursday, December 14, 1961

3 p.m.

Presiding . . . . DR. WORTH B. DANIELS
Chairman, Board of Regents

INVOCATION . . . . . . THE REVEREND WILLIAM R. ANDREW
Chaplain, Clinical Center
National Institutes of Health

ADDRESS . . . . . . THE HONORABLE ABRAHAM RIBICOFF
Secretary of Health, Education, and Welfare

DEDICATION ADDRESS . . . . THE HONORABLE LISTER HILL
United States Senator, Alabama

PRESENTATION . . . . . HIS EXCELLENCY ALEXIS S. LIATIS
Ambassador of the Royal Greek Government

BENEDICTION . . . . . MAJOR GENERAL FRANK A. TOBEY
Chief of Chaplains, U.S. Army

Music by the United States Army Band
Commanded by Lieutenant Colonel Hugh Curry

ARCHITECTS—R. B. O'CONNOR & W. H. KILHAM, JR. New York City
BUILDER—ARTHUR VENNFRI COMPANY Westfield, New Jersey

PROGRAM

Friday, December 15, 1961

10 a.m.

Presiding . . . . DR. FRANK B. ROGERS
Director, National Library of Medicine

THE MILITARY TRADITION OF THE NATIONAL LIBRARY OF MEDICINE
Major General Joseph H. McNinch
Chief Surgeon, U.S. Army, Europe

MEDICAL LIBRARIANSHIP IN THE UNITED STATES
Miss Gertrude L. Annan
President, Medical Library Association

THE BUILDING ARTS IN THE SERVICE OF LIBRARIANSHIP
Dr. Carl W. Condit, *Professor of Humanities and English*
Northwestern University

HISTORY, SCIENCE, AND LIBRARIANSHIP
Dr. Chauncey D. Leake, *President*
American Association for the History of Medicine

PHYSICIANS AND BOOKS
Dr. William B. Bean
Professor of Medicine, University of Iowa

THREE WHO MADE THE LIBRARY
J. S. BILLINGS
ROBERT FLETCHER

F. H. GARRISON

Dr. Frank B. Rogers
Dr. Estelle Brodman
Librarian, Washington University
School of Medicine
Dr. Dorothy M. Schullian
Curator of History of Science Collections,
Cornell University

FIG. 17.3 Dedication ceremonies, National Library of Medicine.

MUSICAL SELECTIONS . . . . BRASS ENSEMBLE
Clark Mitze
Director

INTRODUCTORY REMARKS . . . . . . THOMAS H. ELIOT
Chancellor
Washington University

PRESENTATION OF THE BUILDING . . JOSEPH D. MURPHY
Architect
Murphy & Mackey, Inc.

ACCEPTANCE . . . . ETHAN A. H. SHEPLEY
Chairman, Board of Directors
Washington University

MUSICAL SELECTION . . . . BRASS ENSEMBLE
Clark Mitze
Director

REMARKS . . . . JOHN M. OLIN
Chairman, Executive Committee
Olin Mathieson Chemical Corporation

ADDRESS. . . "The Judging Mind" . . JOHN W. GARDNER
President
The Carnegie Corporation of New York

A Reception and Open House in the Library will follow the ceremonies

FIG. 17.4   Dedication of the John M. Olin Library, Washington University.

17.5   New Rules and Regulations Required by New Facilities

A new library building, as has already been noted, brings problems in its train because of the increased amount of use and the need for a larger staff to provide the service required. Other indirect results are new types of service and new regulations called for by that service, or by changed physical conditions.

New photographic services, audiovisual work of various kinds, checking at exits, book-return slots, arrangements for the use of typewriters, a divisional plan for reading, service areas with new records of various kinds and new staff, and overnight reading rooms are samples of new services.

Plans for these must often be made at just the time the librarian is absorbed with the final details of the building program, the selection of furniture, and the move into the new structure.

Embarrassing moments may be avoided if the librarian keeps these seemingly obvious things in mind and, at least in the case of a large library, assigns to different department heads or other suitable persons the making of plans and the drafting of the required documents. The head of the circulation department may well draft rules in connection with the overnight reading rooms or those operating after the rest of the building is closed. The librarian's secretary might suggest arrangements in connection with typewriter use. If the library is to furnish typewriters, perhaps in the rare-book room where they are to be used in the reading area and must be of the silent variety, one problem presents itself. If the readers are to bring in their own, is there a place to check them in or a form to be filled out which must be presented when they are removed from the building to be sure that an unauthorized person does not take them? Are there to be lockers in which they are to be deposited when not in use, which will have to be furnished by the library, and is a deposit or charge for the locker key or a combination lock to be made? If there is a deposit, is it to be returned when the key is returned? These are simply examples of things that might have to be dealt with.

17.6   High Spots in Library Building Planning

There are many, not just a limited number of high spots in a librarian's life while a new library is in prospect. A few of them are listed below:

Approval by the administration to begin planning

Completion of arrangements for a planning team, sometimes including a consultant or consultants

Completion of the building program

Selection of the architect

Selection of the site

Approval of the schematic or diagrammatic drawings

Approval of the preliminary plans

Authorization for working drawings

Completion of the working drawings and specifications

Calling for bids

Opening of bids

Signing of the construction contract

Preparation of a timetable for construction

Turning over the first spadeful of ground in connection with the building

Laying of the cornerstone and the decision on what to put into it

Agreements in connection with selection of furniture and equipment

Delays due to strikes, labor shortage, or non-availability of essential materials

New rules and regulations required by the new building facilities

Planning for the move

Moving in

The shakedown period

Dedication and celebration ceremonies

It is well to remember that most of these activities involve details that should be carefully planned in advance.

appendix A

Program Examples

No two libraries exactly duplicate each other. No two library building programs should be alike. No one should be content to copy another library program. It is, therefore, with hesitation that program examples, even in abbreviated or outline form, are included here. They are presented in the hope that they will stimulate thought and imagination but will not result in imitation. They should be used primarily to call attention to points that might be considered for inclusion in a particular program.

An outline for a complete program is a suitable starting point. *College and Research Libraries* (21:267–268, July, 1960) summarizes one for Colorado College prepared by Dr. Ellsworth Mason, the librarian, and Dr. Ralph Ellsworth, the library building consultant, under three main headings:

1. The nature of the college
2. General description of the library
3. Specifications of the library area divided into five headings: (*a*) introduction to the library, (*b*) technical processes and administration, (*c*) books and readers, (*d*) miscellaneous, and (*e*) summary of space requirements

The program for the new Tufts University Library, Medford, Massachusetts, prepared by the librarian, Joseph Komidar, is recorded here in abbreviated form.

Foreword by the President Explaining the Educational Philosophy of the University and the Purpose of the Library.

   I. Librarian's Statement
  II. General Objectives and Requirements

 III. Pattern of Library Service
 IV. Outline of Space Needs
  V. Size and Space Needs of the Library Collections
 VI. Accommodations for Readers and Description of Spaces
     A. Vestibules and Entrance Lobbies
     B. Exits and Supervision
     C. Main Desk
     D. Public Catalogue
     E. Reference Collection
     F. Bibliography Collection
     G. Periodical Collection
     H. Reserve Book Room
     I. Documents Collection
     J. Map Collection
     K. General and Special Collections
     L. Crane Reading Room
     M. Exhibits
     N. Browsing Room
     O. Group Study Rooms
     P. Typing Rooms
     Q. Audio-Visual Area
     R. Microtext Reading Area
     S. Curriculum Laboratory
     T. Faculty Studies
     U. Facilities for Smoking
     V. Toilet Facilities
     W. Coat Rooms
     X. Table Sizes
     Y. Chairs
VII. Staff Accommodations
     A. Administration and Department Heads
     B. Book Selection and Processing
        1. Acquisitions
        2. Cataloguing
        3. Mechanical Preparations
        4. Bindery Preparations
     C. Supply Closet

D. Receiving and Shipping Room
E. Storage Room for Equipment
F. Library Staff Room
G. Facilities for Janitor and Maids
VIII. Space Relationships and Traffic Flow
    A. Readers
        1. Reading and Borrowing
        2. Reference
    B. Service Staff
IX. Architectural Problem
    A. Site Planning Conditions
    B. Conditions for the Building Design
        1. Space Requirements
            a. General Distribution by Major Space Categories
                (1) Space for Reading Material
                (2) Seating in Library for Readers
                (3) Work Space for Staff
                (4) Architectural Space
            b. Detailed Allocation of Areas in Library
                (1) Reference Material
                (2) Periodical Indexes
                (3) Bibliographies
                (4) Crane Collection
                (5) Browsing Area
                (6) Reserve Room
                (7) Current Periodicals
                (8) General Collections
                (9) Documents
                (10) Special Collections
                (11) Maps
                (12) Microtext Area
                (13) Audio-Visual Area
                (14) Typing Rooms
                (15) Group Study Rooms
                (16) Extra Seat Allowance throughout Public Spaces
                (17) Main Desk
                (18) Public Catalog
                (19) Preparations Room
                (20) Administration Office
                (21) Other Staff Accommodations
                (22) Seminar Spaces
                (23) Curriculum Laboratory Alcove
                (24) Local Government Collection
                (25) Faculty Studies
                (26) Smoking Area
                (27) Architectural Space
        2. Construction Requirements
        3. Story Heights and Column Spacing
        4. Mechanical Installations
        5. Expansion

Miss Susan A. Schultz, librarian of the Asbury Theological Seminary in Wilmore, Kentucky, prepared a twelve-page program for a library building, and then ingeniously placed the requirements for the five basic physical elements in tabular outline form on one sheet, which is shown as Fig. A.1.

The program for the Francis A. Countway Library of Medicine of the Harvard Medical School and the Boston Medical Library, prepared by Ralph Esterquest, the librarian, is fortunately available on request to Mr. Esterquest at the Countway Library in Boston.

Program Divisions

A library program can properly be divided into five parts as follows:

1. Information about the institution and its objectives

2. The library and a description of its requirements

3. Information about special building areas

4. Basic needs and spatial requirements

5. Spatial relationships

The above arrangement will be followed here. The examples used show some overlapping between the different groups.

1. *Information about an Institution and Its Objectives.* Quotations abbreviated from the program prepared for the University of California at Santa Cruz, a new campus of the University of California. (This is a program for the first stage of what in due course is expected to become a very large library. It is planned to be adequate for seven years after its completion in 1966 or 1967.) The author is Donald T. Clark.

THE LIBRARY AND THE UNIVERSITY IT WILL SERVE

The following features will have a direct bearing on shaping the library organization and building.

1. During this period the student body will be almost exclusively made up of undergraduates, and the first unit should be designed primarily for undergraduate use.

2. During the initial stages there will be emphasis on liberal arts education, with most students majoring in arts and sciences. What laboratories are to the natural and physical sciences, libraries are to the liberal arts.

3. Within the liberal arts the heaviest emphasis will be upon the social sciences and the humanities.

4. A very high percentage of students will be living on campus. This will mean that more than the average number of study spaces should be provided.

5. Much will be done to foster an exciting intellectual climate and with it there will be an emphasis upon independent study.

ASBURY SEMINARY LIBRARY PROGRAM

BASIC ELEMENT	SPACE NO.	FUNCTION	LOCATION–RELATIONSHIP	SPACE QUANTITIES (PRESENT / 15 YRS / 30 YRS)	EQUIPMENT–FURNITURE	REMARKS–QUESTIONS	FLOOR PREFERENCE (GND / MAIN / UPPER)	SPACE REQUIREMENTS
I — READER SERVICE	I‑1	READING & STUDY	CLOSE TO STACKS–SMALL AREAS NATURAL LIGHT	170–200 READERS	TABLES, DESKS, CHAIRS	MAKE LATITUDE SUN STUDY AND CLIMATE ANALYSIS ARE SMALL TABLES	X? / X /	200 X 35 □'/PERSON = 6,000 X 7,000 □' =
	I‑2	RESERVE BOOK	CIRC. DESK MAYBE CLOSED RESERVE–READER	INCLUDED IN ABOVE	USE READING ROOM ABOVE	WHAT IS CLOSED RESERVE ?	/ X / X	15 TO 20 35 □'/PERSON
	I‑3	RESEARCH	OFF STACK AREA WHERE	AS MANY AS POSSIBLE	CARRELS, CHAIRS	WHAT PERCENT OF READERS	/ X /	20 x 35 = 700 = 2 BAYS
	I‑4	BROWSING	NEAR PERIODICALS–VIEW BOOKS CHAIRS THRU STACKS	20±	LOUNGE CHAIRS, STAND‑UP DESKS, TABLES, END TABLES ETC.		X / X /	
	I‑5	STUDY HALL	NEAR ENTRY–OUTSIDE DESK CONTROL AREA NEAR RETURN SLOT	20–30	TABLES, CHAIRS, DESKS, TABLES	WHAT SIZE	/ / X	30 x 35 = 1050 = 2–3 BAYS
II — HOUSING MATERIALS	II‑1	GENERAL BOOKS	FREE STANDING STACKS ADJACENT GENERAL READING AREA	42,000 / 91,000 / 136,000	COMPONENTS	5 VOLS/LIN. FT	/ X /	
	II‑2	REFERENCE BOOKS	WALL AND COUNTER SHELVING NEAR STAFF WORK AREA	4,000 / 6,000 / 8,000	364 / 544	COUNTER HT SHELVES USED AS RM. DIVIDERS, MAPS, ATLAS ETC.	X / X /	
	II‑3	BIBLIOGRAPHY	REF SEAT SERVICE CENTER	285 / 425 / 600	+800 FT 1200 FT 1600 FT. SPECIAL SHELVING FOR L.C. CATALOG ETC.	9–10"	/ X /	
	II‑4	PERIODICALS BND	SHELVES LIKE REF BOOKS & ADJ OR FREE STANDING STACKS 9" DEEP IN GENERAL	1,500 / 3,000 / 5,000	+300 FT 600 FT 1000 FT 50%		/ X /	
	II‑5	UNBOUND & TIED NON‑CURRENT	ROOM LOCKABLE BUT ACCESSIBLE FROM CIRCULATION DESK	380 TITLES / 500 TITLES	1500 L.F 3000 L.F 5,800 L.F		/ X /	
	II‑6	CURRENT	IN SMALL ROOM/AREA NEAR CIRCULATION DESK		SPECIAL SHELVING FOR CURRENT VOLUMES		X / X /	
	II‑7	NEWSPAPERS CURRENT–NON‑CURRENT			NEWSPAPER STAND –	SPECIAL SHELVING W/SLANTED TOP	X / X /	
	II‑8	PAMPHLETS	IN SERVICE AREA		2 LEGAL ½‑8 LEGAL SPECIAL CASES		/ X /	
	II‑9	MICRO‑PRINTS FILMS & CARDS	STORE NEAR SERVICE AREA	600 FILMS / 2000 PTS	½ LEGAL ½ LEGAL SPECIAL CABINETS		/ X /	
	II‑10	AUDIO VISUAL	STORE IN SERVICE AREA	TAPES FOR RECORDER			/ X /	
	II‑11	PICTURES‑MOUNTED	STORE IN SERVICE NEAR PAM. FILE		2 or 3 JUMBO 2 or 3 FILE		X / /	
	II‑12	RELIGIOUS EDUCATION CURRICULUM LAB	SECOND FLOOR		DESK, TABLES, CHAIRS, FILES		/ / X	
III — SERVICE AREA	III‑1	CIRCULATION	NEAR ENTRANCE–VIEW OF STAFF WORK AREA AND READING		CIRCULATION DESK–SWIVEL CHAIRS 2–3 CHAIRS	ARRANGED SO NORMAL NOISE DOES NOT DISTURB READERS – ELEC PLUGS — NEAR CARD CAT. & BIBLIO. RM.	/ X /	
	III‑2	BOOK LIFT	NEAR CIRCULATION DESK–ADJACENT TO RECORDING ROOM	180 TRAYS / 360 TRAYS				
	III‑3	WORK AREA	FOR CIRCULATION AND WORKS		TYPING DESK – REFERENCE DESK – EXEC. CABINET‑STANDING HEIGHT TABLES		/ X /	
	III‑4	CARD CATALOGUE	ACCESS TO PUBLIC & STAFF				/ X /	
	III‑5	EXHIBIT & DISPLAY	MAIN ENTRANCE AND ELSEWHERE		BUILT‑IN AND MOVABLE		/ / X	
	III‑6	BULLETIN BOARDS	MAIN ENTRANCE STAFF AREA				/ X /	
	III‑7	EXIT CONTROL				PLANNED SO CHECKER COULD CONTROL	/ X /	
IV — STAFF WORK AREA / ADMINISTRATION	IV‑1	LIBRARIAN	QUITE ACCESSIBLE TO PUBLIC		EXECUTIVE DESK, SWIVEL CHAIR, 2–3 POSTURE CHAIRS, CABINET, BOOK CASES	EXEC. DESK, SWIVEL CHAIR, BOOK SHELVES AND 2 FILE CASES	/ X /	
	IV‑2	SECRETARY	& STAFF THRU SECRETARY, SUITE FOR 3 PERSONS WITH CONN. OFFICE SERVING LIBRARIAN AND ASSISTANT LIBRARIAN		TYPEWRITER DESK, SWIVEL CHAIR, 4 FILE CASES, TABLE, PIGEON HOLE FOR NOTICES		/ X /	
		ASSIST. LIBRARIAN					X / /	
	IV‑3	CONFERENCE ROOM TABLE & 6 CHAIRS	ADJOINING LIBRARIANS OFFICE – ALSO FOR PREVIEWING SLIDES, FILM ETC.				/ X /	
	IV‑4	ACQUISITIONS PUBLIC SERVICE	EASY ACCESS TO BIBLIOGRAPHY ROOM CAT DEPT. AND CIRC. AREA				X / /	
		PROCESSING LIB MAT CATALOGUER	SPACE BEHIND CIRC. DESK	OFFICE, SEMI‑PRIVATE	WORK TABLE SHELVES EXECUTIVE DESK, SWIVEL CHAIR, BOOK SHELVES, TRUCK		/ X /	
	IV‑3	RECEIVE & SHIPPING	GROUND FLOOR W/LOAD DOCK		TYPICAL DESK, CHAIR, BOOKSHELVES,		/ X /	
		LIBRARY ASSISTANT TYPIST	NEXT TO CATALOGUER TYPIST		WORK TABLE FOR PASTING, SINK,		/ X /	
		LIBRARY ASSISTANT BOOK PREPARATION	NEAR TO CATALOGUER "MESSY" WORK LOCATE OUT OF SITE		BOOK SHELVES, MENDING COUNTER		/ X /	
	IV‑5	PHOTO COPYING	ACCESS TO SECRETARIES AND CIRCULATION STAFF		THERMO‑FAX MACHINERY, TABLE, STOR. PLACE FOR SUPPLIES		/ X /	
V — SPECIAL SERVICES	V‑1	ARCHIVES	STORE AT'S HISTORICAL RECORDS		SHELVING, MAY BE BEHIND		/ X /	
	V‑2	AUDIO‑VISUAL	LANGUAGE STUDY–PREACHING–	15 TO 20 PERSONS	CONSOLE, BOOTHS, STAGING, TABLES		/ X / X	
	V‑3	BUILDING OPERATION AND MAINTENANCE	JANITOR'S OFFICE		JANITOR'S CLOSETS		/ X /	
	V‑4	COAT ROOM OR RACKS					/ X /	
	V‑5	CONFERENCE ROOMS	STUDENT GROUP STUDY CONFERENCES	REMOTE LOCATION 2 ROOMS SEATING 6	TABLES AND CHAIRS		/ X / X	
	V‑6	FACULTY STUDIES	RESEARCH	REMOTE LIBRARY CLOSED			/ / X	
	V‑7	HERITAGE ROOM	NEAR MAIN ENTRANCE GROUND FLOOR	EXHIBIT MOMENTS OF HISTORY			/ X /	
	V‑8	LIBRARY LECTURES	FACULTY FLOOR	ACCESS WITH LIBRARY			/ / X	
	V‑9	MUSIC LISTENING	FOR MUSIC CLASSES	CLOSED A.V. LEARNING CENTER	IND. LIST. IN A.V. CENTER		/ X /	
	V‑10	REST ROOMS					/ / X	
	V‑11	STAFF LOUNGE AND WOMENS REST ROOM	STAFF MEETINGS ACCESS FROM LECTURE ROOM	TO SEAT 12–15	LOUNGE FURNITURE		/ X /	
	V‑12	STORAGE	GIFT BOOKS RECEIVE‑SHIP &		WORK TABLE, BOOK SHELVE, LOCKERS FOR STORE, TYPEWRITER, TABLES, DESKS, CHAIRS		/ X /	
	V‑13	TYPING ROOM	REMOTE				/ X /	

FIG. A.1   Asbury Seminary Library program.

6. New methods of instruction, study, and communication will be encouraged, and the latest developments in communication and programmed learning will have a prominent part in teaching.

7. The library will be a service agency for many non-book types of material—maps, manuscripts, microfilm, film strips, tape recordings, pictures, and so forth, and many mechanical devices will be used to further study activities. Flexibility should be present to provide for inevitable changes that will come with improvements in library technology.

8. In this period the dominant academic unit will be the residential college in which will be combined many educational and curricular student and faculty activities. Each college will have libraries and reading rooms with collections of some ten thousand volumes, but the technical processing of books for the residential college libraries will be done within the university library. Since certain typical study hall activities will be provided by the colleges, more attention can be given to individual study stations in the university library.

9. Santa Cruz is part of the University of California, which means that the resources of other campuses will be available through interlibrary loans and travel. The library will emphasize the collection of bibliographical material, so as to make known the holdings of other institutions. The building should be so designed as to take advantage of newer developments for doing this. We do not know what they are, but we can probably count on greater use of machines.

10. The demands for a new emerging university will differ considerably from those of an older, well-established campus. Space factors derived from the experience of older institutions should not be blindly applied but should be used with recognition of the rapid growth potential. For example, because of the desired rapid buildup in the collection of books, a larger than normal acquisition staff will be needed.

11. The nature of the university will be changing from year to year, from a beginning as a liberal arts college to a full-grown university. Flexibility in building design and in equipment is an essential. There should be a minimum of built-in objects. The library must be so located that it may expand, and the building program should be thought of in units or stages.

Quotations abbreviated from the program requirements for the library of the University of Wisconsin-Milwaukee, by Mark Gormley:

The objectives of the library are based on the objectives of the University itself. They are:

1. To make available the books, periodicals, government publications, and other library materials necessary for conducting a successful university program. This program includes the teaching of undergraduate and graduate courses and research and service programs.

2. To train a competent library staff to service and interpret the library's collections.

3. To provide the physical facilities and equipment that will assist in the use of these library materials.

4. To assist and cooperate with faculty members in their varied instructional and research programs.

5. To instruct students in the efficient and effective use of library materials.

6. To encourage students to develop the habit of self-education.

7. To offer a program of library service that not only will meet but will exceed the requirements and standards of the various professional associations and accrediting agencies.

8. To integrate the library program with local, regional, national, and international library resources.

The basic purpose of a university library is quite simple. It must provide the records of civilization and assist students and faculty to retrieve and interpret them. While this purpose can be expressed simply, neither the function of the library nor its design is a simple problem.

The success of the library will depend upon a clear conception of the true function of this specific library and an architectural solution that will insure efficient operation, provide great flexibility of space, be direct, logical, and easily understood in its arrangement, and provide an environment that is friendly, intimate, warm and pleasant. This library is not to be a static, cold monument; it must be a live, vital place, constantly growing and changing as needs dictate.

The design must be basically a solution of the interior functions. The exterior should reflect the feeling and quality of the interior. Windows are necessary only for relief for the occupants, and should be used cautiously and sparingly. Exterior materials should be chosen in relation to other buildings, either constructed or to be constructed on the campus.

The library should have a special quality that is distinct from classroom buildings and clearly establishes it as the academic heart of the campus.

A library is composed of books and other media for the storage and retrieval of information. Properly planned it is the catalyst in the creation of ideas. Our library is to be a research-oriented library in which undergraduates can be served most efficiently.

Avoid segregating readers too much according to academic level by having certain facilities for undergraduates in one area, and the provision of other areas for more advanced student readers. All materials are to be available to all university personnel. It is only by exposing eager students to a wealth of material that we can develop latent potential in the people that we are pledged to develop intellectually. A library is a place in which the discovery of ideas becomes exciting.

For the faculty the library is a potent teaching instrument. Books beyond the prescribed text of a particular course are the usual rather than the incidental tools of contemporary education. The professor must have access to the materials for research which strengthen him and through him the students whose intellectual background he is developing.

The library is to be one large central building that will house library facilities for all the disciplines on the campus. There will be no organized departmental or satellite libraries in other buildings.

2. *The Library and a Description of Its Requirements.* Selections adapted from the Lafayette College Library building program by Clyde Haselden:

The library at Lafayette College is a central element in the educational program of the College. It should provide a workshop equivalent to the laboratory for students in courses in the humane and social studies. It should supplement the course work of all students and perhaps especially those in the sciences and engineering through facilities and programs that attract and stimulate the individual to broad self-education. Though it can not in a full sense be a research library, it should have sufficient research facilities and resources to allow the faculty, particularly in the humanities and in the social studies to develop as scholars in their fields. The aim of the library program in its various functions must be to cultivate the capacity to enjoy all forms of recorded human experience and achievement and the capacity to use these resources with sound judgment in independent effort that may continue after graduation from college.

To fulfill this function, the new library building must be able to take care of the following broadly defined functions:

1. Supplement the educational program of the college by acquiring, cataloguing and shelving in one central location the necessary books, periodicals and other library materials.

2. Increase knowledge of the basic reference sources by guidance in the use of library facilities.

3. Cultivate interest in and appreciation of books and their value by assistance in the development of the reading habit.

4. Encourage individual and group study by providing carrels, faculty studies and seminars as well as quiet, attractive and comfortable reading areas.

GENERAL CHARACTERISTICS

1. Utility should take precedence over architectural style in planning an effective interior arrangement. While ornamentation and monumentality are to be avoided, an attractive and pleasant interior is essential.

Flexible space relationships are necessary to provide for the rearrangement of units to meet future needs.

The building should be planned for library work with emphasis on efficient and economical service.

Expansion of the building—horizontal or vertical—should be decided now in relation to site, cost, efficiency of operation, and general appearance.

2. Modular construction is essential for economy in construction and flexible, readily-changeable space relations.

3. Open stacks are desired except where there are special collections and items of unusual value.

4. Security is of vital importance since the public will have free access to the stack. Turnstiles will be at the entrance. All stairways should be within the central exit control point.

5. Stacks should be free-standing.

6. Every effort should be made to make the library as quiet as possible through the use of acoustical materials. Soundproofing will be necessary in the Music Library and typing booths. Work area should be located and arranged so that the noise of working and staff conversation will not adversely affect readers.

7. Air conditioning is desired for the protection of books and for the comfort of readers and staff. Adequate ventilation and humidity control is desirable to protect special collections. Thus air conditioning should be planned for and set up on an optional basis. Operable sash is preferred in any case. Adequate ceiling heights should be planned for each level.

8. Illumination in the new building should provide the proper amount of light in terms of the best available research for close continuous reading and to the degree possible with the absence of glare and shadow.

9. Easy access to and from the entire library is necessary. Traffic of patrons and staff from one area to another should be planned, if possible, to eliminate or minimize disturbance of readers and workers. Efficiency and economy in the flow of library materials as well as people must be given high priority.

10. Seating capacity. In terms of the present population of the College, enrollment trends of the immediate future and the emphasis on more and more use of library books in teaching higher level students, the minimum seating capacity of the new library should be 450 readers, plus as many more as can be worked into the plan. With a possible future addition, the total would be over 600 seats, or roughly one-third of the expected future enrollment. As many seats as practical should be included at individual study tables.

11. Book capacity. The library now has 163,000 volumes. Assuming 5,000 volumes are added annually and that it will take three years to complete the library, there will be approximately 178,000 volumes in the present building when the new library is completed. Plan now for space to house 340,000 volumes in the new building but provide shelving initially for only 300,000. Future expansion of the new building should provide for at least 430,000 volumes.

12. Telephones for outside and intercom service will

be installed for all offices and work areas. Public telephones will be located where they can be supervised.

13. Parking facilities should be planned for a library staff. Parking space for off-campus visitors will be considered as part of the overall parking plans for the College.

14. In planning the space the following measurements should be considered as minimum.

a. Students seated at tables or in carrels require at least 25 square feet of space. With more comfortable and informal furniture, these figures might go up to 40 square feet or more.

b. At least 125 square feet is required for each staff member on duty.

c. For shelving books allow 10 volumes per square foot, keeping in mind that this is an undergraduate library and there is a considerable collection of bound periodicals.

15. It is recommended that reading areas should be located with exposure to the north in order to take advantage of northern light, which is more even throughout the year and does not expose readers to the direct sun rays. Windows on the other sides should be protected by drapes or blinds.

Selections from the University of California, Santa Cruz, program:

1. The library shall emphasize the use of materials. The design should provide the greatest possible accessibility to library materials for the largest number of users. The readers and the books should be brought together in an open-shelf type of arrangement.

2. The design of the library should foster something akin to a laboratory situation where through the use of library materials, faculty, students, and librarians can work together.

3. The library shall be a unified, rather than a fragmented collection. The lower cost of operating such a unit and the higher degree of availability of materials and the less need for duplicating expensive materials dictate centrality versus branching.

4. The underlying philosophy of the academic plan, which attempts to encourage inter-disciplinary approaches, suggests, it does not dictate, that departmentalization, particularly in the early stages should be discouraged.

5. Everything should be done to facilitate easy access to books and to encourage reading. This means a mingling of books and students.

6. The library shall be easy for both patrons and staff to use. This calls for an understanding of the functional interrelationships of library departments and a careful ordering of spaces.

7. Because of the openness desired, staff or turnstiles exits are probably a must.

8. In the early stages at least, the library through an audio-visual service center shall be responsible for housing and servicing the university's collections of audio-visual material. This will call for an adequate supply of specialized facilities, both projection rooms, preview rooms, and staff work areas.

9. In Unit 1 a very high percentage of reading tables should be individual seating units with backs high enough to prevent visual distraction at that point.

The University of Wisconsin-Milwaukee program includes these statements:

Concept of flexibility. The basic premise of the plan relationships must be based on growth and change. This will require modular layout for walls, lighting, air conditioning, book stacks, and so forth, to permit an easy interchange between book stacks and seating. Reading areas are to be interspersed with the book stacks to create smaller quieter areas and a better environment for study. Ease of creating new areas by moving stacks and seating furniture is essential.

This is to be an open-stack design. Books will be shelved on free-standing stacks 7'6" high.

Entrance. There is to be a single point of entrance and a separate single point of exit past a control point. This will permit the use of an open-stack system and greater freedom in the location of books and seating areas. Exits required for fire regulations should be equipped with signal devices. A weather vestibule is required.

Floor loading. The floors must be designed for 150 pounds per square foot live load to permit location of book stacks in any location.

Air Conditioning. The entire facility must be air conditioned. Filters of high capacity should be used to filter dust and smoke.

Acoustics. Control of sound is all too often neglected in libraries, and the use of acoustical floor, wall, and ceiling materials must be studied. If solution becomes a serious problem, the services of a competent acoustic consultant must be sought.

Lighting. Fluorescent lighting should be used throughout with serious consideration to locating the ballasts in a remote area. A good light level shall be maintained in the reading areas with higher intensity in the technical processes area and over the card catalogue.

Furniture and equipment should be harmonious with the building and contemporary in design. Contrasts are desirable. A variety of reader facilities are to be provided, such as individual carrels, group study tables, and occasional chairs.

Toilets. There shall be no public toilets on the first floor. A staff men's toilet should be provided near the director's office. A staff women's toilet and rest area should be provided in a convenient location. Adequate public toilets should be provided in secondary areas.

Elevators. It has been the general policy of the University that a student can walk three flights, plus the basement. Elevators are intended to serve the library services, faculty use, and paraplegic patrons.

Excerpts adapted from a program for a large city university library:

RECOMMENDATIONS ON PLANNING AND CONSTRUCTION

1. Acoustical control in a library is not an attempt to achieve a dead silence, but rather to control sudden and extraneous noise and make a pleasant place to work and to study. It will influence all phases of the building. The materials used, the type of structure, the finishing, the air conditioning, and many other factors must be taken into consideration. It is based on three factors: (1) the reduction of sound and the suppression of vibration resulting from the use of the building; (2) the reduction of machinery noise at its source, by appropriate selection of equipment; and (3) reduction of noise that does arise by the proper use of sound-absorbing materials.

2. Air conditioning is a basic requirement in a research library where rare and irreplaceable materials are housed, since its usefulness depends upon its ability to preserve these materials. It is absolutely necessary to exclude elements that cause and accelerate deterioration and decay. There are four factors involved: lights, air pollution and dust, undesirable temperature and relative humidity, and rapid changes in the latter, and finally insects and mold. The last three are definitely a part of air conditioning, and the control of light, sunlight in particular, is closely related to it.

3. Lighting is a very important element in library design. A lighting specialist should be consulted. Light, especially direct sunlight, is detrimental to books and paper. Windows should not be located in walls where direct sunlight can fall on shelving or areas that may be used later for the storage of books.

4. Modular construction is recommended with the weight of each floor supported by columns, rather than bearing walls. Ideally the columns should not be larger than 14″ in either dimension, which would make them fit properly into the stack layouts. The columns must be so placed that they will fit into a stack pattern involving multiples of 3′, providing for stack sections in one dimension and multiples of 4′3″ to 4′6″, the spacing of the stack ranges, in the other. The module should be chosen so that furniture will fit into it without wasted space.

5. Rest rooms should be carefully placed and adequate in size. Each rest room should have individual forced ventilation.

6. Seating arrangements in reading room should provide a combination of individual study tables and larger tables that will accommodate no more than six students. They should allow at least 3′ by 2′ for each student. When less space is provided the students will tend to sit in only every other seat. Individual accommodations are preferred by most persons. Chairs grouped informally can be used to break up the pattern of large numbers of students seated at tables, since not all students wish to take notes. In reading areas students should be divided into groups of not more than forty by screens or partial partitions. Tables for more than two should be located in the center of each area, and single study tables located around the perimeter. Books can be shelved close at hand in a block of free-standing stack. If the entrance to the room is through the stack area, the student will tend to come into the room through the stack, select a book, and then walk to a seat to study. The old method of placing shelves around a reading room causes undesirable distraction as students go to shelves in various parts of the room to select books.

7. Double-faced free-standing stacks with seven shelves 12″ on centers and 7″ or 8″ deep "actual" will take care of most books. On floors where the general book collection is shelved, main access aisles should be at least 4′6″ wide and should run all the way across the stack area, in order to maintain a clear arrangement pattern and prevent patrons from becoming lost in a maze of narrow cross aisles. Aisles other than main access aisles should be 3′ wide.

8. Brick or block walls are easier to maintain than plaster walls. Demountable partitions should be used wherever possible to facilitate future changes in area usages. Aluminum windows are preferred over wood or steel, because there is less maintenance. Light-colored floor coverings, which are easy to clean, durable and quiet to walk and run book trucks on, are most desirable. Serious thought should be given to the use of newly developed coverings. Ceilings should be easy to clean, easy to replace if damaged, noise absorbent and light in color. Finishes which are economical to maintain should be used, even though the initial cost may be somewhat higher. Painted surfaces should be semigloss, rather than flat.

9. Library reading room ceilings have been built as low as 8′1″, but it is recommended that no ceiling be less than 8′6″ in clear height and that the entrance floor be 11′, unless a mezzanine is considered.

10. Coat racks in all major reading areas and coat hooks on carrel partitions should be used instead of coat rooms.

11. Students are to have free access to the general collections of the library. This makes it necessary to have controlled exits. Each patron must pass a control desk where books are checked out before he leaves the library. Ideally there should be only one entrance and one exit. Emergency exits should be provided which are equipped with alarms or other devices and plainly marked so that students and professors will learn that they are to be left shut unless an emergency arises. There will be a service entrance at the rear of the building with an unloading dock that will be large enough to

accommodate two trucks simultaneously. Since books and other materials received by the library are easily damaged by snow or rain, the unloading area should be covered. Heat coils in the concrete walks in front of the entrance would be wise. Recessed perforated mats may be located just inside the entrance to pick up dirt from shoes. Terrazzo or other material that wears smooth and slick should not be used on steps, unless the step nosing has abrasive inserts.

12. A complete directory should be prominently located at the entrance and on each floor.

Selections from the program for a large university library:

General Statement

Because building additions will be needed in the future, the architect should visualize a complete structure at least twice as large as will be required to meet the space requirements given below. The design of the initial structure should be sufficiently independent as not to seem abbreviated or awaiting completion. At the same time it must be part of a harmoniously conceived future completed structure. The architect shall submit elevations and perspective drawing of the completed as well as of the initial structure. The site [which has been selected] provides room for additions to the west and south and the architect shall specify adjacent to the initial structure the approximate areas which should be reserved for future additions.

The design and appearance of the new library, both inside and out, should be determined primarily by its function. Lighting, air conditioning, accessibility of books and of service, the shape, number and size of reading rooms, halls, staircases and elevators should be planned so as to enable students, faculty and library personnel to work comfortably, with the least possible loss of time and patience. It is wise, for example, in planning fenestration to consider the exterior aspect of the building and means of avoiding excessive lighting and heating costs; but the first consideration should be to provide optimum conditions of light for the users of the library. Either insufficient natural lighting or an excessive use of glass can be detrimental to comfortable reading.

The architect should be under no obligation to reproduce the architectural style of other buildings on the campus. On the contrary, a new departure should be most appropriate. The site itself encourages independence in this respect. The sort of monumentality which interferes with the comfortable and efficient use of the library should be avoided. The library building ought by its appearance to invite the passerby to enter, and not intimidate him by cold impersonality. As the heart of the University, the library will combine genuine functionalism with aesthetic imagination and avoid

every sort of aesthetic falsity, pretentiousness, or slovenliness. If the University is to make full use of the opportunity, the new structure will add to the campus a significant example of the best work of modern American architecture.

Modular construction shall be used; for, although internal space assignments will be functionally related and defined in the program, the future will require rearrangements of space. Specifically, there will be in the future changes in the amount of space needed for all operations and services, and these operations and services may need to be relocated in the building. Interior design, therefore, must provide flexibility and the possibility of inexpensive modifications. Bearing partitions should be kept to a minimum. Staircases, elevators, escalators, toilets, custodial rooms, mechanical rooms, vertical shafts, etc., should be arranged and grouped in such a way as not to interfere with future space rearrangements. At the same time, the architect will want to consider the placement of these fixed elements with respect to the efficient operation of the initial structure and its probable additions. Partitions that will be required throughout the structure to separate functions, etc., should, wherever possible, be easily removable, and this should not be at the expense of achieving a pleasing appearance and durability. All floor areas, except those obviously not subject to future book load, should be built to carry the maximum load of a library stack room.

The architect is asked to consider probable traffic patterns on the present and future campus and provide easy, convenient entrances to the building, bearing in mind his planned building addition.

3. Information about Special Building Areas. The questions proposed in Chapter 13 should be answered, giving the requirements for the number of readers, and the types of seating accommodations that should be provided in each public room, the number of volumes, and other material that should be housed, and the spatial and other requirements for the staff. This is one of the more difficult parts of the program to prepare. It requires a great deal of detailed work. No attempt will be made here to provide examples which will answer all the questions, but the following will give some indication as to what might well be done.

a. Printed forms can be prepared, see Figs. A.2 to A.6 for examples used by the University of California, Santa Cruz. Similar sheets may be required for every room in the building.

b. Statements like those on p. 379 which have been selected from the program of a large new university library, might be prepared.

SPACE DESCRIPTION
SANTA CRUZ CAMPUS

SPACE NUMBER ....3...
........1.... Like spaces

PROJECT.......University.Library,..Unit.1..
DEPARTMENT ....

USE OF SPACE
................GENERAL.OFFICE..
................Reception.area;..secretaries,..mail,..clerk-typist....................
....

AREA AND OCCUPANCY
 Assignable area each space in square feet: ....375.................................
 Classroom or Seminar – number of seats: ....
 Teaching Laboratory – number of student stations: ....
 Teaching Laboratory – number of lockers per station: ....
 Other spaces – normal number of occupants:...............3.+.visitors*.....................

ARCHITECTURAL REQUIREMENTS
 Location: ....Adjacent..to.offices..of.the.University.Librarian.and.......
 ...Assistant..University.Librarian;..in.a.location.easily.accessible.to...
 Dimensions: general..public,..faculty,..staff.and.students............................
 Special floor loading: ....
 Special acoustical: ....
 Other: ....
 ....

MECHANICAL AND ELECTRICAL REQUIREMENTS
 Sink with utilities: ....
 Lab utilities: ....
 Special environmental conditions: ....
 Special electric services: ....Outlets.at.each.desk.for.office.machines.............
 Special exhaust: ....
 Other: ....Telephone.outlet;..conduit.for.teletype.cable.......
 ....

COMMENTS
.................*Space.for.people.waiting.to.see.Librarian.or.Assistant........
......Librarian....Space.for.personnel.and.financial.records,.storage.of....
forms, supplies, sorting mail.

EQUIPMENT – FIXED AND MOVABLE

Quantity	Description
3	typist desks, 60x30
3	typist chairs
2	tables, 60x30
2	storage cabinets, 36x78x24
3	side chairs
1	lounge chair
1	couch
6	5-drawer files, 2 with locks
2	wastebaskets
1	wastebasket, large
1	caddy file
1	bookcase
1	TWX teletype unit

Prepared by ——— D. T. Clark ——— Date ——— May 1963 ——— DDP-4
UCSC, 3/63

FIG. A.2   Santa Cruz Library program, general office.

SPACE DESCRIPTION
SANTA CRUZ CAMPUS

PROJECT........University.Library,.Unit.1...
DEPARTMENT ....

USE OF SPACE
...............TECHNICAL.PROCESSES;...ACQUISITIONS...
....
....

AREA AND OCCUPANCY
Assignable area each space in square feet: ....1350...
Classroom or Seminar — number of seats: ....
Teaching Laboratory — number of student stations: ....
Teaching Laboratory — number of lockers per station: ....
Other spaces — normal number of occupants:.................9..

ARCHITECTURAL REQUIREMENTS
Location: ....Contiguous.with.Cataloging,.or.both.may.he.in.one.area;.
....should.be.adjacent.to.Receiving,.Shipping.and.Bindery.Prep....Direct.
Dimensions.access.to.public.catalog....No.through.traffic..................................
Special floor loading: ....
Special acoustical: ....
Other: ....One.micro.film.and.one.micro.card.reader.to.be.shared.with
....Catalog.Department..

MECHANICAL AND ELECTRICAL REQUIREMENTS
Sink with utilities: ....
Lab utilities: ....
Special environmental conditions: ....
Special electric services: ....Wiring.for.eventual.IBM.equipment.(keytronic.sorter)
Special exhaust: ....
Other: ....Electric.outlets.at.each.desk.for.electric.type-
....writers,.adding.machines,.etc,...Telephone.outlets..................................

COMMENTS
.................Single-face..bookstacks.against.walls,..remainder.of.shelving.in
.......corner.near.entrance.to.room..

EQUIPMENT — FIXED AND MOVABLE

Quantity	Description		
5	desks, 60x30	1	supply cabinet, 36x90x24
4	desks, typist	1	microfilm reader
5	swivel arm chairs	1	microcard reader
4	typist chairs	9	wastebaskets
3	side chairs	1	wardrobe cabinet
1	typewriter table		
1	custom built reference book desk and shelves (for Publishers catalogs, CBI, etc.)		
1	adding machine		
6	book trucks		
1	5-drawer file, legal		
3	5-drawer files		
1	15-drawer catalog unit		
4	Kardex units		
12	bookcases, 36x90x10		
1	Thermofax or Verifax		

Prepared by _____ D. T. Clark _____ Date _____ May 1963 _____ DDP-4
UCSC, 3/63

FIG. A.3 Santa Cruz Library program. Technical processes: acquisition.

SPACE DESCRIPTION
SANTA CRUZ CAMPUS

SPACE NUMBER ....19..
.... Like spaces
....1....

PROJECT............ University Library, Unit 1 ....

DEPARTMENT ....

USE OF SPACE

.... RECEIVING AND SHIPPING ROOM ....

..Receiving and shipping room for all materials coming to or leaving the

..Library;.temporary.storage.space.for.acquisitions;.work.area.for.minor.

repairs to library equipment.

AREA AND OCCUPANCY

Assignable area each space in square feet: .... 565 ....

Classroom or Seminar — number of seats: ....

Teaching Laboratory — number of student stations: ....

Teaching Laboratory — number of lockers per station: ....

Other spaces — normal number of occupants:................ 1 ....

ARCHITECTURAL REQUIREMENTS

Location: .... Contiguous.with.the.Technical.Processes.Area;.must.be.....

.adjacent.to.and.on.same.level.as.loading.platform...................................

Dimensions: ....

Special floor loading: ....

Special acoustical: .... Sound.control.of.noisy.operations................................

Other: ....

....

MECHANICAL AND ELECTRICAL REQUIREMENTS

Sink with utilities: .... Sink.with.drainboard.......................................

Lab utilities: ....

Special environmental conditions: ....

Special electric services: ....

Special exhaust: ....

Other: ....

....

COMMENTS

.... Space.for.storing.8.bindery.boxes.(3'x.1').in.2.piles.of.4.........

.... Space.for.parking.book.trucks.and.moving.book.trucks.around........

Doors wide enough to take furniture and equipment.

EQUIPMENT — FIXED AND MOVABLE

Quantity	Description		
1	storage cabinet, 36x78x24	1	5-drawer file
1	gravity-feed conveyor to	1	large paper cutter
	receiving desk, Technical	1	small paper cutter
	Processes area	1	wastebasket, extra large
1	postal scales	1	wastebasket
1	gummed paper dispenser		
1	postal meter		
1	custom-built work table		
1	workbench		
1	small tool cabinet		
8	bookcases, 36x90x10		
3	book trucks		
1	hand truck		
1	dolly		
1	desk, 60x30		
1	stool		
2	typist chairs		

Prepared by _____ D. T. Clark _____ Date _____ May 1963 _____ DDP-4
UCSC, 3/63

FIG. A.4   Santa Cruz Library program. Receiving and shipping room.

SPACE DESCRIPTION
SANTA CRUZ CAMPUS

SPACE NUMBER 25
1 Like Spaces

PROJECT: University Library, Unit 1
DEPARTMENT:

USE OF SPACE: READER STATIONS (Seating Area)

AREA AND OCCUPANCY:
  Assignable area each space in square feet: 29,700 (see next sheet for
                                                          stages of occupancy)

  Classroom or Seminar – number of seats:
  Teaching Laboratory – number of student stations:
  Teaching Laboratory – number of lockers per station:
  Other spaces – normal number of occupants: (See next sheet)

ARCHITECTURAL REQUIREMENTS:
  Location:
  Dimensions:
  Special floor loading:
  Special acoustical:
  Other:

MECHANICAL AND ELECTRICAL REQUIREMENTS:
  Sink with utilities:
  Lab utilities:
  Special environmental conditions:
  Special electric services:
  Special exhaust:
  Other:

COMMENTS:
      Seating shall be interspersed with stack areas; there shall be a high
      percentage of individual seating accommodations. Maximum size of the
      fewer large tables should be 4 seats.

EQUIPMENT – FIXED AND MOVABLE:

Quanity	Description
	(See next sheet)

FIG. A.5 Santa Cruz Library program. Reader stations (seating area), page 1.

REFERENCE SERVICE DESK

1. Suggested size: 400 square feet
2. Use: Desk/counters where patrons may ask for reference help in locating and using library materials.
3. Maximum occupancy at one time: 3 librarians
4. Relation to other areas or rooms: Ground floor. Between public card catalog and reference reading. Near index reference.
5. Special requirements: Vertical files and low shelving. Direct phone from stack levels.

REFERENCE INDEXES

1. Suggested size: 1200 square feet
2. Use: Consultation of periodical indexes, British Museum and Library of Congress catalogs
3. Maximum occupancy at one time: 40 (30 seated)
4. Relation to other areas or rooms: Ground floor. Between public card catalog and reference reading, behind or near reference service.
5. Special requirements: 6 specially constructed index reference tables (60×120). 16 sections of 3' wall shelving, 7' high.

INTER-LIBRARY LOAN

1. Suggested size: 800 square feet
2. Use: Receive requests for inter-library loans, and subsequent operations.
3. Maximum occupancy at one time: 5 library staff and 5 patrons.
4. Relation to other areas or rooms: Ground floor. Reasonably near public card catalog.
5. Special requirements: Counter service to patrons. One small partitioned office within the area.

CARD REPRODUCTION

1. Suggested size: 500 square feet
2. Use: For multilith and other duplicating machinery with possible installation of power cutter and punch.
3. Maximum occupancy at one time: 5
4. Relation to other areas or rooms: Adjoining typists with supervisor office.
5. Special requirements: Power and soundproofing.

BIBLIOGRAPHY ROOM

1. Suggested size: 2,500 square feet
2. Use: Consultation of trade and national bibliographies by library staff and others.
3. Maximum occupancy at one time: 25
4. Relation to other areas or rooms: between cataloguing work area and book order area, but so placed that faculty may enter the room without being obliged to walk through those rooms.
5. Special requirements: Consultation tables for large volumes, standing height counters and shelving (30 3' sections).

READER STATIONS

Stages of Occupancy

Year	Reader Stations	Square Feet
1966	500	12,500
1969	812	20,300
1971	1,188	29,700

Stages of Equipment

1966	500	Reading chairs
	25	Reading tables 36" x 60"
	400	Individual study tables 39" x 24"
1969	812	Reading chairs
	41	Reading tables 36" x 60"
	648	Individual study tables 39" x 24"
1971	1,188	Reading chairs
	90	Reading tables 36" x 60"
	828	Individual study tables 39" x 24"

FIG. A.6 Santa Cruz Library program. Reader stations (seating area), page 2.

4. *Basic Needs and Spatial Requirements.* An example from an Eastern liberal arts college.

SPACE REQUIREMENTS

Seating—public

Lobby	4
General reading room	150
Bibliography area	3
Microfilm room	5
Browsing room	20
Rare book room	4
Reading areas, upper floors	180
Periodicals reading area, basement	70
Faculty studies	10
Conference rooms	48
Typing booths	8
Listening room and booths	20
	522

Seating—staff

Circulation desk	3
Circulation office	2
Reference librarian's desk and office	3
Librarian's office	10
Secretary's office	3
Order department	2
Cataloguing department	5
Receiving room	2
Listening room	1
Periodicals workroom and reading area	3
Janitor's workshop	1
Staff lounge	10
	45

*Book storage capacity**

Reference collection	10,000
Bibliography	1,000
Browsing	4,000
Rare books and special collections	7,000
Basement stack	80,000
Stacks on upper floors	200,000
	302,000

* Excluding temporary shelving in staff offices and workrooms.

SPACE REQUIREMENTS BY FLOOR

The figures below represent no more than an experimental worksheet and are far from exact. Estimates of the size of most facilities are rough approximations in round numbers. Some are incompetent guesses, such as the area in the basement for mechanical equipment and the auditorium. The latter, of course, may be in a separate wing or excluded altogether. No allowance is made for mechanical equipment on the roof, and none is made for the loss of space on each floor due to partitions, columns, and corridors other than stack aisles. There is therefore a considerable margin of error in the totals, probably on the under side.

Basement

	sq ft.
Stacks	5,400
Periodicals display and reading area	2,100
Maps	250
Faculty studies	100
Conference rooms	430
Receiving and shipping	500
Periodicals workroom	450
Janitor's workroom	200
Storage	350
Stairwells, elevator	400
Mechanical equipment	1,000
Auditorium	2,200
Toilets	200
	13,580

Main floor

	sq ft.
Vestibule	360
Lobby	2,200
Circulation desk, etc.	600
Circulation office	200
General reading room and reference collection	5,200
Bibliography collection	150
Browsing room	1,200
Librarian's and secretary's offices	600
Reference librarian	300
Microfilm room	500
Order and cataloguing departments	1,300
Stairwells, elevator	400
	13,010

Second floor

Stack	7,700
Reading area	2,700
Rare book room	900
Conference rooms	430
Faculty studies	200
Staff lounge	500
Stairwells, elevator	400
Toilets	200
	13,030

Third floor

Stack	7,700
Reading area	2,700
Conference rooms	430
Faculty studies	200
Stairwells, elevators	400
Listening room	1,200
Unassigned	430
	13,060

Excerpts from the program of an urban university:

SUMMARY OF FACILITIES

	Seats for readers	Books	Staff	Sq ft.
Lobby				
Circulation dept.			12	1,300
Browsing alcove	10	1,000		500
Card catalog				2,300
Bibliography collection	15	4,200		1,100
Reference room	50	8,000	4	3,050

SUMMARY OF FACILITIES (*continued*)

	Seats for readers	Books	Staff	Sq ft.
Periodical room	60		6	3,300
Technical services area			29	3,420
Reserve book and study area	225	14,500	2	8,200
Stacks				
General stacks		865,000		72,000
General study areas	300			9,000
Carrels	250			4,000
Seminar rooms	130			3,900
Conference & smoking rooms	90			2,700
Faculty studies	75			7,500
Typing rooms	15			450
Special collections area	15	8,000	1	1,400
Audio-visual area	99		2	3,050
Administrative offices			5	1,200
Receiving and shipping room			1	700
Library staff room			45	1,450
Book repair room			1	500
Check room				250
Stock & supply room				150
Equipment storage room				300

Excerpts from the program for a residential suburban college:

SUMMARY OF REQUIREMENTS

1. Public areas	Volumes	Seats	Area
a. General stack area	233,500		15,600 S.F.
b. General reading area		410	10,250
c. Reference & bibliography	6,000	20	1,000
d. Night study area		60	1,400
e. Public catalog			500
f. Periodicals & newspapers		15	400
g. Browsing & new books	1,000	20	600
h. Seminar rooms (4)		40	750
i. Typing rooms (4)		20	400
j. Leverton collection & "Treasure" room	7,500	15	700
Subtotal public areas	248,000	600	32,075 S.F.

2. Staff areas	Volumes	Staff (min-max)	Area
a. Circulation desk & closed reserve	2,000	1–3	400 S.F.
b. Office (shared w/i, c)		1–2	150
c. Technical processing area (1 room)		3–6	900
d. Director and secretary		2–2	400
e. Librarian		1–1	200

SUMMARY OF REQUIREMENTS (*continued*)

2. Staff areas	Volumes	Staff (min-max)	Area
f. Mail sorting magazine rec. gift storage.......	2,000*	1	500
g. Staff lounge locker & toilets			250
h. Vault & fireproof storage			200
i. Mail drop.........			50
Subtotal staff areas	2,000	8–15	3,050 S.F.

3. Service areas	Staff	Area
a. Mechanical room............		1,000 S.F.
b. Superintendent's office........	1	150
c. Janitors' closets (1 per floor) ...	1	100
d. Elevator 3 floors		125
e. Toilet rooms (M & W on each floor)		600
Subtotal service areas	2	1,975 S.F.

4. Summary of areas	Volumes	Seats	Area
a. Public areas	248,000	600	32,075 S.F.
b. Staff areas	2,000	8–15†	3,050
c. Service areas		2†	1,975
d. Subtotal...........			37,100
e. Circulation (7½% of *d*)			2,700
f. Wall thicknesses, ducts, columns, etc. (10% of *d* + *e*)			4,000
Grand total			43,800 S.F.

* Not considered in 250,000 total

† Staff or service personnel

Excerpts from the program for a commuting university:

SUMMARY OF REQUIREMENTS

	Seating	Shelving	Area
Introduction to the Library			
1. Vestibule			120 S.F.
2. Lobby & control...			1,000
3. Circulation desk ...			535
4. Circulation office...			300
5. Ref. & bibliog.	50	25,200	4,750
6. Periodical indexes..	16		680
7. Abstracts area.....		2,520	300
8. Card catalog			1,060
9. Ref. office........			300
Technical processes and administration			
10. Mail room			200
11. Order dept.			1,000
12. Mending			200
13. Catalog dept.			1,080

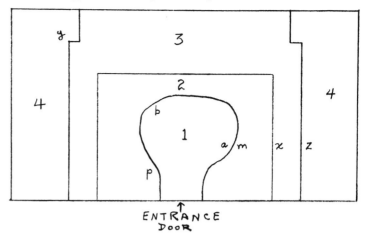

Accessibility Priorites are shown by the numerals 1, 2, 3, and 4. The entrance door gives immediate access to Priority 1 areas. All the areas in Priority 1 are necessarily near each other, e.g., area a and area b. This is not true in the case of Priority 4, e.g., areas y and z. Proximity is possible across Priority lines, e.g., areas a and m, or even areas a and x. Thus, it is possible to have a Priority 4 area like Cataloging staff at z reasonably close to a Priority 1 area like the Public Catalog at a. The diagram shows everything on a single horizontal plane. Possibilities for achieving efficient space relationships are increased by bringing areas into vertical proximity by a wise use of stairs and elevators.

FIG. A.7 Accessibility priorities for the Francis A. Countway Library of Medicine of the Harvard Medical School and the Boston Medical Library.

SUMMARY OF REQUIREMENTS (*continued*)

	Seating	Shelving	Area
14. Documents			250
15. Librarian			200
16. Assistant librarian			200
17. Secretary			175
Books and readers			
18. Periodicals	200	42,588	10,310
19. Reserve books	200	12,096	7,480
20. Curriculum materials	50	6,050	2,640
21. Special collections	24	7,434	1,820
22. Micro-reading	12	630	400
23. Faculty studies	36		1,720
24. Student conference	60		1,000
25. Listening area	computed in bookstacks		
26. Bookstacks	440	168,442	27,784
Miscellaneous			
27. Smoking lounges	36		900
28. Smoking studies	60		1,725
29. Typing rooms	16		360
30. Lock section		5,040	1,140
31. Staff room			1,000
32. Staff indispos.			150
33. Staff toilet			150
34. Supply room			200
35. Public toilets			1,080
Total:	1,200	270,000	72,209 S.F.

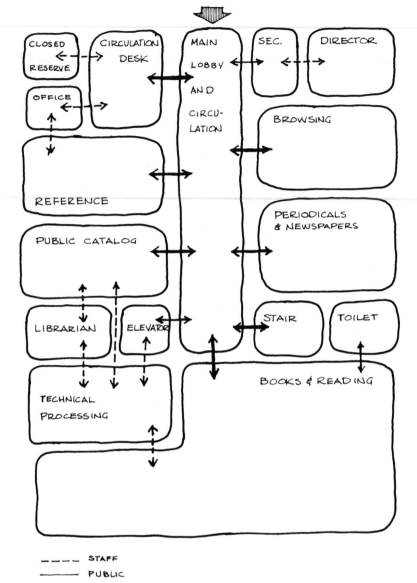

STAFF
PUBLIC

FIG. A.8 Lake Forest College Library. Ground floor. Spatial relationships for ground-floor requirements shown in diagrammatic form.

5. *Spatial Relationships.* Spatial relationships can be presented in various ways in the program prepared for the architect: in writing in the main text; in tabular form; or in diagrams. The library as a whole can be covered in one section of the text, in one column of a table, in one diagram, or scattered through the program in the sections dealing with specific floor levels, or areas of the building. Paragraphs a to e below provide examples of different methods.

a. Fig. A.1, which was referred to earlier, summarizes in the column headed "Location-Relationship" the proposed spatial relationships in the Asbury Theological Seminary Library.

b. Figs. A.2 to A.6, selected from the Santa Cruz program, indicate desired relationships for each library area as the first line *Location* under the heading "Architectural Requirements."

c. Fig. A.7 is a drawing from the program for the Francis A. Countway Library of Medicine of the Harvard Medical School and the Boston Medical Library, and is used to illustrate what are called "accessibility priorities," which do not explain what should be next to what, but only what should be more accessible than something else.

d. Figs. A.8 to A.10 show diagrammatic sketches for spatial relationships in the program for a new building for Lake Forest College, with a sketch for each floor level.

e. Figs. A.11 and A.12, which are diagrammatic sketches taken from the program for a large university library, indicate spatial relationships within limited areas on one floor.

f. Fig. A.13 presents the proposed spatial relationship in a library in Indonesia in a combination of a short written statement and a diagram.

It is suggested that in connection with the preparation of a library building program the following chapters and sections of this volume be consulted:

Section 6.4, on spatial relationships

Section 12.1, on program preliminaries

Chapter 13, on the program for assignable space requirements

Chapter 14, on the program for mechanical facilities, comfort, and other requirements

Appendix D, Selective Annotated Bibliography

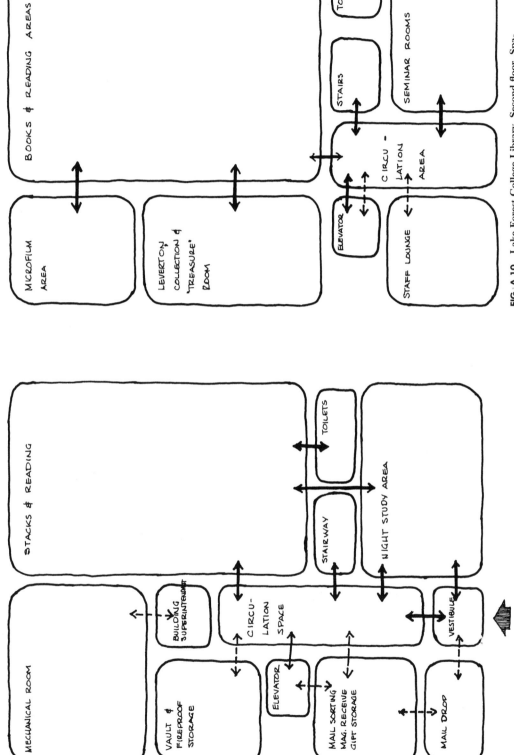

FIG. A.9 Lake Forest College Library. Main floor. Spatial relationships for main-floor requirements. (See Fig. A.8 for ground floor and Fig. A.10 for second floor.)

FIG. A.10 Lake Forest College Library. Second floor. Spatial relationships for second-floor requirements.

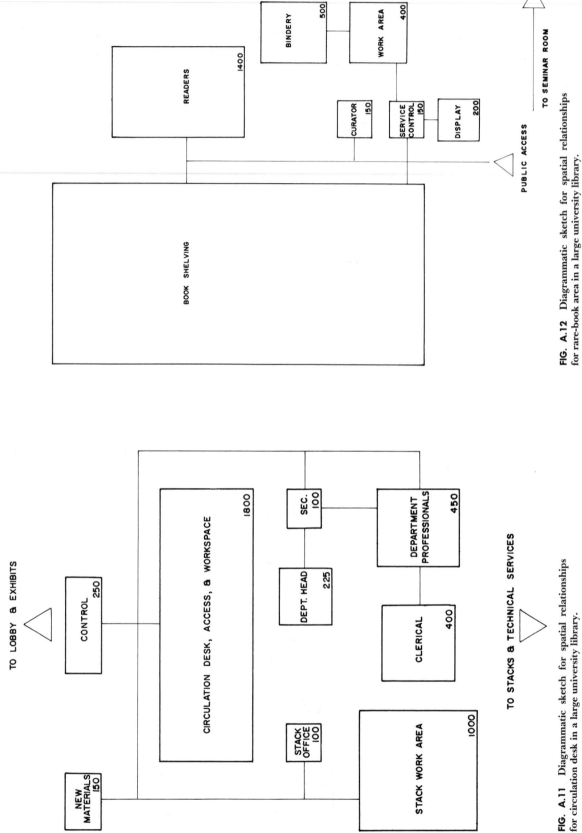

FIG. A.11 Diagrammatic sketch for spatial relationships for circulation desk in a large university library.

FIG. A.12 Diagrammatic sketch for spatial relationships for rare-book area in a large university library.

1. The card catalog is the heart of the library, and three departments MUST be placed close to it, for it is essential to their work:

The Cataloging Department

The Reference Department

The Circulation Department

Note: It is possible to place the catalog within the Reference Departments and the other two Departments close by.

2. The periodical reading room is desirably placed fairly close to both the Circulation Department and the Reference Department, it being slightly more important for it to be near the Reference Department than to the Circulation Department.

3. Since the Cataloging Department must use reference books in their work, it is desirable that the Reference Department and the Cataloging Department be fairly close together.

4. The shipping room MUST be on the ground floor with its own separate entrance and loading platform.

5. The Acquisition (Order) Department is desirably placed near the shipping room but may be directly above it if there is a book lift leading directly between the two.

6. Usual flow of books is as follows: Shipping Room; Acquisition Department; Cataloging Department; Binding and Repair Department; Circulation Department.

7. Auditoriums, projection rooms, exhibit halls, and similar spaces should be placed in such a way as to be capable of being opened separate from the Library.

8. Reserve reading room should be near the main entrance.

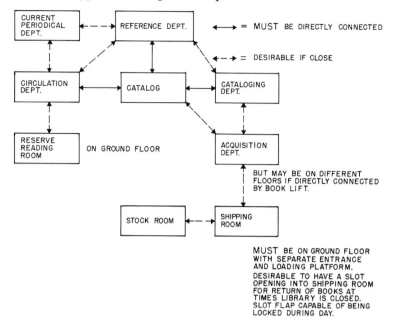

FIG. A.13 Spatial relationships in an Indonesian library shown by a diagram with accompanying text.

appendix B

Formulas and Tables

The figures given here are at best only approximations and may be altered by local conditions; they are not arrived at by exact scientific calculation.

Six groups are dealt with; those relating to:

I. Column spacing. See also Chapter 4.

II. Ceiling heights and floor size areas. See also Chapter 5.

III. Reader accommodations. See also Chapter 7.

IV. Book storage (excluding problems that are affected by column spacing). See also Chapter 8.

V. Card catalogues. See also Sections 11.2 and 16.3.

VI. Government standards.

I. *Column Spacing*

A. *Stack Areas.* No one size is perfect for column sizes or column spacing.

Other things being equal, the larger the bay size, the better, so long as it does not unduly increase construction costs, floor to floor heights, or column sizes.

Column spacing—that is, the distance between column centers—is generally more important in concentrated stack areas than in combined stack and reading areas because in the latter suitable adjustments are easier to make.

Clear space between columns—this is not the space between column centers—in a column range should preferably be a multiple of 3 ft (plus an additional 4 in. to provide for irregularities in the column sizes and for the end uprights in the range).

Range spacing and range lengths have a greater effect on book capacity than the distance between columns in a column range. The reduction of space between range centers by 1 in. increases book capacity by approximately 2 per cent. The reduction of space used for cross aisles at right angles to the ranges is also of importance. (See Figs. 16.19 to 16.23.)

If practicable, columns should be no greater than 14 in. in the direction of a range, and the dimension in the other direction should be kept down to 18 in. If over 14 in. in the direction of the range is necessary, the column might almost as well be 32 in. in that direction. It could then occupy the space of a full stack section and perhaps enclose a heating duct. If a column is wider than the range, it will jut into the stack aisle. Irregular length stack sections are inconvenient, unduly expensive, and can often be replaced to advantage by a lectern or consultation table.

Tables B.1*A* and B.1*B* deal with standard layouts in commonly used module sizes.

The following comments may be useful in connection with Tables B.1*A* and B.1*B*.

1. Spacing 3 ft 9 in. or less should be used for closed-access storage only, with ranges not more than 30 ft long and not more than 18 in. deep.

2. Spacing 3 ft 9 in. to 4 ft 1 in. can be used to advantage for large little-used, limited-access stacks, with ranges up to 30 ft long. Closed-access ranges up to 60 ft long have been used successfully with ranges 18 in. or less deep, 4 ft or 4 ft 1 in. on centers.

3. Spacing 4 ft 2 in. to 4 ft 6 in. can be used for open-access stack, preferably held to 18 in. in

TABLE B. 1*A*. SQUARE MODULES WITH THE COLUMN SPACING A MULTIPLE OF 3 FT (PLUS 1½ FT FOR THE COLUMN ITSELF)*

Bay size	Sections between columns, standard 3′	Ranges to a bay	Range spacing on centers
19′6″ × 19′6″	6	5	3′10⅘″
	6	4	4′10½″
	6	3	6′6″
22′6″ × 22′6″	7	6	3′9″
	7	5	4′6″
	7	4	5′7½″
25′6″ × 25′6″	8	7	3′7⁵⁄₇″
	8	6	4′3″
	8	5	5′1⅕″
	8	4	6′4½″
28′6″ × 28′6″	9	8	3′6¾″
	9	7	4′0⁶⁄₇″
	9	6	4′9″
	9	5	5′8⅖″

* Columns should not be wider than the depth of range. 14 × 14 in. up to 14 × 18 in. is suggested.

depth with the range length based on the amount of use.

4. Spacing 4 ft 6 in. to 5 ft is generous even for heavily used open-access undergraduate stack if ranges are 15 ft long and 4 ft 6 in. on centers, and in some circumstances up to 30 ft if 5 ft on centers.

5. Spacing 5 ft to 5 ft 10 in. is unnecessarily generous for any regular stack shelving and is

TABLE B. 1*B*. SQUARE MODULES WITH COLUMN SPACING A MULTIPLE OF 3 FT*

Bay size	Sections between columns standard 3′	Ranges to a bay	Range spacing on centers
18′ × 18′	5	5	3′7⅕″
	5	4	4′6″
	5	3	6′
21′ × 21′	6	6	3′6″
	6	5	4′2⅖″
	6	4	5′3″
24′ × 24′	7	7	3′5⅐″
	7	6	4′
	7	5	4′9⅗″
	7	4	6′
27′ × 27′	8	8	3′4½″
	8	7	3′10²⁄₇″
	8	6	4′6″
	8	5	5′4⅘″
	8	4	6′9″

* Columns should not be wider than the depth of the range. 18 × 32 in. is suggested.

TABLE B. 2. LONG RECTANGULAR MODULES, 22 FT 6 IN. IN ONE DIRECTION*

Bay size	Ranges to a bay	Range spacing on centers
22′6″ × 18′	4	4′6″
22′6″ × 20′	5	4′
22′6″ × 20′10″	5	4′2″
22′6″ × 21′8″	5	4′4″
22′6″ × 24′	6	4′
22′6″ × 25′	6	4′2″
22′6″ × 26′	6	4′4″
22′6″ × 27′	6	4′6″

*A bay of this size will give seven sections 3 ft long between 14-in. columns in the direction of the column range. The column sizes suggested in Table B.1*A* are suitable here.

often adequate for periodical display cases and for heavily used reference collections.

6. Spacing 6 ft or greater is adequate for newspaper shelving and generous for periodical display cases.

Square bays are more flexible than those that form a long rectangle and are generally somewhat cheaper if the ceiling height is limited. But if the latter are used, the number of suitable sizes can be greatly increased. Table B.2 shows possibilities with 22 ft 6 in. in one direction and different spacing in the other one.

Similar tables can be prepared for long rectangular bays 18 ft, 19½ ft, 21 ft, 24 ft, 25½ ft, 27 ft, and 28½ ft in one direction.

If section lengths are changed from 3 ft to some other size, such as 3 ft 1 in., 3 ft 2 in., 3 ft 3 in., 3 ft 4 in., 3 ft 5 in., or 3 ft 6 in., or in countries using the metric system to 90, 95, 100, or 105 cm, tables comparable to Tables B.1*A*, B.1*B*, and B.2 above should be prepared with those lengths as a base.

Always keep in mind the probable cost advantages available if standard sizes are used. Remember that columns so large that they interfere with aisles are seldom necessary.

B. *Seating Accommodations.* Column spacing is of less importance in connection with seating accommodations than with shelving. Tables B.3 and B.4 show the maximum number of carrels available on one side of standard-size bays and the number of studies available in such bays.

II. *Ceiling Heights and Floor Areas.* Minimum and maximum ceiling heights and floor areas involve basic functional and aesthetic problems. Suggestions from the functional point of view are proposed as an aid in reaching decisions.

TABLE B. 3. CARRELS*

Bay size	Open†	Double- or triple-staggered‡	Small closed§	Large closed¶
18′	4	4	4	3
19½′	4	4	4	3
21′	5	4	4	4
22½′	5	5	5	4
24′	6	5	5	4
25½′	6	5	5	5
27′	6	6	6	5

* A carrel, as used here, is an area in which a reader is cut off from any neighbor who is closer than 3 ft on either side or front and back and one side. The minimum desirable width of an adequate carrel working surface is 2 ft 9 in., which is as useful as 3 ft for each person at a table with two or more persons sitting side by side. Minimum depth suggested is 20 in.

† Distance apart on centers should be not less than 4 ft 3 in., unless the front table leg is set back 4 to 6 in. and armless chairs are used, in which case the distance on centers can be reduced to 4 ft. Any distance over 4 ft 6 in. is unnecessarily generous. A clear space of 27 in. or more between working surface and partition at the rear is recommended. A shelf above the table interferes with overhead lighting and makes a deeper table desirable.

‡ Distance between centers should seldom be less than 4 ft 6 in.; 5 ft is preferred; anything greater is unnecessarily generous. With triple-staggered carrels, the back of the center one should be held down to no more than 10 in. above the table top.

§ The distance between centers should be not less than 4 ft 6 in.; and 5 ft is preferred. Watch out for ventilation. A window is psychologically desirable. Closed carrels are not recommended for undergraduates or any student not actually engaged in writing a dissertation. Glass in the door or grills should be provided for supervision.

¶ A room less than 6 ft long at right angles to the desk will permit shelves above the desk or a bookcase behind the occupant but preferably not both. One less than 6 ft parallel to the desk will not permit a 4-ft long desk, and a second chair, and may make it necessary to open the door outward. See Figs. 7.1, 10.2, and 16.7*B*.

A. *Ceiling Heights.* Ceiling heights greater than functionally necessary may be desirable aesthetically but involve increased cost, unused cubic footage, and larger areas to allow the stairs to reach a higher level. Ceiling heights have desirable functional minimums also, and if reduced beyond them may be unpleasant to the users, may seriously affect book capacity and flexibility, and may needlessly complicate lighting and ventilation. Table B.5 suggests functional minimums and maximums.

B. *Floor Areas.* Both the number of floors in a library and the area of each floor may be important functionally and aesthetically. Decisions in regard to them may properly be influenced by the site surroundings, the slope of the ground, and the value of the property. It is obvious, however, that a skyscraper with only 5,000 sq ft on each floor would be undesirable and that a 250,000 sq-ft area on one floor would involve unnecessary and undesirable horizontal traffic.

Table B.6 makes suggestions, which at best are only approximations, as to the percentage of the gross square footage of a library building which functionally should be on the entrance or central-services level in a typical academic library.

III. *Accommodations for Readers.* Seating accommodations for readers and the service to readers are the largest space consumers in most libraries. The required areas depend on:

A. The number of accommodations provided

B. The types of accommodations and the percentage of each

C. Dimensions of the working surfaces for each type of accommodation

D. Average square footage required for each type of accommodation

E. Additional space required for service to readers

A. *Formulas for Percentage of Students for Whom Seating Accommodations Are Required.* The formula used should depend on:

1. The quality of the student body and faculty. The higher the quality, the greater the library use.

TABLE B. 4. FACULTY STUDIES AND SMALL MULTIPURPOSE ROOMS

Bay size	Small faculty study*	Small conference room or generous faculty study†
18′	3	2
19½′	3	2
21′	3	2
22½′	3	2
24′	4	3
25½′	4	3
27′	4	3

* A room of this size can house a large desk, shelving, a filing case, and permit a door to open in. (See Fig. 7.1.)

† This will provide for conference rooms for four, an adequate small staff office, or a generous faculty study. It should be at least 8 ft in the clear in one direction and have a total area of over 70 sq ft. (See Figs. 7.1 and 7.4.)

Any small room will seem less confining if it has a window, and since window wall space is generally at a premium, a room can well have one of its short sides on the window wall.

TABLE B. 5. CLEAR CEILING HEIGHTS

Area	Suggested minimum[a]	Suggested functional maximum[b]
Book stacks[c]	7'6"	8'6"
Stacks with lights at right angle to ranges[d]	8'4"	8'9"
Stacks with lights on range tops functioning by ceiling reflection	9'0"	9'6"
Reading areas under 100 sq ft . .	7'6"	8'6"
Individual seating in large areas	8'4"	9'6"
Large reading rooms over 100 ft long broken by screens or bookcases[e]	9'6"	10'6"
Auditoriums up to 1,500 sq ft . . .	9'6"	10'6"
Entrance or main level with over 20,00 sq ft	9'6"	10'6"
Floor with mezzanine[f]	15'6"	18'6"

[a] Heights lower than specified have been used successfully on occasion, but ceiling lights should be recessed and good ventilation assured. Financial savings will be comparatively small.

[b] Greater heights may be useful aesthetically and provide added flexibility by making areas available for a wider range of purposes.

[c] 7 ft 6 in. is the lowest height which permits an adequate protective base and seven shelves 12 in. on centers (standard for academic libraries) with suitable clearance at the top. The top shelf will be 6 ft 4 in. above the floor, the greatest height that can be reached without difficulty by a person 5 ft tall. (See Fig. 8.7.) Space above 7 ft 6 in. is not useful for storage of open-access collections and will be confusing if used for other shelving.

[d] This height used with fluorescent tubes, at right angles to the ranges, permits stack ranges to be shifted closer together or farther apart without rewiring, and is high enough so that heat from the tubes will not damage the books on the top shelf. If the fixtures are flush or nearly flush with the ceiling, the clear height can be reduced a few inches.

[e] Fig. 16.4 shows the arrangements for the reading room 131 ft long in the Lamont Library, with a clear ceiling height of 9 ft 6 in.

[f] Mezzanines provide inexpensive square footage if they occupy at least 60 per cent of the floor area (building codes may prohibit them unless mezzanine is partitioned off and made a separate unit), and if the over-all height of the two resulting levels is not much more than 6 ft greater than would be provided if there were no mezzanine.

2. The library facilities provided. The more satisfactory the seating accommodations and the services provided, the greater use.

3. The quality of the collections. Superior collections increase use.

4. The curriculum. In general, students in the humanities and social sciences use the library more than do those in the pure and applied sciences.

5. The emphasis placed on textbook instruction, which tends to reduce library use.

6. Whether the student body is resident or commuting and, if the former, whether the dormitories provide suitable study facilities. Heaviest library use in most residential institutions is in the evening; in commuting ones, during the daytime hours.

7. Whether the location is rural, suburban, or urban. Large population centers tend to decrease evening use because of other available activities and attractions.

8. Whether the institution is coeducational or for one sex only. Coeducation tends to increase library use, particularly in the evening.

9. The emphasis placed by the faculty on the library and on nontextbook reading.

10. The percentage of graduate students and the fields in which they work.

11. The institution's policy in regard to use by persons other than those connected with it.

12. The departmental library arrangements which may make available other reading facilities and reduce the use of the central library. Table B.7 suggests formulas for percentage of students for whom seating is suggested.

B. *Suggestions for Types of Seating Accommodations and the Percentage of Each Type*

1. FOR UNDERGRADUATES:

a. Tables for four or more. Not more than 20 per cent. Should be largely restricted to those in reserve-book and reference rooms.

b. Lounge chairs. Not more than 15 per cent. Should in general be restricted to lounge areas,

TABLE B. 6. SUGGESTED FORMULAS FOR PERCENTAGE OF GROSS SQUARE FOOTAGE FUNCTIONALLY DESIRABLE ON THE CENTRAL-SERVICES LEVEL*

Gross building area in sq ft	Size of collections in volumes	Minimum percentages of gross area on central-services level
Under 20,000	Under 100,000	40–50
20,000–45,000	100,000–250,000	33⅓–40
40,000–80,000	250,000–500,000	25–33⅓
75,000–150,000	500,000–1,000,000	20–30
135,000 +	1,000,000 +	16⅔–25

* Central services as used here include the main control point, circulation and reference services, reference and bibliographical collections, the public catalogue, and acquisition and catalogue departments.

These computations are approximations only, but smaller figures than those in the last column will often necessitate shifting part of the central services to other levels and incidentally may add considerably to staff payrolls.

TABLE B.7. FORMULAS FOR PERCENTAGE OF STUDENTS FOR WHOM SEATING ACCOMMODATIONS ARE SUGGESTED

Type of institution	Percentage
Superior residential coeducational liberal arts college in rural area or small town	50–60
Superior residential liberal arts college for men or women in rural area or small town	45–50
Superior residential liberal arts college in a small city	40–45
Superior residential university	35–40
Typical residential university	25–30
Typical commuting university	20–25

smoking rooms, current-periodical rooms, or used to break up unpleasantly long rows of other types of accommodations. In many libraries 8 to 10 per cent of seating of this kind is adequate.

c. Individual accommodations. Up to 85 per cent. These should provide in most cases for working surfaces cut off from immediately adjacent neighbors, by aisles or partitions on one, two, or three sides. The partitions should be high enough—52 in. for men—so that heads do not bob up or down above them and cause visual distraction. These accommodations may include:

(1) Tables for one. These can be quite satisfactory along a wall or screen if the readers all face in the same direction. When placed in a reading area, as shown in Fig. 7.10, they are not recommended.

(2) Tables for two with partitions down the center. See Fig. 7.11*B*. For limited use only.

(3) Tables for four or more with partitions in both directions. See Fig. 16.12. A great improvement over a table for four without partitions.

(4) Pinwheel arrangement for four. See Fig. 16.12. Satisfactory, but requires more space than (3) above.

(5) Double carrels with readers facing in different directions. See Fig. 16.8. Not as satisfactory as (6) below.

(6) Double-staggered carrels. See Fig. 16.10*A*.

(7) Pairs of double-staggered carrels on both sides of a screen. See Fig. 16.10*B*.

(8) Triple-staggered carrels in place of three stack ranges or in a large reading area. See Fig. 16.11.

(9) Rows of single carrels at right angles to a wall in book-stack or reading area. See Fig. 16.5*A*.

(10) Single carrels in place of last stack section at the end of a blind stack aisle. See Fig. 16.5*B*.

(11) Typing carrels similar to (10) above, but with special acoustic protection. See Fig. 7.6.

(12) Rows of double carrels in a reading area or in place of two stack ranges. See Fig. 7.12*A*, *B*, and *C*.

Closed carrels are rarely recommended for undergraduates. Shelves in carrels tend to encourage undesirable monopolization. A shelf outside the carrel with an open or locked cupboard provides for books and papers to be reserved and makes possible longer hours of carrel use.

2. GRADUATE STUDENT ACCOMMODATIONS:

a. At tables for multiple seating. Not recommended.

b. Open carrels of any of the types proposed in 1 above. Graduate carrels may have shelves over the working surface, but this will require deeper table tops because of lighting problems, unless the shelves are installed at one side. See Figs. 16.6, *A*, *B*, and *C*.

c. Closed carrels. See C and D below for working surface dimensions and square-footage requirements. Closed carrels require special care for satisfactory lighting and ventilation. Unless larger than necessary to provide adequate working surfaces, claustrophobia tends to result. A window for each carrel or an attractive grill on at least one side will help.

3. FACULTY ACCOMMODATIONS: If possible, closed studies should be provided for faculty members engaged in research projects which require the use of library materials. Limited assignment periods are suggested. They should not be used as offices. See C and D below for working surface dimensions and square-footage requirements.

C. *Dimensions of Working Surface for Each Type of Seating Accommodation.* Table B.8 gives suggested minimum and adequate dimensions. No attempt is made to propose maximum or generous sizes.

D. *Average Square Footage Required for Different Types of Accommodation.* The square-footage requirements suggested in Table B.9 are at best approximations, but may be helpful in preliminary stages of planning.

E. *Additional Space Required for Service to Readers.* Space for direct access to seating accommodations is dealt with in Table B.9 and elsewhere.

TABLE B.8. SUGGESTED WORKING SURFACE
AREA FOR EACH PERSON

Type of accommodation	Minimum size	Adequate size
Table for multiple seating..	33″ × 21″*	36″ × 24″
Individual table or open carrel for undergraduate.	33″ × 20″†	36″ × 22″
Open carrel for graduate student without book shelf over it...............	36″ × 24″‡	42″ × 24″
Carrel, open or closed, for graduate student writing dissertation, with a book shelf.................	36″ × 27″§	48″ × 30″
Faculty study	48″ × 30″	60″ × 30″ if there is shelving over it

* Recommended only for reserve-book use or for a college for women.

† A space of 33 × 20 in. goes farther in an individual accommodation than at a large table because others do not intrude on the space.

‡ Shelves are not recommended over open carrels because they make it easier for an unauthorized student to monopolize one.

§ A shelf over a carrel table requires additional depth because it interferes with lighting. A closed carrel should preferably have a window, glass in the door, and more space around the table than an open one, or claustrophobia may result.

Additional space required includes:

ASSIGNABLE AREAS:

The public catalogue.

Space around the bibliographical and reference and current-periodical collections which is required because of heavy use.

Public areas outside service desks.

Special accommodations for microfilm reproductions, maps, manuscripts, archives, and other collections not shelved in the main stack area. These may include audiovisual areas of various types.

Staff working quarters, which were dealt with in section 7.4.

NON-ASSIGNABLE AREAS, discussed in section 16.2:

Entrances, vestibules, and lobbies
Corridors
Areas used primarily as traffic arteries
Stairwells and elevator shafts
Toilets
Walls and columns

It is suggested that not less than 25 sq ft per reader in assignable or non-assignable areas will be required for the services in these groups, and that unless the special accommodations mentioned above are held to a reasonable minimum and careful planning is provided throughout, the 25 may have to be increased to 35 sq ft.

TABLE B.9. APPROXIMATE SQUARE-FOOTAGE
REQUIREMENTS FOR DIFFERENT
TYPES OF SEATING ACCOMMODATIONS[a]

Type of accommodations	Requirements in sq ft		
	Minimum	Adequate	Generous
Small lounge chair[b]....	20	25	30
Large lounge chair[c]....	25	30	35
Individual table[d]	25	30	35
Tables for four[e]........	22½	25	27½
Tables for more than four[f]..............	20	22½	25
Individual carrels[g].....	20	22½	25
Double carrels[h]	22½	25	27½
Double-staggered carrels[i]	22½	25	27½
Triple-staggered carrels[j].	22½	25	27½
Double row of carrels with partitions between, placed in a reading room or in place of two stack ranges[k]	22½	25	27½

[a] The figures used here include: (1) area of working surface if any; (2) area occupied by chair; (3) area used for direct access to the accommodations; and (4) reasonable share of all the assignable space used for main aisles in the room under consideration.

[b] These chairs if in pairs should be separated by a small table to prevent congestion and to hold books not in use. See Fig. 7.14B, C, and D.

[c] Large lounge chairs are expensive, space-consuming, and an aid to slumber. See Fig. 7.14A. Rarely recommended.

[d] Individual tables are space-consuming, are generally disorderly in appearance because they are easily moved, and result in a restless atmosphere from traffic on all sides. See Fig. 7.10. Not recommended except along a wall or screen.

[e] Tables for four are the largest ones recommended, unless pressure for additional capacity is great.

[f] Tables for more than four are space savers, but few readers like to sit with someone on each side. They will avoid using them as far as possible.

[g] Individual carrels are economical in use of space if placed at right angles to a wall, adjacent to an aisle that must be provided under any circumstances. They reduce visual distraction if partitions 52 in. or more in height are provided on at least two of the four sides. See Fig. 7.11A and D.

[h] Double carrels are useful, but the staggered ones described below are preferred. See Fig. 16.8.

[i] Double-staggered carrels are as economical of space as tables for four and reduce visual distraction. See Fig. 16.10A.

[j] Triple-staggered carrels are as economical of space as tables for six or more and reduce visual distraction. See Fig. 16.11.

[k] Double rows of carrels are economical in space use and reduce visual distraction. See Fig. 7.12.

IV. *Book-stack Capacity.* Book-stack capacity is based on:

A. The number of volumes shelved in a standard stack section

B. The square-footage requirements for a standard stack section

A. *The Number of Volumes Shelved in a Standard Stack Section.* The number of volumes that can be shelved in a standard stack section depends on: (1) Book heights and the number of shelves per section; (2) book thickness; (3) the decision in regard to what is considered a full section.

1. BOOK HEIGHTS AND SHELVES PER SECTION: Stack sections in academic libraries are considered standard if they are 7 ft 6 in. high and 3 ft wide. Sections of this height make possible seven shelves 12 in. on centers over a 4-in. base. This spacing is adequate for books which are 11 in. tall or less, which, as shown in Table B.10, include 90 per cent of the books in a typical collection.

It is suggested that most of the remaining 10 per cent will be concentrated in a comparatively few subjects, that 70 per cent of this 10 per cent will be between 11 and 13 in. tall, and that six shelves 14 in. on centers will provide for them.

2. BOOK THICKNESS AND THE NUMBER OF VOLUMES THAT CAN BE SHELVED SATISFACTORILY ON EACH LINEAR FOOT OF SHELVING: No two libraries are alike in this connection. The average thickness will depend on (*a*) The definition of a volume; (*b*) binding policy, particularly for pamphlets and serials and periodicals; (*c*) the collection under consideration.

A commonly used formula for thickness of books is shown in Table B.11.

3. THE DECISION ON WHEN A SECTION IS FULL: In Table B.11 a suggested number of volumes per single-faced section is proposed. It is evident that if books are shelved by subject, it is unwise to fill the shelves completely, and any estimate must be an approximation. For many libraries 125 volumes per stack section is considered safe,

TABLE B.10. BOOK HEIGHTS*

8″ or less	25%	12″ or less	94%
9″ or less	54	13″ or less	97
10″ or less	79	Over 13″	3
11″ or less	90		

* Adapted from Rider's *Compact Storage,* p. 45, which was based to a considerable extent on research done by Van Hoesen and Kilpatrick on the height of books in academic libraries.

TABLE B.11. VOLUMES PER LINEAR FOOT OF SHELF FOR BOOKS IN DIFFERENT SUBJECTS *

Subject	Volumes per foot of shelf	Volumes per single-faced section
Circulating (nonfiction) . . .	8	168
Fiction	8	168
Economics	8	168
General literature	7	147
History	7	147
Art (not including large folios)	7	147
Technical and scientific . . .	6	126
Medical	5	105
Public documents	5	105
Bound periodicals	5	105
Law	4	84

* This table is in common use by stack manufacturers. It was used by Wheeler and Githens, who suggest that 125 volumes per single-faced section be considered practical average working capacity.

although Robert Henderson's cubook formula, which was noted in section 8.2, proposes only 100 volumes per section.

Shelving 125 volumes to a single-faced section, as suggested by Wheeler and Githens, is a practice often used, but it is safer and preferable to estimate the number of standard sections the collection now fills completely and then add 50 per cent to that number to determine the present requirements for comfortable shelving arrangements. This would make the shelves two-thirds full on the average and would leave 1 ft of unused space available on each shelf. If collections are growing each year by 5 per cent of the collection at the end of the previous year, it will take between five and six years for the shelves to become six-sevenths full, and to leave an average of 5 in. vacant on each shelf. By the time this occurs, the annual cost of labor for the constant moving of books that will be necessary, plus the damage done to bindings by the moving, leaving out of consideration the resulting inconvenience, may well be greater than the interest on the capital sum required to provide for additional shelving.

Table B.12 shows the period required for a collection that now occupies two-thirds of available space to reach six-sevenths or between 85 and 86 per cent of absolute capacity at different rates of growth.

Table B.13 shows the period required for a collection that now occupies one-half of the available shelving to grow to the point where it

TABLE B.12. YEARS REQUIRED FOR A COLLECTION
TO INCREASE FROM TWO-THIRDS TO SIX-SEVENTHS
OF FULL CAPACITY

Rate of growth	Years					
	3⅓%	4%	5%	6%	8%	10%
Geometric increase *	7+	6+	5+	4+	3+	2+
Arithmetic increase †	8+	7+	6−	5−	4−	3−

* A geometric increase represents an increase of a given percentage each year of the total number of volumes at the end of the previous year.

† An arithmetic increase represents an increase each year of a given percentage of the total number of volumes at the time used as a base and so does not become larger year by year.

occupies six-sevenths of the shelving, with the growth at various percentage rates. In both tables the rates are figured with the annual increase estimated at a given percentage of (1) the previous year's total, and (2) by a percentage of the total at the time the estimate is made, that is, arithmetically instead of geometrically.

B. *Square-footage Requirements for a Standard Stack Section.* The square-footage requirements for a standard stack section depend primarily on: (1) range spacing; (2) range lengths; (3) the number of cross aisles and their widths; (4) cross aisle area charged against adjacent reader accommodations; (5) non-assignable space.

1. RANGE SPACING: Range spacing should be based on column spacing, which was discussed at the beginning of this appendix; on shelf depths, which are discussed in *a* below; and on stack-aisle widths, dealt with in 2 below.

a. Shelf depths. Depths as used here are based on double-faced bracket shelving with 2 in. between the back of the shelf on one side of the range and the back of the shelf on the other side. Shelf depths specified by stack manufacturers are 1 in. greater than the actual depth, that is, a 7-in. "actual" shelf is called an 8-in. "nominal" shelf, because 8 in. is available if half the 2 in. noted above is assigned to the shelves on each side of a double-faced shelf section.

Table B.14 shows depths of books. If these

TABLE B.13. YEARS REQUIRED FOR A COLLECTION TO
INCREASE FROM 50 TO 85 PER CENT OF FULL CAPACITY

Rate of growth	Years					
	3⅓%	4%	5%	6%	8%	10%
Geometric increase ...	16+	13+	11+	9+	7+	5−
Arithmetic increase ..	27+	18−	14+	12−	9−	7+

TABLE B.14.* PERCENTAGE OF BOOKS IN AN ACADEMIC
COLLECTION BELOW DIFFERENT DEPTHS MEASURED
FROM THE BACK OF THE SPINE TO THE
FORE EDGE OF THE COVERS

5″ or less	25%	9″ or less	94%
6″ or less..........	54	10″ or less	97†
7″ or less..........	79	Over 10″	3
8″ or less..........	90		

* Adapted from Rider's *Compact Book Storage,* p. 45.

† An 8-in. actual, i.e., a 9-in. nominal depth shelf, will house a 10-in.-deep book without difficulty, unless there is another deep book immediately behind it. Most books over 10 in. deep will be more than 11 in. tall and should be segregated on special shelving which is more than 9 in. in nominal depth.

figures are correct (the author believes they represent the average in research and academic libraries), a shelf with 8 in. actual depth, together with the space available between shelves on the two sides of a double-faced section, will provide for practically any book that does not have to be segregated because of its height, and 8-in. actual depth shelves (they are designated

TABLE B.15. SUGGESTED STACK-AISLE WIDTHS
AND STACK-RANGE LENGTHS *

Typical use of stack	Aisle width†		Range lengths‡	
	Min.	Max.	Min.	Max.
Closed-access storage stack	24″	30″	30′	60′
Limited-access, little-used stack for over 1,000,000 volumes	26″	31″	30′	42′
Heavily used open-access stack for over 1,000,000 volumes	31″	36″	24′	36′
Very heavily used open-access stack with less than 1,000,000 volumes	33″	40″	15′	30′
Newspaper stack with 18″ deep shelves	36″	45″	15′	30′
Reference and current-periodical room stacks ..	36″	60″	12′	21′
Current-periodical display stacks	42″	60″	12′	21′

* These are suggestions only and not to be considered definite recommendations. Circumstances alter cases.

† Stack-aisle widths of 24 in. should be considered an absolute minimum and are rarely justifiable. Anything under 26 in. is difficult with a book truck, even when the use is light. The minimum width proposed should generally be used only with the minimum range lengths suggested.

‡ Stack-range lengths are often determined by available space, rather than by their suitability. The maximum lengths shown in the table should generally be used only with the maximum aisle widths suggested.

by the manufacturers as 9-in. shelves) are recommended in place of the 7- or 9-in. actual-depth shelves which are commonly used. In many libraries a 7-in. actual-depth shelf is suitable for a large part of the collections.

2. STACK-AISLE WIDTHS AND STACK-RANGE LENGTHS. Stack-aisle widths should be based on the amount of use by individuals and by trucks and the length of the ranges before a cross aisle is reached. Other things being equal, the longer the range, the wider the aisle should be. Table B.15 suggests desirable stack-aisle widths in conjunction with stack-range lengths under different types and amounts of use.

Do not forget that stack-aisle widths must be based, indirectly at least, on the column spacing, dealt with at the beginning of this appendix, and are affected as well by the shelf depths discussed in 1a above, if columns are not to obstruct the aisles. The distance between column centers should be an exact multiple of the distance between the center of parallel stack ranges within the stack bay, which in turn is determined by the sum of the depth of a double-faced range and the width of a stack aisle.

3. WIDTHS FOR MAIN AND SUBSIDIARY CROSS-STACK AISLES: Cross-aisle widths should be based on amount of use and are inevitably affected by the column spacing. Column spacing often makes it difficult to provide any cross-aisle widths except 3 ft or a multiple of 3 ft. If standard column spacing is altered or if columns 14 in. long in the direction of the ranges are used and the column range is filled out with a lectern, 4 ft 6 in. aisles can be made available. (See Figs. 4.9 and 4.10.)

Table B.16 suggests desirable cross-aisle widths under different types and amounts of use.

4. CROSS-AISLE AREA CHARGED AGAINST ADJACENT READER ACCOMMODATIONS: The effect on square-footage requirements per stack section and volume capacity per net square foot of stack area, resulting from the provision of reader accommodations in the form of stack carrels, is shown in Figs. 16.18 to 16.23. These indicate that the assignment of one-half of the adjacent cross-aisle areas to reader space when carrels are on one side of the cross aisles and book-stack ranges are on the other, may increase rather than decrease book capacity per square foot of net stack area, and in addition provide desirable and economical seating accommodations adjacent to the books. See Table B.17.

TABLE B.16. SUGGESTED CROSS-AISLE WIDTHS *†

Typical use of stack	Main aisle		Subsidiary cross aisle‡	
	Min.	Max.	Min.	Max.
Closed-access storage	3'	4'6"	2'6"	3'6"
Limited-access stack	3'	4'6"	3'	3'6"
Heavily used open-access stack	4'	5'	3'	4'
Heavily used open-access stack for large collection and ranges 30' or more long	4'6"	6'	3'3"	4'6"

* These are suggestions only and not to be considered definite recommendations. Circumstances alter cases.

† In determining minimum or maximum widths, keep in mind the length and width of the book trucks used, as well as the amount of use. Minimum width stack aisles should not be accompanied by minimum cross aisles. From the widths shown in the table, up to 4 in. may have to be subtracted to provide for adjacent stack uprights and irregularities in column sizes.

‡ If open carrels adjoin a subsidiary aisle, they will make it seem wider, but traffic will tend to be disturbing to the carrel occupants. Fig. 16.17 shows a method of reducing undesirable and unnecessary traffic.

If closed carrels open from a subsidiary aisle, they will make it seem narrower.

It is evident that a large number of variables are involved in book-stack capacity. Table B.17 is based on the square footage required for a single-faced standard section in stack layouts, with different range spacing, range lengths, and cross-aisle widths, as well as stack carrels, as shown in Figs. 16.19 to 16.21.

Table B.18 shows stack capacity per square foot of area if 100, 125, 150, or 160 volumes per

TABLE B.17. SQUARE FOOTAGE REQUIRED FOR ONE SINGLE-FACED STANDARD SECTION

Range spacing	Square feet with minimum cross aisles *	Square feet with generous cross aisles †	Square feet with adequate cross aisles combined with carrels ‡
5'0"	8.25	9.00	8.4375
4'6"	7.425	8.10	7.60
4'3"	7.0125	7.65	7.225
4'0"	6.60	7.20	6.75

* Based on Fig. 16.19, with a 15-ft blind-aisle range on each side of a 3-ft center aisle.

† Based on Fig. 16.20, with two 3-ft side aisles and a 6-ft center aisle separated by 30-ft stack ranges.

‡ Based on Fig. 16.21, with 3-ft side aisles between carrels and 30-ft stack ranges, the latter separated by a 4 ft 6 in. center aisle. One-half of the side aisles are charged against the carrels, but even on 5-ft centers the carrels occupy only 22½ sq ft, and square footage for a section is low.

TABLE B.18. VOLUME CAPACITY PER 1,000 SQUARE FEET OF STACK AREA WITH DIFFERENT NUMBER OF SQUARE FEET AND DIFFERENT NUMBER OF VOLUMES PER SECTION

Sq ft per section [a]	No. of sections in 1,000 sq ft	Volumes per 1,000 sq ft with different no. of vols. per section [b,c]			
		100 [h]	125 [i]	150 [j]	160 [k]
10 [d]	100	10,000	12,500	15,000	16,000
9 [e]	111	11,100	13,875	16,650	17,760
8⅓ [f]	120	12,000	15,000	18,000	19,200
7 [g]	143	14,300	17,875	21,450	22,880

[a] Examination of Table B.17 and Figs. 16.18–16.23 should help in determining area to allow for a single-faced section. This matter has been covered in IVB of this appendix.

[b] Volumes per section has been covered in detail in IVA of this appendix.

[c] If a period is used instead of a comma in the volume count in the last four columns shown above, it will give the number of volumes per square foot available under different conditions.

[d] 10 sq ft per section is the cubook formula proposed by R. W. Henderson.

[e] See Table B.17 for an example.

[f] The author suggests that this is a satisfactory and safe figure to use for a large collection accessible to graduate students and a limited number of undergraduates.

[g] Adequate for a very large collection with limited access.

[h] 100 volumes per section is the cubook formula.

[i] The author suggests that this is a safe figure for comfortable working capacity in an average library. See IVA of this appendix and section 8.2 for a full discussion.

[j] The number of 150 volumes per section is too often proposed by architects and librarians. While it is a possible figure, it should be realized that it approaches full capacity and should be used only in cases where additional space is immediately available when capacity is reached. The time to consider what comes next will have passed.

[k] The number of 160 volumes per section should not be considered for most academic libraries, unless the collection has an unusually high percentage of abnormally thin volumes and individually bound pamphlets.

standard stack section is used in connection with 7, 8⅓, 9, or 10 sq ft occupied by each section.

5. NON-ASSIGNABLE SPACE: Non-assignable space was discussed in some detail in section 16.2. It includes, as far as its effect on book capacity is concerned, the floor space occupied by columns, mechanical services, and vertical transportation of all kinds. We mention it here simply to call attention to it. In a carefully designed stack for 25,000 volumes or more on one level, non-assignable space should not amount to more than 10 per cent of the gross stack area, and with a larger installation considerably less than that.

V. *Card Catalogue Capacity.* In planning a card-catalogue room, estimates quite similar to those used for book-stack capacity must be made. They should include:

A. The capacity for each card catalogue unit used

B. The square footage of floor space required to file 1,000 cards comfortably

A. *The Capacity of Each Card Catalogue Unit.* The capacity of each card catalogue unit depends on:

1. The number of trays it contains

2. The depth of each tray and the number of inches of cards that can be filed in it without undesirable and uneconomical congestion

3. The thickness of the card stock, that is, the number of cards that will occupy 1 in. of filing space.

1. THE NUMBER OF TRAYS IN A CARD CABINET: This depends on the number of trays in each direction, that is, vertically and horizontally. Cabinets are made in a great many different sizes, but for large installations six trays wide and 10 to 12 high are considered standard, giving 60 or 72 to a unit.

A cabinet with trays 14 or even 16 high is possible, with fairly low bases so that the top one will be within reach. This will give 84 or 96 trays to a unit.

Cabinets five trays wide of different heights are also available, but may be more expensive per tray unless purchased in large quantities. They have the advantage of fitting into standard 3-ft-wide stack units.

2. THE DEPTH OF THE TRAYS: Trays can be purchased in almost any depth, but just over 15, 17, and 19 in. might be considered standard. A tray under 15 in. is uneconomical in floor space used if the catalogue is large. Those over 19 in. are so heavy when full as to make their use a doubtful blessing.

3. THE THICKNESS OF CARDS AND THE NUMBER THAT WILL OCCUPY 1 INCH OF FILING SPACE: Experience indicates that 100 average cards to 1 in. of filing space is a safe figure to use today. Cards tend to thicken somewhat as they get older. Cards used earlier in the century averaged considerably thicker than those used today.

Table B.19 shows the capacity for cabinets six trays wide with different heights and different tray depths, based on 100 cards to 1 in., with the net available filing space filled to a comfortable

Table B.19. Card Capacity for Standard Card Cabinets Six Trays Wide *

Trays high	Tray length		
	15″ †	17″ ‡	19″ §
10	51,000	60,000	69,000
12	61,200	72,000	82,800
14	71,400	84,000	96,600
16	81,600	96,000	110,400

* Cabinets six trays wide occupy approximately 40 in. in width. Five-tray-wide cabinets occupy approximately 33⅓ in. in width and can be placed in a standard 3-ft-wide stack section. They will probably cost more per tray, but they may fit into the available space to advantage, sometimes combined with the wider units.

† A 15-in. tray is estimated to provide 12 in. of net filing space, which, if filled to 71 per cent capacity, will house comfortably approximately 850 cards which average 1/100 in. in thickness.

‡ A 17-in. tray is estimated to provide 14 in. of net filing space, which, if filled to 72 per cent of capacity, will house comfortably approximately 1,000 cards which average 1/100 in. in thickness.

§ A 19-in. tray is estimated to provide 16 in. of net filing space, which, if filled to 73 per cent of capacity, will house comfortably approximately 1,150 cards which average 1/100 in. in thickness. These trays may be uncomfortably heavy when filled to capacity.

working capacity. The term "tray depth" refers to the over-all depth of the cabinet in which the trays are housed. From it 3 in. should be subtracted to obtain the gross filing space available, and comfortable working capacity can be estimated at between 70 and 75 per cent of the gross filing space, with a somewhat larger percentage usable with the longer trays.

The capacities noted above can be increased by at least 10 per cent before they become completely unmanageable, but it is strongly recommended that the lower figure be used in estimating comfortable working capacity.

B. *Square Footage of Floor Space Required to File 1,000 Cards Comfortably.* The space requirements depend on:

1. The depth of the trays is a somewhat variable factor, as already noted.

2. The height of the cabinets.

3. The space between cabinets set aside for consultation tables and for those who use the catalogue. This should depend on the intensity of use at the time of peak loads. A small catalogue with heavy use requires much more square footage for 1,000 cards than does a large one with light use.

4. The space assigned to main and secondary aisles used to approach the cards.

Figs. 16.29 to 16.32 show different arrangements based primarily on the intensity of use and secondarily on the size of the catalogue which result in all the way from 1,000 to 4,000 cards per sq ft of floor space for the whole area.

Every library building program should indicate the number of cards that should be housed and any available information about the amount of use at the time of peak loads.

VI. *Government Standards.* It is possible and in some cases necessary to base space-assignment figures on standards promulgated by governmental authorities supervising the institutions concerned. These standards can be helpful but, like all formulas and tables, they should be used with caution because, as has been emphasized throughout this volume, situations differ and circumstances alter cases. Do not put yourself into a strait jacket. With this word of warning, standards for three different groups are noted:

A. *California State Colleges Library Standards.* Based upon library volumes to be housed, the following space standards are to serve as guidelines for the design of new buildings or additions to existing buildings:

1. Book-stack areas at the rate of 0.10 sq ft per volume.

2. Readers' stations at the rate of 25 sq ft per station, with stations to be provided for 25 per cent of predicted FTE (full-time equivalent students).

3. Special materials. An additional area equal to 25 per cent of the bound-volume area should be the budget standard for special materials: unbound periodicals, maps, courses of study, and sample textbooks.

4. Special functions:

(These data relate to each person employed in any of these categories)

Square feet

Administration	150
Administrative conference room	150
Secretary-reception	160

Technical services
Division head	150
Department head	110
Asst. catalogue librarian	110
Asst. order librarian	110
Serials librarian	110
Documents librarian	110
Clerical—per position	80

Square feet

Public services

    Division head 150

    Department head 150

    Reference librarian 110

    Special services 110

    Circulation librarian 110

    Clerical—per position 80

Public services points

    Per librarian's station 125

    Per clerical station 80

B. The California State Department of Education in 1955 included this statement in *A Restudy of the Needs of California in Higher Education*.

Libraries.—Total library space requirements, including study halls and all library-staff work areas, were computed on the basis of the following estimates:

1. Reading rooms and study halls, including circulation desks and staff offices: 30 net square feet per station and one station for every four full-time students, or 7.5 net square feet per full-time student.

2. Collections housing the volumes listed below, including work areas, assuming progressively greater use of closed stacks as collections increase in size, and the use of central storage facilities for the larger collections:

First 150,000 volumes . . . . .0.10 net sq ft per volume

Second 150,000 volumes 0.09

Next 300,000 volumes 0.08

Next 400,000 volumes 0.07

Second 1,000,000 volumes. 0.05

(Note: The total floor area allowed by 1 and 2 above will, it is estimated, provide for the necessary carrels, microfilm and audio-visual facilities, etc.)

3. Size of collection:

State college: 30 volumes per full-time student for the first 5,000 students, plus 20 volumes per full-time student beyond 5,000 students.

University: 100 volumes per full-time student for the first 10,000 students, plus 75 volumes per student for the second 10,000 students, plus 50 volumes per student beyond 20,000 students.

C. The United States Veterans Administration has prepared tables to indicate library space assignments which are based on the number of beds in different types of hospitals. They are hoping by the use of these tables to determine through a computer the square footage to be assigned in a library for each group of space users, library staff, hospital staff, patients, shelving equipment, and so forth.

appendix C

A List of Equipment That Might Be Overlooked

"You will [forget] if you don't make a memorandum of it."

The Queen in *Alice in Wonderland*

This list supplements the seventeen chapters of the text.

No attempt is made here to include equipment for audiovisual work, microform readers, photographic installations, maps, archives, manuscripts, music and print rooms. It is suggested that you consider your needs for these and other types of equipment and consult specialists in the various fields about their selection and spatial and physical requirements.

Ash trays and smoking urns: One or the other or both are needed wherever smoking is permitted. Should be deep enough so that a flip of a page will not scatter ashes. If too small or attractive, they will tend to disappear. Urns, if used at building entrances, should be as attractive as possible, probably partially filled with sand to prevent conflagrations. They should not be combined with trash containers.

Bells, buzzers, fire alarms, and gongs: Some simple methods of calling attention of readers to closing time and emergencies and of staff when they are needed at a service desk are desirable. Differentiation between the two is required, and those for staff members should not involve sharp sounds. Telephone bells should be muted. (Do not forget that the use of telephones by staff in public areas can be extremely disturbing unless the instrument is properly placed and protected.) Visual calling systems can sometimes be useful.

Blackboards: Can be very useful in small or large conference rooms for readers or for staff.

Building directory: Should be available in the entrance lobby in all but very small libraries where almost the entire building is visible from the entrance.

Bulletin boards: If suitably placed, can be useful as dispensers of information. If well designed, can be attractive. If cork or other soft surface and thumb tacks are available, they can be easily used. A glass frame that is locked will prevent unauthorized use. Good lighting is a necessity.

Clerestory windows: Can be useful in areas otherwise cut off from outside light or in inner rooms that overtop those adjoining. They can be used between a small room that is without outside light and an adjacent corridor or room, in which case they are more generally termed "borrowed light."

Clocks: Preferably electric clocks should be in all but the smallest offices and workrooms and reading areas, so placed as to be in sight of as large a percentage of the occupants as possible in order to reduce disturbing traffic that would result if they could be seen only from certain areas.

Coat rooms and coat racks: Supervised coat rooms are little used in academic libraries, as rapid change in readers makes them impractical. Unsupervised rooms are hazardous, particularly in large urban institutions and are seldom used. Carefully designed coat racks scattered around the building within sight of the reader are generally preferable. Coat hooks on carrel partitions help to solve the problem. Climatic conditions should affect the decision in regard to their use.

Corners: Should be protected by metal sheets, vinyl tile, buckram, or high projecting bases. This applies particularly to plaster- or wood-covered columns or corners in exposed places.

Cutoffs for water, light, and power: Should be easily accessible to library and maintenance staff but made inaccessible to the public by the use of cupboards and locks, if they are located in a public room. It is of advantage in a multistory library to have the electrical controls for all public areas throughout the building located at or close to the main desk.

Desk and table legs: Can be protected by brass or other types of shoes.

Directional signs and door labels: Should be attractively designed, carefully placed, and easy to read.

Door mats: Are one of the best ways to reduce maintenance costs if they are selected and serviced to meet local conditions. Cocoa mats sunk in the floor are ideal if small enough so that cleaning will not shrink them so much as to result in dangerous cracks. Rubber mats with corrugations are sometimes useful. Some libraries use carpeting on the basis that in spite of cost it will pay for itself in lower cleaning expenditures. In climates subject to snow and slush, a grating close to the main entrance doors through which the snow and slush can fall from the feet, has been found to reduce considerably the maintenance and improve the appearance of the adjacent interior flooring.

Door saddles and sills: Do not use them where book trucks will pass. It is well to avoid them on interior doors in any case. They serve a useful purpose, however, on exterior doors, providing a weather stop which helps to eliminate the penetration of water and drafts into the building.

Drafts: Are not equipment but can be important; should not occur in places such as workrooms and reading areas where staff or readers are sitting down or standing still. Entrances tend to be drafty. Watch out for the problem.

Drinking fountains: Should be placed where spilled water will not damage books or result in dangerously slippery floors.

Electric erasers: Can be very useful in a catalogue department.

Electric fans: Suitable wiring outlets should be provided for them if the building is not air-conditioned. Wall-hung fans save floor space.

Electric outlets: Floor, base, and wall plugs will never be cheaper than in the original wiring installation and may be useful for electric fans and typewriters, electric erasers, reading, dictating and copying machines, vacuum cleaners, buffers, for use with turntables, table and floor lamps, telephones, electronic and computer equipment, carrel installations, and so forth.

Electric typewriters: Are often as essential as telephones. Be sure they can be installed wherever needed without complications arising.

Emergency lights: Required for public buildings by many building codes for use in public areas in case of breakdown, and should generally be made available even if not required. They are often battery-powered and placed so as to make it easy to reach exits if emergencies arise.

Exhibit cases: Provide a place for enough of them, but do not have too many. They should be attractive and well designed, protected from theft and vandalism, and suitably lighted. Some entrance lobbies are suitable for them, as are wide corridors. Separate rooms are expensive in their use of space and may require expensive supervision.

Exit signs: Check their location with building and fire codes.

Fire extinguishers: Provide enough of them in carefully considered locations. Select them with the risks in mind. The CO_2 type is generally preferable to others in libraries. Fire hose and sprinklers should be avoided.

Fire hoses: May be required by building codes and insurance contracts. If they are installed, they should be accessible but placed so as to reduce danger of misuse.

Fireplaces: Rarely desirable in an academic library in spite of being attractive.

Floor lamps: Can be very attractive in a browsing room, but tend to be expensive and difficult to keep in repair.

Floor-plan charts: Are a must on each level of a large building. It is important to orient them so that the user is facing the same direction that is shown at the top of the plan. The architect is equipped to prepare them and will be glad to render this service.

Fly screens: If windows are to be opened and flies are a nuisance in your locality, be sure that screens are provided. If in doubt, at least provide suitable construction for later installation.

Garages: Rarely required in an academic library because generally available elsewhere in the institution.

Gliders (glass or metal): Should be large enough for the task assigned to them. Useful for chairs, tables, and heavy furniture that will be moved frequently. Very heavy pieces can have thick waxed linoleum bradded to the base.

Globes: If you want one, a suitable space should be planned for it. It takes square footage.

Heating coils: Used during rainy and snowy periods under sidewalk or entrance plaza, will lower maintenance costs.

High stools and high swivel chairs: High stools, that can be pushed out of the way under consultation tables, will be appreciated by the reader.

High swivel chairs with suitable footrests for use by staff members serving the public may prevent backaches and tired feet and bring the eyes of a staff member more or less on the level with the reader, a matter of considerable importance and convenience to both, particularly for short staff members.

Incinerators: Rarely desirable in a library. Decision in regard to their use may depend on the institution's policy on waste disposal. They represent a prospective fire hazard, and if used too promptly may result in inadvertent loss of irreplaceable material. All precautions for fire protection should be adopted if they are installed.

Lettering: Exterior lettering identifying the building is important, but should generally be confined to a few words.

Labels at public-service desks with names and sometimes titles may save time and confusion for readers and staff.

Lockers: Should always be available for staff members, and for this use are generally full size, at least 5 ft to 6 ft high.

If installed for readers, adjacent to open carrels, they can make carrel shelves unnecessary and can be much smaller, designed to allow space to store books, notes, and a typewriter.

Mail counter (sorting counter): Be sure to provide one in the shipping room, acquisition department, and in other places where large amounts of material must be sorted. Suitable pigeonholes should be available close at hand.

Mending room: A properly equipped mending room, generally adjacent to the processing areas, is desirable, whether or not the library has a bindery.

Mirrors: Can be used for supervision in critical areas. Rarely required for this purpose in academic libraries.

Outdoor and roof reading rooms: May present a serious control problem. Dust, dirt, and rain complicate matters. But they can be useful, particularly in mild climates if satisfactorily located.

Outside lighting: Desirable at entrances, loading docks, and corners. Can be used for decorative as well as functional purposes.

Pen filler (ink station): If properly located where spilled-ink damage can be kept at a minimum, can be a time saver for readers and staff. Can sometimes be operated as a penny-in-a-slot machine.

Pencil sharpeners: Will be a convenience to readers and staff if easily seen and placed where they will not obstruct traffic or cause a disturbance.

Print shop: Many academic institutions will have installations elsewhere on the campus, but a place in a large library where students can learn typesetting and the principles of book design can be useful and appropriate.

Radiators: If they are installed behind bookcases, be sure proper insulation is provided to protect books. They can also be uncomfortable and even dangerous to adjacent readers, particularly if steam heat is used.

Return-book slot: Be sure that a book placed in one cannot be retrieved by an unauthorized person, and will not drop so far as to damage it or one that preceded it.

If in an outside wall, the slot should be protected from the weather and small animals and should drop the book in a convenient location inside the building. Can be used inside a building on top of or in the front of a desk.

Skylights: Unless well designed, tend to develop leaks. Can be heat producers, but an annual coat of whitewash will help. Sometimes older skylights are replaced with squares of fluorescent lights in fixtures that do not alter the character of the room.

Staff lunchroom: A stove, refrigerator, sink, and cupboards can be made available in one unit. Be careful to avoid encouraging mice and vermin.

Staff quiet room: To be considered essential for a staff of as many as six women. Should be equipped with a cot. Hot and cold water and a medicine chest should be available close at hand. This room can be used for the public in emergency cases.

Sump pumps: Be sure one is provided in the basement if there is danger of flooding. Complete protection can be obtained only with a duplex installation so that maintenance repair or a breakdown will not temporarily complicate matters. Even then it is sometimes desirable to have an adjacent overflow area, for use during flash floods, which can receive any water temporarily in excess of that which can be handled by the pumps.

Supply closets: Do not forget the need for a limited number of small closets in administrative and departmental offices and at least one large one for bulky library and building-maintenance supplies kept under lock and key.

Table lamps: Tend to result in glare and restrict reader's comfort. Too often subject to vandalism in an academic library.

Telephones (public): Are desirable and will be used heavily in most libraries. Place them just off main traffic arteries in order to provide some supervision, but where the noise involved will not disturb readers. Should be adequately soundproofed.

Toilet-room equipment:
Coat hooks
Mirrors
Paper towels or other drying equipment
Sanitary dispensers
Shelves on which to lay parcels
Soap holders or soap dispensers

Trash chutes: May be desirable in or adjacent to janitor's closets on each floor; but watch out for fire hazards.

Trash containers: Useful at building entrances for small bits of paper, wrappers, etc.

Umbrella racks: Until recently unnecessary because umbrellas were little used by students. If coat racks are scattered around the building, umbrella racks may be likewise, but they involve water problems.

Unit air conditioners: Can be useful in offices and perhaps workrooms if building as a whole is not air-conditioned.

Vacuum cleaners: Both portable and building-wide equipment should be considered. Installation costs and the presence of satisfactory air filtering may be factors in the decisions reached.

Vaults and safes: Are expensive and must be adequately ventilated to prevent mold, but can be very useful on occasion. In many cases a screened enclosure in regular book stack will be sufficient, particularly if a small safe for cash and other valuables is available.

Vending machines: Rarely have a place in the library for public use, as food attracts vermin, and wrappers too often do not find their way into containers provided for the purpose. They may be considered for staff lounges and lunchrooms.

Venetian blinds: Horizontal and vertical blinds are available, each with certain advantages. The larger horizontal and most vertical ones can be more prone to present maintenance problems. Cleaning is difficult.

Vertical filing cabinets: Wheeler and Githens call them *major* library equipment. Do not forget to provide suitable space for them in offices and at reference desks, for instance. Select them carefully from the different types (wood or steel) and sizes that are available on the market.

Filing cases standing so that they face each other should be at least 3 ft 6 in. apart to provide for easy access, even when used by only one person at a time.

Wash basins: Are desirable in workrooms where several staff members are on duty, to prevent the loss of time and supervision involved in going to a toilet room.

Waste baskets: An adequate number will reduce maintenance costs. If too light, they will be misplaced. If too heavy and too hard with sharp corners, they will be a hazard. Do not forget suitable ones for paper towels in toilet rooms.

Water coolers: Can be a real boon to the thirsty, but should be so placed that water will not splash onto books or permit readers to reach books with hands that are still wet. A wide stair landing is sometimes a suitable place, but its use is also sometimes contrary to building codes, because it may result in slippery floors and stair treads.

Xerox and other copying machines: Their use will tend to increase rather than diminish. Try to reserve adequate space for them where they and those who use them can be supervised.

appendix D

Selective Annotated Bibliography

This bibliography is a selection of the books and articles published through 1964 which have been particularly useful in the preparation of this volume and which may be useful to its readers for further study of particular aspects of planning.

It is not intended to be a list of the "best" literature on the subject since quality was not the only criterion for selection; accessibility, language, and country of origin were also taken into account. All of the items are in English, and most have an American frame of reference, since the author assumes that readers of the volume, whatever their nationality, will want and expect to get an American approach to the subject. An effort has been made to include works by authors whose points of view differ materially from that of the author of this volume on questions of a controversial nature such as lighting. A long list of building programs would have been included except for the fact that these programs are published in limited editions for local use and are not generally available. A good one which has recently been reprinted and is available is listed under the heading "Programs." Others are quoted in Appendix A and should be useful to the person writing a program or outlining its main sections, but readers are warned of the dangers of copying blindly the program of another institution.

The best approach to current material is through *Library Literature,* The H. W. Wilson Company, New York, published quarterly with annual and three-year cumulations, and *Library Science Abstracts,* Library Association, London,

also published quarterly. The *Proceedings* of the Building Institutes (held nearly every year by the American Library Association's Library Administration Division) deal with buildings that are just being planned or under construction and are especially useful.

The items in the bibliography are arranged in alphabetical order under the following headings:

1. General works
    Bibliographies
    Building institutes
    Other general works
2. Special topics
    Acoustics
    Architects
    Automation and electronic developments
    Book stacks
    Climate
    Color
    Construction
    Consultants
    Contracts
    Fire protection
    Floor coverings
    Furniture and equipment
    Handicapped readers
    Heating, ventilating, and air conditioning
    Lighting
    Moving
    Programs
    Remodeling
    Site selection
    Special collections
    Study facilities

In general, a reference is cited only once in the bibliography under the heading that best describes the item as a whole. It should be noted that many of the references cited under "general works" contain much valuable material that could be listed under the various headings under "special topics."

GENERAL WORKS

Bibliographies

Byers, Mrs. Edna Hanley: *College and University Library Buildings Bibliographies.*
The several bibliographies compiled by Mrs. Byers form a comprehensive listing of articles describing new college and university library buildings in the United States from 1917 to 1955.
 1917–1938 in her *College and University Library Buildings,* American Library Association, Chicago, 1939, pp. 140–152.
 1939–1945 in ACRL Monographs no. 11, 1954, pp. 99–108.
 1945–1953 in ACRL Monographs no. 10, 1953, pp. 81–98.
 1953–1954 in ACRL Monographs no. 11, 1954, pp. 94–98.
 1954–1955 in ACRL Monographs no. 15, 1956, pp. 161–167.

Cowgill, Clinton H., and George E. Pettengill: "The Library Building," *AIA Building Type Reference Guide* (BTRG 3–3), reprinted from May and June, 1959, issues of *Journal of the AIA,* 32 pp.
Useful for its extensive bibliography, which was compiled by Mr. Pettengill, librarian of the American Institute of Architects.

Geer, Helen T.: *Select Readings on Planning College and University Library Buildings,* ACRL Monographs no. 15, 1956, pp. 158–160.
A brief annotated bibliography.

Merritt, LeRoy: "Library Planning: A Bibliographical Essay," in Burchard, David, and Boyd (eds.), *Planning the University Library Building,* Princeton University Press, Princeton, N. J., 1949, pp. 128–141.
A useful general review of the literature of the subject, now somewhat out of date.

Schutze, Gertrude: "Annotated Bibliography," in Chester M. Lewis (ed.), *Special Libraries: How to Plan and Equip Them,* SLA Monograph no. 2; Special Library Association, New York, 1963, pp. 92–102.
An extensive and useful annotated bibliography.

Thompson, Anthony: *Library Buildings of Britain and Europe.* Butterworth & Co. (Publishers), Ltd., London, 1963, 326 pp.
The numerous references at the end of the chapters constitute a comprehensive bibliography on library buildings.

Building Institutes and Conferences

Cooperative Committee on Library Building Plans. Reports of conferences held between October, 1945, and December, 1949, (Various places and publishers). Microfilms available from the De-partment of Photographic Reproduction, University of Chicago Library.
Reports of discussions by librarians, architects, and engineers on a large number of university library building plans; include reproductions of architectural drawings for each building discussed. These early conferences were the forerunners of the Library Building Plans Institutes and had considerable influence on subsequent planning of library buildings.

The First Library Building Plans Institute, sponsored by the ACRL Building Committee: *Proceedings of the Meetings at Ohio State University, Columbus, Ohio, April 25 and 26, 1952,* ACRL Monographs, no. 4, 1952, American Library Association, Chicago, 1952, 81 pp.
This series of Institutes has followed the precedent established by the Cooperative Committee on Library Building Plans which went out of existence in February, 1952. The purpose of the institutes is to provide a clearinghouse for the exchange of ideas on the planning of new library buildings and to make it possible for preliminary plans of libraries of colleges and universities to be critically reviewed. The plans of seven libraries are presented and discussed; floor plans are included.

The Second Library Building Plans Institute, conducted by the ACRL Buildings Committee: *Proceedings of the Meetings at Midwinter ALA Conference, Chicago, Ill., February 1 and 2, 1953,* ACRL Monographs no. 10, 1953, American Library Association, Chicago, 1953, 98 pp.
Presentation and discussion of plans of eight university library buildings.

The Third Library Building Plans Institute, conducted by the ACRL Buildings Committee: *Proceedings of the Meetings at the University of Wisconsin, Madison, Wis., January 30 and 31, 1954,* ACRL Monographs no. 11, 1954, American Library Association, Chicago, 1954, 108 pp.
The plans of seven college and university libraries are presented and discussed.

The Fourth Library Building Plans Institute: See *Planning a Library Building: The Major Steps.*

The Fifth and Sixth Library Building Plans Institutes, conducted by the ACRL Buildings Committee: *Proceedings of the Meetings at Wayne University, January 28 and 29, 1955, and at Rosemont College, July 3, 1955.* ACRL Monographs no. 15, 1956, American Library Association, Chicago, 1956, 167 pp.
The plans of fifteen college and university libraries are presented and discussed. Appendix I contains "Some Comments on Modular Libraries," by Angus Snead Macdonald; Appendix II: "Select Readings on Planning College and University Library Building," by Helen T. Geer; Appendix III: "A College and University Library Buildings Bibliography 1954–1955," by Edna Hanley Byers.

"Guidelines for Library Planners," edited by Keith Doms and Howard Rovelstad, *Proceedings of the Library Buildings and Equipment Institutes sponsored by the ALA, June 18–20, 1959, at the University of Maryland,* American Library Association, Chicago, 1960, 128 pp.

Includes papers by experts on various aspects of library building problems; presentation, criticism, and discussion of the plans of eight college, university, and public library buildings; pros and cons of remodeling and an outline for equipment specification writing.

"Planning a Library Building: The Major Steps," edited by Hoyt R. Galvin, *Proceedings of the Institute sponsored by the ALA Buildings Committee at St. Paul, Minn., June 19–20, 1954,* American Library Association, Chicago, 1955, 80 pp.

Librarians and architects present their points of view in six papers on the three major steps in planning a library building: programming, preliminary planning, and working drawings. A chapter based on the proceedings of the Fourth Library Building Plans Institute sponsored by ACRL includes presentations and discussions of plans of six college and university library buildings. Five brief papers on special aspects of planning and equipping libraries are appended.

"Planning Library Buildings for Service," edited by Harold L. Roth, *Proceedings of the Library Buildings and Equipment Institute, sponsored by the ALA, July 6–8, 1961, at Kent State University,* American Library Association, Chicago, 1964, 127 pp.

Includes several general papers and panel discussions plus presentations of the plans of six college and university library buildings.

"Problems in Planning Library Facilities: Consultants, Architects, Plans, and Critiques," edited by William A. Katz and Roderick G. Swartz, *Proceedings of the Library Buildings Institute, July 12–13, 1963,* American Library Association, Chicago, 1964, 208 pp.

Libraries for Research and Industry: Planning and Equipment, SLA Monograph no. 1, edited by Margaret P. Hilligan, Special Libraries Association, New York, 1955, 58 pp.

Based on a program on library planning and equipment that the Science-Technology Division presented at the forty-fourth annual meeting of the Special Libraries Association at Cincinnati, Ohio, May 16–21, 1954, with the hope "that it would be helpful to those working on plans for a new library, as well as for others who were remodeling or faced with having to make every square inch of area count."

Other General Works

Bleton, Jean: "The Construction of University Libraries: How to Plan and Revise a Project," *UNESCO Bulletin for Libraries,* 17:307–315, 345, November–December, 1963.

A summary article based on the author's considerable experience in planning new university libraries in postwar France.

Burchard, John E., Charles W. David, and Julian P. Boyd (eds.): *Planning the University Library Building,*

Princeton University Press, Princeton, N. J., 1949. Reprinted by the American Library Association, 1953, 145 pp.

A useful work for anyone seriously interested in planning a university library building; it covers most of the problems which are likely to arise in preparing the program and discusses the advantages and disadvantages of the various attacks which have been made on these problems; largely based on discussions of the Cooperative Committee on Library Building Plans from 1944 to 1949.

Byers, Mrs. Edna Hanley: *College and University Library Buildings,* American Library Association, Chicago, 1939, 152 pp.

Contains photographs, floor plans, comparative size and cost data, and critical comment for forty-two buildings erected between 1917 and 1938; covers essentials of planning, selection of site, type of architecture, reading rooms, circulation desk, catalog, workrooms, book stacks, etc.; bibliography of illustrated and descriptive articles; in spite of its age, it is still a useful reference work.

Educational Facilities Laboratories, Inc.: *Bricks and Mortarboards; A Report on College Planning and Building,* Educational Facilities Laboratories, New York, 1964, 168 pp.

Brings together information on current and future trends in planning the four major types of campus buildings—the classroom, the laboratory, the library and the dormitory—and in general campus design.

Ellsworth, Ralph E.: "Library Buildings," *State of the Library Art,* vol. 3, part 1, Rutgers University Press, New Brunswick, N.J., 1960, 151 pp.

A summary of the "state of the art" of library building knowledge from the point of view of the librarian; includes a list of 297 references.

Ellsworth, Ralph E.: *Planning the College and University Library Building,* Pruett Press, Boulder, Col., 1960, 102 pp.

Contains a concise, practical outline of the problems involved in most aspects of planning procedures, especially the early stages, and a more detailed discussion of the basic elements of a library structure; numerous diagrams and floor plans drawn by the author illustrate the various points that must be considered in planning, such as stack arrangement, audiovisual layout, central exit-control points, and the subject divisional library.

Fussler, Herman H. (ed.): *Library Buildings for Library Service; Papers Presented before the Library Institute at the University of Chicago, August 5–10, 1946,* American Library Association, Chicago, 1947, 216 pp.

Contains a dozen papers by leading librarians and architects on various aspects of library planning, including historic development of library buildings, functions, role of the architect, lighting, air treatment, building design, etc.; an important, and still very useful collection of papers, but should be supplemented by more recent material.

Galvin, Hoyt R., and Martin Van Buren: *The Small Public Library,* UNESCO, Paris, 1959, 133 pp.

Contains useful material and points of view for those concerned with planning academic libraries.

Gerould, James T.: *The College Library Building: Its Planning and Equipment,* Charles Scribner's Sons, New York, 1932, 116 pp.

Still a basic work, although some chapters are completely outdated.

Lewis, Chester M. (ed.): *Special Libraries: How to Plan and Equip Them,* SLA Monograph no. 2, Special Libraries Association, New York, 1963, 117 pp.

A collection of fourteen papers on planning and equipping special libraries, and descriptions of ten recently completed installations with floor plans and illustrations. An extensive annotated bibliography and a directory of manufacturers and suppliers are appended.

Library Journal, "Architectural Issue," R. R. Bowker Company, New York.

Issued annually on December 15, 1954, and before, and on December 1 thereafter. Contains articles on various aspects of library planning and equipment as well as numerous brief descriptive articles on recently completed buildings.

Library Planning, Bookstacks and Shelving, Snead and Company, Jersey City, N. J., 1915, 271 pp.

Contains much material of historical value as well as numerous plans and photographs of major libraries in the United States.

Lodewycks, K. A.: *Essentials of Library Planning,* Melbourne, 1961, 136 pp. Processed.

Based on the author's research and experience in planning the Baillieu Library at the University of Melbourne; not a finished text on library planning but compresses into one volume a wealth of detail and information which is not readily available elsewhere; will be of value to anyone planning a large library.

Lyle, Guy R.: *The Administration of the College Library,* 3d ed., The H. W. Wilson Company, New York, 1961, 415 pp.

The chapter on library building and equipment covers the basic elements of planning a building and includes material on the planning team, programming, and space requirements for various functions.

Macdonald, Angus Snead: "New Possibilities in Library Planning," *Library Journal,* 70:1169–1174, Dec. 15, 1945.

A significant article by one of the pioneers of modular construction in libraries; contains plans, photographs, and a list of eight desirable objectives to be reached in library buildings.

Palmer, R. Ronald, and William Maxwell Rice: *Modern Physics Buildings,* Reinhold Publishing Corporation, New York, 1961, 324 pp.

A comprehensive guide for college and university administrators, architects, and members of physics departments; the chapter on libraries contains a useful check list and other information, but the book is cited here primarily as an example of what has been done in another but closely related field.

Ranganathan, S. R.: "University Library Building," *Annals of Library Science,* 5:22–32, March, 1958.

A concise summary from an Indian point of view of the basic principles of good library design; prescribes standards for area per reader, volumes per square meter in stack rooms, and specifications for furniture and fittings.

Reece, Ernest J.: "Building Planning and Equipment," *Library Trends,* 1:136–155, July, 1952.

Summarizes trends and developments in college and university library building planning since 1940; includes a substantial list of references.

Reynolds, Helen Margaret: "University Library Buildings in the United States, 1890–1939," *College and Research Libraries,* 14:149–157, 166, April, 1953.

An historical and architectural review of thirty-eight buildings; an interesting background article.

Schunk, Russell J.: *Pointers for Public Library Building Planners,* American Library Association, Chicago, 1945, 67 pp.

Contains useful data for academic library planners; especially pertinent is Chapter 4, "Team Play in Planning the Large Library."

Soule, Charles C.: *How to Plan a Library Building for Library Work,* Boston Book Company, Boston, 1912, 403 pp.

One of the first modern works on planning a library; though largely outdated, it is still useful and remains a classic.

Thompson, Anthony: *Library Buildings of Britain and Europe,* Butterworth & Co. (Publishers), Ltd., London, 1963, 326 pp.

A useful reference work; part I summarizes the problems of creating a library building; part II traces in outline the history of library buildings and gives detailed analyses of a large number of buildings erected since 1930; examples are mostly from Britain with some from Europe and overseas; includes photographs and plans on uniform scales; numerous bibliographical references at the ends of chapters and accompanying descriptions of particular buildings.

Wheeler, Joseph L., and Alfred Morton Githens: *The American Public Library Building,* Charles Scribner's Sons, New York, 1941, 484 pp.

A comprehensive treatise in six parts and forty-two chapters; profusely illustrated with photographs, drawings, plans, tables, and charts; while it deals primarily with public libraries much of the material is also pertinent to academic libraries; it is still one of the most useful books on the subject, but it should be supplemented by more recent material.

Wilson, Louis Round, and Maurice F. Tauber: *The University Library,* 2d ed., Columbia University Press, New York, 1956, 641 pp.

Chapter 14, "Buildings and Equipment," pp. 481–525, is a good summary of the state of the art; covers all major aspects of the subject from selecting the site to equipping the library.

SPECIAL TOPICS

Acoustics

National Research Council, Building Research Institute: *Noise Control in Buildings,* National Research Council Publication 706, Washington, 1959, 136 pp.

Analyzes the noise-control problems arising in all types of buildings because of the increased use of lighter weight construction for exterior walls, interior partitions, and floors; noise problems created by mechanical equipment are also discussed; recommendations for noise control and a complete model specification for the control of noise from mechanical equipment provide practical guidance for the building designer.

Architects

American Institute of Architects: *Architect's Handbook of Professional Practice,* Washington, 1963, loose-leaf.

Contains twenty chapters in individual brochure form, plus thirty-eight AIA Documents in a binder. Chapter I is a circular of information on the AIA *Handbook* and a catalogue of publications and documents; other chapters deal with selection of an architect, owner-architect agreements, consultants, contracts, etc. The institutes of some other countries publish similar material.

Architectural Services and Compensation, A Statement and Recommendations of the Massachusetts State Association of Architects, a Chapter of the American Institute of Architects, adopted Oct. 31, 1951, revised Jan. 12, 1961.

Because of differences in local conditions the AIA delegates to its local chapters the determination of rates of recommended fee schedules. This is cited as an example of the kind of information that may be available from local AIA chapters.

"Building Together," *Library Association Record,* 65:440–452, December, 1963.

Two papers, one by an architect (D. W. Dickenson) and the other by a librarian (E. M. Broome) discussing the teamwork that is necessary for a successful library building.

Code for Architectural Competitions, AIA Document B-451, 1960 edition, The American Institute of Architects, Washington, 1960, 15 pp.

A complete guide to the selection of an architect by competition with special emphasis on the code of ethics which the AIA has formulated; discusses three types of competitions, question of programming, building committees, legal advice, etc.

Facts about Your Architect and His Work, American Institute of Architects, Washington, 1963, 23 pp.

A brief introduction to the subject of owner-architect relations.

"Standard Regulations for International Competitions in Architecture and Town Planning," *RIBA Kalendar,* 1962–1963, London, 1962, pp. 30–31.

These regulations were the subject of a recommendation to the member states adopted during the ninth session of the General Conference of UNESCO, New Delhi, 1956.

Automation and Electronic Developments

Automation and the Library of Congress, a Survey Sponsored by the Council on Library Resources, Inc., submitted by Gilbert W. King, and others, Washington, Library of Congress, 1963, 88 pp.

Report of a survey of the feasibility of mechanization of research library activities and of requirements for such mechanization; has serious implications for library planners.

Bolt, Beranek and Newman, Inc.: *Toward the Library of the 21st Century; A Report on Progress Made in a Program of Research Sponsored by the Council on Library Resources,* Cambridge, Mass., 1964, 41 pp.

Deals with the role that the science of information handling can play in solving the problems of the library of the future.

Morse, Philip M.: "The Prospects for Mechanization," *College and Research Libraries,* 25:115–119, March, 1964.

Discusses the feasibility of mechanizing the various activities of large research libraries.

Stein, Theodore: "Automation and Library Systems." *Library Journal,* 89:2723–2734, July, 1964.

An independent consultant, formerly with IBM, outlines the arguments for and against automation and data processing in libraries, with conclusions that are not encouraging as far as the immediate future is concerned.

Book Stacks

Harrar, Helen Joanne: "Cooperative Storage Warehouses," *College and Research Libraries,* 25:37–43, January, 1964.

This article is a summary of a doctoral dissertation accepted by the faculty of the Graduate School of Library Service, Rutgers University, in 1962. The dissertation is a thorough analysis of the economics of the three types of cooperative storage facilities in the United States today.

Hill, F. J.: "The Compact Storage of Books: A Study of Methods and Equipment," *Journal of Documentation,* 11:202–216, December, 1955.

The various systems are described and their advantages, disadvantages, and costs are analyzed and compared.

Kaplan, Louis: "Shelving," *State of the Library Art,* vol. 3, part 2, Rutgers University Press, New Brunswick, N. J., 1960, 41 pp.

A survey of the literature on shelving and storage of books, microcopies, and other library materials.

Muller, Robert H.: "Evaluation of Compact Book Storage Systems," ACRL Monographs no. 11, 1954, pp. 77–93.

An analysis of various systems including Remington Rand, Ames, Hamilton, and Art Metal, etc.; contains illustrations, plans, and tables; an abridged version of this study was published in *College and Research Libraries,* 15:300–308, July, 1954, with the title "Compact Storage Equipment; Where to Use It and Where Not."

Rider, Fremont: *Compact Book Storage,* Hadham Press, New York, 1949, 90 pp.

An original contribution to an important subject; discusses the need for, and various methods of, storing books compactly including conventional shelves.

Schunk, Russell J.: "Stack Problems and Care," *Library Trends,* 4:283–290, January, 1956.

Summarizes the main requirements of a stack system and describes typical equipment; discusses stack administration, types of stacks, control of access in closed and open stacks, control of atmospheric conditions, cleaning, efficient service, lighting.

Van Buren, Martin: "What to Look for When Buying Shelving," *Library Journal,* 90:1614–1617, April 1, 1965.

Climate

Plumbe, Wilfred J.: "Climate as a Factor in the Planning of University Library Buildings," *UNESCO Bulletin for Libraries,* 17:316–325, November–December, 1963.

A brief introduction to the subject followed by a list of addresses where additional information may be obtained and a bibliography.

Color

Birren, Faber: *New Horizons in Color,* Reinhold Publishing Corporation, New York, 1955, 200 pp.

An expert and readable introduction to the use of color in architecture.

Bryan, James E.: "Building Planning and the Use of Color in the Library," *Wilson Library Bulletin,* 28:570–573, March, 1954.

A good brief introduction to the use of color in libraries; discusses its use on floors, walls, furniture, and equipment; lists conclusions based on the author's experience and gives pointers on selecting a color scheme.

Construction

Architectural Record: *Time-Saver Standards; A Manual of Essential Architectural Data for Architects, Engineers, Designers, Builders, Draftsmen, and Other Technicians,* 3d ed., F. W. Dodge Company, a Division of McGraw-Hill, Inc., New York, 1954, 888 pp.

A fourth edition edited by J. H. Callender will be published by McGraw-Hill in 1965.

McGavin, Charles T.: "Asphalt Paving for Parking Areas, Driveways, and Walkways." *Cornell Hotel and Restaurant Administration Quarterly.* (In preparation.)

A report on construction, maintenance, and layout.

Means, Robert Snow: *Building Construction Cost Data,* Annual, Duxbury, Mass.

Provides average unit prices on a wide variety of building construction items for use in making up engineering estimates.

Merritt, Frederick S. (ed.): *Building Construction Handbook,* McGraw-Hill Book Company, New York, 1958, various paging.

A useful reference work for library planners; text is presented in easily understood language so as to be useful to the student and nonspecialist as well as to the specialist in the field.

Ramsey, Charles G., and Harold R. Sleeper: *Architectural Graphic Standards,* 5th ed., John Wiley & Sons, Inc., New York, 1956, 758 pp.

A handbook of construction details and requirements for architects and builders.

Consultants

Ellsworth, Ralph E.: "Consultants for College and University Library Building Planning," *College and Research Libraries,* 21:263–268, July, 1960.

After a brief historical sketch of the development of the library consultant as a member of the planning team, the author describes the duties of the consultant, the most important of which is to help the institution prepare a written program; he then tells in detail how to proceed with the program. A model outline of a successful program written by Ellsworth Mason for Colorado College is reprinted here.

Contracts

Marke, Julius J.: "Construction and Maintenance," *Library Trends,* 6:459–468, April, 1958.

The author shows how the laws of contract apply to the relationship between librarian, "owner," and architect; detailed discussion of the owner-architect contract, the difference between a private institution negotiating with a contractor and a government agency entering into such a relationship; fees, and legal forms are mentioned and illustrated by actual case references; fully documented in thirty-six footnotes.

Fire Protection

Protecting the Library and Its Resources: A Guide to Physical Protection and Insurance, Report on a study conducted by Gage-Babcock & Associates, Inc., Library Technology Project Publications no. 7, American Library Association, Chicago, 1963, 322 pp.

The first section of the book dealing primarily with

fire and to a lesser degree with other types of physical losses and their prevention is required reading for library planners. Fire-defense measures and equipment—including the pros and cons of sprinkler systems —in existing buildings and in relation to the planning of new buildings are discussed in considerable detail.

Floor Coverings

Armstrong Technical Data, 1964-65, Armstrong Cork Company, Floor Division, Lancaster, Pa., 1964, 56 pp.

Particularly useful for the comparative data on the physical characteristics and cost of various types of resilient floors.

Berkeley, Bernard, and Cyril S. Kimball: *The Care, Cleaning and Selection of Floors and Resilient Floor Coverings,* Ahrens Publishing Company, New York, 1961, 45 pp.

A thorough and authoritative manual with tables comparing the physical characteristics of various types of floor coverings.

Berkeley, Bernard, and Cyril S. Kimball: "The Selection and Maintenance of Commercial Carpet," *Cornell Hotel and Restaurant Administration Quarterly,* 3(4):47–78, February, 1963.

Useful for anyone contemplating the use of carpeting in a library; contains illustrations, tables, references, and a glossary.

Plaister, Cornelia D.: *Floors and Floor Coverings,* American Library Association, Chicago, 1939, 75 pp.

Describes the various types of floor covering available, giving advantages and disadvantages of each; includes methods of laying and instructions for maintaining floors. A good summary of the subject but should be supplemented by more recent material.

Snell, Foster D., Inc.: *Floors and Floor Coverings,* Library Technology Project, American Library Association, Chicago. (In preparation.)

Furniture and Equipment

"Library Buying Guide 1964," *Library Journal,* 89:1518–1571, Apr. 1, 1964.

A comprehensive list of products and supplies; appears annually in the April 1 issue.

The catalogues and house organs of the four or five major library-supply houses are invaluable sources of information on various types of equipment.

"Library Furniture and Equipment," *Proceedings of a three-day institute conducted at Coral Gables, Florida, June 14-16, 1962,* sponsored by the Library Administration Division, ALA, in cooperation with the University of Miami. American Library Association, Chicago, 1963, 68 pp.

Contains papers on furniture and book-stack selection, specification writing, bidding procedures, and photocopying equipment.

Salmon, Eugene N.: "Resources in Library Technology," *Library Journal,* 89:1495–1502, Apr. 1, 1964.

An essay on the sources of information available to assist in the solution of technical problems; includes a list of associations and organizations and a selected bibliography.

Van Buren, Martin: "Interior Planning of College and University Libraries," *College and Research Libraries,* 17:231–235, 238, May, 1956.

Stresses the importance of proper use of materials and color and care in selection of equipment and furnishings.

Van Buren, Martin, and Stephen D. Pryce: *Manual of Library Furniture,* Library Technology Project, American Library Association, Chicago. (In preparation.)

Handicapped Readers

American Standard Specifications for Making Buildings and Facilities Accessible to, and Usable by, the Physically Handicapped, Approved Oct. 31, 1961, American Standards Association, Inc., New York, 1961, 11 pp.

An important aspect of library planning which should not be neglected.

Heating, Ventilating, and Air Conditioning

American Society of Heating and Air Conditioning Engineers: *Heating, Ventilating, Air Conditioning Guide,* 37th ed., New York, 1959, 476 pp.

Divided into a technical data section of reference material on the design and specification of heating, ventilating, and air-conditioning systems and a manufacturers' catalog section.

Grad, I., and A. Greenberg: "Air Conditioning for Books and People," *Architectural Record,* 121(7): 231–234, June, 1957.

A good summary article.

Lighting

Berens, Conrad, and C. L. Crouch: "Is Fluorescent Lighting Injurious to the Eyes?" *American Journal of Ophthalmology,* 45:47–54, part 2, April, 1958.

The thesis of the article is that when fluorescent tubes are installed and maintained with proper shielding so that they are not glaring, they have no harmful effects on the eyes or skin of healthy individuals. Contains a good bibliography.

Blackwell, H. R.: "Development and Use of a Quantitative Method for Specification of Interior Illumination Levels on the Basis of Performance Data," *Illuminating Engineering,* 54:317–353, June, 1959.

The IES recommendations for lighting levels in libraries are based on the author's studies, which show that 30 foot-candles are needed for printed materials and 70 foot-candles for reading involving the taking of penciled notes. Should be supplemented by his series "Vision Engineering" in *Lighting,* 1963–1964. (See below.)

Blackwell, H. R.: "Vision Engineering," *Lighting,* 79–80, various pages, July, 1963–April, 1965 and continuing.

An important series of articles in which the author, one of the leading authorities on the subject, develops methods for evaluating all aspects of lighting quality and quantity, and their effects upon the ease of seeing, visual comfort, and aesthetic pleasantness, in terms too technical for the layman.

Carmichael, Leonard, and Walter F. Dearborn: *Reading and Visual Fatigue,* Houghton Mifflin Company, Boston, 1947, 483 pp.

The most comprehensive study of the subject currently available; includes a bibliography of over four hundred items.

Crouch, C. L.: "New Method of Determining Illumination Required for Tasks," *Illuminating Engineering,* 53:416–422, August, 1958.

Summarizes the methods and studies of H. R. Blackwell.

Hopkinson, R. G.: *Lighting: Architectural Physics,* Great Britain, Department of Scientific and Industrial Research, Building Research Station, H.M.S.O., London, 1963, 360 pp.

A textbook for architectural students based on principles which give first consideration to the needs of the individual in the context of his environment; an outstanding work for architects and librarians seriously interested in the problems of lighting; contains an extensive bibliography.

Illuminating Engineering Society: *IES Lighting Handbook; The Standard Lighting Guide,* 3d ed., New York, 1959.

An essential reference work for library planners.

Jordan, Robert T.: "Lighting in University Libraries," *UNESCO Bulletin for Libraries,* 17:326–336, November–December, 1963.

A nontechnical survey of the "state of the art" written for librarians; contains a select bibliography.

Ketch, J. M.: "Library Lighting," *Light,* published by the Lamp Division of General Electric, 23(2):15–21, March–April, 1954.

This is an article of pictures; discussed are the various types of modern lighting fixtures for library buildings; also shows what new lighting can do for older buildings in the remodelling process.

Lam, William M. C.: "Lighting for Architecture," reprinted from *Architectural Record,* June, July, October, 1960 and January, 1961, 48 pp.

Emphasizes the architectural aspects of lighting.

Larson, Leslie: *Lighting and Its Design,* Whitney Library of Design, New York, 1964, 228 pp.

A designer with an architectural background analyzes and questions the illuminating engineering approach to lighting and prefers the point of view of aesthetics and design, the ophthalmologist, the psychologist, and the psychiatrist. The sections on lighting and vision; recommended levels of illumination; on fluorescent, incandescent and mercury vapors compared; and on luminous surfaces, pp. 15–35, are of special interest to librarians, and challenge the high intensity recommendations prevalent in recent years.

National Research Council, Building Research Institute: *Building Illumination: The Effect of New Lighting Levels,* a research correlation conference conducted by the Building Research Institute, May 20 and 21, 1959, Cleveland, Ohio. National Research Council Publication 744, 1959, 93 pp.

Eight papers on the effects of the new IES lighting level based on the studies by H. R. Blackwell. Includes papers by Blackwell, C. L. Crouch, and other well-known authorities. Charles D. Gibson, an authority on school lighting, cautions against establishing one recommended foot-candle level for classroom tasks, indicating that the over-all design of the lighting systems, the quality and the quantity of tasks to be performed, etc., must be taken into consideration.

Phillips, Derek: *Lighting in Architectural Design,* McGraw-Hill Book Company, New York, 1964, 310 pp.

Bridges the gap between architects and illuminating engineers.

Moving

Kephart, John E.: *Moving a Library,* University of Illinois Library School Occasional Papers, no. 21, Urbana, Ill., May, 1951, 8 pp.

Analyzes the moving of seventeen libraries in the United States between 1921 and 1950; common factors are discussed: when to move, transport problems according to location of the library, plan of operations, space to be left for expansion, manpower required, methods of moving. Bibliographical footnotes.

Spyers-Duran, Peter: *Moving Library Materials,* Library Associates of University of Wisconsin-Milwaukee, Milwaukee, 1964, 51 pp.

Deals in detail with moving problems in public and academic libraries; includes illustrations and bibliography.

Programs

Esterquest, Ralph T.: *Building Program for the New Francis A. Countway Library of Medicine of the Harvard Medical School and the Boston Medical Library,* working edition, revised March, 1961, 90 pp.

An example of a library building program which is available on request.

Macdonald, Angus Snead: "Building Design for Library Management," *Library Trends,* 2:463–469, January, 1954.

Outlines the program that should be established by library management to serve as a guide to the architect;

such factors as planning of areas, equipment, and aesthetic features are discussed.

Reece, E. J.: "Library Building Programs: How to Draft Them," *College and Research Libraries,* 13:198–211, July, 1952.

Stresses the importance of a program and consultation and team work between architect and librarian; the program should be "the simplest possible statement of the problem, as definite as it can be in all matters dealing with the purpose, function and conditioning of the building, and as free as possible in all matters dealing with plan arrangements and design." A good treatment of the subject.

Remodeling

Bryan, James E.: "Remodeling of Library Buildings," *ALA Bulletin,* 43:77–81, February, 1949.

How to make remodeling studies; the article, although written for public library situations, contains a "check list for remodeling" which can be used in any library.

Site Selection

Wheeler, Joseph L.: *The Effective Location of Public Library Buildings,* University of Illinois Library School Occasional Papers, no. 52, Urbana, Ill., July, 1958, 50 pp.

The author's thesis is that the public library should be located at the center of the major pedestrian shopping and office area and that it should have a street level entrance and facade which is brightly lit, colorful, and allows the activities and services offered to be seen from the street. While the location of academic libraries is not discussed, the point of view and the approach to the problem should be of interest to academic library planners.

Special Collections

American Standard Practice for Storage of Microfilm, American Standards Association, New York, 1957, 11 pp.

Duckles, Vincent: "Problems of Music Library Equipment," *MLA Notes,* 11:213–223, March, 1954.

Based on his experience in planning the Music Library at Berkeley the author discusses shelving for music scores, books, and records, service equipment, and listening facilities; much of the equipment described here is now largely obsolete.

LeGear, C. E.: *Maps: Their Care, Repair and Preservation in Libraries,* rev. ed., Library of Congress, Washington, 1956, 75 pp.

Includes discussion of map storage equipment, drawer dimensions, capacities, and room layouts.

National Education Association: *Planning Schools for Use of Audio-Visual Materials: no. 4, Audio-Visual Centers in Colleges and Universities,* Washington, 1955, 140 pp.

Pickett, A. G., and M. M. Lemcoe: *Preservation and Storage of Sound Recordings,* Library of Congress, Washington, 1959, 74 pp.

While most of this report deals with the chemical and mechanical properties of discs and tape, chapters 2. B, "Handling and Storage," 2. G, "Predicting Shelf Life," and 3. E, "Summary of Conclusions and Recommendations for Storage of Phonograph Discs," are more directly concerned with architectural problems, selections of shelving, air conditioning, etc.

Study Facilities

Student Reactions to Study Facilities, with Implications for Architects and College Administrators, a report to the Presidents of Amherst College, Mount Holyoke College, Smith College, and The University of Massachusetts, prepared under the auspices of The Committee for New College, by Stuart M. Stoke and others, Amherst, Mass., 1960, 60 pp.

The Committee's study confirms what has been common knowledge among librarians—that students prefer intimate or individual study facilities and that the traditional vaulted reading room is obsolete.

appendix E

Glossary

No attempt has been made to make this a complete glossary of library or building construction terms. It includes only those that are used in the volume, those that have not been defined in detail in the text, and that might not be understood by members of the groups for whom it was written. As an effort has been made to avoid technical jargon and abstract terms, the list is shorter than might have been expected.

Addendum (contract): A written amplification of the contract documents after they have been issued to the bidders but before the bids have been received.

Air conditioning: Sometimes called *Climatization.* The term is used for the artificial control of humidity, temperature, purity, and motion of air within buildings. In libraries the objective may be to secure either human comfort or the proper environment for the preservation of library materials.

Aisle: A passageway between furniture or equipment; for instance, between ranges of shelving in a book stack, between rows of reading accommodations (chairs or chairs and tables), or between tables and shelving in a reading area. As used in this volume, an aisle at right angles to stack ranges is called a cross aisle. A main cross aisle is the "Main Street" of a book stack and generally will have book ranges on both sides and will be wider than a subsidiary or secondary cross aisle, which may have ranges on one side and carrels or faculty studies on the other. An aisle between two parallel ranges is called a range or stack aisle.

Alcove: An area enclosed on three sides by walls, partitions, or bookcases, or a combination of these, normally large enough to accommodate a table and from one to four readers.

Architectural space: (See *Non-assignable space.*)

Audiovisual materials: Aids to teaching "through ear and eye," e.g., phonodiscs, tape recordings, films, and filmstrips. Plastic models, show panels, etc., are also included, and the various mechanical devices for programmed instruction are sometimes referred to by the term.

Bay: (See *Module*).

Book truck: A small cart consisting of a set of shelves on wheels used for transporting books within the library. Called a book trolley in many countries.

Building code: The civil regulations governing the construction and alterations of buildings in a given locality, setting forth requirements and restrictions as to the use, safety, size, and type of building in certain zones and areas.

Caisson: A watertight metal compartment open at the bottom, used for the construction of foundation piers, particularly when the subsoil conditions require these piers to be extended below the ground water level.

Canopy top: Slightly projecting rooflike cover over sections of shelving. (See Fig. 8.4.)

Cantilever: A beam or slab projecting beyond the vertical column or wall construction so that it is supported on one end or side only and is capable of carrying weight throughout its projection.

Carrel: A small room or alcove in the book stack, in which the reader may be permitted to retain the books on which he is working. Open carrels often consist of desks with visual barriers formed by open book shelves or low partitions. Closed carrels have doors and often soundproof semipermanent walls. (See Fig. 16.7B.)

Casement windows: Window units hinged vertically so that they open outwards or inwards. They can be operated either manually or by means of a mechanical crank attachment.

Catalogue: Library catalogues exist (1) in the form of book catalogues, and (2) as card catalogues. The catalogue most often found in American libraries is the dictionary catalogue on cards. (See also *Official catalogue.*)

Catalogue department: The administrative unit of a library where books are catalogued and classified. (See also *Technical services.*)

Centers, or on Centers: The distance between the centers of two pieces of similar equipment or construction placed parallel to each other. Generally used in connection with stack ranges, carrels in a reading area, tables in a reading room, desks in a workroom, parallel rows of catalogue cases for the library's catalogue, or with columns or windows.

Circulation department: Service department for loan transactions, often also responsible for the supervision of the book stacks. (See also *Readers' services.*)

Closed-access stacks: Stacks to which only members of the library staff normally are admitted.

Closed-circuit television: A type of television in which the signal is not broadcast as in ordinary television but is transmitted by wire to one or more receivers. Existing telephone lines have been used in experimental installations. Possible applications of closed-circuit television in libraries include (*a*) transmission of educational programs to auditoriums and classrooms; (*b*) transmission of documents—pages of books or manuscripts—and of bibliographical information from a central service point to distant monitoring stations. In a large library system use of closed-circuit television might reduce the need for departmental or branch libraries and minimize duplication of catalogues and bibliographical collections. It can also be used as an aid to supervision.

Collateral reading: Suggested or recommended reading designated by the teaching faculty to supplement required reading. (See also *Reserve books.*)

Commercial shelving: Inexpensive metal shelving which can be supplied by a dealer. Adjustable with the use of nuts and bolts. (See Fig. 8.1.)

Contingency figure: A safety factor included in cost estimates to cover any anticipated inflation and to provide for expenses which may occur at a later date, the amounts of which are unknown at the time of estimating.

Cubicle: (See *Carrel*).

Cubook: A term devised by Robert Henderson of the New York Public Library for a book of average size. He estimated that 100 cubooks could be housed in a standard single-faced stack section 3 ft wide and 7 ft 6 in. high.

Curtain wall: A thin exterior wall, between and often in front of the main structural members of steel or of reinforced concrete, bearing no load.

Dado: The lower part of a wall faced with wood or colored differently from the upper part.

Deck: Area occupied by one level of a book stack, referred to in this volume as a stack level.

Divisional plan: (See *Subject-divisional plan*).

Double-faced section: Two sections back to back, generally attached to the same upright. Also called a *compartment.*

Drawings: Schematic drawings and sketches, preliminary, working, and usually many detail drawings to illustrate specifications, included in the architect's professional services.

Schematic plans are drawings for proposed floor layouts. Sometimes several sets must be prepared before one is accepted. These are used as the basis for the preliminary plans.

Preliminary plans are drawings developed in much greater detail. These drawings show not only structural building elements but location and space requirements for everything to be contained in the building. Together with outline specifications preliminary plans serve as the basis for preliminary cost estimates.

Working drawings, together with specifications, are the detailed contract documents used for the preparation of bids and for the erection of the building; they show architectural, structural, and mechanical work.

Detail drawings are produced by the architect to explain, enlarge, and clarify sections of his working drawings or specifications.

Shop drawings are prepared by the manufacturers or the suppliers of special building equipment and are provided to the contractor for his use in preparing its installation. They illustrate in detail the size, operation, and features of the special equipment and should be approved by the architect before use.

Elevation (*drawing*): A vertical representation of a building drawn to a scale. (See section 16.4.)

Elevator: A platform for the mechanical transportation of passengers, books, or freight, vertically from one level of a building to the others. When used for passengers, the platform should be completely enclosed by walls and roof. Called a lift in many countries. (See also *Two-to-one roping.*)

Ellison doors: Trade name for heavy balanced swing doors with hinges placed about 6 in. from the side frame at top and bottom. Doors swing both in and out at the same time because part of the swinging action goes in the reverse direction. They use less space than ordinary doors with hinges directly on the side frame. Their use is especially applicable to wide outside doors where wind problems exist and for interior parts of the building where the suction between air-conditioned and non-air-conditioned rooms makes the operation of more normal hardware difficult.

Facsimile: (1) A facsimile reproduction of a manuscript or printed document made by lithographic or photographic processes; *not* a reprint. (2) Transmission of photographic images of documents by a patented telegraphic process. (See also *Closed-circuit television; telautograph.*)

Flashing: A material, usually copper or impregnated fabric (today rarely lead or zinc), generally used as a protective covering to prevent water penetration into the building at joints between horizontal and vertical building surfaces (such as roofs, floors, and walls), at the head of sills or exterior wall openings, and on all sides of roof openings for gables, dormers, skylights, glass domes, pipes, drains, etc.

Fluorescent light: (See *Light sources*).

Foot-candle: Unit of illumination equal to one lumen per square foot, which is the amount provided by a light source of one candle at a distance of one foot. Full sunlight with the sun in the zenith is of the order of 10,000 foot-candles on a horizontal surface. This term is often replaced by the use of "lumen per square foot."

Fore edge: The edge of a book, opposite the binding edge or spine, i.e., the front edge.

Foundations: The supporting members of a building or structure at the ground or its underpinning if it is supported by columns; the piers at the bottom of each column are its foundations. The type of foundation required for a building depends on its structural system and on the ground and climate. In soft soils, piles may have to be driven down 100 ft or more. On rocks, little more than dowels may be necessary to anchor the building. If a building has no basement but is erected directly on a concrete slab, that is the foundation. If a building has bearing walls supporting the roof, the foundations are the lowest divisions of these walls.

Free-standing stacks: Library stacks whose principal support is the floor of the story they occupy. Stack manufacturers do not regard a stack as free-standing unless its bases are so broad that they do not require strut bracing running from one range to another or other methods to provide stabilization, such as fastening to the floor. (See *Multitier stack.*)

Furring (walls, ceilings): The application of a layer of thin wood, masonry, or metal to a surface to level it, as for lathing, plastering, etc., or to make an air space.

General contractor: A builder who is prepared to be responsible for all the work necessary in building a structure.

Gross space: The total area enclosed by a building expressed in terms of cubic footage or square footage of floor area, including walls. Gross space generally includes roof houses, projections, and mechanical spaces and also one-half of all spaces not enclosed with walls, but provided with a roof and a floor. To the floor-to-floor heights used in computing cubic footage 1½ ft is generally added below the lowest floor to allow for foundations.

Incandescent light: (See *Light sources*).

Intercom system: A telephone system providing direct communication between stations on the same premises. Local systems may be independent of or associated with the nationwide telephone network. The equipment often has such features as provision for conference calling, hands-free talking, and for switching of executive phones to public-address systems.

Lally columns: Columns made of a cylindrical steel pipe shell filled with concrete. The standard type is reinforced with only the steel pipe shell; special types have additional reinforcement consisting of steel bars.

Layout: The plan for distribution of equipment in a building. (See section 16.3.)

Lift: In American library usage the term often denotes the book elevator, not the passenger elevator. Lifts are operated by electric motors or by hand.

Light sources:

Incandescent light is produced by a light bulb in which a metallic substance glows at white heat.

Fluorescent light is generated by an electric-discharge lamp in which the radiant energy from the discharge is transferred by suitable materials (usually phosphors) into wave lengths giving high luminosity.

Mercury vapor lamps are tubular lamps in which mercury vapor is made luminous by the passage of an electric current.

Mezzanine floor: A level of a building extending over only a part of the area available to it and leaving the remainder with additional height. (See section 5.2.)

Microreproductions: Also known as *microforms.* They are microphotographic copies of printed or manuscript matter. The principal forms are: microfilm on reels, "microfiche" (sheet microfilm), microcards (opaque paper positives), and microprint (paper opaques which are duplicated in large editions by a photomechanical process.

Mock-up: A full-sized replica or dummy of a part of a building, often made of a substitute material, such as wood or plaster.

Modular construction: A system of building construction in which the floor area is divided into equal rectangles defined by structural columns at the corners, instead of by load-bearing walls. This system makes it possible to provide or to extend areas for the different departments as desired. A modular library is one constructed on this principle.

Module: One of the rectangular units of space into which a modular construction is divided; also called a *bay*.

Multitier stack: A type of multistory stack construction which before the Second World War was by far the most popular type and which is found in most large research libraries. The principle of multitier stack consists of vertically and horizontally interconnected sections and ranges of shelving, "stacked" one on top of another, which are self-supporting and support the total weight of the books stored. Their installation makes it unnecessary to have load-bearing floors in the building itself, which can be of a loft type. The same columns which accept the shelves support the thin stack floors also. Multitier stacks ensure maximum capacity, but the stack area lacks flexibility.

Net space: The part of the gross space left after deducting the non-assignable space.

Non-assignable space: Non-assignable space in a library, also called architectural space, is that not available for direct library purposes, that is, for seating accommodations, book storage, and areas used for staff quarters and library services to readers.

Official catalogue: A catalogue maintained for the use of the library staff. The entries in this catalogue often include details for the guidance of cataloguers.

On centers: (See *Centers*).

Open-access stack: Stack to which readers are admitted.

Parging (walls): The lining of the layers in outer walls with mortar or plaster to give a smooth surface for greater insulation and to reduce fire risks and water penetration.

Periodical shelving: Shelving constructed to display current issues of unbound periodicals, sometimes with space on lower shelves for storage of back numbers.

Plans: (See *Drawings*).

Pneumatic tubes: Used for the transportation of books or of call slips. Cartridges containing books or call slips are propelled by air pressure or by vacuum.

Public services: (See *Readers' services*).

Range (shelving): A row of sections of bookcases, called a *press* in British usage; can be single-faced or double-faced with uprights or shelf supports common to both sides. (See also *Aisles* and *Centers*.)

Readers' services: The departments of a library which deal with the public directly, such as the *circulation department*, the *reference department*, the interlibrary loan office. Photographic reproduction service is often included in this group. (See also *Technical services*.)

Reference department: The department of a library which helps the reader use the library's resources and provides assistance in the search for information. The department usually supervises and maintains the collection of reference books which are not for circulation but for consultation in the library only.

Reserve books: Books for assigned or collateral reading removed from their regular positions in the stacks and placed on open reserve shelves or closed reserve shelves. If the latter, they are available only by signing a call slip. They are sometimes withdrawn from the shelves by a stack attendant and given to the reader over a counter and sometimes selected from restricted shelves by the reader who then gives a signed call slip to the attendant before leaving the restricted area.

Riser (stair): The upright piece of a step, from tread to tread. (See also *Tread.*)

Sash: The wooden or metal framework in which panes of glass are set for installation in windows or doors. Double-hung windows have upper and lower sash; casement windows have sash that open on hinges fastened to the upright side of the frame. Fixed sash do not open. They may be used in connection with opening sash, or all the sash in an air-conditioned building may be fixed.

Section (architectural): A drawing illustrating the graphic picture resulting from a theoretical cutting along a predetermined line, through the building or a portion of it. The expressive French term for this type of drawing is *coupe.*

Section (shelving): The vertical division of a set of shelves between uprights, usually, in the United States, 3 ft wide and 7 ft 6 in. high (called a *tier* in British usage).

Specifications: Written documents in which an architect enumerates and describes the quality of the materials to be used and the level of the workmanship. (See section 16.4.)

Spine: The sewn or binding edge of a book; the back.

Stack (book): Space for the storage of books. (See also *Free-standing stack; Multitier stack.*)

Stack uprights: Vertical members or uprights which act as shelf supports and divide sections or compartments. In a *multitier* stack they carry the load on the levels above.

Stall: (See *Carrel*).

Storage libraries: Three distinct types of storage arrangements for less-used books have developed among libraries in the United States: (1) local storage in buildings or parts of buildings owned by the parent institution; (2) co-operative storage in warehouse-type buildings owned jointly by several libraries, each of which is retaining ownership of the materials it is storing; (3) cooperative-storage libraries, into which books are released from the individual contributing libraries and become jointly owned property.

Stroboscopic effect: The flickering created by light periodically interrupted as in a strobo-scope.

Subject-divisional plan: Form or organization which many academic libraries in the United States have adopted. Under this plan resources and services are subdivided according to subject content of the collection. Subject trained librarians are responsible for the technical and readers' services in typical areas, such as humanities and social sciences, physical sciences, life sciences, etc. Under the full subject-divisional plan no centralized functional departments exist in the library. There are several variants of the plan; often it includes readers' services only, while the technical services are operated in a centralized fashion and there is a single public catalogue.

Technical services: The departments of a library responsible for the planning and development of resources as well as their maintenance and bibliographical control, e.g., acquisitions, cataloguing and classification, binding and preparing the book for the shelf (labeling, etc.). Photographic reproduction is sometimes included in technical services. (See also *Readers' services.*)

Telautograph: A facsimile telegraph for reproducing handwriting. The motions of the transmitting pencil are reproduced by a receiving pen controlled by electromagnetic impulses.

Thermopane: Trade name for an insulating double-glazing pane for windows or doors. Another trade name is *Twindow.*

Tier: [See *Section (shelving).*]

Tread (stair): The upper, horizontal board of a step.

Trolley: (See *Book truck*).

Truck: (See *Book truck*).

Two-to-one roping (elevators): Electric traction elevators have either 2:1 or 1:1 roping. With 2:1 machines the cab speed is only half the rope speed, whereas with 1:1 machines the cab speed is the same as the rope speed.

Two-way radio: Radio communication carried on between several localities with portable equipment which permits receiving and transmitting of messages.

Vapor barrier: Vapor barriers are designed to prevent passage of moisture through a wall and to avoid condensation within. They consist of thin sheets, usually of metallic foil, impenetrable by moisture, or are applied in liquid form hardening into a similarly impenetrable sheathing.

Weeding: The practice of withdrawing books from the collection, either by discarding superfluous copies or transferring infrequently used books to storage or to other libraries.

Index